p183

ADVANCED
MARKETING
STRATEGY

ADVANCED MARKETING STRATEGY:

Phenomena, Analysis, and Decisions

Glen L. Urban
Massachusetts Institute of Technology

Steven H. Star
Massachusetts Institute of Technology

PRENTICE HALL, Englewood Cliffs, New Jersey 07632

Library of Congress Cataloging-in-Publication Data

Urban, Glen L.
    Advanced marketing strategy : phenomena, analysis, and decisions /
    Glen L. Urban, Steven H. Star.
         p.   cm.
    Includes bibliographical references and index.
    ISBN 0-13-851940-4
    1. Marketing—Management.   2. Strategic planning.   I. Star,
Steven H.   II. Title.
HF5415.13.U73   1991
658.8'02—dc20   90-35900
                                           CIP

Editorial/production supervision: Eleanor Perz
Interior design/cover design: Linda J. Den Heyer Rosa
Manufacturing buyer: Bob Anderson

Cover: Jasper Johns, *Target with Four Faces* (1955).
 Assemblage, encaustic on newspaper and cloth over canvas, surmounted
    by four tinted plaster faces in wood box with hinged front. Overall di-
 mensions with box open, 33⅜ × 26 × 3″ (85.3 × 66 × 7.6 cm)
Collection, The Museum of Modern Art, New York.
Gift of Mr. and Mrs. Robert C. Scull.

Printed in the United States of America
10 9 8 7 6 5 4 3 2 1

ISBN 0-13-851940-4

Prentice-Hall International (UK) Limited, *London*
Prentice-Hall of Australia Pty. Limited, *Sydney*
Prentice-Hall Canada Inc., *Toronto*
Prentice-Hall Hispanoamericana, S.A., *Mexico*
Prentice-Hall of India Private Limited, *New Delhi*
Prentice-Hall of Japan, Inc., *Tokyo*
Prentice-Hall of Southeast Asia Pte. Ltd., *Singapore*
Editora Prentice-Hall do Brasil, Ltda., *Rio de Janeiro*

From Glen
to
ANDREA
AND OUR 25 INCOMPARABLE YEARS TOGETHER

and
from Steve
with love to
BRENDA,
ALEXANDER, and ANTHONY

BRIEF CONTENTS

PART THREE
STRATEGIC DECISION MAKING   281

PART FOUR
IMPLEMENTATION   457

viii

CONTENTS

ix

PREFACE

This book stands for the synthesis of the managerial and the analytic approaches to marketing. During the past three decades, these two points of view have diverged sharply. Model-building analysts said that ''case-based managerials'' were good at problem definition, but could not generate optimal solutions; managerials said that ''management science analysts'' could solve any problem, but could not find the right problem.[1] The analysts argued, in effect, that the managerials couldn't see the trees for the forest, and the managerials argued that the analysts couldn't see the forest for the trees.

The training and careers of the two authors of this book reflect this split in the marketing field. One of us has been primarily a model builder and developer of new research methodologies, an author of books and articles on marketing science and analytic approaches to new products, and an entrepreneur who co-founded a successful business devoted to the application of scientific approaches to marketing problems. The other, an archetypal product of the Harvard Business School in its heyday, has been a prolific developer of managerially-oriented cases, a classic case method teacher, and a consultant on marketing strategy issues to numerous firms and organizations.

During the 1983–84 academic year, the two of us began to work together in the marketing group at the M.I.T. Sloan School of Management. Perhaps a bit wary of each other at first, we soon came to realize that we had many common interests and concerns. In particular, as we found ourselves working increasingly on issues of marketing strategy rather than tactics, we each felt a need to supplement our own experience with the other's perspective. Moreover, we were both teaching marketing strategy courses—to Masters students and to executives, respectively. As we discussed our courses, it became apparent that both types of students would benefit from a combination of theory and models, on the one hand, and managerial cases, on the other. While our courses continued to differ significantly in focus and pedagogy, each came to be based on a combination of the two approaches. We tried to teach applied marketing science analysis to managers and the broad perspectives of marketing to analysts, in hopes of developing complete marketing strategists.

---

[1] ''Case'' is used here to refer to a comprehensive description of a managerial situation calling for action. Many analytically-oriented marketing courses do employ short, mini-cases that essentially function as enhanced problem sets, but are not true cases in our sense of the word here.

This book is an outgrowth of the collaboration. It is based on an original paradigm for the application of analytic methods to strategic issues in marketing. Approximately half of the text is devoted to the development of this paradigm, while the other half consists of ten challenging cases that call for the student to apply both managerial judgment and higher level analytic approaches to complex marketing strategy problems.

As we developed this book, we soon came to realize how much we owed to our respective individual mentors, John D. C. Little of M.I.T. (Urban) and Ted Levitt of the Harvard Business School (Star). Not only were they instrumental to our early training and development, but they also have provided us with inspiration throughout our careers. Our colleagues John Hauser, Arnoldo Hax, Len Lodish, John Roberts, and Eric Von Hippel and our students and business associates provided the range of perspective and insight that made our integrative effort productive.

Our thanks also to the following reviewers: Dipankar Chakravarti, University of Arizona; Susan Douglas, New York University; James M. Lattin, Stanford University; Michael P. Mokwa, Arizona State University; Marian Chapman Moore, Duke University; Dan Toy, Penn State University; and Robert B. Woodruff, University of Tennessee-Knoxville.

In the years we have been working on this book, we have been encouraged (indeed, prodded) by our editor at Prentice Hall, Whitney Blake, to whom we are most grateful. Our secretaries, Barbara Davis de Urea, Annie Cooper, and, especially, Linda Pierpont, have contributed mightily to the preparation of the manuscript. Most recently, Whitney's successor, Chris Treiber, and Prentice Hall production editor Eleanor Perz have undertaken the very welcome task of helping us bring this book to completion. Thanks to all of you.

Finally, the many hours that went into the writing of this book were borrowed largely from time we would otherwise have spent with our families, whose support and encouragement were unwavering. One of the most important rewards of this project is the fact that in the process we have all become close friends.

G.L.U.
S.H.S.
March 21, 1990

ADVANCED MARKETING STRATEGY

PART ONE

MARKETING STRATEGY FORMULATION PROCESS

MARKETING STRATEGY AND DECISION MAKING

THE IMPORTANCE OF MARKETING STRATEGY

The formulation of effective marketing strategies is critical to the achievement of an organization's goals. Consider these examples of successful marketing strategy:

- *IBM*: IBM's success is largely based on its ability to help customers solve problems through the use of computers and information systems. IBM account teams seek to understand the needs and buying behavior of the various members of a customer's decision-making unit, and to position IBM as the customer's partner in analyzing and proposing solutions. Because of this approach, IBM is often viewed as uniquely qualified to be the customer's information systems supplier. Customer needs are satisfied by IBM with training, technical service, and account team support. IBM's valued-added strategy delivers additional benefits through people who understand customer needs. This strategy distinguishes the company from its competitors and has become a critical success factor for IBM. It has protected the company's franchise from low-cost hardware competitors, and built enduring and growing customer relationships that have paid off in substantial sales and profit levels.

- *Procter & Gamble*: The consumer is queen (king) at P&G. The company's policies insist that P&G products fit customer needs and be viewed by customers as superior to competitive products on a scale of evaluation that is important to the customer. Large budgets are established for market research to understand consumer decision processes, evaluate P&G products relative to competitors, and identify unfulfilled consumer needs. Once an opportunity has been identified and a superior product developed, P&G commits heavy advertising and promotion budgets so that it can gain the dominant competitive position in that market. After dominance has been achieved, it is defended by aggressive advertising, promotion, and point-of-purchase programs, as well as by widening the product line to meet the unique needs of each

3

segment of the market. P&G dominates the U.S. detergent market, for example, with brands such as Tide, Era, Cheer, and Bold.

- *Northrop*: The largest-selling jet fighter in the world, the Northrop F-5, was not built under contract to the U.S. Department of Defense. Rather, Northrop designed this aircraft to fit a particular segment of the market—smaller NATO and developing nations—and was able to sell over 3,500 aircraft for more than $3 billion. Although the F-5 was not the equal of U.S. front line fighters such as the F-16, it was competitive in combat performance with the Russian MIG 21 and was inexpensive, easy to learn to fly, and easy to maintain. It did not fit U.S. Department of Defense preferences (the United States bought fewer than fifty F-5s, largely to simulate MIG 21s in training exercises), but it did fit the needs of countries like Taiwan, Korea, Norway, and Greece. This positioning led to sustained success for over fifteen years, contributing significantly to Northrop's profitability.

- *Polaroid*: Polaroid's introduction of instant photography was based on proprietary, patented technology that delivered a significant benefit to consumers and satisfied a previously unmet need: immediate delivery of a photographic image. The product was effectively advertised, packaged, and distributed, leading, over time, to a line of cameras (priced from $30 to $200) that spanned the requirements of multiple market segments. Polaroid achieved outstanding earnings primarily through follow-on film sales. Technological improvements stimulated continued growth in sales, while aggressive legal defense of Polaroid's patent position kept direct competition to a minimum. Polaroid became a major corporation on the basis of a unique product coupled with an extremely effective comprehensive marketing strategy.

These examples illustrate some of the factors critical to effective strategy formulation. Unfortunately, many marketing strategies are far less successful. Consider the following:

- *IBM*: IBM was late in entering the minicomputer market. Although it ultimately achieved substantial sales in this market, it never achieved (vis-à-vis DEC, Data General, and other companies) anything like the dominance it holds in the mainframe computer market. Similarly, IBM was late in recognizing the importance of the work station market, allowing Sun and DEC to take leadership positions, and stumbled with its PC/Jr. and Satellite Business Systems ventures—in each case by misunderstanding a yet-to-develop market.

- *Procter & Gamble*: After pioneering the disposable diaper market with Pampers, P&G lost almost one-third of this market to Kimberly Clark's Huggies. Huggies appealed to a segment that desired more comfort and absorbency, and was willing to pay a premium price. In another example, P&G, although it invented ready-to-eat soft-center cookies, was upstaged by competitors who read the P&G test market, developed their own marketing programs aimed at this segment, and went national before P&G. P&G ultimately went national with its Duncan Hines brand, but Almost Home by Nabisco and Soft Batch by Keebler were already entrenched in the market.[1]

- *Northrop*: In 1984, Northrop introduced the F-20 Tigershark, an updated model of its F-5. The Tigershark was also targeted at the export market segment. By this time, however, the Defense Department had changed its policy to permit sales of the more advanced F-16 to many countries that had previously purchased the F-5 (e.g., Pakistan and Venezuela). By 1989, Northrop had not yet obtained any orders for the Tigershark, despite aggressive marketing to the export markets where the F-5 has been so successful, as well as to the United States, whose Congress was increasing its emphasis on both value and performance in budgeting funds for new

---

[1] P&G prevailed ultimately, however, when it accepted an out-of-court settlement of $125 million for patent infringement from Nabisco, Keebler, and Frito-Lay. *New York Times,* September 13, 1989.

weapons systems. Northrop is reputed to have lost over $1 billion on its Tigershark program.

- *Polaroid*: Instant still photography was a winner, but when instant camera sales matured (partly because of the success of Japanese 35mm cameras and the rapid proliferation of "quick" film-developing laboratories), Polaroid was not ready with new products that could sustain growth in sales and profits in the consumer market. When it tried to apply the original consumer benefit of instant images to home movies, the resulting product, Polarvision, launched just as home video was taking off, was a failure that resulted in losses of hundreds of millions of dollars.

We have cited examples of both success and failure from the same companies to emphasize the complexity and risk involved in formulating marketing strategy. A good strategy is invaluable, but the development of such a strategy is exceedingly difficult. A disciplined strategy formulation process is needed to minimize the chances of failure and maximize the returns from a successful strategy.

The goal of this book is to provide you with the perspectives and tools necessary for sound strategy formulation and implementation, as well as the ability to understand the critical features that distinguish effective from ineffective marketing strategies.

THE STRATEGY FORMULATION PROCESS

Marketing strategy requires a definition of the market domain in which the company will compete and a statement of how utility and value will be created for customers through product and service offerings. Recognizing customer needs and filling them better than competitors is the core of successful marketing strategy. When customer needs are satisfied by effective marketing programs, long-term competitive advantage can be achieved and financial goals can be met.

We view the development of successful strategies as a process. A simplified view of the marketing strategy formulation process is shown in Figure 1.1. Strategic analysis should be carried out *before* decisions are made or programs are implemented, because otherwise there is a high risk that corporate, stockholder, and societal resources will be used inefficiently. Careful analysis provides a solid basis for intelligent decision making and strategy formulation. Analysis should be updated on the basis of results from the marketplace, and strategic decisions should be revised to achieve the firm's goals.

Learning is critical to the success of this process. Management must seek to understand *why* a particular strategy succeeded or failed. Strategic analysis should be based on an in-depth understanding of the phenomena that underlie effective marketing strategy. This understanding offers a powerful means for assessing the firm's strengths and weaknesses, as well as the threats and opportunities it faces. The most appropriate place to begin is with an understanding of the behavioral determinants of consumer decision making. Concepts from psychology, sociology, and social psychology, integrated into a comprehensive model of how individuals collect and process information in making purchase decisions, are useful in developing quantitative models that identify where the firm's products are in their respective life cycles. We must ask what phase of the life cycle each product is in, whether too many of our products are in the mature phase to sustain business growth at the desired level, and whether we need more resources to support growth.

Segmentation and differentiation also require careful diagnosis. Have we attacked growing and profitable market segments? Are we uniquely positioned in our targeted market segments? Are there opportunities for new products? Does our product line cover the market without unjustified duplication of effort?

Market response models that predict how sales will respond to changes in such marketing variables as price, advertising, promotion, sales effort, and distribution are valuable in increasing the productivity of marketing resources. Are our marketing-mix variables at the profit-maximizing level? Are there opportunities for gaining more output from the input within our marketing budget?

Modeling competitive behavior requires the integration of underlying phenomena into a comprehensive understanding of marketing strategy. How will we surpass our competition? How can we create advantages from our understanding of customer decision making as reflected in life-cycle, segmentation, positioning, and market response analysis? How will competitors react to our offensive moves? How should we respond to their actions?

Understanding the role of market share in competitive strategy and the effects of

FIGURE 1.1
Marketing Strategy
Formulation Process

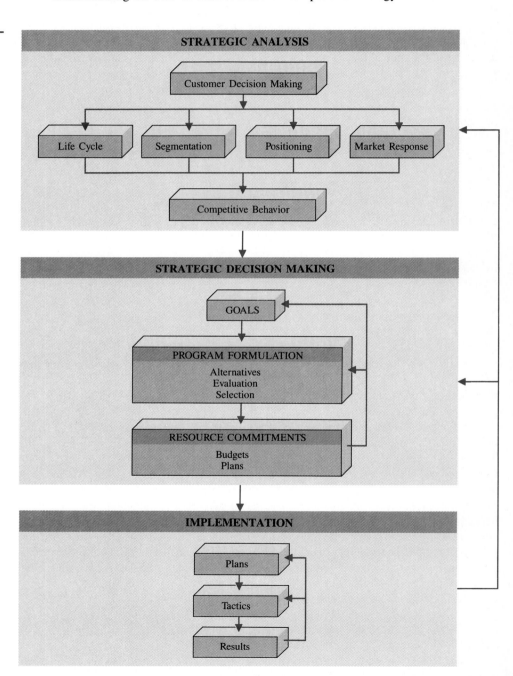

experience are critical to an understanding of our market position. Is share a critical success factor in our business? Does experience lead to reduced costs as cumulative volume grows?

Finally, we must carry out a comprehensive diagnosis of the marketing strategy we have developed. This diagnosis will use the analytic insights and learning gained from studying behavioral, market, and competitive phenomena. It will seek to identify our company's strengths and weaknesses, the threats and opportunities it faces, and its potentially unique competitive advantages in serving customers. (This diagnosis can also be used to provide inputs to the corporate strategic planning process.)

After our comprehensive analysis is completed, the stage is set for effective strategic decision making. In broad terms, the decision-making steps we shall follow are: (1) goal specification; (2) program formulation; (3) resource commitment; and (4) detailed planning. Goals should be specified in terms of the product/markets served, sales growth and market share to be achieved, and financial rewards expected (e.g., margins, profits, return on investment). Program alternatives, formulated to meet analytically determined goals, must be evaluated systematically to select the best candidates for corporate resource allocation. This may require reinspection of goals to be sure they are both realistic and ambitious enough to push the organization toward superior performance. Creativity and insight are key elements in generating ideas for new programs, while analytic models are especially useful for evaluating such programs. A combination of sound managerial judgment and rational analysis is essential if a firm is to achieve consistently high levels of program and resource utilization. Specific goals, programs, and commitments need to be converted into detailed plans for new products, existing products, and entire product lines, as well as for the worldwide enterprise.

In order to implement strategic programs and plans, it is necessary to translate strategies into detailed tactics. For example, in consumer packaged goods, the specifics of advertising copy and the media plan must reflect the overall positioning strategy. In industrial products, details of sales force training and telemarketing sales support should build upon the overall strategy. In services, technology and people must be combined to deliver the benefits customers expect consistently. After the tactics have been specified, detailed plans and budgets should be established so that results can be measured and compared to explicit goals. A decision support system is often a useful aid in this process.

The control process should act as a feedback mechanism leading to appropriate revisions in tactics and, in some cases, modification of original goals and strategies. In Figure 1.1, this strategic control mechanism is represented by the arrow coming out of the implementation box and feeding back into previous stages of the strategy formulation process.

Although we have described the strategy formulation process as consisting of three major activities, in reality it is much more complex and iterative. If, for example, a firm is caught offguard by a competitor's entry into its market, its first reaction may be a tactical price adjustment. This would be perfectly appropriate if a strategic analysis is also undertaken. The firm could conduct an in-depth analysis of competitive reaction rules and assess the advisability of formulating a new segmentation and differentiation strategy. Using this updated analysis, goals could be reexamined, new creative program alternatives formulated, resources committed, and plans laid. The firm would, in effect, have used the implementation and control steps of the strategy formulation process to develop a planned strategic response.

LEVELS OF STRATEGIC ANALYSIS

The analysis that precedes the development of good, sound strategy can range in complexity from clear thinking to a formal mathematical model. In our view, a useful way of thinking about types of analysis is to organize them into three levels:

- *Level I* involves a clear structuring of the questions and issues and understanding of interrelationships. Creative alternatives are generated. Inputs of phenomena and outcomes are based on judgment.

- *Level II* consists of simple mathematical models to aid in understanding complex interactions. Both judgment and market research inputs go into this analysis. Simulations are used to explore the implications of strategies.

- *Level III* uses sophisticated mathematical models and statistics to provide in-depth quantitative representation of phenomena. Research data are empirically based and some market experimentation is done. Optimization algorithms are used to find profit-maximizing strategies.

All marketing strategy problems demand Level I analysis, and most benefit significantly from Level II analysis. Although Level III analysis is often expensive and time-consuming, it can pay off where major resource commitments are required.

In order to make these distinctions clearer, we can consider a commonly used procedure called "gap identification." This procedure is applied to (say) the next five years in order to compare the forecast of sales of the firm's current products to the firm's goals. A Level I approach to this problem consists of judgmentally drawing a graph such as that shown in Figure 1.2. This graph shows a gap developing in year 3 (1990) and increasing thereafter. The forecast is based on judgmentally projected sales in each line of business. Estimates reflect managers' views of the stage of the life cycle for each existing product, the arrival of new products on the market, and their rate of successful acceptance. Major creative inputs may be needed to fill the gap.

Level II analysis uses a mathematical life-cycle forecasting model (see Chapter 6) to enhance managerial judgment. The model identifies the phase of the life cycle for each product, and projects future sales of existing products. Sales of new products are forecast through use of premarket forecasting models that draw on consumer research to predict the diffusion of innovation (see Chapter 14). The effects of new strategies are judgmentally derived, but the underlying forecast and representation of phenomena are based on the output of simple mathematical models.

Finally, Level III analysis is accomplished through the utilization of a comprehensive computer-based model that not only generates forecasts but also optimizes the application of resources to new and existing products over the planning period.

We emphasize Level I and II analyses in this book. Every manager must be proficient in Level I analysis in order to function effectively. We maintain, however, that a substantial increase in the productivity of marketing decision making can be obtained by use of Level II analysis. We emphasize Level II methods for understanding underlying phenomena,

FIGURE 1.2
Gap Identification

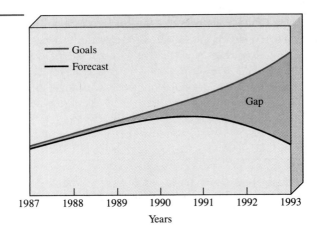

Years

creating alternatives, and encompassing selected advanced issues in decision making and control. Since Level III analysis can be a powerful adjunct to the strategy formulation process, we have also outlined state-of-the-art Level III methods as applied to each phase of that process. This book does not attempt to teach ''marketing science'' model building, but does provide a perspective that will enable the reader to determine when complex models are appropriate and how to assess their managerial value.

There are three rules to observe when doing analysis:

1. Always do Level I analysis.
2. Never do Level II analysis before you have carried out a comprehensive Level I analysis.
3. Never, never do Level III analysis without having completed effective Level I and Level II analyses.

OBJECTIVES OF THIS BOOK

Specifically, we want you to:

1. Learn a framework for strategy formulation and implementation.
2. Understand the concepts and analytic methods underlying advanced marketing decision making.
3. Acquire the ability to apply quantitative and qualitative thinking to marketing strategy problems in complex environments.
4. Be aware of the state of the art and appreciate the role of advanced quantitative methods in strategic analysis and decision making.

We use text, chapters, cases, and computer exercises to achieve these objectives. The text emphasizes analytic methods, models of underlying phenomena, and state-of-the-art analytic approaches. Computer exercises are provided to give you a better understanding of quantitative methods and their appropriateness in strategy formulation. Cases stress problem recognition and integration of underlying concepts in creating and implementing solutions to problems. The cases are not intended to teach specific mathematical techniques, but rather to teach you how to analyze and develop effective strategies in environments characterized by complexity, ambiguity, and rapid change. We want you to be able to employ *quantitative and qualitative approaches*; we want you to be able to *identify the correct problems as well as to formulate their solutions*.

Chapter 2 contains an exposition of the strategic planning process outlined in Figure 1.1. Then, in Chapters 3 and 4, we present two cases (Godfather's Pizza and GE UDF jet engines); in analyzing these cases, you should consider each of the issues in strategy formulation. By the end of Part One, you should have obtained a good grasp of the challenges of dealing with the uncertainties, risks, and resource commitments characterizing marketing strategy. In Part Two of the book, we address the phenomena underlying such strategy. This discussion emphasizes conceptual frameworks and Level II analytic techniques. Although we do not expect you to be able to utilize these methods on your own, you should know when to direct your marketing research or strategic planning staff to conduct such analyses. And you should be aware of what they can and cannot do.

Next we integrate these underlying techniques into the diagnosis of a specific managerial situation, considering strengths versus weaknesses and threats versus opportunities, and then use case studies to advance your understanding of the complex role of analytic support. The appropriate level(s) of analysis and the specific techniques to be employed, of course, vary with the situations presented in each case. Determining the appropriate level of analysis and techniques to be employed is often a major part of the challenge in confronting a strategic marketing problem.

After strategic analysis, we consider selected issues in the strategic decision areas of new products, established products, product lines, and corporate and worldwide management (Part Three). Since it is impossible to deal comprehensively with all of these areas, we review the basics and then select issues in each area that are the most critical to marketing management as it approaches the twenty-first century. For each area selected, we consider the nature of the issue, appropriate analytic methods, and strategic implications. We use cases to embed the issues in a wider context and to advance your understanding of the role of advanced methods of problem determination and solution generation. Throughout Part Three we stress the transition from analysis to goal, program, and resource commitment decisions.

Implementation and control topics are addressed in Part Four. Clearly, we could not cover all the many important tactical decisions that must be made in marketing. Instead, we have directed our attention toward translating strategy into detailed action plans and maintaining strategic coherence throughout implementation.

We close the implementation section with an integrated marketing plan (Chapter 23). Often one of the first tasks a marketer faces at the beginning of his or her career is that of writing the marketing plan for a product or product line. In this discussion, we emphasize the analysis of the underlying phenomena and the relationship between a longer-range strategy and the annual financial plan.

The final case, which deals with IBM's strategies in typewriters and PC printers (Chapter 24), is comprehensive and raises most of the issues discussed throughout the book—strategic analysis, decision making, and implementation.

Finally, we end the text with observations on the future of advanced marketing strategy formulation and decision making.

QUESTIONS FOR DISCUSSION

1. What do you think is the greatest success in marketing in the last ten years? What marketing strategy was used? Why was it successful? What lessons can we learn from this success?

2. What do you think is the greatest failure in marketing in the last ten years? What marketing strategy was used? Why was it a failure? What lessons can we learn from this failure?

3. Given the fact that marketing analysis takes time and money, is it not easier and just as effective to use marketing intuition to formulate marketing strategies?

4. Under what conditions would Level II analysis be appropriate in addition to Level I analysis?

5. What characterizes decisions and problems that warrant Level III analysis?

6. Why is it important to formulate alternatives when making strategic decisions rather than to develop only one effective solution?

FORMULATING MARKETING STRATEGY

In Chapter 1, we introduced a three-stage process for strategic planning: analysis, decision making, and implementation (see Figure 1.1). In this chapter, we examine these stages in greater detail in order to provide an overall framework for the chapters that follow. Our approach is to view the strategy task from a broad perspective and then to focus on specific marketing dimensions.

   This chapter gives you a set of issues to consider when you study the Godfather's Pizza and General Electric cases. It should sensitize you to the role of analysis in the complex and sometimes confusing strategic decision-making process.

STRATEGIC ANALYSIS

The first step in formulating a strategy is to conduct a comprehensive diagnosis of the marketing phenomena relevant to a particular situation. Diagnosis should be driven by a clear understanding of the underlying marketing phenomena: consumer decision making, position in the life cycle, segmentation, positioning, market response, and competitive behavior. These phenomena are the building blocks for market diagnosis leading to an understanding of the size and growth of the market and its competitive environment. Once we understand the phenomena that underlie the behavior of our markets, we can assess our *strengths and weaknesses* relative to those phenomena. *External threats and opportunities* need to be carefully examined so that we can apply our strengths to areas with high potential and avoid major environmental pitfalls. Finally, we must link the resulting diagnosis to our *corporate capabilities, strategies, and constraints* in order to ensure a good fit between our marketing strategy and major corporate goals and objectives. These diagnostic components must be integrated if they are to provide an effective basis for strategy formulation (see Figure 2.1).

   In Chapters 5 to 9, we consider the marketing phenomena in depth; here we look at the three key diagnostic components and how they fit into the overall strategic planning framework.

11

FIGURE 2.1
Analysis and Diagnosis

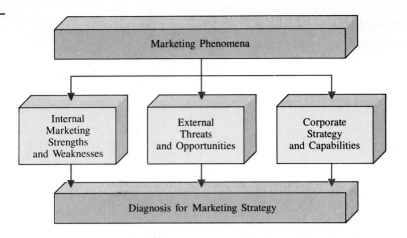

Strengths and Weaknesses

It is useful to begin by identifying the key marketing strategic success factors for a given business, and then to rate ourselves on them relative to the competition. It is critical that managers at all levels of the organization devote considerable attention to this task since it will provide the basis for subsequent diagnosis and strategy formulation.

Table 2.1 lists the more common strategic marketing success factors. Some of these may not be relevant in a given situation; others may be required. For each factor, we need to rate ourselves relative to the strongest competitor we face. Our objective should be to develop our strengths and overcome our weaknesses. Then if our strengths are greater than those of our primary competitors, we can be said to have a strategic advantage. If we maintain this advantage, we will have a basis for a sustainable, successful long-term strategy.

TABLE 2.1   Strengths and Weaknesses—Success Factors

STRATEGIC SUCCESS FACTOR	RATING VS. COMPETITION				
	Much Worse	**Worse**	**Equal**	**Better**	**Much Better**
Leverage from Phenomena					
Sensitivity to changing market needs					
Understanding of how and why customers buy					
Innovative response to customer needs					
Consumer loyalty					
Linkage of technology to market demand					
Link marketing to production					
Investment in growth markets					
Knowing when to shift resources from old to new products					
Long-term view of market development and resources					
Ability to target and reach segments of market					
Identify and exploit global market					
Product-line coverage					
Short time to market for new products					
Lack of product-line overlap					

TABLE 2.1 (continued)

13

FORMULATING
MARKETING STRATEGY

STRATEGIC SUCCESS FACTOR	RATING VS. COMPETITION				
	Much Worse	Worse	Equal	Better	Much Better
Identification and positioning to fulfill customer needs					
Unique positioning advantage					
Strong brand image and awareness					
Understanding of competitors' capabilities and decision rules					
Sensitivity to cues for cooperation					
Prevention of price wars					
Aggressive commitment when required					
Willingness to form interfirm coalitions					
Maximizing payback from marketing response to resources					
Marketing Variables					
Distribution coverage, delivery speed, and prominence					
Cooperative trade relations					
Advertising budget and copy effectiveness					
Promotion magnitude and impact					
Sales force size and productivity					
Customer service and feedback					
High product quality					
Patent protection					
Low product cost					
Ability to deliver high value to user					
Large marketing resource budget					
Decision Making					
Marketing research quality					
Information system power					
Analytic support capability					
Develop human resources					
Attract the best personnel					
Managerial ability and experience					
Quick decision and action capability					
Organizational effectiveness					
Learning systematically from past strategies					

Three sets of factors are included in this table. The first reflects the organization's ability to leverage its understanding of underlying marketing phenomena into well-designed and executed marketing strategies. The second relates to the effectiveness of specific marketing-mix elements. The third set of factors reflects the organization's decision-making and organizational capabilities, stressing information and analytic support as potential competitive advantages.

The rating of the success factors can be done for the corporation or business unit as a whole, but we have found that it is more effective to rate a tightly defined product/ market sector. This sector may be one in which we currently have substantial business, or one that we are considering entering. In carrying out this diagnosis, our objective is to identify unique competitive strengths that can be sustained to achieve high levels of profits. Weaknesses that are identified through this process need to be rectified or balanced by corresponding advantages. Alternatively, we would avoid such product/market sectors altogether. A firm seeking success in a given product/market sector ought either to have a significantly higher rating than competitors on one especially critical factor or a superior average profile across all success factors.

Once we have arrived at a comprehensive view of our marketing strengths and weaknesses for each product/market sector, we can match our profile to specific market opportunities and environmental threats in order to specify a platform for market selection, program generation, and resource allocation.

Threats and Opportunities

Major changes that are likely to occur in our existing markets should be identified by a careful examination of trends in the environment. Emerging opportunities should be balanced against developing threats to our position. We recommend the use of a formal rating procedure to ensure that this diagnostic step is carried out comprehensively (see Tables 2.2 and 2.3). If possible, the rating should be done first on an overall basis, and then for each existing and potential market.

Threats: The threats listed in Table 2.2 reflect only some of the dangers likely to impact the success of a marketing strategy. Managers must be careful not to be blindsided by unexpected developments. In markets characterized by rapid and/or discontinuous environmental and technological changes, it is essential to employ very sensitive monitoring techniques and to have comprehensive contingency plans in place. Fortunately, major changes generally occur at a relatively slow, steady pace, and thus can be readily anticipated by alert managers. Most significant technological changes, for example, can be forecast by managers who regularly inspect academic journals, interview research leaders in public institutions, and fully exploit their professional contacts.

TABLE 2.2   Threats to Business or Market Segment Success

THREAT	MAGNITUDE			
	Very Small	Small	Large	Very Large
Reactions from existing competition				
New competition likely to enter				
Competition by vertical integration				
Channel cooperators begin competing				
Decreased entry costs				
Price/promotion war				
Change in consumer tastes and values				
Increasing power of buyers				
Increasing segmentation				
Technological change				
Material availability and supplier prices				
Economic stagnation				
Inflation				
Regulatory changes				
Foreign exchange fluctuation				
Political/social changes				
Environmental pollution				
Takeover/merger				

TABLE 2.3   Business and Market Segment Opportunities

OPPORTUNITY	MAGNITUDE			
	Very Small	Small	Large	Very Large
Merger				
Technological change				
Political, economic, social trends				
Size of market				
Growth of market				
Unfulfilled customer needs				
Gaps in existing product positions				
Market not segmented				
High margins				
Few or weak competitors				
Stable price structure				
Vulnerable to entry				
Low entry cost				
Low exit barriers				
High response to sales, advertising, promotion				
Transfer cost experience				
Low investment				
Low risk				
Matches our strengths				

An astute manager is especially sensitive to competitive threats. Traditional competitors may react as they have in the past, or changes in their managements or strategies may cause a fundamental shift in their competitive behavior. Potential entry by new competitors, with either equivalent offerings or functional substitutes, is often a major threat. This is particularly true when the firms currently in a market have achieved tacit cooperation. In scanning the environment for potential entrants, it is critical to consider not only other domestic manufacturers but also channel members and suppliers, who may seek to integrate vertically, and foreign firms, which may come to view their markets as global. Moreover, managers should remain alert to the possibility that a stand-alone product or service will be replaced by an expanded systems offering. In the 1980s, for example, the trend in medical diagnostics was toward an electronic, computer-based systems business.

Political and economic changes can also represent major threats. Massive oil price increases during the 1970s caused U.S. consumer preferences to shift to smaller cars. Japanese automobile manufacturers capitalized on this shift in preferences; they greatly increased their market shares by emphasizing high-quality, fuel-efficient small cars. It is interesting to note that even after oil prices had (in real terms) dropped to pre-1970 levels in the mid-1980s, most Americans appeared to retain their preference for smaller cars. A careful understanding of the effects of environmental changes on customer buying behavior is essential if we are to map the marketing implications of economic, political, and social trends.

A final external threat comes in the form of takeovers and mergers. A company that fails to aggressively pursue its markets and its stockholders' interest may find itself the target of a hostile takeover. If your company is acquired in this way, you may find yourself out of a job. If a key competitor is acquired, the competitive environment in which you operate may be fundamentally transformed.

Structural Analysis of Industries: A powerful conceptual approach to understanding competitive threats and opportunities is to analyze the structure of rivalry in the industry. Porter's (1980) paradigm is shown in Figure 2.2. The intensity of rivalry among firms in the industry is determined not only by their strategies but also by the potential impact of new entrants, suppliers, substitute goods, and customers.

A structural analysis of this rivalry is based on the economics faced by each participant as well as on the pace of technological change. The rivalry among existing firms will depend upon the number and balance among firms, industry growth, fixed costs, experience and scale effects, and the height of exit barriers (e.g., specialized production plants that cannot be converted or sold, labor agreements, links to other businesses of the company, emotional commitments of managers, and government and social restrictions). An industry made up of few firms with high exit barriers and slow industry growth is likely to be characterized by high rivalry, depressed margins, and low profits. Easy exit, rapid industry growth, and few competitors frequently represent high profit potential.

New entrants, however, will often be attracted to an industry with high profits, good growth prospects, and a comfortable competitive environment if the cost of entry is recoverable through future sales and profits. Barriers to entry may be present in the form of proprietary technology, requirements for large investments, economies of scale born of the experience curve, customer loyalties, customer switching costs, distribution channel power, raw material supply, government licensing, or defensive strategies by existing competitors (deterrent pricing or retaliation). Understanding such economies and barriers will allow a clear assessment of the threats from new entrants. When entry barriers are high, our threat and opportunity analysis can be directed solely at the firms presently in the industry, but in most markets, there is a real threat of new entrants. At the same time, low entry barriers can provide opportunities for us to enter other markets if our firm's goals cannot be fulfilled within our current business scope. When entry barriers are low, profits are also likely to be low. When entry barriers are high, profits will be higher, unless exit barriers are high enough to cause intense rivalry and reduced margins.

Rivalry can also be influenced by the power of suppliers and buyers. Suppliers may be able to control the supply and therefore the price of raw materials or components, or they may threaten to integrate forward into the industry. Conditions like these will cause industry profits to be lower as suppliers use their bargaining power to extract premium

FIGURE 2.2
Forces Driving Industry
Competition
Source: Reprinted with
permission of The Free Press, a
Division of Macmillan, Inc.,
from *Competitive Strategy:
Techniques for Analyzing
Industries and Competitors* by
Michael E. Porter. Copyright ©
1980 by The Free Press.

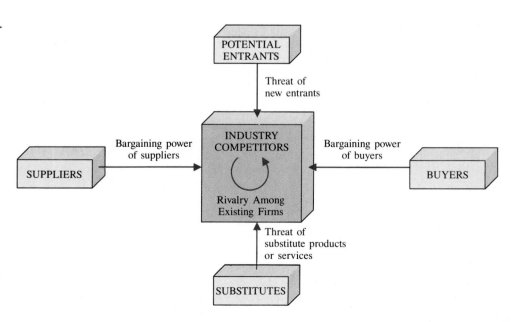

prices. Buyers can similarly influence profits. If there are few buyers and many suppliers, or if a single buyer represents a significant proportion of the firm's business, margins are likely to be lower. If buyers have the capability of integrating backward, their bargaining power will be increased.

Substitute products from outside the industry can significantly influence the competitive structure. When substitutes are available, they may set a price ceiling and strongly impact the nature of the industry. For example, the technical evolution of packaging from steel can, glass, and paper boxes to aluminum, plastic containers, and composite bags dramatically changed the nature of rivalry in the packaging industry, leading to the emergence of a new, wider set of suppliers offering alternate technologies.

Understanding how rivalry is structured by economic and technical determinants provides an invaluable perspective in isolating threats to current business and identifying opportunities in other businesses.

Opportunities: Table 2.3 lists a number of factors that represent opportunities. Note that the first such action listed as a strategic opportunity, "Merger," is also listed as the last threat in Table 2.2. A threat in one situation can be an opportunity in another. The possibility that your company might be raided and then dismembered and stripped of its assets is clearly a threat. If, however, a merger provides your company with needed skills and resources, and if you are able to keep your job, you should view the merger as a strategic opportunity. Technological, political, economic, and social changes can also have either positive or negative effects.

In some countries, for example, the role of women has changed little, while in others, it has undergone a major shift. The role of women in the United States has changed dramatically in recent years, with over 50 percent of women now working outside the home. For some industries (e.g., floor wax and sewing machines), this development has been a major threat, while for others (e.g., fast foods, timesaving appliances, female business attire), it has created major opportunities. In formulating marketing strategies, managers must recognize major trends and fully understand their implications, both for the industry in which they operate and for their own particular strategy.

When considering entry into a new market, we need reliable information concerning market size, market growth, potential margins, and competitive structure. If the market is not now segmented or if there is a positioning gap, we may be able to enter it by carving a niche where we can establish a unique advantage. Low entry and exit barriers reduce the risk in entering a new market, and may make the opportunity more attractive financially. But low entry and exit barriers are a double-edged sword in that they encourage other new competitors to enter. In many cases, we would be better off selecting market opportunities with high entry barriers (despite the greater risk and investment required) so that we can enjoy the advantage of fewer potential entrants. This is especially true under the following conditions: (1) exit barriers are low; (2) we have a comparative advantage in a critical resource (e.g., control of a distribution channel); *and* (3) a strong market position, once achieved, is likely to be sustainable (e.g., a market characterized by high advertising or sales force–induced product loyalty).

Market opportunities often are available for only a limited period of time. If we do not get in quickly, a competitor may preempt the market or a rival technology may become so entrenched that it will be difficult to displace. An accurate estimate of the "window of opportunity" for market entry is critical. If the "window" is narrow, as it frequently is in high-tech and high-fashion markets, timing may turn out to be the most important strategic success factor.

The last factor listed in Table 2.3 reflects the importance of integrating our diagnosis of strengths and weaknesses with our identification of strategic opportunities. If our unique skills match the critical success factors in an otherwise appealing market, there is a high probability that that market will turn out to be attractive to us. The objective of strategy formulation is to build unique and enduring competencies and then select markets where these competencies provide a sustainable competitive advantage.

Corporate Capability

The third element in a comprehensive marketing diagnosis (Figure 2.1) is the incorporation of output from the firm's overall strategic plan. Marketing is an important *input* to the corporate strategic planning process, but it also derives specific goals, perspectives, and constraints from that process. The two frameworks must be fully integrated if both corporate and marketing strategies are to be truly effective.

Capability: The analysis of strengths and weaknesses we outlined in Table 2.1 focuses on marketing. Additional competitive advantages (or disadvantages) that may be present at the corporate level must also be identified and integrated into the diagnosis. Our firm may have significant corporate strength in the production area, for example. If our manufacturing processes are flexible, we may be able to increase product variety and make frequent changes in production schedules (thereby meeting the specific needs of multiple customer segments) without incurring a heavy cost premium. In contrast, if we operate with a "fixed" production line that utilizes "just-in-time" inventory control, we may enjoy lower costs but be constrained by rigid product specifications and production schedules.

Similarly, a parent corporation with "deep pockets" may provide an important competitive advantage. Its financial power may allow us to surmount high entry barriers to enter a new market, or permit us to raise the marketing stakes (e.g., higher advertising expenditures, more price promotion) in a market crowded with more competitors than we deem desirable. Conversely, if our parent corporation's financial resoures are restricted, it would probably be prudent for us to target smaller markets with low entry costs and high margins.

Since marketing tends to be a people- and skills-intensive function, human assets are a very important source of advantage. (In Japan, the human resource director is often the most important manager after the president of the firm.) Corporate research and development can also provide a significant long-run advantage, although many organizations have found it difficult to link corporate R&D (as distinct from business unit R&D) and marketing as effectively as they desire. In some instances, corporate R&D is simply too remote from the market to be adequately responsive to customer needs and decision criteria.

Constraints: Managers must clearly understand the corporate constraints under which their strategy will operate. If corporate management demands 12 percent ROI (return on investment), low risk, and five-year payback, it makes little sense to devote resources to the development of hypersonic aircraft or holographic television sets. Corporate ethical policies may also constrain marketing strategy. One major pharmaceutical firm with which the authors are familiar will not market high-dosage vitamins because it believes they are ineffective for most consumers, perhaps even harmful. Corporate style may also dictate available options. Where top management is highly conservative and operates in a bureaucratic fashion, managers would probably be wasting their time and resources considering entry into markets characterized by fickle consumers and short life cycles. Marketing management has an ongoing responsibility to keep management apprised of the implications of corporate policies and practices for marketing strategy. When telecommunications in the United States became deregulated and demonopolized, key marketing managers at AT&T argued vociferously that a virtually complete change in corporate culture would be required if the company was to compete effectively in the new environment.

Product/Market Business Definition. A critical output of corporate strategy is definition of the business. Do we define our business by designating selected customer needs and specifying particular products or markets, or do we focus on the exploitation of a particular technology? Is our market scope (1) the market for instant film and cameras, (2) the recording and display of images in the home, or (3) the application of instant photographic technology? In the first case, the definition is by product, in the second by function, and in the third by technology. The charter for a particular business unit may be defined according to any one, or any combination, of these dimensions. Such a "business definition" should be one of the major concerns of the corporate strategy formulation process (see Abell, 1980). Marketing diagnosis must effectively interface with corporate strategy in order to ensure that whatever marketing strategies are developed are fully consistent with corporate perspectives.

Once we have an overall definition of our business, we need to understand the markets that compose it and decide where we will participate in the offering of products. We need to know how the market is structured and the nature of the competition in each product/market segment. We may elect to concentrate our marketing on specific segments where we have a competitive advantage, or we may decide to cover all business opportunities with a comprehensive set of product offerings. The decision will depend heavily on our analysis of the phenomena of market segmentation, life cycle, and competitive response. This analysis, together with our analysis of our strengths and weaknesses and threats and opportunities, should figure in corporate decisions concerning which markets to target and how fully to cover them.

Another issue in product/market strategy is whether we want to grow by taking our existing products to new markets, by adding new products to serve our existing markets better, or by attacking new markets with new products. If we elect to take our existing products to new markets (e.g., new countries in a global expansion), our emphasis will be on distribution, selling, advertising, promotion, and pricing to reach targeted markets. If we decide to add products to serve our current markets, our emphasis will be on product development. If we choose to enter new markets with new products, we must be willing to undertake major product design and marketing implementation programs and to incur a considerable degree of risk.

To be effective, marketing needs to ask: What are the bounds of the market territory we can explore? Can we move into new product areas in the pursuit of customer functional needs? Are all segments of the market to be considered? Should we be interested in both the industrial and consumer implications of our technology (e.g., can we move beyond computer processing into fields such as the reproduction and dissemination of computer analysis)? How widely should we construe the total system that we will seek to provide (e.g., in the office of the future, will we attempt to be a total system provider or restrict our attention to word processing and file keeping)?

In assessing our strengths, weaknesses, threats, and opportunities, we should produce ratings for both the overall market and specific submarkets in which we are interested. A product/market business definition derived from corporate strategy is useful in limiting the number of submarkets to be considered. Nevertheless, it is generally a good idea for marketing managers to explore adjacent submarkets that do not fit their business's current market definition. It is marketing's responsibility to advocate doing whatever is required to serve customer needs fully, even if this means modifying the definition of the business.

Marketing should resist focusing too hard on product or technology in the business definition. While corporate strategy provides critical inputs into the formulation of marketing strategy, marketing strategy should likewise provide feedback leading to revisions of corporate strategy and business definitions.

Diagnosis for Marketing Strategy

While it is useful for analytical purposes to disaggregate the three components of marketing diagnosis, the power of the methodology we are employing lies in its ability to take the whole picture into account when formulating marketing strategies. The next step in our process is, therefore, one of synthesis. A useful approach to this task is to prioritize both corporate and marketing strengths according to their ability to generate competitive advantage. This prioritized inventory of our competitive advantages should then be used as a framework for developing programs that build upon and strengthen our distinctive competencies. Identified weaknesses must be similarly prioritized, and either eliminated or finessed by selecting product/market opportunities where they do not figure as strategic success factors.

Major environmental threats have important implications for the strategies we develop. Failure to avoid such threats, or to develop programs that surmount them, is a recipe for disaster. Similarly, environmental opportunities should be exploited in as timely a manner as possible in order to preempt competition and obtain maximum positive leverage for our strategic market position.

Frequently companies find that an overall diagnostic synthesis is not precise enough to encompass the differences among the many markets in which they operate. Strategic success factors, threats, and opportunities may vary widely among individual product/market sectors. One method for addressing this diversity is to synthesize strategic diagnoses for each product/market sector in which we are interested.

Figure 2.3 is an example of synthesis by product/market sector. Analysis of our strengths vis-à-vis the strategic success factors for each sector allows us to evaluate the degree of our competitive advantage in that sector while taking into account the relative attractiveness represented by the opportunity. If we portray the existing and potential sectors on a grid, we can then prioritize them. The most desirable are those in the cell representing a combination of high attractiveness and major competitive advantage (cell 1). Highly attractive markets where we have no competitive advantage (cell 2) are not as desirable, but programs to develop unique capabilities in these markets might have a high long-term payoff. Major competitive advantage in moderately attractive markets (cell 4) could offer opportunities if we are able to isolate the most desirable segments, but we may prefer to allocate scarce resources to markets with higher potential. The cells on the diagonal (cells 3, 5, 7) should generally be given lower priority, although it may prove worthwhile to develop programs to improve strengths relative to strategic success factors or to cause the market to become more attractive (e.g., advertising to accelerate industry

FIGURE 2.3
Attractiveness and
Competitive Advantage of
Markets
Note: Points represent markets.

Note: Points represent markets.

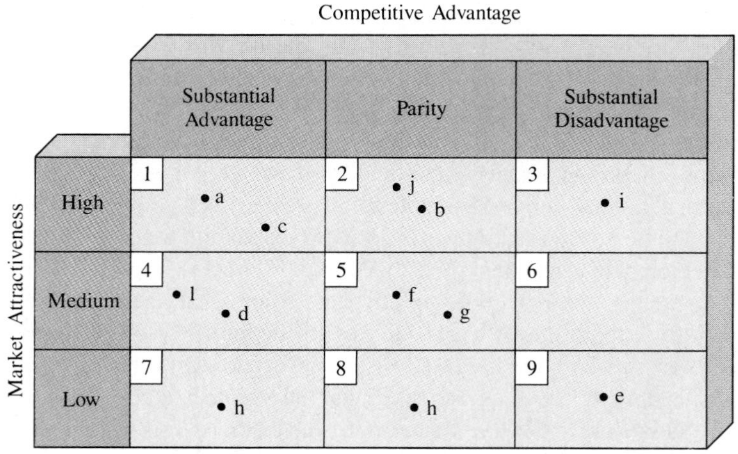

growth). Otherwise, resources currently allocated to these cells should probably be shifted toward cell 1. Cells 6, 8, and 9 represent unattractive markets where our skills do not generate a competitive advantage. Therefore, it probably makes sense to develop programs to reallocate resources from these cells to more advantageous market opportunities.

Market attractiveness and competitive strength matrices of this type were first used at General Electric in the 1960s and have since been widely adapted by other companies (see Lorange, 1975; Robinson, Hickens, and Wade, 1978; Hax and Majluf, 1984; and Day, 1984). While in the past this technique has been used most often to specify strategies, we prefer to use it primarily for summarizing the diagnostic process. In our experience, the relationships among strategies for individual product/market sectors are often far more complex than suggested by matrices of this type. Individual product/market sectors may turn out to be highly interdependent in customers, technology, or manufacturing.

Moreover, shifting resources from one cell of the matrix to another may require expenditures that outweigh the theoretical benefits of the reallocation. Techniques of this sort are useful to the manager in summarizing and crystallizing key strategic issues, but they are no substitute for managerial judgment and analysis.

In our view, the leading cause of failure in strategy formulation is poor or insufficient analysis. Inappropriate higher-level analysis, not based on sound Level I analysis, can, however, be as dangerous as no analysis and may misdirect efforts to find a competitive advantage. In formulating strategies, organizations often exaggerate their strengths and minimize their weaknesses, at the same time underestimating their competitors' abilities and the speed with which they can respond or attack. The only effective remedy for this tendency is comprehensive, explicit Level I analysis backed by targeted Level II or Level III measurement and modeling. We believe that an analysis of the marketing phenomena underlying strategic diagnosis is so important in formulating effective strategy that we have devoted half of this text to the analytic process. We have yet to encounter a strategic marketing situation that would not have benefited from explicit analysis.

STRATEGIC DECISION MAKING

This section provides an introductory view of the major steps in sound marketing decision making that *follow* the analysis step. Strategic analysis should lead to the subsequent steps of (1) goal definition, (2) program formulation, (3) resource commitment, and (4) implementation (review Figure 1.1). This section briefly discusses steps 1 to 3. The next section of this chapter considers the major issues of implementing marketing strategies, including motivation, evaluation, and control.

Goals

No business function, including marketing, can operate completely independently. To be effective, the marketing process must operate within a hierarchy of goals. At the top are corporate goals, which should reflect the interests of the firm's major stakeholders, especially stockholders. This level in the hierarchy generally defines the product/market scope of the business and establishes key targets for the corporation as a whole. Corporate policy goals need to be translated into specific, measurable criteria. In the United States, stock price and earnings per share (and their growth rates) occupy the highest position in the hierarchy, with return on assets (or investment) close behind. Because financial markets and corporate raiders typically pay close attention to these measures, top management understandably tends to give them very high priority. In Japan, adequate returns, building market share, and providing premium products are more likely to be paramount goals.

Within the hierarchy of corporate goals, "marketing" is usually responsible for sales revenue, market share, and operating profit. Thus, marketing strategies are formulated to achieve specific sales, share, and profit objectives. It is critical that "marketing" recognize it has a responsibility for profits, not just for sales and share. In many leading companies, marketing is responsible not only for absolute profits (in dollars) but also for achieving target ROA and ROI results.

The "gap analysis" presented in the first chapter of this book is an example of the strategic use of explicit goals. You will recall that when projected sales levels over time fail to reach sales growth goals, a "gap" between forecasted sales and goals is identified. A similar approach could be used to assess the likelihood of achieving goals defined according to various measures of profitability. In either case, when a gap has been identified, the next step is to develop programs to increase sales (whether through increased share of existing businesses or entry into new businesses), reduce costs, or both.

It is useful to employ the diagnosis of strengths and weaknesses and threats and opportunities reflected in the market attractiveness and competitive advantage matrix (Figure 2.3) as a framework to establish goals for individual businesses within the firm. Attractive markets where we have competitive advantages should generally receive top priority in resource allocation, while attractive markets where we can build a competitive advantage should be viewed as opportunities. Before we can define specific share, sales, and profit goals for each business unit, however, we must consider the likely effects of allocating various levels of resources to these businesses. If we increase advertising and promotion by 50 percent in an existing business where our competitive advantage has already led to very high share, it is unlikely that we would earn very much incremental profit. Rather, we need to evaluate the outcomes of various levels and mixes of resources, and then use these evaluations in an iterative goal-setting process. We begin by setting target levels of share, sales, and return on investment. Next we assess the probability of achieving these goals with specific programs, and then, if necessary, we reexamine the goals that we started with.

If the "best" program we can come up with exceeds the goals we initially established, we should adjust the goals upward (although some managers have a tendency to "sandbag"[1] under these circumstances). Conversely, if we are unable to come up with a program that is likely to achieve the preestablished goals, we should lower those goals (or perhaps we should be replaced by a manager who can create new programs that will achieve the goals). It is far better to admit the probable outcomes of a particular marketing program early than to permit an organization to operate under false delusions that put it on a collision course with failure. There is a delicate balance between setting goals that "inspire" an organization and proposing unrealistic objectives that cause managers to write plans they know to be meaningless. When unrealistic goals are set, the whole strategic planning process becomes merely a game. Effective goal setting causes an organization to stretch to achieve its full capability, but is realistic enough to generate commitment on the part of its managers.

Program Formulation

In seeking the best way to achieve a given set of goals, it is usually appropriate to generate a number of alternative programs and then evaluate and prioritize them. Two generic strategies that can inspire specific alternatives are cost leadership and differentiation (Porter, 1985). Cost leadership is based on building volume so that, given economies of scale in production, the lowest cost will be achieved. Differentiation is based on identifying a segment in the market and developing a product for that segment that is significantly

---

[1] To underbudget in order to improve measured results.

different from products offered by the competition. The latter strategy avoids direct price competition. Even though costs may not be low, the positioning allows premium margins to be earned.

Many programs can be formulated around these generic strategies, but you should not feel constrained by them. The basic understanding generated by analysis of the underlying marketing phenomena should trigger the generation of many creative program alternatives.

Programs can be analyzed through the use of models that forecast the impact on share, sales, and profits of various combinations of marketing actions under various market response assumptions. Forecasts developed in this way can be used iteratively to select the "best" program, possibly to fine-tune it further, and also to evaluate how well its expected outcome achieves the goals established for the business.

A program represents a major strategic thrust for the business. Here are some examples:

1. Allocation of $10 million to R&D and marketing to develop a performance advantage in telecommunications equipment and service that would allow entry into NASDAC electronic stock trading. The $10 million would cover fifty person-years of effort over three years, the generation and market testing of four product concepts, the creation and evaluation by customers of two prototype products, and the development of a comprehensive marketing strategy (physical product, communication execution, and distribution channel) for premarket forecasting.

2. Increase the size of the sales force by 25 percent (thirty additional representatives at $150,000 each, including overhead costs) to allow direct selling of raw materials to automotive component suppliers and manufacturers previously sold by distributors, and the expansion of the product line by 10 percent. The program would also involve retraining the existing sales force to be materials science–oriented problem solvers rather than product pushers.

3. Reduction by 50 percent in the advertising and promotion budget for a line of toothpastes, while lowering food and drug channel trade margins and reducing the number of SKUs (stock keeping units) in the product line by eliminating half the flavor varieties and package types.

Note that these programs are described with respect to specific shifts in resources (funds, people, and/or facilities) and changes in past practices. The first is an example of a program to fill a gap in future sales and profits through the development and introduction of a new product. The second reflects additional commitment to an existing business and a shift to direct customer service and toward building long-term customer relationships. The third is a milking strategy that cuts resources in the expectation that, while sales will drop, profits will increase because of more-than-proportional cost reductions. These programs can be delineated by the resources required, the nature of the strategic change desired, and the business unit(s) most affected.

Programs should be generated to create competitive advantage in existing or new markets or to counter competitive or environmental threats. Competitive advantage will be obtained by directing the firm's strengths toward market opportunities where those strengths represent key success factors.

The diagnostic process discussed earlier in this chapter provides an important input to the generation of effective programs. Managers should be careful not to become too committed to a particular program too early in the process. In formulating a marketing strategy, the first step should almost always be to think widely about alternatives.

After an alternative has been generated, the next step is to evaluate that alternative on its potential to achieve the desired goals, the degree of risk involved, and how well it matches the firm's corporate and marketing strengths. In carrying out this task, it is helpful to list factors that are considered important and to rate the alternative with respect to each factor on a 5-point scale. These ratings, in turn, can be incorporated into a PC spreadsheet model showing sales and profit results. Level II models that simulate the outcomes of the programs can also be built and utilized at this stage. Subsequent chapters will present Level II models that can be helpful in selecting among alternative marketing programs.

Resource Commitments

After we have decided on our overall strategy and developed the marketing programs to carry it out, the next step is to convert those programs into specific budgets and plans. Typically, these lay out in considerable detail the specific actions to be undertaken, the spending associated with each action, and the results anticipated for each time period.

For the first program example outlined above, the more detailed plan might contain the following items:

- Assigning a senior project manager from the existing pool of R&D managers to the new project. Hiring a new project manager at $90,000, plus bonus, to fill the senior project manager's current position.

- Hiring one senior (fifteen years experience) and two junior electrical engineers trained in computer science. Salaries to be $75,000, plus bonus, at the senior level, and $47,500 at the junior level. Hiring three technical assistants at $25,000 each.

- Hiring one new product/market manager (trained in marketing research and product development) at $60,000.

- Allocating 2,000 square feet of office space and 1,000 square feet of lab space in R&D lab building to the project. Project to be charged $50,000 per year for this space.

- Budgeting $500,000 for customer contact, travel, and marketing research projects.

- Making a capital expenditure of $900,000 for computers and communication equipment.

This budget reflects specific decisions on resources to be allocated to achieve program objectives. The plan includes specific timing for the application of resources to the project, as well as the milestones against which the project's progress will be evaluated. In practice, such milestones tend to be more difficult to define for R&D than for, say, upgrading the sales force. An R&D program may call for the development of two finished concepts and the completion of 25 percent of the basic computer programming for the network by the end of the first six months, but the exact timing may depend on technical breakthroughs that are difficult to predict. A sales program, conversely, can be very specific in setting targets, such as hiring thirty sales representatives in the first quarter, completing both their training and the retraining of the old sales force by the end of the second quarter, phasing out the ten existing distributors by the end of the third quarter, and adding the proposed new products to the line before the end of the year.

Models are often very helpful in evaluating alternate levels of funds that might be allocated to each item in the budget and the plan. In our third example of a program, where it had been decided to "milk" a toothpaste product line, we might want to look at the relative costs and payoffs of cutting the promotional budget for consumer coupons versus reducing expenditures for point-of-purchase promotions. There are models that can help us do this. In Chapter 15, we will describe several models that can be used to simulate the effects of such promotion changes. These models work with variables such as the levels of various types of promotion for each brand, size, flavor, and specific month of implementation. Today the availability of electronic checkout data (derived from UPC-scanning cash registers) makes precise modeling and the comparison of predicted and actual results possible in package goods. While this level of detail and precision is not yet feasible in industries lacking such rich data sources, the use of models to evaluate the level and timing of resource allocation is becoming increasingly widespread.

After completing our detailed budgets and plans, we may find that the predicted results fall well below our goals. In this case, we would reconsider our original goals and programs (see the feedback loops in the diagram in Figure 1.1) and then either develop more effective programs or renegotiate the goals. In the iterative application of this process, our objective should be to establish realistic, achievable goals that are both meaningful in motivating managers and useful in monitoring and controlling the program.

IMPLEMENTATION

The best strategy in the world is of negligible value unless it is implemented effectively. The history of both business and warfare is replete with examples of superior strategy losing out to superior implementation.

Implementation involves two separate types of activity. The first consists of converting plans into tactics, carrying out the tactics, and controlling the results. The second is the strategic decision-making process itself, which shapes the ways in which the organization actually implements the decision activities shown in Figure 1.1.

Tactics from Strategies and Plans

To translate strategy into tactics requires developing even more highly detailed programs, budgets, and plans. Very specific actions are now defined, and the time frame becomes shorter. The program and plan may span five years, but the tactical specifications are typically for only a year or two.

In the sales force expansion program described above, a sales training activity is planned. Tactics in support of this plan would include defining the sales training method (e.g., contracting with an outside firm to conduct a professional selling skills workshop), deciding who is to be trained (e.g., all district sales managers [three days], as well as the national sales manager [one day]), selecting the site for the workshop (e.g., the Atlanta Hyatt Conference Center), and specifying its timing (e.g., the third week of May 1991).

Working on the assumption that both the proposed sales force expansion and the training activity will be completed as planned, the next step would be to set specific sales goals (by product and by customer) for the new sales force. Each sales representative would be given a customer list, which would include some customers who had been previously served by distributors and some who had been called on by the direct sales force. Once these account assignments have been made, it would be appropriate to establish specific sales objectives for the sale force (e.g., the conversion of all previous distributor customers during the next three months, the expansion of business with existing customers by 10 percent per quarter for the next year, and the addition of two new customers per month in the last six months of the year).

Control

The tactical objectives derived from plans become the control standards. Actual sales and intermediate results are compared to these standards, both on an aggregate basis and for individual products and customers. If the agreed-upon objectives are not achieved, the reasons for the shortfall must be examined and corrective actions taken. We might, for example, wish to conduct additional sales training, replace our least effective sales representatives, or create new sales incentives. Or we might decide that new tactics are needed to counter unanticipated competitive actions.

Tactical adjustments of these kinds are the most common response to a shortfall, but the underlying strategy should also be reviewed. Is the replacement of the distributors working? Are our new problem-solving approaches turning out to be as effective with our customers as we had hoped? Is there, in fact, as much of a market for materials substitution as we had envisioned?

Confronting such "hard" questions is a critical first step in achieving *strategic control*. Answers to these questions may be sought through a number of approaches, including analysis by management, interviews with customers, and the application of more formal models. Whatever the means, achieving strategic control as soon as possible will give us an early warning system as to the strategy's effectiveness. If the strategy is wrong, it is foolish to waste tactical resources implementing it. Instead, we should seek new strategies by reviewing our underlying assumptions and analyses and repeating the strategy formulation process described above. This activity is depicted in Figure 1.1 by an arrow from implementation back to strategic analysis.

Failure to achieve goals forces the organization to change its ways. Willingness to engage in strategic revision should not, however, be limited to cases where shortfalls have occurred. It is possible that our situation may have changed for the better; in this instance, revised strategies can lead to much better results than had been anticipated. If, for example, a key "opinion leader" customer has found our new product by accident and discovered important new uses for it, it makes sense for us to modify our strategy significantly to take advantage of this fortunate occurrence. Capturing the benefits of such serendipity requires close customer contact, sensitivity, and a flexible strategy. We will return to this important subject in the final section of this book.

Implementing the Strategic Planning Process

Although the sequential process of analysis, program formulation, goal definition, resource commitment, and strategy implementation is logical and compelling, it is difficult to carry out in practice. Numerous factors conspire to prevent effective strategic planning. Many businesses do not take time to develop strategies. Others write detailed strategic plans but fail to follow them. The most common excuse for this failing is that short-run pressures overwhelm long-run issues. Managers continually involved in "putting out fires" find it difficult to consider actions that will produce a payback in three to five years. Pressure to "make the numbers" and deliver promised quarterly sales and profit levels to stockholders often leads to a short-term focus. Under this kind of management, long-term thinking and investment planning are discouraged.

Although top managers often do retain a strategic perspective even under such pressures, at lower organizational levels harried managers typically consider demands for inputs into the strategy formulation process a diversion from what they perceive to be more critical short-term activities. Their reluctant participation can result in a "Five Year Plan" that is vacuous and largely irrelevant. Such plans, often handsomely bound, are put on the shelf to gather dust, unread, let alone acted upon. We discuss in more detail why this happens in the final section of this book, but we note here that an important part of every effective strategy is a plan for its dissemination, understanding, and acceptance throughout the organization.

Effective strategic planning requires commitment from all levels of management in order to gain meaningful input for analysis, creative ideas for programs, reasonable requirements for budgets, and tactical action alternatives. Iteration of goals, budgets, and plans is necessary as the strategy flows from corporate headquarters to business units, and from business units to product groups. An effective strategy reflects operating managers' shared perspectives on where they are going, why they are going there, and how they will get there. When this perspective is complemented by an organizational structure and reward system that is linked to the strategic objectives, the probability of successful strategy formulation is greatly increased.

CONCLUSION AND TRANSITION

We illustrated the strategic development process in a neat and structured way in Figure 1.1. In the real world, it does not happen quite so cleanly. Typically, the process is more iterative, while many activities take place at the same time. Program ideas may, for example, emerge in the course of developing tactics for other programs. Goals may be revised downward in one business unit because of disappointing results, and revised upward in another business unit because of a promising new acquisition. Many activities may be going on at any one time, and it is important to pull together the pieces regularly (at least once a year) through a comprehensive strategic reassessment and detailed reviews of programs, budgets, and plans.

Working with the cases in Chapters 3 and 4 will give you a deeper understanding of the complexity of the strategy formulation process, as well as of the difficulties imposed by time pressures, incomplete information and models, uncertainty, and human factors.

In this chapter, we have explored a strategy formulation process consisting of analysis, strategic decisions, and implementation. We have argued that the strategist's notions of strengths, weaknesses, threats, and opportunities are best comprehended by thorough analysis of underlying strategic phenomena: customer decision making, life cycles, segmentation, positioning, market response, and competitive strategy. We devote a chapter to each of these underlying marketing phenomena (Chapters 5 to 10) and provide three cases that allow you to work with these phenomena in strategic marketing decision-making environments (Chapters 11 to 13). In each case, you will want to identify the underlying marketing phenomena and gauge their primary implications for marketing strategy. When you have completed this analysis, you should have a solid grasp of the diagnostic processes that form the basis for sound strategic judgments. You should be able to determine where we are, how we got there, and how the environment in which we operate is likely to change. Only when you are confident of your ability to answer these questions will you be ready to address the central strategic issues: (1) where do we want to go? (2) how do we plan to get there? and (3) why do we think that we will be able to attain our goals?

While the basic logic of the strategic process applies to virtually all types of decisions in marketing, the focus in subsequent chapters will be on key strategic issues that concern the development and introduction of new products (Chapter 14), established product management (Chapter 15), product-line management (Chapter 16), and corporate and worldwide marketing (Chapter 17). For each of these topics, the basic issues will be reviewed, and selected state-of-the-art decision-making approaches will be addressed. Chapters 18 through 21 are comprehensive cases selected to provide experience with the strategy formulation process and a focus on one of the decision areas. Implementation issues are discussed further and linked to the annual marketing plan in Chapters 22 and 23. The IBM case laid out in Chapter 24 provides an opportunity for integration. The text closes with some observations on the future of marketing.

QUESTIONS FOR DISCUSSION

1. How does our understanding of the basic marketing phenomena affect our assessment of strengths/weaknesses and threats/opportunities?

2. How does marketing strategy relate to corporate strategy? What is in corporate strategy that is not in marketing strategy?

3. In a matrix of market attractiveness and competitive advantage, what specific factors would you use to measure attractiveness and advantage?

4. Should goals be set before considering programs and resource commitments or after?

5. What is the difference between a generic strategy and a program?

6. Describe the differences between a program, a plan of resource commitments, and tactics.

7. Compare and contrast "tactical" and "strategic" control.

8. What factors might account for a failure of the strategic planning process that would result in changes in the tactics implemented in the market?

REFERENCES

AAKER, DAVID. 1988. *Developing Business Strategies*. New York: John Wiley & Sons.

ABELL, DEREK F. 1980. *Defining the Business*. Englewood Cliffs, NJ: Prentice Hall.

DAY, GEORGE S. 1984. *Strategic Market Planning*. St. Paul, MN: West Publishing Co.

———. 1986. *Analysis for Strategic Market Decisions*. St. Paul, MN: West Publishing Co.

GELB, BETSY D., AND GABRIEL M. GELB. 1986. "New Coke's Fizzle—Lessons for the Rest of Us." *Sloan Management Review*, Fall: 71–76.

HAX, ARNOLDO, AND NICOLAS MAJLUF. 1984. *Strategic Management: An Integrative Perspective*. Englewood Cliffs, NJ: Prentice Hall.

KOTLER, PHILIP, WILLIAM GREGOR, AND WILLIAM RODGERS. 1977. "The Marketing Audit Comes of Age." *Sloan Management Review*, Winter: 25–44.

LORANGE, PETER. 1975. "Divisional Planning: Setting Effective Direction." *Sloan Management Review*, Fall: 77–91.

McGINNIS, MICHAEL A. 1984. "The Key to Strategic Planning: Integrating Analysis and Intuition." *Sloan Management Review*, Fall: 45–52.

PORTER, MICHAEL E. 1980. *Competitive Strategy*. New York: The Free Press.

———. 1985. *Competitive Advantage*. New York: The Free Press.

ROBINSON, S. Q. J., R. E. HICKENS, AND D. P. WADE. 1978. "The Directional Policy Matrix: Tool for Strategic Planning." *Long Range Planning* 17: 8–15.

GODFATHER'S PIZZA

Developed in collaboration with James Hawes III[1]

In early September 1988, Herman Cain, president of Godfather's Pizza, and a member of the management group that had just purchased the company from the Pillsbury Company in a leveraged buyout, was trying to shape a course of action for the troubled fast-food chain. In the twenty-eight months since he had joined Godfather's Pizza, Cain had achieved what more than one industry observer had characterized as a miracle, but he knew that Godfather's Pizza was still far from being out of the woods. While franchisee relations had been greatly improved and a number of new products and initiatives had been launched, what had been achieved, in Cain's view, was essentially a process of consolidation. Godfather's Pizza had fallen to a number five ranking in the pizza segment of the fast-food industry, and had not kept up with the industry growth rate in recent years. The key question in Cain's mind was how Godfather's Pizza should be positioned in light of slowing industry growth, intensifying competition, and Godfather's Pizza's limited size and resources relative to the competition.

COMPANY HISTORY

Several years prior to starting Godfather's Pizza, its founder, William "Willy" Theisen, had earned his living by collecting bills for a finance company and parking cars for a downtown Omaha parking lot. In the early 1970s, he got a job as manager of an apartment complex, and soon afterward opened Wild Willy's, a bar that rapidly became popular with his young tenants. A friend of Theisen's, Greg Johnson, who had been a Pizza Hut manager, opened a pizza restaurant next door to the bar. This restaurant served a new type of pizza (see Exhibit 3.1) which Theisen and Johnson had developed in an apartment

---

[1] This case is based largely on and incorporates considerable material from Mr. Hawes's M.I.T. M.S. thesis (1988), which should be consulted for specific notes and sources. Certain data have been disguised, and details of the LBO alluded to in the case have been omitted. Mr. Cain's thought processes at the time of the LBO have been inferred from published accounts.

kitchen, allegedly using the "self-cleaning" oven setting in order to obtain high enough temperatures. By 1973, the two enterprises were engaged in a booming business relationship. Willy's patrons were able to order pizza through a passageway between the two establishments, an arrangement that caused the sales of both operations to skyrocket. Theisen and Johnson joined forces to form Godfather's Pizza, and shortly thereafter the twenty-year-old Theisen bought out his partner. Within ten years, Godfather's Pizza had become the country's second-largest pizza operation, surpassed in sales only by Pizza Hut.

Unwittingly, Theisen and Johnson had come in on the ground floor of a trend toward thicker pizza. Research conducted for Pizza Hut, the largest pizza franchiser with about 3,100 restaurants, had suggested that 40 percent of their customers wanted a thicker crust. It was not until 1975, however, that Pizza Hut began offering a thick "pan pizza," which soon came to account for 35 percent of their business. By that time, Godfather's Pizza had perfected the thicker-crust pizza and was growing rapidly.

Theisen and Johnson disagreed over the reasons for their initial success. (One former executive described the first venture as a gold mine that opened at 4:00 P.M. and closed at 1:00 A.M.). Johnson claimed that they got customers by advertising free delivery to nearby apartments. Theisen said Wild Willy's bar drew crowds of young people who craved "thick and juicy" pizza with their beer. John Chisholm, one of the first franchisees and later the owner of thirty-seven outlets, attributed their success to a good product, lack of competition, and the personal magnetism of Theisen. Several of Theisen's other associates contended that he could "sell ice cubes in the Arctic."

Shortly after buying out his partner, Theisen embarked on an aggressive franchising program. Whatever the causes of Godfather's Pizza's initial success, there could be little question that Theisen's personality was directly related to the company's success as a franchisor. "Under Willy, it was like tent religion," recalled a former Godfather's Pizza executive. The franchisees, he said, wanted to touch the man. Theisen was said to have once borrowed a snowmobile in a blizzard to haul supplies from a stalled truck to his restaurants. As Theisen himself noted, "At Godfather's Pizza, our attitude has always

EXHIBIT 3.1
**Godfather's Pizza's
"Combo"**
Courtesy of Godfather's Pizza, Inc.

EXHIBIT 3.2
Godfather's Pizza's Wall
Menu Layout

SEATTLE ADI

GODFATHER'S PIZZA				S P E C I A L T Y T R A N S L I G H T	LUNCHEON BUFFET		
Original (Thick Crust) or Golden (Light, Buttery Flavor)					All You Can Eat Pizza and Salad		
	Large	Medium	Small		1 Medium Slice	2 Medium Slices	
Deluxe Cheese					1 Medium Slice, One Trip Salad & Drink		
Toppings					BEVERAGES		
Specialty						Pitcher Large	Regular
Super Combo (with descriptions)					Soft Drinks		
					Beer		
GOLDEN CRUST DOUBLES					Iced Tea, Coffee or Milk		
2 Cheese Pizzas					OTHER (or blank slat)		
Added Toppings (Both Pizzas)					Salad Bar (With Pizza)		
Mini Pizza (Cheese plus 2 toppings)					Sandwiches Hot Ham & Cheese or Meatball		
Toppings: Meatballs	Sausage	Pineapple			Garlic Bread	Cheese Bread	
Pepperoni Mushroom	Beef	Jalapeno			Kids Meal - Mini Pizza, Soft Drink & Cookie		
Ham Black Olive	Onion	Green Pepper			Mon-Tues Nite Buffet		

been positive, sometimes even blindly positive.'' Four hundred people were invited to Theisen's thirty-fifth birthday party, which featured a huge cake in the shape of a plane and music by a high school band. For his thirty-seventh birthday, entertainment was provided by the Pointer Sisters. On his fortieth birthday, "Willy Theisen's Great Trans-atlantic Birthday Olympics" treated ninety-eight guests to a chartered Concorde flight and five days of London partying and sightseeing. Ground transportation over a twelve-mile route from London's Heathrow Airport to the city was via forty Rolls-Royce limousines, which prompted one airport worker to speculate that it must be either the king of Saudi Arabia or Bruce Springsteen.

Godfather's Pizza restaurants featured a limited menu of pizza, sandwiches, salads, and beverages (see Exhibit 3.2), with pizza normally accounting for more than 80 percent of sales. The restaurants ranged in size from 2,500 to 5,000 square feet, seating 80 to 250 customers in a self-service format. Each unit required an investment of $60,000 to $120,000 in leasehold improvements, and $60,000 in furniture, fixtures, and equipment. Unlike many other fast-food chains, the Godfather's Pizza concept lent itself to a wide variety of building types and locations, such as strip shopping centers, former gas stations, and the premises of failed restaurants. One of the most successful Godfather's Pizza units was a converted mortuary in Sioux Falls, South Dakota.

The interior of a typical Godfather's Pizza restaurant featured raised dining areas accented with rough-hewn wooden posts, beams, and wall paneling, carpeted dining areas, and earth-tone graphics and plants (see Exhibit 3.3). Most units had several video and pinball games for use by customers waiting for their food to be served.

The typical Godfather's Pizza outlet achieved sales of between $400,000 and $500,000, compared with $270,000 for the average pizza chain outlet. It was not uncommon for a new Godfather's Pizza unit to net $75,000 in its first year. The combination of a limited menu, self-service format, and the ability to use low-cost locations enabled Godfather's Pizza outlets to put more money into the product, resulting in a cost of sales considerably higher than for most competing pizza chains. The most popular pizza, accounting for approximately one-third of sales in a typical Godfather's Pizza restaurant, was the Combo, which featured several different toppings. The Large Combo, which weighed almost five pounds and normally served four to six people, sold for $9.75 to $11.50.

The widely publicized success of early Godfather's Pizza units contributed significantly to the rapid growth of franchises in the late 1970s and early 1980s. At the end of 1982, there were 56 company-owned outlets (company stores) and 720 franchises, many of which were held by multiunit operators, the largest of which owned just under 80 units.

31

Each franchisee paid franchise fees consisting of an initial area franchise fee, a license agreement fee of approximately $15,000 per unit, and a continuing fee of 3–5 percent of gross revenues. In addition, each franchisee was required to spend 3 percent of revenue on advertising (a 2 percent contribution to national and regional campaigns, and 1 percent for local advertising). In 1982, fees paid by franchisees represented approximately 35 percent of Godfather's Pizza's corporate revenues.

While Godfather's Pizza had by 1982 become (temporarily) the second-largest pizza chain in both number of restaurants and total sales, company management felt that there was still considerable potential for growth. Roughly 30 percent of the United States was totally untapped, and consumer awareness of Godfather's Pizza appeared to be low even in those areas where the chain did have outlets. In a nationwide survey conducted by *Restaurants and Institutions* magazine, 83 percent of the representative sample of 2,000 households were not familiar with the chain. Of those who did know Godfather's Pizza, however, the overwhelming majority ranked it as their favorite pizza chain. Godfather's Pizza management believed that this study supported their belief that the chain had strong

EXHIBIT 3.3
Typical Godfather's Pizza
Exterior and Interior
Courtesy of Godfather's Pizza, Inc.

growth potential, and planned to open 200 or more units per year over the next several years. It was decided at this time, however, not to seek new franchisees. Instead, the company would accelerate its program of building new company-owned stores and would offer additional franchises to current operators.

In April 1982, Godfather's Pizza went public, with Theisen receiving almost $14 million for a portion of his holdings, but retaining almost 75 percent of the common stock. It soon became apparent that the nature of the company was changing. As ongoing operations (as distinct from franchising) increased in importance, problems began to surface. Theisen, who was convinced that further expansion would dilute the personality of Godfather's Pizza, announced in September 1983 that he was turning over his duties as president and chief executive officer to Charles L. Boppell, a former rival who had been a top executive at Pizza Hut before becoming head of Taco Bell, a chain of Mexican fast-food restaurants. (Both Pizza Hut and Taco Bell were divisions of Pepsico.) Boppell, described as "a numbers guy" with a good track record in the industry, had been considered a rising star at Pepsico.

In January 1984, Godfather's Pizza was acquired in a friendly takeover ($312 million in stock) by Chart House, a Louisiana-based operator of more than 500 restaurants, including Burger King franchises, Cisco's Mexican Food Restaurants, and Luther's Bar-B-Q outlets. Donald Smith, who had been Boppell's boss at Pepsico and had recently joined Chart House, became president of Diversifoods, the new company formed by the merger of Chart House and Godfather's Pizza. According to Theisen, the reunited Pepsico team was "as good as you could get. . . . We felt that if they were not going to do it, it was not going to be done." Theisen became vice chairman of Diversifoods, while the former head of Chart House, William E. Trotter II, became chairman.

Even before the merger, there had been signs that Godfather's Pizza was losing market share to Pizza Hut, whose deep-dish pan pizza seemed to compete directly with Godfather's Pizza's thick, juicy pizza. Pizza Hut had spent several years developing and testing its new product (which resembled Ike Sewell's legendary "Chicago" pan pizza), and then had backed it with massive advertising and promotion expenditures. By 1983, it was believed to represent 70 percent of the chain's pizza sales.

Godfather's Pizza's new management felt it imperative to respond to Pizza Hut's attack with a Godfather's Pizza deep-dish pan pizza, which would be thicker, deeper, and juicier than Pizza Hut's entry. Godfather's Pizza's traditional pizza, a thick-crusted pie loaded with toppings, was relatively easy for restaurant personnel to prepare. By contrast, the new Godfather's Pizza pan pizza significantly increased labor costs and required nearly $10,000 in new equipment per store. Moreover, managers now had to open the restaurants at 5:30 A.M.—four hours earlier than previously—to prepare the deep-dish dough, place it in new "proofing" ovens, and then partially bake the shells.

Supported by heavy promotion, Godfather's Pizza's new pizza at first seemed successful. Then the unexpected happened: rather than paying an extra dollar for an equivalent-sized pan pizza, Godfather's Pizza customers began trading down from large traditional pizzas to cheaper, smaller-sized (but richer and more filling) pan pizzas. Profit margins began to shrink, while sales revenue stayed flat at best. It soon became clear that the new product was a failure. According to one disenchanted franchisee, Godfather's Pizza would have been better off simply copying Pizza Hut's successful pizza, and then inventing some other new product that it could have used to win new customers. Theisen believed that Godfather's Pizza should have simply repackaged its original thick and juicy pizza and served it in a pan. We had a deep-dish and didn't even know it," he lamented.

Internal management strife, compounded by increasingly aggressive competition from Pizza Hut, soon sent Godfather's Pizza into a tailspin. Operating earnings plunged 94 percent in 1984 to $978,000. Some franchisees, rebelling against management, started withholding royalty fees. Theisen resigned, charging that management routinely ignored his advice. Shortly thereafter, the board of directors asked for the resignations of Smith and Boppell.

John M. Creed was hired as Diversifoods' president in January 1985. His first actions were to shelve all expansion plans, dismiss 25 percent of Godfather's Pizza's corporate staff, close a number of unprofitable company-owned stores, and hire Henry V. Pettis as Godfather's Pizza president. Pettis was to improve relationships with franchisees and to pare costs at the unit and corporate levels. He was apparently beginning to have some success with these tasks when—in July 1985—Pillsbury, a diversified international food company that owned Burger King, the second-largest hamburger-oriented fast-food chain, acquired Diversifoods. Most observers believed that Pillsbury was primarily interested in Diversifoods' 378 Burger King franchises, and would soon sell Godfather's Pizza. Apparently because it did not receive an adequate offer for the troubled chain, Pillsbury instead decided to try to turn it around, appointing one of its most promising young executives, Herman Cain, to head Godfather's Pizza in early 1986.

Cain had been raised in a working-class neighborhood in Atlanta, Georgia. His mother was a domestic worker and his father a chauffer. The product of a family with a strong work ethic, Herman graduated salutatorian of his high school class and went on to earn a degree in mathematics from Morehouse College and a degree in computer science from Purdue. First he took a job with the Navy as a civilian mathematician, and then he worked for Coca-Cola for several years before joining Pillsbury in 1977. In early 1982, he was assigned to Pillsbury's restaurant division, where, as described in the *Minneapolis Star & Tribune*:

> The fast track started in the back end of a restaurant. "I was making $70,000 plus," Cain said with a chuckle, "and next thing I knew I was working in a Burger King restaurant in Hopkins, Minnesota." Pillsbury put him on an intense 18-month training program, from flipping burgers to understanding the vagaries of franchisee relations. But within nine months, 36-year-old Cain was named vice president of Burger King's troubled Philadelphia region [which, with 470 units and $440 million in sales, with considerably larger than the entire Godfather's Pizza chain].

Cain had turned the Philadelphia region into one of Burger King's top performers, when Jeffrey Campbell, the president of Burger King, called him in San Francisco to ask him to take on the Godfather's Pizza challenge. Cain's recollection of the remainder of the conversation was as follows:

> I said, "Godfather's Pizza?" He said, "Yeah, and I'd like to talk to you about it. Today is Wednesday. Can we meet on Friday?" I said, "Well, I'm on my way to Colorado. I'm going skiing after the meeting for a week." He said, "Can you come through Miami?" I said, "Jeff, Miami isn't on the way to Colorado." And so we laughed, and I said, "Okay, when do you want me there?" He said, "Is Friday too soon?" So, anyway, I changed my reservations and I went down there and I talked to him. We talked for hours and one of the things that I remember him saying was, "I know that we should be in the pizza business; I just don't know if Godfather's Pizza is the vehicle because I don't know if it is too far gone. A lot of people believe that it is too far gone and if you were to go to Godfather's Pizza and turn it around, it would be the turnaround of the century in the restaurant business. If you can't turn it around, it would probably be a situation where it was too far gone anyway, and your credibility and track record would still be intact."

Cain met Theisen shortly thereafter. Theisen was quite favorably impressed:

> He's one of the smartest guys I've talked to. A new president's a start, but he's really got to take control from day one. If it's do-able, he's going to do it. And if he can't, it's gone.

The fast-food industry, which developed rapidly in the United States during the 1960s and 1970s, owed its origin to the hamburger stands, drive-ins, and soft ice-cream stores of an earlier era. In contrast to traditional "family restaurants," fast-food outlets were typically characterized by at least partially pre-prepared dishes, self-service, extreme informality, a "good value" image, and efficient, rapid service. Carefully devised formats, methods, and advertising gave chains (generally consisting of both franchised and owned units) significant competitive advantages over local "mom and pop" restaurants, with the top ten chains accounting for 62 percent of restaurant sales by 1988. During this period, changes in family lifestyles, in part stimulated by the influx of women into the work force, led to "eating out" and "takeout" accounting for a rising percentage of American food expenditures. ("Fast foods" alone represented 12 percent of the food dollar in 1988.) Spearheaded by McDonald's ("over __ billion sold") and Colonel Sanders' Kentucky Fried Chicken), the fast-foods business had become a $50 billion industry (in the United States alone) by the mid-1980s.

Traditionally, the industry had been segmented by type of food. The largest category was hamburgers (dominated by McDonald's and Burger King); next was pizza (Pizza Hut, Domino's and Godfather's), followed by chicken (Kentucky Fried Chicken and several strong regional chains) and Mexican food (Taco Bell). During the past decade, the pizza and Mexican segments had been growing faster than hamburgers and chicken, but still represented less than 20 percent of fast-food sales (see Exhibit 3.4).

In recent years, the growth of the fast-food industry had been largely a function of new outlet openings (i.e., sales per unit had remained relatively flat). It was becoming increasingly difficult to take additional business away from the few remaining independents or to significantly improve location convenience. According to a 1987 study conducted by Burger King, the fast-food business had moved into the mature phase of the product life cycle, but would continue to grow somewhat faster than other segments of the food industry. There would be considerable differences in the growth rates of various categories, with pizza, seafood, Oriental, and ethnic fast foods growing the fastest, and steak, full menu, chicken, and pancakes falling behind. Increasingly, there would be a blurring of traditional distinctions among food retailers. The restaurant sector would rely more heavily on the takeout and delivery portions of its business, while supermarkets and convenience stores, in an effort to regain their share of the total food dollar, would place much more

	1976	1981	1986	1991
Hamburger	$8.0	$14.3	$25.6	$36.5
Chicken	1.6	2.8	4.5	6.3
Pizza	1.1	3.2	6.9	10.9
Seafood	0.4	0.9	1.3	4.1
Mexican	0.3	1.1	2.6	4.1
Other*	3.2	7.7	10.6	13.8
Total	14.6	30.0	51.5	75.7

* Includes sandwich, steak/full menu, and pancake/waffles categories.

Source: Franchising in the Economy, *U.S. Department of Commerce; TPC Forecasting and Economic Analysts.*

EXHIBIT 3.4
Fast-Food Revenues by Category

emphasis on ready-to-eat items, such as prepackaged salads, fully cooked entrees, and shrink-wrapped sandwiches. It appeared that the fast-food industry faced slower growth, declining productivity, and lower profit margins. The battle would increasingly be over market share, with advertising and product proliferation the primary weapons in the war. Distinctions between fast-food categories would continue to break down (i.e., there would be more cross-category products such as Chicken McNuggets) and there would be greater efforts by all chains to expand their ''dayparts'' (e.g., get into the breakfast market). The Burger King study concluded that the fast-food industry would have to go through a transformation from an undercapitalized, rapid-growth, entrepreneurial, ''seat of the pants'' business to a well-capitalized, less risky, professionally managed, ''branded prod-uct'' business.

Prospects for the pizza category appeared to be somewhat brighter than for fast foods in general. In 1986, pizza was served by approximately 38,000 restaurants (11 percent of all restaurants), with sales of approximately $7 billion. Chains represented 40 percent of pizza sales, a much smaller percentage than for hamburgers or fried chicken. Pizza chain sales had recently been growing at about 10 percent per year, roughly twice the rate for the overall fast-food industry. According to one widely respected industry forecast, pizza sales would grow from $6.9 billion in 1986 to $10.9 billion in 1991, resulting in an increase in pizza's share of the fast-food market from 10.7 percent to 14.8 percent.

Growth of the pizza category seemed to be strongly related to increases in consumer traffic. Between 1983 and 1986, for example, customer traffic at pizza outlets increased from 91.7 million to 127.4 million (by 11.6 percent), while overall fast-foods traffic had increased by only 4.6 percent. (See Exhibit 3.5).

EXHIBIT 3.5
Customer Traffic
(in millions per category)

	1983	1986	% CHANGE	SHARE 1983	1986	CHANGE
Total						
Fast Food	613,264	701,736	4.6%	100.0%	100.0%	0.0
Hamburger	240,127	261,804	2.9	39.2	37.3	−1.9
Pizza	91,694	127,414	11.6	15.0	18.2	+3.2
Chicken	47,929	55,512	5.0	7.8	7.9	+0.1
Seafood	15,067	14,969	−0.2	2.5	2.1	−0.4
Mexican	16,509	23,699	12.8	2.7	3.4	+0.7
Oriental	4,233	8,543	26.4	0.7	1.2	+0.5
Other	197,705	209,784	2.0	32.1	29.9	−2.2

Source: Crest Household Report, 1983–86.

Various studies suggested that the typical pizza customer had at least some college education (67 percent) and was under fifty years old (86 percent versus 80 percent for hamburgers), and that 36 percent of consumers were from two-income families. According to a recent Gallup study, 56 percent of American adults had ordered pizza in a restaurant during the past three months, although there were considerable difference among age groups in this regard:

AGE	% OF SAMPLE ORDERING PIZZA DURING PAST 3 MONTHS
18–24	74%
25–34	76%
35–49	66%
50–64	40%
65 and older	30%

According to *Pizza Segment Report*, published by Burger King, Americans viewed pizza as a "fun food" that encouraged social interaction. The average party size (2.48) ordering pizza was larger than for other fast foods, families with children were more likely to eat at a pizza establishment, and pizza was more likely to be a late-night snack. Moreover, pizza fit trends in consumer lifestyles: it was an appropriate food for "grazing," and was considered nutritional compared to other fast foods. According to the Center for Science and the Public Interest:

> Nutritionists have to note that pizza, though commonly considered junk food, is not junk food at all. . . . At its best, pizza is a balanced meal that teenagers actually eat.

Pizza was regarded as a good value providing excellent variety by many consumers. A family of four could be well fed for as little as $10 to $11. Pizza could have an infinite variety of toppings, crusts, cheeses, spiced sauces, and serving sizes.

The success of pizza had attracted the attention of other food marketers. McDonald's was known to be testing a convection oven-baked McPizza, while Taco Bell had introduced the Pizzaz Pizza (a tortilla shell topped with a layer of beans, meat, pizza sauce, salsa, cheddar cheese, and pepperjack cheese) in 1985. ARA's campus dining division had introduced Itza Pizza (with free delivery on campus) to seventy-five colleges and prep schools. Convenience stores were rapidly adding freshly prepared, frozen, and micro-wavable pizza products to their fast-food offerings. The 7-Eleven chain, for example, was testing both fresh-baked French bread pizza and thin and crispy frozen pizza, selling for .69 cents to .99 cents per slice, with a choice of three toppings. Not to be outdone, a number of supermarket chains were experimenting with new pizza concepts (such as "take and bake centers," where customers could select their toppings and observe the preparation of their pizzas, obtaining a fully cooked pizza in eight to fifteen minutes for $4.50).

The pizza chains were responding to these environmental and competitive trends in a number of ways. The percentage of fast foods actually eaten inside fast-food restaurants had been declining for several years as drive-through windows and home delivery grew in popularity. Increasingly, fast-food units were being referred to as "supply points" rather than "restaurants," with approximately 60 percent of their output being consumed off the premises. Home delivery was becoming more important as consumers (moving into a form of behavior described by some observers as "cocooning") demanded more and more convenience. This trend seemed to be especially important to the pizza industry: Domino's, a heavily delivery-oriented chain, had recently attained the number two ranking behind Pizza Hut, and virtually all the major chains were either offering or experimenting with some form of delivery.

Traditionally, dinner had been the dominant daypart for pizza, representing approximately 79 percent of sales (versus 38 percent for hamburgers). Daypart development was being given high priority by the pizza chains, in the expectation that development of the lunch market would (1) broaden their customer base, (2) build frequency, and (3) increase facility productivity. Innovations such as lighter pizza, pizza-by-the-slice, the use of convection ovens to speed cooking time, and ''luncheon specials'' were intended to increase the pizza chains' share of the lunch market.

The pizza chains were also experimenting with a variety of new product forms, which typically had been pioneered by local establishments. New crusts made from whole wheat flour and sourdough were being developed, while toppings were beginning to include gourmet ingredients such as clams, goat cheese, and even caviar. A vogue seemed to be developing for ''wood-burning'' ovens and for what some observers characterized as ''designer pizzas.'' As the market approached saturation, it seemed likely that innovations aimed at brand differentiation would become increasingly important.

HERMAN CAIN ARRIVES

Herman Cain, Godfather's Pizza's new president, arrived in Omaha on April 1, 1986. Almost immediately he called a meeting of Godfather's Pizza's headquarters staff, telling them:

> I'm Herman Cain and this ain't no April Fools joke. Our objective is to prove to Pillsbury and everybody else that we will survive.

At Campbell's urging, Cain had already begun to develop what he called his ''100-day plan.'' He knew that pizza was one of the fastest-growing segments of the restaurant business:

> I figured that there had to be something internal to the company as to why it wasn't succeeding. It wasn't because the segment was dying, since most of the other competitors in the segment were making a whole lot of money. It had to be how the company was being run. So it wasn't a flat or declining market. It was simply that you had a business here that just wasn't running right. We first had to prove ourselves relative to the basics of business before Pillsbury was going to allow us to spend large sums of capital. The first milestone we had to achieve was to reverse our three-year negative sales trend. It had been negative for three consecutive years. Negative on top of negative on top of negative. Could we reverse that? That would indicate that we could get people back into our stores, could begin to build our average volume back up to where we would start flowing cash like maybe we were worth it.

Cain felt that the managers knew how to turn the company around; they just needed leadership.

> When I got here, the first thing I did was to go through the normal preliminaries. But even prior to that, I identified from the organizational listing the top people in the company in terms of rank and responsibility—all the vice presidents and all the directors—and I conducted nearly twenty one-on-one interviews with those people. I basically asked them two important questions: first, what excites you about your job, what excites you about your work, and what type of person are you? I wanted to get to know the individuals from their perspective and to know a little about what made them tick. I had to assess whether or not these people would fit with my management style and what I wanted to do. The second question I asked every one of them was: If you were president, what would you do? What would be your three top priorities for fixing Godfather's? I wanted to get their perspectives—from various disciplines, various functions, and different levels.
>
> When I got through asking the two questions, I boiled down what everybody said. They all said essentially the same thing, maybe using a little different wording, maybe expressing it a bit differently, but the net was this: the existing base of people were good,

not great, but good. With regard to our strategic and tactical focus—something that the restaurant manager and the hourly employees can say, this is what this company is about, this is where this company is going—they basically came back and said that none existed. They told me that leadership and decisiveness were weak; that our image was blurred; that corporate, field, and franchisee morale were poor; and that the company's infrastructure—training systems, programs and resources, standards, procedures and specifications—all of the infrastructure was weak.

The franchisees, however, were still hopeful. They hadn't thrown in the towel, although they knew things were pretty bad.

I don't claim to be a rocket scientist, so I took my 100-day plan, and I took the result of these interviews, and I merged the two together. I then came back to my management and said, "Okay, this is what you told me, and based upon how I see things, this is what I think we ought to do. This is the direction I think we ought to go and these are some changes we need to make. We are trying to do too much with too little. We have to decide what we are going to do and throw all our resources behind that."

I went on to say, candidly, that "everybody in this world figures we are going to fail." And that addressed the whole morale issue right there. It was the rallying point that we used to get everybody motivated to get this system turned around. And you've always got to have a rallying point. The architect of purpose is responsible for general morale and is responsible for establishing, articulating, effective rallying points for the organization. If you don't, people in an organization will create their own, and they may be negative.

So basically what we did was focus all the resources in every area. We stopped trying to be everything. We just had too much stuff going on. Nobody knew what we were doing. We focused and mobilized all of our resources, including our people, and got the organization enthusiastic about survival. The rest of it was sticking to the basics.

During that process, we worked hard, and we were able to develop several new products, some more successful than others, but if we didn't have that drive to succeed, and didn't have the belief in the company, we might not have tried as hard to make these products successful, and they might not have turned out to be as successful as they were.

We took a lot of chances, we took some risks in terms of capital investments, in terms of marketing programs. We changed agencies overnight because the existing advertising agency wasn't doing the job. I saw that. I had to make a gut call on that the day I walked in here. I went to the Marketing Department and said, "Show me the creative that we're using." They showed me all of the creative. And this is where I exercised my prerogative, and made a decision based on how it came across to me. With no evaluation. That is just a prerogative you have as a leader of the organization. The execution of the creative didn't impress me, the message, if there was one, it didn't impress me. When I talked with the people who were affiliated with that advertising agency, they didn't impress me. So we said, "Let's go out and interview other agencies."

I think we interviewed three or four different agencies. They came in and made a pitch, and we told them what their assignment was. Several very good agencies wanted this account. Here was a company that was the walking dead man of the industry and these advertising agencies were coming out of the woodwork. They wanted to work on this account because they saw it as an opportunity to help turn it around.

And we were able to do that. We were able to reverse the sales trend. [Case writers note: See Exhibit 3.6 for recent financial statements.] We increased sales during the first twelve months I was here; we went from minus 13 percent to plus 10 percent in our core company store base. Our franchisees didn't do quite so well, because they were not implementing the new products in the program as fast as we were.

We didn't have time to test every new product. We didn't have time to test every idea. When you are dying and you've already been down for two of your last gulps—you've got one more to go—you don't evaluate whether that air is clear or dirty, you just go ahead and breathe it and hope it doesn't kill you.

So we basically just kind of threw a lot of stuff on the wall, and said let's see what works. It wasn't panicky, but we had to identify some of the things we wanted to do.

EXHIBIT 3.6
Recent Income Statement
for Godfather's Pizza

Godfather's Pizza, Inc., and Subsidiaries Consolidated Statements of Operations		
	53 WEEKS ENDED MAY 31, 1987	47 WEEKS ENDED MAY 25, 1986
Net sales	$94,475,010	$71,081,092
Other revenues, net	2,023,132	2,393,548
	$96,498,142	$73,474,640
Costs and expenses:		
Cost of sales	76,703,618	60,149,917
Selling, general, and administrative expenses	19,705,773	14,746,012
Interest expense	317,345	375,343
	96,726,736	75,271,272
Loss before income tax credit	(228,594)	(1,796,632)
Income tax credit	14,000	983,400
Net loss	$ (214,594)	$ (813,232)

Source: Company records.

We had a lot of lawsuits facing us, and we resolved every last one of them. Every one of them was resolved or settled in some way, form, or fashion. We had lawsuits—if all of them had gone against us in judgments, it would have represented close to $50 million in liabilities. If we had lost any one of those lawsuits, this company would have gone under. It wouldn't have been able to survive. We would have had to declare bankruptcy.

Cain described his management style as one based on common sense, employee participation in the decision process, and a willingness to make the critical calls. His rallying point was to create "more-than-a-paycheck environment." Cain's commitment to this philosophy was, he believed, illustrated by an action he took in late 1987, when he fired Godfather's Pizza's vice president of finance. According to Cain:

[This executive was] one of the brightest technical financial people around. He was with me during the turnaround and during the hard long days of trying to figure out the turnaround strategy. He was with me for twenty months as right-hand man. But he was not creating, in his own department, a "more-than-a-paycheck environment." People felt intimidated and did not feel good about their environment. It manifested itself in little things like not being flexible on the general leave policy, too many internal policies on absenteeism, lunch breaks, how many breaks could be taken, and so on. It got to the point that some people in the department were too intimidated even to talk to the human resources vice president.

CAIN'S TURNAROUND STRATEGY

The major elements in Cain's strategy were: (1) to improve relations with franchisees; (2) to restructure corporate management; (3) to introduce new products and services; (4) to make more effective use of a limited advertising budget; (5) to streamline the system by eliminating poorly performing units, and then expand on a market-by-market basis; and (6) to settle all pending lawsuits.

Franchisee relations were Cain's first priority. An early endorsement by V
was a very positive starting point. According to some observers, Cain's outgoi
and decisive leadership style had been very important in turning around franchisee and
employee morale. It was said that there was never a dull minute in any group he was in,
and that he had the unique ability to entertain a group of employees or franchisees and
at the same time keep Godfather's overall purpose and mission ahead of the fun.

Franchisee morale was also enhanced by the early success of several Cain-era
innovations. Godfather's Pizza's company-owned stores had replaced the deep-dish pizza
with a double-crusted Stuffed Pie, added a new Hot Slice product to their menus, and
(in selected cases) retrofitted delivery service into existing sitdown units. Delivery soon
generated 20 percent of sales for company-owned units offering the service, with most
of the business being incremental. The stronger franchisees, with very little urging, adopted
these new products and services, and began to show real sales and profit gains.

Management restructuring was also a critical ingredient in Cain's strategy. While
Cain felt after his initial assessment that no massive changes were needed, at least right
away, he had fired the vice president of operations after only two days on the job, and
the vice president of marketing shortly thereafter. According to Cain, these decisions were
based, in part, on prior research through his "network" at Godfather's Pizza, Burger
King, and Pillsbury, but nevertheless were essentially subjective:

> Such decisions are the prerogative of the president, and, although it may seem unfair and
> cruel, you can't be looking over your shoulder if you're going to turn a situation around;
> you have to know that the troops are behind you. Effective leaders must often make instinctive
> calls. The right chemistry must be present with key employees. There were some people that
> I immediately knew would not fit with my management style. So I just went to them and
> said, "I think it best that you pursue another alternative." There were some who were
> borderline in my mind, so I decided to give them three to six months. . . .
>
> I did not make these decisions by simply looking at and evaluating individuals. I visited
> many of our company stores, for example. The morale of the restaurant managers wasn't
> what I thought it should be. A lot of the conditions within the stores were totally unacceptable
> to me. So if this was the net result of his [the vice president of operation's] efforts, he had
> failed.
>
> I also eliminated the five or six regional VPs who were running 140 stores. Wasn't
> that absolutely ridiculous? I hired a new vice president of operations, and expanded his role.
> My goal was to realign for efficiency, not primarily to reduce costs, although costs were
> reduced. Prior to the realignment, our vice president of operations had two vice presidents
> under him, and five regional vice presidents with area managers reporting to them, and district
> managers reporting to the area managers, and restaurant managers reporting to the district
> managers. This structure caused too much filtering of communications and inhibited line
> feedback. We now have three management layers instead of six!
>
> This approach works both ways, I might add. Our franchised operations, in all honesty,
> looked a lot better than our company stores. So the franchise operations guy is still here
> today, and he is gaining even more responsibility.

Cain had been able to recruit a number of experienced fast-food executives from
Burger King (vice presidents of marketing, operations, finance, and human resources),
while Godfather's Pizza's new vice president of research and development came from
Pillsbury.

New Products and Services

New products and services were central to Godfather's Pizza's turnaround strategy. The
Hot Slice, which was available only at lunch, was aimed at Pizza Hut's five-minute express

lunch (see Exhibit 3.7). It was guaranteed to be ready in three minutes or customers would receive their money back. It soon came to account for 20 percent of all lunch sales, and was helping Godfather's company-owned and franchised units to make significant inroads into the lunch daypart.

Godfather's Pizza's deep pan pizza had continued to be a source of contention at many franchise locations. It was eliminated and replaced with a "stuffed pan pizza," which rapidly came to account for between 20 and 22 percent of sales, despite a price premium of $1 to $2 over the top-of-the-line "combo." Cain referred to it as a "gourmet pizza," and felt that it was both superior as a product and easier to prepare than the pan pizza it replaced.

At this time, Godfather's Pizza eliminated the salad bars it had installed in many units, replacing them with prepackaged salads, which, according to the vice president of marketing, were "not a sales success yet, but would enhance the chain's reputation for speed and convenience."

Cain had felt that Godfather's Pizza had to respond to the increasing expectation among consumers that pizza be delivered quickly, fresh and hot, to their homes. In his view, if Godfather's Pizza was going to compete in delivery, it had to bring something "new to the table." He chose the chain's largest market, Seattle-Tacoma, where the chain had fifty-two units, to experiment with a one-number system, in which a customer anywhere in the market could call 223-1111, and have his or her order routed to the closest unit with a guaranteed delivery within thirty minutes. This system was estimated to have cost several million dollars to install, but was considered cost effective given Godfather's Pizza's outlet density in this market. Cain believed that one-number delivery would be an intergral part of Godfather's Pizza's business in the future. He noted that the system would make possible the development of a powerful consumer data base, which could be used for direct marketing and promotion, and speculated that it might eventually be possible to promote a single nationwide toll-free number.

EXHIBIT 3.7
The "Hot Slice"
Courtesy of Godfather's Pizza, Inc.

Consolidation and Expansion

Consolidation and expansion were also hallmarks of Cain's strategy. Approximately 250 of the less profitable units were to be eliminated, as the company embarked on a more rational expansion plan. The expansion plan called for greater concentration of ownership and increasing density through the clustering of stores in selected markets. The first objective was to add units in those markets where Godfather's Pizza already had a presence—wherever possible, through professional multiunit franchisees who wanted to grow their own businesses. In addition, the chain would enter new markets, but only where multiunit ''saturation'' was practical.

In both old and new areas, efforts would be made to tailor the overall concept to specific characteristics of the market or site. Godfather's Pizza opened its first mall unit in Minneapolis' Nicollet Center, for example, to fit that market's understandable preference for connected indoors shopping and eating. Because of the lunch market potential in a downtown shopping mall, this unit was designed with an oven that could cook 1,000 Hot Slices per hour. In Las Vegas, Godfather's joined forces with two other Pillsbury companies, Burger King and Häagen-Daz ice cream, to form a food court at Del Webb's Mint Casino and Hotel.

Standardization

Increased standardization was a key element in Cain's strategy for Godfather's Pizza. To ensure consistency in such key operational areas as quality, service, and cleanliness, new procedures were established and disseminated to all franchisees. Cain felt that some items such as product mix should vary with local conditions, but that quality, service, and cleanliness standards, as well as the prompt payment of royalties and fees, were not negotiable. According to John Chisholm, a multiunit franchisee, one of the reasons for the failure of some Godfather's Pizza's units that earlier had been successful was that absentee investors had attempted to increase margins by scrimping on ingredients. To deal with problems of this sort, Cain had recruited Michael J. Stanley, a former transportation manager at Pillsbury, to serve as director of materials management and synergy. His immediate task was to develop ingredients specifications and a list of approved suppliers and distributors in order to achieve greater standardization and higher quality levels throughout the chain.

Advertising

Effective advertising would be essential to the future success of the chain in Cain's view. The pizza industry was characterized by heavy expenditures on consumer promotion, with most of the major chains spending heavily on short-term discounts (''Only $3.95—this week only'') and cents-off or dollars-off coupons. According to Charles (Charlie) Henderson, Godfather's Pizza's vice president of marketing, the heavy emphasis on promotions had led to a situation where there was virtually no brand loyalty, and people went wherever the best deal happened to be during a particular week. In Henderson's opinion, only chains that were able to obtain brand loyalty and build frequency of purchase would survive ''in the long run.''

Accordingly, Godfather's Pizza had deemphasized discounts and coupons,[2] and was attempting to build on its reputation for quality by stressing convenience, consistency, and speed in its media advertising. Its advertising budget had been running at a fraction

---

[2] It was estimated, for example, that only 20 percent of company stores were currently using coupons.

EXHIBIT 3.8
Godfather's Pizza's New TV Campaign

Television Copy

CLIENT: Godfather's Pizza
DESCRIPTION: "NEW Meatball Pizza II"
LENGTH: (0:30)
BROADCAST ID: GFTV2

VIDEO	AUDIO
GF HEARS DRUMS AND GIVES CUT SIGN	(DRUM ROLL) (0:01) HIMSELF: Look, no one else has the audaciousness as to invent a brand new pizza topped with. . .(0:05)
CUT TO 4-SHOT OF GF AND AS HE LIFTS UP A MEATBALL PIZZA	(DRUM LICK) Meatballs! (0:025) (BUTTON)
DISSOVLE TO SERIES OF CLOSE-UPS, PULL SHOTS, FINISH WITH SLICE COMING AT LENS	Introducing Godfather's Pizza's new Meatball Pizza! A virtual profusion of savory succulence. Each meatball simmering in my singular sauce and then smothered in 100% real mozarella cheese. (0:14)
GF MCU	I oughta get a noble prize. . .(0:02) CHORUS: GODFATHER'S PIZZA NEW MEATBALL! PIZZA! (0:04)
DISSOLVE TO CLOSING SIGNATURE WITH LOGO AND INSERT OF PIZZA	
KEY BOX INSERT OF GF	HIMSELF: DO IT! (0:01) (MUSIC OUT --29:50)

Television Copy

CLIENT: Godfather's Pizza
DESCRIPTION: "NON-NEW Meatball Pizza"
LENGTH: (0:30)
BROADCAST ID: GFTV3

VIDEO	AUDIO
	(MUSIC UNDER)
GF MCU - CAMERA TRACKING IN AS HE HOLDS UP MEATBALL PIZZA	HIMSELF: Hey! Waddayamean you ain't tried my Meatball Pizza? You need an invitation?
DISSOLVE TO SERIES OF CLOSE-UPS, TO INCLUDE FRESH, INGREDIENTS, SAUCING A CRUST, PULLING PIE WITH PADDLE, CUTTING CLOSE-UPS, PULL SHOTS, AND ECU'S OF PIZZA FROM VARIOUS ANGLES	Look, you're starin' at a veritable paradise. I start with my sensational sauce made only from the choicest ingredients on top of which I place an abundance of meatballs -- each seasoned to perfection -- then slow cooked to savory succulence while smothered in 100% authentic mozarella cheese.
DISSOLVE TO GF MCU	There oughta be a law against a pizza this great. . .(0:24)
DISSOLVE TO CLOSING SIGNATURE WITH LOGO AND INSERT OF PIZZA	CHORUS: GODFATHER'S PIZZA MEATBALL! PIZZA! (0:04)
KEY BOX INSERT OF GF	HIMSELF: DO IT! (0:01) (MUSIC OUT -- 29:00)

EXHIBIT 3.8 (continued)

Television Copy

CLIENT: Godfather's Pizza
DESCRIPTION: "Doubles"
LENGTH: (:30)
BROADCAST ID: GFTV4

VIDEO	AUDIO
GF MCU	HIMSELF: Look, puttin' my Godfather's Doubles Pizza offer up against anything else on the street is like comparin' Hamburgers to filets. Ain't no contest.
DISSOLVE TO SERIES OF CLOSE-UPS FINISH WITH SLICE COMING AT LENS	HIMSELF: My golden crust made fresh daily. . . (MUSIC BUTTON) My singular sauce. . . (MUSIC BUTTON) The choicest toppings and more of 'em. (MUSIC BUTTON) HIMSELF: 100% per-cent authentic mozarella cheese.
DISSOVLE TO GF MCU	Hey, get a bigger bang for your buck. (GENERIC 0:10 TAG)
DISSOLVE TO CLOSING SIGNATURE WITH LOGO AND INSERT OF PIZZA	HIMSELF: Want it delivered? Pick up the phone and call. I know your neighborhood. . .
KEY PRICE INFO ON SPECIFIC TAGS	CHORUS: GODFATHER'S PIZZA -- DOUBLES
KEY BOX INSERT OF GF	HIMSELF: Do it!

Television Copy

CLIENT: Godfather's Pizza
DESCRIPTION: "Takeout Special"
LENGTH: (0:30)
BROADCAST ID: GFTV5

VIDEO	AUDIO
GF MCU	HIMSELF: Hey, 'cause I got a heart a gold I'm gonna make ya a deal on your next Take-out order from Godfather's Pizza. Call now. (PHONES RING)
GF DOES TAKE TO LENS DISSOLVE TO SERIES OF CLOSE-UPS, PULL SHOTS	Listen, there ain't enuf superlatives to describe my singular sauce. . . The choicest ingredients and more of 'em. . .100% real mozerella and more of it.
DISSOLVE TO GF	Look, since you're willin' to get off your duff to pick up your Take-out, here's what I'll do for ya. . .(0:13) (0:20:50)
DISSOLVE TO CLOSING SIGNATURE WITH LOGO AND INSERT OF PIZZA BOX TO GO	HIMSELF: (TAKE-OUT SPECIAL TAG) CHORUS: GODFATHER'S PIZZA TO GO. . .
KEY INSERT OF GF	HIMSELF: Do it! (MUSIC OUT -- 29:50)

EXHIBIT 3.9
Godfather's Pizza's New
Radio Campaign

:30 RADIO   "DELIVERY"

GODFATHER: So, there ya are, just sittin' on your duff when you could be sittin' on your duff <u>and</u> wrappin' your chops around a Godfather's Pizza. Call now!

(PHONE RINGS)

GODFATHER: Yeah, I'll deliver whatcha want and soon you'll be swoonin' over my singular crust. Only the choicest toppings -- and more of 'em. Only one hundred percent real mozarella cheese -- and more of it. Baked to perfection. It's Godfather's Pizza, delivered. Hey, call -- I know your neighborhood.

SINGERS: Godfather's Pizza.

GODFATHER: DO IT!

:30 RADIO   "SUPER COMBO"

GODFATHER: Hey, you stuck in a rut? Well, trot your chops to Godfather's Pizza and get more of what ya want with one a my speciality pizzas. Got a capacious craving? Then order up my Super Combo. An outrageous blend of pepperoni, ham, beef, sausage, mushrooms, onions, black olives, green peppers, tomatoes and extra cheese. It'll set ya on yer ear. Look, I put more toppings on more pizzas ... if it ain't at my place, it probably ain't been thought of.

SINGERS: Godfather's Pizza.

GODFATHER: DO IT!

:25/:05 RADIO   "DOUBLES"

GODFATHER: Look, puttin' my Godfather's doubles pizza offer up against anything else on the street is like comparin' hamburgers to filets. Ain't no contest. My golden crust made fresh daily ... my singular sauce ... the choicest toppings and more of 'em ... and 100% real mozarella cheese. Hey, get a bigger bang for your buck.

(5-SECOND INTERVAL FOR OFFER)

SINGERS: Godfather's Pizza ... doubles.

GODFATHER: DO IT!

of its competitors'. While Godfather's Pizza was able to concentrate its expenditures in a somewhat smaller geographic area than its larger competitors, there was considerable concern that it would be increasingly difficult "to get heard" in the midst of so much competitive advertising.

Most tactical advertising decisions were the responsibility of the franchisees, who operated ten regional advertising cooperatives for this purpose. Using company-supplied materials, they could choose among a variety of media, including television, radio, direct mail, and newspapers. (Company stores participated in a similar program, seeking to achieve as much consistency as possible with the franchisees at the local level.)

Godfather's Pizza had employed several different advertising approaches since its acquisition by Pillsbury. According to the trade journal *Restaurant Business*, when the Pillsbury team took over, the market theme for the chain had been: "Godfather's Pizza. Find one. It's Worth It." This theme had played up relative smallness as a strength, implicitly contrasting Godfather's Pizza with the giant chains.

The new management team worked with its newly appointed agency to develop several new copy themes: first "What Are You Waiting For?" (complete with its own musical score), and then the "Pizza Emergency" campaign. In this campaign, individual advertisements featured somewhat weird people undergoing a "pizza emergency" that could only be remedied by the *immediate* consumption of a Godfather's Pizza. Sirens then sounded, and a Godfather's pizza delivery car with a police car's flashing lights would race to the scene to the accompaniment of the "What Are You Waiting For?" theme.

These commercials were intended to be funny, with a "Far Side Gallery" quality to them. One spot, which had received a lot of attention, featured two brothers—one white and one black—testifying as to the benefits of a Godfather's Pizza "two-for-one" special. "That is a gimmick that only a company with a black president could get away with," Henderson chuckled.

Most recently, the agency had recommended a new campaign (see Exhibits 3.8 and 3.9).

CONCLUSION

By mid-1988, it was clear that Cain's strategy was having many of the desired results. The chain now consisted of 600 units (180 company stores, 45 of which had been purchased from franchisees in 1987, and 420 franchised outlets), down from a peak of 911 units in 1984 (see Exhibit 3.10). While system-wide sales had declined slightly in 1987, average unit sales had increased from $368,000 to $402,000, with the average company store averaging just under $500,000. The current advertising campaign appeared to have been successful in increasing consumer awareness; operations and product quality both seemed to have improved considerably; and the vast majority of franchisee problems had been sorted out. Nevertheless, the chain had fallen to a fifth-place ranking in the pizza segment (behind Pizza Hut, Domino's, Little Caesar's, and Pizza Inn; see Exhibit 3.11), and many of its weaker franchisees claimed to be losing money.

In looking forward to the leveraged buyout, Cain recognized that the chain's financial performance would have to improve considerably if it was to both meet the interest payments on its debt and have sufficient resources to invest in Godfather's future. With the company currently operating at approximately break-even, it appeared that an increase in revenues of 15 to 25 percent per operating unit would be required. While this target appeared ambitious, especially in light of intensifying competition in the industry, Cain noted that average per-unit revenues had reached $432,000 in 1983, the last year in which "Wild Willy" Theisen had run the company.

EXHIBIT 3.10
Units Open and Unit Sales, 1983–1987

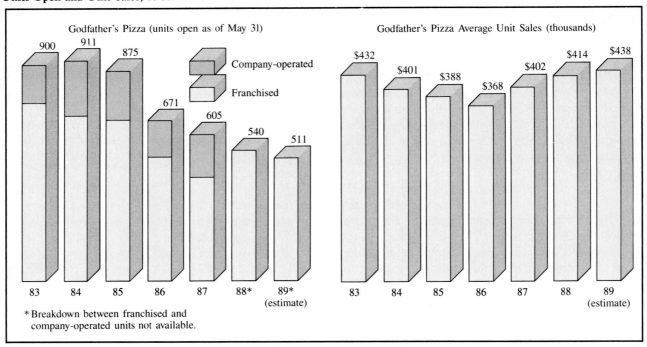

Godfather's Pizza (units open as of May 31)

Company-operated

Franchised

900 911 875 671 605 540 511

83 84 85 86 87 88* 89*
(estimate)

*Breakdown between franchised and company-operated units not available.

Godfather's Pizza Average Unit Sales (thousands)

$432 $401 $388 $368 $402 $414 $438

83 84 85 86 87 88 89
(estimate)

EXHIBIT 3.11
Top 25 Pizza Chains

| | RANKING | | | | NUMBER | TOTAL | GROWTH | |
'88	'87	'86	'85	TOP 25 FRANCHISES	OF UNITS	SALES	UNITS	SALES
1	1	1	1	Pizza Hut, Inc.	5,600	$2.8 billion	−	+
2	2	2	2	Domino's Pizza	4,148	$2 billion	+	+
3	3	3	5	Little Caesars Pizza	2,375	$1 billion	+	+
4	4	4	4	Pantera's Corp.	780	$350 million	*	*
5	5	5	3	Godfather's Pizza, Inc.	583	$245 million	−	−
6	6	6	6	Round Table Franchise Corp.	550	$260 million	+	+
7	8	8	9	Mr. Gatti's	337	$215 million	**	**
8	9	10	10	Mazzio's Corp.	282	$ 66 million	+	−
9	10	9	8	ShowBiz Pizza Time, Inc.	274	$226.3 million	+	+
10	11	13	*	S'barro, Inc.	270	$116.3 million	+	+
11	7	7	7	Shakey's, Inc.	228	$228 million	−	+
12	12	11	12	Dino's/Crusty's USA, Inc.	206	$ 50 million	+	−
13	14	16	20	Rocky Rococo Corp.	131	$ 50 million	+	−
14	*	*	*	Breadeaux Pisa, Inc.	111	$ 20 million	*	*
15	17	*	*	Fox's Pizza Den, Inc.	110	$ 24 million	+	+
16	15	17	18	Peter Piper Pizza	110	$ 60 million	**	+
17	16	14	14	Noble Roman's	99	$ 49 million	−	+
18	23	*	*	Four Star Pizza	90	$ 30 million	+	+
19	18	19	17	Happy Joe's Pizza & Ice Cream	85	$ 26 million	−	**
20	21	*	19	Papa Aldo's	83	$ 15 million	+	+
21	19	18	15	Pasquale's Pizza	81	$16.8 million	−	**
22	25	23	*	Little King Restaurant Corp.	73	$16.5 million	+	**
23	*	*	*	Jerry's Subs & Pizza	68	$ 50 million	*	*
24	*	*	*	Lamp Post Pizza	62	$ 29 million	*	*
25	24	*	22	Numero Uno Pizza	60	$ 30 million	−	−

+ increase   − decrease
* not included in survey   ** no change

Source: Pizza Today, July 1988.

1. How would you characterize the U.S. market for "fast foods"? How is this market segmented? Where is it in its life cycle?

2. How would you characterize Godfather's Pizza's position in the fast-food market? Why has Godfather's Pizza achieved the success that it has?

3. How would you appraise Herman Cain's efforts to date? How would you evaluate his leadership style? What do you consider to be his most significant accomplishments?

4. What do you think are Godfather's Pizza's most critical threats and opportunities?

5. What are Cain's major alternatives? Which would you select? Why?

4

GENERAL ELECTRIC COMPANY
Aircraft Engine Business Group

Developed in Collaboration with Donald Hooper[1]

In late March 1986, senior executives at General Electric's Aircraft Engine Business Group (AEBG) were meeting to decide whether to proceed with the development of the radical unducted fan engine (UDF) on which AEBG engineers had been working for more than a decade. To date, AEBG had invested approximately $50 million in the new technology. It was estimated that an additional $1.2 billion to $1.4 billion investment would be required to complete product design and bring the new engine to the market. While an investment of this magnitude would require the approval of GE's CEO and board of directors, AEBG management was confident that approval would be forthcoming if they could make a strong enough case for the project.

In essence, GE's UDF design removed many of the speed, thrust, and noise constraints that had therefore limited the application of otherwise highly efficient turboprop engines to smaller, slower aircraft. The major benefit of UDF technology was expected to be very large improvements in fuel efficiency. Carrying the same number of passengers the same distance, a state-of-the-art early 1990s aircraft powered by UDF engines would be expected to use 70 percent less fuel than a 1970 vintage Boeing 727, and 40 percent less fuel than a mid-1980s aircraft powered by a state-of-the-art high-bypass fan jet engine.

The UDF's appearance and mode of operation were so radically different from "accepted practice," however, that some resistance to the new concept by aircraft manufacturers and their customers, the airlines, seemed likely. The critical questions seemed to be whether enough UDF engines would be sold despite these considerations; what the timing of such purchases might be; and what share of UDF-type business AEBG could expect to command.

---

[1] This case is largely based on and incorporates considerable material from Mr. Hooper's M.I.T. M.S. thesis (1986), which should be consulted for specific notes and references. All data in this case that are not publicly available (e.g., manufacturing cost data) have been disguised, and certain aspects of General Electric's decision process and reasoning have been simplified.

General Electric was one of the world's largest industrial companies, with revenues of approximately $29 billion and net earnings of $2.3 billion in 1985. A highly diversified corporation, GE competed in industry segments as varied as home appliances, engineered plastics, power generation equipment, aircraft engines, and financial services. In 1985, no industry segment represented as much as 20 percent of GE's sales or earnings, although technical products and aircraft engines had each markedly increased their percentages of corporate revenues over the past five years. (See Exhibit 4.1 for GE sales revenues and net income by industry segment for 1981–1985.)

Between 1981 and 1985, GE's sales had been relatively flat, increasing only from $27.9 billion to $29.3 billion. Net profits, however, had grown by 41 percent, from $1.65 billion in 1981 to $2.34 billion in 1985. Virtually all of this earnings growth had come from a combination of price increases and cost reductions, sources that, in the view of a number of analysts, were unlikely to make as significant contributions to profit improvements in the years ahead.

	1985	1984	1983	1982	1981
Revenues (Sales Plus Other Income)					
Consumer products	3,569	3,858	3,741	3,943	4,202
Major appliances	3,617	3,650	3.078	2,751	3,132
Industrial systems	4,571	4,274	4,228	4,705	5,364
Power systems	5,552	6,010	5,878	6,093	6,015
Aircraft engines	4,712	3,835	3,495	3,140	2,950
Materials	2,459	2,241	2,060	1,791	2.050
Technical products and services	5,197	4,803	3,823	3,546	3.005
Financial services	499	448	397	286	239
Natural resources	—	609	1,579	1,575	1,722
Corporate items and eliminations	(904)	(792)	(598)	(638)	(825)
Total	29,272	28,936	27,681	27,192	27,854
Net Earnings					
Consumer products	217	228	163	146	225
Major appliances	224	223	156	79	82
Industrial systems	143	73	84	148	212
Power systems	449	486	439	384	242
Aircraft engines	381	251	196	161	149
Materials	266	262	182	148	189
Technical products and services	261	232	210	218	144
Financial services	406	336	285	203	145
Natural resources	—	117	301	318	284
Corporate items and eliminations	7	72	8	12	(20)
Total	2,336	2,280	2,024	1,817	1,652

EXHIBIT 4.1
General Electric Company Revenues and Net Earnings by Industry Segment, 1981–1985*
(in thousands $)

* Years end December 31.
Source: General Electric Company, *Annual Report 1985* (Fairfield, CT: 1986), p. 34.

GE's dynamic young chairman Jack Welch was publicly committed to the concentration of GE resources in those businesses that were clearly "winners." According to a number of sources, Welch had essentially told the managers of GE's several hundred business units that unless a business was first (or a close second) in market share in its product category (or had plans for becoming number one or two) *and* also highly profitable (or had the potential for well-above-average profitability), it would be a prime candidate for divestiture. In the five years since he had become chairman, Welch had, in fact, overseen the sale of GE's natural resources and housewares business units, as well as the curtailment of a number of smaller ventures and facilities.

In a widely quoted speech titled "Beyond Incrementalism," Welch had argued that one of the major weaknesses of U.S. business was its tendency to pursue modest, low-risk ventures rather than to tackle the big problems where solutions would be likely to lead to big payoffs. According to Welch, "Nothing less than reorientation to the culture of big institutions is needed—away from incrementalism. Quantum thinking must become a way of life. Not a one-year, one- or two-product program, but a decade-long, total-company process."

THE AIRCRAFT ENGINE BUSINESS GROUP

The Aircraft Engine Business Group (AEBG) was one of GE's largest business units, representing approximately 16 percent of both sales and earnings in 1985. Since 1981, when AEBG had accounted for only 10 percent of GE's revenues and profits, the group's sales had grown at a compound annual rate of 12 percent, well above the corporation's overall growth rate of slightly less than 1.5 percent per year.

By 1985, AEBG's sales of $4.7 billion were approximately evenly divided between military and commercial jet engines. Since the early 1970s, when AEBG had been only a very minor player in the commercial jet engine business, that segment of the group's business had grown explosively, with AEBG surpassing the Pratt & Whitney division of United Technologies as the industry leader by 1985.

During the 1970s and early 1980s, AEBG had benefited by being the airlines' first choice on several aircraft (the Boeing 737, McDonnell Douglas DC-10, and Airbus Industrie A-300) that turned out to be the "best-sellers" during that period, as well as a frequent (although minority) choice on such aircraft as the Boeing 747 and 767. AEBG served the commerical aircraft market with two families of high-bypass turbofan engines: the CF6 family, used on the DC-10, A-300/310, and 747/767; and the CFM56 family, used on new 737's and retrofitted DC-8's.

The CF6 and CFM56 engine families were both derived from General Electric's military engine designs. This "modification" approach to engine development was very attractive from a financial point of view, since the bulk of the heavy development costs for a new engine (as much as $1 billion or more) would be paid for by the government. (AEBG did, however, invest approximately 20 percent of its total revenues in company-funded R&D, an exceptionally high R&D/sales ratio, even in the high-technology sector.) In return for allowing designs it had funded to be modified for commercial use, the government received a "recoupment fee" (essentially a royalty) on each commercial engine sold, as well as benefiting from the experience of the commercial airlines, which would "fly" an engine far more hours than its military counterparts.

Looking forward, AEBG executives expected a flattening (at best) in the military jet engine business as a result of congressional limits on military spending; the diversion of procurement funds to nonaircraft defense systems (e.g., the Strategic Defense Initiative ["Star Wars"]); and the increased tendency for the government to split an engine production contract between two or more manufacturers, with little preference being given to the vendor whose design had been selected. Moreover, a number of observers believed that it would be much more difficult in the future to derive commercial jet engines from their military counterparts, as the performance requirements of the two markets diverged even more sharply. For all these reasons, AEBG executives were considering the development of a totally new engine (''from scratch''), even though such a course represented a radical departure from the derivative development strategy that had served GE so well over the preceding decade.

THE COMMERCIAL AIRLINE INDUSTRY

Prior to the introduction of jet-powered aircraft, only about one in ten Americans had ever used a commercial airline. The speed and convenience afforded by jets, however, caused a significant shift from surface to air travel, with the result that over 65 percent of Americans had flown on a commercial jetliner by the mid-1980s.

One of the primary reasons for this growth in the popularity of air travel was the increase in speed achieved by jetliners in comparison with propeller-driven aircraft. A regression model, developed by a market forecaster at Rolls Royce, concluded that the effect of decreased travel time was an increase in revenue passenger miles of about 42 percent compared with what they would have been at prejet speeds.

The fact that jet-powered aircraft generally were able to carry more passengers and fuel than propeller-powered aircraft also made a major contribution to the growth of the air travel market. Jet aircraft could carry more people over longer distances more quickly, greatly increasing the productivity of an aircraft. As a result, airlines were able to reduce fares significantly, contributing further to primary demand for air travel (see Exhibit 4.2).

Lower fares also led to a change in the demographics of commercial air travel. In the mid-1950s, business travelers accounted for about 80 percent of domestic and 90 percent of transatlantic travel. By the mid-1980s, 50 percent of domestic and 90 percent of transatlantic travel were for leisure purposes. Since many of these new ''leisure'' travelers were highly price sensitive, anything that adversely affected either operating costs (and therefore fare structures) or consumer disposable income, or both, had a substantial negative impact on airline profitability.

Because the demand for air travel was so price and income sensitive, airline profits had been highly volatile since the early 1970s. The oil price shocks of 1973 to 1974 and 1979 to 1980 resulted in significant worldwide economic downturns, unprecedented inflation, and a deep erosion of discretionary income. At the same time, skyrocketing fuel and labor prices greatly increased airline operating costs. In an effort to keep revenues from dropping below day-to-day operating expenses, most airlines lowered their fares considerably, resulting in record losses (which were followed by record profits during periods of economic recovery). As John Newhouse noted in his 1982 book on the commercial airlines industry, *The Sporty Game*:

> . . . perhaps no other industry has endured as many ups and downs—as much ''cyclical shock,'' as it is called. The volatility of the airlines' finances is reflected in their earnings and stock prices. In the early 1960s [before the full positive impact of jetliners had been felt], the average price of airline stock was a little over $5; by 1966, it had soared to $47, but in 1970 [in the midst of a major recession] had fallen 75% to $13. The major, or trunk, airlines earned over $1 billion in 1978 and $400 million in 1979, and lost $225 million in 1980.

Prior to the Airline Deregulation Act of 1978, the Civil Aeronautics Board (CAB) had controlled the airlines' route and fare structures and limited new entrants in an effort to maximize industry stability. Following airline deregulation, the situation changed markedly, with the industry passing through three major stages by the mid-1980s:

1. New nonunion carriers (e.g., People Express) entered the industry by offering lower prices, precipitating the fare wars of the early 1980s. This phase, during which the number of certified U.S. carriers increased from 30 to 130, coupled with the aftereffects of the 1978–1979 oil price shock, caused profits for most airlines to drop precipitously during 1980–1983.

2. Major airlines began to gravitate toward ''hub and spoke'' route structures in which ''numerous flights (the spokes) fed passengers into a large central airport (the hub), where they changed flights (same carrier) to other cities.'' Under this system, airlines often flew less productive, less profitable routes into a hub to feed the longer, more profitable routes—in effect, taking a ''systems approach'' rather than looking at the profitability of each leg of their route structures in isolation.

3. Beginning in 1984, the industry underwent a shakeout and consolidation, with the weaker players going out of business or being acquired by the stronger airlines. In general, the new ''no fringe'' airlines flew older, less efficient aircraft than the majors, which made them vulnerable to competitive pricing actions as the stronger

EXHIBIT 4.2
**Price and Income Elasticity
of Air Travel**

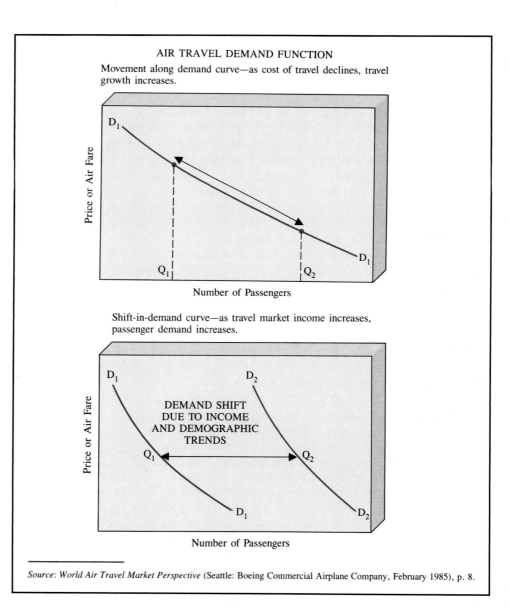

Source: *World Air Travel Market Perspective* (Seattle: Boeing Commercial Airplane Company, February 1985), p. 8.

carriers reduced their own costs through two-tier wage structures, more efficient route networks, and the placing in service of new, more fuel- and labor-efficient aircraft. Moreover, the major trunk carriers seemed to have learned how to compete effectively under deregulation: they used "hub and spoke" routing and "frequent flyer" programs to increase customer loyalty, and cut fares selectively on only those routes under attack by the "no fringe" airlines at a particular point in time.

By early 1986, it seemed probable that both the U.S. and international airline industries would emerge from this period of shakeout and consolidation in relatively healthy condition. In 1985, the U.S. airline industry earned $2 billion (net), while the corresponding figure for other "free world" carriers was about $3 billion. According to some analysts, barring a major recession or oil shortage, these profit levels could be expected to rise as much as three fold by the late 1980s, as demand for air travel began to significantly outstrip capacity.

AIRFRAME MANUFACTURERS

The British-built DeHavilland Comet, which entered commercial service in 1952, was the first jet-powered commercial airliner. Several early crashes plagued this aircraft, however, and it was not until the U.S.-built Boeing 707 began to serve transatlantic routes in 1958 that commercial jet aviation became viable. By the mid-1980s, over 20 models of large commercial jet airliners had been produced, totaling about 8,500 aircraft with more than 1.25 million seats. (See Exhibit 4.3.) According to Boeing Company estimates, the cumulative market value of these aircraft was $181.5 billion (in 1984 dollars), or about $150,000 per seat.

Unfortunately, the cost of developing, certifying, and manufacturing these aircraft had been considerably more than $150,000 per seat. As of 1982, when John Newhouse wrote *The Sporty Game*, only two models were known to have broken even: the Boeing 707 and 727. The resurgence in sales of the Boeing 737 and the McDonnell Douglas DC-9/MD-80 series in 1984 and 1985 may have brought these two models to the break-even point, if one ignores the opportunity cost of the money invested in these programs over such a long period of time.

Boeing, with three of these four profitable aircraft, was one of only two remaining U.S. airframe manufacturers. The other, the Douglas Aircraft division of McDonnell Douglas, had been weakened considerably by the destructive head-to-head competition between its DC-10 and Lockheed's L-1011 in the late 1970s. (Lockheed subsequently withdrew from commercial jet aircraft manufacture to concentrate on its military aerospace business, following a bail out by the U.S. government.) By the early 1980s, DeHavilland, Vickers, Hawker Siddeley, Dassault, and Convair had also withdrawn from the commercial airline business, leaving the field to Boeing, McDonnell Douglas, and Airbus Industrie, a heavily subsidized European consortium.

As this list of casualties suggests, building and selling commercial airliners had proved to be a very risky business. It typically cost a company as much as $2 billion in design, development, certification, and tooling costs to launch a new aircraft program. Superimposed on these nonrecurring costs were even greater operating costs, such as wages and facilities upkeep. The peak cumulative cash outlay generally occurred five to six years after program launch, at which point the cumulative loss often exceeded $5 billion (not including interest). As *The Economist* magazine explained, a new aircraft program could only succeed if it sold "well enough early enough to overcome the burden of interest payments on the initial investment. If 400 aircraft are sold within the first seven or eight years of production (i.e., 12–13 years after the decision to go ahead with the program), the company may break even on its investment."

EXHIBIT 4.3
Unit Sales of Jet Aircraft—Commercial Jet Airliner Scoreboard

Delivering the Jets	1958	'59	'60	'61	'62	'63	'64	'65	'66	'67	'68	'69	'70	'71	'72	'73	'74	'75	'76	'77	'78	'79	'80	'81	'82	'83	'84	Total
707	8	77	91	80	68	34	38	61	83	118	111	59	19	10	4	11	21	7	9	8	13	6	3	6	8	8	8	969
727						6	95	111	135	156	160	115	54	33	41	92	91	91	61	67	118	136	131	97	26	11	8	1834
737										4	105	114	37	29	22	23	55	51	41	25	40	77	92	111	95	82	67	1070
747												4	92	69	30	30	22	21	27	20	32	67	73	58	25	23	16	609
DC-8		21	91	42	22	19	20	31	32	41	102	85	33	13														556
DC-9/MD-80								5	69	152	203	121	54	44	32	29	48	42	50	22	22	39	23	73	44	50	44	1166
DC-10														13	52	67	67	43	19	14	18	36	40	23	11	4	2	379
L-1011															17	39	41	25	16	11	8	14	24	29	14	6	4	248
880/990			14	33	33	16	4	2																				102
757																									2	25	18	45
767																									20	55	29	104
US Manufacturers Subtotal	8	98	196	156	122	75	157	210	319	470	681	498	289	211	202	281	325	280	223	167	251	369	386	397	243	264	196	7082
Comet	7*	19	20	14	13	2	2	1		1																		112
Caravelle		18	39	39	35	23	22	18	18	21	14	11	9	4	6	3												279
Trident							12	18	11	1	11	9	2	13	11	7	4	6										117
VC-10							14	11	7	10	9	2	1															54
BAC-111								34	46	20	26	40	22	12	7	2	4	2	17	6	3							231
F-28												9	11	10	13	19	9	20		13	11	13	13	13	11	19	17	218
Mercure																	6	4										10
A300																	4	9	13	16	15	24	40	45	46	21	19	252
A310																										17	29	46
BAo 146																										7	11	18
VFW-614																		1	4	5								10
Concorde																		1	6	2			3	2				14
Non-US Manufacturers Subtotal	7*	37	59	53	48	25	50	74	82	53	60	71	45	39	36	31	27	43	49	49	33	38	59	62	59	64	76	1361
Total	15*	135	255	209	170	100	207	284	401	523	741	569	334	250	238	312	352	323	272	216	284	412	445	459	302	328	272	8443

* Plus 33 Comets delivered 1952–1957.

Source: Boeing and Company reports. See "The Big Six: A Survey of the World's Aircraft Industry," *The Economist*, London, June 1, 1985, survey p. 8. Copyright © 1985, The Economist Newspaper Ltd. All rights reserved.

A manufacturer's high cumulative investment in a new aircraft was, in part, a function of the fact that marginal costs were extremely high in the early stages of production. On the assumption that at least 500 to 600 aircraft would be built, prices were based on projected costs at, say, the 250th unit. (Costs were expected to decrease about 20 percent with each doubling of cumulative production volume.) Consequently, manufacturers generally experienced very heavy losses in the early years of a new aircraft program. As John McDonnell, president of McDonnell Douglas, explained, "You rationalize each additional cut in price, because with each additional airplane sold, you are further down the learning curve."

In an effort to avoid such ruinous price competition, aircraft manufacturers sought to identify "holes," or high potential niches in the market. However, as a leading industry analyst, Wolfgang Demisch of the First Boston Corporation, pointed out:

> [T]he trouble is there's only room for one manufacturer in the niche, at most two, but not three. Someone loses, and big! The current hole in the market is considered to be a 150-seat plane. But niche holes can bring disaster. One old aerospace executive used to say, "Sure, there is a hole but that doesn't mean we have to fall into it." It was falling into the same hole with McDonnell Douglas on a giant widebody that put Lockheed out of the commercial business.

In recent years, aircraft manufacturers had tended to follow one of two basic development approaches. Boeing and Airbus Industrie opted for the "clean-sheet-of-paper" approach, in which they would design an all-new aircraft for a given niche. McDonnell Douglas, conversely, believed that derivative airplanes (i.e., modifications to existing designs, such as adding a plug to the fuselage to expand seating capacity, or a new engine to improve performance and fuel economy) provided the most benefits for the least cost at the lowest risk. In the view of some observers, the outcome of this battle between two totally different design philosophies would largely determine the shape of the aircraft industry in the 1990s.

AIRCRAFT ENGINE MANUFACTURERS

The aircraft engine industry was similar in many respects to the airframe industry. Its products were based on extremely sophisticated state-of-the-art technologies, requiring staggering lead times (about seven years from initial design to market introduction) and very large investments (over $1 billion to design, develop, and certify a new engine and to tool up for production). A typical engine development schedule is shown in Exhibit 4.4.

Production costs for commercial aircraft engines tended to follow an 80 percent learning curve, very much like that for the aircraft they powered. Engine manufacturers did, however, have a somewhat greater probability of recovering their investments than did airframe manufacturers since there were two to four times as many engines installed as there were aircraft. Moreover, airlines typically purchased an additional lot of spare engines (usually totaling about 20 percent of the number of installed engines), which, along with the parts sales, added significantly to an engine manufacturer's revenue potential. (Installed engines represented between 20 percent and 30 percent of the total purchase price of a new aircraft. Spare engines and spare parts typically raised this percentage to almost 100 percent over the thirty-year life of the aircraft. Because of improvements in engine reliability, however, the cost of spare parts over the typical fifteen-year life of a new engine would probably not exceed its purchase price.) In general, manufacturer gross margins on spare parts were considerably higher than on the engines themselves, with margins in the 60 percent range not uncommon.

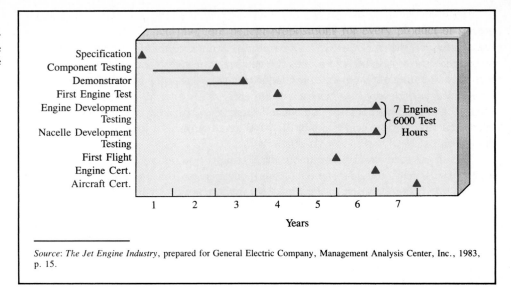

EXHIBIT 4.4
Typical Engine
Development Schedule

Specification
Component Testing
Demonstrator
First Engine Test
Engine Development Testing
Nacelle Development Testing
First Flight
Engine Cert.
Aircraft Cert.

7 Engines
6000 Test Hours

1   2   3   4   5   6   7
Years

Source: *The Jet Engine Industry*, prepared for General Electric Company, Management Analysis Center, Inc., 1983, p. 15.

The high-risk nature of the commercial airframe business carried over directly to the commercial engine business, with the result that, by the 1960s, there were essentially only three major engine manufacturers building engines for large commercial aircraft: Pratt & Whitney, a division of United Technologies, and General Electric's Aircraft Engine Business Group (AEBG), both of which were U.S. firms; and Rolls Royce Limited, in Great Britain.

In the 1960s, Pratt & Whitney (P&W) held 90 percent of the commercial engine market, and Rolls Royce about 7 or 8 percent. GE entered the market with its CF6 engine, designed for the Douglas DC-10 tri-jet, in 1970. At that time, a given aircraft was offered with only one engine: the DC-10 could only use the CF6; the Lockheed L-1011 was fitted with the Rolls Royce RB211 engine; and all Boeing aircraft were powered by P&W's JT8D or JT9D engines.

In 1971, however, P&W broke tradition by offering the financially strapped Douglas Aircraft Company approximately $150 million to modify its DC-10 to accept a P&W engine and to recertify the aircraft with the P&W engine option. Douglas accepted the offer, and the P&W engine became available on the DC-10. Boeing then contacted GE and indicated it would consider installing a GE engine on the 747. GE paid Boeing $12.5 million for installation and recertification work, and the CF6 became an available option for that aircraft. By the 1980s, there were usually two, if not three, competing engine options for every commercial jetliner (see Exhibit 4.5).

Consequently, the negotiating leverage of the airlines increased considerably, as did price competition in the engine market and the "riskiness" of the business. Engine manufacturers sought to reduce their risks through conservative new-product strategies that offered relatively small, incremental improvements in performance over previous models. Differences in performance among competing models came to be very minor, with the winner of an engine competition determined by such factors as price and financing terms.

Pratt & Whitney had sales in 1985 of about $4.5 billion (about 33 percent of United Technologies' total). Harry Gray, United Technologies' CEO, was said to be highly sensitive to market share. One of P&W's managers noted, "With Harry Gray, there's only one market share that's OK: 100 percent." In 1985, P&W had cut prices fiercely and offered very innovative financing plans to the airlines in an effort to win back its traditional market leadership. GE had responded in kind, however, and had been able to maintain a narrow lead.

Rolls Royce (RR), with 1985 revenues of about £2.5 billion, was state-owned, ranking second in the United Kingdom to British Aerospace in both high-tech jobs and exports. Rolls Royce was generally considered to have capable engineering talent, and had been the first company to introduce a number of major engine innovations. In recent years, RR had suffered high losses, in large part because of the industry recession but also because the company's fortunes had been closely tied to those of the ill-fated Lockheed L-1011. In early 1986, it was rumored that Britain's Conservative Thatcher government, which was seeking to "privatize" as many state enterprises as practical, was putting pressure on RR to improve its financial performance.

GE's market leadership was partly based on its strategic alliance with SNECMA, the French aerospace manufacturer. In 1984, an exceptional year in which AEBG captured

Type of Aircraft		No. of Engines	In Service	No. of Seats (approx.*)	Range (nautical miles)	Engine Maker
Boeing (U.S.A.)						
Narrow body	737–200	2	✔	110	1,900–2,500	P&W
(single aisle)	737-Lite	2	Under study	100	1,500–2,500	P&W; CFM(?); R-R(?)
	737-300	2	✔	128	1,900–2,800	CFM
	727-200	2	✔	156	1,900–2,700	P&W
	757-200	2	✔	186	2,600–4,000	P&W; R-R
Wide body	767-200	2	✔	216	3,300–4,000	P&W; GE
(twin aisles)	767-200ER	2	✔	216	5,300	P&W; GE
	767-300	2	Late 1986	261	4,000	P&W; GE
	767-300ER	2	Offered	261	5,000	P&W; GE
	747SP	4	✔	331	6,000	P&W; GE; R-R
	747-200	4	✔	452	6,100	P&W; GE; R-R
	747-300	4	✔	496	5,600	P&W; GE, R-R
McDonnell Douglas (U.S.A.)						
Narrow body	MD-81	2	✔	142–155	1,560	P&W
(single aisle)	MD-82	2	✔	142–155	2,050	P&W
	MD-83	2	✔	142–155	2,360	P&W
	MD-87	2	Late 1987	100–130	2,370–2,830	P&W
	MD-89	2	Under study	170	2,135	IAE
Wide body	DC-10-10	3	✔	250–380	3,300	GE
(twin aisles)	DC-10-15	3	✔	250–380	3,780	GE
	DC-10-30	3	✔	250–380	5,090	GE
	DC-10-40	3	✔	250–380	4,995	P&W
	MD-IIX	3	Offered	277–337	4,500–6,200	P&W; GE; R-R
Airbus Industrie (France, West Germany, Britain, Spain)						
Narrow body	A320	2	Spring 1988	150–164	1,900	IAE; CFM
(single aisle)						
Wide body	A300 B2	2	✔	251	1,550–1,910	GE; P&W
(twin aisles)	A300 B4-100	2	✔	251	3,050	GE; P&W
	A300 B4-200	2	✔	251	3,300	GE; P&W
	A300-600	2	✔	267	3,550–3,750	GE; P&W
	A310-200	2	✔	218	2,850–3,800	GE; P&W
	A310-300	2	End 1985	218	4,650	GE; P&W
	TA9-200	2	Under study	243–288	4,000–6,000	GE; P&W
	TA9-300	2	Under study	328–420	4,000	GE; P&W
	TA11	4	Under study	220–280	6,000–6,600	CFM; IAE

* Based on manufacturers estimates of first and economy class mix. IAE = International Aero Engines consortium of Pratt & Whitney, Rolls Royce, Japanese Aero Engine Corporation, MTU (West Germany), Fiat (Italy). P&W = Pratt & Whitney (USA). GE = General Electric (USA). R-R = Rolls Royce (Britain). CFM = Joint company of General Electric and Snecma (France).

Source: "The Big Six: A Survey of the World's Aircraft Industry," *The Economist*, June 1, 1985, survey p. 9.

EXHIBIT 4.5
Engine/Aircraft Choices Available to the Airlines

57 percent of the large commercial engine orders, the engine accounting for the greatest number of those orders was the CFM56, an engine jointly produced with SNECMA. Collaboration between AEBG and SNECMA dated back to the late 1960s, when GE agreed to allow SNECMA to participate in the production of AEBG's CF5-50 engine (and its derivatives) for the Airbus A300B and the Boeing 747. SMECMA assembled and tested a proportion of these engines and produced certain component parts. In December 1971, AEBG and SNECMA organized a joint venture, CFM International, which produced the highly successful CFM56 family of engines. This jointly produced engine accounted for the bulk of AEBG's sales in 1984, when airlines ordered 117 737-300's powered by CFM56-3's.

P&W, faced with a shrinking market share after having invested heavily in two new engine lines—the PW2037 and PW4000—had recently entered into a consortium with RR, MTU of West Germany, Fiat of Italy, and the Japanese Aircraft Engine Company (JAEC) to produce a new 20,000-to-30,000-pound thrust engine to compete with GE's CFM56. This consortium, the International Aero Engine Company or IAE, would produce the new V2500 high-by-pass fan jet engine, which was expected to represent the state of the art in the late 1980s.

In 1983, an outside consultant for GE summarized the competitive dynamics of the aircraft engine industry as follows:

> Both [P&W and RR] have responded [to the GE challenge] with increased R&D spending; younger, more aggressive management teams; and more attention to product quality and support. Each has emulated GE's successful international team approach, including a joint venture with each other. Neither had been slow to adopt successful GE technical ideas. With the full attention and resources of both the largest and most innovative engine competitors now focused on maintaining [or improving] their existing market shares, . . . the competitive situation has never been more demanding. . . . There will be a premium on picking and developing the right products at the right time, teaming up with the right partners for market access and technology, and innovating in airline financing and support.

THE UDF PROJECT

It had long been known that turboprop engines were considerably more efficient (i.e., used less fuel to carry a given payload a given distance) than pure jet (or even fan jet) engines. The reasons for this were complex (see Appendix 4A for a primer on engine technology), but essentially were a function of a propeller's ability to accelerate a relatively large mass of air with a relatively low expenditure of energy.

The efficiency advantages of turboprop engines were, however, limited to speeds below approximately 350 miles per hour. At higher speeds, the rate of discharge of air near the propeller blade tips approached Mach 1.0, and considerable energy began to be lost in the form of severe airflow disturbance. Moreover, in the case of turboprop engines, it was necessary to incorporate a gearbox between the gas turbine, which had a high optimal rotational speed, and the propeller, which typically had a much lower optimal rotational speed. This gearbox added weight to the engine and tended to increase noise and vibration, especially at high speeds. Consequently, in the mid-1980s, turboprops were confined largely to private and corporate aircraft and air taxis, for which 350 miles per hour was usually sufficient speed.

The 1970s and 1980s had been characterized by numerous improvements in turbojet engines. In particular, the incorporation of a second turbine, or fan, in the engine had significantly increased fuel efficiency. Still, increases in the efficiency of fan jet engines appeared to be limited to, at best, about a 10 percent improvement per engine generation. With development costs for each new generation of engines increasing (and now ap-

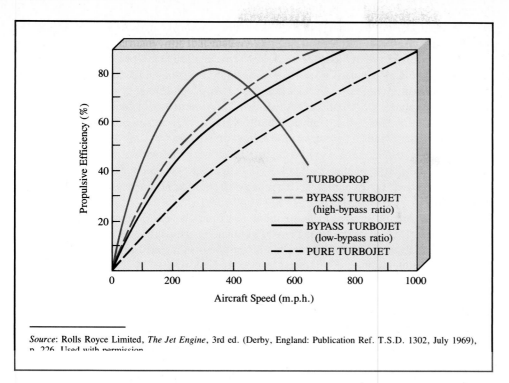

Source: Rolls Royce Limited, *The Jet Engine*, 3rd ed. (Derby, England: Publication Ref. T.S.D. 1302, July 1969), p. 226. Used with permission.

EXHIBIT 4.6
Theoretical Efficiency at Various Aircraft Speeds by Engine Type

proaching $1 billion), industry observers wondered whether such small incremental improvements in efficiency would generate sufficient sales, or make possible enough of a price premium, for engine manufacturers to recover their heavy development costs.

As Exhibit 4.6 illustrates, huge theoretical improvements in engine efficiency could be achieved if a way could be found to prevent the efficiency curve for turboprop engines from turning downward in the typical cruising speed range of a commercial transport (about Mach .8, or 500 miles per hour). In the mid-1970s, at NASA's behest, engineers at General Electric (and other engine manufacturers) began to use advanced computer technology in efforts to design a new type of propeller blade that would not lose energy to blade tip turbulence at high flight speeds. By 1983, General Electric engineers had, in fact, designed such a propeller blade (see Exhibit 4.7), a blade that, when incorporated on a state-of-the-art turboprop engine, could be expected to achieve efficiency levels

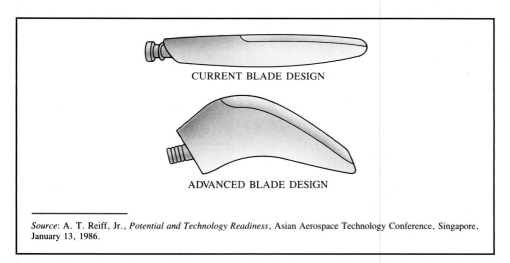

EXHIBIT 4.7
Advanced Propeller Design

Source: A. T. Reiff, Jr., *Potential and Technology Readiness*, Asian Aerospace Technology Conference, Singapore, January 13, 1986.

61

almost 15 percent higher than those of the most advanced turbofan engines (e.g., the V2500) expected to be available in the 1990s.

In the view of AEBG management, however, an efficiency improvement of at least 25 percent would be required to justify the development, manufacture, and introduction of a new turboprop engine to the market. In search of an efficiency improvement of at least this magnitude, GE engineers turned their attention to an old concept whose origins could be traced to the 1940s: counterrotating propellers. In this configuration, a second stage of propeller blades would be placed behind the first, but would rotate in the opposite direction. This second stage would recapture the energy that would otherwise be lost in the swirling discharge of the first stage. This two-stage approach, when applied to the propfan, could, in theory, produce very large improvements in engine efficiency (see Exhibit 4.8).

Counterrotation also led to an important secondary benefit. The torque of the second stage counteracted that of the first, thereby eliminating the net torque experienced by the engine mount system. The engine could thus be "soft mounted" on rubberlike mounts, significantly reducing the vibration transmitted to the airframe.

A third benefit of counterrotation was that it permitted the blades to be more highly loaded (i.e., absorb more power per square foot of swept area). With a single row of blades, the loading had to be limited to reduce the swirl coming off the blades. The incorporation of a second stage resulted in the recovery of the energy that would otherwise have been dissipated in this slipstream swirl. Since engine loading could thus be increased, it became possible to reduce the diameter of the propeller for a given power input. This reduction in propeller diameter made an aft fuselage mounting scheme viable. Aft mounting

EXHIBIT 4.8
Efficiency Advantage of Two Counterrotating Propeller Blades versus Alternative Propeller Configurations

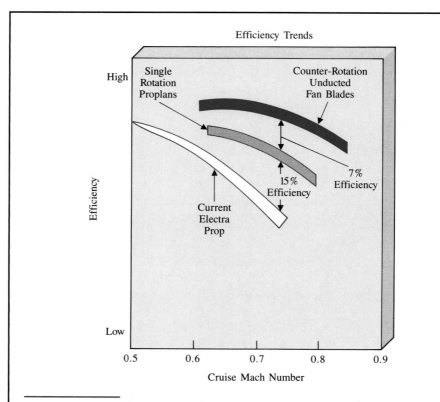

Source: Illustration excerpted from M.I.T. Sloan School Master's Thesis written by D. M. Hooper (Sloan Master's Degree 1986), courtesy of G.E. Aircraft Engines, Lynn, Mass.

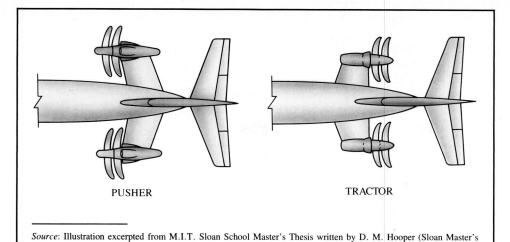

Source: Illustration excerpted from M.I.T. Sloan School Master's Thesis written by D. M. Hooper (Sloan Master's Degree 1986), courtesy of G.E. Aircraft Engines, Lynn, Mass.

EXHIBIT 4.9
Alternate Propfan Configuration

PUSHER

TRACTOR

reduced cabin noise and lessened hazards to ground personnel by moving the plane of rotation away from aircraft service points. (Exhibit 4.9 shows a top view of the tail of an aircraft with alternative "pusher" and "tractor" counterrotating *propfan* configurations.)

In order to keep the far-field noise levels of the prop at acceptable levels, the rotational tip speed of the blades could not exceed about 800 feet per second. The smaller the diameter of the blades, the slower the rotational speed of the blade tips at a given hub speed. GE engineers found that they could increase disc loading, and thus reduce the prop diameter to the point where the rotational speed of the propeller blades approached the efficient range of rotational speeds of the turbine driving the propeller. As a result, a speed reduction gearbox was no longer required, thus eliminating another source of noise, weight, and vibration, as well as a major maintenance headache for the operator.

The direct-drive approach ultimately selected by GE placed the prop blades at the aft end of the engine in the plane of rotation of the turbine, in a pusher configuration (see Exhibit 4.10). AEBG's proposal called for GE to provide the complete propulsion system, including the air inlet, exhaust, and nacelle (the shell in which the engine was enclosed),

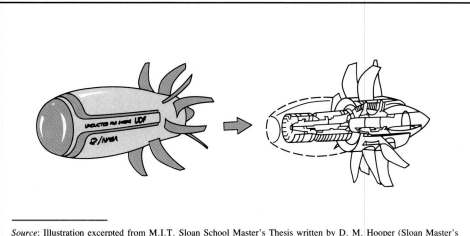

Source: Illustration excerpted from M.I.T. Sloan School Master's Thesis written by D. M. Hooper (Sloan Master's Degree 1986), courtesy of G.E. Aircraft Engines, Lynn, Mass.

EXHIBIT 4.10
The UDF Engine

as well as the mounting system. The entire "system" was named the UDF (or *un*d*u*cted *f*an) engine.

The propulsive efficiency of the UDF and of modern technology turbofans are compared in Exhibit 4.11. Exhibit 4.12 translates the UDF's greater efficiency into its fuel burn advantage vis-à-vis various aircraft/engine combinations. On a 1,700-nautical-mile flight, for example, an advanced technology aircraft powered by the UDF would

EXHIBIT 4.11
UDF versus Turbofan (TF)
Propulsive Efficiency

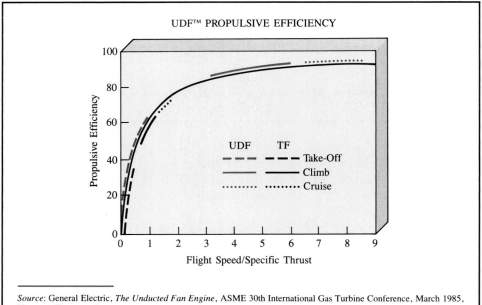

Source: General Electric, *The Unducted Fan Engine*, ASME 30th International Gas Turbine Conference, March 1985, Houston, Texas, p. 8.

EXHIBIT 4.12
Advanced Aircraft with
UDF versus Alternative
Engine/Aircraft
Configurations

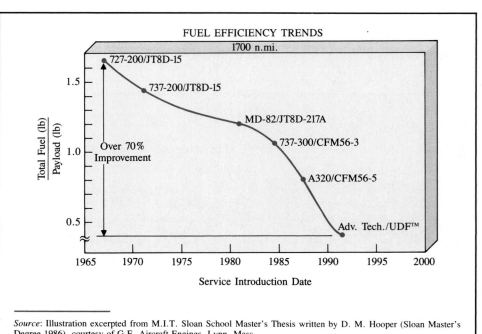

Source: Illustration excerpted from M.I.T. Sloan School Master's Thesis written by D. M. Hooper (Sloan Master's Degree 1986), courtesy of G.E. Aircraft Engines, Lynn, Mass.

require 70 percent less fuel per pound of payload than a 1980 vintage 727, and 40 percent less than an A320 powered by the CFM56-5.

AEBG disclosed its revolutionary new design in December 1983 before a NASA-organized gathering of senior technical personnel from both the airlines and the airframe manufacturers. NASA responded to AEBG's presentation with a $20 million grant to design a demonstrator engine, while Boeing agreed to provide a 727 aircraft and technical support for a flight demonstrator program. Somewhat later, McDonnell Douglas agreed to a similar test program, using a modified MD-80 aircraft. Airbus Industrie, however, which was about to launch its own 150-passenger A320 aircraft design and development program with conventional turbofan engines, was very critical of the UDF concept.

AEBG executives were, of course, highly encouraged by the responses of Boeing, McDonnell Douglas, and NASA to their UDF program. Nevertheless, as one GE executive noted:

> $1.25 billion to $1.5 billion, just for development costs, is one hell of a lot of money. If we go for this, the future of AEBG, as well as many of our own careers, may damn well be on the line. We'd better be sure, and I really mean sure, that the demand will be there, *and* that we will get enough of whatever demand there is to make this project pay off.

FORECASTING UDF SALES

The AEBG proposal was based on the premise that there would be a considerable demand for new 150-passenger short-range aircraft in the 1990s. Most passengers seemed to prefer more frequent schedules to the greater comfort of large, wide-body aircraft. Moreover, lower-capacity aircraft provided a better fit with the increasingly popular "hub and spoke" route structures. It seemed likely, therefore, that airlines would be replacing their aging fleets of Boeing 727s and 737s and McDonnell Douglas DC-9s with planes having similar capabilities, as well as adding whatever aircraft would be needed for the growth in air travel expected in the late 1980s and 1990s.

Demand for GE's proposed UDF engine would, in the view of AEBG managers, depend on a number of factors:

1. What would be the demand for air travel during the later 1980s and early 1990s?

2. What would be the financial condition (ability to buy) of the airlines during the "market window" for the new engine?

3. At what rate would the airlines replace and/or add "seats" to their fleets during the period in question?

4. What proportion of such new "seats" would be on new 150-seat aircraft that *could* use UDF-type engines?

5. What proportion of these aircraft would, *in fact*, utilize UDF-type engines (at various price premiums over state-of-the-art fan jet engines)?

6. What share of the resulting UDF-type market would GE be able to obtain, and retain?

7. What would be the timing of sales of the new engine (for calculating the present value of the project's cash flows)?

AEBG planners were aided in their efforts to answer these questions by the wide availability of aircraft sales forecasts disseminated by the major airframe manufacturers and other industry participants. Boeing, for example, made use of a complex set of models to forecast aircraft delivery requirements at various points in time:

Boeing's Forecast of Aircraft Deliveries, 1986–1995

YEAR	DELIVERIES	CUMULATIVE	CUMULATIVE %
1986	395	395	10.1
1987	426	821	21
1988	426	1247	31.9
1989	386	1633	41.7
1990	334	1967	50.3
1991	315	2282	58.4
1992	413	2695	68.9
1993	424	3119	79.8
1994	408	3527	90.2
1995	382	3909	100
Total	3909		

AEBG planners had been told informally that Boeing expected about 55 percent of these aircraft to be short-to-medium-range aircraft that could use UDF-type engines, provided the aircraft was designed to employ the radical new engine technology.

AEBG's own forecast was that 3,810 aircraft would be sold between 1986 and 1995, with 2,143 aircraft (56 percent) likely to be delivered during the critical 1991–1995 period. Breaking down and extending this forecast further, GE expected 2,360 short-range aircraft to be sold worldwide between 1992 and 2000 (see Exhibit 4.13).

As a reality check, AEBG compared its forecast with the published forecasts of a number of other industry participants and observers. As may be seen in Exhibit 4.14, there was a remarkably close fit among these presumably independent forecasts. AEBG planners noted, however, that the various players had obviously gotten a look at one another's forecasts, and therefore, there was probably a lot more "cross-contamination than any of us would like to admit."

AEBG forecasters had also attempted to gauge the typical product life cycle for a new aircraft or engine. In studying the first eight years of the 727, 737, and DC-9 aircraft, for example, they had found the following pattern of deliveries (in aggregate):

EXHIBIT 4.13
Market for Short-Range Aircraft, 1992–2000

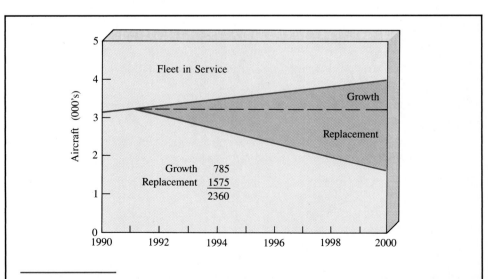

Source: Illustration excerpted from M.I.T. Sloan School Master's Thesis written by D. M. Hooper (Sloan Master's Degree 1986), courtesy of G.E. Aircraft Engines, Lynn, Mass.

PRODUCTION YEAR	CUMULATIVE % OF DELIVERIES	ANNUAL %
1	1	1
2	15	14
3	35	20
4	55	20
5	71	16
6	83	12
7	93	10
8	100	7

Noting that these data reflected a typical life-cycle curve, the forecasters concluded that, in the absence of arguments to the contrary, they would assume a similar curve for the UDF engine if it were introduced and proved successful.

AEBG was thus relatively confident that almost 4,000 aircraft would be delivered between 1990 and 1999, and that at least half of these would be short- or medium-range aircraft that could use the UDF engine. In their view, the most important remaining questions were: (1) Which aircraft would be designed to incorporate UDF-type technology? (2) How many aircraft would, in fact, be ordered with UDF-type engines by the airlines? (3) What share of such UDF-type business would accrue to General Electric?

Boeing and McDonnell Douglas, in discussions with AEBG executives, had both expressed "cautious enthusiasm" with respect to the new engine technology. Both companies were planning new 150-seat, short- to medium-range aircraft for the early 1990s (the 7J7 and a new version of the DC-9, respectively), but had not yet "finalized" their design concepts. While both airframers were currently "thinking in terms of" advanced fan jet engines such as the V2500 or CFM56-5, neither considered itself to be "locked into" a particular engine concept. Executives of the two aircraft comapnies had noted, however, that the cost of the new engine and its date of availability (Airbus Industrie's fan jet–powered A-320 was expected to be the most technologically advanced aircraft on the market following its first deliveries in 1988 or 1989) would be important considerations in their aircraft design decisions. Moreover, it was common industry practice for an

Source	1986	1987	1988	1989	1990	1991	1992	1993	1994	1995	Total	Short-Range %
Boeing/1	395	426	426	386	334	315	413	424	408	382	3909	55.3
MD/2	165	219	329	387	397	358	506	489	430	458	3738	53.3
GE/3	390	305	285	325	360	387	385	397	493	483	3810	61.1
RR/4	280	384	421	431	432	405	402	398	346	319	3818	48.1
Rohr/5	354	445	304	345	379	421	529	391	433	479	4080	50.0
TRW/6	390	433	422	373	356	361	384	404	434	462	4019	58.0
ML/7	394	444	460	375	450	490	505	490	490	490	4588	51.4
(Amalg.)	338	379	378	375	387	391	446	428	433	439	3994	53.9

EXHIBIT 4.14
Aircraft Delivery Forecasts, 1986–1995

Sources: "World Travel Market Perspective and Airplane Equipment Requirements," *Boeing Current Market Outlook* (Seattle: February 1986), p. 70; *1985–1999 Outlook for Commercial Aircraft*, p. 45; General Electric Airline Marketing Division, *Commercial Market Outlook* (Cincinnati: November 1985), p. 4; *Market Potential for Commercial Jet Engines*, Sect. 4, p. 2; Chart from Rohr's "Chart Room," dated November 7, 1985; Interview with William Wilder, Market Analysis Specialist, TRW Aircraft Components Group, March 5, 1986; Merrill Lynch Industry Review, *Aerospace—Commercial—1985*, October 1985, pp. 8 and 12.

airframer to insist on a minimum number of firm orders from airlines (e.g., 100 aircraft) before committing itself to manufacture a particular airframe/engine configuration.

AEBG executives believed that "if we really move into high gear on this right now," the UDF engine could be operational on a new generation of aircraft by early 1992. Current plans called for the UDF to be priced at $5 million per engine, approximately $600,000 more than the announced price ($4.4 million) for the V2500. In the view of AEBG executives, the $5 million price represented "good value" to the airlines. At the current price for jet fuel (81.6 cents per gallon, at approximately $20 per barrel of crude oil), a 150-passenger aircraft operating at a 65 percent load factor[2] would save approximately $160,000 worth of fuel per engine per year if it was powered by a UDF engine rather than a V2500. At different fuel prices, savings would be proportionally higher or lower.[3]

The $5 million proposed price for the new engine was based partly on its estimated "value" to the airlines, and partly on the anticipated costs of developing and manufacturing the new engine. AEBG planners estimated that a total investment of almost $1.25 billion (in 1986 dollars) would be required to develop, certify, and tool up for production of the new engine. Approximately $50 million of this investment had already been incurred, with future expenditures (assuming an immediate "Go" decision), expected to be as follows:

Projected UDF Investment

	R&D EXPENSE ($ million)	CAPITAL INVESTMENT ($ million)	TOTAL ($ million)
1986	60	15	75
1987	225	25	250
1988	100	150	250
1989	75	175	250
1990	75	175	250
1991	25	100	125
Total	560	640	1200

While, as one manager noted, "these projects do take on a life of their own," the UDF program could, at least in theory, be aborted at any point prior to actual introduction.

As was typical on a project of this type, production cost estimates for the new engine were still "rather tentative." Assuming an 80 percent experience curve for the first 200 units and an 85 percent experience curve thereafter, direct manufacturing costs at various levels of *cumulative* production would be as follows:

---

[2] Most analysts agreed that a 65 percent industry load factor represented approximate "long-run equilibrium." If average load factors fell much below 65 percent, airlines would lose money and aircraft would be withdrawn from the market. Conversely, if average load factors were much above 65 percent, many flights would be sold out, generating considerable passenger ill-will and, presumably, an increase in seat capacity.

[3] There was considerable disagreement among energy economists and other analysts concerning future oil prices. A summary of their views in early 1986 would suggest a range of plus or minus 50 percent of the 1986 fuel price (about $20 per barrel), with approximately equal probabilities of its being higher or lower than that price.

TOTAL UDFs PRODUCED	AVERAGE CUMULATIVE DIRECT COST/ENGINE* ($ million)	MARGINAL DIRECT COST/ENGINE† ($ million)
100	6.60	6.60
250	5.40	4.60
500	4.80	4.20
1000	4.20	3.60
2000	3.70	3.20
3000	3.48	2.83
4000	3.30	2.73
5000	3.15	2.54

* To be read: After 3,000 engines have been manufactured, the average direct cost per engine for the total 3,000 engines would be $3.48 million.

† To be read: After 2,000 engines have been manufactured, the marginal cost per engine of the next 1,000 engines (up to 3,000 units) would be $2.83 million.

Indirect costs, including imputed interest on working capital, were estimated at 20 percent of revenue, regardless of volume.

AEBG executives knew that P&W, the Allison Division of General Motors,[4] and—to a lesser extent—Rolls Royce were all engaged in at least some development work on UDF-type engines. None of their projects seemed to be getting much priority, however, presumably because these companies already had too much on their plates, and perhaps because they were skeptical about the technical feasibility and/or market acceptance of the new type of engine. Nevertheless, in the view of AEBG executives, one or more of these firms (perhaps in a consortium) would be able, in a crash program, to bring a UDF-type engine to the market within twenty-four to thirty months of GE's first shipments.

CONCLUSION

It was against this background that AEBG executives were considering whether to recommend "going full blast" on the UDF project to corporate management. Clearly, a great deal was at stake—not only money, but AEBG's reputation and relationships with its key commercial customers as well.

AEBG was intensely proud of having finally passed P&W and achieved leadership in the commercial jet engine market. Was the time now ripe for GE to seek to increase its momentum by introducing a major innovation in technology, or would it make more sense to consolidate its gains by upgrading its CFM-56 family of engines to match or modestly exceed the specifications of the V2500?[5]

---

[4] Allison was best known as a manufacturer of military helicopter engines. According to industry rumors, it planned to modify one of its helicopter engines and fit it with a gearbox to power an advanced turboprop configuration. The resulting engine would sell for as little as $3.5 million, but have thrust considerably below GE's proposed UDF engine.

[5] AEBG executives expected that such an upgrade could be accomplished for an investment of approximately $500 million, with first deliveries by early 1989.

QUESTIONS FOR DISCUSSION

1. How would you characterize the market for commercial jet aircraft engines? What are the roles of the major decision-making units in this market?

2. How would you explain the strategies and performance of the major competitors in this market?

3. What are AEBG's principal objectives for the UDF engine? What will success depend on?

4. As a senior executive of AEBG, would you favor the UDF project?

5. If you were Jack Welch or a member of the GE board of directors, would you approve the project?

4A

JET ENGINE PRIMER[1]

AN HISTORICAL PERSPECTIVE

The earliest applications of jet propulsion actually predate the advent of mankind, as denizens of the deep such as squid and cuttlefish jet-propelled themselves through the primordial seas. The first human application of the principles of jet propulsion is credited to Hero of Alexandria, who in about 100 B.C. invented a device known as an aeolopile. This device, pictured in Exhibit 4A.1, converted water into steam, which it directed through two jet nozzles on a spherical vessel. The nozzles were arranged and the sphere mounted in such a manner that the escaping steam caused the vessel to rotate. More than a millennium later, in about A.D. 1200, the Chinese invented gunpowder, which they used to propel their rockets and fireworks displays. In the early sixteenth century, Leonardo da Vinci developed a machine called the chimney jack, which used the energy from hot air rising from an open fire to spin a turbinelike wheel that drove a roasting spit.

The laws of motion upon which all jet propulsion devices are based were developed in 1687 by Sir Isaac Newton. Newton is also credited with the design of a jet-propelled horseless carriage that was driven by steam escaping through a nozzle facing rearward. Although throughout recorded history there are numerous examples of the use of Newton's reaction principle, there was a gap of 2000 years from the first recorded use to the point at which technological advancements in engineering, metallurgy, and manufacturing made jet-propelled flight a reality on August 27, 1939, when the HE-178, a German aircraft, lifted off.

America entered the jet age in October 1942 with the first flight of the Bell XP59A aircraft, which was powered by a General Electric IA turbojet engine. The IA engine was developed from plans carried to this country from England by Sir Frank Whittle, generally considered to be the father of the jet engine (even though the Germans were the first to actually fly a jet-powered aircraft). America provided safe haven for the development of the Allies' jet engine, and General Electric was selected to work with Whittle to develop the engine because of its experience under Dr. Sanford A. Moss with turbosuperchargers

---

[1] This appendix was written by Donald Hooper as part of his Sloan Fellow M.S. thesis, "Marketing Strategy in the Commercial Engine Business," Massachusetts Institute of Technology, 1986.

Source: Rolls Royce Limited, *The Jet Engine*, 3rd ed., Publication Ref. T.S.D. 1302 (Derby, England: July 1969), p. 2. Used with permission.

(very similar devices to jet engines, lacking only the combustion chamber and associated systems). For security reasons, Whittle carried the plans for his design to this country in his head. The story goes that he dictated the specifications for his engine to his secretary while sitting on the beach in Swampscott, Massachusetts, a few miles from the General Electric facility at which the engine would eventually be produced.

BASIC THEORY OF OPERATION

The underlying principle of jet propulsion is Sir Isaac Newton's Third Law of Motion, which states that for every unbalanced force applied to a body, there is an equal and opposite reaction. There is a simple analogy to jet propulsion of aircraft with which virtually everyone is familiar: when a balloon is inflated and released with the stem unsecured, the balloon moves in a direction opposite to the escaping air.

It is commonly misinterpreted that the escaping air pushes against the atmosphere, thereby propelling the balloon forward. In fact, the reaction of the balloon is due solely to forces acting on the balloon, not on the air outside the balloon. When inflated, the pressure inside the balloon is greater than that of the outside air. Let us call this pressure differential P_d. If the stem is tied, the internal pressure pushes equally on the entire inside surface of the balloon, as depicted in Exhibit 4A.2A. However, if the stem is opened, a force imbalance is created, i.e., there is no internal pressure being felt by the balloon at the point of the opening, while there is still a force applied to the opposite surface. This unbalanced force (equal to P_d times the area of stem opening) is evidenced by the balloon moving in a direction opposite to the opening and the escaping air, as shown in Exhibit 4A.2B.

The movement of the balloon is relatively short-lived because the pressure inside the balloon quickly reaches equilibrium with the pressure outside it (i.e., P_d goes to zero), and the unbalanced force disappears. If air could somehow be continuously pumped into the balloon at a sufficient pressure and flow, the movement of the balloon could be sustained. A jet engine is similar to such a balloon in that it carries its own compressor to maintain the necessary flow and pressure to sustain the propulsive thrust.

The thrust (reactive force) produced by a jet engine can be expressed in terms of Newton's Second Law of Motion (more commonly known in the form $F = ma$) by the following formula:

$$F = \dot{m}\, \Delta v$$

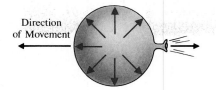

Direction
of Movement

When the stem is tied, the
forces within the balloon are
balanced.

Untying the stem opens a hole which causes
the internal forces to become unbalanced.
This unbalance of forces helps the balloon
to move to the left in the direction away
from the hole.

A

B

Source: N. E. Borden, Jr., Pratt & Whitney Aircraft, *Jet-Engine Fundamentals* (New York, Hayden
Book Company, 1967), p. 11.

where $\dot{m}$ is the mass flow rate of air through the system, and Δv is the change in velocity
of the air between the points at which it enters and exits the system.

Thus, there are two dials, if you will, that can be adjusted to produce thrust, i.e.,
mass flow or change in velocity of air through the system. It should be noted that the
same fundamental relationship applies to the thrust produced by a propeller. In the case
of a propeller, the change in velocity is relatively small, but the mass flow is enormous.
In the case of a turbojet engine, the opposite is true.

TYPES OF JET ENGINES

There are three generic forms of jet engines—or, more properly, gas turbine engines—
that have been used to power commercial aircraft: the turbojet, turboprop, and turbofan.

Turbojet

A turbojet engine is the simplest form of a gas turbine engine. The basic Whittle-type
turbojet engine is composed of a five-component ''gas generator,'' which includes an air
inlet, a compressor, a combustion chamber, a turbine, and an exhaust nozzle (see Exhibit
4A.3). Atmospheric air is sucked in through the inlet by the compressor, which raises
its pressure to many times that at which it enters. The compressed air then enters the
combusion chamber, where it is mixed with fuel and burned to produce a hot expanding
gas. This hot gas rushes out the back of the engine through the exhaust nozzle, but not
before it passes through a turbine that extracts sufficient energy to drive the compressor
to which it is mechanically linked through a common rotating shaft. As mentioned earlier,
the thrust of a turbojet engine is due primarily to the Δv component of the thrust equation.

Turboprop

The core of the turboprop is fundamentally the same as the gas generator described above.
To this core is added a second ''compressor'' in the form of a propeller. The propeller
is driven either by the same turbine that drives the core compressor or by a second ''free''
turbine. In either case, most of the remaining energy in the hot escaping gases not used
by the core compressor is used to drive the propeller. Therefore, very little thrust is derived
from the exhaust of the gas generator. The propeller uses the energy to accelerate a large

73

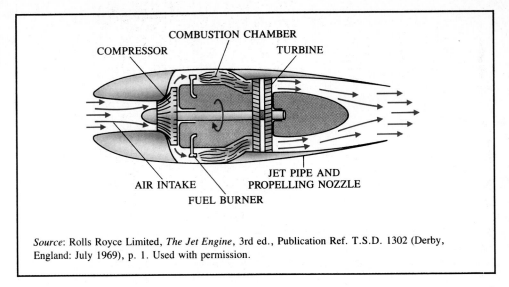

Source: Rolls Royce Limited, *The Jet Engine*, 3rd ed., Publication Ref. T.S.D. 1302 (Derby, England: July 1969), p. 1. Used with permission.

mass of air, and although the change in velocity of that air is not great, the mass flow of air is sufficient to produce considerable thrust.

Before leaving this discussion of the turboprop engine, it is important to note that the most efficient rotational speeds of the propeller and turbine are typically quite different, the turbine running significantly faster. A gearbox is, therefore, incorporated between the turbine and propeller to allow both to operate in their respective optimal rotational speed ranges.

Propulsive Efficiency

Prior to describing the turbofan engine, let us digress for a moment to define and discuss propulsive efficiency. The performance of an aircraft propulsion system depends not only on the amount of thrust produced but also on how efficiently the system converts kinetic energy into propulsive work. Propulsive efficiency may be expressed by the following relationship:

$$\eta \propto \frac{2V}{V + v_j}$$

where V = velocity of the aircraft and v_j = velocity of the gases exiting the propulsion system (e.g., the hot exhaust gases from a turbojet or the airstream behind a turboprop's propeller). Therefore, when the velocity of the exiting gases is high, so too must be the velocity of the aircraft in order to achieve a high propulsive efficiency. This is the case with a turbojet engine. The lower the velocity of the gases exiting the system relative to the aircraft velocity, the higher the propulsive efficiency at a given airspeed. This would imply that a turboprop engine should have a higher propulsive efficiency than a turbojet over the entire spectrum of possible airspeeds. However, in the case of a turboprop, the relationship does not hold at forward velocities greater than about 350 mph at typical cruising altitudes (or about Mach 0.5). Above this speed, the so-called helical velocity of the propeller discharge air near the blade tip begins to approach Mach 1.0 and significant energy begins to be lost in the form of severe airflow disturbance.

If this somewhat technical dissertation on propulsive efficiency leaves the reader confused, Exhibit 4.6 in the chapter should clarify the matter. It shows that a turboprop is more efficient than a turbojet only at the lower end of the aircraft flight speed regime, while the turbojet is more efficient at higher velocities. Exhibit 4.6 also shows that there is a third type of gas turbine engine that offers a good compromise between the high-speed, high-altitude capability of a turbojet and the high efficiency and high thrust at low speeds and altitudes of a turboprop. This is the so-called bypass turbojet or turbofan engine.

Turbofan

In operation, a turbofan is similar in principle to a turboprop in that the $\dot{m}$ component of the thrust equation dominates, although not to the extent that it does with a turboprop. However, as shown in Exhibit 4.6, a turbofan does not suffer from the same cruise speed limitation as a turboprop. The turbofan avoids the airflow disturbance problem at the blade tip by replacing the propeller with a duct-enclosed fan whose blades are similar to, but much larger than, those of the core compressor. The fan on a turbofan engine is like a turboprop on which the propeller is driven by a separate free turbine. However, unlike a turboprop, which requires a speed-decreaser gearbox between the turbine and the propeller, the fan on a turbofan engine is driven directly by the free turbine in the same manner that the core compressor is driven by the gas generator turbine. The air mass accelerated through the fan on the high-bypass turbofans in commercial service today is typically six to eight times that which passes through the core. The ratio of bypass flow to core engine flow is called the bypass ratio or BPR. As can be seen in Exhibit 4.6, the higher the BPR, the higher the propulsive efficiency. The problem with increasing the BPR to much more than the current levels is that the size of the duct that shrouds the fan becomes so large that the weight and drag penalties become limiting factors.

PART TWO

STRATEGIC ANALYSIS

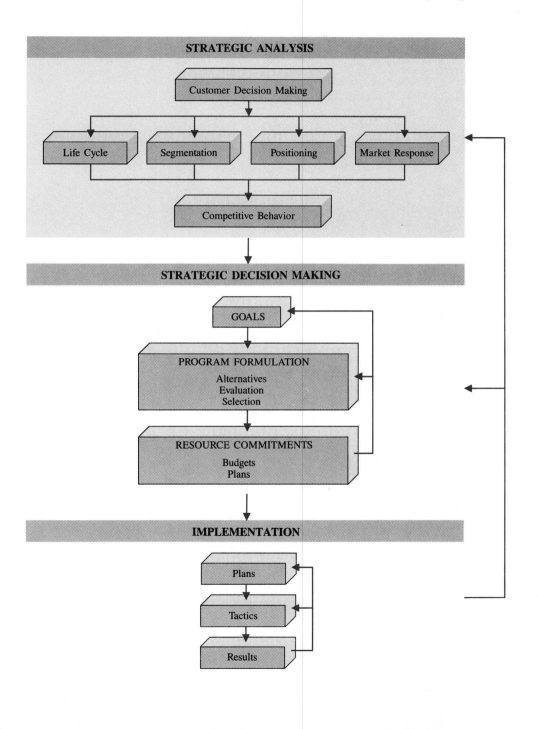

CUSTOMER DECISION MAKING

CUSTOMER RESPONSE AS A KEY MARKETING ELEMENT

The success of any organization is based on its ability to satisfy the needs of its target customers or constituents. The organization fulfills *its* goals by developing products or services that customers value enough to buy instead of competitive offerings. Sound marketing decisions require a clear understanding of customer desires and how consumers decide what, if anything, to buy. Only with such an understanding will we be able to define product attributes, communication, distribution, and pricing strategy to create a ''bundle of utility'' that the customer will select in lieu of competitive offerings. Good marketing strategy seeks to satisfy customer needs and to fit the process used by buyers in making buying decisions. For these reasons, ''customer'' is the first phenomenon to be examined in the analysis phase of the strategy formulation process (review Figure 1.1 on page 6).

We begin this chapter by using an information-processing model to view the behavioral foundations of individual buying decisions, and then consider the implications of that model for marketing strategy. Recognizing that in many industrial markets the process of choice is complicated by the involvement of multiple participants in the decision-making process, we then discuss a number of concepts that are available to help managers who face markets where more than one dominant influencer is involved in the choice of a product or service. Finally, we outline several levels of analytic support that can be employed in using the individual consumer behavior model and multiperson decision concepts.

INFORMATION PROCESSING

Understanding consumer decision processes is extremely difficult because of the diversity among buyers. No two people are exactly alike. They may differ in terms of demographics (age, income, education, marital status, geographic location), values and attitudes (inner-versus outer-directed, liberal versus conservative, high versus low self-esteem), and preferences. Variation across people will cause individuals to behave differently according to the buying situation (e.g., buying a car versus purchasing a dozen eggs.) Diversity across people and situations is increased by the number of purchase alternatives available. For example, there are over 300 models of cars and trucks available worldwide in combinations to appeal to virtually any preference; when option combinations are considered, there are literally thousands of choice alternatives.

In the face of such extreme diversity, how does a manager gain an understanding of the consumer decision process that will facilitate intelligent marketing management decisions? Important steps in the process are the development of behavioral science models of individual decision making and the support of those models through analysis and testing. Building on an adequate individual model, the manager can aggregate individual consumers into market segments. In this chapter, we describe an individual information-processing model. In Chapter 7, we discuss market-segmentation methods to group people who are similar to one another.

Information processing in its simplest form comprises three activities: (1) input, (2) decision making, and (3) output (see Figure 5.1). Each of these steps includes many behavioral phenomena and related issues. At the first level of analysis, it is important for managers to ask: How do consumers obtain information? How do they interpret and consolidate this information to reach a decision? How do they learn from their experience and influence others?[1]

Input

Marketing managers expose potential customers to a constant barrage of information (TV and radio advertising, billboards, sales calls, telemarketing, and point-of-sale displays) about products and services, but how does this affect purchasing decisions? The first question to ask is: Does the sensory stimulation provide input to the decision-making process? The second is: How is this sensory stimulation used in choice behavior? We consider the first question below and the second in a later section.

Limited Information Processing: Customers do not internalize all the information they are exposed to. The information-storage and -processing capabilities of the mind are limited, and these limits are reflected in the amount of stimulus consumers are willing to admit and the effort they will expend to utilize such stimuli for decision making. In other words, consumers filter available information, admitting only a small portion of the total into their mental processes. The salience, vividness, and relevance of the information will affect whether or not it is taken as input. Internalized information functions as a frame of reference for new information. Since past information is updated by new information, the effect of the new information depends not only on its content but also on prior attitudes stored in memory.

Exposure and Attention: Obviously, marketers who want their messages to enter a consumer's information processes must expose buyers to these messages. In advertising, the correct media must be chosen and adequate budgets established to reach the target market. In personal communication, sales calls must be made to deliver the information. Enough personal calling capacity must be present to gain exposure within the target group.

But exposure is not enough in today's information glut; the message must attract the customer's *attention* if it is to be processed. One or more sensory receptors (sight,

---

[1] See Bettman (1979) and Sternthal and Craig (1982) for an in-depth discussion of information-processing theory.

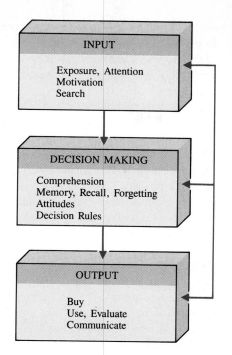

FIGURE 5.1
Information-Processing
Model

INPUT

Exposure, Attention
Motivation
Search

DECISION MAKING

Comprehension
Memory, Recall, Forgetting
Attitudes
Decision Rules

OUTPUT

Buy
Use, Evaluate
Communicate

sound, touch, smell, or taste) must be aroused. An ad must have something special to stand out in today's advertising clutter.

Motivation: When involvement with a product is low, it is usually more difficult to gain consumers' attention. Since the purchase of a packaged consumer good (e.g., a laundry detergent) is not likely to represent a high level of personal involvement, ads in these categories must go to considerable lengths to gain attention or build involvement.

When consumers judge information to be relevant to their important current or future decision needs, their motivation to take in that information will be high. Their attention levels will be correspondingly high, and they will more readily recognize and accept input. Selecting a prepaid health care plan is a good example of a decision characterized by high involvement.

Active Search for Information: When involvement is high, consumers are not passive receptors, but rather active searchers for information to fill their decision needs. The risk of making a wrong decision is perceived as great, and is amplified if low levels of prior information are present. Much of the input used in the decision-making environment is the result of an active search of alternative information sources by the buyer. This goal-oriented search may include shopping trips, talking to friends, scanning consumer publications, reading newspaper articles, talking to repairmen, and consulting experts. Surveys of consumer durable purchasing often indicate that friends and relatives are the most important source of information for buyers.

The search will be limited by the customer's ability and willingness to process additional information. If the customer is able and willing to process more information, and that information has high value relative to the costs (in time or dollars) of obtaining it, the search will continue. In industrial markets, the value of information may be so high that consultants will be hired to collect the relevant data and make recommendations.

Advertising and personal selling efforts are important tools for marketers, but they are only one element in the consumer's total information-input process. Even when the advertising and selling for a product are outstanding, if the product itself is of poor quality,

81

leading to negative word-of-mouth recommendations from peers, consumers are not likely to purchase it. It is a mistake to underestimate the ability and desire of consumers to search for information when they are motivated and face a decision they perceive as important. Consumers will pursue even incomplete and inaccurate information if they feel it will have utility for them.

The input phase thus raises several important questions. Managers need to ask: What information sources do the consumers in our target market use? What is the role of advertising and personal selling? How important are peer recommendations? How many outlets does the consumer visit before making a choice? How many competitive bids are solicited by the industrial buyer? Is the correct information provided at each step in the purchase process? Does editorial material in consumer and trade publications play an important role in supplying information? How much time and effort are spent by consumers on information gathering? What are the search activities and how can we be sure our product is represented in them?

Decision Making

After the buyer has collected the requisite information, he or she must then process that information in order to make an appropriate buying decision. A number of phenomena are critical to an understanding of how information inputs are comprehended, stored in and retrieved from memory, and integrated into the buying process. It is imperative that managers understand the steps in the mediating of input to output decisions.

Comprehension: After a consumer's attention has been obtained, the consumer must understand the input stimulus if it is to become "information" capable of influencing a buying decision. Whether the input is comprehended correctly will depend both on how well the message is crafted and on how accurate the consumer is in encoding and understanding that message. Biases may be present; selective perception may make the consumer see only what he or she wants to see, rather than what the producer desires. Since the filters consumers apply to messages may severely distort the intended communication, marketers need to design and test their messages to increase the probability that they will be correctly comprehended.

Interpersonal communication is more difficult to evaluate and control. Comprehension in this kind of communication depends on both the perceptual biases of the potential buyer and the selective perception filters utilized by word-of-mouth recommenders or detractors of the product. Rumors may develop that adversely affect consumer opinion of a product or service (see Tybout et al., 1981). The content of this communication path is important to monitor because discussions among individuals may lead not only to arousal and attention but also to higher levels of comprehension.

Memory, Recall, and Forgetting: Once an input has been comprehended, it is stored in memory along with past information (from media, interpersonal communication, and personal experience) for use in decision making. Contemporary cognitive psychology conceptualizes two types of memory: short-term and long-term. Short-term memory is active memory and contains information that is used to make current decisions. It usually includes a limited amount of relevant information that is forgotten rather quickly. Long-term memory is a much larger storehouse of information that can be drawn into short-term memory for the purpose of active decision making.

Psychologists conceive of long-term memory as organized into "nodes," each surrounded by a network of information. These structures, called "schema" guide access to information. For example, we may have a schema organized around the node of "Korean" autos. The associated information could be: low in cost, reliable, simple, economical, similar to "Japanese" cars. The "exemplar" or typical representative of this schema might be the Excel by Hyundai.

These schema are organized within a hierarchical structure, with large topics (e.g., transportation) that break down into finer classes (e.g., autos versus airplane, then autos into foreign and U.S., and U.S. autos into Ford, GM, and Chrysler, and GM into family, truck, and sporty cars). This hierarchical storage structure will control which information is transferred to short-term memory when a decision is being made. It is likely that the accessibility of the information will depend upon its place in the memory structure. If a marketer knows the hierarchy in which information is stored and accessed, he or she can achieve more effective communication through the appropriate selection of message and media.

Information in memory is sometimes forgotten over time. The rate of decay is rapid in short-term memory, but current theory suggests that long-term memory is permanent. Although information is not lost, it is often difficult or impossible to retrieve: the information is there, but we "forgot" it because we cannot access it. Thus, marketers must renew their messages if they do not want them to be forgotten. If the interval between decisions is long, either new information must be made available for input and processing or information in long-term memory must be made accessible.

Attitudes: The process of information acquisition, comprehension, storage, recall, and analysis leads to the formation of cognitions. In cognition, information is organized and attitudes are formed for decision making. Judgments are made about what attributes a product possesses and attitudes are formed based on feelings and beliefs about the attributes of the product (Fishbein, 1975). We may, for example, develop a judgment that foreign cars are high on attributes of quality and reliability, based on discussions with friends or on our own experience. These beliefs at the foreign/U.S. level of our memory structure reflect an attitude when we attach an evaluative judgment to them. Attitude is an intervening factor affecting our final decision.

Not all attitudes are directly linked to attributes. If we feel negatively about "foreign cars," and even though we do not have specific attribute evaluations for a car, we will have an overall "affective response" that would deter us from buying a foreign car. This feeling is an attitude component, which is likely to influence our final decision.

Beliefs and feelings are important determinants of choice. Marketers must seek to understand the attributes that customers associate with their product and with the class of products in which it is grouped in memory. Attitudes that represent wider moral obligations are called "normative beliefs" (see Ryan and Bonfield, 1975). Thus, a U.S. auto buyer may feel it is right to buy a small foreign car to help fight pollution or, conversely, a U.S. car to help American industry and employment.

Marketing managers need to understand normative beliefs as well as cognitive product attributes and affective reactions. The attitudes that producers want a consumer to have toward their product may not, in fact, exist in the consumer's mind. The consumer's selective information exposure and perceptual filtering of communication and experience may result in a radically different attitude set vis-à-vis the product.

Affect Referral: Given the reservoir of feelings and beliefs organized within memory, how do customers combine these inputs to form preferences and make choices? The simplest process is "affect referral" whereby the consumer accesses the stored feeling about the product and acts upon it without any other information processing (Wright, 1975). This may occur in low-involvement, repetitive-purchase decisions.

Weighing Attributes: The most commonly accepted model of choice involves cognitive information processing. This model is one in which buyers are presumed to weigh their beliefs about each attribute by the judged importance of that attribute, and then sum the weighed values to identify their preferred choice (Wilkie and Pessemier, 1973). For a simple example, assume there are two attributes of primary importance to consumers when buying an auto—reliability and power. If the ratings on a 1–7 scale (7 being the best value) are 4 for reliability and 6 for power, and the importance of reliability and power are equal (weights of .5 each), the utility score would be 5 (.5 × 6 + .5 × 4 = 5). Such models are called *linear* because they simply sum the product of the importances times belief ratings. Many more complex weighing systems have been proposed (see Urban and Hauser, 1980, chaps. 10 and 11). Some of these weigh attributes nonlinearly, while others, called *lexicographic* models, sequentially consider attributes or check to see that minimum levels are satisfied.

Simple weighing or linear models have received much attention because they appear to be robust and useful for managers. The relative importance of attributes is critical when designing a new product or developing a communications program. If a product is to be differentiated by an attribute, that attribute should be one of critical importance to the buyer. Ideally, a brand would be equal to its competitors on most attributes, and better on one or more that are especially important to consumers. Often, however, trade-offs must be made to position the product to attract buyer segments whose weighed preferences favor a particular set of attributes. In these cases, the weighed attribute advantage must compensate for any inferiority relative to the competition on other evaluative dimensions.

Elimination Heuristics: In complex consumer decision situations where many stimuli and attributes are present, buyers may not engage in compensatory weighing of all attributes because it would require too much effort to process the plethora of information available. Under such circumstances, heuristic rules are usually employed to simplify the buyer's task. One method used to simplify the choice is to eliminate alternatives that do not meet the buyer's minimum requirements with regard to selected attributes. (See Tversky, 1972, for an example of an elimination-by-aspects model.) Elimination strategies result in consumers evaluating only a small set of products when making choices. Such "consideration sets" are typically much smaller than the number of brands on the market. In autos, buyers typically consider only 3 or 4 car models out of over 300 possibilities. In package goods such as deodorants, an average consumer considers 3 brands out of over 30 available. For manufacturers, this is a particularly important behavioral phenomenon, because if a product is not in a potential buyer's consideration set, it will not be chosen no matter how desirable its attributes.

Another possible simplifying heuristic involves consumers classifying a product into a schema based on its similarity to other products, and then transferring the associated information and attitudes to the brand (Tyversky and Kahneman, 1974). A new Cadillac Allante may be classified as a Cadillac rather than a foreign sports car, even though it is very similar in engineering, style, and price ($48,500) to the Mercedes-Benz 450SL. If the associated cognitive attitudes (inefficient, too large, for old people, decadent) and affective response to Cadillac are negative, the Allante will not be considered further. Cadillac may, however, try to use the cue of "body by Pinafarina" and the fact that Allante bodies are air-freighted from Italy to break the classification scheme or modify its associated attributes.

Risk: Perceived risk is another factor that complicates the buyer's decision-making process. If a consumer believes there is a significant risk of making a wrong decision, he or she will reflect this in buying behavior. The consumer may be concerned about buying an unsafe product or one that does not work, or about experiencing unexpected side effects. This may result in an active search for information input, as well as in a more complex decision process.

One approach to modeling decision making in this situation is to treat risk as an attribute and weigh it against other attributes. Another is to use more complex utility theory models that explicitly consider risk in choices (Hauser and Urban, 1979), and a third is to consider elimination models based on risk. If a firm is selling a product that consumers tend to see as having risk elements, management must either develop modifications to assure consumers there will be no unpleasant side effects or communicate lower risk.

Another risk is the reduction of price over time. Customers can deal with this risk by delaying purchase, but they will have to give up the utility of use of the product while they wait. Price and performance expectations are important when marketing a new product with economies of scale and experience effects that will result in lower costs and prices, especially when continual technological advances are likely to make additional features available. Personal computers and compact disc players are good examples of product areas where the formation of expectations and evaluation of risk are key behavioral phenomena that can control the success or failure of a new product.

Iteration: The customer's ultimate choice may not be made after just one evaluation, and may, in fact, vary over successive reevaluations. New information may cause beliefs and feelings to change, forcing revision of the decision. A preliminary choice may change, for example, because of new information obtained while shopping or the receipt of word-of-mouth or media communication. The process is iterative and the sensitivity to media or interpersonal input is high. The consumer may continue searching for more information or new alternatives until he or she is confident of having made a ''good'' decision.

The intensity of a consumer's search for information and the extent of his or her effort in decision making tend to increase proportionally to increases in the consumer's involvement and perception of risk, the value of information in improving the decision, and the consumer's ability to process information. In complex decisions, simplifying heuristics are likely to be used even under these conditions. Managers who understand the dynamics of the decision process will be better equipped to supply consumers with the information they require, thereby increasing their product's share of consumer choices.

Output

After consumers have obtained inputs and engaged in their decision-making processes, several postpurchase phenomena take place. As consumers use a product, they gain new information about how the product performs and learning occurs (see arrow from output to decision-making box in Figure 5.1). Memory is updated for revised beliefs and feelings, or the classification of the product in the hierarchical memory structure may change. The post-use evaluation is critical for repeat-purchase products. If a product does not fulfill expectations, attribute perceptions and affective responses will decrease, and it is not likely to be purchased again. The process of assigning the causes of observed outputs by updating beliefs and attitudes after product experience is called *attribution.*

Some psychologists have argued that consumers may rationalize their negative experiences with a product by selectively perceiving only the positive attributes. Although attribution may be complex and unexpected, managers should be extremely cautious in relying on this alleged phenomenon to minimize the impact of weakness in their product offerings. In most cases, the direct effect of unfulfilled promises is a lower probability of repeat purchase because of a reduction in the perception of desired product attributes. It is thus critical in most cases to build high-quality products and have postpurchase service available to guarantee that the product delivers on its implied promises. Since consumers actually buy the product's benefits rather than the product itself, purchase is only the first step in delivering utility to consumers. Understanding attribution based on experience is important in building customer loyalty and a long-term business franchise.

Another important postpurchase phenomenon is interpersonal communication. Buyers may recommend the product to others if they like it; if the product is flawed, they may provide negative information to others. This feedback from past purchasers to prospective buyers is an important information input to the buying process (see Figure 5.1). It may result from requests from potential buyers, spontaneous recommendations by previous buyers, or simply conversation that leads to a two-way discussion of the product.

Often opinion leaders serve their social groups by supplying media and usage information and recommendations for specific product classes. This phenomenon is particularly important in new-product situations where considerable information is needed by customers. Through interpersonal communication, opinion leaders create awareness among potential customers, supply attribute information for storage in memory, reduce perceived risk, and facilitate adoption of the new product. Often, but not always, the opinion leader is also an innovator or an early adopter.

Feedback in the case of an industrial product may involve specific product attributions as well as an evaluation and revision of the buying process. Management may want to ensure that at least two qualified vendors survive in the market so that bidding will remain competitive. This could lead to a "splitting of the business" in order to preserve low long-run prices. The dynamics of such a situation might require continual monitoring of the buying process by marketing management to make sure that its assumptions about purchasing remain correct.

Feedback and learning complete our model of consumer information processing. Although simple, this model is a powerful way of focusing managerial attention on customers. It asks the manager to consider how consumers collect, process, and update information in deciding to exchange money for a particular product or service. Sound strategy can be formulated and good decisions made only by managers who understand consumer response.

MULTIPERSON DECISION MAKING

We discussed the information-processing aspect of individual decision making in the last section. But sometimes more than one person participates in product selection. In these situations, we must know not only how each participant processes information but also how participants interact with one another in making a final product decision. These people form a decision-making unit or DMU.

The most common example of a DMU occurs in industrial buying, where end users, purchasing agents, and management may all be involved in the choice of a supplier. Multiperson decision processes and DMUs can also occur in many consumer markets. Auto purchases, for example, may involve several members of the family. The choice of a health maintenance organization (HMO) is even more complex; it may involve not only the family but also the employer (who offers only a restricted set of options to the employee).

In formulating a marketing strategy, managers must determine whether a multiperson DMU situation is present. They must also distinguish the multiperson situation where the ultimate buying decision is dominated by one person. A research engineer who needs a single low-cost part may be able to make the final choice by herself or himself, knowing that it will be approved by the purchasing agent and general management. In such a case, the presence of a "dominant influencer" simplifies the multiperson decision problem for a vendor. Wherever several people significantly influence the final decision, however, the vendor must identify the key players in the DMU and understand the process through which they make a choice. This is critical not only for selling and advertising strategies but also for product design. The importances of product attributes may vary across decision participants, with the best attributes for one person not necessarily the best for another member of the decision-making group. For example, engineering may feel that incremental performance is most important, while production may think that reliability is the most critical factor and purchasing may be most sensitive to cost.

If more than one person is involved in the buying decision, the seller needs to identify the functions performed by each member of the DMU. Among the most important such functions in industrial buying situations are:

1. *Specification*: defining the need and specifying the necessary attributes and performance requirements for the product or system. Often this function is performed by the final user.
2. *Gatekeeping*: controlling the input of information into the organization. This activity determines whether a supplier will be recognized and qualified for consideration.
3. *Budgeting*: allocating funds for the purchase of a specific product or for the project in which the product is to be employed.
4. *Generation of alternatives*: identifying solutions, products, and qualified bidders who have the potential to fill the organization's needs.
5. *Evaluation*: considering, in detail, bids and proposals in order to select the one that best meets requirements. Price/benefit trade-offs are generally made at this point.
6. *Selection*: choosing, finally, the source to supply the product or service.
7. *Approval*: obtaining an OK from top management.
8. *Monitoring*: assessing whether the product or system performs ''to specs.''

Each of these functions may not be carried out by a separate person. Typically, more than one person is involved at each functional step in the buying process, and a single individual may be active in more than one function. Identifying who is involved in accomplishing each function is the next step in diagnosing the DMU.

After functions and participants are identified, it is necessary to understand the dynamics of the decision process. Where does the information flow? What is the formal procurement process? What is the role of informal meetings and inputs (discussions in the hall or over lunch)? How long does the decision process take? When is the timing of various types of input most critical? Can the decision be reopened by appeal to higher levels in the organization? These are difficult questions, and although behavioral science theory is useful in modeling individual decision making, multiperson decision theory is not so well developed. Nevertheless, marketing managers must comprehend the process if they are to make sound decisions.

The complexity of this process is exemplified by recent changes in how companies buy information systems. Following the advent of personal computers and their related software, many local managers found that they had budget authorization limits that permitted them to procure their own machines. This greatly increased the importance of end users in the buying process. Instead of going to the information systems department for approval and procurement, the manager often went to a retail outlet and purchased the PC directly. This shift caused information systems departments to become more sensitive to end-user requirements, even to the point of opening their own internal stores to service PC demand. Eventually, however, top management in many large organizations decided that better coordination and controls were needed, and so began requiring authorization of new PC purchases by the information systems department. Thus, in effect, PC buying patterns reverted to the more traditional processes that had characterized mainframe system purchases.

Definitions of the buying functions, participants, and process must be continually updated for changes in the environment, products, and people. This difficult and demanding task is critical to understanding the phenomena that drive purchase decisions. Ultimately, it is this understanding that controls the ability of the organization to achieve its sales and profit goals.

ANALYTICAL SUPPORT

The first level of analytical support in understanding customer decision making is direct contact with buyers. Many organizations have a policy that top executives must spend at least one day each week in direct contact with customers or potential customers. Understanding begins with first-hand contact and experience with users.

More formal market research methods can also be useful. One might, for example, bring in a group of customers to discuss a particular "problem." Such "focus group" sessions with customers are common in both consumer markets (e.g., group discussion on how colds are treated in the family) and industrial markets (e.g., chief administrative officers' discussion of their needs in telecommunication systems). Typically, managers directly observe such groups, listen to audio transcripts, or view videotapes of the sessions. In some companies, such videotapes, which have been edited to portray realistically customer needs, desires, and information processing, are disseminated widely throughout the organization as educational tools.

The sales force is another source of information on buying processes. These are the people who are in most frequent contact with customers. Often the best salesperson is the one with the clearest understanding of which people in the customer organization are important, when they are active in the decision process, and what they are most sensitive to in the product offering. Increasingly, firms are using account teams to service their industrial customers. Because different members of the decision-making unit have greatly varying needs and capabilities, no one person can cover all the bases. An effective team, however, should be able to develop a clear view of the decision process.

A useful way of portraying a customer's information-processing procedure is to develop a flowchart describing its steps in the acquisition and processing of information. Figure 5.2 is a Level I flowchart of the decision processes in a consumer choice of refrigerators and laundry appliances (Wilkie and Dickson, 1985). The complex sequential process is evident.

Prior attitudes on brands, retailers, and product features were strong, but a precipitating event (appliance failure, move, redecoration, appliance not working well) triggered an active information search. This search included friends, media, and catalogs. Newspaper ads and friends were the most common source (approximately 40 percent of buyers indicated using each of these sources).[2] Consumer advisory services such as *Consumer Reports* were used by 20 percent of buyers, while 14 percent consulted appliance repairpeople.

After requirements for the appliance were initially specified, consumers decided which retailer to visit. Here the salesperson became a dominant influencer and supplied information on features, price, delivery, and service (41 percent of customers said the salesperson was the single most important source of useful information). This often led to a respecification of the desired product. After identifying the best alternative available, a decision was made to continue shopping or to make a purchase. This was the result of a specific cost/benefit trade-off: Is the cost of shopping worth the expected benefit (i.e., is the extra driving, time, and inconvenience worth the benefit of a lower price or a better product)? For many buyers, prior information, initial retailer selection, and point-of-purchase information led to an end of the search at this point, and a purchase. Thirty-seven percent shopped at only one store, and seventy-four percent of these only considered

---

[2] See Wilkie and Dickson (1985) for further discussion of empirical data reported in this paragraph.

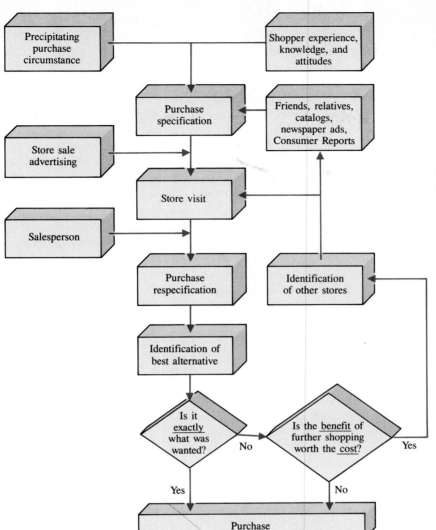

FIGURE 5.2
A Dynamic-Adaptive Model
of Shopping Behavior for
Refrigerators and Laundry
Appliances
Source: Reprinted with
permission from ''Shopping for
Appliances: Consumers'
Strategies and Patterns of
Information Search,'' working
paper. Copyright © 1985 by the
Marketing Science Institute,
Cambridge, MA.

one brand. Nineteen percent found it worthwhile to go to two stores, and sixty-three percent of these considered two brands. Fourty-four percent went to three or more stores and typically considered three or more brands. Consumers differed on the amount of information they required before making a purchase. Three-quarters made purchases at special low prices. Sale prices were not only effective in inducing the purchase process but also affected the choice of retailer and shortened the consumer's search by reducing the benefits of further shopping.

Figure 5.2 represents a simplification of the decision process. Explicit decision rules are not stated, and the joint husband-and-wife nature of the decision is not outlined (in 52 percent of the cases, both husband and wife were involved; in 40 percent, the female was solely or primarily involved). Although the figure is simplified, and individuals differ widely in their processes, it is a useful first step toward conceptualizing the information processing done by customers. With this flow model, the impacts of advertising, past purchasers, distribution, and price can be better understood.

Similar flowcharts can be used in industrial markets where a sequence of steps leads to a purchase decision. Here the multiperson phenomenon may be more evident. A simple conceptual technique for capturing the multiperson effects is a decision matrix that arrays participants in the DMU in columns and decision-process functions in rows. The entries in the cells indicate the relative influence of each individual at each stage. Table 5.1 shows a decision matrix for the purchase of lithographic plates based on interviews with twenty-five general commercial printers. The four types of participant and the median managerial ratings on influence at each of three stages in the decision process are shown. The ratings were on a 1–5 scale, where 5 indicates higher involvement and influence.

The results indicate that the pressman and the foreman are most important in initiating a change of plate supplier, all participants are highly involved in evaluation, and the general manager and foreman are most influential in the final decision. In constructing such matrices, one should recognize that all participants may not agree as to who is most important at each stage. Therefore, ratings should be taken from several informants in the organization, and multiple measures of influence and participation should be collected. (See Silk and Kalwani, 1982, for further discussion of the reliability and validity of matrix measures.)

Although the decision matrix does not represent the dynamics of the process and is dependent upon accurate assessments of influence, it does help us to structure the complexity of multiperson decision making and can be a component in a wider information-processing flow diagram analogous to the one in Figure 5.2.

Level II analysis formalizes the understanding obtained through Level I analysis, and integrates simple data and models with the conceptual framework. Often this is done within the context of specific decisions or phenomena.

Our consideration of life cycles in the following chapter is based on capturing the behavioral phenomenon of diffusion of innovation in a quantitative model to forecast sales over the life cycle. We extend this to a quantitative flow model that describes information acquisition and its influence on purchases. This model includes measures of the impact of word-of-mouth communication. In Chapter 8, we discuss specific analytical techniques for the measurement of attitudes and their representation in perception and preference models that aid in product positioning and the design of a communications program. Throughout the remainder of this book, we will draw on behavioral concepts to develop Level II analytical support tools for improved marketing strategy formulation.

Level III analytical support would include behavioral experimentation to test specific hypotheses involved in information processing. For example, research on memory may seek to determine how "family" and "sports" sedan cues affect the categorization and preference for these cars (see Marlino, 1985). Another activity at this level might be a detailed protocol analysis to specify the type of flowchart shown in Figure 5.2. Consumers may be given a tape recorder and asked to describe their actions and thoughts as they walk through a store. A decision net model may result (Bettman, 1979). A computer-based simulation of information processing in multiperson decision making would, in our view, be especially useful, given the complexity of these phenomena.

While Level III modeling is enticing because of its potential to enhance our understanding of highly complex phenomena, the costs of such an analysis are likely to be high and the results (at this stage) quite uncertain. Consequently, managers would be

TABLE 5.1   Relative Influence of Participants in DMU for Purchasing Lithographic Plates

	PRESSMAN	PLATEMAKER	FOREMAN	MANAGER
Initiate change	5	4	5	3
Evaluate	4	4	4	4
Make final decision	3	2	4	4

Source: Reprinted from *Journal of Marketing Research*, published by the American Marketing Association. From Alvin J. Silk and M. U. Kalwani, ''Measuring Influence in Organization Purchase Decisions,'' Vol. 2 (1982), pp. 165–181.

wise not to attempt this level except for critical, long-term decisions, and then only as part of a major, continuing research program.

Level I analysis is required to develop sound marketing strategy. Level II procedures often reward relatively small resource expenditures with large gains in understanding and improved decision making. In the next several chapters, we present a number of examples to support this proposition. Later in the book, we provide further examples of the integration of analytical support and managerial creativity and judgment for specific decision areas. However elaborate such analysis, it is critical to remember that the first step in good marketing strategy development is to obtain a clear understanding of the customer decision process.

QUESTIONS FOR DISCUSSION

1. Take a recent purchase decision you made (e.g., stereo, toothpaste, record, movie) and draw a flow diagram of the steps you went through in gaining input, making a decision, and updating information based on experience. How does it correspond to the processes outlined in this chapter?

2. Under what conditions will a customer spend large amounts of effort to search for information to support a decision? Under what conditions will a consumer seek little or no new information?

3. How does the buying process for industrial products differ from that for consumer products? Is the decision-making unit (DMU) concept equally applicable to both?

4. How can manufacturers affect the level and content of word-of-mouth communication about their products?

5. Why do customers use heuristic decision processes? Think of an instance in which you used a heuristic in making a decision. What was the basis of simplification and why did you use it? Did you practice selective perception?

6. What is the most important information source in the selection of a deodorant? A personal computer? An auto? A college?

7. How can a manufacturer ensure that the benefit proposition or "bundle of utility" it offers to customers is correctly perceived and evaluated?

8. What do you think are the three most important behavioral phenomena identified in this chapter? How do they affect the way in which effective marketing strategies are formulated?

REFERENCES

BETTMAN, JAMES R. 1979. *An Information Processing Theory of Consumer Choice*. Reading, MA: Addison-Wesley.

————. 1986. "Consumer Psychology." *Annual Review of Psychology* 37: 257–289.

BONOMA, THOMAS V. 1982. "Major Sales: Who *Really* Does the Buying?" *Harvard Business Review*, May/June: 111–119.

FISHBEIN, M. 1975. *Belief, Attitude, Intention and Behavior: An Introduction to Theory and Research*. Reading, MA: Addison-Wesley.

HAUSER, JOHN R., AND GLEN L. URBAN. 1979. Assessment of Attribute Importances and Consumer Utility Functions: Von Neumann-Morgenstern Theories Applied to Consumer Behavior." *Journal of Consumer Research* Vol. 5. pp. 251–262.

HOCH, STEVEN J., AND JOHN DEIGHTON. 1989. "Managing What Consumers Learn from Experience." *Journal of Marketing* 53: 1–20.

JOHANSSON, JOHNY K., AND IKUJIRO NONAKA. 1987. "Market Research the Japanese Way." *Harvard Business Review*, May/June: 16–22.

MARLINO, DEBORAH. 1985. "Heuristic Processing in the Formation of Judgments by Consumers." *Working Paper*. Cambridge, MA: Alfred P. Sloan School of Management, M.I.T.

MCQUISTON, DANIEL H. 1989. "Novelty, Complexity, and Importance as Causal Determinants of Industrial Buyer Behavior." *Journal of Marketing* 53: 66–79.

QUALLS, WILLIAM J., AND CHRISTOPHER P. PUTO. 1989. "Organizational Climate and Decision Framing: An Integrated Approach to Analyzing Industrial Buying Decisions." *Journal of Marketing Research* 26: 179–192.

RYAN, M., AND E. H. BONFIELD. 1975. "The Fishbein Extended Model and Consumer Behavior." *Journal of Consumer Behavior* 2: 118–136.

SILK, ALVIN J., AND MANOHAR U. KALWANI. 1982. "Measuring Influence in Organization Purchase Decisions." *Journal of Marketing Research* 19: 165–81.

STERNTHAL, BRIAN, AND C. SAMUEL CRAIG. 1982. *Consumer Behavior*. Englewood Cliffs, NJ: Prentice Hall.

SUJAN, MITA, JAMES R. BETTMAN, AND HARISH SUJAN. 1986. "Effects of Consumer Expectations on Information Processing in Selling Encounters." *Journal of Marketing Research* 24: 346–353.

TYBOUT, ALICE M., BOBBY J. CALDER, AND BRIAN STERNTHAL. 1981. "Using Information Processing Theory to Design Marketing Strategies." *Journal of Marketing Research* 18: 73–79.

TVERSKY, A. 1972. "Elimination by Aspects: A Theory of Choice." *Psychological Review* 79: 281–299.

TVERSKY, A. AND D. KAHNEMAN. 1974. "Judgment and Uncertainty: Heuristics and Biases." *Science* 185: 1124–31.

URBAN, GLEN L., AND JOHN R. HAUSER. 1980. *Design and Marketing New Products*. Englewood Cliffs, NJ: Prentice Hall.

WILKIE, W. L., AND P. R. DICKSON. 1985. "Shopping for Appliances: Consumers' Strategies and Patterns of Information Search." Working Paper. Cambridge, MA: Marketing Science Institute.

WILKIE, W. L., AND E. PESSEMIER. 1973. "Issues in Marketing's Use of Multi-attribute Models." *Journal of Marketing Research* 10:428–441.

WRIGHT, P. L. 1974. "The Harassed Decision Maker: Time Pressure, Distraction and the Use of Evidence." *Journal of Applied Psychology* 59: 555–561.

6
LIFE CYCLES

Now that we have a good set of insights into customer information processing and decision making, we can address some of the phenomena that reflect the aggregation of individual consumers at the product or industry level. In the next four chapters, we consider life-cycle, segmentation, positioning, and market response phenomena. We then examine their integration within the organization's competitive environment and strategic positioning.

LIFE-CYCLE ANALOGY

The so-called life cycle, in which a product or industry passes sequentially through phases of introduction, growth, maturity, and decline, has been observed for many products, product classes, and industries. The notion is drawn from the biological model of plants and animals being born, growing, reaching maturity, and then dying. Could not product dynamics be represented by the same model? Casual examination of past sales of products suggests some correspondence with this analogy. Figure 6.1 shows the theoretical shape of the life cycle; Figure 6.2 shows the sales of Citizen Band (CB) radios, which seem to follow the same pattern. Both start slowly and then show rapid growth, followed by leveling off and, finally, decline. The model can also be used to describe the profits a firm should expect in each phase. Profits are negative before introduction owing to development costs, and low in the earliest phases because of investments to develop the market; they increase in the growth phase, reach a maximum at maturity, and drop as decline sets in and margins fall.

Analogies can be powerful because they serve as useful benchmarks in new situations, but one must be careful not to ascribe to an analogy a degree of correspondence that is not valid. A considerable amount of care should be exercised when seeking to use biological models for nonbiological phenomena, such as product or market life cycles. Aging is an inalienable progression in plants and animals; but is the life cycle for products a natural

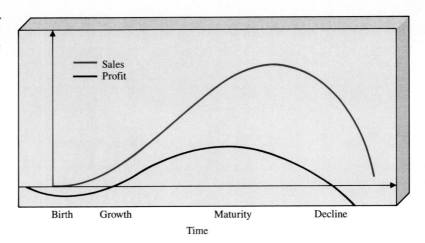

FIGURE 6.1
Idealized Life Cycle

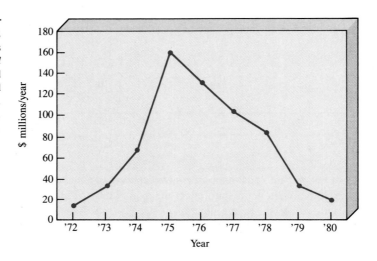

FIGURE 6.2
Sales of Citizen Band Radios
Source: Current *Industrial Reports*, MA-36N, Selected Electronic and Associated Products, Bureau of the Census, U.S. Department of Commerce, Washington, DC.

process over which the manager has virtually no control? The analogy with biology would suggest a positive answer to this question, but we should examine this proposition before accepting it.

In this chapter, we study the life-cycle model and the underlying determinants of this particular sales pattern. Some of the determinants are directly controllable, while others are "natural" phenomena that are largely outside the manager's control. With an understanding of the determinants of the life cycle, we can forecast sales and use these dynamic sales patterns as a basis for formulating a sound marketing strategy. We can then go on to consider the strategic implications of the life cycle and review the formal models that can provide analytic support for the forecasting of life-cycle sales dynamics.

DETERMINANTS

Technology

Figure 6.3 shows the historical sales pattern of steam locomotives. Sales started slowly, rose rapidly, reached a peak, and then declined. In this case, decline was due to the replacement of steam power by diesel and electric engines. Technological substitution

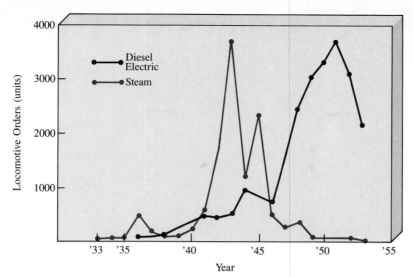

FIGURE 6.3
Replacement of Steam Locomotive by Diesel-Electric Locomotives
Note: Locomotive units include switcher, passenger, and freight locomotives.
Source: A. Cooper, E. Demuzzio, K. Hatten, E. Hicks, and D. Tock, ''Strategic Response to Technological Threats,'' Inst. Paper No. 431, Krannert Graduate School of Management, Purdue University, November 1973, by permission of the authors.

caused the dynamic sales pattern to correspond to the life-cycle shape. An accurate forecast of the decline phase for steam engines, would, of course, have required an ability to predict the time of arrival of new technologies.

A company called Baldwin dominated the steam locomotive market in the United States. Although Baldwin built the finest steam engines, it is little known today because it failed to predict the shift to diesel power and thus was not able to compete in the new market technology, which came to be dominated by General Motors. It is easy to condemn Baldwin for failing to recognize the technological threat to its business, but only three years before steam engine sales disappeared almost completely, there had, in fact, been a surge in demand. Baldwin management may well have viewed this surge as evidence of a return to the ''mature'' level of prewar sales.

Another example of a life cycle driven by technology in transportation is provided by the commercial jet aircraft market in the 1954–1965 period. Douglas had over 50 percent of the market with its line of propeller-driven planes when Boeing pioneered the commercial jet in 1959, subsequently becoming the largest supplier. Although Douglas ultimately responded with its own jet, Boeing has continued to dominate the market.

As we saw in the case cited in Chapter 4, the commercial aircraft market today faces a new technological opportunity with the unducted fan jet (UDF). The key question in this case is: Will the UDF replace jet and turboprop propulsion systems, and if so, at what rate? Forecasting the future sales pattern for the UDF depends largely on the answer to this question. The case provides one life cycle based on jet aircraft program sales dynamics. Managers could use this forecast of the diffusion rate or prepare their own life-cycle forecast as an input to rate-of-return calculation and a Go/No Go managerial decision.

Technological life cycles also occur in services. Figure 6.4A shows the growth of cable TV in the United States. This growth, combined with the growth and maturity in VCR machines, has caused major shifts in entertainment habits. Network viewership is down, a rental home movie market has developed, and the tendency of households to record one TV show for later viewing while simultaneously watching another has changed the competitive structure of programming. Understanding and predicting the life cycles in this instance are critical to successful diagnosis of the strategic environment.

A final example of technological life cycles is shown in Figure 6.5. Each succeeding RAM size was replaced by a new, larger-capacity chip. Each chip experienced rapid growth, a leveling off, and then a sharp decline in sales. The figure shows that maximum levels are increasing and time from first entry to replacement is shortening. Substitution

95

FIGURE 6.4
Life Cycles of Two Home
Entertainment
Technological Innovations
Source: Adapted from
Predicasts Basebook (1988),
pp. 655, 760.

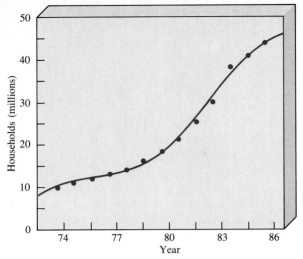

A. Cumulative households Subscribing to Cable TV

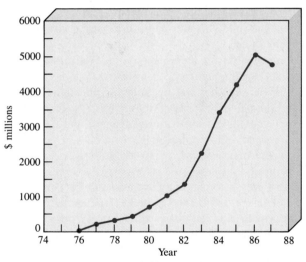

B. Annual shipments of VCRs

FIGURE 6.5
Technological Life Cycles—
RAM
Sources: Adapted from:
"Semiconductor Memory Chip
Peak Sales and Prices,"
Fortune, May 16, 1983, p. 154;
"IC Memory Chips Sales
Projected 1990," *Electronic
Marketing Trends*, April 1982,
p. 19; "Solid-state Memory
Devices Shipments Projected,"
*Telephone Engineering &
Management*, March 1, 1980, p.
22.

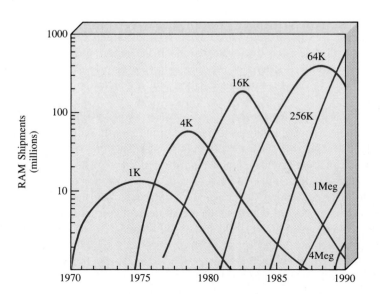

is now moving so rapidly that the development time may be too long to take advantage of the technological window for the next-size chip. In this market, it would appear that a firm not having a 1 megabyte bit chip on the market by 1990 would be wise to skip this generation and concentrate on a 4 megabyte bit chip.

Diffusion of Innovation

A decline in sales for a given product after rapid growth may occur for reasons other than the substitution of a new technology. The behavioral phenomenon of diffusion of innovation can produce a similar pattern. According to diffusion theory, innovators adopt first and then communicate the product's benefits to others through word-of-mouth interaction. Recall from Chapter 5 that interpersonal communication often plays a major role in consumer decision making by portraying information that can change attribute beliefs and reduce the customer's perceived risk. Papers at professional meetings, referrals, and direct observation of use are other methods innovators use to disseminate information to later adopters. Diffusion is characterized by a slow start, but a subsequent rapid increase in sales as the innovation is accepted by the majority of the market. If the market has a finite limit, there comes a point when most of those inclined to buy the product have already purchased it. Saturation sets in, leading to a decline in annual sales.

A graph of the historical sales of CT (Computer Tomography) head scanners used for diagnosis of cancer and brain disease is shown in Figure 6.6. Innovative medical school hospitals were the first to adopt this new technology. Only after the technology

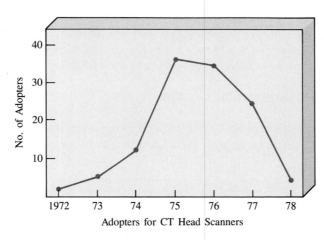

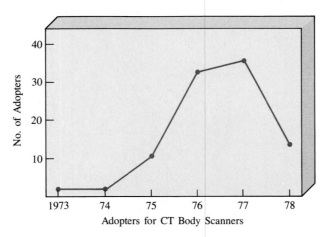

FIGURE 6.6
Actual and MLE Fitted Number of Adopters for CT Body Scanners
Source: Reprinted with permission from David C. Schmittlein and Vijay Mahajan, "Maximum Likelihood Estimation for an Innovation Diffusion Model of New Product Acceptance," *Marketing Science*, Vol. 1 (1982), pp. 57–78.

was proven and communicated did other hospitals purchase it. Sales flattened because the number of hospitals that could buy such expensive machines was limited by government "certificate of need" requirements. As the market of hospitals eligible to buy became saturated, annual sales began to decline. While a related technology produced the full body scanner, it did not turn out to be a replacement for the head-only scanner. As Figure 6.6 shows, both had high sales levels in 1976 and 1977, while sales of both fell in 1978. Hospital usage studies confirm that both devices were utilized by many hospitals as complements rather than as substitutes, in the context of rising demand for diagnostic services. Similar diffusion patterns may be expected for the new imaging technologies (magnetic resonance and radio isotope), which are superior to CT scanning technology in some applications.

Understanding diffusion processes and information flows is critical to predicting sales patterns in many new-product marketing situations. In a later section of this chapter, we will examine the use of mathematical models to describe and predict diffusion-of-innovation rates.

Consumer Preference

A product's sales may also drop because of <u>consumer preference</u> for new competitive products. Figure 6.7 shows the sales of red light-emitting diode (LED) and black or white liquid crystal diode (LCD) watches. Both types of display followed the life cycle, but by 1980, consumer preferences had shifted from LED to LCD; LCDs were dominant throughout the 1980s.

The decline phase of sales of a particular automobile model is usually the result of new competitive entrants that are preferred to the existing car. That is, the model's decline in sales is not primarily a function of saturation or new technology, but of the fact that when a car is to be replaced, a newer and preferred model is available.

Environmental Change

A wide variety of environmental changes can affect the life cycle of a product. Massive increases in the price of oil during the 1970s caused the sale of many products to decline.

FIGURE 6.7
Sales of Light-Emitting Diode (LED) and Liquid Crystal Diode (LCD) Watches
Source: "Digital Watch Sales for 1978–1979," *Merchandising*, May 1979, p. 42 (New York: Billboard Publishing).

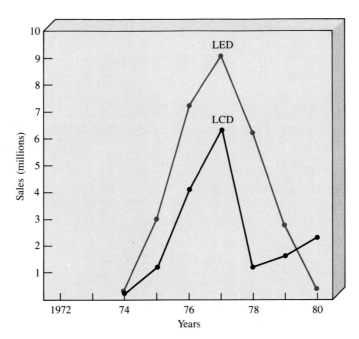

For example, sales of large cars fell rapidly, as did those of many energy-intensive products. Changes in government regulations, social values, styles, and fashions, and fluctuation in international exchange rates provide other examples of environmental factors likely to impact life cycles significantly.

The effect of changes in government regulations can be especially profound. Figure 6.8A shows the drop in sales of oral diabetic drugs in 1975 after an FDA report cited them as ineffective. A sharper drop occurred in the use of clofibrates for the reduction of cholesterol when a government study reported dangerous side effects (see Figure 6.8B).

In the 1970–1985 period, U.S. government regulation of cigarette advertising and warnings did not cause a rapid decline in total consumption, but there was a large shift from regular to filter and ultra-high-filtration cigarettes. Brand shifts took place as well.

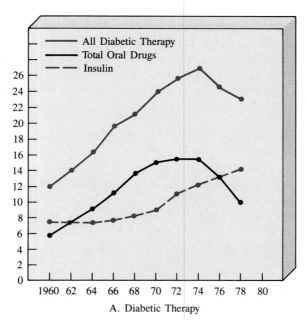

A. Diabetic Therapy

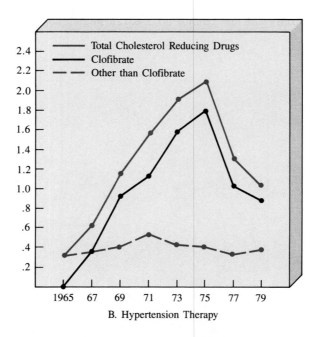

B. Hypertension Therapy

FIGURE 6.8
Ethical Pharmaceutical Sales Patterns
Source: Adapted from Stan N. Finkelstein and Dana L. Gilbert, ''Scientific Evidence and the Abandonment of Medical Technology: A Study of Eight Drugs,'' Sloan Working Paper (Cambridge, MA: MIT, 1983, p. 11).

When examining life-cycle phenomena, it is important to consider industry, product class, and brand effects. In this case, total industry sales were stable, those of filter cigarettes grew, and brands of filter cigarettes varied in their performance (Kent and Winston declined, while Marlboro, presumably because of the strength of its "Marlboro Man" image, improved its market position). The cigarette industry is beginning to decline in the United States because of restrictions on smoking in public enacted in the 1980s; smoking is not permitted in most public places in Cambridge, Massachusetts, for example, and smoking on U.S. airlines has been virtually banned altogether. This decline has led cigarette manufacturers to concentrate on markets in the rest of the world, where growth potential continues to exist.

Trial and Repeat Purchasing

Sales patterns similar to life cycles can occur in product classes characterized by trial and repeat purchasing. Typical examples are consumer package goods such as shampoos, analgesics, and breakfast cereals. A new product in one of these categories may experience a rapid buildup during the trial phase, but the potential for initial purchases may be exhausted in a year or two. After trial, repeat purchases show growth, but at a rate that depends on frequency of purchase and repeat-purchase probabilities. In products where

FIGURE 6.9
Trial and Repeat Sales
Pattern

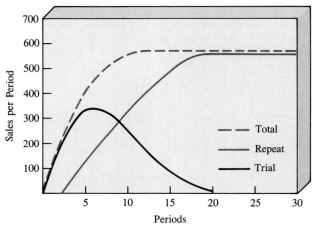

A. Short Purchase Interval

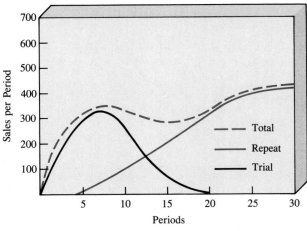

B. Long Purchase Interval

the purchase interval is long, repeat sales build slowly. If the interval between purchases is short, sales build rapidly to a steady-state level. Figure 6.9 shows two patterns of total sales that can develop in trial and repeat-purchase environments with different purchase intervals. In the short-interval case, sales rise rapidly to a mature level, while in the longer-interval case, they rise, drop, and then build to the mature level.

Such patterns are not restricted to consumer package goods. They can occur in industrial buy/rebuy situations (e.g., new writing instruments, new fasteners for fabrication) and services where resubscription is necessary (e.g., HMO membership, financial information reporting). In pharmaceuticals, doctors try a new drug for their patients and continue prescribing it if it is effective and shows few side effects.

Trial and repeat levels can be affected by marketing actions. Trial is stimulated by advertising, promotion, and sampling. Repeat purchases are similarly influenced by marketing practices. In one study of ethical drugs (Cox, 1967), sales systematically increased (reversing a decline phase) when manufacturers significantly raised their promotion levels (advertising and "detailing" by salespeople).

New Uses and Redesign

Decline can be delayed by creating new uses or new customer markets for a product. This rejuvenation of the life cycle can often be achieved through product innovations. Nylon, produced by DuPont for parachutes and women's hosiery in the 1940s, would probably have followed the traditional life cycle, reaching maturity and decline, if DuPont had not developed new uses for nylon in broad woven fabrics, tire cord, and sweaters. With these new applications, nylon was kept in a growth phase for over twenty years.

Rejuvenation to meet consumer needs is a powerful marketing action. In the face of rising oil prices, some firms refused to accept the decline phase of the life cycle for their oil-dependent products, but instead redesigned those products to renew their life cycles. Figure 6.10 shows Boeing's redesign of the 727 to achieve greater fuel economy. Sales of the 727 entered a new growth phase, in contrast with the decline of the 747 from 1971–77. Note, however, that the 747 also had a rejuvenation in the period 1978–82. In your consideration of the UDF engine case in Chapter 4, you may have forecasted a rejuvenation of the life cycle in 1999 after the initial decline phase.

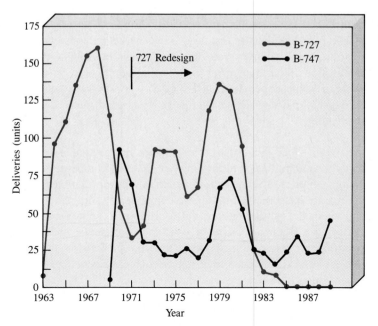

FIGURE 6.10
B-727 Rejuvenation
Source: World Jet Airplane Inventory, 1988, p. 7, Boeing Commercial Airplane Group, The Boeing Co.

Strategy over the Life Cycle

A number of managerial implications can be drawn from the position of a product in the life cycle. Critical success factors and strategic choices are different at each stage. The following paragraphs describe the generally accepted managerial prescriptions for each phase in the life cycle, as well as the complexities often experienced in applying these generic strategies to specific marketing situations.

Introduction: Emphasis is generally placed on expanding the market. Heavy expenditures for advertising, selling, sampling, promotion, and distribution are made to facilitate initial purchases and to stimulate diffusion of innovation. Efforts are undertaken to achieve awareness and positive purchase attitudes in the target market. Innovators are given priority in order to maximize positive feedback after use, thus increasing the rate of diffusion. Product performance must be good at introduction, and must be constantly improved so that the innovating company can continue to preempt competitors who might be considering entering.

Negative cash flow and initial losses are likely during this phase. The firm should be prepared to invest in the market. At the introduction phase of the life cycle, an entrepreneurial manager is highly desirable to overcome the many obstacles that exist within the organization and the market. Flexibility, sensitivity to feedback, and the ability to take quick action are the key organizational success factors.

Profitability will be affected by the introductory marketing budget. Pricing is a key strategic decision that will affect life-cycle return on investment. Should price be set high to ''skim'' the market demand, with resultant slow sales growth but high profit levels; or should price be set low to ''penetrate'' the potential market, encourage diffusion, build share, and achieve greater profits later in the life cycle? In today's market, the skimming strategy is often ineffective because it allows competitors to enter under the price umbrella and build market position. They can copy the innovation and not suffer the time penalties usually experienced by later entrants. Only if the originator is protected from competition (by a strong patent, for example), or if the strategy is to take profits and then move on to other markets, would skimming be recommended. Penetration is an aggressive strategy; pricing below initial cost is especially risky because if costs do not decline with volume, profits may never be earned. We will discuss these issues further in later chapters on market share, competitive strategy, and market response phenomena. Our approach will be to define alternative strategies, use models to evaluate their long-term profit and ROI implications, and then select the one that seems best given a particular firm's strategic goals and objectives. (In the UDF case, you may have noted that initial prices were less than costs, and considered alternative prices and their effect on the rate of diffusion of innovation.)

Growth: Once initial market acceptance has been achieved, the innovator firm's focus shifts to holding and building market share as competitors enter. Product improvement continues, prices decline as production costs drop, more product variants are introduced, the market is segmented into basic components, competitors differentiate their products, and channels of distribution widen. Emphasis switches from stimulating diffusion to capturing a dominant share of consumer preference and choices. Primary managerial requirements move from those of the entrepreneur to those of professional marketing management. Cash flow may approach break-even, and profits begin to accrue. The organization becomes larger and more formal.

Maturity: In the mature phase, competition intensifies and price erosion is likely. Price promotion is common. More segmentation occurs in an attempt to find higher-margin sales opportunities, and efforts are made to differentiate within each segment. Emphasis must be placed on production-process improvement; major product innovation is less likely. Firms earning high profits are likely to be both low-cost producers *and* effective marketers.

Cash flow and profitability should be at their highest levels at this point in the life cycle. The achievement of this potential profit requires good administration to reduce costs and increase revenues. Careful budgeting, planning, and control are critical. The manager who is successful in this phase may not be the entrepreneur or marketing manager who guided the product through the early phases of its life cycle. The emphasis now is on efficiency and on holding share. This is the phase where profits must be earned to reward earlier innovation and risk taking.

Decline: In the decline phase, prices fall further and some competitors drop out of the market. Only a few can survive when faced with falling industry sales. As sales decline, a firm has two basic strategic choices: it can milk the product to obtain whatever profit potential remains, or it can rejuvenate it to begin the growth phase of a new life cycle.

Milking the product entails reducing marketing expenditures and depends on consumer loyalty to maintain high margins. This harvesting strategy allows the product to die gracefully and profitably. It avoids the pitfall of overspending to maintain volume levels at a time when sales potential is declining. If expenditures stay high, profits and return on investment may drop precipitously in the wake of falling volumes.

The milking strategy produces a self-fulfilling forecast. If sales are forecast to decline and marketing expenditures are accordingly reduced, sales will decline. Viewed in retrospect, both the forecast and the decision will appear to be correct. Sales were forecast to decline and they did!

Often a dictatorial managerial style is required to implement major expense reductions. Tough budget cuts may have to be made and enforced in the face of resistance from subordinates who continue to believe in growth. In some companies, certain managers have reputations as ''harvesters.'' Their appointment as general manager of a particular business may be unwelcome to many subordinates and may give competitors an important piece of competitive intelligence.

Rejuvenation is a pure marketing strategy. It entails finding new needs or uses for the product and fitting the product to them to produce a new spurt of sales. The shape of the life cycle can be modified by this strategy, as we saw in the Dupont and Boeing examples cited earlier. A firm may be overlooking major profit opportunities if it fails to carefully evaluate the ''reinnovation'' option, cycling back to the first phase of the life cycle in a search for new product attributes or segments where consumer value can be created.

Managers who are efficiency oriented generally show little interest in rejuvenation. The danger here is failure to recognize signs that a reinnovation strategy could recycle the product to the growth phase of the life cycle. If the manager in charge is not changed, a rejuvenation strategy is unlikely to be proposed or implemented. An entrepreneurial marketing manager is needed to manage ''reinnovation,'' and this person must have the support of top management.

Issues in Life-Cycle Management

Although the strategies just discussed are intuitively appealing, a number of difficult questions must be addressed before the prescriptions for each phase of the life cycle can be evaluated. We need to define the life cycle properly, determine the degree to which we can control it, and establish where we are on the curve.

At What Level Should We Define the Life Cycle? Should we examine the life cycle at the industry, product class, or brand level? Research indicates that life cycles are especially evident at industry or product class levels (Polli and Cook, 1969). But we are much more in control at the brand level. Sales of VCRs, for example, demonstrate much more volatility at brand level than at product level, where a traditional product life cycle is evident. The overall home entertainment industry is highly aggregated and will show only a long life cycle, if it shows any at all.

Another issue in defining the life cycle is the information lag in the distribution channel. Customer effects are first felt at retail or at point of final sales and order. Because of delays resulting from ordering procedures at wholesalers and distributors, manufacturers may not sense the life-cycle change until much later. As a result, the decline phase may occur later at the manufacturer level, but with a much steeper falloff. Consumer sales gradually decline, but the manufacturer may not sense this until reorders cease. Some manufacturers of CB radios and video games were caught by surprise when orders from distributors dropped to zero, even though evidence of decline at the retail level had been evident for some time. For some companies, this shock produced losses that forced them out of business (e.g., Intelevision). If managers are to diagnose the life cycle correctly, they must obtain information directly from the consumer level.

To see if life cycles are evident, it is best to examine sales patterns at all levels. First we must find out which of the determinants is driving the sales patterns at each level. Then we can forecast levels of future determining factors and act on the resulting life cycle. Usually, the life cycle is most relevant for the product class (e.g., VCRs); brand shares within it are modeled by explicit market response functions, brand-level diffusion phenomena, and focusing on variables that managers can use to control the sales pattern.

Can We Control the Life Cycle? From our discussion thus far, it is evident that some of the determinants of the life cycle can be controlled, while others display a strong inertia that makes them nearly impervious to managerial action. Technological change is partially a function of our R&D, but is more heavily determined by the cumulative effect of academic and industrial research by many organizations. In each industry, management should ask to what degree it controls the rate of technological advancement. If the level of control is low, management can assume that life-cycle decline due to technology is a given, and plan and respond to it accordingly. Although Intel affects the rate of advance in RAM capacity, for example, it would be wise to forecast that the technology will advance and make lower-capacity RAMs obsolete even if Intel is not the innovator responsible for such advances.

Diffusion of innovation, on the other hand, is a natural phenomenon that can be influenced by our actions. If we advertise heavily, we will increase awareness of the new product, which should benefit us. It should also increase the rate of diffusion of the product class—for example, the advertising of our brand of compact disc player will increase awareness of compact disc players in general as well as recognition of our brand. If competitors are sensitive to our increases in advertising expenditures, the result may be an overall increase in product-class advertising and a further acceleration of the diffusion of innovation. Similar effects would be observed at brand and product-class levels should one competitor drop price and others follow. Managing the life cycle when it is strongly influenced by a process of diffusion of innovation requires the blending of natural and controllable effects. Diffusion progresses in a specific pattern, but our marketing strategy can influence that pattern.

Changes in consumer preferences and environmental factors are largely outside our control, although the availability of products is what makes consumer preference possible. Consumer preference for LCD watches was not evident until both LED and LCD watches were on the market. While declines due to new preferences or entry by new competitive products are difficult to predict, they may change life-cycle patterns, so management must devote attention to understanding and forecasting them. New market research methods may allow earlier assessment of these shifts (see Chapter 14 on new-product development). Government regulation can be affected by lobbying and political influence, but this factor is often uncontrollable in terms of life-cycle forecasting. Should the FDA find that heavy use of aspartane-based artificial sweeteners has adverse side effects, many brands will suddenly find themselves in the decline phase.

The pattern of trial and repeat purchases is another example of a life-cycle determinant where the underlying structure is natural but the parameters of the structure can be changed. Providing free samples of a product gives people a trial experience and moves them on to the potential purchase state. Likewise, promotion by in-pack coupons can increase the repeat-purchase rate. Special displays may shorten the time between purchases or increase the purchase quantity. Competitive responses may amplify these effects to the product-class level.

From this review of the determinants of the life cycle, it is clear that marketers frequently possess substantial influence and control. In contrast to the natural progression of the biological analogy, the firm and its competitors have significant control over the level and timing of the life cycle. In our view, the marketer would do better to think of "dynamic sales patterns" (DSP) and how to affect them than to focus unduly on the allegedly inevitable "life cycle."

What Phase of the Life Cycle Are We in? Assuming that dynamic patterns affect the sales of our brand as described by the life-cycle model, we need to identify what phase of the life cycle we are in before we can employ the generic strategies outlined above. It is easy to look back at the complete sales history of a product and define the phases of introduction, growth, maturity, and decline; it is much more difficult to recognize the phases as they unfold. With five years of experience in the market, how do we know when growth will end? How long will maturity last before decline?

In the next section, we examine analytic approaches that can, in our view, provide considerable assistance in answering these questions.

ANALYTIC SUPPORT AND LIFE-CYCLE MODELING

The most basic analytical support procedure is based on collecting accurate sales and product histories. These should include records of marketing expenditures, competitive actions, technological advances, and environmental changes. With good historical data, managers can often diagnose the determinants of the dynamic patterns they observe through the intelligent use of judgment and insight. Based on the conclusions drawn from such analysis, the manager then seeks to forecast future patterns and to select an optimal marketing strategy.

While managerial judgment is clearly the place to start in defining and predicting the phases of the life cycle, stronger analytical tools are also available. Quantitative models help to designate which phase of the life cycle we are in and to forecast future sales levels. In this section, we describe two types of quantitative models frequently used for this purpose. The first represents the life cycle by a single equation and predicts the future based on early market sales results. The second disaggregates the consumer purchase process into awareness, shopping, choice, and interpersonal communication in order to forecast the life cycle *prior to* market introduction. After describing these Level II analysis tools, we indicate some of the extensions available for Level III analytic support.

Aggregate Diffusion Modeling

When (1) the diffusion of innovation is a major determinant of the life cycle, (2) our concern is primarily with initial rather than repeat purchases, and (3) there has been at

FIGURE 6.11
Probability of Purchase and
Cumulative Adoption

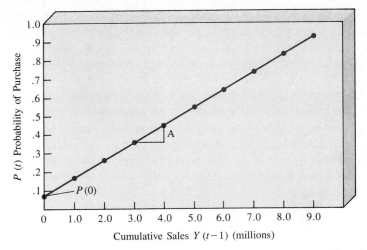

Cumulative Sales $Y(t-1)$ (millions)

least five years of sales experience, a relatively simple model can be employed to forecast the pattern of future sales. It is based on representing the initial trial, the rate of diffusion, and the total market potential in a mathematical model (see Bass, 1969, for full derivation).

Model: Probability of initial purchase is shown in Figure 6.11. The vertical axis is the probability of purchase for people in the potential market who have *not* purchased by the designated period t. The horizontal axis is the *cumulative* number of past buyers who have purchased by period t (i.e., the sum of buyers from introduction through the beginning of period t). One must take care to understand these definitions. The vertical scale is *not* the total probability of purchase, but rather the probability for those who have not yet purchased. The horizontal axis is *not* time since introduction, but rather the total number of customers who have made initial purchases by period t. The lower left portion of the figure shows a purchase probability when cumulative sales are zero (denoted as $P(0)$). This reflects period 1 purchases by early innovators. After these people have bought, we enter a value for the number of past buyers on the horizontal axis. As the cumulative number of past buyers increases, the model posits that the probability of purchase increases for those who have not yet bought. Implicit here is the notion that intensifying word-of-mouth communication and rising social acceptance increase the probability of purchase as diffusion of innovation takes place.

Consider the early compact audio disc players. In 1985, some sales were made to innovators. Based on their experience, they recommended the product to others. ("It really does sound better"). If the initial probability of purchase was .01, the model would suggest that the probability of purchase for those who had not purchased in 1985 would be higher—say, .015. Sales in 1986 would thus be .015 times the number of people remaining in the potential market after customers who purchased in 1985 are removed. In 1987, the cumulative past buyers would be the sum of 1985 and 1986 buyers, and Figure 6.11 would specify an increase in purchase probability to .023. The rate of increase in the probability is controlled by the slope of the line.

The equation to represent the initial trial purchase is:

(6.1) $P(t) = P(0) + A Y(t - 1)$

where:

$P(t) = $ probability of purchase in period t for those who have not yet purchased

$P(0) = $ initial probability of purchase in period $t = 0$,

106

$$Y(t - 1) = \text{cumulative number of customers who have purchased through the end of period } t - 1$$

$$A = \text{slope coefficient}$$

In order to calculate the sales in any period, we need to multiply this probability times the number of people who have not purchased. This is the total potential market (M), less the cumulative past buyers ($Y(t - 1)$):

(6.2) $S(t) = (M - Y(t - 1))P(t)$

where:

$$S(t) = \text{sales in period } t$$

$$M = \text{total number of customers who will ever buy}$$

We get our final equation by substituting equation (6.1) into equation (6.2). At the same time, we reexpress the slope of the purchase probability curve as $A = Q/M$ so that the diffusion parameter Q can be compared across product classes where the potential market differs. Simple algebraic manipulation produces:

(6.3) $S(t) = P(0)M + (Q - P(0))Y(t - 1) - (Q/M)Y(t - 1)^2$

where:

$$Q = \text{diffusion parameter}$$

This equation says that sales in any period are the initial sales ($P(0)M$), plus a component that increases with past buyers and is dependent on the diffusion process ($Q - P(0)$), less a component that is a function of the square of the number of past buyers. The result is shown in Figure 6.12 and resembles the theoretical life-cycle shape.

Inputs: In order to forecast with this model, we need three values: $P(0)$, Q, and M. We can use judgment based on experience to set them, or we can do a statistical analysis of historical sales data. Estimates of the initial sales probability ($P(0)$) can often be based

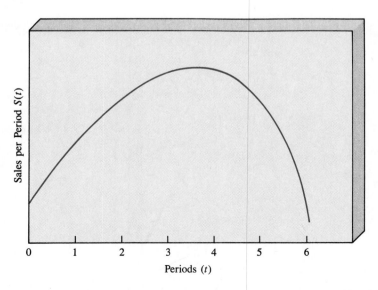

FIGURE 6.12
Bass Curve

on concept tests with customers and past sales of similar new products. The value is usually small, and the overall forecast is generally not too sensitive to it. The Q value is the main factor determining the rate of growth for a new product. It is not easy to set by judgment, but it may be helpful to examine diffusion rates from analogous products. For reference, Figure 6.13 gives the Q values that have been found most appropriate in forecasting the life cycles of selected classes of products. Systematic studies of many categories indicate that the typical P is .02 (higher for consumer durables than for industrial products) and Q is typically .4 to .5 (lower for consumer durables than for industrial products). (See Schmittlein and Mahajan, 1982; Srinivasan and Mason, 1986; Sultan, Farley, and Lehmann, 1990; and Montgomery and Srinivasan, 1989.)

The most difficult parameter to estimate is the total size of the potential market (M). Is it 10 million households for a new compact disc player, or is it 50 million? Sales can be calculated for a range of M values and judgment applied to find the best forecast.

One of the best ways to set the parameters of the model is to make sure that the model incorporating the selected parameters does, in fact, describe the known sales history for the product. We can do this by trying different values that seem reasonable until we achieve a good fit between the model and actual results. Or we can use more formal methods, such as regression of the model equation against actual sales results. If we do this regression over the complete sales history, we can usually be certain of obtaining a good fit. Figure 6.14 shows the actual and fitted values for CT head and body scanners. Across a range of consumer durables, the percent of the variation explained by such regressions is about 80 percent.

A forecast of the future life cycle with regression that is based solely on *early* results is subject to large errors unless enough data are available (Heeler and Hustad, 1980; Srinivasan and Mason, 1986). To ensure statistical adequacy, at least five years of sales data are required (as much as eight years if the life cycle is long). Where judgment can be used to pare the range of possibilities, however, it is possible to obtain reasonably good forecasts with considerably less data.

FIGURE 6.13
Life-Cycle Model Q Values
Source: From K. D. Lawrence and W. H. Lawton, "Application of Diffusion Models: Some Empirical Results," in Wind et al. (eds.), *New Product Forecasting Models and Applications* (Lexington, MA: Lexington Books, 1981).

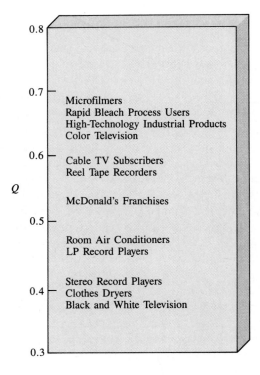

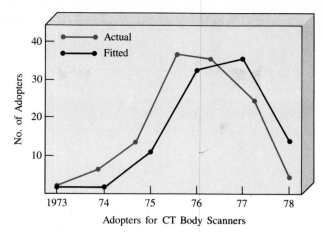

Adopters for CT Body Scanners

FIGURE 6.14
CT Head and Body Scanner
Fits
Source: Reprinted with
permission from David C.
Schmittlein and Vijay Mahajan,
''Maximum Likelihood
Estimation for an Innovation
Diffusion Model of New
Product Acceptance,''
Marketing Science, Vol. 1
(1982), pp. 71–72.

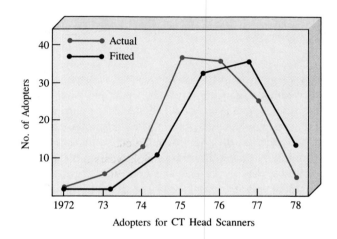

Adopters for CT Head Scanners

Managerial Use: When the primary determinant of the life cycle is diffusion of innovation and managers are confident of their judgment, or when there are enough historical sales data, an aggregate diffusion model can be used. This model can predict future sales patterns and identify the phase of the life cycle for the product class.

The aggregate model represents innovator purchasing, diffusion, and saturation, but does not explicitly represent the other determinants of the product life cycle. It is, however, possible to extend the model in Level III analysis to include such factors. A simple extension can be done by adding replacement purchases to the initial purchase model described by equation (6.3). Table 6.1 shows replacement buying lagging seven years after first purchase, and assumes all buyers will replace their units at that time. The new input required is the time between purchase and replacement and the fraction of people who will replace their initial purchase at the specified time. Other extensions include advertising and price effects, growth in the target group, and word-of-mouth communication (see Mahajan and Wind, 1986; and Mahajan, Muller, and Bass, 1989, for a summary). The most recent extension includes technological substitution (Norton and Bass, 1987), and has been successfully applied to the semiconductor industry. These extensions expand the richness of the model, but demand more parameter estimates than the simple basic model. Managers who want to estimate statistically the model's parameters must either have access to more data or employ a greater amount of judgment.

TABLE 6.1   Original and Replacement Sales

YEAR	ORIGINAL PURCHASE	REPLACEMENT PURCHASE	TOTAL
1982	12.1		12.1
1983	16.7		16.7
1984	22.6		22.6
1985	29.9		29.9
1986	38.2		38.2
1987	46.6		46.6
1988	54.1		54.1
1989	59.1		59.1
1990	60.4	12.1	72.5
1991	57.7	16.7	74.4
1992	51.7	22.6	74.3
1993	43.7	29.9	73.6
1994	35.2	38.2	73.4
1995	27.2	46.6	73.8
1996	20.4	54.1	74.5

Aggregate diffusion models can be useful tools in answering the critical questions of where products are in the life cycle and what will be the characteristics of demand in the future. Managers should, however, be sure that the key determinants affecting their products are captured in the model before they use the forecasts, or else be prepared to modify the forecasts for critical effects that have not been incorporated. Such models are particularly powerful when diffusion of innovation is important, a reasonable amount of historical data is present, and norms for the parameters have been established through comparison with products that are much farther along on their product life cycles.

Premarket Forecasting of Life Cycles

Managers often face the problem of having to forecast dynamic sales patterns before product introduction or solely on the basis of early national sales data. In these cases, the value of aggregate diffusion models is limited. In this section, we describe a disaggregated "consumer flow model" and consumer clinic measurement system that provide a powerful forecasting and management tool prior to market entry or very early in the life cycle. After we describe the basic model, we offer a mini case study of its application.

Customer Flow Model: In contrast to the aggregate diffusion model shown in equation (6.3), a flow model uses many equations to track the *individual* consumers who flow from one stage in the buying process to another. If there were 10 million people aware of our product and 1 million of them went shopping for it, the flow between "awareness" and "shopping" would be represented by the simple multiplication of 10 million aware individuals times the fraction of them who become "shoppers" (10 percent), resulting in 1 million shoppers.

Figure 6.15 depicts such a flow model for consumer durable goods purchasing. It represents awareness in the target group as being the result of advertising, word-of-mouth communication, or both. A fraction of aware individuals will flow from the awareness state and enter the market (i.e., buy in this product class) during this period. Some fraction of these buyers will go shopping for the product in an outlet that carries it. Some fraction of these customers in the store will buy the product. If they buy, they will be able to provide word-of-mouth communication to prospective buyers. The number of potential customers they bring to a state of awareness will depend on how many recommendations

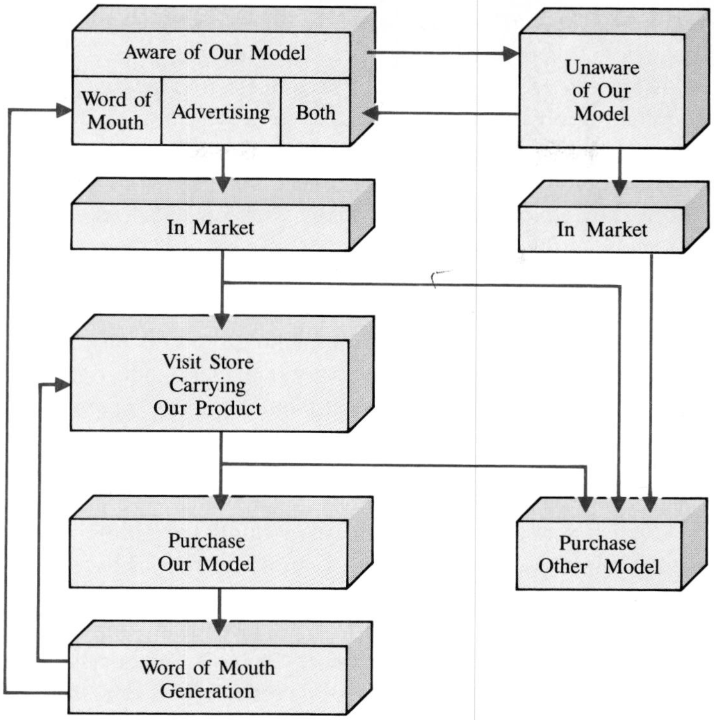

FIGURE 6.15
Macro Flow Model

they make in the next period. Another flow reflects forgetting; people move from an aware state to one of unawareness of our product. Finally, some flows lead to states in which consumers purchase competitive products.

If one can estimate the flow from one state to another, dynamic sales patterns can be calculated. These flows will reflect the consumer buying process and diffusion through interpersonal influence. It is possible to program such a model on a PC. If done, this model will provide you with the opportunity to simulate sales of new consumer durables (e.g., automobiles). If you make alternative simulations, you can get a good idea of the sensitivity of the forecasts to varying assumptions. By altering the flow rates into "awareness" for varying levels of advertising expenditures, for example, the implications of strategic changes in the "communications mix" can be examined. Distribution changes could be reflected through modifications in the fraction of consumers who find the product when shopping. The effects of word-of-mouth recommendation can be simulated by increasing the number of people each buyer talks to, or the fraction of consumers who flow from word-of-mouth awareness to visit a dealer and actually make a purchase.

A flow model such as that in Figure 6.15 can be extended to include other behavioral phenomena. For example, a customer's search for interpersonal recommendations after shopping could be captured by a new state that reflects the number of shoppers who are successful in getting input that subsequently revises their purchase probability (see Urban, Roberts, and Hauser, 1990). Extensions have been developed for individual risk, multiattribute evaluation at the choice stage (Roberts and Urban, 1988), and consumer budget constraints (Hauser and Urban, 1986). In essence, there is ongoing progress in extending the flow model to represent the behavioral process of choice outlined in Chapter 5, and thus to improve our ability to forecast life cycles accurately.

Inputs: The inputs needed to implement a flow model are the fractions of people who will flow from one state to another. We need to estimate the fraction who will buy our product given the fact that they are aware, in the market, and in a store carrying our product. In effect, we must estimate the conditional probabilities that a consumer will move from one box in the flow model to another (i.e., from various information levels *to* awareness of the product *to* exposure to it at retail *to* involvement in interpersonal communication).

A major advantage of flow models is that the conditional flow probabilities can be estimated on the basis of market research conducted in a clinic where alternate levels of information are provided. After making respondents aware of advertising for our product (by showing them a print or TV ad), we can ask them about the probability that they would go shopping for this product. Next we can put them in a simulated store environment and expose them to a product demonstration. The resulting probability of purchase would be applicable to the flow of people who are aware of advertising for our product *and* frequent a store stocking it. Word-of-mouth communication can be simulated by showing customers videotapes of typical users talking about the product as they would to a friend or neighbor. These tapes might employ professional actors using scripts derived from focus group sessions or other feedback from people who have actually used the product long enough to evaluate it.

Such a clinic study is expensive ($100,000 or more), but would be more than justified for high-investment products by its ability to forecast accurately the life cycle for a new product before launch or early in the diffusion process. Moreover, managerial judgments can be used to reduce the measurement costs or to simplify the simulation.

Disaggregated analysis provides the basis for understanding the consumer's buying process and probable response to the product. This is essential knowledge for managers if they are to carry out their marketing responsibility effectively. Given the flow model structure and inputs, forecasts can be made and simulations conducted to help managers create and evaluate improved marketing strategies. The following case describes the application of such a flow model to the life-cycle forecasting of a new automobile.

Application—1985 Buick Electra: In late 1982 and early 1983, the Buick Motor Division was laying plans for the launch of the 1985 Buick Electra. The Electra and its sister, the Park Avenue, were top-of-the-line Buick luxury models. The new Electra had been downsized, and some executives were concerned that the car would not sell the desired number of units (about double the old model volume). A life-cycle forecast would be useful for formulating marketing strategy and establishing production levels.

A consumer clinic was conducted with 336 potential luxury car buyers. Ads were shown, preproduction autos were made available for test drives, and word-of-mouth videotapes were used to simulate positive and negative interpersonal communication. Purchase propensities were measured after each conditional information exposure. Two-thirds of the respondents drove the new Electra and viewed its advertising. The other one-third of the sample, who served as a control group, were exposed to old Electra advertising and given the current-model Electra for their test drives.

The new car achieved higher preferences than the old at all levels of information (ads, test drive, and word-of-mouth video). This was good news, suggesting that sales for the new model could be higher than those for the old Electra. It applied to a subsample of past Buick owners as well as to other U.S. and foreign car owners. The concept of the new downsized and efficient luxury car was attractive across the market.

The impact of the test drive was to increase preferences for the new car by a further 15 percent, indicating that a program that induced potential customers to test-drive the new car had high potential benefit. Following the test drive, the new Electra not only fulfilled advertising expectations, it received even higher ratings. Positive word-of-mouth messages reinforced the test-drive results and produced a further 5 percent increase in preferences.

Negative communication was measured by showing one-half the respondents a negative simulated word-of-mouth video, while the other half saw a positive video. The negative interpersonal simulation caused a significant drop in preference even after the test drive—over 14 percentage points. This implied that if the car did not demonstrate quality and reliability to buyers after use, the diffusion of innovation would be impeded. The importance of reliability was also evident in consumer ratings of this attribute for the new car. Consumers felt it would not be highly reliable, even though GM engineering had devoted a great deal of attention to this factor. Perception of quality was low, even though actual reliability was expected to be good.

When the flow model was run with the clinic values and the initial marketing plan, it forecast that the Electra would achieve sales 10 percent higher than the old model, provided that a diffusion process based on positive word-of-mouth recommendation took place. Peak sales would occur in the third year, but sales would be lower than those for the old car while awareness and positive attitudes were developing. This forecast was substantially below management's goals, so efforts were made to improve the marketing strategy. After using the model to evaluate many alternatives, management identified an improved strategy that was forecast to generate sales 50 percent greater than the old model. This strategy was based on: (1) new copy that stressed reliability (see Figure 6.16 for the

FIGURE 6.16
Innovative Electra
Advertising

copy, which was dramatically different for a luxury car); (2) higher advertising expenditures; (3) a dealer training and incentive program to promote test drives, called "selling from the inside out" (it was based on getting the customer "in" the car and driving it, and then selling the "outside" of the car); (4) targeting the foreign car market for incremental sales; and (5) ensuring that quality was high before introduction. These actions were derived from the research data and simulations using the flow model. They showed management that: (1) perceived reliability had to be improved; (2) increased advertising was necessary to accelerate the rate of diffusion; (3) the car was rated higher after drive experience; (4) previous Electra buyers were pleased, and foreign car buyers were responsive; and (5) the impact of negative word-of-mouth would be devastating.

Thus, a life-cycle model provided forecasts that triggered action on management's part and resulted in an improved strategy for targeting advertising and selling. After a six-month delay to be sure the new Electra transmission was free of flaws, the new car was successfully introduced. Initial production capacity restricted growth, but the car was one of the most successful recent introductions by the division.

STATE OF THE ART

As we have said, viewing the life cycle as strictly analogous to biology is inappropriate. Although some determinants are uncontrollable and some phenomena have a natural structure, management has considerable ability to influence and control the life cycle. Marketing actions can change the rate at which the natural processes occur and, except in a few cases, can influence their determinants. Nevertheless, managers should not ignore the life cycle, since sales rarely continue at current rates. An effective marketing manager must take a wider view of the dynamics underlying sales, and understand the determinants that produce the observed *dynamic sales patterns* and how managerial actions can influence them. Judgment and inspection of past data are critical first steps in such an analysis, but more formal models that forecast future patterns and the results of planned strategies often add value to the marketing process. In many cases, Level II analysis models, such as aggregate diffusion and consumer flow models, prove very useful in forecasting future sales and evaluating the impact of future strategies. Where large resource commitments are involved, it may be worthwhile to implement even more elaborate measurement and model extensions.

QUESTIONS FOR DISCUSSION

1. What is natural about the life cycle? What elements are controllable? On balance, are there more natural or controllable determinants of the life cycle? Does your answer depend upon whether the life cycle is defined at the industry, product-class, or brand level? How?

2. Select a product currently on the market and research its sales history in published literature (consult *Predicast*, trade journals, and the business press). What phase of the life cycle is the product in? What strategies are firms in the industry using at this point in time? Do their strategies match the life-cycle strategy recommendations? Why or why not?

3. Under what conditions would a penetration pricing strategy be appropriate for the birth phase of the life cycle?

4. When should you spend money to rejuvenate a product life cycle and when should you milk the brand?

5. What makes a milking strategy sales forecast self-fulfilling?

6. Why is it important in high-tech consumer electronics to estimate the life cycle on the basis of retail sales rather than manufacturing shipment data?

7. What assumptions underlie the Bass model? What are the limits of this model? How can they be overcome?

8. Compare and contrast the Bass model and the macro flow model as methods of new-product life-cycle forecasting.

REFERENCES

BASS, FRANK M. 1969. "New Product Growth Model for Consumer Durables." *Management Science* 15: 215–227.

COX, W. E., "Product Life Cycles as Marketing Models," *Journal of Business*, (October 1967), 375–384.

HAUSER, JOHN R., AND GLEN L. URBAN. 1986. "The Value Priority Hypotheses for Consumer Budget Plans." *Journal of Consumer Research* 12: 446–462.

HEELER, R. M., AND T. P. HUSTAD. 1980. "Problems in Predicting New Product Growth for Consumer Durables." *Management Science* 2: 1–18.

LAMBKIN, MARY, AND GEORGE S. DAY. 1989. "Evolutionary Processes in Competitive Markets: Beyond the Product Life Cycle." *Journal of Marketing* 53: 4–20.

MAHAJAN, VIJAY, EITAN MULLER, AND FRANK M. BASS. 1990. "New Product Diffusion Models in Marketing: A Review and Directions for Research." *Journal of Marketing* 54: 1–26.

MAHAJAN, VIJAY, EITHAN MULLER, AND RAJENDRA K. SRIVASTAVA. 1990. "Determination of Adopter Categories Using Innovation Diffusion Models." *Journal of Marketing Research* 27: 37–50.

MAHAJAN, VIJAY, AND YORAM WIND. 1986. *Innovation Diffusion Models of New Product Acceptance*. Cambridge, MA: Ballinger Publishing.

McKENNA, REGIS. 1988. "Marketing in an Age of Diversity." *Harvard Business Review*, September/October: 88–95.

MONTGOMERY, DAVID B., AND V. SRINIVASAN. 1989. "An Improved Method for Meta Analysis: With Application to New Product Diffusion Models." *Working Paper*. Stanford, CA: Stanford University Graduate School of Business.

NORTON, J. A., AND F. M. BASS. 1987. "A Diffusion Theory Model of Adoption and Substitution for Successive Generations of High-Technology Products." *Management Science* 33: 1069–88.

POLLI, R., AND V. COOK. 1969. "Validity of the Product Life Cycle." *Journal of Business* 42: 385–400.

QUALLS, WILLIAM, RICHARD OLSHAVSKY, AND RONALD MICHAELS. 1981. "Shortening the PLC—An Empirical Test." *Journal of Marketing* 45: 76–80.

ROBERTS, JOHN H., AND GLEN L. URBAN. 1988. "Modeling Multiattribute Utility, Risk, and Belief Dynamics for New Consumer Durable Brand Choice." *Management Science* 34: 167–185.

SCHMITTLEIN, DAVID C., AND VIJAY MAHAJAN. 1982. "Maximum Likelihood Estimation for an Innovation Diffusion Model of New Product Acceptance." *Marketing Science* 1: 57–78.

SRINIVASAN, V., AND CHARLOTTE H. MASON. 1986. "Nonlinear Least Squares Estimation of New Product Diffusion Models." *Marketing Science* 5: 169–178.

SULTAN, FARENNA, JOHN U. FARLEY, AND DONALD R. LEHMANN. 1990. "A Meta-analysis of Applications of Diffusion Models." *Journal of Marketing Research* 27: 70–77.

URBAN, GLEN L., JOHN H. ROBERTS, AND JOHN R. HAUSER. 1990. "Pre-Launch Forecasting of New Automobiles: Models and Implementation." *Management Science* 36: 401–421.

WERNERFELT, BIRGER. 1985. "The Dynamics of Prices and Market Shares over the Product Life Cycle." *Management Science* 31: 928–939.

WIND, YORAM, THOMAS S. ROBERTSON, AND CYNTHIA FRASER. 1982. "Industrial Product Diffusion by Market Segment," *Industrial Marketing Management* 11: 1–8.

MARKET SEGMENTATION

As we discussed in Chapter 5, customer decision making is individual and highly idio-syncratic, but mangers have to develop useful aggregations of individual customers in order to create an effective strategy. Segmentation involves dividing the market into parts and devising alternative strategies for some or all of these parts. Differences in consumer preferences and needs are the primary reason for segmentation. If preferences vary and we can design a product to fit a subset of these heterogeneous preferences, we create additional utility for customers in that segment. Consumers are willing to pay more for a product tailored to their needs than for one designed to fit the average preference, and this willingness allows the manufacturer or service provider to charge a higher price and to earn additional profit.

Although heterogeneity in preferences is the major driving force in segmentation, marketing program differentiation can also be based on cost differences. For example, large and small accounts are traditionally treated differently in sales strategy; large accounts are sold directly by the manufacturer, and small accounts through middlemen. The sales potential of the small account may be too low to justify the cost of a personal call by the manufacturer's salesperson, so even if the large and small accounts have the same pref-erences, such cost differences will dictate distinct marketing efforts. The complexity of devising a system of segmentation increases when costs and preferences are both different; but with a correctly designed segmentation strategy, sales can be increased, costs lowered, and/or margins improved.

Segmentation as a strategy offers other benefits as well. It may reduce competitive pressure when competitors do not have a product tailored to a particular segment's needs. A competitor with one product that fits average preferences will lose share to a firm with multiple products fitted to particular segment needs, assuming similar prices. Within the segment, the tailored product is relatively insulated from the effects of price wars, and can generally maintain a price premium.

117

Given the advantages of segmentation, why not treat each consumer individually? Why aggregate customers at all? If needs are different, the maximum utility is generated by a customized product for each person. Obviously, cost is the problem. If custom products are built, the unit production cost goes up and prices, therefore, must be higher. Consumers then face a price/value trade-off: Should they pay more for a tailored product or less for a product that does not fit their needs as well? Thus, manufacturers try to keep costs down by standardizing marketing programs as much as possible, but with enough variation to earn a high market share in each market segment and maximize profits.

Manufacturing costs are not the only expenses that rise with segmentation. Inventory and service costs also multiply. Management time requirements go up because decision making is more difficult: advertising, selling, pricing, and distribution must be planned, controlled, and coordinated within and across segments.

The trade-off between the increased costs and the potential sales gains to be made from offering products targeted at specific segments is a fundamental managerial concern. Two key questions that must be addressed are: (1) How many segments should we define? (2) How should customers be grouped in them to best describe a market? To answer these questions, we must first understand our strategic alternatives, and then select the best one.

SEGMENTATION STRATEGIES

Let us assume that the market can be adequately described by three segments and examine our strategic choices. We could focus on these segments in our planning and offer differentiated marketing programs to each segment or, alternatively, we could ignore the segments and offer only one program. The latter is the lower-cost and simpler solution, of course, but it increases our vulnerability to competitive entry. In almost all of today's markets, competition has forced segmentation and the offering of many product variants. It is difficult to think of any markets (except, perhaps, pure commodities) where multi-product segmentation strategies are not practiced. Modern marketing managers must be skilled at recognizing and exploiting segmentation opportunities.

Given that there is meaningful segmentation in the market and that it will provide the basis for our strategy, we must decide whether to target only one segment or to offer a product line to span segments. If the preference differences are large, it can be profitable to offer products for each segment. This is especially true if some of the production and marketing costs can be shared by one or more products. If costs cannot be shared because expertise is unique to each segment, it may be more effective to target only one or a few segments. We may, for example, offer premium-quality homes and not participate at all in the low-cost, low-quality subdivision segment of the housing market.

If we decide to offer benefits selectively to more than one segment, we have the choice of varying both the physical product and its "nonproduct" attributes (price, distribution, advertising, selling effort) or of varying only the nonproduct attributes. Usually we would vary both the product and nonproduct aspects (i.e., the bulk of the marketing program), but if maintaining a standard product means substantial economies, it often makes sense to vary only the nonproduct attributes. Automobile manufacturers do this when they offer the same basic car with minor trim, brand, and advertising differences. For example, the Buick Somerset, Pontiac GrandAm, Oldsmobile Calais, and Buick Skylark are built from the same basic frame, drivetrain, engine, and body.

Implementing a segmentation plan requires the ability to reach that segment efficiently. If the media or channels of distribution needed to reach a segment selectively do not exist, the notion of targeting is not viable. If we want to sell videotape instruction material to sail boat owners (e.g., on navigation and engine repair), the availability of selected media (*Sail*, *Yachting*, *Cruising World*) and channels (marine supply stores and catalogs) is critical to our success. It would be difficult to reach this segment economically if we had to sell through general book stores or advertise in *Sports Illustrated*. The more selective we can be in our use of marketing variables, the tighter effective segmentation can be. The recent growth of specialized journals and distribution systems is a major force pushing toward increased segmentation.

As more and more segments are defined, overlap between them increases. With few segments, groups can be insulated from one another, enabling employment of distinct strategies. The same dress may be sold at both a designer store and a discount factory outlet at different prices if customers shop only at one of these retail distributors and are exposed to independent information sources.[1] But if there is overlap in media exposure or shopping patterns, price differences between segments may not be viable. As pressures build for more segmentation, overlap between segments increases the difficulty of designing and maintaining differences, thus reducing the number of segments that can be profitably served.

The goal is to segment the market for the purpose of achieving maximum profits. This is a challenging task because there are so many ways to segment markets: it is often difficult to access segments selectively; there is frequent overlap between segments; and segments can change markedly over time. We need to define the criteria for grouping customers, specify the number of groups, and decide how to vary our product offering across segments. Let us now review a number of common bases for segmentation and the analytic tools available to support segmentation strategy.

BASES OF SEGMENTATION

The strategic alternatives discussed in the preceding section are based on aggregating customers into discrete segments that can be selectively addressed. One of the most important decisions in segmentation is the designation of the dimensions upon which customers will be grouped in an effort to find homogeneous segments. In autos, should it be age, attitudes toward car ownership, product feature importances (fuel economy, stereo quality, safety), or something else (number of children, how the car is used, or products it competes with in the consumer's choice process)? It is difficult to answer these questions because there are so many different criteria that can be used to divide the market into segments.

There is no one correct segmentation. A best grouping can often be found through the use of statistical criteria to define similarity between customers, but in the final analysis, effective segmentation is based on good managerial decisions. In this section, we discuss the most common bases for segmentation, suggest when each is most appropriate, and argue that a combination of criteria provides a comprehensive view of market segmentation possibilities.

Demographics

The most obvious and clearly measured differences between customers are often demographic. Sex, age, marital status, family size, age of children, income, occupation, geographic location, mobility, home ownership, education, race, religion, and nationality are all candidate variables for the definition of segments. Where young persons (say, teens) have different preferences from older customers, this can be the basis for defining a segment. Soft-drink manufacturers, for example, know younger people like a sweeter taste. This was an underlying reason for the introduction of New Coke and Cherry Coke.

---

[1] Off-price (bargain) outlets selling branded merchandise (e.g., factory outlets, Marshall's, Loehmann's) generally do not advertise specific items.

Where demographic variables are good surrogates for preference differences, they provide an easily obtainable source of segmentation data and facilitate grouping of consumers in a straightforward manner (see the analytic discussion of clustering methods in the next section of this chapter).

Demographic segmentation is useful because it can aid in identifying market changes that represent either a future threat or opportunity. In the next thirty years, the fastest-growing age segment will be the over-fifty-five group, which is forecasted to increase more than 50 percent (from 20.9 percent of the population in 1990 to 30.9 percent in 2020). Because people are living longer and have healthier lives and higher levels of discretionary income, the over-fifty-five segment will provide major opportunities to many firms.

In industrial markets, commonly used demographic variables are size of company (sales volume or number of employees), SIC code business designation, number of manufacturing plants, geographic location, and years of operation. It is common in industrial markets to designate large companies as national accounts and service them with special teams, while selling to smaller accounts through wholesalers. Priorities for personal selling are often defined by demographics. Government-owned hospitals, for example, have faster adoption rates of CT head and body scanners (Wind, Robertson, and Fraser, 1982). Large hospitals have the highest ultimate penetration rate, but small hospitals reach ultimate penetration levels sooner. Therefore, though the first priority for a manufacturer of these scanners would be large government-owned hospitals, small hospitals that are qualified as potential adopters may also deserve immediate attention because of their possibility for quick sales results.

Attitudes

Demographic data are generally easy to collect, but they may not lead to the best groupings for marketing strategy formulation. Attitudes may be a better basis for identifying differences in response, and therefore offer better criteria for market segmentation.

Attitudes can be measured with established market research questions (see Oppenheim, 1966; and Churchill, 1976). Attitudes may relate to overall social issues (religion, politics, work, drugs, women's rights, sex, and the like), personal interests (family, home, job, food, self-achievement, health, clubs, friends, shopping), or specific product attitudes ("the highest-quality product is usually the best long-run buy" or "Mercedes-Benz is for rich people").

Grouping customers by attitudes can be a powerful way of identifying opportunities for segmentation. As mentioned in Chapter 5, attitudes are intermediaries between information inputs and decision outcomes. They can be good discriminators of behavior differences. The stress on the work ethic in Miller beer advertising ("It's Miller time" after a tough day's work) is an example of successful utilization of a consumer attitude and its link to consumption.

Importances

The most direct measure of differences in preferences between customers is the importances they attach to product benefits and characteristics. In our model of consumer decision making, we outlined how importances of attributes might be combined in choice rules (see Chapter 5). If the importances can be estimated at the individual level, customers can be grouped according to their similarity with respect to importances. Such a system of segmentation has been called "benefit segmentation" because it uses the importance of the benefits to group people. For toothpaste, those who think decay prevention is most important are a segment likely to chose Crest, while those who weigh taste most highly are more likely to choose Aim. Recently, the benefit claim of tartar reduction has segmented the market on a new appeal; those who value this attribute highly choose plaque-reduction brands.

Another importance is reflected in sensitivity to changes in price. Those who think price is important will have high price elasticities, and may represent a possible segment. Similarly, promotion, channel, preference, or advertising sensitivity could be utilized as a segmentation variable.

Another way to group customers is on the basis of their similarities and differences in decision-making processes. Here, not only are importances considered, but also input, screening, and decision rules. In industrial marketing, this could result in buyers of copiers being segmented into one group in which the administrative officer is dominant, and another in which users, administrative officers, and purchasing agents are all heavily involved.

Usage

Importances are not always easy to estimate. Sometimes observed behavior is a more practical correlate to preference differences. Heavy users of a product may represent a meaningful segment because they account for such a large proportion of sales. In many markets, the top 20 percent of customers in usage account for 80 percent of sales volume.

Another purchase variable is brand loyalty. In consumer goods, this is measured by high repeat-purchase probabilities, while in industrial products, a high (preferably majority) share of the business in a buying unit is a common indicator of brand loyalty. Manufacturers may give price reductions or special service to loyal buyers to protect this segment from competitive encroachment.

When a product has a number of possible uses, segmentation as a function of use may be appropriate. It might, for example, make sense to market differently to customers for pre-engineered steel buildings used for schools, auto dealerships, and barns.

Competitive Products

So far we have defined groups on the basis of individual characteristics. An alternative to individual preference grouping is to group products that compete in specific markets and to define segments based on product identities rather than on individual consumer attributes. This kind of segmentation, in effect, defines the market. Competitive structure can be approached directly by asking customers to identify the products they would consider buying as alternatives to the product they last bought. For example, do foreign cars represent a separate segment of the auto market? If buyers of foreign cars shopped only for other foreign cars and buyers of U.S. cars only for U.S. cars, we would have evidence of two distinct segments. Product segmentation can yield new insights by causing managers to look at opportunities in different ways.

Selection

Clearly, there is a bewildering array of possible criteria for use in segmentation. The most common method of defining the basis for segmentation is to select one dimension as the priority designator. Lufthansa Air Lines, for example, has segmented the market for business travel, and, instead of stressing low prices, employs on-time service as its core benefit proposition. This use dimension represents Lufthansa's priority in defining segments in both its product and its communication strategies. In contrast, Continental's strategy is based on low costs and prices, and is directed at the price-sensitive segment of the market that is willing to give up some amenities in order to obtain a lower price.

Research has not defined any one criterion as being best for segmentation, but some decisions are more effectively supported by certain criteria than by others. Attitude segmentation, or what is sometimes called "Psychographics," is most commonly used in generating advertising copy. The design of products is usually based on segmentation by alternative uses or importances. Allocation of selling effort is commonly tied to demographics. Product-line composition and competitive strategy can be examined insightfully through competitive product segmentation.

Segmentation decisions need not be restricted to one of the criteria. In fact, a combination of demographics, attitudes, importances, and uses may provide the richest view of segmentation opportunities. Often a profile of typical customer attributes is used to define a segment. A new imported beer may be targeted toward professional women who want to be seen as individuals and like a light, sharper taste, for example. Such profiles are commonly based on demographics or attitudes (see the next section, Analytic Support), but in principle, one could use any of the bases of segmentation we have outlined.

The notions of priority and profiles can be combined into a hierarchy of criteria. Figure 7.1 shows a hypothetical representation of the market for PCs in the home, with demographics as the highest priority, and attitudes, importances, use, and brand preference as profile descriptors. In this example, strategy would be driven by demographics, but the profile in each segment would be used to create differentiated marketing programs (e.g., advertising copy and media, in-store display materials).

With so many alternative segmentation schemes available to the manager, it is natural to ask: What is the one true segmentation of our market? It would be nice if we could settle on one segment designation and use it for all decisions, but this is simply not possible in most markets, since multiple criteria are significant. All people are different. If there is a natural segmentation, it is at the level of the individual. Segmentation is a summing up of the preferences of heterogeneous individuals. It is done, fundamentally,

FIGURE 7.1
Hypothetical Demographic Segmentation of Home PC Market

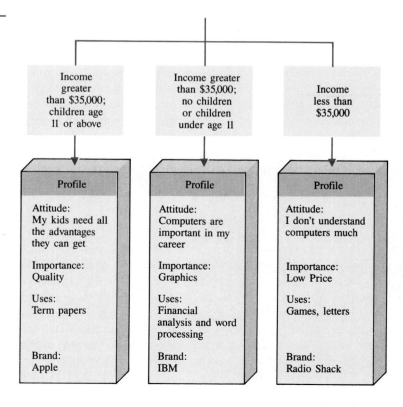

to foster better managerial decision making. Segmentation is a method to help managers decide which dimension or combination of dimensions will lead to the best overall strategy and to specific sales, advertising, price, product, and channel decisions.

A useful approach to this challenging task is to develop a multidimensional system that defines similar customers and is capable of changing the priority dimension depending on the decision being made. In the home PC market, for example, a priority dimension could be defined on the basis of the brands that consumers see as competitive (see Figure 7.2), rather than on demographics (see Figure 7.1). The other variables would then be used as profile descriptors in the product segments.

Both Figures 7.1 and 7.2 contain the same variables and both could represent valid segmentations of the market, but each would be most helpful for a different type of decision. Figure 7.1 would be most useful in establishing distribution, communication, and pricing strategy, while Figure 7.2 would be better employed to support product/market strategy formulation. If we are entering the PC market, should we be IBM compatible? Should we target only this segment, or should we offer a broad line to span the competitive product segments?

Looking at the market with different priority dimensions can be useful, but only if they are based on a consistent underlying representation with common underlying descriptor variables and similarities. This approach to segmentation is like looking at a three-dimensional object from different perspectives. The real object is the same, but it looks different from various angles (see Figure 7.3 for several orthogonal views of a solid object). With alternative priority segmentation dimensions, the market may look very different depending on the decision to be supported. It is acceptable to have different

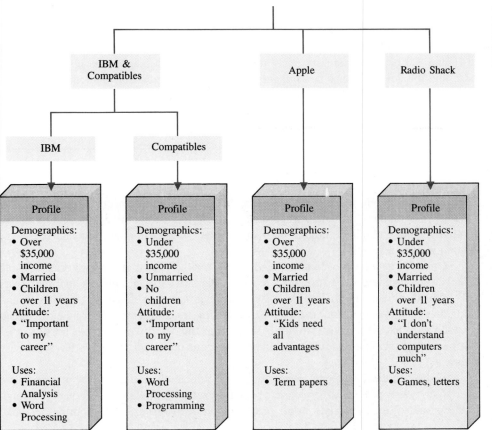

FIGURE 7.2
Hypothetical Product Segmentation of Home PC Market

FIGURE 7.3
Two-Dimensional Views and
Solid Object

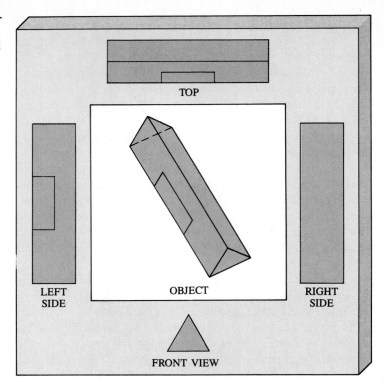

views of the market for different decisions so long as the underlying multidimensional representation of the market does not change as the priority dimension is altered. The same data base should be used and the best segmentation should be selected for each dimensional priority viewpoint.

In marketing, the object (i.e., market) is more complex than the object represented in Figure 7.3 because there are many more than three dimensions, the hierarchies may have multiple levels, and some segments may overlap. Fortunately, a number of analytic support tools now offer considerable help in segmenting complex markets.

ANALYTICAL SUPPORT

Level I Analysis

Level I analysis begins with gathering data on the attributes with respect to which customers differ: demographics, attitudes, importances, uses, and competitive products. This information can be obtained through first-hand contact with customers, secondary data, or custom market research.

Once the data have been assembled, one can either select a single priority variable or develop a profile of key attributes. A simple classification into buyers and nonbuyers will often result in a useful profile. Any dimension can be defined as "priority," and using that priority dimension, the average values for the other variables can be calculated for each segment. If price sensitivity is selected as the priority dimension, for example, other consumer attributes would be tabulated for segmented high and low price-sensitivity segments.

If the resulting segments can be accessed selectively and do not show excessive overlap, they may provide an appropriate basis for strategy formulation. Although judgment is the primary Level I analytic tool, segmentation decisions are too important to make without using data that have been carefully collected, and without considering alternative segmentation schemes.

Level II Analysis

The aggregation of customers into homogeneous groups can be formalized by a simple statistical technique called *cluster analysis*.

Input to this method comes from the set of individual responses and attributes. These may be very diverse: age, income, years of education, urban/suburban, agree/disagree scores on attitude questions (e.g., agree or disagree on a 5-point scale with the statement, "I feel we all have a responsibility to support our president"), product consumption rates. The data are arrayed in a matrix where each consumer is a row and the columns represent the attributes. Each cell contains an individual's value for a particular attribute.

Clusters of consumers are formed by matching those who have similar responses to the questions asked. That is, two consumers are grouped together if their row values are similar. Similarity between two consumers can be gauged according to the sums of the differences between their scores on each question. If the value is low, the individuals are assigned to the same cluster. To minimize overlap, the computational algorithms attempt to group individuals so that the variation within each group is small and the variation between groups is large. The programs calculate a measure of goodness of fit of the clustering for each of 2,3,4, . . . cluster representations of the market. This measure is the percentage of the variation in the data explained by the cluster memberships (see Everitt, 1974, for a technical discussion of clustering).

Though clustering is undoubtedly a valuable tool, its use is subject to some caveats. Generally, the percentage of variation explained is less than 50 percent, and there is considerable variation within clusters as well as between them. Managers must recognize this limitation of cluster analysis before they use it to formulate segmentation strategies.

Demographics: Clustering methods have been used by commercial research and consulting firms to analyze demographic data. One system, called PRIZM, clusters a reduced set of 1,000 possible demographic measures.[2] In this system, ZIP code areas rather than individuals are used as micro data inputs. Each ZIP code represents a row of the data matrix; demographic attributes define the columns. PRIZM develops ten and forty cluster solutions, and provides a profile of attributes for each cluster. Table 7.1 shows an example: Cluster 28. It is much higher in the professional/managerial career attribute: 51.2 percent in this cluster versus 22.7 percent in the U.S. population (the index is the ratio of these and has a value of 222 percent). The cluster profile reflects higher incomes (38.1 percent of those in Cluster 28 have incomes over $50,000 versus 4.6 percent of the U.S. population, or an 829 index), education, home ownership, likelihood of being middle age, and average household size. For these reasons, Cluster 28 has been termed "Blue Blood Estates." Although it represents only .7 percent of the U.S. population, it would be critical if we were selling luxury goods.

Contrast Cluster 28 with Cluster 4 (see Table 7.2). Cluster 4, "Heavy Industry," is blue collar, low income, and low education. It constitutes 2 percent of the population.

Clusters can be very useful in targeting opportunities where demographics are a key driver in the segmentation strategy. By correlating consumption with such clusters, we can identify the groups now buying and examine the others as potential targets. This can be done in detail, for example, by using specific ZIP code cluster assignments to reach desirable target segments with direct mail.

---

[2] PRIZM is the registered trademark of Claritas, Inc.

TABLE 7.1 PRIZM Cluster No. 28—Blue Blood Estates

KEY DEMOGRAPHIC INDICATORS

	% Composition U.S.	Cluster	Index		% Composition U.S.	Cluster	Index
Occupations				*Age Distribution*			
Professional/Managerial	22.7	51.2	226	Under 18 yrs.	28.1	27.5	98
All other white-collar	30.3	32.0	106	18–34 yrs.	29.6	20.4	69
Blue-collar	31.2	9.1	29	35–54 yrs.	21.4	30.9	144
Service	12.9	6.9	54	55–64 yrs.	9.6	12.0	125
Farming/Forestry/Fishing	2.9	0.8	27	65+ yrs.	11.3	9.2	81
Household Income				*Race/Ethnic Origins*			
Less than $5,000	13.2	3.2	24	Black	11.7	1.3	11
$5,000–$14,999	31.2	9.9	32	Oriental	0.9	2.5	272
$15,000–$24,999	26.6	13.6	51	Hispanic	6.4	2.4	38
$25,000–$34,999	15.7	14.8	94	Foreign born	6.2	10.2	163
$35,000–$49,999	8.7	20.4	236	*Household Size*			
$50,000+	4.6	38.1	829	One person	22.7	14.1	62
Educational Levels				Two persons	31.3	32.4	103
Some high school or less	33.5	7.9	24	Three or four persons	32.8	39.0	119
4 years high school	34.6	20.0	58	Five or more persons	13.2	14.5	110
1–3 yrs. college	15.7	21.4	137				
4+ yrs. college	16.2	50.7	313				

Base Population Counts—1980 Census

	Count	% of U.S
Housing Characteristics		
Households	494,852	0.6
Owner-occupied — Population	1,486,743	0.7
Renter-occupied — Adults	1,078,179	0.7
Single-unit — Adult males	515,617	0.7
2–9 units — Adult females	562,562	0.7
10+ units — Median household income	$41,094	n/a
Mobile units — Median home value	$145,975	n/a

Housing Characteristics	U.S.	Cluster	Index
Owner-occupied	64.5	83.2	129
Renter-occupied	35.5	16.8	47
Single-unit	71.2	87.1	122
2–9 units	13.8	5.7	41
10+ units	10.1	6.8	67
Mobile units	5.0	0.4	8

Source: Claritas Corporation, Alexandria, Virginia. Used with permission.

Attitudes: Clustering methodology can also be applied to attitudinal responses. Commercial services have clustered attitude measures obtained from large samples to determine segments. One of the best known of such services is called VALS.[3] It is based on attitudes toward issues such as the importance of work, the effectiveness of free enterprise, concentration of power, women's role, strength of religious belief, personality (''I like to be outrageous'' or ''I prefer a quiet evening at home to a party''), and satisfaction with life. Cluster-analyzing 800 of these kinds of measures across 2,713 individuals produced 9 clusters: survivor, sustainer, belonger, emulator, achiever, I-Am-Me, experiential, socially conscious, and integrated. Detailed value and lifestyle profiles were developed for each group. Survivors and sustainers are need driven and just hanging on in what they see as a hostile world. Belongers, emulators, and achievers are outer directed. Achievers are action oriented, work within the system, and enjoy good living. Emulators want to make it big, but have not yet. Belongers are conservative, middle-majority individuals. Experientials and socially conscious people are inner directed, with the experientials trying what life has to offer, and the socially conscious dominated by social responsibility. The integrated groups combine the best of inner- and outer-directed attitudes.

This kind of attitude segmentation (often called *psychographic segmentation*) provides a different perspective on market structure. It is particularly useful in creating advertising and image-related product attributes.

[3] VALS is the registered trademark of SRI, Inc.

TABLE 7.2   PRIZM Cluster No. 4—Heavy Industry

KEY DEMOGRAPHIC INDICATORS

	% Composition U.S.	Cluster	Index		% Composition U.S.	Cluster	Index
Occupations				*Age Distribution*			
Professional/Managerial	22.7	12.7	56	Under 18 yrs.	28.1	27.2	97
All other white-collar	30.3	27.9	92	18–34 yrs.	29.6	28.3	96
Blue-collar	31.2	43.6	140	35–54 yrs.	21.4	19.1	89
Service	12.9	14.9	115	55–64 yrs.	9.6	11.4	119
Farming/Forestry/Fishing	2.9	0.9	31	65+ yrs.	11.3	14.0	124
Household Income				*Race/Ethnic Origins*			
Less than $5,000	13.2	18.6	140	Black	11.7	8.6	74
$5,000–$14,999	31.2	36.7	118	Oriental	0.9	0.4	48
$15,000–$24,999	26.6	26.2	99	Hispanic	6.4	13.9	217
$25,000–$34,999	15.7	12.0	76	Foreign born	6.2	12.5	201
$35,000–$49,999	8.7	5.0	57	*Household Size*			
$50,000+	4.6	1.5	33	One person	22.7	27.2	120
Educational Levels				Two persons	31.3	29.8	95
Some high school or less	33.5	51.4	153	Three or four persons	32.8	29.9	91
4 years high school	34.6	32.6	94	Five or more persons	13.2	13.1	100
1–3 yrs. college	15.7	9.5	61	**Base Population Counts—1980 Census**			
4+ yrs. college	16.2	6.5	40			Count	% of U.S
Housing Characteristics				Households		1,677,675	2.1
Owner-occupied	64.5	52.4	81	Population		4,525,152	2.0
Renter-occupied	35.5	47.6	134	Adults		3,294,448	2.0
Single-unit	71.2	57.7	81	Adult males		1,517,124	2.0
2–9 units	13.8	34.1	248	Adult females		1,777,324	2.1
10+ units	10.1	7.2	72	Median household income		$13,407	n/a
Mobile units	5.0	1.0	19	Median home value		$32,203	n/a

Source: Claritas Corporation, Alexandria, Virginia. Used with permission.

Attitudinal and demographic segmentation can be merged if demographic data are collected along with attitudinal responses. Clustering such data gives a more comprehensive profile of customers, and, if the sample is large enough, makes possible finer segmentation schemes (e.g., geographic ''micromarketing'').

In both of the demographic and value approaches just described, the segments are very general. A firm could do an attitude and demographic survey of its own market and develop a more detailed segmentation scheme based on questions targeted to issues relevant to consumption in this specific market. Custom clustering of responses is not difficult (off-the-shelf computer programs are readily available), and can be done on a set of attributes viewed as most representative of differences between customers and most valuable in profiling market segments. Figure 7.4 shows an attitude segmentation scheme for four groups of stomach remedy users (Wells, 1975). Based primarily on symptoms and attitudes toward treatment, this scheme results from clustering eighty product-specific items and then judgmentally describing the average member of each cluster in terms of symptom frequency, benefits provided by brands, attitudes toward treatment, beliefs about ailments, and personality. Table 7.3 shows that brands differ in their appeal to these segments—that is, the psychographic differences appear to be reflected in behavior.

Hierarchies: An extension of clustering called *hierarchical clustering* can be used to group subclusters into larger groups. For instance, the forty PRIZM clusters can be grouped into ten larger clusters, and further into three groups. Hierarchical groupings facilitates

FIGURE 7.4
Psychographic Segmentation of Stomach Remedy Market
Source: Reprinted from the *Journal of Marketing Research* published by the American Marketing Association. From W. D. Wells, ''Psychographics: A Critical Review,'' Vol. 12 (May 1975), p. 203.

The Severe Sufferers

The Severe Sufferers are the extreme group on the potency side of the market. They tend to be young, have children, and be well educated. They are irritable and anxious people, and believe that they suffer more severely than others. They take the ailment seriously, fuss about it, pamper themselves, and keep trying new and different products in search of greater potency. A most advanced product with new ingredients best satisfies their need for potency and fast relief, and ties in with their psychosomatic beliefs.

The Active Medicators

The Active Medicators are on the same side of the motivational spectrum. They are typically modern suburbanites with average income and education. They are emotionally well adjusted to the demands of their active lives. They have learned to cope by adopting the contemporary beliefs of seeking help for every ill, and use remedies to relieve even minor signs of aliments and every ache and pain. In a modern product they seek restoration of their condition and energy, mental recovery, and a lift for the active lives. They are influenced by a brand's reputation and by how well it is advertised. They tend to develop strong brand loyalties.

The Hypochondriacs

The Hypochondriacs are on the opposite side of the motivational spectrum. They tend to be older, not as well educated, and women. They have conservative attitudes toward medication and a deep concern over health. They see possible dangers in frequent use of remedies, are concerned over side effects, and afraid of remedies with new ingredients and extra potency. To cope with these concerns, they are strongly oriented toward medical authority, seeking guidance in treatment and what products they should use. They hold rigid beliefs about the ailment, and are disciplined in the products they use and how frequently they use them. They want a simple, single-purpose remedy that is safe and free from side effects and backed by doctors or a reputable company.

The Practicalists

The Practicalists are in the extreme position on this side of the motivational spectrum. They tend to be older, well educated, emotionally the most stable, and least concerned over their ailment or the dangers of remedies. They accept the ailment and its discomforts as part of life, without fuss and pampering. They use a remedy as a last resort, and just to relieve the particular symptom. They seek simple products whose efficacy is well proved, and are skeptical of complicated modern remedies with new ingredients and multiple functions.

alternate levels of segmentation and identifies the most critical differentiating variables.

This type of clustering describes aggregated profiles, but it does not define a priority dimension and then develop a profile within it. We can readily do this, however, by selecting one dimension a priori, dividing the sample based on this single criterion, and then clustering within each group. Another statistical technique, the *automatic interaction detector*, selects a dependent measure (e.g., usage rate) and then derives attribute clusters hierarchically in order to discriminate best between levels of the dependent measure.

TABLE 7.3 Brand Use of Stomach Remedy Segments (Percent Use Brand Most Often)

BRAND	SEVERE SUFFERERS	ACTIVE MEDICATORS	HYPOCHONDRIACS	PRACTICALISTS
A	6	3	1	1
B	32	23	10	8
C	16	17	12	5
D	16	19	24	8
E	5	29	37	51

Source: Reprinted from the *Journal of Marketing Research*, published by the American Marketing Association. From W. D. Wells, ''Psychographics: A Critical Review,'' Vol. 12 (May 1975), p. 203.

Urban, Johnson, and Hauser (1984) proposed a hierarchical method for testing alternative competitive structures of a market. This method segments the market by the products buyers see as competitive, and then develops a profile of consumer attributes within each competitive sector of the market. This methodology first asks customers (1) what brands they would consider and then (2) what their first-choice product would be. Finally, either in response to questioning or by means of a simulated buying opportunity (e.g., exposure to a store shelf containing competitive products), respondents indicate what products they would buy if their first choice were not available. They also report their probability of buying each of the others. With this information, alternate distributions of the products among segments are tested until one is found where consumers have the highest probability of remaining in the segment also containing their second-choice brand under the condition that they are forced to switch from their first-choice brand. If, for example, we were testing a segmentation of caffeinated versus decaffeinated coffee, we would assign customers to the segment that contains their most preferred brand, and then calculate the probability that they would choose another product in that segment if they were forced to switch. If the probability was high (say, 80 percent in each segment), the hypothesized segmentation scheme would be supported. If it was low or if an alternate segmentation scheme was better (e.g., ground versus instant coffee), the original segmentation scheme would be rejected. If ground versus instant turned out to be the best scheme, for example, the next step would be to profile other attributes for the ground and instant segments.

The following industrial product case is an illustration of this approach to market segmentation.

Application—Heart Pacemakers: As the market for heart pacemakers has grown steadily over the last twenty-five years, the range of available pacers has increased. The original models worked by sending impulses to a single chamber of the heart. They were preset before implantation in the chest. More recently, technological innovation has resulted in programmable variable-pacing, two-chamber stimulation and sensing (see Figure 7.5), automatic pacing with micrologic components, and lithium battery power. Product lines

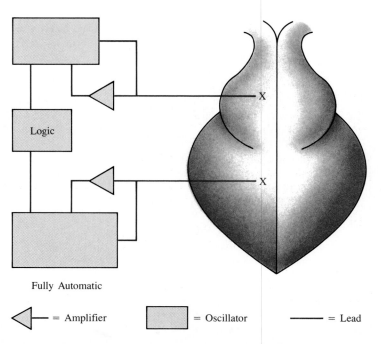

FIGURE 7.5
Sophisticated Dual-Chamber Pacemaker

Logic

X

X

Fully Automatic

◁— = Amplifier   ▭ = Oscillator   —— = Lead

are offered by many manufacturers—Cardiac Pacemakers, Cordis, Intermedics, Medtronic, Pacemaker, and Telelectronics being among the leaders. These manufacturers seek to meet the needs of cardiologists and thoracic surgeons, and to build brand loyalty. Their salesmen are exceptionally highly trained, even assisting surgeons in the operating room on some occasions. Aggressive promotion is used to build sales (e.g., contributions to medical schools and research, various perquisites for doctors).

The key segmentation issue faced by firms in this market is whether the market is segmented by brand loyalty, type of pacer, or medical symptomatology (e.g., use). If the market can be divided by type of pacer, we must ask whether there are different segments for single- and dual-chamber, or for "simple" (preset or simple programmable) and "sophisticated" (dual-chamber and advanced programmable) pacers. Answering these questions leads to product-line and marketing support decisions. If symptomatology is the best method of segmentation, pacers designed for each use would be appropriate. If segmentation is based on the type of pacers, having multiple pacers in a product segment might result in unwarranted overlap and duplication. If brand turns out to be the key dimension, marketing efforts aimed at maximizing one's overall brand franchise should receive the highest priority.

In order to shed light on these issues, a mail survey of cardiologists and thoracic surgeons was conducted. (A 50 percent response rate was achieved, suggesting high respondent interest in the topic.) The survey asked for the doctors' pacemaker preferences in each of three symptomatologies (average, older, and younger patients); asked them to note the pacers they would consider; and finally, on a 1–10 scale, requested that they indicate the probability of use of each of the pacers they would consider (see Figure 7.6 for an excerpt from the questionnaire).

Every alternative segmentation scheme (brand, symptomatology, and type) was evaluated by assessing from the survey data the probability that each respondent would

---

FIGURE 7.6
Pacemaker Questionnaire
Component

CASE REPORT

A younger patient, 55 years old, used to be quite active, sick sinus rhythm, partial heart block, may benefit physiologically from hemohynamic contribution of the atrium, is not paced currently.

(Check all the pacemakers that you would *consider* using. Rate the likelihood that you would *use* the pacemakers that you checked.)

____ Vivalith 5 (Pacesetter)
____ Enertrax (Medtronic)
____ ThinLith, Medium-lived (Intermedics)
____ Cyberlith IV (Intermedics)
____ Stamicor Gamma (Cordis)
____ Programalith 6 long-lived (Pacesetter)
____ Multicor Gamma, Medtronic Connector (Cordis)
____ Spectrax-SX-HT (Medtronic)
____ Omni-Stanicor Gamma (Cordis)
____ ThinLith, long-lived (Intermedics)
____ Vivalith 10 (Pacesetter)
____ Command-P5 (CPI)
____ Microthin-P1 (CPI)
____ Omni-Atricor Lambda (Cordis)
____ Spectrax-SXT (Medtronic)
____ Spectrax-VM (Medtronic)
____ Cyberlith I (Intermedics)
____ Multicor Gamma, 33 grams (Cordis)

____ InterLith-RP (Intermedics)
____ Spectrax-VL (Medtronic)
____ Byrel (Medtronic)
____ Programalith 3, long-lived
____ Microthin-D1 (CPI)
____ Spectrax-VS (Medtronic)
____ Spectrax-SX (Medtronic)
____ Microthin-D2 (CPI)
____ Programalith 6, medium-lived (Pacesetter)
____ Quantum (Intermedics)
____ Cyberlith (Intermedics)
____ Multicor Gamma, Cordis connector (Cordis)
____ Programalith 3, medium-lived (Pacesetter)
____ Optima MP (Telectronics)
____ Microthin-P2 (CPI)
____ Multicor Gamma, 41 grams (Cordis)
____ Optima (Telelectronics)
____ Some Other Pacemaker

purchase again in the segment that contained his or her most preferred brand if that brand were unavailable. Figure 7.7 shows the analysis for sophisticated versus simple pacers, and gives the probability of buying in each segment under the forced switching scenario. A doctor whose first preference was a sophisticated pacer had an 89.6 percent chance of buying another sophisticated pacer if his or her first-choice pacer were not available (labeled as *PB* in Figure 7.7), and only a 10.4 percent chance of shifting to a simple pacer. Similarly, those doctors who had a first preference for a simple pacer had a 63.7 percent probability of using another simple pacer if their most preferred pacer were not available. This segmentation scheme turned out to represent switching criteria better than segmentation schemes based on brand or use.

If we profile the doctors in each of these product segments, we find that the sophisticated segment has a higher fraction of high-volume implanters (i.e., doctors who implant many pacers per year). Further analysis shows that these doctors are most likely to use sophisticated pacers for younger patients.

The sophisticated product segment can be further divided into the two classes of dual-chamber and advanced programmable pacers, while the simple segment can be divided into preset and basic programmable sections. This market structure was found to be statistically significant, indicating that each of the four segments could be considered as a separate market.

Since many of the costs and much of the expertise across the product segments are shared, one strategic implication of this study is that a full product line should be offered. The old type of preset single-chamber pacer still appeared to be a viable segment, even though it was in the later phases of its life cycle. It was used for older patients where price was a concern. Similarly, simple programmable pacers were preferred for specific symptoms by certain doctors who did not include sophisticated pacers in their competitive sets. Sophisticated pacers ranged from established dual-chamber pacing to advanced programmables, which were in the early phases of their life cycles. A firm seeking a strong position in this market should almost certainly have an entry in each segment and concentrate on adding new segments through technical innovation (radio-controlled reprogramming by the doctor of an implanted pacer).

Although product segmentation turned out to be better for marketing pacemakers than brand, use, volume, and other product segmentations, it does not follow that the priority segmentation dimension should not be varied for specific decisions. Product segments were most helpful in establishing overall product-line strategy, but allocation of sales force efforts might better vary among segments based on volume. The sales force would, under these circumstances, continue to allocate most of its efforts to high-volume implanters. Moreover, analyzing the overall data by volume segments, and then profiling within them, reveals that high-volume users tend to require more sophisticated pacers and treat younger patients with more complex symptoms.

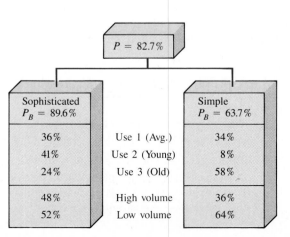

FIGURE 7.7
Product Segmentation of Pacemaker Market

This study contained only a restricted set of identifiers; in an actual company, a much larger set of profile attributes would be used. But the lack of segmentation by brand loyalty and the continuing range of product segments are important inputs to the formulation of segmentation strategies. Using market research and simple grouping criteria can help managers test alternative segmentation schemes and understand the dimensions of customer aggregation.

Level III Analysis

Level III analysis would include formal models to simulate the profit impact of alternate segmentation strategies. It would model the preference and cost of differences between alternative segmentation schemes. Costs would have to include shared production, distribution, and marketing components. Preference differences would include importances by segments, as well as full attitudinal, usage, and demographic profiles linked to choice rules. The objective would be to enable managers to forecast sales results for various combinations of product and nonproduct marketing variables. A comprehensive Level III analysis would also have to consider the effects of overlap between segments and the choice rules of consumers who face a choice between two or more of the firm's offerings.

Measures designed to ascertain the categorization structure in consumers' memory and to understand the consideration step in information processing may provide the basis for an improved Level III representation of segmentation and its effect on decision making.

There are as yet no validated simulation models that fully support segmentation strategy, but research is under way and progress can be expected. Currently managers must rely on their judgment, supported by Level I and Level II analyses, to select the dimensions of segmentation, define the number of segments, and develop an effective marketing program for each segment that is to be served.

CONCLUSION

Segmentation offers the firm important opportunities for increased profitability. A comprehensive data base of demographic, attitudinal, importance, usage, and competitive products, as well as alternative segmentation schemes, should be collected and used to support specific strategy decisions. The primary dimension of segmentation may vary by decision area: product for overall product market strategy, attitudes for copy formulation, demographics for allocation of sales force effort. But the underlying multidimensional representation must be a constant.

Once segments have been defined, firms can decide how many segments they should target with tailored products and marketing programs. If multiple segments are to be served, various combinations of marketing variables can be tailored for individual segments. Analytic support is available to help managers in this critical dimension of marketing strategy, but experienced judgment still describes the present state of the art.

QUESTIONS FOR DISCUSSION

1. Why segment markets? Would it not be simpler to offer only one product? What are the most important forces leading to increasing segmentation?

2. Take a product you are familiar with and, using your own knowledge or research into the advertising and marketing strategies firms employ, describe how the market is segmented. What basis of segmentation are firms apparently using? How does this affect their marketing programs?

3. Which is the most important of the five bases for segmentation described in this chapter? Why? Which basis is most commonly used?

4. Take one basis for segmentation and outline at least ten measures that could be used to implement this kind of segmentation. (For example, you could use income as a segmentation variable to implement demographic segmentation.)

5. Is there one true segmentation for a market? Why might you want to describe segments differently in different situations?

6. In developing a hierarchical segmentation scheme, how do you decide which variables characterize the branches in the hierarchy and which should be placed in the profile of customers within a branch? Take a specific example and try alternative hierarchies.

7. How should one manage overlap between segments? What if media and channels cannot uniquely address each segment? If there is leakage between segments (that is, customers that fit into more than one segment), how would this change your strategy?

8. When should a firm target one segment? When should it cover all segments?

9. What are the advantages and limitations of the Level II analytical support tools for segmentation?

REFERENCES

CHOFFAY, JEAN-MARIE, AND GARY L. LILIEN. 1980. *Market Planning for New Industrial Products*. New York: John Wiley.

CHURCHILL, G. A. 1976. *Marketing Research: Methodological Foundations*. Hinsdale, IL: The Dryden Press.

CLARITAS INC. 1986. *How to Use PRIZM*. Arlington, VA: Claritas, Inc.

DICKSON, PETER R., AND JAMES L. GINTER. 1987. "Market Segmentation, Product Differentiation and Marketing Strategy." *Journal of Marketing* 51: 1–10.

DOYLE, PETER, AND JOHN SAUNDERS. 1985. "Marketing Segmentation and Positioning in Specialized Industrial Markets." *Journal of Marketing* 42: 24–32.

EVERITT, B. 1974. *Cluster Analysis*. London: Heinemann Educational Books.

FRANK, R. E., W. F. MASSY, AND Y. WIND. 1972. *Market Segmentation*. Englewood Cliffs, NJ: Prentice Hall.

GOBELI, DAVID H., AND WILLIAM RUDELIUS. 1985. "Managing Innovation: Lessons from the Cardiac-Pacing Industry." *Sloan Management Review*, Summer: 29–43.

KASINKAS, M. 1980. "Competitive Structures in Industrial Markets: A Modeling Approach to Hierarchical Segmentation in the U.S. Pacemaker Industry." M.S. thesis. Cambridge, MA: Sloan School of Management, M.I.T.

OPPENHEIM, A. N. 1966. *Questionnaire Design and Attitude Measurement*. New York: Basic Books.

URBAN, G. L., P. L. JOHNSON, AND J. R. HAUSER. 1984. "Testing Competitive Market Structures." *Management Science* 3: 83–112.

WELLS, W. D. 1975. "Psychographics: A Critical Review." *Journal of Marketing Research* 12: 196–213.

WIND, Y., T. S. ROBERTSON, AND C. FRASER. 1982. "Industrial Product Diffusion by Market Segment." *Industrial Marketing Management* 11: 1–8.

CHAPTER

8
PRODUCT POSITIONING

POSITIONING VERSUS SEGMENTATION

Segmentation analysis tells us how the market is defined and allows us to target one or more market opportunities. Product positioning takes place within a target market segment and tells us how we can compete most effectively in that market segment. If we are to make good positioning decisions, we need to know: (1) What dimensions do consumers use to evaluate competitive marketing programs—how many are there and what should they be named? (2) How important is each of these dimensions in the decision process? (3) How do we and the competition compare on these dimensions? (4) How do consumers make choices on the basis of this information? Answering these questions requires a clear understanding of the customer decision process (Chapter 5), and benefits from the use of proven analytic market research procedures.

In our analysis, it is important to realize that what we are positioning is the *complete* product offering, not just advertising and its psychological evaluation or just physical product features. We are concerned with the consumer's evaluation of the complete "bundle of utility": physical product attributes, image, service, distribution, and price. Before we can formulate effective positioning strategies, we must understand how consumers evaluate multiattributed product offerings and how they choose among competitive products.

In the pacemaker case described in Chapter 7, we learned that product segments could be defined according to the sophistication of the pacer. Suppose we targeted the sophisticated dual-chamber segment. Next we would try to position our product within it, and to do this, we would have to answer the four questions posed at the beginning of this chapter. For this example, assume that a doctor's dimensions of evaluation are: (1) functional capability (e.g., programmability, range of logic functions); (2) reliability (e.g., low failure rate, long life, lack of side effects); and (3) "ease of implantation" (e.g., size, shape, attachments, company surgical assistance). In this example, price is not an issue (although it probably would be if we were positioning in the simple preset pacemaker segment of the market). In the sophisticated pacer segment, all three dimensions are

134

TABLE 8.1   Evaluations for a Selected Doctor

DIMENSION	IMPORTANCE	RATINGS FOR BRANDS CONSIDERED		
		Medtronic	Cordis	Pacesetter
Functional capability	.4	4	3	5
Reliability	.3	5	4	3
Ease of implanting	.3	5	3	3
	1.0			

important, but functionality is most dominant in a doctor's choice process. Positioning of the competitive alternatives on the three dimensions can be done by comparing the ratings of the competing products on each dimension. Table 8.1 shows the ratings and importances for *a* selected doctor, and the three brands of sophisticated dual-chamber pacers he or she is considering.

This doctor rates—on a 5-point scale—the Pacesetter brand as having the most functionality, but rates Medtronic highest on reliability and ease of implanting. With the relative importances shown and assuming a simple weighing of the ratings by their importances, we predict that this doctor would choose Medtronic.

If all doctors were similar to this one, the example suggests that Medtronic is well positioned, but may be able to improve sales by adding more functionality; Pacesetter could compete more effectively by improving reliability and ease of implanting; while Cordis has opportunities on all dimensions. In the real world, of course, doctors vary with regard to the brands they consider, the relative importance they assign to each dimension, and their evaluations of competing brands.

In this chapter, we examine perceptual mapping and choice modeling as methods for understanding positioning issues. We consider differences in preferences among individuals within a target segment and how physical features can be used to shift positions. Key factors in selecting a positioning are outlined and complicating managerial issues are presented. The final sections of the chapter review the state of the art of analytic support for positioning decisions.

PERCEPTUAL MAPPING AND CHOICE

Perceptual Maps

While tables can be used to represent product positionings on several dimensions, a graph or "map" is often more effective in portraying the options. Figure 8.1 shows a two-dimensional perceptual map for selected cars in the luxury car market in 1984. Consumers rated cars from extremely poor to excellent on nine attributes: (1) luxury and comfort; (2) style and design; (3) reliability; (4) fuel economy; (5) safety; (6) maintenance cost; (7) quality; (8) durability; and (9) road performance. These nine attributes were combined into two perceptual dimensions (see the analytical support section later in this chapter for a discussion of the statistical procedure) that were named "appeal" and "rational." Appeal represented primarily the evaluations on luxury, style, and performance, while the rational dimension reflected ratings of reliability, fuel economy, maintenance cost, quality, and durability. The Buick Riviera is positioned highest on the appeal dimension, while Honda Accord is highest on rational. The other models are shown as reflecting various trade-offs between the appeal and rational positionings.

A perceptual map can be used to identify gaps that may represent opportunities for new products. At the time these data were collected (1984), no existing car enjoyed the

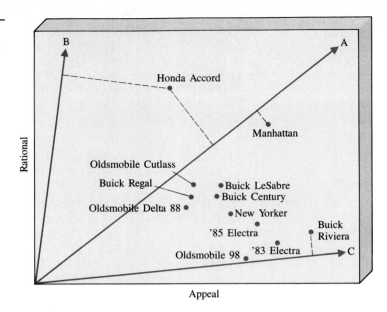

FIGURE 8.1
Perceptual Map for Selected Luxury Autos in 1984

best position on both the appeal and rational dimensions. More recently, Honda with its new Accura has been trying to achieve this position by adding more luxury, style, and performance to its high ratings on the rational dimension. Recall our discussion of the 1985 Buick Electra in Chapter 6. It is shown on this map, along with the old 1983 Electra. Ratings by consumers after driving the test cars showed that the new 1985 model was viewed as lower on appeal but higher on the rational dimension. Buick advertising stressed durability in an attempt to position the Electra in the gap represented by high values on both dimensions.

Importances and Choices

Let us hypothesize that a car was developed that did very well on both dimensions—the new "Manhattan" shown in Figure 8.2. Would all people in the luxury car market buy it? For those buyers who want both appeal and rational utilities, the Manhattan is the

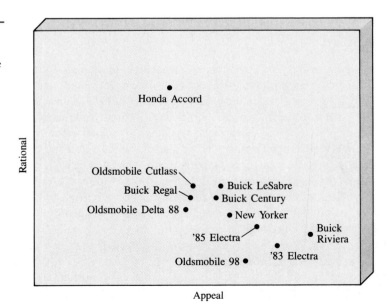

FIGURE 8.2
Perceptual Map for Selected Luxury Autos, Including the Hypothetical "Manhattan"

most attractive alternative. But buyers for whom the rational dimension is the overiding consideration and appeal has little utility would choose Honda over the new Manhattan because it has a higher position on the rational dimension, even though it is lower on appeal. Similarly, people who only considered appeal in their selection would choose the Riviera because the Riviera is superior on this dimension and this utility outweighs its low rational rating. The importances assigned by consumers to the dimensions in choosing between alternatives is a critical input in the positioning decision.

We can represent the importances by arrows on the perceptual map. For example, people who weigh both dimensions equally will have an arrow at 45 degrees (arrow in Figure 8.2*A*). They would choose the brand farthest out on this arrow if they multiplied the ratings on the dimensions by their importance weights and chose the highest value (see Chapter 5 and Table 5.1 for another example of this linear weighing). Technically, this means we draw a perpendicular line from each brand to the arrow on the map, and choose the brand whose perpendicular intersects farthest out on the vector. In Figure 8.2, Honda is the predicted choice for these consumers.

Consumers who view the rational dimension as dominant could be represented by arrow *B*. They assign much higher importance to rational aspects than to appeal, and they, too, would choose Honda because its projection is farthest along the vector. Consumers who consider appeal much more important could be represented by arrow *C*. Because the Riviera, projected perpendicularly, intersects the most extreme point, we would predict that it would be these people's choice.

Now let us represent the preferences of the market by a collection of arrows. Let each vector represent the importances of 10 percent of the market. Figure 8.3A shows one collection of ten arrows, based on the assumption that most people want both appeal and rational characteristics, but vary somewhat in their weighing of them. Figure 8.3B depicts the situation where half the market wants rational characteristics and the other half want appeal. The implications of these importances for positioning are significant. If Figure 8.3A truly represents tastes in the market, the Manhattan would be a big success, while if Figure 8.3B is more accurate, the Manhattan's sales would be much lower.

FIGURE 8.3
Importance Vectors (Each Vector Represents 10% of the Market)

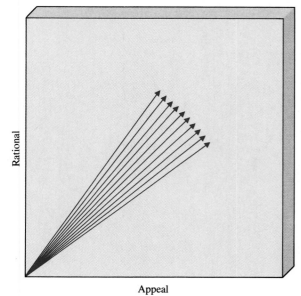

A. Value Both Dimensions

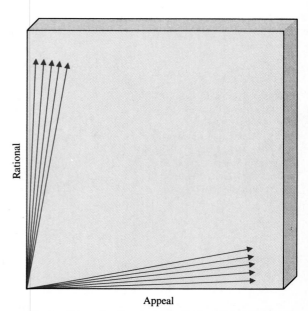

B. One Dimension Dominant for Each of Two Subgroups

It is necessary to understand preference differences within the targeted market segments because they are important in selecting a position for a brand and in determining the competitive structure within the segment. When preferences vary within a segment, positions and physical product features may vary considerably. If preferences are relatively homogeneous within a segment, the positions of competing brands will be relatively similar, and the quantity of advertising and promotion will be the critical competitive weapons.

Price and Maps

If the Manhattan costs $75,000 and the Honda costs $10,000, the Honda may be purchased by customers represented in Figure 8.3A, even though their importance vectors are directed at the Manhattan. Price was not explicitly considered in the auto maps in Figures 8.1 and 8.2. To complete our positioning analysis we must consider the effects of price on the final choice.

Price can be represented in two ways in perceptual maps. The first is to create an additional dimension in the perceptual map to represent price. In the auto example, the map would become a cube, with the prices of the cars as the third dimension. The importance vectors would then represent the trade-off among appeal, rational, and price characteristics in the final choice.

The second approach is to divide both dimensional coordinates of each brand by that brand's average price. Figure 8.4 shows a map of the mouthwash category without price. Figure 8.5 shows the same brands with the coordinates being the Figure 8.4 values divided by price. These are known as the "per dollar coordinates." From Figure 8.4, it is difficult to understand how Signal could get any sales because other brands are better on the dimensions of "fighting bad breath" and "pleasant taste." Examining Figure 8.5 reveals that Signal is the best in "fights bad breath per dollar." Because its price is lower, it improves its positioning to a competitive level. Listermint with anticavity rinse is a higher-priced brand, so on Figure 8.5 it no longer enjoys a dominant position on the two dimensions. In price-scaled maps such as Figure 8.5, the brands tend to arrange themselves along a "frontier." That is, if you connect them, they form an outer boundary; brands cannot exist for long inside the boundary. The importance vectors will now represent the trade-offs of the per-dollar scaled dimensions, and therefore the combined trade-offs of the original dimensions and price.

FIGURE 8.4
Mouthwash Market
Unadjusted for Price
Source: Based on S. M.
Shugan, "Estimating Brand
Positioning Maps Using
Supermarket Scanning Data,"
Journal of Marketing Research,
Vol. 24 (February 1987), Table
2, p. 8.

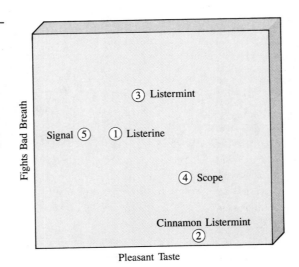

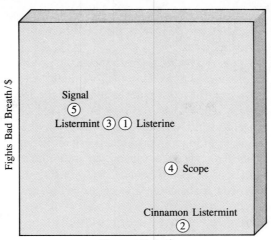

FIGURE 8.5
Mouthwash Market
Adjusted for Price
Source: Based on S. M.
Shugan, Estimating Brand
Positioning Maps Using
Supermarket Scanning Data,''
Journal of Marketing Research,
Vol. 24 (February 1987), Figure
3, p. 10.

Features and Positioning

Should the new Manhattan auto have leather seats? Should the suspension be adjustable? These are questions about the choice of features. The perceptual maps represented overall dimensions of evaluation and not detailed features. Feature selection is critical in positioning, however, because features are an important determinant of overall perception and choice.

We can think of features as driving the positioning on each dimension. Leather seats will probably lead to an increase in the rating of luxury and comfort, and therefore enhance the Manhattan's position on the appeal dimension. An adjustable suspension would probably lead to an increase in consumer ratings on road performance, and therefore enhance the Manhattan's position on the rational dimension. The inclusion of features may increase cost, so the effects of price must be considered by one of the procedures outlined earlier.

Another way to view features is as direct influencers of choice. In following this course, we would try to combine the most valued features into general attributes. This is a sound approach, but a complete positioning analysis should also consider the intermediate effect of features on perceptual map positions and resulting choices. When the features are related to perceptual dimensions, the role of advertising and the consumer's ability to perceive engineering differences can be better understood.

SELECTING A POSITIONING

Profit and Share

The criterion for selecting a best positioning is long-run profitability and return on investment. This is often achieved by maximizing share of choices through positioning in a dominant location. We can maximize share by adding features and advertising to achieve high coordinate values on the map dimensions in the direction of most of the importance vectors. But if the costs of this positioning are very high and price is low, the resulting profits may be unsatisfactory. We must balance the costs of positioning with price and share changes to identify the strategy that will achieve maximum long-run profitability.

Profitability will also depend on the competitive environment. If we can set price without competitive reaction, the decisions are much simpler. However, if competitors react to our price and positioning actions, the long-run profit implications of strategies are much more complex. We will address these complexities in Chapter 10, but we must recognize from the outset that the best position is the one that meets financial as well as marketing goals.

One way to represent the profit implications on a perceptual map is to show alternative positionings with anticipated profits indicated in parentheses. Figure 8.6, which illustrates a hypothetical set of repositionings for the 1985 Electra, also indicates the relative price of each positioning. Position E1 is based on more expensive components and an improvement in reliability and durability. Sales rise, but so do costs, with the result that the profit increase is marginal. Position E2 is achieved by advertising that stresses social status and body style—again, the profit improvement is only modest. Position E3, which reflects better components and advertising designed to build perceptions that match the improved engineering, appears to be the most profitable of the strategies.

Capability and Fulfillment

One way to achieve a more preferred position is by making strong advertising claims and backing them with effective copy. We could claim, for example, that a new mouthwash called ''Everfresh'' is longer lasting than any other brand in fighting bad breath and has an improved mint and cinnamint taste. This strategy might earn us a preferred perceptual position in Figure 8.5 and result in considerable trial purchasing. But if our product does not fulfill its claim, consumers will lower their evaluations and Everfresh will drop to a low level on both dimensions. Repeat-purchase probabilities will be low and success unlikely. Before implementing a positioning strategy, we must be sure that the physical product can fulfill the positioning.

Similarly, in our car example, the new Electra advertising stresses reliability, but if the car is not truly reliable, word-of-mouth communication among customers and magazine ratings (e.g., *Car and Driver* or *Consumer Reports*) will lead to a reduction in the positioning coordinates. Introducing a car that has some residual bugs can have an equally devastating effect on perceptions. The quality of dealer service and the manufacturers' policies on guarantees can affect the postpurchase evaluations of product satisfaction relative to expectations. Once the market has formed perceptions, it is often difficult to change them, so if reliability is a key positioning claim, both the product and postpurchase service system must be effective.

FIGURE 8.6
Perceptual Map for Selected Luxury Autos: The 1985 Buick Electra

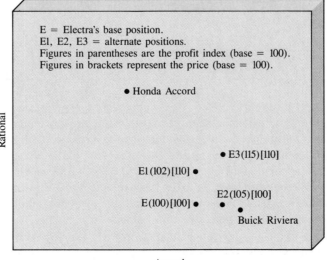

E = Electra's base position.
E1, E2, E3 = alternate positions.
Figures in parentheses are the profit index (base = 100).
Figures in brackets represent the price (base = 100).

• Honda Accord

Rational

• E3 (115) [110]

E1 (102) [110] •

E2 (105) [100]
E (100) [100] •   •
                    •
              Buick Riviera

Appeal

In marketing pacemakers, we should be very aware that doctors communicate informally through friends and formally through papers and speeches. If we were claiming our pacemaker had no side effects, but doctors found this was not true, sales would drop very quickly (recall life-cycle declines for two ethical drugs in Chapter 6, Figure 6.8). All of these cases reinforce the tenet that good marketing is based on products that are advertised and sold honestly and generate real value by filling customer needs.

Quality

While "quality" means fulfilling a product's specifications with no defects, it is actually a much wider concept. Total quality includes the design of the product and customer service. The quality concept begins with design, carries through production, distribution, and service, and ends in total customer satisfaction. In product positioning for quality, we must understand how engineering decisions are linked to feature creation; how features are related to the perceptions, preferences, and choices of customers; and how costs, prices, and profits are affected by engineering decisions. The best quality level is the one that meets the needs of customers, can be produced defect free, and earns profits for the firm. Quality is an integral part of creating benefits and positioning a product in a target market segment.

Unique Benefit Proposition

The final output from positioning is a profit-maximizing strategy for physical product design, advertising, distribution, service, and pricing. We earn sales by offering a product that has a better combination of utility-generating attributes than the competition. This is often done by identifying our own unique competitive advantages: flavor formulation in mouthwashes, dealer service in autos, advanced chip logic in pacemakers. By using our unique competitive advantage in positioning, we can reduce our vulnerability to competition. It is difficult for competitors to match our product-positioning attractiveness without resorting to price-cutting. If we develop a unique competitive advantage on a dimension of importance to a significant portion of the market, we can enjoy a substantial share and high margins. We differentiate our product from competition in a way that generates utility for customers and profits for us.

Maintaining the resulting competitive advantage should be a major priority in our strategy. Thus, we will continue to innovate in flavor sensation for our mouthwashes, service for our autos, and state-of-the-art computer technology for our pacemakers. As competitors strive to match our capabilities, we will need to work hard to maintain leadership in our unique consumer benefit area.

MANAGERIAL ISSUES

Creating a Dimension

Since most products are evaluated within the perceptual structure of the segment, the most common positioning question is where to place our product in that space. Sometimes, however, a more revolutionary approach based on creating a new dimension may be our best choice. If we can create a new dimension that is important to consumers and position uniquely upon it, we can enjoy high market share and profits.

Creating a new dimension is difficult. The use of micrologic chips in pacemakers created the dimension of functional sophistication. In soft drinks, the use of saccharin and aspertane created the low-calorie dimension. Most new dimensions result from major product innovations. Minor product changes, though they may be intended to create a new dimension, are often reflected instead in the existing perceptual structure. For example, introducing a retractable hardtop on a car may not create a new dimension, but rather lead to a change of position on the appeal dimension. Likewise, a new remote radio reprogrammable heart pacemaker may not create a new dimension, but lead to a change in position on the reliability dimension through its subattributes of lack of side effects and long life.

Sometimes an innovation is so major that it creates both a new dimensional structure and an entire new segment. In pacemakers, the use of micrologic components segmented the market into simple and sophisticated pacers, besides creating the dimension of functional capability in the sophisticated segment. On the other hand, the use of microcomputers in autos did not create a new segment or dimension, but rather enhanced perceptions of reliability.

The final result of innovation may be either a new positioning within the current structure or the creation of a new dimension or an additional segment. When a firm sees no opportunities for improvement in the existing positioning structure, it should strive to add a dimension. If the firm has spanned all segments and is well positioned in each, it should try revolutionary approaches to developing new segments.

One caution here is that managers often think they are revolutionizing a category when consumers feel nothing but a mild perceptual perturbation. Customer reaction must be measured to determine what is really occurring. This can be done informally by contact with key customers or by more advanced analytical methods such as those discussed in the Analytic Support section below.

Positioning Across Segments

Segments often overlap, making it difficult to position products in different segments independently. The overlap may result from a group of customers who shift between segments or from media or channels of distribution that impact both segments. In these circumstances, positioning claims must not conflict across segments. For example, positioning on low price in the preprogrammed pacemaker market may lead to a reduction in the perception of reliability in the sophisticated pacer segment for doctors who are active in both segments.

One way to avoid this problem is to have different brands in each segment. Procter & Gamble uses this strategy effectively in detergents. By keeping the P&G identification low, the company can position optimally for each segment without contaminating the perception of its other brands.

Another strategy is to adopt an umbrella appeal across segments and texture the positioning within each segment. Goodrich's line of T/A radial tires is based on the overall appeal of technical advantage, but the advertising claims and copy are different for individual segments. For the sports and racing-oriented driver, the ads show racing cars and stress the T/A performance advantage. In the suburban/executive segment, luxury cars are featured, with claims of durability and safety. This differentiation is possible because the media are also differentiated for these segments (*Motor Trend* for the sports segment and *Business Week* for the suburban segment).

Dynamics

Perceptual structures and importance of dimensions are not static. The importance of the rational dimension in auto choice increased during the oil crisis 1972, for example, while in 1985–1986, when oil prices (in real terms) fell to their 1970 level, consumers did not shift their preferences back to large cars, although they did become more interested in powerful cars. The dynamics of perception, preference, and choice can be best understood by longitudinal studies of these complex phenomena. A strategic posture that is flexible enough to respond to possible shifts is generally the best course when faced with rapidly changing structures.

Category dynamics occur as the life cycle proceeds. Initially, products compete on the efficacy or performance dimension. Then new dimensions emerge as new brands enter the market and consumers refine their ability to differentiate. Psychological factors (e.g., appeal in cars), ease of use (e.g., ease of implanting in pacemakers), and solution of in-use problems (e.g., improved reliability in pacers) often appear as the product market matures.

Additional segmentation is also evident as aging takes place. A single pacemaker market for preset pacers divided into four segments as technology advanced. Complexity increases as segmentation and positioning opportunities change. Recognizing and coping with such change is a critical function of marketing. Unless a company learns to accurately diagnose change and implement timely and effective responses, its market share and profits can quickly disappear as competitors use technological and marketing innovations to improve their position in the market.

ANALYTIC SUPPORT

Level I Analysis

Certain questions about customers' dimensions of evaluation, the importance of these dimensions, and the differences across customers are basic to effective marketing. Personal experience in the business and direct consumer contact are invaluable starting points in seeking answers to these questions. Many companies (e.g., IBM, Xerox, and Lanier) encourage all their senior executives to maintain frequent direct contact with customers. Some go so far as to assign top executives to client service teams. This helps increase sales, as well as to develop a customer-based perspective and a shared understanding of the most important market response mechanisms.

While such customer contact is essential, we must be careful that it is not biased. If it is too oriented to existing customers, we may lose needed input from noncustomers. Care should be taken to understand why some consumers are not buying our product as well as why others are.

Focus groups are often used to provide more representative input on positioning opportunities. In some firms, focus groups are run regularly and videotape summaries are presented to top managers to keep them in touch with changing customer requirements.

At Level I, simple data inputs and experience can be used to identify positioning opportunities. Perceptual maps can be drawn judgmentally: First, select two or three dimensions, name them, and place your brand and competition on the map. Then add importance vectors to reflect subsections of the market (say, four arrows, each representing 25 percent of the market). Examine the points and vectors and predict which products each group of customers will choose (those that project perpendicularly farthest out on the vectors). Think about what is driving your position and how features and advertising can be used to change it. Estimate the share gains and costs for shifting your position. Finally, look for opportunities to increase your profits.

Level II Analysis

Level II analysis is directed toward the same questions as Level I, but utilizes market research measures, statistics, and simple models to answer them. We do not attempt to teach these techniques here, but simply describe how they work and the judgments managers should exercise in using them.[1]

---

[1] See Urban and Hauser (1980) for a complete description of the technical procedures of mapping and choice modeling procedures outlined in this section.

TABLE 8.2   Steps in Positioning Analysis

STEPS	MANAGER'S ROLE
1. Define target market	Be sure correct segment definition is used.
2. Design survey	Specify decision requirements.
3. Attribute generation	Assure completeness.
4. Statistical mapping	
Name dimensions	Use judgment to provide input.
Number of dimensions	Examine additional dimension for relevance.
Coordinates of brands	Review for reasonableness.
Importance vectors	Decide on number of subgroups.
5. Features	Select features and levels, link to preference and/or perception.
6. Evaluate alternative strategies	Be sure any contemplated shift can be achieved, confirm with concept/product tests.

Table 8.2 lists the steps in a Level II analysis to support positioning and notes the issues marketing management should be involved with at each point. The first step is to define the target market for the positioning research. It is important here that management clearly define the segment and make sure that the market research department or supplier accurately transfers this definition into a screening questionnaire to qualify respondents for the study. The analytic procedures outlined in Chapter 7 should be helpful at this stage.

Designing the survey, step 2, will be the responsibility of the research group, but managers should ask what they are going to do with the results of this study before the research is designed. They should set clear guidelines on the possible marketing actions and decisions that should be supported so that the needed information will be collected. Too much research generates interesting findings but does not provide the input critical to taking action.

Step 3 is generating attributes for evaluation by consumers. Respondents will be asked to rate the products they would consider purchasing on each of the detailed attributes. In the auto study, the nine attributes listed in the first column of Table 8.3 were used. The marketing manager should be sure that all important attributes are included and that this wording is meaningful. For example, should luxury be separated from comfort in the attribute rating in Table 8.3? What about durability and resale? Should a scale be added for the quality of dealer service? Should the importance of price be investigated directly, or should a scale such as "inexpensive" be used? One consideration is the nature of the decision to be supported. If, for example, advertising is considered critical, psychological

TABLE 8.3   Factor Loadings

	DIMENSIONS	
Attribute	**Appeal**	**Rational**
Luxury and comfort	0.86	0.10
Style	0.72	0.08
Reliability	0.45	0.63
Miles per gallon	0.24	0.64
Safety	0.52	0.31
Maintenance	0.10	0.67
Quality	0.48	0.64
Durability and resale value	0.38	0.60
Performance	0.67	0.35

scales should probably be emphasized; if physical product revisions are contemplated, more detailed instrumental attributes would be included. Sometimes more scales are desirable than can be feasibly measured. In this case, a subresearch study should be undertaken with consumers to reduce the set of attributes. This subsurvey could also be used to ensure that all the consumer evaluative criteria have been identified. Management involvement in this process is at a rather detailed level, but unless the correct attributes are included, the maps will not be meaningful and subsequent action may be inappropriate.

In step 4, a statistical procedure called *factor analysis* can be used to reduce brand ratings on the attributes to an underlying set of perceptual dimensions. This procedure is not completely automatic, however; judgment must be used in naming the dimensions and selecting the number of dimensions.

Table 8.3 shows the correlations (called *factor loadings*) between each of the original attributes and the underlying perceptual dimension. The name attached to the dimension is a judgment based on the correlations (loading values greater than or equal to .6 are underlined in table). The first dimension is most highly correlated to ratings on luxury and comfort, style, and performance, and was named ''appeal'' by the product manager. It could have been named ''image'' by another manager. The second dimension in this study is highly correlated to ratings on reliability, maintenance, quality, and durability, and was named ''rational.'' It could also have been called ''functionality.'' The important point is to know which detailed attributes are associated with the dimension and to label these with a relevant name.

An additional dimension can always be drawn out of the data with factor analysis. Statistical measures can help in determining if the dimension is significant, but managers should also examine it to see if it is interpretable (i.e., are there high correlations with meaningful attribute scales; is the added dimension helpful?).

Once the number of dimensions has been determined, factor analysis can be used to define the coordinates for each brand on each dimension. Managers should check the coordinates to see that they are reasonable, and be sure that the interpretation of the dimensions is consistent with the brand positions. The resulting perceptual map for these data was shown in Figure 8.1.

Next, the importance vectors are generated, either on the basis of the importances as reported by consumers or on the basis of statistical regression. The equation is a simple linear one in which the brand coordinates on each dimension are multiplied by the importance of that dimension and summed over dimensions to describe observed preferences. For a two-dimensional map:

(8.1) $P(b) = a(1)*C(b,1) + a(2)*C(b,2)$

where:

$P(b)$ = consumer preference for brand b

$C(b,d)$ = coordinate on map of brand b on dimension d

$a(d)$ = importance of dimension d

The importances could be obtained from consumers directly, but a better procedure is to estimate them. We can measure preference (first choice, second choice, etc.), derive the coordinates by factor analysis, and use linear regression to estimate the importances (a). The ratio of the importances ($a(1)/a(2)$) is the slope of the importance vectors shown in Figure 8.2. When the importances of both dimensions are equal, the ratio is 1 and the angle of the vector is 45 degrees. If dimension 1 is twice as important as dimension 2 (i.e., $a(1)$ is twice $a(2)$), the slope is .5 and the angle is 26.6 degrees. Projecting the coordinates perpendicularly (as we did earlier in this chapter) is equivalent to calculating preference with equation (8.1).

If the target market contains subgroups with different trade-offs, their vectors and individual consumer descriptor profiles should be examined to determine their appropriateness for decision making. Simulations can be utilized to estimate the choice effects of shifting the brand positions.

Some Level II analyses include an examination of the link of features to perceptual dimensions and preferences (step 5 in Table 8.2) to aid in understanding how brands can be shifted. In this step, the relevant features are identified and combinations of the features are presented to consumers. For example, Figure 8.7 shows a combination of auto features. In this study, ten body styles, six brands, five prices, three fuel economy levels, three horsepower levels, two door configurations, three resale values, three maintenance costs, three financing rates, and three option packages were designated for analysis. Six hundred and forty different descriptions in the format of Figure 8.7 were drawn up, and potential buyers rated a subset of them (four per respondent). This allowed the importance of each feature to be statistically estimated across the sample. Figure 8.8 shows the relative importance of each feature over the range tested. This type of research, called *conjoint analysis,* is commonly applied in industry (see Green and Srinivasan, 1978, for a summary of the state-of-the-art in this area). Design and manufacturer are most important, but other factors are also significant. These are averages of individual values. Subgroup analysis

FIGURE 8.7
Feature Combination

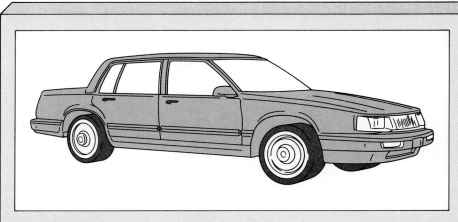

MANUFACTURER	: Buick
PRICE	: $15,000
EPA MILEAGE (city)	: 23 mpg
ENGINE/POWER	: 6 cylinders, 3.8 litres (232 cu. in.)
DOORS	: Four doors
ESTIMATED RESALE VALUE AFTER 3 YEARS	: 75% of price paid
ESTIMATED MAINTENANCE COST PER YEAR	: $200
FINANCING AVAILABLE	: 7.9%
FEATURES	: Automatic transmission with overdrive range, power brakes, power steering, power doorlocks, tape and AM/FM stereo, defroster on all windows, remote-control mirrors, air conditioning, cruise control, digital instrument pane, six-way adjusting front seats, carpeting, light group (trunk, hood, doors, map light, glove compartment)

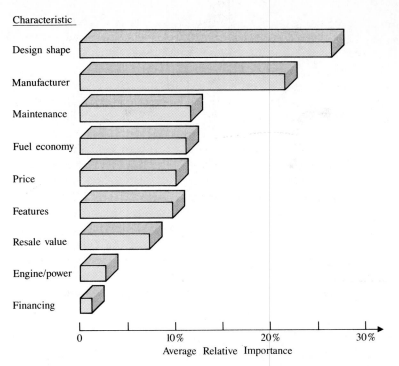

FIGURE 8.8
Relative Importance of Features

showed that import owners had higher importances for fuel economy, resale value, small engines, and price. Figure 8.9 shows the utility gains and losses by shifting the feature levels. It suggests that consumers, on the average, would be willing to pay an additional $3,000 and give up 1 utility point if maintenance cost were reduced from $600 to $400 a year, increasing utility by 1 point.

Managers need to be involved in conjoint analysis, specifying the feature variables and the levels of each feature to be evaluated. Usually, fewer features are investigated than in this study. Limits should be based on managerial relevance. Managers should also specify whether the linkages should be to preference, as in this study, or to perceptual dimensions, or to both. Overall importances should be examined, as well as importances within relevant subgroups of the target segment to obtain a feeling for the diversity within the market.

When implementing a total product quality program, one more level of detail must be considered in step 5: the specific links between engineering decisions and feature creation. In our example, this level of detail would be represented by specific engineering improvements that would result in less maintenance (e.g., stainless steel muffler systems or plastic body panels to reduce corrosion). In a procedure called *quality function deployment* (QFD), complete and sometimes exhausting linkages are made between product specifications and customers' desires (see Hauser and Clausing [1988] for more information). Detailed matrices are specified to link engineering characteristics and their objective measures to customer attributes; customer attributes to customer perceptions; and engineering characteristics to each other with respect to interaction and creativity. These matrices lead to specific engineering targets intended to achieve the best positioning for the product.

The final step in the positioning analysis is the evaluation of alternative strategies. If we change our features or advertising and selling message, what are the sales and profit implications? With the preceding analysis, a sales model can be built by multiplying the total segment sales times the share of choices we obtain with our positioning relative to competition (our preference value divided by the sum of other brand preferences). Here

147

FIGURE 8.9
Utility Points at Feature
Levels

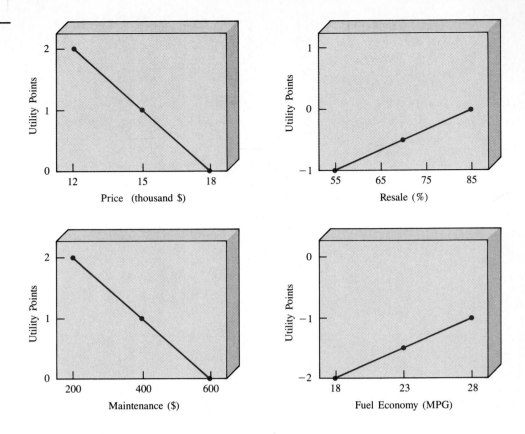

management is using the analysis as a tool to identify positioning opportunities and high-leverage feature and attribute changes. This may trigger new advertising copy generation, new physical formulations, price changes, improved distribution incentives, or expanded service capability. The costs of each option when compared with the sales and revenue gains will allow a profit calculation (recall Figure 8.6).

As noted earlier, if profit goals cannot be achieved by repositioning, consideration should be given to creating a new dimension or a new segmentation of the market. Concept tests with consumers should be carried out to see if the desired changes would, in fact, occur or if the brand would merely shift within the current perceptual frame of reference.

A monitoring of the positioning through a longitudinal analysis is useful in most markets because of shifting perceptions and preferences, the entry of new brands, or competitive shifts of position.

Level III Analysis

Advanced analysis follows the same general steps shown in Table 8.2, but more complex models are used. Instead of the linear preference model shown in equation 8.1, for example, one might use nonlinear discrete choice models. The most commonly employed such model, which is called Logit, models choice probability as the utility of one brand divided by the sum of the utilities of all brands an individual considers. Estimates of the coefficients for each dimension are based on a statistical procedure applied to observed choices and perceptual or feature input.[2]

---

[2] See Urban and Hauser (1980) for a discussion.

Other models simultaneously estimate the map coordinates and the distribution of importance trade-offs across individuals so as to fit best observed choices (Hauser and Shugan, 1983; and Shugan, 1987). These approaches allow maps and importances to be estimated with a minimum of input data.

Level III models have also been developed to simulate the effects of shifting positioning (Hauser and Simmie, 1981). With explicit cost functions and feature linkages, cost and profit implications can be outlined.

The newest approach to positioning is based on the information-processing concepts outlined in Chapter 5. First, categorization is studied to ensure correct segmentation assumptions. Then the process of consideration is addressed to understand the mechanisms that lead to a product being evoked for purchase. Perceptions and individual decision heuristics are measured. The resulting sample of individual models is then consolidated in a computer base against which alternate strategies can be simulated.

Even with these and other advanced procedures that will become available in the future, managers still must become involved in the issues outlined in Table 8.2. Key managerial review and specification functions should never be delegated to the analyst or to a mechanical procedure.

STATE OF THE ART

The competitive structure in many markets demands that managers devote more attention to the positioning of their products. Unique benefit propositions and sustainable advantages must be sought. Basic understanding of consumers' dimensions of evaluation, competitive positions, and choice rules are necessary for sound strategy formulation.

Fortunately, there is an array of proven market research and simple modeling tools available to support these managerial decisions. Factor analysis based on consumer ratings, importances based on preference, and feature analysis provide the building blocks for a good analysis. When these are combined with managerial judgment, good positioning decisions can be reached.

Such analytical tools are valuable, but new dimensions or segments are usually identified as the result of creative effort rather than analysis. Analysis, judgment, and innovation are the critical ingredients in formulating profitable positioning strategies.

QUESTIONS FOR DISCUSSION

1. Take a product class with which you are familiar and use your judgment to specify a perceptual map. Define the number of dimensions, name them, position competitive products in the space, and draw importance vectors. What features substantiate the positioning? What are the product-positioning implications for each product based on your map?

2. How do you determine which attributes to use in defining a perceptual map? How many attributes should be measured? Why should managers be involved in specifying the attributes for a market research–based perceptual mapping study? What other technical aspects of perceptual mapping should managers be involved in?

3. When you draw a perpendicular line from a product point to an importance vector on a perceptual map, what can you learn about the preference for that brand relative to others?

4. How can importance vectors be used for benefit segmentation? What is the role of importance vectors in defining the best positioning for a brand?

5. How can a price reduction be represented on a perceptual map?

6. What are the major similarities and differences between conjoint analysis and perceptual mapping? Discuss both the technical and the managerial aspects of this comparison.

7. When is it best to try to add a new dimension to a perceptual map rather than to position within an existing perceptual space?

8. How do perceptual maps vary over the life cycle? What are the managerial implications of these changes?

REFERENCES

BLATTBERG, R. C., T. BUESING, AND S. K. SEN. 1980. "Segmentation Strategies for New National Brands." *Journal of Marketing* 44: 59–67.

CATTIN, P., AND D. R. WITTINK. 1982. "Commercial Use of Conjoint Analysis: A Survey." *Journal of Marketing* 46: 44–53.

GREEN, PAUL E. 1984. "Hybrid Models for Conjoint Analysis: An Expository Review." *Journal of Marketing Research* 21: 155–169.

––––––– AND V. SRINIVASAN. 1978. "Conjoint Analysis in Consumer Research: Issues and Outlook." *Journal of Marketing Research* 5: 103–123.

––––––– AND YORAM WIND. 1975. "New Way to Measure Consumer's Judgements." *Harvard Business Review* 53: 107–117.

HAUSER, JOHN R., AND DON CLAUSING. 1988. "The House of Quality." *Harvard Business Review* 66: 63–73.

HAUSER, JOHN R., AND S. M. SHUGAN. 1983. "Defensive Marketing Strategies." *Marketing Science* 2: 319–360.

HAUSER, JOHN R., AND P. SIMMIE. 1981. "Profit Maximizing Perceptual Positioning." *Management Science* 27: 33–56.

HOLBROOK, MORRIS B., AND WILLIAM J. HAVLENA. 1988. "Assessing the Real-to-Artificial Generalizability of Multiattribute Attitude Models in Test of New Product Designs." *Journal of Marketing Research* 25: 25–35.

KAMAKURA, WANGER A. 1988. "A Least Squares Procedure for Benefit Segmentation with Conjoint Experiments." *Journal of Marketing Research* 25: 157–167.

KOHLI, RAJEEV, AND RAMESH KRISHNAMURTI. 1987. "A Heuristic Approach to Product Design." *Management Science* 33: 1123–34.

LEVITT, THEODORE. 1981. "Marketing Intangible Products and Product Intangibles." *Harvard Business Review*, May/June: 94–102.

–––––––. 1980. "Marketing Success Through Differentiation—Of Anything." *Harvard Business Review*, January/February: 83–91.

REIBSTEIN, DAVID, JOHN E. G. BATESON, AND KENNETH BOULDING. 1988. "Conjoint Analysis Reliability: Empirical Findings." *Marketing Science* 7: 271–286.

SHUGAN, S. M. 1987. "Estimating Brand Positioning Maps Using Supermarket Scanning Data." *Journal of Marketing Research* 24: 1–18.

URBAN, GLEN L., AND JOHN R. HAUSER. 1980. *Design and Marketing New Products.* Englewood Cliffs, NJ: Prentice Hall. pp. 155–360.

MARKET RESPONSE

MARKET RESPONSE AND PROFITABILITY

In the last chapter, we emphasized how important it is to understand life cycles, segmentation, and product positioning. One more ingredient is critical to formulating an integrated marketing strategy—market response. We need to know how the market within our target segments, at the current life-cycle phase and with our positioning, will respond to changes in controllable marketing variables such as price, advertising, sales effort, and distribution. In this chapter, we outline the major phenomena that cause a market to respond to changes in marketing variables. These include single-period elasticities, as well as more complex dynamics due to the decay of a variable's impact (e.g., forgetting an advertising message), changes in inventory levels at various levels of distribution (including the consumer's cupboard), the impact of a consumer's expectations concerning future prices and product features, and the relationship between a product or service's position in its life cycle and the way in which its sales will respond to various marketing actions.

The primary objective of our analysis is to provide a basis for maximizing the productivity of marketing resources. Prices, as well as sales effort, advertising and promotion expenditures, and intensity of distribution, should be calibrated to achieve as high a return as possible on resources utilized. As it becomes increasingly necessary to get ''more bang for the buck'' from our marketing investments, such optimization of marketing expenditures is especially critical. How much in incremental sales and profits did a promotion generate? Should we distribute more coupons? Would it be worthwhile to enlarge our advertising budget to increase consumer trial of our new product and obtain leverage from our heavy investment in point-of-purchase displays? What would happen if we shifted some of our personal selling resources to telemarketing? Would it pay to provide special incentives to distributors to induce them to do more local advertising and give our product preferential sales attention?

151

In this chapter, we consider a number of models and measurements that have proved especially useful to managers seeking to answer these and similar questions. Fortunately, established analytic techniques are now available to help us understand market response and to model the effects of alternative deployments of marketing resources. New data sources and analysis methods offer the promise of further improvement in the calibration of sales and profit responses to changes in marketing variables. Managers who thoroughly understand such response functions can combine them in a "model" that facilitates "what if" analyses to determine the most profitable level for each variable, both individually and in combination with the others.

MARKET RESPONSE FUNCTION PHENOMENA

Individual versus Market Response

To be able to set appropriate levels for the various marketing variables, we must estimate (explicitly or implicitly) the relationship between the level of each variable and aggregate sales and profits. While it is often useful to express this relationship in the form of an elasticity coefficient, graph, or mathematical function, we must remember that market response is not a sterile mathematical value but rather the result of many *individual consumer decision processes*. Effective response analysis begins with an understanding of how the buying decisions of individual consumers are affected by changes in our marketing variables. We then combine the actions of these individuals into an estimate of aggregate market response. In this section, we describe a hypothetical individual's decision process and responses to various types of marketing actions. We then identify the key response phenomena reflected in the example and indicate how they can be represented in an aggregate market response function. (You may also want to review Chapter 5 on customer decision making.)

Managerial Scenario: A manufacturer of stereo components must decide what price to charge, what levels of customer and trade promotion to utilize, how much advertising to budget, and which media to use for a new product—cordless stereo headphones that receive programming via infrared waves from an add-on stereo component. The manufacturer wishes to estimate how changes in price, promotion, or advertising will affect the aggregate market for its new product. Clearly, the overall response of the total market to a change in these marketing variables will reflect the aggregate responses (or non-responses) of a large number of individuals. Let us consider one such individual.

Imagine that you are a likely customer for the new cordless stereo headphones. A music buff whose musical tastes and preference for high-volume sound conflict strongly with the desires of other members of your household, you have been using headphones for several years, but have been frustrated by the physical and psychological constraints of being hooked up to your stereo like another component.

The cordless headphones described above seem custom-designed to satisfy your needs. *But* will you buy them? And if so, when? You might, for example, leap at the opportunity to buy the product at a price of $100, not even consider it at a price of $200, and procrastinate for a considerable length of time before making a purchase at $150. The price set by the manufacturer will certainly affect your probability of purchase.

Clearly you will not buy the new product unless you know that it is available, have some idea of what it can do, and know where to get it. How big an advertising budget will it take to provide you with all this information? You subscribe to specialized high-fidelity publications as well as to special interest magazines such as *Rolling Stone*, *Cosmopolitan*, and *Esquire*. Since you probably do not read every issue of each of these magazines, an advertising campaign in various magazines over several months would have to be run to catch your awareness and raise your interest sufficiently to impel you to search out the product. Expenditures on public relations, if successful in obtaining editorial support (e.g., favorable mention in an *Esquire* new electronics products feature), are likely to amplify the impact of such advertising.

Similarly, trade promotion could be used both to create awareness of the new product and to induce you to buy it. If trade incentives cause the stereo retailer in the shopping mall you frequent to display the new product prominently in its window, you may see it and be interested enough to enter the store and ask for a demonstration (and sales presentation). Alternatively, you may have been intrigued by advertisement you saw in *Cosmopolitan*, but not enough to go shopping for the product. But now you pick up the daily newspaper and see an ad placed by the local stereo dealer that says, "For this weekend only, a special price of only $129." This advertised local price promotion may be the impetus you need to visit the retail outlet and purchase the new product.

Your individual decision process is subject to change over time. You may forget the advertisements you saw. Your price response may change, perhaps as a result of unexpectedly large auto repair bills. You might have a general policy of not buying new electronics products on the expectation that their prices will come down and their functionality improve in time, but be induced to violate your policy after trying the new headphones at a friend's and concluding that you must have them at once!

Moreover, your individual responses to variables tend to be interrelated. How much you are willing to pay for the product will depend, in part, on how convincingly it has been extolled in advertisements and articles you have seen, and how effectively it is demonstrated and sold by the stereo retailers you visit. The overall probability of your purchasing the new headphones might actually be higher if the manufacturer charged a higher price, and used the resulting increased margin for advertising and trade promotion, than if it charged a lower price, and failed to advertise and promote the new product heavily.

Response Function Representations

These individual response phenomena must be captured somehow if the manufacturer is to use them in making appropriate price, promotion, distribution, selling, and advertising decisions. In this chapter, we review some of the most effective methods of developing models of market response. While varying considerably in approach and technique, they are all based on identifying the phenomena represented in individual decision processes and then aggregating them to reflect overall market response.

Three major components of market response can be identified in the cordless headphones buying scenario just described: (1) immediate (direct, one-period) sales results; (2) dynamic market phenomena; and (3) interaction effects. In the following sections, we consider each of these components and then discuss how they can be measured and captured in managerially useful models.

Single-Period Response

In the customer decision process described, we considered the effect of setting the price of the new headphones at $100, $150, and $200. The probability of purchase by our hypothetical consumer was 100 percent at $100, zero at $200, and somewhere in between at $150. If we can estimate individual probabilities of purchase (see the analytic support section on page 159), we can then add up all the individual customer values to develop a graph that shows the number of unit sales that will occur at each price level.

Figure 9.1 is such a graph. It shows a linear price response (solid line). Sales increase from 10,000 units to 12,000 units when the price drops from $150 to $135. The average

FIGURE 9.1
Price Response

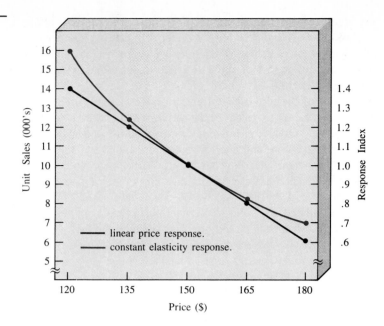

elasticity in this example is −2.0 (a 20 percent increase in sales results from a 10 percent drop in price). The sales response function does not, however, have to be linear. Figure 9.1 also shows a nonlinear response (dashed line) that represents a *constant* price elasticity of −2.0.[1] In aggregate market response analysis, it is necessary to determine the shape of the curve and the parameters that define it. In this instance, should the price response function be linear or nonlinear? What is the elasticity?

In our cordless headphones example, as with most new products, advertising played a major role in influencing sales. The greater the amount of advertising seen by a target consumer, the greater will be his or her level of information, motivation, and likelihood of purchase. If we graph the market response to advertising, we generally end up with a curve that is quite different in shape from the price response curve in Figure 9.1. Advertising response curves tend to slope upward to reflect higher individual probabilities of purchase as advertising increases, but are typically nonlinear, representing diminishing returns to additional expenditure. In most situations, the first advertisement for a product that we see has a higher incremental impact on our decision to buy than the tenth. At high levels of spending for advertising, the next increment of spending will almost always generate a smaller increase in sales than the previous increment. (See the solid line in Figure 9.2 for a curve that reflects constantly diminishing return to spending.) Since most products obtain some sales even with no advertising, an S-shaped curve (such as the dashed line in Figure 9.2) may be the best estimate of sales response to advertising. Sales start out at a minimum threshold level, increase slowly for a time, and then experience large marginal returns before the curve flattens. This form of the response curve is consistent with the notion that an advertising campaign has to fight its way through media clutter before it begins to work, but eventually wears out as frequency of exposure among those exposed to the campaign becomes so large that little incremental effect is obtained from still more exposure. Similarly, an S-shaped response curve is often observed when graphing the market response to increased personal selling efforts. There is a minimum sales level from customer reorders or channel efforts that will occur even with no direct selling

---

[1] Note that the difference between the linear and nonlinear effect over the range of a 10 percent change in price is small, while outside this range the deviations are large.

activities by the manufacturer, and even the best salesperson can make only so many calls, or load the customer with so much effort, before his or her welcome wears out.

Our cordless headphones example suggested that consumer sales might be increased considerably by a retailer's promotional price of $129 (resulting from trade incentives). In much the same way as we did with price level, advertising expenditures, and selling effort, we could draw a graph showing the estimated relationship between such promotional incentives and consumer sales. For each marketing variable, whether it be promotion, distributor's margin, or number of salespeople, a graph showing the estimated market response to a change in that variable (at various levels) should be drawn. In preparing such graphs, it is usual for the horizontal axis to represent a measurable value for the variable (e.g., dollars of advertising, percentage retail margin, or number of sales calls) and the vertical axis to show sales or market share. Once we have drawn such a graph, it is a relatively straightforward procedure to calculate sales and profit levels for alternative levels of the decision variable.

Market Dynamics

Simple single-variable response graphs such as those described above show the estimated effects of a change in a decision variable for a single period, but do not reflect the more complex dynamic effects resulting from consumer forgetting, changes in customer and channel inventory levels, customer expectations concerning future changes in one or more marketing variables, and changes in customer buying behavior over the course of a product or service life cycle.

Awareness: Single-period advertising response functions describe the effect of advertising expenditures on immediate sales, but this effect represents only part of the response because advertising generally has a delayed impact on future sales as well. If we conceptualize the role of advertising to be the generation of awareness, and assume that the probability a given consumer will make a purchase is a function of his or her awareness, we have a basic structure to represent dynamic response to advertising.

Assume, for example, that awareness in a single period increases with advertising expenditure, as shown by a response function, but that awareness decreases over time

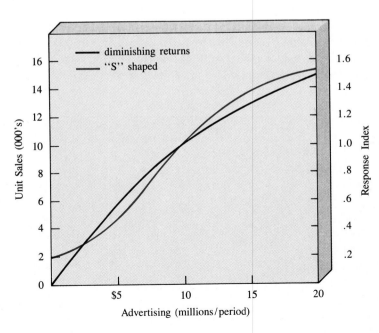

FIGURE 9.2
Advertising Response

because of forgetting. Figure 9.3 shows period 1 advertising generating awareness at the 40 percent level, but a nonlinear decline as forgetting takes place over periods 2 and 3. It is common to delineate forgetting on a graph of this type by specifying the percentage of this period's awareness level that will be retained in the next period. In Figure 9.3, we show a retention rate of 70 percent (i.e., a forgetting rate of 30 percent). In period 4, however, new advertising causes a vertical rise in awareness to the 30 percent level, but then forgetting resumes. The level of awareness thus depends on both the amount of expenditure for advertising, which controls the degree of vertical rise, and the forgetting rate, which determines the speed at which awareness will decay.

Sales for each period can be calculated by multiplying the awareness level for that period by the probability of purchase given awareness. (This assumes the sales rate, given awareness, is constant, which seems reasonable for many established products.) It is, of course, also possible to estimate sales dynamics directly by graphing over time the estimated relationship between advertising and sales. We recommend using awareness as an intermediate variable, however, since doing so encourages a deeper understanding of consumer behavior and provides an additional measure of advertising performance.

Inventory: The aggregate pattern of sales over time often shows discontinuities when price promotion is used. If, in our stereo example, a retail chain placed a large order at promotion prices of $89, some of the resulting sales might be truly incremental, but others would represent no more than stocking up for future demand. The promotion might then appear to be profitable on a direct single-period basis, but if what seem to be incremental sales are in fact no more than an earlier booking of sales that would have occurred anyway, the true profitability of the promotion would be questionable at best.

Increases in inventory at the customer location or within a channel of distribution are common mechanisms through which interperiod shifts occur. Figure 9.4 shows a time path that represents a big sales increase in period 3 (50,000 units), followed by a significant decrease in period 4 (20,000 units) as a result of this type of interperiod shift. In this case, 40 percent of the single-period effect reflects sales that would have occurred in the next period (20,000/50,000 = 40 percent, assuming a stable underlying sales rate of 100 units per period). These kinds of inventory effects are most readily observed in factory shipment or wholesale withdrawal data, but consumer sales patterns may also show a dip after a promotion of this type. For example, a factory rebate of $1,000 on new autos is likely to induce some buyers to replace their old cars sooner.

Response templates can be used to calculate the incremental profitability of a particular marketing action. In this example, a gain of 50,000 units occurred in period 3, but the net gain was only 30,000 units. The question is whether the product's unit contribution at the promotional price, multiplied by 30,000, is large enough to compensate

FIGURE 9.3
Awareness Patterns with Spending and Forgetting

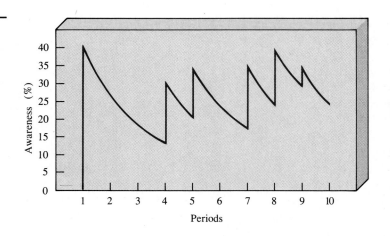

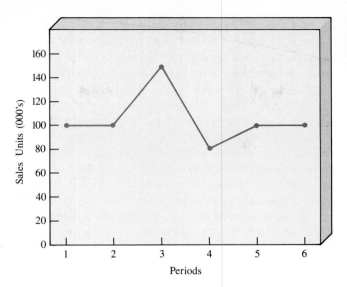

FIGURE 9.4
Promotion and Inventory
Effect

for the cost of the promotion, including lost contribution from nonincremental units sold at the promotional price. Thus, the true desirability of a promotion action can only be evaluated by calculating the cumulative profit for a long enough period to take account of such interperiod effects. Moreover, this task can be very difficult when frequent promotions generate large, sometimes overlapping fluctuations in sales (e.g., plus or minus 30 percent of the mean sales level). Under these conditions, identifying the true incremental effect of a particular promotion can be quite complex. (See the analytic support section on page 159 for an additional discussion of this problem.)

Expectations: Expectations can also cause discontinuities in response. In our cordless headphones scenario, for example, the customer was planning to wait for a lower-priced, more fully featured unit until given a demonstration at a friend's home. If consumers expect a price rise, sales may increase dramatically before the expected date of the price change. Conversely, if consumers anticipate a drop in prices, sales may be delayed. A similar pattern often results from expectations concerning product characteristics. When Osborn (the first company to market a portable PC computer) announced that it had developed an improved model with many new features, sales of its original model virtually stopped. Because the new model was announced far in advance of its actual shipment date, Osborn soon found itself in a position in which it was receiving revenues from neither the old nor the new model, resulting in a fatal cash flow gap.

Many high-tech products are characterized by continual price declines and performance improvements. It is challenging to estimate response functions for such products, as some consumers choose to wait, while others deem the product's current utility sufficient to warrant purchase, even though they anticipate lower prices and additional features. The most useful tool available to the marketer under these circumstances is disaggregation— estimating the number of potential units represented by customers in each segment and forecasting the purchasing behavior of each segment under alternative price/feature configurations.

Life Cycles: Customer expectations concerning price reductions and product improvements are only some of the factors that vary over the course of the life cycle. Advertising response primarily takes the form of product category awareness early in the life cycle, but becomes more of a weapon in earning market share later. Price response is likely to be especially sensitive late in the cycle as the number of competitive alternatives increases.

157

While the "innovators" who contribute the bulk of a new product's sales during its introductory phases may not be very price sensitive, early price reductions might nevertheless accelerate the diffusion of innovation. In our cordless headphones example, a price cut three years after introduction would likely have its primary effect on market share, while a similar cut during the first six months would mainly impact the rate at which the new type of headphones was adopted.

Personal selling is critical to establishing distribution and reaching innovators early in the life cycle. Most pharmaceutical companies use their sales force to "detail" (i.e., present) a new product to doctors at the time of its introduction, but do not find that this personal selling effort is cost justified after the product has matured. In other industries (e.g., data-processing and telecommunications systems), personal selling is the primary weapon in the competitive battle and is heavily relied on throughout the life cycle.

Distribution and retailer support are important to new packaged goods such as detergents and coffee because point-of-purchase display and local feature advertising are powerful trial generators. If the product is a type that is frequently purchased and obtains good repeat purchasing rates, investments in trade promotions aimed at retailers may pay off. Later in the life cycle, such promotions might also be profitable, but their objective would be largely to induce brand switching rather than to attract new triers for the product category. Similarly, in industrial products and services where wide availability, rapid delivery, and technical backup are important to customers, channels are deserving of an allocation of promotional resources.

Interactions

The single-period and dynamic effects of changing individual variables are important, but, as our example demonstrated, the marketing environment is far from simple. A combination of advertising by the manufacturer and promotion by the dealer results in a different amount of impact than the mere sum of their individual effects. The market response to a change in one variable generally depends, at least to some degree, on the levels set for other variables.

Consider again the price and advertising response graphs in Figures 9.1 and 9.2. Will advertising have more of an effect at a lower price than at a higher price? Probably so. The combination of advertising increases and price decreases typically has more of an impact than either one alone, or even than the sum of their independent effects. If we reduce price 10 percent and increase advertising 33 percent, the result of the independent effects is a 20 percent increase in sales due to price and a 20 percent increase due to advertising, or a 40 percent increase in total. If the advertising effect is more powerful at the lower price level, however, the synergistic result may be an increase in sales of 45 percent.

One simple way to capture this effect is to create response indices that have values of 1.0 at the reference conditions and 1.0 plus the percentage change at other levels (see the right-side vertical axes of Figures 9.1 and 9.2). Multiplying these indices produces an interaction effect. In our example, the response index is 1.2 for the 10 percent price reduction and 1.2 for the 33 percent advertising increase; the product of these is 1.44, suggesting that reducing price by 10 percent while increasing advertising by 33 percent will lead to a 44 percent increase in sales, rather than 40 percent that would occur if we add the two 20 percent effects.

The presence of interaction effects causes managers to search for the best mix of marketing variables. Should we conduct a consumer price promotion in concert with a sales contest and an extended warranty, or should we increase advertising, lower price, and give the trade a special price deal? One way to handle interactive response effects of this type would be to develop several marketing programs consisting of alternative combinations of variables, and then assess the single-period and dynamic effects of each on sales and profits. Another approach would be to decompose the individual effects, and then combine them to allow for response interaction. The multiplying of response indices cited above is a simple example of this procedure.

An extension of this basic approach is to analyze the buying process for a particular product, and then assign a variable to each stage. Consider a simple three-step buying process: (1) gaining awareness; (2) finding the product; and (3) selecting a brand. If we multiply the target group size by the fraction of awareness in that group, and then multiply the result by the percentage of stores carrying our product and the probability of purchase given that an average consumer is aware of our product and in a store carrying it, we will have an estimate of sales. If we assume that (1) advertising affects awareness, (2) dealer margin affects distribution, and (3) price affects the probability that a particular brand will be selected, we will have a simple structure to explore interactions among marketing variables. Under these assumptions, putting all our money into advertising would not be attractive, because without distribution and price promotion, the impact on sales of such advertising would be sharply limited.

If we have a response graph for each of the three variables, it is a relatively straightforward task to estimate their combined interactive effects. Assume that a 33 percent increase in advertising has a 1.2 response index on awareness, that a 5 percent increase in retailer margins has a 1.25 effect on distribution coverage (i.e., 5 percent more retail margin increases distribution 25 percent from current levels), and that a 10 percent price reduction has a 1.2 response index on brand choice, given awareness and distribution. The combined result of these actions would be a 1.8 sales response index ($1.2 \times 1.25 \times 1.2$), or an 80 percent increase in sales. If the response functions did not interact, sales would only increase by the sum of their response indices, or 65 percent ($20 + 25 + 20$).

This simple structure for thinking about marketing mixes represents the beginning of our efforts to develop formal models of market responses to various combinations of marketing variables. In the analytic support section below, we will look at a number of more elaborate models that attempt to capture considerably more complex response and interaction effects, as well as the impact of competition.

Competition

In market response analysis, we focus on single-period response, dynamics, and inter-actions. We must not, however, neglect the impact of competitive actions on the response of a market to various combinations of marketing actions. Although we understand the direct effects of our actions, we may be misled if our analysis does not take the effects of competitive response into account. In the next chapter, we will outline a decision structure to incorporate the interaction of market response analysis and competitive analysis. Once again, we will begin by formulating response estimates and then integrate them in a matrix that reflects alternate results as a function of other firms' actions. With this matrix we examine alternate competitive strategies and set the variables to achieve the "best" results given the competitive market dynamics.

ANALYTIC SUPPORT: MEASUREMENT, ESTIMATION, AND MODELS

One of the most critical issues in response analysis is estimating the impact on sales resulting from a change in a variable. The graphs in Figure 9.1 and 9.2 are deceptively simple. In reality, determining the magnitude of the marginal increase in sales due to a change in a variable is a highly challenging task, often leading to imprecise results. In this section, we review the use of judgment, past empirical data, and experiments in estimating response functions. Then we describe how these response estimates can be combined in an integrated model that can be used to establish an appropriate level for each of the marketing-mix variables and to improve the productivity of marketing resource utilization.

Judgment

Direct judgment of the sales effect of implementing a set of marketing actions is the simplest and fastest method of obtaining a response estimate. We can ask a set of managers to estimate what sales will result from several alternative marketing programs, and then either select the one that seems to maximize profits or use their estimates to generate even stronger alternatives.

In allocating sales force time among customers, a critical response input is the expected sales level at a specified call frequency. Lodish (1971) used direct judgment concerning this response as an input to a model that recommends the number of calls a specific salesperson should make on each of his or her accounts in order to maximize profit. Lodish asked each salesperson to estimate the amount of business that would be generated by an existing account over a one-year period at each of five discrete levels of call intensity: (1) essentially no calls; (2) half the current rate; (3) the current rate; (4) one and a half times the current rate; and (5) a saturation rate of calling. Similar questions were asked about the probabilities of gaining business from a prospective client at different levels of calling intensity. These inputs were then incorporated in a model, CALLPLAN, which was tested on United Airlines' freight and passenger sales forces. Twenty salespeople, the experimental group, made judgments and employed the calling patterns recommended by the model. Ten other salespeople, the control group, followed their usual calling frequencies. After six months, the experimental group had obtained an 11.9 percent increase in sales, while the control group had only been able to raise its sales by 3.8 percent. Lodish's technique for utilizing the judgmental responses from experienced salespeople thus appears to have considerable promise as a method of increasing the productivity of a given set of marketing resources.

Figure 9.5 shows the judgments of three managers (brand, market research, and advertising) concerning the probable effect on sales of alternative advertising spending

FIGURE 9.5
Example of a Judgmentally Determined Curve of Sales Response to Advertising

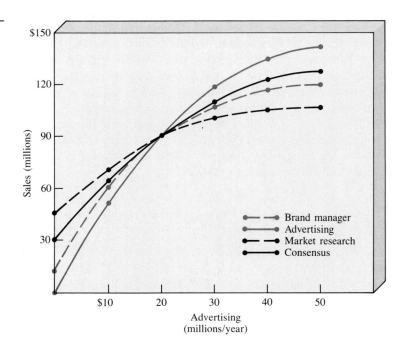

levels. Two managers agree, but the third (advertising manager) estimates a much greater impact. Under these circumstances, the average or median response could be used or the group could be asked to review the results and reach a consensus judgment. As in Lodish's work, the resulting response function could then be used to calculate the profit after advertising at each spending rate, assuming no competitive reaction.

In direct judgments of these sorts, the dynamic effects are captured in cumulative results on a response graph. An alternate approach is to estimate single-period responses and dynamics separately, and then combine them in a simple model. This process is illustrated in the model support section on page 166.

Past Empirical Data

Judgment is the least costly and fastest method of estimating response, but it may not be the most accurate. Given the large potential payoff of accurate response estimation, it is often productive to apply statistics to past market data to see if useful response parameters can be identified.

Cross-Sectional Analysis: Examining differences across markets can be informative if marketing spending levels vary but the markets are similar in other respects. In this situation, a log linear regression of sales against advertising (e.g., $ln(\text{Sales}) = a + b \log(\text{Advertising})$) can yield a diminishing returns curve similar to the one in Figure 9.2.

Figure 9.6A shows sales per capita in several geographic areas when plotted against advertising per capita. This S-shaped graph was produced by analysis in each area to

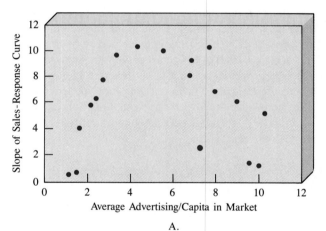

A.

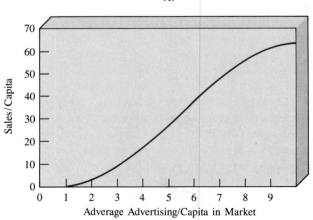

B.

FIGURE 9.6
Cross-Market Advertising-Response Analysis
Source: Reprinted with permission from John D. C. Little, "Aggregate Advertising Models: The State of the Art," *Operations Research*, Vol. 27, No. 1 (1979), p. 639. Copyright 1979, Operations Research Society of America. No further reproduction permitted without the consent of the copyright owner.

obtain an estimate of the marginal response to changes in advertising, or the slope of the overall response curve at each level of spending (see Figure 9.6B). The slopes then dictated the overall shape of the curve.

If areas are systematically different, finding matching areas is a possible method for estimating marginal response. Alternatively, the differences can be included as independent variables in the analysis. For example, the use of per capita advertising and sales in Figure 9.6 takes population differences into account. Similarly, if distribution varies across market areas, it can be normalized (e.g., sales per capita per percentage of all commodity distribution) in a regression analysis to estimate advertising effects.

Time Series Analysis: Differences in independent variables (e.g., advertising) and dependent variables (e.g., sales) over time are also used to estimate response functions. These data can be analyzed by time series econometric methods. If the levels of the relevant variables changed significantly over time, econometric methods may find a response effect. The most elementary regression models use sales in a time period as a dependent variable, and marketing spending per period (e.g., advertising, promotion, sales effort) as an independent variable in conjunction with other variables that may account for a change in sales (e.g., interest rates, GNP, price index). Competitive effects are often included by the use of market share as the dependent variable and relative marketing spending (our spending divided by the sum of our competitors' spending) as the independent measure. Carryover effects can be included by using past expenditures as variables to explain current sales or by estimating the effect of past sales on current sales (see Clarke, 1976, for a review).

Econometric analysis is a highly technical subject and fraught with many pitfalls (see Parsons and Schultz, 1976). The model may not include the correct variables, or there may be considerable error in the measurement of the variables; some observations may be "outliers" exerting undue leverage on the response estimates (see Belsley, Kuh, and Welsch, 1980); statistical assumptions may be violated; or the results may be misinterpreted. Managers should be sure that they receive expert advice when using econometric techniques. Pushing a button on a PC with a regression program and data base is dangerous for the untrained. Even though the results may be printed out as statistically "significant," there are so many opportunities for error that the alleged response function may well be misleading.

Individual Data Analysis: One of the underlying problems in the statistical analysis of cross-sectional and time series data at the level of the total market is that sales variations often are not measurably sensitive to changes in marketing variables. Another common problem occurs when the variation in sales is large relative to the probable effect of the marketing variables. It is difficult in such a case to obtain a precise estimate of response because the unexplained variation swamps the analysis. Fortunately, we are now able to employ data that are statistically valid for much smaller markets or time periods.

Consider the marketing of packaged consumer goods. As a direct result of the electronic scanning of universal product codes (UPC), we now have access to weekly store-level data—a significant improvement over the bimonthly data covering a relatively large market area to which we were previously limited. Figure 9.7 shows how this new, rich data base makes response effects easier to identify. At the bimonthly market data level, no price response is evident. As the data are displayed on a weekly basis, however, changes begin to appear. At the store level, clear fluctuations are present. When statistical procedures are applied to such individual store data, response parameters can be much more accurately and confidently estimated.

Syndicated data sources now collect weekly data from a sample of food and drugstores with regard to unit and dollar sales, prices, advertising, promotions, display, and distribution by stock-keeping unit (SKU). In some markets, such store data are now

FIGURE 9.7
Data Disaggregation
Source: Information Resources, Inc. Used with permission.

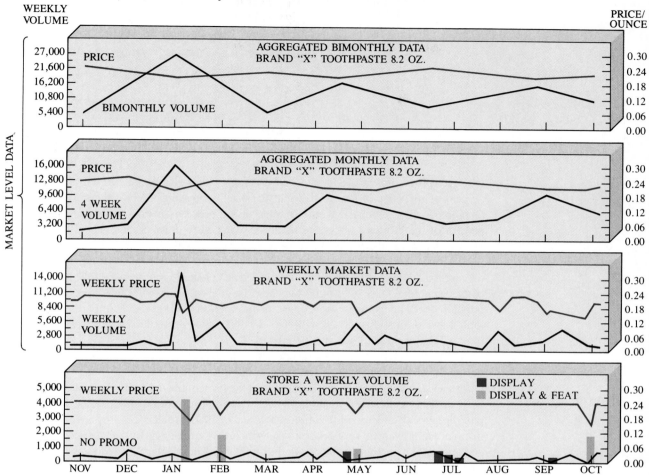

supplemented by individual purchase panel data. Members of consumer panels present a card when they check out and all of their purchases are recorded electronically. Information Resources, Inc. (IRI), for example, collects data from 100,000 panelists in addition to weekly sales data from 2,300 stores on 20,000 SKUs.

New mega data bases of these types provide powerful insights into consumer behavior and response. It is now practical to identify the effectiveness and source of promotional sales. Table 9.1 compares three different promotions with regard to their ability to attract new buyers to a particular brand. While all three increased total sales considerably, the

TABLE 9.1 Promotion Evaluation in a Panel

	TRIAL SIZE	PRICE-OFF PACKAGE	COUPON IN NEWSPAPER
Immediate sales gain	+25%	+32%	+20%
Percent new buyers	68%	46%	60%

163

TABLE 9.2   Gain and Loss in Sales During Promotion Based on UPC Panel Data

	BRAND A GAINS AND LOSES (% of last period sales)		
Competitor	**Switching In from Brand**	**Switching Out to Brand**	**Net Change**
B	30	30	0
C	30	5	+25
D	6	2	+4
E	5	20	−15
Total	71	57	+14

trial-size promotion attracted the most new customers. Table 9.2 shows that while 71 percent of the sales of brand A during the promotion were to consumers who switched to brand A after purchasing other brands in the previous period, at the same time, 57 percent of the previous buyers of brand A switched to other brands. Thus, the net gain of 14 percent was the result of two large switching effects. It is also revealing to analyze the interplay between brand A and each of its major competitors. Brand A gained 25 percent at the expense of brand C, but experienced a net loss to brand E during the period of the promotion. Clearly, insights like these are of great value to the marketers of frequently purchased packaged goods where consumer promotion is an especially important marketing tool. Later in this chapter we will consider the use of these new, productive data bases in even more powerful statistical analyses.

Unfortunately, marketers of consumer durables, services, and industrial goods do not yet have access to mega data bases utilizing the UPC technology, but even in these industries, the trend toward collecting data at the level of the individual is evident. Retailers such as Sears collect information on each purchaser of durable goods electronically; in pharmaceuticals, doctor prescription panels and retail sales data at pharmacies are available; insurance and financial services companies record customer data by social security number; and industrial marketers are increasingly automating client order files and sales call records. These data sources should lead to a considerable increase in the sophistication of marketing decision making in a wide variety of industries.

Experimentation

The availability of store-level and individual data makes estimation of the response effects easier, but we frequently find that there has not been enough variation in marketing variables to obtain good estimates of their effects. Sometimes so many changes have taken place simultaneously that it is hard to isolate the effect of one variable, even if it has changed significantly. When we are asked to evaluate new products or new promotional methods, past data are generally of little or no use, except when we can reason by analogy (estimate the response to something new on the basis of an earlier response to something similar). In cases where analogies do not hold, variation has been small, or interactions are present, it is often appropriate to use controlled market experimentation to obtain a meaningful estimate of market response.

In most experimental designs, one essentially compares changes in the dependent variable of interest in one or more "test" cells with the results occurring in "control" cells where the independent variables are held constant or are otherwise systematically varied from those in the test cell. Figure 9.8 shows the ratio of sales in test areas divided by the control areas in an experiment to determine the impact of increased advertising expenditure. Sales increased rapidly during the experiment, and decayed slowly thereafter.

Sometimes more elaborate designs are used. Urban (1975) changed advertising levels and test and control roles systematically over twelve market areas for eight quarters and found significant direct advertising and carryover effects. In cases where market response is undergoing change, it is often beneficial to establish a program of continuing experimentation and updating of response estimates. Such adaptive systems (see Little, 1966), in addition to responding to changes, have the advantage of improving response estimates over time as experimental evidence accumulates.

The availability of improved data in the packaged-goods field has led to more reliable and valid experimental settings. Calibrated markets, where advertising exposure can be controlled at the household level, are especially promising in this regard. In Behaviorscan markets operated by Information Resources, Inc., an electronic unit on the television set of each experimental household permits the insertion of a test advertisement during regular programing on instructions from a central facility. Such "targetable" TV capabilities allow experimental designs to be executed at the household level. Household meters report exposure to normal and test advertisements each five seconds, while scanner-equipped supermarkets and drugstores report virtually all purchases made by each experimental household.

Calibrated test markets can be used to measure market response to a wide variety of marketing variables through consumer purchasing and retail sales data. Comprehensive data at the individual or household level make possible the design of powerful experiments to measure advertising copy and spending-level effects. Whether in a single market or across markets, retail promotions (e.g., price deals, coupons), advertising (copy and intensity), packaging, and even product features can be varied systematically. This methodology is, of course, especially fruitful for new products lacking historical data bases. Data on trial and repurchase rates, as well as on frequency of purchase, by market segment, for alternative introductory marketing programs, are already proving to be a major boon to marketers of new products.

The trends among leading marketers are clearly toward more data, improved statistical capabilities to analyze past data, and more reliable and valid controlled experiments in calibrated markets. Although these trends are more evident among marketers of frequently purchased consumer goods, they are likely to occur in other industries as well.

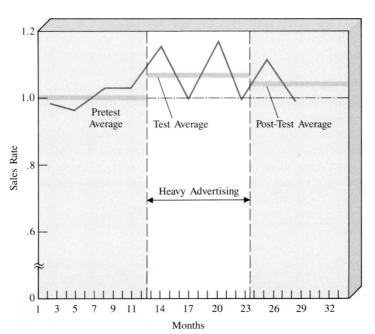

FIGURE 9.8
Heavy-Up Advertising Experiment
Source: Reprinted with permission from John D. C. Little, "Aggregate Advertising Models: The State of the Art," *Operations Research*, Vol. 27, No. 1 (1979), p. 634. Copyright 1979, Operations Research Society of America. No further reproduction permitted without the consent of the copyright owner.

Using richer data to improve our estimates of response functions, especially when such functions are incorporated into models that facilitate evaluation of the profitability of alternative marketing actions, obviously has exceptionally high potential payoff. Let us now turn to a discussion of such models.

Decision Calculus Marketing Response Models

A wide range of models exist to aid managers in setting marketing variables at optimal levels. Some are simple and based on judgment and basic measures, while others are highly technical and designed to take advantage of the new, rich data sources discussed above. In this section, we sample the variety of approaches, and then close with a manager's view of response analysis.

Managerial judgments on market response to changes in price, advertising, selling, or distribution variables can be incorporated into simple models to evaluate the profit impact of such actions. These models can be designed so that they are complete in representing the underlying phenomena, easy to use (one is able to revise inputs and get outputs quickly), controllable (one is able to determine readily which inputs result in what outputs), robust (outputs will fall within managerially meaningful ranges), and adaptive (such models can be updated easily as new data become available). Models meeting these criteria have been termed a "decision calculus" by Little (1979).

Advertising Budgeting: To understand the concept of a decision calculus, consider two key elements in advertising budgeting: direct response and dynamics. Little has developed what he calls the ADBUDG (advertising budgeting) model to integrate managerial judgments on advertising response and evaluate the profitability of alternative strategies. He assumes an S-shaped response such as the dashed line in Figure 9.2, and asks managers to provide an estimate of: (1) the amount of spending to maintain share; (2) the minimum share next period if no advertising is done; (3) the maximum share next period if spending is increased to its limit; and (4) the share next period if advertising is increased 50 percent. These inputs give the direct response. An estimate of the long-run minimum share with no advertising is the final response input required. Sales are calculated as the long-run minimum, plus the sales that would result if no advertising were implemented (the fraction of the difference between the long-run minimum and the last-period sales that would persist with no advertising), plus the effect of spending to increase share in the period (from the S-shaped response).[2] This model has been designed in a simple interactive format so that a manager can use it to conduct "what if" analyses of alternative advertising schedules. Its output provides an improved understanding of the effects of alternate response judgments, an ability to integrate single-period and dynamic advertising effects, and a calculus for evaluating the profit implications of alternative advertising expenditures.

A decision calculus model is the first step in combining judgments concerning underlying response phenomena in order to determine the desirability of changing marketing variables. It is more attractive than the use of pure judgment, and provides a basis for learning and integrating the judgments of multiple managers. Once the model is

---

[2] The equation is:

$$S(t) = a + b(S(t-1) - M) + c\,F(A(t))$$

where

$$S(t) = \text{share in period } t$$
$$M = \text{long minimum share}$$
$$F(A(t)) = \text{single-period "S" response to advertising}$$
$$= A(t)^e/(d + A(t)^e)$$
$$a,b,c,d,e = \text{parameters calculated from judgmental input values}$$

formulated, statistical and experimental findings can be used to refine and improve the response estimates. While judgment is the starting point, it is usually worthwhile to do additional analysis to provide a convergent basis for estimating the sales responses. Ultimately, the model can be extended to include other variables and competitive effects. (See Chapter 15 for a discussion and application example in the context of product management.) Such an evolution of the model structure allows the complexity of response to be captured without losing the understanding critical to managerial acceptance.

Industrial Communication Mix: Many models have been built to assist in the sales force management task (see Lilien and Kotler, 1983, for a review). CALLPLAN was mentioned earlier as one method of setting call norms for individual salespeople and accounts. This model has more recently been extended to include territory design and overall budgeting. Others have attacked the territory design problem (Zoltners, 1976; and Zoltners and Sinha, 1980) and examined the profit implications of adding more salespeople. Under all of these approaches, it is necessary to estimate the response to additional sales effort in order to compare incremental contribution with incremental costs, determine profit impact, and produce a set of recommendations.

Let us now look at a case that illustrates response interaction effects in an industrial market.

Situation: Assume that your company is selling an office productivity system (workstation and software) to lawyers. Your current sales are $14 million. Your sales force consists of twenty-eight people and costs $3.5 million per year. Your product, which is priced at $16,000, provides a contribution margin of $5,000 per system. Fixed costs other than the sales force are $750,000 per year. The market is 10,000 legal practices nationwide, and you have divided them up into five equally sized segments based on size and legal specialty.

AT&T has approached you with a proposal that you use telemarketing in addition to direct personal selling. They point out that your salespeople each make an average of four calls per day at a cost of $125 per call ($125,000 per year for salary and expenses). The AT&T telemarketing specialist estimates that trained telemarketing salespeople could make eight calls per day at a cost of $37.50 per call ($75,000 per salesperson per year). According to AT&T, if you use telemarketing to target your personal sales calls and advertising to build awareness, your total sales productivity will go up considerably. Advertisements are expensive, however, at $30,000 for a full page in a business publication. One advertisement would reach only 10 percent of the target group; if a campaign of ten advertisements were employed, reach would increase to 65 percent. According to readership studies conducted by the business publication, about one-half of those exposed to the advertisement would actually read it.

This situation raises a number of questions. Should we use telemarketing? Is it worthwhile to advertise, and if so, at what level? How many salespeople should we have? If we do employ telemarketing, should we reduce the size of our direct sales force, or should we instead try to take advantage of the greater efficiency achieved through telemarketing to build market share?

Model: A simple model employing judgmental response estimates was used to examine these issues. Figure 9.9 shows its structure. An overall communication resource pool level is established, and divided into advertising, personal selling, and telemarketing. Next, this resource pool is allocated across the five segments. Advertising builds awareness that may generate a specific request for a sales visit or create positive attitudes that predispose the customer to react positively to sales efforts. Telemarketing may lead directly to sales, but more often performs the functions of qualifying and preselling customers, who will actually be sold (perhaps after receiving a direct-mail piece requested during the tele-

FIGURE 9.9
Communication Mix

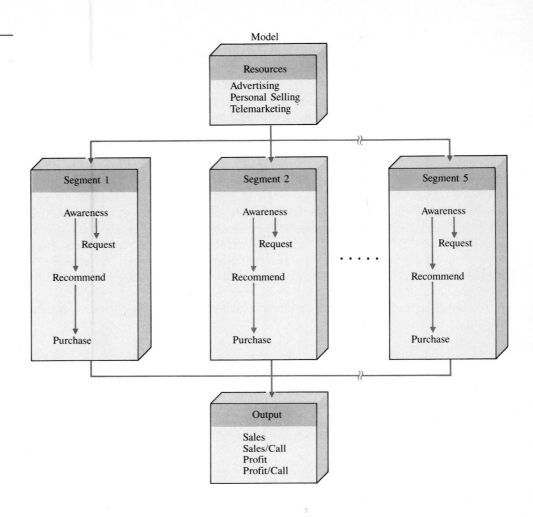

marketing contact) by the direct sales force. We assume in our model that salespeople answer referrals from telemarketing first, and then allocate their remaining capacity to making cold calls on potential customers distributed equally among the five segments. Thus, personal selling can be used to do the complete communication job (awareness, attitude formation, recommendation), or it can build on what has already been accomplished through advertising and telemarketing. If advertising and telemarketing are used, we would anticipate that the probability of making a sale on a given call would go up and/or that the time spent on each sales call would go down.

Response Estimates: Estimates of the direct responses to sales efforts in each segment were based on managerial judgment (see Figure 9.10). As the average number of visits per customer per year in each segment was increased, the probability that the person contacted by our sales force would recommend purchase of our system also increased, but to a diminishing degree. If personal selling alone was used, the probability of a positive recommendation to buy would increase to .5 in segment 1 (the highest-potential group), .45 in segment 2, .33 in segment 3, .25 in segment 4, and .1 in segment 5. Similar response functions were estimated for advertising and telemarketing working alone. We assumed further that the probability that an actual sale would occur, given that a positive recommendation was made by the contact person, would be .6. That is, assuming we got our message across, we would get an order in 60 percent of the cases.

Next, probabilities were estimated for each segment for combinations of direct sales calls, advertising exposure, and telemarketing contacts. Figure 9.11 shows a typical form of the input. The probability that a sale will be made increases at each level of personal selling intensity, as a function of the number of advertisements to which the segment had been exposed. In addition, it was estimated that 3 percent of those reading an ad would call or write for more information. If a potential customer requested information, a 50 percent higher probability of making a purchase was assigned than for the typical customer in the segment. (See Table 9.3 for the probabilities of one exposure and the saturation levels for combinations of the three communications vehicles in segments 1 and 5 [the other segments took on intermediate values].)

Simulation: Given the response estimates (direct and interactions), the model structure (Figure 9.9), contribution margins, and fixed costs, we can calculate profits for alternative levels of advertising, personal selling, and telemarketing. Table 9.4 begins with the base case in which we allocate all of our communications resources to our direct sales force. At $14 million in sales, profits are $870,000. If advertising is used to support our direct sales efforts, a computer simulation conducted using the model suggests that maximum profit is earned at a rate of seven advertisements per year. This level of advertising support increases the sales and contribution by a small amount ($45,000), and also allows the sales force to be reduced by one person. While our net communications budget is increased,

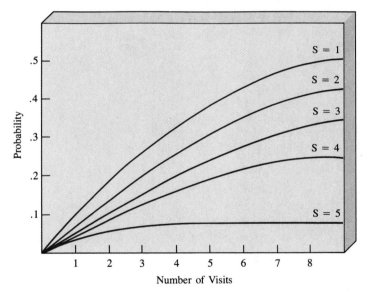

FIGURE 9.10
Personal Selling Response by Segment

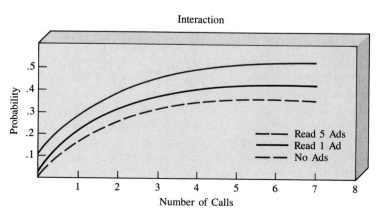

FIGURE 9.11
Advertising and Personal Selling Interaction

TABLE 9.3 Probability of Recommendation by Mix and Segment

	SEGMENT 1		SEGMENT 5	
	One Exposure	Saturation Level	One Exposure	Saturation Level
Advertising	.07	(.25)	.014	(.05)
Telemarketing	.09	(.40)	.018	(.08)
Personal selling	.11	(.5)	.022	(.10)
Ad and personal selling	.17	(.6)	.034	(.12)
Personal selling and telemarketing	.19	(.8)	.038	(.16)
Ad and personal selling and telemarketing	.25	(.85)	.05	(.17)

TABLE 9.4 Communication-Mix Strategy

	ALL PERSONAL SELLING	BEST WITH ADS	BEST WITH TELEMARKETING
Number of ads	—	7	—
Number of personal calls	22,000	20,140	11,040
Number of telemarketing calls	—	—	29,200
Total sales	$13,984,000	$14,056,000	$20,710,000
Communication budget	$2,750,000	$2,727,000	$2,475,000
Profit	$870,000	$915,000	$3,215,000
Profit/personal call	$40	$45	$291
Profit/communication budget	$.32	$.34	$1.30
Profit per hour of total selling effort	$1.97	$2.20	$8.76
Sales per hour of total selling effort	316	348	560

our profit per call, profit per hour of personal selling, and sales volume per hour each go up by a small amount. Nevertheless, advertising alone is clearly not a high-leverage variable in improving profits in this case.

Our simulations suggested that adding telemarketing to our communications mix offered greater potential for improving sales and profits. We obtained maximum profits with fourteen direct salespeople (11,040 calls) and eighteen telemarketing salespeople (29,200 calls). The number of salespeople increased from twenty-two to thirty-two, but our total costs decreased $275,000 because a telemarketing salesperson costs considerably less than a salesperson in the field. In this simulation, when we optimized our communications mix, sales increased 48 percent and profits by a factor of 4. The productivity measures of profit and sales per sales hour likewise showed dramatic improvements. Using telemarketing, 1,200 requests for sales visits were generated, with the result that the sales force only had to make cold calls on the two highest-priority segments. The response inputs indicated a positive interaction effect and suggested that using telemarketing to qualify and presell clients in this market would be highly effective.

In this case, advertising does not seem to pay off, even when used in conjunction with telemarketing. According to the judgments of managers familiar with the market, the target group can be most efficiently and effectively reached and sold by a combination of phone contact and direct sales efforts.

Decisions: According to this simulation, the potential gains from modifying our communications mix seem evident. Combining telemarketing and personal selling increases profits, and does a better job than either of them alone. The response estimates used in the simulation were all judgmental, however, so some caution should be exercised. We could implement the proposal directly, but an experiment may be our best next step. We could add telemarketing to personal selling in selected geographic areas and compare the results to those for a balanced control group to determine whether the judgmental inputs were more or less correct. If they were, the magnitude of the potential productivity increase is so large that we could confidently move ahead with the decision to add telemarketing.

As marketing variables are changed, monitoring systems should be put in place to check the response assumptions and to adapt to changes in the market. As experience is gained, the parameters of what appear to be high-potential variables should be investigated in greater detail. In our communications-mix example, while advertising in a national publication did not appear to be profitable, this may have been because the cost of reaching such specialized market segments was too high relative to the response. Local media, the trade press, or direct mail may, however, have turned out to be profitable because of their ability to target narrow market segments. Targeted advertising and direct mail may make the telemarketing more effective, and therefore contribute to even more productive selling strategies.

Advanced Models: These two models demonstrate the basic concept of combining sales response estimates with prices and costs to calculate profit results. They are primarily judgment based, and use simple model structures. Experiments and statistical analysis can be employed to improve the estimates incorporated in such models. The models themselves can be structurally modified to include additional phenomena (e.g., more variables, periods, competitors, or products). As these extensions are made, the models become technically complex.

Many models have been developed in the area of response analysis (see Lilien and Kotler, 1983). They are comprehensive, and increasingly utilize the newly available sources of individual data, as well as sophisticated choice models (see Guadagni and Little, 1983, for examples).

Statistical and management science expertise *and* a sound managerial perspective are needed when venturing into the realm of advanced models. If all of these ingredients are present, the potential for significant competitive advantage and high returns is enormous. But if one is present and the others are not, the danger of misusing these new technologies is also enormous. Consequently, the utilization of contemporary response analysis is very much a managerial as well as a technical process.

MANAGERS AND RESPONSE ANALYSIS

Having considered a number of important and sometimes technical issues in this chapter, it is now appropriate to review the manager's role in market response analysis. Although the manager is not expected to be a statistician or an operations researcher, he or she should know when to request a response analysis and how to use the results to improve decisions. Here are a few key managerial guidelines.

Ask What You Are Getting for Your Marketing Expenditure. It was once commonly believed that the results of marketing spending could not be isolated. "I am wasting half my advertising budget, but I don't know which half," was a common complaint. Today managers can determine the relationship between advertising and sales with considerable precision. Statistical analysis of past data and experimentation can provide these answers. This is also true for price, promotion, distribution, and personal selling. Managers should ask what the payback is from changes in marketing variables. They should direct their attention at refining judgmentally based estimates and developing a systematic program for learning how the market responds.

Look at the Profit Implications. Once you know what the sales results will be from changes in marketing variables, calculate the profits. Consider the short term, but concentrate on the longer-term payoff. Ultimate success is not measured in sales and share, but in profits and return on investment. Models can be helpful in making profit calculations. Simple PC-based models can calculate the profit impact of changes in marketing variables and unit sales. More sophisticated models are available from consultants, advertising agencies, and market research firms, or they can be developed internally. If these capture the relevant phenomena in your market, they can be very useful in formulating an effective marketing strategy.

Develop Good Staff Support. Since market response analysis is increasingly technical and complex, managers need good staff support to get precise response estimates. A manager's judgment is complemented by a good statistician. Find a good model builder, and make sure he or she understands the notion of a decision calculus, as well as your business, goals, and evaluation system. Learn what the model can and cannot do. Let the model evolve as you become familiar with it and gain confidence in the data it provides. Do not give up control and attempt to market on autopilot. Do not hesitate to modify the recommendations of the model if you feel that the assumptions on which they are based (including response estimates) are not realistic or that all the important phenomena operating in your market have not been captured.

Experiment if a Big Opportunity Is Present. Although managerial judgment and evaluation of past data are useful approaches to response estimation, conduct market experiments (e.g., test markets) when sales and profitability are highly sensitive to a variable on which large expenditures are concentrated. Investment in experimental learning has a high probability of being repaid if (1) the probable market response to the variable is large, (2) the proposed investment in the variable is significant, and (3) the accuracy of the experiment is high. If the market is changing, a continuing program of experimentation may represent both a prudent insurance policy and an excellent window through which to view new market opportunities.

Consider the Competitive Dynamics. Even if a large market response is identified, it may not be wise to increase spending if doing so will trigger a strong reaction from competitors. As we discuss in the next chapter, if competitors respond forcefully, we may be lucky to end up with the same sales and only slightly lower profits. In highly competitive markets, especially those with entrenched competitors, response estimates should be considered in the context of competitive reactions before embarking on an aggressive change in marketing strategy.

Create New Marketing Impact Mechanisms. While it is important to understand how and why your market responds to the variables currently being employed by you and your competitors, the greatest opportunities often lie in creating new marketing approaches rather than in fine-tuning traditional tactics. Creating new advertising copy that is 10 percent more effective may be more valuable than fine-tuning the budget to improve profits by 10 percent. New types of sales force incentives may have greater payoffs than higher expenditures on traditional approaches. Consumer promotions may have worked well in the past, but a new retailer deal and display may yield substantially better results.

Outstanding managers both create new, more effective mechanisms *and* adjust the level of spending to maximize profits. Understanding market response can help set the optimal levels for the major marketing variables, as well as provide the critical insight for a creative breakthrough. In the 1990s, marketing managers will require both analytic *and* creative skills to compete successfully and earn high profits.

1. "We cannot accurately measure the sales, let alone the profit impact, of advertising, so we should stop pursuing the myth of determining the incremental sales generated by advertising spending and use our intuitive judgment to establish advertising budgets." Do you agree or disagree with this statement? Why?

2. Why is an S-shaped market response curve appropriate for advertising but not for price?

3. Why would you expect the dynamics of market response for a toothpaste promotion (e.g., a 25¢-off coupon) to be different from those for a change in the suggested price?

4. How would you combine a single-period advertising response graph (Figure 9.2) with forgetting over time (Figure 9.3) to calculate the effect over one year of an advertising budget increase of 25 percent? What other information do you need to build a simple model to do this calculation?

5. Why might it be better to have a short intense expenditure (called a pulse) in advertising rather than to have a uniform level of spending for the same total budget? What response function would support a pulsing decision?

6. Why might there be an interaction effect between personal selling effort and price in industrial products?

7. How has the advent of scanner data (UPC data) changed response analysis in consumer packaged goods? What industries may have access to analogous individual customer data in the future? How could they use it?

8. If the addition of ten telemarketing personnel has increased our sales by 30 percent, should we increase our telemarketing effort further? Should we reduce our personal selling staff? Discuss the conditions that would favor either or both of these alternatives.

9. Is it more important to have good creative copy for an advertising campaign or to set the budget spending level and media allocation optimally?

REFERENCES

BAWA, KAPIL, AND ROBERT W. SHOEMAKER. 1987. "The Coupon-prone Consumer: Some Findings Based on Purchase Behavior Across Product Classes." *Journal of Marketing* 51: 99–110.

BELSLEY, DAVID A., EDWIN KUH, AND ROY E. WELSCH. 1980. *Regression Diagnostics*. New York: John Wiley.

BLATTBERG, ROBERT C., AND ALLEN LEVIN. 1987. "Modeling the Effectiveness and Profitability of Trade Promotions." *Marketing Science* 6: 124–146.

BLATTBERG, ROBERT C., AND SCOTT A. NESLIN. 1990. *Sales Promotion*. Englewood Cliffs, NJ: Prentice Hall.

CLARKE, DARRAL G. 1976. "Econometric Measurement of the Duration of Advertising Effects on Sales." *Journal of Marketing Research* 18: 345–357.

CORNELIUS, A. DE KLUYVER, AND EDGAR A. PESSEMIER. 1986. "Benefits of a Marketing Budgeting Model: Two Case Studies." *Sloan Management Review*, Fall: 27–38.

FARRIS, PAUL W., AND DAVID J. REIBSTEIN. 1979. "How Prices, Ad Expenditures and Profits are Linked." *Harvard Business Review*, November/December: 173–184.

GUADAGNI, PETER M., AND JOHN D. C. LITTLE. 1983. "A Logit Model of Brand Choice Calibrated on Scanner Data." *Marketing Science* 2: 203–239.

HOLAK, SUSAN L., DONALD R. LEHMANN, AND FAREENA SULTAN. 1987. "The Role of Expectations in the Adoption of Innovative Consumer Durables: Some Preliminary Evidence." *Journal of Retailing* 39: 243–259.

IBRAHIM, MAGID M., AND LEONARD M. LODISH. 1987. "PROMOTER: An Expert Promotion Evaluation System." *Marketing Science* 6: 101–124.

LILIEN, GARY L., AND PHILIP KOTLER. 1983. *Marketing Decision Making: A Model Building Approach*. New York: Harper and Row.

LITTLE, JOHN D. C. 1966. "A Model of Adaptive Control of Promotional Spending." *Operations Research* 14: 1075–1097.

――――. 1979. "Aggregate Advertising Models: The State of the Art." *Operations Research* 27: 629–667.

LODISH, LEONARD M. 1971. "CALLPLAN: An Interactive Salescall Planning System." *Management Science* 18: 25–40.

――――. 1986. *The Advertising and Promotion Challenge*. New York: Oxford University Press.

PARSONS, LEONARD J., AND RANDALL L. SCHULTZ. 1976. *Models and Econometric Research*. New York: North Holland Publishing.

QUELCH, JOHN A. 1989. *Sales Promotion Management*. Englewood Cliffs, NJ: Prentice Hall.

QUELCH, JOHN A., AND K. CANNON-BONVENTRE. 1983. "Better Marketing at the Point-of-Purchase." *Harvard Business Review*, November/December: 162–169.

QUELCH, JOHN A., S. A. NESLIN, AND L. B. OLSON. 1987. "Opportunities and Risks of Durable Goods Promotion." *Sloan Management Review*, Winter: 27–38.

TOTTEN, JOHN C., AND MARTIN P. BLOCK. 1987. *Analyzing Sales Promotion*. Chicago: Commerce Communications.

URBAN, GLEN L. 1975. "Allocating Ad Budgets Geographically." *Journal of Advertising Research* 15: 7–18.

WALTERS, ROCKNEY G., AND SCOTT B. MACKENZIE. 1988. "A Structural Equations Analysis of the Impact of Price Promotion on Store Performance." *Journal of Marketing Research* 25: 51–63.

ZOLTNERS, ANDRIS A. 1976. "Integer Programming Models for Sales Territory Alignment to Maximize Profit." *Journal of Marketing Research* 13: 426–430.

ZOLTNERS, ANDRIS A., AND P. SINHA. 1980. "Integer Programming Models for Sales Resource Allocation." *Management Science* 26: 1197–1207.

10

COMPETITIVE BEHAVIOR

COMPETITIVE REACTIONS

In the last four chapters, we have explored life cycles, segmentation, product positioning, and market response. All of these phenomena are rooted in the customer decision-making process. Life cycles depend on an underlying process of adoption and diffusion; segmentation is based on customer heterogeneity and customers' differing perceptions of competitive products; positioning decisions flow from psychological perception, preference, and choice processes; and market response is a function of how controllable variables affect each information-gathering and trade-off point in the decision-making protocol.

We are now ready to bring these phenomena together in an investigation of competitive dynamics (see Figure 10.1). In doing so, we will use the analysis to create unique benefit propositions and to build sustainable competitive advantages. Each of our previous discussions has alluded to the competitive issues. In the chapter on market response, for example, we called attention to the danger of establishing a promotion program without explicitly considering competitive reaction. Elsewhere we have noted that the use of perceptual maps and choice models for positioning is essentially static because it does not take into account the ongoing dynamics of competition. The maps reflect market structure as it has been, not as it will be after competitors have had a chance to respond to our market entry or our change in positioning. Similarly, since competitors may choose to compete in our segments or to define an alternative segmentation scheme, we need to take *their* alternatives into account when formulating *our* strategies.

Any action we take may be construed as an offensive move by our competition. In an effort to resist our attempts to increase market share, competitors may reposition their products, add new products, revise their segmentation strategies, or change prices. Thus, the sales and profit results of our positioning will be highly dependent upon how they react, and upon the dynamics of competition between our strategy and their *new* strategies.

Even if we do not modify our marketing strategy or act aggressively, competitors may attack our established products. When this occurs, it puts us on the defensive, and

175

FIGURE 10.1
Phenomena Underlying
Strategic Analysis

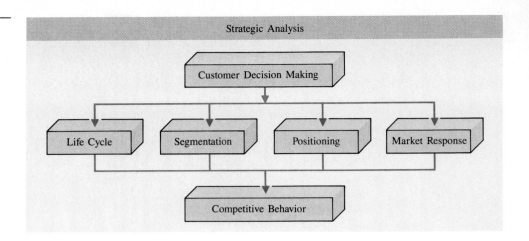

we must decide whether to allow our share to erode or to fight back with price, product, or other marketing actions. If we do fight back, it is probable that one or more of our competitors will react to our response, escalating the battle to an all-out war for consumer choice.

What is a firm's best strategy for dealing with such dynamic competitive behavior? Should it adopt an aggressive stance and defend its share to the last point? Should it regard competitive activity as a "war" and go all out to win? Or should it be more moderate and conciliatory in an effort to prevent a price war and to encourage stability, thus (hopefully) increasing profits?

In this chapter, our concern is with how to formulate a sound marketing strategy in situations where strong competitive reactions can be expected. Under such circumstances, decision making is difficult because the outcomes depend not only on our actions but also on the actions of our competitors. We begin by asking how much a gain (or loss) in market share is really worth. We then consider the payoffs from various combinations of competitive decisions in a potentially destructive game, and suggest that analogous situations often occur under real-world business conditions. We go on to outline several alternative generic, competitive strategies, and recommend a method for evaluating and selecting the most effective. Finally, we review the few analytical models available to help managers cope with the myriad complexities of intensely competitive markets.

THE ROLE OF MARKET SHARE

Conventional marketing wisdom holds that the best strategy is the one that results in the highest market share, and that managers should therefore strive to maximize the market shares of their brands. Implicit in this "wisdom" is the assumption that higher market share leads to higher profits and return on investment (ROI). If this assumption is true, the process of strategy formation is relatively straightforward. If it is not true, however, or if it is true only under certain conditions, it becomes necessary to test alternative strategies against both market share and profitability criteria. What, then, is the effect of market share on short- and long-term profitability?

Empirical Support

The notion that there is a direct link between share and return on investment has been studied in considerable depth by a number of research projects. The PIMS (Profit Impact on Marketing Strategy) project, for example, collected data from approximately 3,000 independent business units belonging to 450 industrial, consumer, and service companies (Buzzell and Gale, 1987). For each business unit, PIMS collected historical information concerning both marketing variables (e.g., market share, sales history, competitive prices, advertising and selling expenditures, relative quality) and profitability variables (e.g., net profit, return on sales, return on assets, return on investment). A cross-sectional statistical regression suggested that there was a strong correlation between market share and ROI. According to this study, a 10-percentage-point difference in market share was, on average, accompanied by a 5-percentage-point difference in ROI (Buzzell, Gale, and Sultan, 1975) (see Figure 10.2).

This was a major finding, allegedly explained by traditional notions of scale economy as well as by the newer concept of the experience curve. According to the latter, costs decline as the *cumulative* volume of production increases (in contrast with scale economies, where costs decline with volume in a particular time period). Since cumulative volume increases when market share goes up, it follows that, all other things being equal, higher market share should lead to lower costs *and* the cost leader should have both higher overall profits and higher returns on investment and assets.

The unit cost decline is not viewed as linear. Rather, the equation for this curve is:

(10.1) $\quad C(Q) = C(I)(Q/I)^{-b}$

where:

$$Q = \text{cumulative number of units produced}$$
$$I = \text{initial number of units}$$
$$C(Q) = \text{unit cost at } Q \text{ units of cumulative production}$$
$$b = \text{experience parameter } (b \text{ greater than zero})[1]$$

As production increases from the initial value, the unit cost decline is controlled by the value of b. For example, if cumulative production is twice the initial value (($Q/I) = 2$) and $b = .152$, the costs decrease to 90 percent of their initial value. If $b = .322$, the costs decline to 80 percent of their initial value as cumulative volume doubles. The cost decrease is a constant fraction for each doubling, but the greatest rate of cost decrease occurs at smaller volumes.

---

[1] The curve is a straight line when logs are taken of each side of equation (10.1) or if the values are plotted on log-log graph paper.

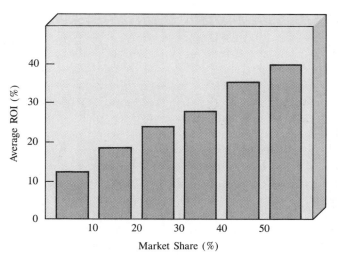

FIGURE 10.2
Market Share and ROI
Note: Based on four-year averages of pretax, preinterest ROI for 2,611 business units in the PIMS data base.
Source: Reprinted with permission of The Free Press, a Division of Macmillan, Inc., from *The PIMS Principle: Linking Strategy and Performance* by Robert D. Buzzell and Bradley T. Gale. Copyright © 1987 by The Free Press.

Figure 10.3 shows the cost decline of the Model T Ford from 1907 to 1926. During this period, Ford's costs were systematically driven down through labor efficiency (learning), new processes and methods (e.g., production-line improvements), product standardization, economies of scale, vertical integration, and substitution of lower-cost materials. These reduced costs made it possible for Ford to lower prices, which, in turn, led to its achievement of a dominant market share during these years. Similar experience curves have been observed in many industries (e.g., jet aircraft, video recorders, electronic components, computers).

Both the PIMS findings and the experience curve concept imply that a firm should strive for maximum market share. This is, in fact, a reasonable "first approximation" in formulating a marketing strategy, but a number of caveats are in order. Application of the "maximize market share" dictum is much more complex than its original proponents envisioned, and can often lead to results precisely opposite to those anticipated (i.e., lower, rather than higher, profits).

Caveats

Share of What? One of the most difficult challenges in implementing a strategy of increasing market share is to answer the question: Share of what? If we manufacture automobiles, for example, should we focus on our share of all autos? U.S. autos? Mid-sized U.S. autos? Four-door mid-sized U.S. autos? If we define the market widely, we will have a low share; if we define it narrowly (as a market segment), we will have a high share.

The importance of this issue may be seen clearly in a comparison of the PIMS data concerning the proposed relationship between market share and ROI and the diametrically

FIGURE 10.3
The Ford Experience Curve in 1958 Constant Dollars
Source: Reprinted by permission of *Harvard Business Review*. An exhibit from "Limits of the Learning Curve" by William J. Abernathy and Kenneth Wayne, September/October 1974. Copyright © 1974 by the President and Fellows of Harvard College; all rights reserved.

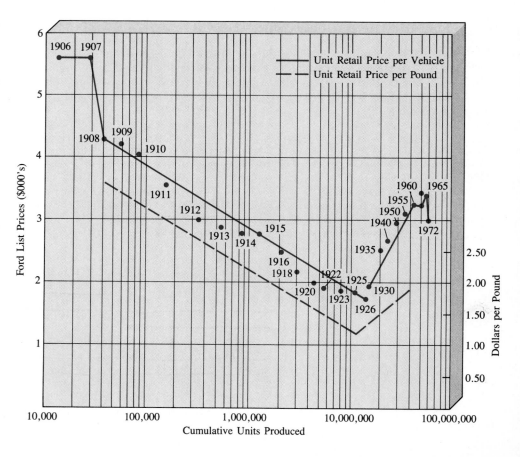

opposed data presented by Michael Porter in his well-known book *Competitive Strategy* (1980) (see Figure 10.4). A comparison of Figures 10.2 and 10.4 suggests a rather critical difference. In the PIMS data base, low market share correlates with low ROI, while Porter's conceptualization suggests that low market share correlates with high ROI. The apparent reason for this seeming contradiction is that in the PIMS data the managers supplying the data defined their own ''served markets,'' while Porter's graph reflects share of ''total market.'' Porter and the advocates of the PIMS finding would agree that high market share of a particular segment tends to lead to high ROI, even if the resulting share of the total market is, in fact, quite low (as reflected in Porter's plot as shown in Figure 10.4).

It is therefore critical to define the relevant market correctly when assessing a firm's market share. The product-segmentation methodologies described in Chapter 7 are useful in this process inasmuch as they group products that compete for consumer choices, and thus provide the manager with a hierarchical description of the competitive structure in which he or she is operating. Nevertheless, the manager must determine what level of the hierarchy represents the relevant market. In the product hierarchy for pacemakers shown in Figure 7.7, for example, should the manager view the market as consisting of two segments (as shown), or should the market be further divided into four segments, as supported by statistical analysis? In our view, it is usually best to focus on a managerially relevant segment that is consistent with consumer definitions of alternative choices. Whatever the market definition, consistency in planning and implementation is critical. It is unsound, for example, to claim that one has a high share (of a small segment) when competing for corporate resources, and a small share (of the total market) when trying to motivate a sales force or distribution network.

Statistical Adequacy: While the PIMS results showed a significant correlation between market share and ROI, subsequent statistical analyses of the same data suggest caution in interpreting this finding. First, although the results are statistically significant, market share accounts for only 5 percent of the variation in the observed ROI of the various business units (Jacobson and Aaker, 1985, p. 14). Much of the remaining variation occurs among business units reporting low market shares. For example, 6.2 percent of the low-share business units had an ROI greater than 20 percent (Woo and Cooper, 1982). This may be due to the ''low share of what?'' issue or to the innate variability of success determinants. Second, if we consider past as well as current market shares, the resulting regression equation suggests that the direct effect of share on ROI is weaker than original estimates indicated (Jacobson and Aaker, 1985), and if unobserved events are modeled, share is not significantly linked to ROI (Jacobson, 1988). Third, a statistical analysis of data from the Federal Trade Commission, using statistical models of market share and profits, suggests that such share is not significantly correlated to profits (Anterasian and Phillips, 1988). It does not follow that we should completely reject the notion that share can lead to higher ROI, but it does seem likely that the relationship is not a simple causative

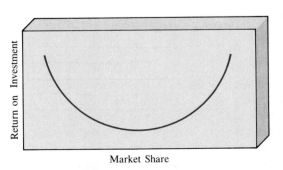

Return on Investment

Market Share

FIGURE 10.4
Porter's Share/ROI Relationship
Source: Reprinted with permission of The Free Press, a Division of Macmillan, Inc., from *Competitive Strategy: Techniques for Analyzing Industries and Competitors* by Michael E. Porter. Copyright © 1980 by The Free Press.

function, but only indicative. Other factors must be modeled to unravel the complex links between share and profitability.

The experience curve is also subject to a number of caveats. Care must be used to adjust for inflation when estimating cost declines. Different cost components may be subject to different experience effects and thus require separate experience curves. Some costs may be a function of the production of other products and thus decline as the result of a shared experience curve. These effects make accurate estimation of the experience parameter (b in equation [10.1]) difficult.

There have been few rigorous statistical studies of cost versus cumulative volume; most experience curves have, in practice, been drawn on the basis of inspection and judgment. One rigorous study was reported by Stobaugh and Townsend (1975). In their study of eighty-two petrochemical companies (before the 1974 oil crisis), they found a significant price reduction associated with cumulative volume; even so, most (over 65 percent) of the variation in the data was not explained by the relationship. They found that almost 35 percent of the price reductions were due to experience effects—cumulative volume increases. The remaining reductions were due to increased competition, standardized quality, more output per producer, and other time-related factors. Again, there is a statistically significant relationship, but it turns out to be not as strong as implied by earlier proponents of the theory.

Thus, both experience and share effects should be viewed as no more than hypotheses. They should be investigated thoroughly for each specific market before making strategic decisions.

Managerial: Many pitfalls lie waiting for firms that base their strategies to too great a degree on experience curve considerations. Projecting an experience curve ahead assumes that the estimate of the parameter is correct and accurate. Sometimes a history of cost and production data suggests learning when what, in fact, has occurred is technological advancement. In this case, projected cost declines are not a function of volume, but rather of technological progress (which may not recur). In other cases, costs do decline with cumulative volume, but since the learning is not proprietary, other firms can later "share" in the experience by purchasing the latest production machinery and implementing the most modern methods.

The Ford data shown in Figure 10.3 demonstrate another pitfall. Impressive as the cost decline is, it did not lead to *sustained* market dominance. In the 1920s, as Ford's prices continued to decline, its market share simultaneously dropped from over 50 percent to less than 25 percent. Why did this happen? Ford's price reductions were important to consumers, but other factors (e.g., style, power) also came to be important determinants of consumer choice, and on these dimensions, General Motors was the clear industry leader. After 1926, Ford had to shut down its factory to convert from Model T to Model A production. Even with the new car and annual model changes, Ford never regained its share dominance. (See Figure 10.3 for data on the 1927–1965 period, when costs increased with annual model changes and more features were being added.) Clearly, the experience curve is only one factor in marketing strategy. Cost and price advantages surely need to be considered, but such consideration should be in the context of the multiple factors that, in concert with price, lead consumers to select one product over another.

One must also be careful not to take action to increase share without considering how competitors are likely to react and what the effects of *their* reactions on *our* profits are likely to be. Although aggregate historical data may show a linkage between achieved market share and profit, there is no reason to assume a similar relationship between attempted gains in market share and profits. If we lower prices (or raise promotional spending), for example, and competitors match our actions, the resulting price or promotion war may result in the same market shares but reduced profits for all of us. In the early 1980s, People Express gained market share in the air travel market through very low prices. Other airlines then cut their prices in order to maintain passenger loads. The final result was not increased share for People Express, but near bankruptcy and, in 1986, takeover by one of its chief competitors, Texas Air. People Express and many other firms have learned (too late) that blind adherence to the strategic objective of maximizing market share can have disastrous consequences, regardless of what PIMS data and experience curve theorists may suggest.

181
COMPETITIVE BEHAVIOR

PRISONER'S DILEMMA AND MARKETING COMPETITION

Managers need ways to evaluate the likely short- and long-term market share and profit consequences of their marketing strategies and actions. Making such evaluations can be highly challenging inasmuch as they are so dependent upon the anticipated actions of competitors. One tool that managers have found useful in thinking about competitive actions is game theory. Game theory describes the immediate payoffs from various combinations of actions by individual competitors, and then examines where alternative decision rules employed by the competitors are likely to lead over time.

One well-known exercise of this sort is the so-called prisoner's dilemma game, in which two persons (say, you and your accomplice) have been caught just after committing a crime. At the police station your attorney explains that if you both remain silent, you will both get off with ninety-day sentences. But if you confess while your accomplice remains silent, you will be given a ten-day sentence and your partner will receive a sentence of ten years. If, on the other hand, your partner confesses and you do not, your partner will get a ten-day sentence and you will go to jail for ten years. Finally, if you both confess, you will both spend eight years in jail. You are not permitted to communicate with your partner. What should you do?

Think about it. The best overall outcome is for both of you to remain silent, but you could do even better by betraying your partner *provided that* your partner does not simultaneously betray you. Needless to say, your partner would also be better off betraying you, *if* you remain silent. If you betray each other, the worst outcome results: both of you go to jail for eight years. This is called the prisoner's dilemma: cooperation produces a good result, both parties acting in their self-interest gives a poor result, and there are strong incentives for each party to betray the other.

There is a clear analogy between the prisoner's dilemma and competitive pricing strategy. Figure 10.5 shows the consequences of price cuts by either or both of two

FIGURE 10.5
Two-Firm Pricing Dilemma

Firm A Results / Firm B Results	Firm B	
	Lower Price	Hold Price
Firm A Lower Price	(50)* 50† / (50) 50	(75) 200 / (25) 0
Firm A Hold Price	(25) 0 / (75) 200	(50) 100 / (50) 100

* <u>XX</u> = market share.
† (XX) = profit.

competitors. Each can gain significant market share and double profits if it reduces price, provided the competitor does not. Shares remain constant, while profits decline by one-half for both firms, however, if both firms cut price. What should the two firms do? Think about it. If they cooperate and keep prices constant, "good" profits result. If one attempts to increase share by price-cutting and the other does not, the price-cutter significantly improves its position. Consider what happens to Firm Two's profits if Firm One cuts price: they go down—dramatically—to zero. Under these circumstances, what should Firm Two do? Unless it is willing to live with no profits and low share, it would cut price in an effort to improve its situation. But both competitors would now be worse off than they were before the price war. Moreover, there is no obvious way to get back to the original situation without collusion, especially if both competitors are seeking to maximize profits in the short run.

Under these circumstances, actions to maximize share are unlikely to increase ROI. A ruinous price war is a much more likely outcome. Consider airline competition following deregulation. Lower prices generated big immediate sales gains for the price-cutting airlines, but competitors, seeing their load factors and profits decline, responded with aggressive price cuts of their own, thus stabilizing market shares and lowering profitability for everybody.

Price is not, of course, the only marketing tool available to the aggressive competitor. Advertising, product features, positioning, selling effort, promotion, distribution, and service can all be "raised" in an effort to improve share. A unilateral change in one of these variables will probably increase short-term share and profit but, if matched by competitors, will lead to smaller gains and perhaps even negative consequences. In 1986, for example, auto manufacturers decided to use low financing rates as a competitive weapon. Rates declined to 7.9 percent, then 5.9 percent, and then 2.9 percent, until finally, American Motors offered 0 percent interest! While industry sales increased in the short term and manufacturers were able to clear out their excess inventory, market shares remained relatively constant and industry profits declined.

Most market environments contain both more variables and more competitors than can be reflected in a simple game such as the prisoner's dilemma. The competitive lineup may change as competitors enter and exit the market. Levels of advertising, promotion, product modification, and the like are revised constantly. But while the resulting "game" is far more complex than the prisoner's dilemma, the principles and issues involved are remarkably similar.

DYNAMIC COMPETITIVE STRATEGIES

Aggression or Cooperation?

A fundamental question faced by every firm is how it should deal with competitors. Should it play "to win," or should it try "to accommodate," seeking to do well even if it does not actually win?

In several recent studies, researchers have simulated a dynamic process in which competitive decisions are made, over multiple periods, in an environment with "prisoner's dilemma" characteristics (Axelrod, 1980a, 1980b). In these studies, each player was to specify a set of decision rules. An entrant's decision rule might, for example, be always to take the action that would maximize his or her outcome in the next period, on the assumption that the competition would not respond (an aggressive or betrayal strategy). Another rule might be simply to keep everything the same (i.e., not respond or stir things up). An especially interesting rule, known as "Tit for Tat," consisted of following whatever the competitor did.

Computer simulations were used to play the entrants' rules against each other. The object was to determine which rule would do best against all the other competitors in paired evaluations. The outcome was interesting. The aggressive strategies did not do well; in fact, they often led to the worst result. The best strategy overall was "Tit for Tat," even though it did not do especially well against aggressive strategies. In the first period, the aggressive strategy would win, but then "Tit for Tat" would match the aggressive strategy, leading to equal but unsatisfactory results for both parties. However, "Tit for Tat" showed the best results vis-à-vis the full range of strategies entered. It tended to encourage cooperative solutions, and did not initiate actions likely to precipitate a price war.

Based on this decision-rule "tournament," Axelrod proposed that effective competitive strategies had five key properties:

1. *Nice:* Did not take actions first in an effort to make unilateral gains (e.g., "Tit for Tat" does not initiate self-serving moves).

2. *Forgiving:* Did not try to punish competitors for actions they took (e.g., "Tit for Tat" matches, but does not exceed, competitive actions).

3. *Provocable:* Responded when competitor took damaging action (e.g., "Tit for Tat" responded immediately by matching the competitor's move).

4. *Not Envious:* Focused on your own results, not on whether competitor did better than you (e.g., "Tit for Tat" rarely "won" relative to its direct competitor, but was able to achieve the best overall results).

5. *Clear:* Enabled competitors to forecast your responses to their actions (e.g., "Tit for Tat" is easily deciphered by competitors, given its consistent pattern of response).

These notions have been further tested in a somewhat more realistic marketing game by two scholars at M.I.T. (Fader and Hauser, 1988). In this study, there were three competitors whose sales were a nonlinear function of the prices of all firms in the market.[2] Forty decision-rule strategies were entered by marketing managers and academics. Even under these conditions, the top four places went to "Tit for Tat"–type strategies that sought implicit coalitions. Several of the "winning" strategies were more complex than simple mimicking, but they clearly were "nice" (as defined in Axelrod's list) rather than "envious." A subsequent study with a more complex profit model confirmed the value of cooperation.

The results of these studies employing game theory are quite noteworthy. They suggest that aggressive strategies that seek maximum market share rarely turn out to be the most profitable. Under conditions approximating the "prisoners dilemma," "forgiving" and "nice" strategies appear to lead to higher profits and ROI over the long run.

Avoiding Destructive Competition

Cooperation is only one way to avoid price wars and their consequences. One could also retreat. Under certain circumstances, a strategic retreat that allows the deployment of resources in other, more attractive markets may be the best course. General Electric, for example, recently withdrew from the small electric appliances business (selling its operations to Black and Decker) because it could not earn adequate profits in this "cutthroat

[2] The equation was $Q(1) = K P(1)^{**}(-a) P(2)^{**}b P(3)^{**}b$, where $Q(1)$ is the sales of firm 1, $P(i)$ is the price of firm i, and $a = 3.5$ and $b = .25$. Profit was $R(1) = (P(1) - 1) Q(1) - 3375$. ** denotes exponentiation.

competitive'' market, and had, in the view of top management, much better alternatives elsewhere.

Other strategies often used to minimize head-to-head destructive competition are to segment the market differently from the competition and/or to differentiate the position of one's product from the competition. Both strategies reduce the chance of a prisoner's dilemma by avoiding direct confrontation in the market. Analytic methods such as those described in the last two chapters are often helpful in defining such ''protected'' segments and positions.

Under some conditions, it is possible to hide under the marketing umbrella of a dominant firm. A smaller firm may be able to charge lower prices without precipitating a reaction from the larger firm, *provided that* the smaller firm does not get too greedy and the dominant firm has a strong interest in maintaining its margins. The long-term profitability of the smaller firm under these circumstances would depend, in part, upon its being able to approach the production efficiencies of the larger firm through a shared industry experience curve. Manufacturers of compatible clones were able to prosper under IBM's price umbrella in the early 1980s, for example. When they began to take too much of the market (circa 1985–1986), however, IBM's forceful retaliation brought all but the strongest of them to their knees.

One variant of the umbrella strategy is the ''guerrilla'' strategy, in which a smaller firm enters, earns good profits, and withdraws before the larger firm retaliates. This strategy requires extreme flexibility and a price/cost relationship that provides decent margins without the benefits of experience curve or scale economy effects.

Unique Competitive Advantage

A unique competitive advantage is clearly the best way to avoid the disastrous consequences of a prisoner's dilemma. A firm may use its distinct competence in R&D to produce products with better features or reliability; its advertising may be more persuasive; its sales force may be better at solving customer problems; its automated production facilities may give it cost leadership; or its channels may provide better delivery time. If competition cannot readily match such distinctive capabilities, it may be possible to maintain a profitable business that is relatively immune to destructive competition, even if it is necessary to settle for less than maximum market share, and not be ''envious.'' High consumer satisfaction, profits, and return on investment are themselves meaningful rewards for an effective strategy.

MANAGERIAL IMPLICATIONS

Strategy Selection

The selection of an optimal competitive strategy is difficult at best. Nevertheless, a rational, analytic approach can be of great assistance to the manager. One rational approach to this problem is a three-step process that we have found to be very effective in a wide range of competitive situations.

The first step is to specify the payoff matrix. For various combinations of competitive variables (e.g., prices and positions), we ask what the payoff would be for each competitor. What levels of market share and profits would each firm achieve in each period? Figure 10.5 illustrated one such matrix—a prisoner's dilemma. Figure 10.6 shows a similar but more complex situation in which results are highly sensitive to price and to volume-related manufacturing costs. Assume that Firm One and Firm Two are each now charging a price of $110. Firm One could reduce its price to $100, thus increasing its profits (from $1,500 to $1,867) and its market share (from 50 to 59 percent), provided that Firm Two does not modify its actions. If Firm Two matches Firm One's price cut, however, Firm One's

FIGURE 10.6
Payoffs to Firm One with
High Price Response and
Large Experience Effect

(Share) Profit	Firm Two				
	80	90	100	110*	120
80	(50) 0	(61) 871	(73) 1814	(86) 2828	(100) 3910
90	(41) −301	(50) 500	(60) 1369	(70) 2302	(82) 3298
100	(34) −550	(42) 194	(50) 1000	(59) 1867	(68) 2792
110*	(29) −760	(36) −64	(43) 690	(50)† 1500 ‡	(58) 2365
120	(25) −940	(31) −285	(37) 424	(43) 1187	(50) 2000

(left axis label: Firm One)

Note: $E = -1.7$; $B = .7$.
    * = starting prices.
† (YY) = market share.
‡ XXX = profits.

FIGURE 10.7
Payoffs to Firm One with
Moderate Price Response
and Large Experience Effect

(Share) Profit	Firm Two				
	80	90	100	110*	120
80	(50) 0	(57) 543	(64) 1093	(71) 1650	(79) 2212
90	(44) −37	(50) 500	(56) 1044	(62) 1594	(69) 2150
100	(39) −70	(45) 462	(50) 1000	(56) 1545	(61) 2095
110*	(35) −99	(40) 427	(45) 961	(50)† 1500 ‡	(55) 2045
120	(32) −126	(36) 396	(41) 925	(45) 1460	(50) 2000

(left axis label: Firm One)

Note: $E = -1.1$; $B = .7$.
    * = starting prices.
† (YY) = market share.
‡ XXX = profits.

market share remains at 50 percent, while its profits drop to $1,000. This would be a classic price war under conditions of the prisoner's dilemma.

The development of such a matrix requires the estimation of sales responses to changes in marketing variables and of the relationships between costs and volumes, as well as a method for making the appropriate profit calculations. The values in Figure 10.6 were derived from a demand function that holds that share is a function of the ratio of prices between the two firms raised to a power called the elasticity (E). Profit is calculated as unit sales multiplied by price less unit costs, which decrease as volume increases. This is the experience curve with a learning parameter (B).[3] Figure 10.7 uses the same equation, but assumes less price elasticity. In this instance, as price is reduced relative to competition,

---

[3] The market share equation is: $S(1) = 50(P(1)/P(2))^E$, where $S(1)$ = market share and $P(i)$ is the price of firm i and E is the elasticity. The profit calculation is: $N(1) = S(1)(P(1) - 80S(1)^{-B}) - 3,741$, where $N(1)$ equals net profit in thousands of dollars of Firm One and B is the learning or experience curve parameter.

185

there is less impact on market share. Firm One will still increase its profits by reducing its price from $110 to $100, but only by 3 percent ($1,500 to $1,545). Thus, a prisoner's dilemma may still be said to be present, but both competitors have fewer incentives to cut price. Unless Firm One is virtually certain that Firm Two will not match its price cut, it would clearly have little to gain (relative to risk) in cutting prices.

The prisoner's dilemma does not always exist. Figure 10.8 is based on the same equations as those underlying Figures 10.6 and 10.7, but in this case, price sensitivity is very low. Under these conditions, there is no incentive for either firm to lower its current price of $110. In fact, Firm One could raise its profits by unilaterally *increasing* price. Its share loss (50 percent to 47 percent) would be more than made up for by margin increases, even in the face of increasing unit costs. If Firm Two were astute enough to follow this price increase, profits for both firms would increase dramatically.

Finally, consider Figure 10.9, where price sensitivity is moderate and the experience effect on costs is small. A price reduction from $110 to $100 for Firm One would result

FIGURE 10.8
Payoffs to Firm One with Low Price Response and Large Experience Effect

(Share) Profit		Firm Two				
		80	90	100	110*	120
Firm One	80	(50) 0	(55) 363	(59) 716	(63) 1060	(68) 1397
	90	(46) 127	(50) 500	(54) 864	(58) 1219	(62) 1567
	100	(42) 242	(46) 626	(50) 1000	(54) 1365	(57) 1722
	110*	(39) 350	(43) 743	(47) 1126	(50)† 1500 ‡	(53) 1866
	120	(37) 450	(40) 852	(44) 1244	(47) 1626	(50) 2000

Note: $E = -.75$; $B = .7$.
* = starting prices.
† (YY) = market share.
‡ XXX = profits.

FIGURE 10.9
Payoffs to Firm One with Moderate Price Response and Small Learning Effect

(Share) Profit		Firm Two				
		80	90	100	110*	120
Firm One	80	(50) 0	(57) 489	(64) 987	(71) 1493	(78) 2006
	90	(44) −12	(50) 500	(56) 996	(62) 1499	(69) 2010
	100	(39) −20	(45) 506	(50) 1000	(56) 1501	(61) 2009
	110*	(35) −24	(40) 508	(45) 1000	(50)† 1500 ‡	(55) 2008
	120	(32) −27	(36) 509	(41) 999	(45) 1496	(50) 2003

Note: $E = -1.1$; $B = .41$. Values scaled so profit is 1500 at starting point.
* = starting prices.
† (YY) = market share.
‡ XXX = profits.

in a very small gain. If the price reduction were matched by Firm Two, profits for both firms would decline. Neither firm would have an incentive to reduce prices further, since doing so would cut profits. Similarly, a price increase would not lead to increased profits. If both competitors have the same cost structure, neither would have a unilateral incentive to change its price—a situation likely to result in price stability, or in what is technically called an ''equilibrium.''

Thus, a given market situation may turn out to be a prisoner's dilemma or, conversely, an equilibrium. Each possibility calls for a diametrically different strategy. The first step in the rational formulation of a sound competitive strategy is to make sure one has a basic analytic understanding of the demand and cost structure of the market and of the firm. The market response techniques outlined in the last chapter are very useful in estimating the elasticities. With good elasticity estimates, the payoff matrix has real value as a method of simulating competitive strategies.

The second step is to develop mechanisms for forecasting competitive initiatives and responses. ''Know thy competition'' is a sound adage. What are your competitors' goals and aspirations? What are their current states? Are they ''fat and sleepy'' or ''lean and mean''? How do they see the market? What are their assumptions about your firm? What are their strengths and weaknesses, relative to each other and to you? How have their strategies evolved over time? How are they likely to evolve in the future?

Next we need to convert our insights into our competitors' strategies and behavior into reaction functions that predict how each competitor will respond under a variety of conditions. How capable is each competitor of reacting to price or product actions on our part? How aggressive is each competitor? Will it follow our changes immediately or ''wait and see''? How good are our competitors at market intelligence? Are they ''reasonable,'' seeking a stable environment, or do they have a ''go for the jugular vein'' mentality? What public statements have they made? Perhaps more importantly, how have they acted in the past?

The third step in strategy formation is to evaluate the alternatives and select the ''best'' strategy. One way of doing this is to model probable competitive responses, link them to the payoff matrix, and simulate ''what ifs'' for each alternative strategy we wish to consider. In Figures 10.6 and 10.7, such a simulation would suggest that we should lower our prices if we do not expect competitive retaliation, but that we need to be very careful if we expect competitors to respond to our moves.

The structure of Figure 10.7 characterizes many markets. The sensitivity to changes in marketing variables is high and there are significant economies of scale. We can simulate the effects of an aggressive strategy under various assumptions concerning our competitor's likelihood of response and ability to survive at various levels of competition. If we can force our major competitor out of the market and no new competition enters, the long-run effect of a price war may be beneficial to us, leading to high share and increasing margins. Competitors' willingness to retreat will, of course, depend on their economic barriers to exit as well as on their managerial commitment to the market. If, for example, they have a large production facility that cannot be used for other purposes or be sold, they may have little choice but to tolerate minimal profits. Or if top managers' egos are highly involved in a particular business, they may persist in that business indefinitely despite poor financial results.

We must never assume that new competitors will not enter our markets. If we successfully force out our chief rival and margins return to high levels, new entrants, with war chests primed for a new price war, may come into the market in pursuit of some of the premium profits.

Whether or not we are faced with new entrants will depend largely on the apparent attractiveness of our market and on the presence or absence of barriers to entry (e.g., high capital requirements, proprietary technology, experience curve effects, exclusive distribution channels, customer loyalties). One way to guard against new entrants is to reduce the attractiveness of our market by engaging in a *deterrent* strategy. We could cut profits to a minimum whenever a new entrant appears on the horizon. If potential competitors learn (and believe) that this is our "decision rule," they may be deterred from entry.

If we are able to forecast our competitors' likely initiatives and responses and estimate their competitive intelligence capabilities, we can simulate the effects of a "Tit for Tat" strategy. How many times would we have to follow a competitor's price cuts before it realized that this is our policy, recognized the destructive nature of the process, and began to return to higher pricing levels? Depending on the outcome of this simulation, we might wish to implement a "nice" strategy. If the simulation indicates a high potential for destructive competition, however, we would want to employ a strategy intended to extricate us from the prisoner's dilemma and/or to force our competitor(s) from the market.

Achieving a unique competitive advantage is generally the "best" strategy, even under these conditions. Such advantages can be represented by increased share and profit levels throughout the payoff matrix. Given these higher values, we may be able to achieve a high ROI position even though we do not have a dominant share. This position may insulate us from competitors and produce premium profits—in effect, allowing us to sit out the battle and still "win."

Eliciting Cooperation

If we are in a situation where our competitor is aggressive and we are unable to develop a unique competitive advantage, it generally makes more sense for us to promote a cooperative environment than to participate in a marketing war that will probably lead to mutual low profits.

The obvious method of gaining cooperation is by collusion, a process that is, for better or worse, illegal in some countries. In the United States, executives have been sent to jail for price collusion. There is, however, nothing illegal about acting unilaterally in a fashion that maximizes your firm's performance in a particular competitive environment.

"Tit for Tat" is legal in all countries, and appears to be an effective way of teaching competitors that aggressive behavior will be mutually destructive to profits in the long run. A clear and consistent set of responses is likely to be understood by an intelligent competitor, who should then be able to see the results of its competitive practices. Developing a reputation for matching any and all price reductions is often a strong deterrent to such actions. The effective implementation of a "Tit for Tat" strategy requires clear demonstration that one will follow, but *not* initiate, ruinous competitive moves.

Cooperation can also be facilitated through effective use of public information channels. Media statements such as "We will match any price reductions by our competitors, but strive for price stability" may cause competitors to pause before initiating a price reduction. Plant tours may help competitors understand how much capacity we have available and how much our cost structure depends on volume. Trade associations, as well as consulting and research firms, often publish reports on capacity, prices, and market shares. Studies of critical issues frequently promote a common understanding of the industry and allow competitors to learn a great deal about one another. Meetings allow competitors to get to know one another on a personal basis. This sharing of perspectives and values can lead to nonaggressive strategies.

Sometimes firms informally share technology. Von Hippel (1986) found that in the steel industry process engineers often shared production know-how on an informal and reciprocal basis. According to this study, ten of eleven "mini" steel mills (which process scrap iron into structural shapes) shared their production know-how. Such cooperation is "rational" if the proprietary benefit of the know-how is less than the net benefit from implementing other firms' know-how, which would otherwise be unavailable. In this case, the industry appears to believe that the competitive advantage of proprietary knowledge is outweighed by the common gain from sharing. Similar examples of cooperation are evident in joint R&D contracts and the licensing of technology.

A competitive strategy thus need not be based on a warfare model. In prisoner's dilemma payoff situations, cooperative strategies are often more likely to meet a firm's goals. In a rational industry, patterns of cooperation tend to emerge once the mutual benefits of such actions become evident.

Performance Evaluation

What measures should be used to evaluate marketing managers? Share is an important measure of relative position, but one should be cautious in making share maximization a goal. Market share is a good objective if it correlates with higher-order firm goals, but, as we have seen, maximizing market share may not maximize dollar profits or ROI. In the prisoner's dilemma, a marketing manager may achieve higher share but lower profits (e.g., in Figure 10.6, notice the cell with prices of $90 for Firm One and $100 for Firm Two). Even worse, one might end up with the same share but drastically reduced profits (e.g., see cell with prices of $80 for each firm in Figure 10.6). Marketing managers should certainly be evaluated on the basis of financial performance, but market share measures should be used as secondary indicators of the firm's strategic position. We would not, for example, want a marketing manager to maximize short-term profits by reducing advertising expenditures, and thus market share, if doing so is likely to be at the expense of our long-term profit potential.

Measurement of performance reflects how management sees the competitive task. Is it like a football game, where the objective is to win the game and it does not make any difference whether the score is 7 to 3 or 34 to 31? If so, share is a good measure. Or should our objective be to get as many points as possible, without caring how many points the other player has? If so, profit is the best measure. Which would you rather have in the long run: low profits, but more share than your competitor, or high profits, but less share than your competitor?

We believe that managers should, under most conditions, use profitability, or return on investment, to measure performance. These measures encourage the efficient use of resources and discourage "envious" behavior likely to lead to destructive responses. They deemphasize winning the war and focus on maximizing long-term profitability. Firms will continue to compete, of course, and should use share as an indicator of long-term viability, but cooperative as well as aggressive strategies should be rewarded. Ideally, the primary bases of competition would then shift from price and promotion to innovation aimed at developing unique competitive advantages that maximize benefits for both the firm and its customers.

ANALYTIC SUPPORT

The last section described a three-step approach to selecting an optimal competitive strategy: (1) estimate the payoff matrix, (2) define competitors' reaction functions, and (3) simulate "what if's" and select the best strategy. The analytic support available to help managers employ this process is, unfortunately, not well developed. Management science technology has not evolved in this area to the same level as it has in, say, positioning and segmentation. Therefore, managers must rely primarily on their experience and judgment to identify competitive payoffs, responses, and strategic options.

This task is particularly difficult when the number of competitors is large. Then entry and exit are probable, conditions are subject to rapid change, many marketing tools are available to competitors (e.g., price, promotion, product features, distribution channels, service, advertising, personal selling), and competitors are likely to employ several different segmentation strategies. In these circumstances, the pattern-recognition skills of managers must be high, for the game is likely to be complex and to require elaborate strategies, anticipation of competitive response, and sophisticated contingency planning.

One promising Level II analysis tool is the use of price-scaled perceptual maps to simulate the competitive dynamics resulting from competition based on price and positioning in a market where attributes differ markedly in importance. Figure 10.10 shows a map for three brands of automated industrial robots; the dimensions are "power per dollar" and "ease of use per dollar." These perceptual dimensions encompass electromagnetic hardware, information-processing hardware, and software. They are scaled by dividing customer ratings by price.

Let us assume that customers vary in the importance they give to each of the dimensions, and that they are equally distributed with regard to the relative weights they place on the two dimensions (i.e., their attribute weight vectors are equally spaced over the quadrant in Figure 10.10).

If prices and costs are held constant, it can be shown that competitive efforts to maximize profits will lead to all three brands shifting their product positions along the circle shown in Figure 10.10 to the point on the 45-degree line where each obtains an equal share, and an equilibrium where none of the firms can increase its profits by unilaterally moving from this point exists. If we allow prices and positioning to change (i.e., each brand can move along the radius as well as around the circle), the situation quickly deteriorates into destructive competition, with prices and positioning becoming equivalent and profits for all firms falling to zero.

If one firm had a competitive advantage, however, the result might be quite different. Assume, for example, that Rocon has a structural cost and positioning advantage such that it can command a position 5 percent farther out on the radius than its competitors. It might, perhaps, have a 5 percent cost and price advantage. Robologic and I, Robot can move *around* the circle, but they cannot match Rocon's movement along the radius. In this competitive situation, all firms do not converge at the 45-degree line and all profits do not fall to zero. In fact, if Robologic and I, Robot move to the 45-degree position, they will get no sales because Rocon is farther out on the ideal vector. Under these conditions, we would expect Rocon to achieve premium profits and dominant market

FIGURE 10.10
Price and Positioning
Competition
Source: Adapted from John R.
Hauser, "Competitive Price and
Positioning Strategies,"
Marketing Science, vol 7, no. 1
(Winter 1988), p. 82.

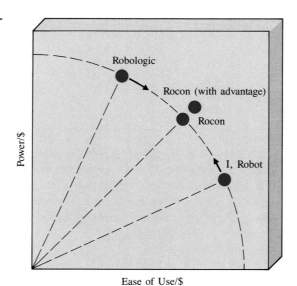

Power/$

Robologic

Rocon (with advantage)

Rocon

I, Robot

Ease of Use/$

share, while Robologic and I, Robot would move toward the 45-degree line but stop considerably short of it. Rocon would obtain sales from customers who weigh the dimensions approximately equally, and Robologic would sell to those who consider power most important, while I, Robot would be favored by those who weigh ease of use most heavily. Note that this is a segmentation of the market based on the importance that customers associate with the various dimensions.

This example demonstrates the value of having a unique competitive advantage (see Hauser, 1988, for more discussion). This advantage earns the firm premium profits and also causes competitors to back away from the segment of the market that values the unique advantage. This simple case also demonstrates how perceptual maps help us to understand complex competitive situations. While such maps do not identify the best competitive strategy, they can be useful in aiding managers to understand the richness of the competitive responses and consumer choice rules existing in a market.

The study of competitive equilibrium is receiving high research priority from marketing scholars and economists (Eliashberg and Chatterjee, 1985; Eliashberg and Jeuland, 1986; Moorthy, 1985). We can expect new Level II tools and Level III analytic models in the near future. Until such time, however, Level I judgment-based approaches, supplemented by consumer and competitor response models, represent the most effective methodology in this complex area.

Another area of needed research concerns the social welfare implications of cooperation. We need to ask if our current policies in this regard are best for society as a whole. Is it better to restrict all forms of cooperation, thus encouraging competitive price wars and rapid exit and entry, or should stability be encouraged, with competitive entry and government regulation serving as the primary means of ensuring both efficiency and viable long-term prices?

CONCLUSION

The importance of competitive strategy has been increasingly recognized in recent years. Traditional prescriptions that one should strive for maximum share and exploit the experience curve have evolved into a game-theoretic view of the world where competitive reactions and the cost associated with earning share are also taken into account. High market share can result in high ROI when experience effects are important and the prisoner's dilemma does not characterize the market. In many markets, however, maximum profitability is likely to be achieved at moderate share levels, levels that reflect cooperative rather than aggressive strategies.

We now have completed our study of the most critical phenomena underlying marketing strategy. Analysis is the key to transforming these phenomena into useful inputs to the strategy formulation process. Level I understanding is the minimum; but in almost all cases, Level II data and simple models are necessary for a fuller comprehension of the decision implications of the concepts. In some cases, the full power of Level III management and behavioral science analysis can be useful. In any event, our understanding of underlying marketing phenomena should be reflected in our diagnosis of our organization's strengths and weaknesses, the environmental threats and opportunities it faces, and our corporate capabilities. (Review Chapter 2 and specifically Figure 2.1.)

We are now ready to consider how to make effective strategic decisions and implement them to achieve our goals. In Chapters 14–21 we study the state of strategic decision making, and in Chapters 22–25, we examine the implementation and integration of strategy into the marketing plan. But first we close out Part Two with three cases illustrating strategic marketing phenomena.

QUESTIONS FOR DISCUSSION

1. Under what conditions is it wise to maximize market share? Name some industries where these conditions apply.

2. What do you conclude from the recent statistical evidence on the relationship of share and ROI? Should the concept be rejected? Do you have enough confidence to base your strategy on the share and profitability relationship?

3. Pick a product class where a prisoner's dilemma or destructive competitive game exists. Trace recent competitive moves and characterize competitive behavior. What is your forecast for competitive interactions in this industry in the future?

4. When would an aggressive strategy of price-cutting work? When would it be better to seek a cooperative competitive environment?

5. How does the outcome of a competitive game in business depend on price elasticity and experience curves? Why is it important to have a good estimate of market response when formulating a competitive response rule?

6. How can product positioning and segmentation be used to avoid destructive price competition? How can they be used to create a unique competitive advantage?

7. How do entry and exit barriers affect the likelihood of a destructive competitive scenario?

8. Is not a nice or forgiving strategy contrary to the need for a good market manager to ''go for the jugular'' and build share?

9. Should marketing managers be evaluated on share and sales or on profit results?

10. If a firm's announced strategy is: ''We will be number one or two in industry or get out of that business,'' how could a competitor with a long-term view maximize its profit?

REFERENCES

ABERNATHY, W. J., AND K. WAYNE. 1974. ''Limits to the Learning Curve.'' *Harvard Business Review* 52: 109–119.

ALBERTS, WILLIAM W. 1989. ''The Experience Curve Doctrine Reconsidered.'' *Journal of Marketing* 53: 36–49.

ANTERASIAN, CATHY, AND LYNN W. PHILLIPS. 1988. ''Discontinuities, Value Delivery, and the Share-returns Association: A Reexamination of the 'Share-Causes-Profits' Controversy.'' Research Monograph. Cambridge, MA: Marketing Science Institute.

AXELROD, R. 1980a. ''Effective Choice in the Prisoner's Dilemma.'' *Journal of Conflict Resolution* 24: 3–25.

———. 1980b. ''More Effective Choice in the Prisoner's Dilemma.'' *Journal of Conflict Resolution* 24: 379–403.

———. 1984. *The Evolution of Competition*. New York: Basic Books.

BUZZELL, ROBERT D., B. T. GALE, AND R. C. SULTAN. 1975. ''Market Share—A Key to Profitability.'' *Harvard Business Review* 53: 97–106.

BUZZELL, ROBERT D., AND BRADLEY T. GALE. 1987. *The PIMS Principles*. New York: The Free Press.

CARPENTER, GREGORY S. 1989. ''Perceptual Position and Competitive Brand Strategy in a Two-Dimensional, Two-Brand Market.'' *Management Science* 35: 1029–1044.

DAY, GEORGE S., AND ROBIN WENSLEY. 1988. ''Assessing Advantage: A Framework for Diagnosing Competitive Superiority.'' *Journal of Marketing* 52: 1–20.

ELIASHBERG, J., AND R. CHATTERJEE. 1985. "Using Game Theory to Model Competition." *Journal of Marketing Research* 22: 237–261.

ELIASHBERG, J., AND A. P. JEULAND. 1986. "The Impact of Competitive Entry in a Developing Market upon Dynamic Pricing Strategies." *Marketing Science* 5: 20–37.

ELIASHBERG, J., AND THOMAS S. ROBERTSON. 1988. "New Product Preannouncing Behavior: A Market Signaling Study." *Journal of Marketing Research* 25: 282–292.

FADER, P. S., AND J. R. HAUSER. 1988. "Implicit Coalitions in a Generalized Prisoner's Dilemma." *Journal of Conflict Resolution* 32: 553–582.

HAUSER, JOHN R. 1988. "Competitive Price and Positioning Strategies." *Marketing Science* 7: 76–91.

JACOBSON, ROBERT. 1988. "Distinguishing Among Competing Theories of the Market Share Effect." *Journal of Marketing* 52: 66–80.

JACOBSON, ROBERT, AND DAVID A. AAKER. 1985. "Is Market Share All That It's Cracked Up to Be?" *Journal of Marketing* 49: 11–22.

———. 1987. "The Strategic Role of Product Quality." *Journal of Marketing* 51: 31–44.

KUMAR, K. RAVI, AND D. SUDHARSHAN. 1988. "Defensive Marketing Strategies: An Equilibrium Analysis Based on Decoupled Response Function Models." *Management Science* 34: 805–815.

MOORTHY, K. S. 1985. "Using Game Theory to Model Competition." *Journal of Marketing Research* 22: 262–282.

PORTER, MICHAEL E. 1980. *Competitive Strategy*. New York: The Free Press.

STOBAUGH, R. A., AND P. L. TOWNSEND. 1975. "Price Forecasting and Strategic Planning: The Case of Petrochemicals." *Journal of Marketing Research* 19: 19–30.

VON HIPPEL, E. 1986. "Cooperation Between Competing Firms: Informal Know-How Trading." M.I.T. Working Paper. Cambridge, MA: Alfred P. Sloan School of Management, M.I.T.

WOO, C. Y., AND A. C. COOPER. 1982. "The Surprising Case for Low Market Share." *Harvard Business Review* 60: 106–113.

11
CENTRAL BELL PUBLISHING, INC.

Developed in collaboration with Linda Isenhour[1]

Peter Powers, marketing vice president of Central Bell Publishing, listened intently as Jim Spencer, his assistant vice president for marketing planning and strategy, summarized the alternative strategies by which CBPI might more effectively deal with the competition that had recently appeared in two of its most profitable geographic markets. Powers had asked Spencer and his staff to analyze the company's current business plan and recommend revisions in light of the external market changes CBPI was experiencing. Powers would be discussing the alternatives and his proposed strategy with President Bill Denson at an afternoon meeting. During the following weeks, Denson and Powers would present the new plan to CBPI's parent company, Central Bell, Inc.

"As soon as I looked at the product life-cycle analysis for the yellow pages, I knew that there was only one way to go," Spencer was arguing. "This is a classic case of a mature product that is losing market share to competition. We should plan to spend as little money as possible to maintain our cash flow from yellow pages and prepare to get into other businesses."

Spencer's matter-of-fact assessment stunned Powers. He had known that revenue had grown only 6 percent (compared to a normal 15 percent) in the two markets that recently had been attacked by major competitors, but he found it hard to believe that this signaled the demise of such a profitable product. Even worse, it was the company's *only* product! "Thanks very much, Jim. I'll review the details and call you with any questions," Powers muttered as he ushered the younger man from the office. Returning to his chair with a grimace, he opened the planning document and settled back to read through the staff report.

---

[1] This case is largely based on and incorporates considerable material from Ms. Isenhour's M.I.T. M.S. thesis (1985), which should be consulted for specific sources and references. The name of the Regional Bell Operating Company and certain confidential data have been disguised at the company's request.

CBPI was an infant company, born on January 1, 1984, to provide its parent, Central Bell, Inc., with a position in the advertising and publishing industries. Its only products at the time of its formation were the white and yellow pages directories for the geographic areas served by the former AT&T operating companies in its region. A strong growth area, CBPI's region comprised 13 million households in 1980, a number expected to increase to 15 million by 1990.

CBPI was a wholly owned subsidiary of Central Bell, Inc., one of the seven regional companies formed following the 1981 settlement of the American Telephone and Telegraph (AT&T) antitrust suit. Before 1984, employees of CBPI had been members of the directory departments of the three Bell telephone operating companies that were combined to form Central Bell. These operating companies had provided local telephone services in their franchised areas, including white and yellow pages directories, as wholly owned subsidiaries of AT&T. After the divestiture, they continued to provide regulated local exchange telephone services, minus the directories, as wholly owned subsidiaries of Central Bell.

From its inception, telephone service had consisted of an instrument in a home or business that was connected via a particular company's lines to instruments in other homes and businesses. Initially, when making a call, the calling party lifted the receiver from the hook and was connected to an operator who made the physical connection to the called party. This type of arrangement continued until 1878, when the first commercial switch was introduced in New Haven, Connecticut. Then customers could call within the same town without involving the operator by simply dialing the other party's number—usually three or five letters or digits.

To encourage use of this new feature, the local telephone company published the first telephone directory, listing the numbers of all subscribers in the local area. The directory proved to be so popular that businesses, wishing to attract new customers, asked to put special messages in the unused spaces, such as the margins. As the number of subscribers grew, however, this space became insufficient. The R. H. Donnelley Company offered a solution to this problem (in Hartford, Connecticut) by publishing a special section for businesses wishing to advertise. To distinguish this section from the regular number listings, they printed it on yellow paper.

The "Yellow Pages" proved to be so successful that telephone companies throughout the United States began printing their own yellow pages directories. One attractive aspect of the yellow pages was the fact that advertising rates were set by each local telephone company rather than by the state regulatory bodies that established telephone rates. The regulators did require, however, that revenues from yellow pages advertising, along with those from long-distance and business accounts, be used to subsidize local rates for residential customers. This process of regulation and use of yellow pages revenues to subsidize "universal service" continued until AT&T and the United States Department of Justice settled the long-standing antitrust suit.

In the modified final judgment (MFJ) that finalized this settlement, AT&T agreed to divest itself of its operating telephone companies, while retaining control of its long lines (interstate) network, manufacturing arm (Western Electric), and research and development organization (Bell Laboratories). In return, AT&T would be freed from 1956 restrictions that had kept it from entering the data-processing and information markets. The divested operating companies were prohibited from selling equipment that they had manufactured, from entering interstate long-distance markets, and from going into the information-processing business. As part of the reorganization, the financial viability of the twenty-three telephone operating companies, which would continue to be responsible primarily for regulated local exchange service, would be improved by combining them into seven regional holding companies. As of January 1, 1984, the regional companies would be individual corporations with no ties to AT&T or to one another except via their shared ownership of the Bell Communications Research Group, an organization established to provide coordination for national defense purposes and to engage in jointly funded research and development.

During the negotiations between AT&T and the U.S. Justice Department, one of the items of contention was what would happen to AT&T's highly profitable yellow pages business. AT&T argued vigorously that the yellow pages were not a part of local telephone service, and that therefore AT&T should be permitted to retain the $5 billion in annual revenue from these directories. While the court ultimately did agree to allow AT&T to engage in electronic directory services as part of its freedom to enter the information services business, traditional directory services were designated as part of "exchange access" and assigned to the operating companies.

The former operating companies were prohibited from providing electronic directory services as part of the general prohibition against their entering the "information services" business. The newly formed regional holding companies, such as Central Bell, were not, however, excluded from any business, provided they received a waiver from the court and found a way to ensure that regulated rate payers did not subsidize unregulated business ventures. Before approving unregulated businesses, the court was expected to demand that separate subsidiaries be formed to ensure that regulated and unregulated revenues were separated. It was primarily for this reason that Central Bell decided to establish a separate publishing and advertising subsidiary, Central Bell Publishing, Inc. (CBPI).

CBPI MARKETING STRATEGY

CBPI's initial products were the 513 white and yellow pages directories that had been assigned to it when the old directory departments were transferred from the regulated telephone companies to Central Bell's new, unregulated publishing subsidiary. The white pages consisted of alphabetical listings of residence and business subscribers for a specific geographical area, providing addresses and telephone numbers as well as more general public service information (e.g., police, fire, and other city departments' telephone numbers, telephone company rates). The yellow pages directory, which generally covered the same geographical territory as the white pages directory, contained, under various descriptive headings, a free alphabetical listing of business addresses and telephone numbers as well as paid advertising messages. In addition, most yellow pages directories had begun to include more "consumer service" information, such as area ZIP codes and city transportation maps, to increase their attractiveness to users and advertisers alike.

Advertising rates varied according to the size of ad, type style, graphics, and so on. Additional fees were assessed for extra or bold-type white pages listings, as well as for red highlighting in yellow pages advertisements. During the past decade, the telephone companies in CBPI's region had increased their yellow pages rates by approximately 15 percent per year. (See Exhibit 11.1 for typical configurations and advertising rates.)

In its contracts with the regulated telephone company subsidiaries of Central Bell, CBPI agreed to publish the white pages, as well as the yellow pages, for all of the regulated companies' markets in exchange for the exclusive use of the regulated companies' names, associated "goodwill," and after-sales service and billing representation. Under its agreement with Central Bell, CBPI paid total licensing fees of $356 million in 1984, with annual fee increases of 14.5 percent through 1989. In addition to its use of the regulated companies' names, CBPI was to receive the list of names, addresses, and telephone numbers for all current subscribers as well as ongoing access to new subscribers and

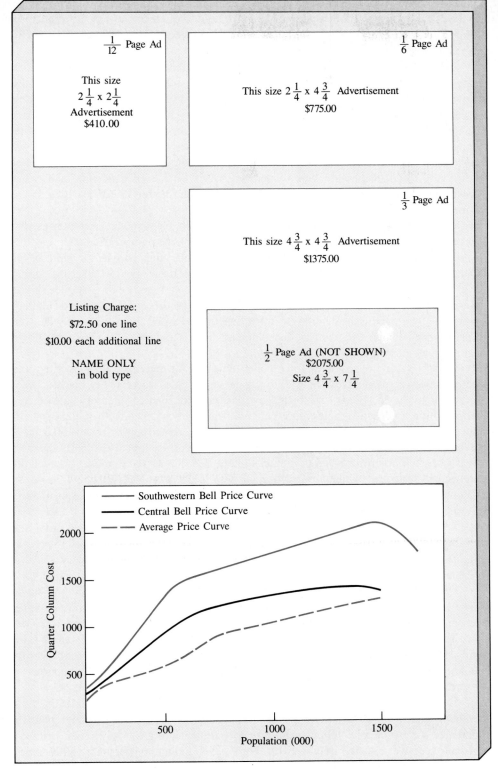

EXHIBIT 11.1
Typical Ad Sizes and Rates

$\frac{1}{12}$ Page Ad

This size
$2\frac{1}{4}$ x $2\frac{1}{4}$
Advertisement
$410.00

$\frac{1}{6}$ Page Ad

This size $2\frac{1}{4}$ x $4\frac{3}{4}$ Advertisement
$775.00

$\frac{1}{3}$ Page Ad

This size $4\frac{3}{4}$ x $4\frac{3}{4}$ Advertisement
$1375.00

$\frac{1}{2}$ Page Ad (NOT SHOWN)
$2075.00
Size $4\frac{3}{4}$ x $7\frac{1}{4}$

Listing Charge:

$72.50 one line

$10.00 each additional line

NAME ONLY
in bold type

EXHIBIT 11.1
(continued)
Price as a Function of Population

Southwestern Bell Price Curve

Central Bell Price Curve

Average Price Curve

Quarter Column Cost

2000

1500

1000

500

500   1000   1500

Population (000)

updates associated with address and telephone number changes. Any other firm that wished to publish a directory in CBPI's territory had a right to ''equivalent access'' to subscriber listings in return for the payment of an ''equivalent'' fee to the regulated telephone company operating in the area.

CBPI had developed highly efficient, mechanized data bases that facilitated its use of these data to publish white pages directories and to schedule sales contacts for the yellow pages. Under its contracts with the regulated telephone companies, CBPI was to provide both a white pages and a yellow pages directory to each subscriber at no extra cost upon installation of telephone service, and annually thereafter as long as service continued. (Prior to divestiture, the number of directories a subscriber had received depended on the quantity of telephone sets leased from the local telephone company. After divestiture, leased telephones were owned by AT&T, and each residential subscriber received only one white and one yellow pages directory, often combined in a single volume.)

CBPI's day-to-day interface with the three regulated telephone companies consisted of receiving service orders for all new and changed telephone numbers and addresses via mechanized data links. These service orders automatically updated CBPI's white pages data base. The system then extracted the service orders for businesses, whether containing old or new information, and updated the yellow pages data base. Finally, service orders for new businesses were routed automatically to the responsible yellow pages sales representatives. Using this lead, either a telemarketing or a premise sales call would be initiated during annual sales canvas, depending on the size and type of the business shown on the service order.

CBPI's yellow pages sales force consisted of 3,000 unionized telemarketing and premise sales representatives. In addition, sales contacts in some of its markets were carried out by L. M. Berry, one of the two leading independent directory sales firms. Compensation for company sales representatives was set by a collective bargaining agreement that was due to expire in August 1986. Salaries represented approximately 50 percent of a sales representative's compensation and commissions accounted for the remainder. It was not uncommon for sales personnel to earn $25,000 or more annually under the commission structure, which rewarded each new or increased advertising sale on an escalating percentage-of-revenue-earned basis. For example, a sales call that resulted in only maintaining the current advertising level would earn a commission of 5 percent, while a call that increased the amount of new revenue through sales of a larger ad or one with special features, such as red highlighting, would generate a commission of 15 percent or more. CBPI paid L. M. Berry a 20 percent fee in those areas where Berry acted as its sales agent.

CBPI's intensive recruiting and screening processes facilitated the hiring of many highly motivated college graduates for its sales force. Requirements included previous sales experience and completion of a rigorous training course. Those who were not successful in completing the course were dismissed. As part of the training, new sales representatives were schooled in techniques specifically designed to help them listen to and understand the needs of a variety of advertisers while overcoming objections to increased rates.

Eighty-two percent of CBPI's revenues were obtained from local advertisers (e.g., plumbers, attorneys, beauty salons) that offered services primarily to a geographically segmented part of the total yellow pages directory audience (e.g., an advertiser's primary customer base was situated in only two suburbs, even though the regional yellow pages in which it advertised covered ten suburban communities). According to CBPI research, many small businesses spent the majority of their advertising budgets on the yellow pages for one or more of the following reasons:

• Their competition was listed there.

- Their new clients came largely from among people who had just moved into the area and had had no previous contacts for their service and from those who were disgruntled with their current suppliers.

- Yellow pages advertising was relatively inexpensive for the 24-hour-a-day, 365-days-a-year coverage provided when compared to newspapers, radio and television, and direct mail.

- They had confidence in the circulation numbers and the marketing research data provided by CBPI, which showed universal awareness and frequent use of the yellow pages.

Contacts with all businesses having telephone service were made during the annual sales canvas. Scheduling of the canvas for a particular directory market was determined by the publication schedule for its updated white pages directory. Approximately six months before the directory "closeout" (i.e., the date when the completed listing had to be ready to be sent to the printer to ensure meeting the specified publication schedule), the appropriate sales force and its managers were given a target revenue objective level. This target was based on the "annual commitment view" of the budget, which specified the total net income to be provided to the parent company in the form of "dividends" on CBPI's stock. It was anticipated that Central Bell would expect a 15–20 percent annual increase in these dividends, at least for the next several years.

Once the revenue goal for a given geographic market was set, a canvas of an appropriate length of time—two weeks to two months—was launched. Sales calls on all existing and new business telephone subscribers were completed, either by premise visits or by telephone. Sales representatives were randomly assigned to their sales contacts each year, partly to preclude perceptions of unfair advantage in meeting sales commitments on "easy" versus "hard" sales accounts, and partly to minimize client-salesperson rapport that might interfere with the sales force's willingness to push the larger sizes and special features that meant large annual rate increases. In addition, the company felt little need to match sales representatives with clients, since the salespersons were not responsible for "customer service." Indeed, once the sale was made, the sales representative moved on to another canvas, and any adjustments or complaints were handled by a separate service/adjustment group at each regulated telephone company.

In preparing for a sales call, the sales representative would review the customer's current advertisement to determine possible selling points. A common sales technique was to ask a customer whether its present advertising copy fulfilled the needs of consumers who used the yellow pages directory. Citing statistics from recent national yellow pages usage studies (see Appendix 11A), sales representatives would suggest that yellow pages copy should feature a firm's:

1. *Reliability*: years established, size, company policies, and national brands.
2. *Authorized products/services*: well-known products, names, services.
3. *Special features*: hours, promptness of service, parking, credit terms.
4. *Completeness of line*: products, services, range, variety, special types, availability.
5. *Illustrations/slogans*: image building, telling a story, gaining attention.
6. *Location*: area served, nearness, and convenience.

Using the customer's own assessment of how well its current copy met these criteria, the sales representative would proceed to make suggestions for improvement. Sales personnel were trained to listen for special areas of concern (e.g., competitors who had larger, more informative or colorful advertisements) as clues to the customer's "hot buttons." For example, an advertiser's concerns about the size of its competitor's advertisements could frequently be leveraged by the sales representative into increased expenditures on yellow pages advertising. Reservations concerning the cost effectiveness of more expensive advertisements would be met with specialized user studies that purported to demonstrate the effectiveness of alternative size/content/color configurations in the client's particular category. Finally, the salesperson closed the sales call by having the client indicate the desired changes on a prescribed form, promising to return via mail a photocopy of the revised advertisement, and having the client sign the order form approving the sale. (See Exhibit 11.2 for one customer's critical view of this sales process.)

After completing the sale, the sales representative would return to his or her office, fill out the sales report, and prepare a description of the agreed-upon changes in the advertisement, which would then be forwarded to an outside firm for development of final copy. At the end of each day during the canvas, the group sales manager would hold a meeting at which each sales representative would announce his or her revenue achievement for that day. A comparison of each representative's earned revenue with the cumulative goal for that day of the canvas would be posted on the office sales board (in graphical format). This standardized procedure was used to motivate less effective sales

EXHIBIT 11.2
One Customer's View of CBPI's Sales Campaign

Recently the local Yellow Pages salesman stopped by to renew my ad for the next year. I get a different salesman each year, but I always know who they are before they introduce themselves—they all drive late model Buicks; they all wear a large diamond on their little finger; and all have a golf suit hanging in the back seat. These are all standard equipment issued by their company, and I suspect that the reason for this may be that they want to create the impression that they could take our accounts or leave them. Which, of course, is meant to intimidate us into not questioning their rate structure.

Having been in business for a while, the value of advertising becomes proportionately smaller as repeat business fills your calendar. The talk of recession has caused more business to cut prices or at least hold steady, but when you are a monopoly you aren't burdened with such trivial matters, or at least according to my salesman. "Why aren't you guys having an ad sale?" I asked. "With business being down, you should have a rebate program!"

"Ha, ha," he chuckled condescendingly. "That's funny. I'll have to remember that one. Now, about your ad."

"Well," I said, "I don't know if I need as much advertising as last year. How much does the smaller ad cost?"

He hesitated for a moment and said resignedly, "I'm afraid last year's small ad has increased in price."

"How much?" I asked casually. "It's about the same price as your big ad last year," he said. "Can I list you under Safes and Vaults with a picture ad?"

"Wait a minute!" I interrupted, "you mean I pay the same price for a smaller ad this year as my large ad last year? Didn't you guys ever hear of Supply and Demand?"

"Ha, ha" he chuckled. "I'll have to remember that one. Yes, Joe, may I call you Joe? . . . Since business is getting scarce, let's pretend it is like a pie . . . now, if a pie is shrinking, you have to take a bigger piece of it just to stay at the same level, therefore, you have to advertise more than usual. . . . Do you understand?"

"I understand," I sighed. "You are going to eat all my pie!"

"You missed the point, Joe. If you are going to compete with all of these companies" (showing me the other ads in the book), "you have to have a larger ad just to keep the same amount of calls. How about red? . . . Do you like red? . . . Our studies prove that red sells. . . ."

"Hold it" I yawned. "How do I know you aren't telling the other locksmiths the same things you're telling me?"

"Joe, I'm shocked!" he gasped, and proceeded to read the tatoo emblazoned on his forearm. "Each client is treated equally and I cannot divulge any information relating to their business and/or their decisions. . . . Do you want to be listed under Burglar Alarms, or how about Door Closures?"

"That's door closers!" I corrected. "How about just a column ad, with bold type. That way my phone bill will match my house payment."

"Ha, ha," he laughed. "I'll have to write that down. Do you mind if I tell the other salesmen that one? Now, seriously, let's think big!"

"I never did like pie" I said. "Let's go with a column ad."

"You're making a big mistake, Joe," he warned. "I hate to see a nice fellow like you suffer because of a bad decision."

"I think the only one to suffer will be you," I said. "You'll probably have to come back from Tahiti a day early."

"If you change your mind, Joe, you still have a couple of weeks," he admonished. "I'll be glad to come back out. . . ."

"Thank you," I said sweetly, as he drove away in a huff.

The new phone books are out, and for the first time in five years I haven't choked on my phone bill, and better yet, the kids call me Daddy, instead of the UPS man. I have time now to sell better security to my existing customers, and by taking good care of them, my referral rate has kept new repeat customers coming in.

Now . . . if we only had a local association that could work together, all of us could save our customers money, by putting a ceiling on the size of our phone ads—but that is another article. . . .

Source: Joseph A. Locke, *National Locksmith*, Summer 1983.

EXHIBIT 11.2
(continued)

representatives, while recognizing those who were successful, an approach that was reinforced through annual award-filled sales meetings.

Completing the sales campaign ended the first phase of publishing a new directory. The next step was to coordinate outside printers, photocopiers, and distributors, as well as to ensure the quality of the data bases, special information pages, and cover design. Advertisers would then be billed on a monthly or quarterly basis. Prior to divestiture, yellow pages invoicing was included in a business's telephone bill, with the implicit threat of telephone service termination for nonpayment. After the establishment of a separate publishing subsidiary, however, completely separate invoices for directory advertising were required. In the view of some CBPI executives, this change mandated that the company do a much better job of customer service than it had in the past. If, for example, a sales representative "oversold" and a customer did not feel it was getting its money's worth for its yellow pages advertisement, it might simply refuse to pay its bill. Even though it had signed a binding contract and thus could be sued for nonpayment, such suits were neither cost effective nor beneficial to Central Bell's corporate image.

By American business standards, CBPI was quite successful. During 1985, its pretax income had been $84 million on sales revenues of $800 million (see Exhibit 11.3), an operating margin of 10.5 percent. Return on assets had been 23 percent, slightly above the industry average.

CBPI's revenues had been derived from the following sources in 1984:

- Local white pages advertising: 9%

- Local yellow pages advertising: 82%

- National Yellow Pages Services (NYPS) advertising and commissions: 8%

- Miscellaneous: 1%

Local white pages advertising included products such as bold type and extra information (e.g., "physician"). Local yellow pages advertising consisted of all copy appearing in the yellow pages that resulted from sales contacts with businesses in the local geographical area (or scope) of the directory. National Yellow Pages Services (NYPS) referred to revenue from national accounts such as Sears or Eastern Airlines, which placed their yellow pages advertising through NYPS. NYPS was responsible for ensuring that the advertisement appeared in directories across the country, without each directory sales organization having to be contacted individually. (In its territory, CBPI acted as the NYPS agent for some national accounts, receiving commissions on the advertisements placed for these accounts in directories in other geographic areas.)

EXHIBIT 11.3
Central Bell Publishing,
Inc.: 1985 Income
Statement (Partial)

	$ MILLION	
Revenues	800	
Local white pages advertising	72	
Local yellow pages advertising	656	
National yellow pages advertising		
and sales commissions	64	
Other revenues—rent/custom work	8	
Less: Uncollectible revenue	(4)	
Publishing fee	(384)	
Total revenues		412
Expenses—Product/Project	275	
Local Sales Expense	96	
National Sales Expense	2	
Sales Promotion	16	
Production Expense	35	
Manufacturing Expense	86	
Delivery Expense	14	
Mechanization Expense	6	
Other Expense	6	
General Administration Expense	11	
Rent Expense	6	
Pensions/Benefits	18	
Other Expense	8	
Total Expense		328
Taxes		39
Net Income		45

Prior to divestiture, the Bell system (AT&T and its subsidiaries) had dominated the yellow pages advertising industry. The Bell system had maintained approximately an 80 percent market share of the $5 billion market, a market that had experienced a 15 percent compound annual growth rate between 1975 and 1984 (see Exhibit 11.4). The industry's pattern of development resembled the growth stage of a typical product life-cycle curve (see Exhibit 11.5). Among other advertising media, only television could approach the astonishing growth rate achieved by the yellow pages.[2] Indeed, yellow pages advertising growth outstripped that of all other print media between 1980 and 1984 (see Exhibit 11.6).

After divestiture, at which point the seven regional companies assumed responsibility for yellow pages advertising, the industry's structure took on an entirely different shape. It was now fragmented, with ten major players, including former AT&T companies,

---

[2] Total U.S. advertising expenditures (all media) were estimated to have reached $95 billion in 1985, having grown at a 13.5 percent compound annual rate between 1975 and 1985.

SEGMENT	1975	1980	1981	1982	1973	1984
			($ million)			
AT&T/Bell System	1,085	2,450	2,695	3,375	3,755	4,095
All others	215	490	545	670	750	910
Total	1,300	2,940	3,240	4,045	4,505	5,005

Source: Communications Trends, Inc.

EXHIBIT 11.4
Yellow Pages Market Growth, 1975–1984

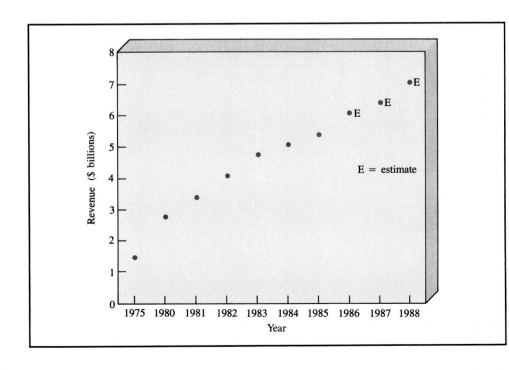

EXHIBIT 11.5
Life-Cycle Curve for Yellow Pages Industry
Source: Communication Trends, Inc.

independent or non–Bell-affiliated telephone companies, and former contract sales agents that had begun to transform themselves into integrated yellow pages publishers. By 1984, no single company controlled more than 15 percent of the national market (see Exhibit 11.7).

While the former AT&T operating companies continued to dominate the industry, there were many other participants, including L. M. Berry and R. H. Donnelley (a subsidiary of Dun & Bradstreet), the two largest contract directory sales agents. Prior to divestiture, directory sales agents had received commissions of 20–25 percent of gross billings. By acting as contract publishers (i.e., providing a "total package" to the local telephone company), however, they could increase their revenues to 50 percent of gross billings. If they went even further and published a directory in competition with the local telephone company, their profit potential would, of course, be even higher. Donnelley's yellow pages revenues for 1984 totaled $240 million. Berry's were about $175 million.

EXHIBIT 11.6
Growth in Yellow Pages Revenues versus Other Print Media, 1980–1984

SEGMENT	1980	1982	1984	% CHANGE 1980–1984
		($ million)		
Newspapers	17,963	21,280	26,690	48.6
Periodicals	8,965	11,525	14,661	63.5
Books	6,114	7,723	9,362	53.1
Yellow pages	2,940	4,045	5,005	70.2
Total, 4 segments	35,982	44,573	55,718	

Source: Communication Trends, Inc., based on U.S. Commerce Department and other sources.

EXHIBIT 11.7
Largest Yellow Pages Publishers Ranked by Revenue, 1984

COMPANY	TELECOMMUNICATIONS REVENUES	DIRECTORY
	($ million)	($ million)
Central Bell	9,874	728
Southwestern Bell	6,184	622
Bell South	8,186	533
Pacific Telesis	6,728	445
Ameritech	7,178	438
GTE	7,796	433
US West	6,261	429
Bell Atlantic	6,958	428
Nynex	8,176	330
United Telecom	1,845	63
Contel	1,330	51
Total: top 11	70,519	4,500
Total: industry	96,000	5,005

Source: Complied from company reports and estimates.

Before the divestiture, Donnelley had largely confined its directory business to acting as sales agent for telephone companies in the states of New York, Pennsylvania, and Illinois, while Berry's primary contracts had been with United Telecom, Wisconsin Bell, and Ohio Bell. (Berry also published AT&T's directory of toll-free numbers.)

The remaining independent yellow pages publishers were generally small firms with revenues of less than $5 million. During 1984–1985, Donnelley enhanced its position in the industry by acquiring several such independents, thus becoming the largest independent publisher of directories. (See Exhibit 11.8 for estimates of the market shares of each major category of yellow pages publisher.)

Besides segmenting the market geographically, divestiture opened up the way for competition among the newly established regional Bell operating companies (RBOCs). Permitted by the consent decree to enter markets outside their traditional geographic territories, many of the RBOCs began to expand their operations.

Several of them immediately announced that they would enter the specialty directory markets; for example, Southwestern Bell published *Silver Pages* (directed at senior citizens) and Ameritech produced purchasing directories (directed at corporate purchasers). Others, such as Pacific Telesis, announced they would expand into general publishing, such as city tourist guides. Before long, expansion into other geographical markets began, with US West acquiring Trans-Western Publishing (publisher of directories in California and Florida), Southwestern Bell acquiring Mast Advertising and Publishing (a $67 million publisher of directories in forty-two states), and Bell South acquiring TechSouth (a firm selling telephone directory layout and typesetting services). Southwestern Bell even forayed into international directory markets, winning a contract to sell yellow pages advertising for Australia's telephone company.

Within a matter of months, the structure of the yellow pages industry had been transformed markedly. At the same time, industry executives found themselves increasingly concerned with longer-range changes likely to result from a variety of new electronic media such as teletext, videotext, and electronic yellow pages. While still in their infancy, these media held much promise for advertisers, especially those seeking to move from mass to targeted marketing. According to Lawrence Strauss in his book *Electronic Marketing* (1984), "Videotext provides the user with unique 'on-demand' video capability to access large amounts of information and to take immediate follow-up action. No other medium can make this claim." To CBPI executives, however, this claim seemed amazingly close to that made by the yellow pages industry, which proclaimed that "the customer looks here when he is ready to buy."

Internationally, France's Teletel system had already met with considerable success after introducing electronic directory service. Teletel gave terminals to its customers in order to get them to try its computerized services and two-way communication offerings. With 1.3 million terminals installed, its most widely used service, the electronic directory,

CATEGORY	REVENUES	SHARE
	($ million)	**%**
11 largest phone companies	4,500	90.0
All other phone companies	330	6.6
Independent publishers	175	3.5
Total	5,005	100.1

EXHIBIT 11.8
Share of Yellow Pages Revenues by Publisher Category, 1984

Source: CBPI, Communications Trends, Inc.

received 8 million calls a month in early 1986. Other services, such as home banking and shopping, also profited from considerable demand as the number of free terminals in the hands of the public grew. One especially popular service was an "electronic singles bar" in which users described their characteristics, interests, and preferences, and—if a "match" was made—agreed to meet at a particular time and place.

Concerned about the future of their classified advertising revenues, U.S. newspapers had engaged in a number of videotext experiments, such as the ill-fated Viewdata joint venture between Knight-Ridder Newspapers, the nation's second-largest newspaper group, and AT&T, in Coral Gables, Florida. This venture had failed for a number of reasons, including the high cost of the AT&T-supplied terminal and the lack of a critical mass of services on the system. More recently, CompuServe[3] and the Newspaper Advertising Bureau had initiated a national classified advertising service whereby CompuServ subscribers could access information on jobs, homes, and cars. According to a number of industry observers, the use of videotext for classified advertising—either by newspapers or by "electronic yellow pages"—was likely to be the most effective way to introduce users to the new electronic media. Advertisements could be updated immediately, sparing buyer and seller wasted time and effort; listings could be indexed and cross-referenced easily by key words to facilitate search and retrieval. Moreover, the limited graphics associated with current videotext technology, which discouraged television and nonclassified print advertisers, would be much less relevant in the classified and yellow pages advertising classifications. According to several recent industry studies, the new electronic media had the potential to obtain as much as 25 percent of classified and yellow pages–type advertising revenues by 1990.

Newspapers had not been alone in their desire to enter the potentially lucrative electronic marketing arena. Prior to divestiture, the Bell system and other telephone companies had argued, in Strauss's words, that "going electronic with their publications was their birthright in an electronic world—in effect an extension of their multi-billion dollar Yellow Pages publishing business." Newspapers were understandably concerned about the ability of electronic yellow pages publishers to update their advertisements daily, since yellow pages enhanced in this way might siphon off newspaper classified advertising revenues. In 1981, the American Newspaper Publishers Association (ANPA), through an intensive lobbying effort, successfully blocked an attempted electronic yellow pages test market by Southwestern Bell (then part of AT&T) in Austin, Texas. Citing among their reasons AT&T's plan to offer "sales/special advertisements designed to provide supermarkets, department stores and other businesses with a vehicle to highlight merchandise on a frequently changing basis," the ANPA was able to delay the test market until divestiture, when the modified final judgment blocked the former Bell operating companies from entering the information business, including electronic classified or yellow pages–type publishing. While the court had left AT&T free to enter the electronic directory business, as part of its freedom to engage in "information services businesses" broadly, the telecommunications giant had not yet made any visible move to do so.

Even before videotext became available, a number of companies had begun to offer yellow pages–type listing information over the telephone. Classified Information Services, Inc. (CLAS), in Houston, Texas, for example, was offering a 24–hour, 7-day-a-week "free" service to consumers. Advertisers paid CLAS for promoting their firm only after consumers called for the name of a particular type of business and had been given their names. If, for instance, a consumer called CLAS asking for a plumber, the CLAS operator would read the name, address, and telephone number of the plumber who had "rotated" to first position on his or her list, as well as up to 300 words of advertising copy. CLAS emphasized the currency of its information compared to that in printed yellow pages, which was often out-of-date by the time of publication. Another key selling point used

---

[3] A firm selling a number of telecommunications-based information services on a national basis to computer users.

by CLAS was that advertisers could measure the degree to which their advertisements were bringing in customers, while with printed yellow pages, they had to assume they were getting referrals as a result of their advertising expenditures.

National electronic yellow pages had been offered for several years by Market Data Retrieval (MDR) in Westport, Connecticut. According to MDR, their service provided a listing of 4,800 yellow pages phone directories plus data from over 1,000 other sources accessible by town, industry, or company. Claiming to have data on more than 10 million businesses in the United States, MDR suggested a variety of uses for the electronic directory, including telemarketing, creating prospect lists, identifying potential employers in a particular town, developing fund-raising lists, and finding suppliers of various services (e.g., theaters, museums, and hotels). Although the service did not provide advertising copy along with its listings, it did include related business information such as size, type and form of business, and trade names.

While originally projected to reach 20 million households in the United States by 1988, forecasts of electronic yellow pages growth had by 1986 been revised downward to recognize the slower-than-expected proliferation of videotext systems and home computer terminals. Nevertheless, experts projected revenues of $3.5 billion by 1996, with $1.1 billion coming from consumers and the remainder from advertisers.

CURRENT STRATEGIC ISSUES

CBPI had, from its inception, followed a strategy of producing high-quality, premium-priced directories. Located in a growing region of the United States, CBPI was expected to provide its parent company with major infusions of "unregulated" profits and cash flow that could be used to fund new, unregulated ventures. According to Central Bell's 1984 strategic plan, for example, CBPI was expected to increase its operating profits by 15–20 percent per year, while raising its return on equity from 24–48 percent by 1989.

This profitability target, while ambitious, had seemed "realistic" when the company was incorporated. All that would be required was to raise advertising rates 15 to 20 percent per year, control costs, continue to trade advertisers up to "bigger packages," and obtain as much "gravy" as possible from new ventures and forays into new geographic areas. At the time these goals were set, however, the magnitude of the transformation the industry would undergo had not been foreseen. Eighteen months after CBPI's strategic plan had been formulated, the force of events had created considerable uncertainty in the minds of CBPI and Central Bell management as to whether its strategy was, in fact, realistic.

Since divestiture, CBPI management had been faced with a number of disappointments and concerns. CBPI had, for example, quickly set up new sales offices outside its region in an effort to begin the process of establishing a national presence. It had soon learned, however, how difficult it was to introduce new products to new customers in new territory. Moreover, accustomed as they were to overseeing their sales force from nearby, CBPI managers had difficulty maintaining control over employees located in distant cities, a problem that was exacerbated by information systems that had been designed for a limited geographic area.

CBPI management was increasingly concerned about its relationship with its contract suppliers. For years, CBPI and its predecessor directory departments had contracted out most of the actual design, photocopying, publishing, and directory delivery to independent firms. Some of these firms had already been acquired by other regional Bell holding companies. If this trend continued, most, if not all, of CBPI's major suppliers would soon be subsidiaries of its largest potential competitors. Already, Southwestern Bell had purchased Mast Publishing, while US West had acquired Trans-Western Publishing. Some scenarios envisioned steep price increases for publishing the large directories typical of CBPI's metropolitan markets, while others predicted intolerable schedule delays as suppliers favored their parents rather than their customers. CBPI could, in theory, buy its own set of suppliers, but such a course would require the investment of "unregulated" funds that might otherwise be used by Central Bell for other purposes. Moreover, the profitability of the functions being performed by its contract suppliers was considerably lower than CBPI's current profit levels.

CBPI had also begun to have difficulty with its long-standing delivery contract agent. This agent received the directories for CBPI's region as they were published, hired the necessary labor to distribute them, and generally handled all problems associated with storage and transportation. Since the divestiture, however, the agent had increasing difficulty meeting schedules because of its expansion into other markets. In addition, delivery of directories to new subscribers was a growing problem, as telephone company installers, who had traditionally done this job, made fewer visits to customer premises.

THE COMPETITIVE CHALLENGE

Yellow pages competitors were not new in CBPI's region. The old telephone company directory departments had, over the years, seen a variety of "fly-by-night" firms attempt to make market inroads. With very low barriers to entry—a few salespeople and a contract with a printer could put a company in business—anyone could go to local businesses and sell "Yellow Pages"[4] advertising. Some local businesses would always "give the new directory a try" because of the lower rates offered by these firms, their disgruntlement for one reason or another with the telephone company, or simply their desire to try something new. However, after seeing the relatively poor quality of the new directory (if one was actually printed) and recognizing its limited circulation and readership, the advertiser would almost always return to the "real" yellow pages. Thus, yellow pages competitors would be born and die in one or two years, with no measurable impact on telephone company revenues or profits.

Since the divestiture, however, the characteristics of CBPI's key competitors had changed markedly. Mast Publishing, the Southwestern Bell subsidiary, and R. H. Donnelley, the Dun & Bradstreet subsidiary, were well-financed, knowledgeable firms that could indeed have a significant impact on CBPI's market share and profitability. In the last several months, each of these firms had entered one of CBPI's major markets. While neither had yet been especially successful with respect to revenues or profits, the books that they had "canvassed" and published were already acting as "spoilers" with regard to CBPI's revenue and profit targets.

Moreover, these large competitors represented only one new form of competitive challenge. After the divestiture, independent "cutters," frequently previous yellow pages advertising salespeople, began calling on advertisers and offering, as independent consultants, to "cut" their yellow pages advertising bills in half. In return for their service, the "cutters" would charge fees of up to 30 percent of the "saved" expenditures. Advertisers, confused by the divestiture in general, were often quite responsive to "objective recommendations" from "yellow pages experts" whom they had known in the "good old days." While the "cutters" had not yet impacted CBPI's revenues significantly, they had a steadily growing presence in CBPI's major markets. CBPI had established three separate task forces to deal with the "cutter" problem, but had yet to find a solution that looked like it would be effective.

Competitors traditionally had entered a market by "rescoping" the local telephone company's yellow pages. They would, for example, identify "communities of interest" among several outlying towns surrounding a metropolitan area, and publish a separate yellow pages directory for just those communities. In many cases, subscribers found these

---

[4] The "Yellow Pages" name and walking fingers logo had never been copyrighted, and so were considered to be in the public domain.

"targeted" directories more convenient than the yellow pages directories that were published by the telephone company, which included all advertisers in the metropolitan area and were frequently quite massive in size.

Faced with competition of this sort, CBPI had in some cases rescoped its own directories, both as a defensive tactic and as a way of increasing revenue. Nevertheless, it had proved to be less flexible than its smaller competitors; was less willing to rescope given its policy of "cost control through standardization"; and considered "targeted" directories to be peripheral to its core directory business. Compared to the $80 million in revenues it received from its largest metropolitan directory, for example, the $6 million it obtained from the "targeted" directories it published for the surrounding suburbs was paltry.

In addition to rescoping, the tactics that competitors in the past had found most effective included:

- Undercutting rates, often by as much as 40–50 percent.

- Seeking "exclusive" placement of their directory in commercial establishments such as hotels and restaurants.

- Running a sales campaign immediately before the "real yellow pages' " planned canvas (the dates of which were public knowledge).

- Assigning a representative to an account on a permanent basis, and having this representative "drop by" regularly to establish rapport and gain greater understanding of the account's problems and opportunities.

- Claiming to have "superior" circulation in a geographic area of particular interest to an advertiser.

- Claiming that their directory was of "superior quality," emphasizing features such as better graphics and more consumer service pages.

- Selling advertising on a cash-in-advance, one-time payment basis (in contrast to CBPI's policy of billing monthly over the course of the year in which a particular directory would be active).

- Emphasizing their flexibility compared to CBPI's traditionally more heavy-handed sales approach.

CBPI management had been quite familiar with such competitive tactics for many years, but since no competitor had ever gotten very far, they had generally chosen to ignore such activities and continue with "business as usual." Even the announcements by Mast and Donnelley that they intended to publish competitive directories in CBPI's region had not caused CBPI top management much concern at first (although CBPI's local sales managers had expressed considerable alarm). It was only when the preliminary results of CBPI's canvas in the Youngsville metropolitan area were reported that top management began to recognize the magnitude of the problem.

Youngsville was one of the CBPI's most lucrative markets, accounting in 1984 for $80 million in revenues from the metropolitan yellow pages and ancillary white pages, and an additional $6 million from the surrounding suburban directories. Revenue goals for the 1985 canvas had been established at $99 million, of which $92 million was expected to come from the metropolitan books. Youngsville and its surrounding area had been growing at a rate of 8 percent annually, with tourism, banking, and construction (commercial and residential) heading the list of major industries. CBPI managers had felt comfortable with the 1985 goal, even though Donnelley had just published a competitive metropolitan directory in Youngsville.

As the canvas got under way, however, reports from sales representatives began to create concern. Advertisers were clearly confused. Many said that they could not afford to advertise in two or more metropolitan directories, and were angered by what they perceived as multiple sales visits. They had believed that they were advertising in *the* yellow pages by placing insertion orders with Donnelley, only to learn that what they had traditionally known as the telephone company yellow pages was a totally different product. One advertiser was trying to begin a movement to get the state to prohibit the publishing of more than one yellow pages directory for an area.[5] Others touted the low rates charged by Donnelley, gleefully exclaiming that at last they had someone to deal with other than, as one put it, "a monopoly which did not care about its customers and charged outrageous prices."

The managers of the Youngsville canvas scrambled to find ways to overcome the resistance their sales force was meeting in the market. They developed a program, for example, to "bundle packages" by offering a free small advertisement under a supplemental heading as an inducement to increase the size of an advertisement in the account's primary classification. Promotional materials extolling the advantages of advertising in "the product most used by consumers in the area" were handed out freely. Nevertheless, salespeople frequently found that they had to spend much more time than planned to close a sale, even one that resulted merely in the same advertisement as had been placed the previous year.

Ultimately, revenues from the Youngsville canvas had increased only 6 percent instead of the expected 15 percent, a severe blow to an organization accustomed to meeting and exceeding its sales goals. While CBPI executives now recognized that the new competitors were formidable opponents, and were likely to become even more formidable in the future, they still had no comprehensive strategy for dealing with these new types of competitors.

CONCLUSION

Powers put down the planning document, rose stiffly from his chair, and walked to the large plate-glass window overlooking the office park in which CBPI's headquarters was located. Of the thirty-two years he had spent in the directory business, he could remember none as pivotal as 1986 promised to be. The direction that he and president Bill Denson laid out next week would greatly influence the future of what was currently an exceptionally successful business. Staring out at the brown landscape and bare trees, he struggled to formulate the long-term marketing strategy that he would recommend.

QUESTIONS FOR DISCUSSION

1. What kind of medium is the "yellow pages"? Why do businesses advertise in it? How would you explain the extraordinary growth of yellow pages revenues over the past decade?

2. What are the major changes in the environment affecting CBPI in the short run? In the longer run?

3. How would you compete with Donnelley and Mast (Southwestern Bell) in markets such as Youngsville? What would you do about the "cutters"?

4. What is your evaluation of the threat posed by "electronic yellow pages" and similar new media?

5. Do you agree that the growth phase of the yellow pages product life cycle has run its course and profits should now be used to fund other ventures with higher growth potential? If not, what would be your strategy to rejuvenate the medium?

---

[5] According to CBPI attorneys, it was difficult to conceive of a legal basis for such an action.

11A

YELLOW PAGES RESEARCH DATA

TABLE 11A.1   **The 1985 National Yellow Pages Usage Study: First-Quarter 1985 Estimates of Past 7-Day Usage of the Yellow Pages[1]**

		POPULATION (000'S)	% OF POPULATION	PAST 7-DAY YELLOW PAGES USAGE (AVERAGE FREQUENCY)	PAST 7-DAY USES (000'S)	% OF USES	USAGE INDEX*
Total	Adults 18+	170,429	100.0	1.87	318,702	100.0	100
Sex	Males 18+	81,028	47.5	1.86	150,672	47.3	100
	Females 18+	89,401	52.5	1.88	168,030	52.7	100
Age	18–24	28,977	17.0	2.36	67,301	21.1	124
	25–34	40,405	23.7	2.61	103,784	32.6	138
	35–49	41,709	24.5	1.89	76,758	24.1	124
	50–64	32,972	19.3	1.60	51,918	16.3	85
	65+	26,366	15.5	0.73	18,941	5.9	38
Education	Less than high school graduate	33,052	19.4	0.86	28,081	8.8	45
	High school graduate	66,377	38.9	1.79	117,376	36.8	95
	At least some college	71,000	41.7	2.47	173,245	54.4	131
Household Income	Under $10,000	28,632	16.8	1.28	33,684	10.6	63
	$10,000–$24,999	61,014	35.8	1.60	89,724	28.2	79
	$25,000–$39,999	48,231	28.3	2.59	114,813	36.0	127
	$40,000+	32,552	19.1	2.69	80,481	25.2	132

* Index = % users/% population.
Source: Statistical Research, Inc.

[1] This table provides the key findings from the 1985 National Yellow Pages Usage Study. Based on the first quarter of 1985 (12 measurement weeks during January, February, and March 1985), a total of 2,960 telephone interviews were conducted among a random sampling of persons aged 18 and over residing in telephone households in the continental United States.

TABLE 11A.2 Yellow Pages Usage Study Highlights

98.8%	of all adults indicated familiarity with the Yellow Pages, hence awareness of the Yellow Pages is virtually universal.
76.5%	of all adults referred to the Yellow Pages during the typical month in the first quarter 1985.
55.8%	of all adults in the United States referred to the Yellow Pages in a typical week.
3.35	references to the Yellow Pages were made, on the average, by adult *users* in the average week, or 46 million references in the typical day. Among *all* persons, average frequency of usage is 1.87 references.
18.6%	of all adults used the Yellow Pages on the typical day during the first quarter of 1985.

TABLE 11A.3 Yellow Pages Reference Behavior Findings

55.0%	referred to at least one Yellow Pages advertisement (the average was 3.2 advertisements); 42.5% looked at the listings only.
56.9%	had the name of a store, firm, or establishment in mind prior to looking in the Yellow Pages; however, 40.2% did *not* have a name in mind.
82.5%	of all Yellow Pages references resulted in a contact of a store or business.
45.0%	of these Yellow Pages references resulted in the purchase of a product or service (that's 20.7 million purchases on the typical day). Among those who did not make a purchase, 75.2% indicated they were either very or somewhat likely to make a purchase. Of those adults who did make a purchase: —29.7% spent $25 or less on that purchase. —28.6% spent from $25 to $100. —15.6% spent from $100 to $500. —6.8% spent over $500. —19.3% did not know how much was spent or had not been billed at the time.

TABLE 11A.4 Types of Information Sought by Respondents Who Turned to the Yellow Pages Advertisements for Information

INFORMATION	NUMBER OF RESPONDENTS	PERCENT DISTRIBUTION
Types of goods or services offered	351	46.9
Availability of branded products	115	15.4
Location of firms or organizations	90	12.0
Price information or availability of credit	58	7.7
Hours of operation	27	3.6
Delivery information	14	1.9
Other information about specific practices and policies	94	12.5
Total Responses	749	100.0

Source: Feldman & Halterman, 1963, Table 2.7.

USE	USE OF THE YELLOW PAGES	
	Agree That Ever Used This Way	Agree That Usually Used This Way
To find a dealer who offers specific products, brands, services	89	77
To call ahead to find if a specific product is available	87	65
To find the phone number of a dealer I already know about	85	61
To check the address of a dealer I intended to visit	82	60
To call ahead for the price of a product	78	56
To get a store's phone number to call about the hours	85	55
To get a store's number to call to get directions to the store	73	33
(Base = 200)		

Source: Foote, Cone & Belding/Wahlstrom, 1981, p. 44.

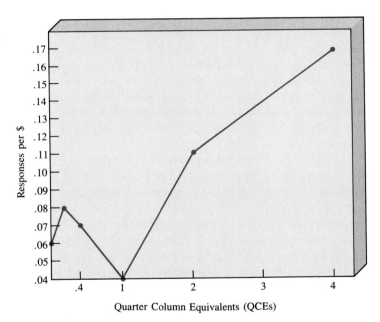

Quarter Column Equivalents (QCEs)

FIGURE 11A.1
Responses per Dollar as a
Function of Ad Size
Source: Feldman & Halterman,
1963, and NYPSA, *Rates and
Data*, 12/82.

12

AMERICAN EXPRESS COMPANY
Credit Card Marketing

Developed in collaboration with Alex Savich and Paul Smith[1]

In January 1986, Janet Frost, who had recently been appointed marketing vice president—retail of the Travel Related Services (TRS) subsidiary of the American Express Company (Amex), was seeking to formulate a new marketing strategy for the American Express® Card's retail market segment. In her new position, she was responsible for maximizing American Express card billings for retail purchases, a use that had long been dominated by the so-called bank cards (Visa and MasterCard) and individual retailers' proprietary "house cards."

TRS, which first introduced the Amex® Card in 1958, had seen the number of its cards outstanding grow to more than 20 million by 1985. TRS believed that with its other financial products—in particular, traveler's checks—it offered an unmatched selection of payment and travel products designed to meet the lifestyle and business needs of its individual and company clients. The American Express Card faced increasing competition from other "general purpose" cards, however, including Visa, MasterCard, Citicorp's Diners Club and Choice cards, and Sears' new Discover card.

The recent loss of a number of significant retail accounts, including Filene's department stores in Boston, had led Frost to the conclusion that a comprehensive reevaluation of Amex's strategy for dealing with the retail market was needed. In considering how TRS should defend its U.S. market share, Frost noted that TRS charged its franchises a higher average discount[2] than its competitors did; charged card members a higher annual fee than its competitors did; and did not offer most of its card members a credit line.[3]

---

[1] This case is largely based on and incorporates considerable material from Savich's and Smith's M.I.T. M.S. theses (1986), which should be consulted for specific sources and references. While believed to be representative of the events and issues it describes, this case has been prepared for pedagogical purposes, and should not be utilized as a source of research data. Nonpublic information and data may be disguised.

[2] The "discount" was the percentage fee charged by a card company on a sales transaction (e.g., a 5 percent discount on a $100 sale would provide the card company with a $5 fee on the transaction).

[3] Amex Card invoices were "due upon receipt," except for the Gold Card (see below) and under special circumstances (e.g., Amex's Sign & Fly program). In practice, a cardholder with a good payment record could generally pay his or her Amex Card bill as much as three weeks following receipt without receiving a "reminder."

While each of these policies had been a central tenet of Amex's traditional card marketing strategy, Frost wondered if it were not time to initiate a new approach.

COMPANY HISTORY

The American Express Company was formed in 1850, through a merger of the three major express companies of that time: Wells & Co., Livingston & Fargo, and Wasson & Co. Henry Wells was elected president. The westward expansion resulting from the California gold rush provided an opportunity for rapid growth. American Express quickly became the nation's foremost express operation, with an extensive business handling shipments of coin and gold for banks. A fast-freight service was added as far west as St. Louis, and goods in bond were transported into Canada. At the outbreak of the Civil War in 1861, American Express made its services available to the U.S. government, and by 1862, there were 890 offices and agencies employing 1,500 men traveling more than 9,000 miles of railroad each day.

At the end of the Civil War, competition increased and business declined. In particular, American Express faced competition from New York merchants who formed their own express service, the Merchants Union Express Company. In 1868, however, the two companies merged to become the American Merchants Union Express Company, with a new president, William Fargo. The company dropped the "Merchants Union" from its name in 1882, when Fargo died. The man who succeeded William Fargo, James Fargo, was to run American Express like an autocrat for the next thirty-three years. He was responsible, in 1881, for the introduction of the American Express Money Order in response to the United States Post Office's new postal money order. It was immediately successful and was still being used by many people more than a century later. In 1891, Fargo, while traveling in Europe, encountered difficulty with the cumbersome letter of credit travelers used at that time. He instructed his staff to "come up with something" that would be as safe as the letter of credit but easier to use. The result was American Express Travelers Cheques. By 1901, sales of the company's traveler's checks had reached over $6 million; in 1985, sales were some $15 billion. About the time of the introduction of the traveler's check, commerce with Europe was expanding. American Express significantly enlarged its transatlantic freight business as this trade grew, opening shipping offices in principal port cities. These offices soon became involved in the travel business, and by 1909, the company began offering European tours.

In 1914, Fargo resigned and was succeeded by George Taylor as the First World War began. The war emergency saw the nationalization of the express industry, leaving American Express with a number of smaller but nonetheless valuable businesses: Money Orders, Travelers Cheques, foreign remittances and foreign exchange, travel, a small foreign banking operation, and an international freight business. The company continued to expand, and by 1950, under a new president, Ralph Reed, it had significant interests in the travel, travel-related services, and international banking businesses. The 1958 introduction of the American Express Card was a logical extension of these services, building on the travel and financial businesses of the company. Within three months of its introduction, the card was being used by 500,000 people.

In 1960, Ralph Reed retired and Howard Clark began to lead American Express into an era of new growth. Clark's goal was to establish a broadly balanced international earnings base. The company's international expansion was driven by consumer demand as Americans increased their overseas vacation and business travel. As the travel and international banking services grew at phenomenal rates, the company acquired a major insurance organization, Fireman's Fund. Increasing monetary requirements for large-scale industrial and natural resource projects overseas also led to the establishment of merchant and investment banking subsidiaries, commencing in late 1973. The largest, Amex Bank

Limited, operated outside the United States as a full-service merchant bank headquartered in London. Others served the Middle East and the Far East. The acquisition of Shearson/ Lehman and IDS provided the company with major positions in investment banking and mutual funds. To serve these myriad businesses, American Express had, by the 1980s, developed one of the most sophisticated and comprehensive information systems networks in the world. (See Exhibit 12.1 for the Amex organization chart, and Exhibit 12.2 for a financial profile of the company.)

EXHIBIT 12.1
American Express Corporate Organization Chart

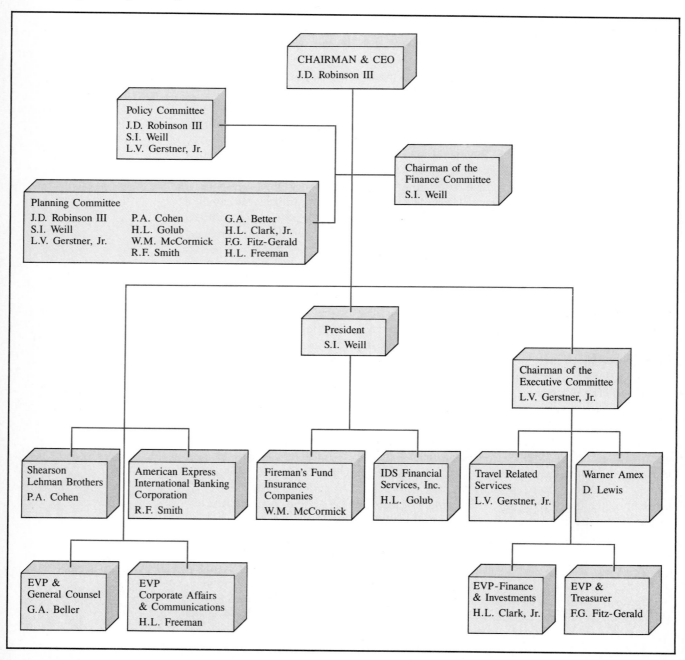

EXHIBIT 12.2
American Express Financial Highlights

AMERICAN EXPRESS COMPANY

(dollars in millions, except per share amounts)

	1984	1983	Percent Increase
Revenues	$ 12,895	$ 9,770	32%
Net income	$ 610	$ 515	18
Common share cash dividends declared	$ 276	$ 252	10
Per share amounts:			
Net income	$ 2.79	$ 2.53	10
Common share cash dividends declared	$ 1.28	$ 1.26	2
Book value	$ 20.21	$ 18.95	7
Average number of common shares outstanding (millions)	217	203	7
Total assets	$ 61,848	$ 43,981	41
Shareholders' equity	$ 4,607	$ 4,043	14
Return on average equity	14.4%	14.5%	
Pretax investment income (tax equivalent basis)	$ 2,156	$ 1,417	52
Assets owned, managed and/or administered	$139,679	$103,939	34
Life insurance in force	$ 37,436	$ 28,717	30
Number of employees	76,447	70,456	9
Total American Express offices worldwide including representative offices	2,282	2,153	6

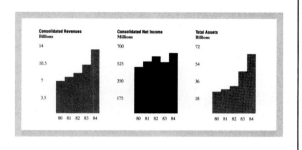

EXHIBIT 12.2
(continued)
American Express At-a-Glance

AMERICAN EXPRESS: TOP RATED BY INDEPENDENT STUDY

American Express products and services hold the confidence of millions of people. They look to American Express brand names for better ways to make, use and protect their money. In a survey in 1984, the *American Banker* found that people rate American Express products and services higher than those of any other top financial services firm in the United States.

Who Consumers Know (%)*

American Express	75
Prudential Insurance	72
Bank of America	70
Merrill Lynch	66
Beneficial Finance	55
Sears Roebuck	54
Citicorp	53
Chas. Schwab	21

*Multiple Responses Permitted. Reprinted with permission of *American Banker.*

TRAVEL RELATED SERVICES

Travel Related Services
An American Express company

Travel Related Services began the American Express tradition of reliable service in 1850 by moving freight. Today, it moves people and their buying power around the world. People know the quality of the American Express Card, Travelers Cheque and Travel Services.

(millions, except percentages)

	1984	1983	Percent Increase
Revenues	$ 3,620	$ 2,889	25%
Net income	$ 387	$ 301	29
Card charge volume	$47,638	$38,356	24
Travelers Cheque sales	$15,116	$13,862	9
Total assets	$12,542	$10,226	23
Average Travelers Cheques outstanding	$ 2,634	$ 2,437	8
Cards in force	20.2	17.3	17
Return on average shareholder's equity	25.3%	24.1%	

INTERNATIONAL BANKING SERVICES

International Banking Corporation
An American Express company

At American Express International Banking Corporation, the accent is on "international." The Bank helped American Express expand internationally following World War I. Today, 82 offices in 39 countries offer export financing, private banking and other select services.

(millions, except percentages)

	1984	1983	Percent Increase (Decrease)
Net income from International Banking Services	$ 156	$ 136	15%
Loans and discounts	$ 6,272	$ 6,290	—
Reserve for loan losses	$ 165	$ 162	2
Total assets of American Express International Banking Corporation	$13,875	$13,309	4
Customers' deposits and credit balances	$10,517	$10,328	2
Shareholder's equity of American Express International Banking Corporation	$ 897	$ 819	10
Primary capital to average assets	7.64%	7.05%	
Return on average assets	1.15%	1.04%	
Return on average shareholder's equity	17.81%	17.67%	

EXHIBIT 12.2
(continued)
American Express At-a-
Glance

INVESTMENT SERVICES

SHEARSON LEHMAN BROTHERS
An American Express company

Shearson Lehman Brothers Inc. evolved from strategic acquisitions—most recently, Lehman Brothers. Today, Shearson Lehman melds this investment banking franchise with strong trading and distribution capabilities.

(millions)

	1984	1983	Percent Increase (Decrease)
Revenues	$ 2,280	$ 1,826	25%
Pretax income	$ 168	$ 326	(49)
Net income	$ 103	$ 175	(41)
Total assets	$22,735	$ 9,060	151
Total capital, including subordinated debt, of Shearson Lehman Brothers Inc.	$ 1,896	$ 1,057	79
Assets managed and/or administered	$64,939	$47,144	38

Note: Investment Services 1984 amounts include the effect of the acquisition of Lehman Brothers Kuhn Loeb Holding Co., Inc., accounted for as a purchase as of May 11, 1984.

IDS FINANCIAL SERVICES

IDS
An American Express company

IDS Financial Services Inc. and its subsidiaries have earned people's trust, through outstanding financial advice and services, since 1894. The 4,400 representatives of IDS provide financial plans and products that stand the test of time.

(millions)

	1984	1983	Percent Increase (Decrease)
Revenues	$ 1,576	$ —	—
Pretax income	$ 95	$ —	—
Net income	$ 62	$ —	—
Individual life insurance in force	$13,818	$11,424	21%
Assets owned and/or managed:			
Assets managed for institutions	$ 3,080	$ 3,650	(16)
Assets owned and managed for individuals:			
Owned assets	$ 6,411	$ 5,410	19
Managed assets	$ 9,812	$ 9,162	7

Note: The acquisition of IDS Financial Services was accounted for as a purchase effective December 31, 1983. Therefore, revenues, pretax income and net income for 1983 are not presented.

INSURANCE SERVICES

FIREMAN'S FUND INSURANCE COMPANIES
An American Express company

Fireman's Fund Insurance Companies was born in San Francisco in 1863 to provide protection against the frequent fires that ravaged the city. Today, Fireman's Fund is an industry leader in developing new products and new approaches to marketing.

(millions, except percentages)

	1984	1983	Percent Increase
Fireman's Fund Insurance Companies			
Revenues	$ 4,025	$ 3,784	6%
Net income	$ 43	$ 30	42
Total assets	$ 7,735	$ 7,057	10
Shareholder's equity	$ 1,485	$ 1,304	14
Return on average shareholder's equity	3.1%	2.2%	
Property-Liability Companies			
Premiums written	$ 2,834	$ 2,781	2
Underwriting ratio	121.1%	126.0%	
Loss and loss expense ratio	86.4%	86.5%	
Expense ratio	32.2%	36.6%	
Policyholder dividend ratio	2.5%	2.9%	
Life Companies			
Premiums written	$ 655	$ 539	21
Life insurance in force	$23,133	$15,493	49

THE TRS DIVISION

The TRS division and its products were among the oldest components of Amex, with roots reaching back to 1850 when the parent company was founded. TRS was split off from the rest of Amex and established as a separate subsidiary in 1983 to operate the American Express Card, Travelers Cheques, travel, transaction processing, and communications businesses. In 1984, it had operations in 131 countries and 26,427 employees worldwide. More than 1,200 owned and representative travel agency offices made it one of the world's largest travel companies. In 1984, revenues were $3.6 billion and net income was $387 million.

A third of all TRS employees were employed in the United States, and this work force was growing at about 15 percent per annum. (See Exhibit 12.3 for the TRS organization chart.) Because of the rapid growth within TRS, few "professionals" stayed in any position for more than a year, leading, in some employees' views, to a decision-making process that was not, perhaps, quite as deliberate as it might have been.

Within TRS, the Service Establishment (SE) marketing group was responsible for convincing service establishments (e.g., airlines, hotels, restaurants, and—increasingly—retailers) to honor the American Express Card. The SE marketing organization was originally set up to serve the lodging, travel, and entertainment segments. It did this through a matrix in which specialized groups were organized along market segment and functional dimensions. The lodging group, for example, was assisted when required (e.g., in de-

EXHIBIT 12.3
TRS Organization Chart (1986)

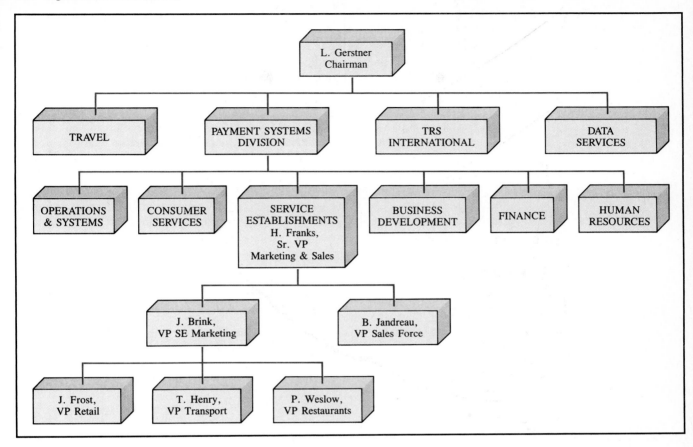

veloping a promotion) by marketing specialists who also consulted with the travel group. As competition among Amex's customers intensified (e.g., increasing price competition among car rental companies) and markets became less well structured (e.g., following airline deregulation), the marketing organization responded by increasing its size (essentially doubling its work force between 1983 and 1985), adding new industry segment groups (e.g., retail), and providing each industry group with a greater complement of dedicated functional resources.

THE CREDIT CARD INDUSTRY

Credit card companies traditionally segmented the credit card market into travel and entertainment (T&E) and general purpose segments. Each product segment filled a particular need: T&E cards gave the business traveler a more convenient form of payment than cash or checks; general purpose cards offered the retail customer a more convenient form of revolving credit to finance major purchases. In recent years, the distinction between the T&E and bank card segments had become increasingly blurred. The American Express Card, the dominant T&E product, had recently entered the retail market, for example, while MasterCard and Visa had added premium cards and sought to expand their international presence.

Without clear distinctions between the T&E and general purpose segments, most credit card marketing now addressed, not the type of use, but the type of user. By the mid-1980s, the fundamental segmentation scheme being used in the industry was to distinguish between the convenience user and the "revolver." Convenience users typically paid off their credit card bills before incurring interest charges, while revolvers carried finance balances on their credit lines. About 70 percent of cardholders did not pay their outstanding balances in full at the end of the month, a segment that was growing significantly in the mid-1980s. Revolving credit balances at commercial banks doubled from $32.1 billion in May 1982 to $66.3 billion in May 1985; consumers paid close to $6 billion in finance charges in 1984.

Amex had traditionally dominated the convenience user segment by attracting upscale and prestige-seeking cardholders. By 1985, however, the overall credit card market was heavily saturated. Eighty percent of those eligible for credit cards already held some form of bank card. Almost 50 percent of the 4.3 million households earning more than $50,000 per year already had an American Express Card. The average cardholder carried seven different credit card products. According to Robert Burke, vice president of First Chicago's bank card division, "The whole game today is trying to make your card more appealing, so people will pull it out before they pull out the other guy's card."

Although consumers carried an ever-larger array of credit cards, a recent credit study had found that 47 percent of consumers would have preferred a "universal" plastic card that would consolidate all credit and debit transactions onto one billing statement. In the mid-1980s, the major "players" in the industry all seemed to be trying to position themselves to become as close to this one "universal card" as possible.

In 1984, there were approximately 20.3 million Amex cards outstanding (17 million Personal, 3.3 million Gold, and 50,000 Platinum). Major competitors had almost 265 million "cards-in-force," including Visa's 121 million (118.5 million regular and 2.5 million preferred), MasterCard's 103 million (101 million regular and 2 million preferred), and Sears' 40 million.[4] (See Appendix 12A for comparative data.) Billings per card varied considerably among the four, however:

CARD	CARDS OUTSTANDING	ANNUAL BILLINGS	PER CARD
Amex	20 million	$47 billion	$2315
Visa	121 million	$61 billion	$500
MasterCard	103 million	$50 billion	$490
Sears	40 million	$15 billion	$375

The credit card industry had recently been characterized by considerable technological innovation. This innovation was driven primarily by card issuers' efforts to reduce operating costs and by the desire of retail service establishments (SEs) for faster, cheaper, "hassle-free" credit card handling. This desire for "cash-equivalent" handling was reflected in the increasing number of SEs using point-of-sale (POS) terminals. These POS terminals, which were electronically connected to one or more card issuers, obtained automatic authorization for the sale, while simultaneously crediting the SE's account and debiting the customer's. Such POS terminals were typically owned by either a credit card issuer or a third-party processor. (In 1984, 56 percent of specialty stores used third-party processors for their card sales.)

POS terminals could also be used to collect valuable marketing information (e.g., average dollar purchases for card issuers, SEs, and cardholders), which could then be sold by the "collector." There were economies of scale in processing and the opportunity

---

[4] Data are for the Sears retail "charge card" prior to its introduction of the Discover card in January 1986 (see page 228).

for card issuers to offer the retail SE additional services (e.g., in-store banking) once their POS terminals were installed. As a result, both credit card companies and banks were competing to install as many of their own POS terminals as possible by offering lower discounts, faster transaction times, and quicker payment to the SEs.

Many retail SEs were interested in combining authorization and transaction processing. Debit cards, which debited the customer's bank account directly at the time of purchase, seemed especially promising, as did the recent development of "smart cards," whereby a customer's account or credit balance could be stored on a chip. There was considerable concern in the industry, however, about (1) how consumers would respond to the loss of bill-paying "float," (2) rising levels of fraud with all types of cards, and (3) the cost of debit card POS terminals or "smart" cards.

Many in the industry were also concerned about the continuing pressure by some SEs for a change in federal legislation to permit "surcharging" on credit card transactions. Although it was currently illegal for most SEs to add a surcharge to credit card purchases, there were some "exemptions" (e.g., gas stations were allowed to offer discounts on cash sales). TRS research indicated that one in seven SEs would be likely to add a surcharge to credit purchases if allowed to do so.

AMERICAN EXPRESS

When Lou Gerstner arrived from McKinsey (a large management consulting firm) to become head of TRS in 1978, the Amex Card had appeared to be a mature business. Almost all traveling executives had the Card, and it was accepted by most airlines, travel agencies, car rental agencies, hotels, and "better" restaurants. Service establishment marketing efforts concentrated on increasing activation rates rather than on increasing market penetration.

Under Gerstner, however, TRS had achieved an average compound growth rate of 25 percent a year. This had been accomplished largely by focusing cardholder acquisition strategy on the nonbusiness traveler and by expanding the types and numbers of service establishments that honored the Amex Card. The company ran advertising campaigns aimed at women, for example, with the result that the number of cardholders who were women had risen from 16 percent to 29 percent between 1981 and 1985. In a similar vein, Amex had reemphasized a program that solicited graduating college students to become cardholders and establish credit records. Gerstner pushed the Amex Card out of the confines of its traditional travel and entertainment segment into the retail market. By signing retailers ranging from Saks Fifth Avenue to Zayres, American Express entered into direct competition with bank cards in their traditional stronghold.

At the same time it was expanding the scope of its cardholders and service establishments, Amex increased the vertical segmentation of its cardholders by clearly differentiating its Personal, Gold, Platinum, and Corporate Cards. Each card was packaged to offer specific levels of services and prestige.

Personal Card

In 1958, Amex introduced its Personal® Card product—commonly referred to as the Green Card. The card was intended as a defensive measure against the recently introduced Diners Club card, which threatened to damage Amex's lucrative Travelers Cheques market. The American Express Card was, from the outset, positioned as a premium product over the Diners Club card. Amex charged an annual fee of $6 versus $5 for the Diners product. Although there was some media advertising for the Personal Card, most of the marketing was done at the point-of-sale of Amex Travelers Cheques. In fact, within three months, the Personal Card was being used by 500,000 cardholders, and Amex's major concern was handling the unexpectedly high demand for the card. Throughout the 1960s, the American Express Card experienced increases in membership volume and spending per cardholder. By 1976, the Personal Card was available in sixteen currencies, had 17 million members worldwide, and had become an important profit center within the company.

Advertising for the Personal Card was handled by Ogilvy & Mather, a leading New York–based advertising agency. The Personal Card was the only Amex Card advertised on radio and television, and was the sole card to be featured in cooperative advertisements and promotional campaigns with Amex service establishments, such as car rental and hotel organizations. According to Amex advertising executives, this policy was intended to protect the higher prestige of the Gold and Platinum Cards, while not offending Personal cardholders.

Amex advertising sought to enhance the prestige of the American Express Card. Cardholders were encouraged to think of Amex as an "exclusive" card. Amex encouraged this through charging a higher enrollment fee than its competitors ($45 per year for the Personal card versus typically $25 per year for Visa and MasterCard), imposing a minimum income requirement, and not specifying an explicit limit on the amount that could be charged. The fact that the American Express Card was not technically a credit card was considered important by some cardholders, who believed that payment by an American Express Card indicated to SEs that the cardholder could pay for all of his or her purchases without credit. As a CEO of a failing company is reported to have said, "I may manage a company that faces certain bankruptcy, but with an American Express Card, my creditors know I can still pay *my* bills each month."

Amex had spent slightly over $20 million on Personal Card television advertising in 1985, and was planning to spend considerably more than that amount in 1986. Amex was currently running television campaigns featuring the long-lived "Do You Know Me?" theme, as well as the newer "Interesting Lives" theme, which emphasized the lifestyles of American Express cardholders. Print ads stressed vacation risks, buying power, and receipts. (See Exhibit 12.4 for examples of Personal Card print advertising.)

One example of an advertising campaign directed as much at SEs as at consumers was the retail group's print advertisements showing celebrities (such as Tom Seaver in "How do you buy a pitcher?") using the card for retail purchases. The dual aim of this campaign was to inform cardholders (present or potential) of the new uses of the card and to convince retail establishments that accepting the card would bring in additional sales.

Gold Card

Prior to 1966, the American Express Card had been positioned as a travel and entertainment card for consumers who did not need a line of credit. This positioning was not fully voluntary, since TRS did not have a domestic bank charter, and thus was prohibited from offering either intra- or interstate consumer credit. A loophole in the banking regulations was found, however, and Amex introduced the Gold® Card, initially restricted to high-income consumers (with household incomes greater than $35,000 per year) through agreements with local banks in each state. Because of the different agreements reached with each bank, however, the credit terms for individual customers varied considerably.

By 1985, there were 3.3 million Gold Cards outstanding. Advertising for the Gold Card was handled by a separate advertising agency (McCann-Erikson) in order to encourage its differentiation. The Gold Card was positioned as being slightly more upscale and prestigious than the Personal Card, with an annual membership fee of $65 (versus $45), as well as being more difficult to acquire. (American Express chose, however, not to be explicit about the requirements for obtaining a Gold Card.)

Advertising for the Gold Card was limited to upscale print media such as *Travel & Leisure*, *Time*, *The New Yorker*, *Golf Digest*, and *Food & Wine*. Advertising copy was

EXHIBIT 12.4
**American Express Card
Advertising**

intended to appeal to the ego of the reader: ''It merely reaffirms what you already know about yourself.'' The advertisements attempted to achieve a balance between accessibility and prestige. According to one marketing research manager at Amex, the trick was for Gold Card advertising to project exclusivity without discouraging prospective cardholders from applying for the card.

The average holder of a Personal or Gold Amex Card had a household income of approximately $35,000 and a 71 percent probability of being in a professional or managerial job. The Gold cardholder used his or her card six times more often than the average Personal cardholder, however, generating billings that were much higher than those of the average Personal cardholder.[5]

---

[5] A variant of the Gold Card was the Premier Services Program (or ''Black Card'') offered by the American Express International Banking Corporation (AEIBC) to foreign Gold cardholders. To qualify for the program, a person had to be a non-U.S. citizen,

EXHIBIT 12.4
(continued)

Platinum Card

The Platinum® Card was introduced in the summer of 1984 at an annual fee of $250. The goal was to sign up between 200,000 and 300,000 Platinum members by 1987. The extra services provided by the card included free 24-hour, worldwide travel service, $10,000 check-cashing privileges, $500,000 in travel insurance, and nonresident membership privileges at twenty-five private clubs in the United States and abroad. According

---

a Gold cardholder, and have a personal banking relationship with AEIBC valued at $500,000 or more. The Black Card enabled its estimated 1,000 holders to dial hotline numbers and request AEIBC to arrange a wide array of services—anything from renting a jet to buying the entire ''house'' at a concert or theater performance. All of these services were then charged to the individual's Gold Card account.

EXHIBIT 12.4
(continued)

to Lou Gerstner, Amex had developed the new card because the company's research showed that cardholders wanted the new services: "This card is designed for a group of people who have very real needs. What we've concluded is that the Platinum Card is an enormous value at its price."

The Platinum Card was marketed solely via direct mail (a high-quality, prestigious "invitation to join") to what would ultimately be 5 percent of Amex cardholders, selected on the basis of annual charge volume and payment records. The aim of the Platinum program was to address the "special" needs of those who qualified for the card. A typical Platinum cardholder would presumably not be interested in the cheapest room or flight, but would wish to be recognized by service establishments that might then tailor their services to his or her "special needs." By confining its marketing efforts to highly selective direct mail, Amex hoped to minimize damage to the prestige of its Personal and Gold Cards.

Corporate Card

Amex employed a special marketing package designed to make its Personal Card appealing to corporations. This "corporate card" service consolidated all business-required expenses onto one reporting format. Using TRS's travel resources, Amex also offered corporate Travel Management Services (TMS) that promised to rationalize and reduce corporate travel expenses. The Corporate® Card was offered alone or in conjunction with TMS. While supported by some advertising, it was marketed primarily through a direct sales force.

VISA INTERNATIONAL

Visa was the outgrowth of Bank of America's BankAmericard, which had been established in 1958. By 1986, Visa was the world's largest credit card issuer, with over 100 million cards in force. Visa International was a member-owned umbrella organization consisting of 15,000 members in 100 countries. This umbrella organization was owned by member banks, which exercised control through their seats on its board of directors. Each bank issued its own Visa cards and was responsible for soliciting customers and collecting fees and other payment revenue. Each bank was also free to compete to provide processing service to those SEs that agreed to accept the card. The fee for this service normally took the form of a discount from the face amount of the charge slip—usually 1–3 percent of the dollar value of the transaction.

The Visa umbrella organization was responsible for three key activities: (1) advertising the product to form a single worldwide image; (2) running and maintaining a credit authorization service, through which an SE could verify that a customer was using a valid card, regardless of which bank had issued the card to the customer (SEs were charged an average of $0.134 for each authorization request); and (3) operating an automated clearing service that provided settlement services between the SE's bank and the bank that had issued the customer's Visa card.

In 1981, Visa began to maintain selected cardholder information in its own computers and to authorize low-risk transactions without querying the cardholder's bank. "Low risk" was typically defined as a charge below the "floor limit" of $50. In 1982, Visa began distributing cardholder bulletins directly to merchants—circumventing the need for most on-line verifications. At the beginning of 1986, Visa started encoding additional information on each card's magnetic strip. If an SE was equipped with a compatible electronic terminal, many card transactions could now be authorized at the point-of-sale (POS).

With 86.4 million cards in the United States, Visa had more than five times as many domestic cards outstanding as Amex. Visa president Charles Russell pointed out, however, that "research showed that Visa was looked down upon compared with American Express; therefore we took the strategy of comparing Visa with the image leader." In early 1985, Visa unveiled a new $20 million advertising campaign directed at American Express. Using the tag line "It's Everywhere You Want to Be," the campaign featured three 30-second television commercials describing interesting merchants (or service establishments) where Visa was accepted, but American Express was not. The target market for the campaign was said to be households with more than $20,000 in income and cardholders aged twenty-five to fifty-four.

According to *Advertising Age*, the goal of this campaign was to emphasize merchant utility—the number of service establishments that accepted each card. Visa maintained a ten-to-one advantage over American Express in this regard. The campaign was also trying to change the perception of Visa as a "shoppers' card" by highlighting its travel and entertainment uses. In a related effort, Visa was said to be planning to launch a cooperative advertising program between Visa bank members and local service establishments.

In 1982, Visa had issued its Premium card, aimed at affluent households. According to *Marketing Communications*, the target market for the new card was adults aged twenty-five to fifty-four with an income of more than $25,000. The print advertisements were limited to upscale magazines such as *Ski*, *Newsweek*, *Time*, and *The New Yorker*. But with less than 2 million Premium cards outstanding, the product was not a major success. According to *The Nilson Reports* (a credit card industry newsletter), preferred cards such as Visa's Premium were not doing well because it was hard to sell the idea of another status card.

Increased competition between Visa member banks also affected Visa's marketing strategy. As large banks such as Citicorp expanded their Visa marketing efforts, other banks responded by increasing the size of their insignias while shrinking the Visa logo (a practice allowed by Visa International) and offering card enhancements that attempted to differentiate their products. These enhancements ranged from travel insurance to card registration programs. According to several recent consumer surveys, however, there was scant evidence that these actions had had much of an effect on consumer perceptions. To most consumers, a Visa card was a Visa card, regardless of what bank issued it.

MASTERCARD INTERNATIONAL

Although MasterCard has traditionally been viewed as Visa's primary competition in the credit card field, according to its president, Russell Hogg, the two organizations maintained a "friendly" rivalry since both were owned by many of the same banks.

Like Visa, the MasterCard organization wanted to facilitate the interchange of card privileges worldwide and to allow banks of any size to enter into a large-scale credit card program. In 1986, MasterCard had 27,000 financial institutions in 140 countries as members. As with Visa, banks in the MasterCard network owned their own cards, were permitted to emphasize their own logos and enhance their cards' functionality, and assumed all the credit risks. The MasterCard International organization was a nonprofit cooperative that provided national and international advertising, new-product development, and technological services to members.

In the early 1980s, after Russell Hogg became president, MasterCard moved quickly to improve the image of its card and to expand internationally. In 1981, MasterCard introduced its gold card product and also launched the "So Worldly, So Welcome" advertising campaign for its standard card. The goals of these two moves were to attract executive and professional users and to expand the association's retail merchant coverage. MasterCard's attempt to capture a piece of American Express's affluent customer base was considerably more aggressive than Visa's efforts to market a premium card. The MasterCard gold card was issued almost a full year before the Visa Premium card, with a target market of men over thirty-five whose net worth was between $100,000 and $150,000. The gold card advertisements echoed Amex Gold card advertising, utilizing muted colors and rich tones in scenes containing no people.

The recent introduction of Sears' Discover card had apparently forced MasterCard to rethink its approach to the market. In February 1986, it launched a new $30 million advertising campaign: "Master the Possibilities." According to *Advertising Age*, this campaign sought to position MasterCard against Amex and Visa, while protecting it from the challenge raised by Sears' new Discover card. Advertisements in the "Master the Possibilities" series emphasized the utility of MasterCard's 4.2 million service establishments, in comparison with the much lower number of SEs that honored the American Express and Discover cards.

The new campaign reflected MasterCard's contention that consumers were tired of status-oriented credit cards and now wanted real value and benefits from card ownership. The new advertisements addressed this issue with statements such as: "I choose it because

I use it'' and ''Don't talk to me about impressions. Give me possibilities.'' Forthcoming print advertisements would feature short essays by sociologists and futurists about consumers' heightened demand for real values—stressing that ''substance and freedom have replaced style and status.''

MasterCard Technological Strategy

A large part of MasterCard's strategy to offer ''real value'' to the cardholder was based on providing improved electronic systems. The goal of this information-processing emphasis was to reduce transaction time, lower processing cost, and improve the ability of SEs (especially those outside the United States) to access the network. In 1985, MasterCard opened a new communication network that enabled a foreign bank's telex terminal to verify international transactions by communicating directly with MasterCard computers. Previously, overseas banks that made authorization checks for local merchants had to call MasterCard and then wait while operators at MasterCard manually rekeyed the information into the computers. By increasing the speed of these transactions, MasterCard sought to make their card more convenient for both cardholders and merchants. The increased speed would also facilitate merchant authorizations on a wider range of transactions, hopefully reducing fraud losses from small-dollar-value transactions.

THE SEARS DISCOVER CARD

In January 1986, Sears, Roebuck and Company, the largest retailer in the United States, launched Discover, the first new general purpose credit card since the 1960s. During the previous five years, Sears had created the Sears Financial Network, which included Dean Witter Reynolds (a stock broker), Coldwell Banker (a national real estate agency), Sears Savings Bank, Allstate Insurance, and the Greenwood Trust company. Eventually, Discover was to be its cardholders' complete link for accessing this array of financial services. Initially, though, Discover was to establish itself by competing directly with existing card products and emphasizing its unique enhancements (a savings account and a 1 percent yearly rebate on purchases). Sears' strategy for Discover was to build on its existing cardholder base and its strong national brand loyalty. It planned to mail preapproved applications to 26 million U.S. households, primarily holders of its store card, and to support those mailings with a blitz of television, newspaper, and magazine advertisements. Industry observers estimated that Discover's rollout costs could be as high as $40 million, especially if the advertising intensity of its Atlanta test market (97 percent reach, 24 frequency over a three-month period) was retained for the national launch. Several analysts estimated that Sears' total cumulative investment in the new card could easily reach $200 million before it had any possibility of becoming profitable.

Sears planned to charge no fee for its Discover card, at least initially. (Bank cards charged an average fee of $19, while the fee for Amex's Green card was $45.) Discover would offer a bonus of $150 worth of discounts on Sears auto service, as well as discounts from major SEs that had agreed to accept the Discover card. Once a year, cardholders would receive rebates of up to 1 percent of their charge volume in cash, Sears merchandise, or credits against their balances.

Sears' introductory advertising campaign for Discover emphasized the low cost of using the new card. Typical advertising copy used themes such as: ''The card that saves you money every time you use it'' and ''Get the new credit card that pays you back every time you use it.'' According to an Ogilvy & Mather analysis (prepared for Amex), Discover was targeting the mass market of men and women between twenty-five and forty-nine, emphasizing that the card makes the ''good life'' more affordable and attainable. As the report concluded:

The broadscale commercials confirm the belief that Discover is targeting to a mass audience, with emphasis on the middle to lower-end segment. While the "good life" is familiar to American Express Cardmembers, they have either achieved it or are well on their way. As a result, we believe this advertising does not present a direct competitive threat to the Amex franchise.

Sears' strategy appeared to be to sign up a large quantity of SEs, including leading department and specialty stores, in order to enhance consumer perception of widespread acceptance and high utility. As an incentive to SEs, Sears was charging only a 1–1.25 percent discount, in contrast to the 2.5 percent average discount for bank cards and the 3.75 percent average discount for American Express. Nevertheless, some industry observers questioned whether Sears would be able to sign up enough SEs "soon enough," noting that Sears competed with virtually every major U.S. retailer. Even though Sears pledged to keep Discover billing information from its retail stores, many large retailers were reportedly worried that the information could be used against them. Neither large department store in the Atlanta test market, for example, had accepted the Discover card. Competitors had also questioned Sears' policy of offering Discover cardholders discounts on certain Sears services—a policy that appeared to be directly competitive with their own businesses.

CITICORP

Citicorp, a large, diversified financial services corporation, was seeking to expand aggressively from its strong base in commercial banking, and represented a major threat to Amex on a number of fronts. In early 1986, it offered seven credit cards: MasterCard and MasterCard gold; Visa and Premium Visa; Diners Club, Carte Blanche,[6] and Choice (see Exhibit 12.5). Citicorp was estimated to have spent between $150 million and $200 million to market its cards in 1985.

MasterCard/Visa

Citicorp had been one of the most aggressive marketers of cards bearing the MasterCard and Visa logos. The aggressiveness was seen not only in Citicorp's nationwide advertising ("It's the bank that makes them better") but also in the range of enhancements offered on Citicorp cards. The "CitiDollars" program, for example, offered 20 CitiDollars (redeemable for services or merchandise) for every $100 charged on the card. This program encouraged the cardholder to charge more purchases on the Citicorp card, and helped Citicorp differentiate its Mastercard and Visa products from those offered by competing banks.

The wide array of credit cards offered by Citicorp appeared to be part of a corporate strategy to establish a strong national presence for Citicorp's retail banking services. According to *Fortune*, Citicorp's plan was to place millions of cards bearing the Citicorp name in the hands of consumers throughout the United States, and then to cross-sell mortgages, student loans, and other financial services to their cardholders.

Diners Club

In 1981, Citicorp acquired the Diners Club card, a product that had been losing money since 1974. In 1983 and 1984, Citicorp spent over $70 million to relaunch the card.

---

[6] Citicorp marketing efforts in support of its weak Carte Blanche card were relatively quiescent in the mid-1980s, and thus will not be discussed in this case. According to industry observers, Citicorp seemed to be holding Carte Blanche in reserve, perhaps for use as a "fighting brand" if competition continued to intensify.

EXHIBIT 12.5
Citicorp Credit Cards

	1984–1985 ESTIMATES
Total domestic cards	9.7MM*
Visa/MasterCard	6.0MM[†]
Diners Club	2.2MM[†]
Carte Blanche	0.3MM[†]
Choice	1.2MM[‡]
Total worldwide cards	12.8MM*
Diners Club	5.0MM[‡]
Carte Blanche	0.5MM[§]
Merchant acceptance[‖]	
Diners Club	650,000[§]
Carte Blanche	500,000[§]
Choice	60,000[§]
Domestic charge volume	
Visa/MasterCard	$ 3.66B*
Diners Club	$ 4.76B[†]
Carte Blanche	$ 0.4 B[†]
Choice	$ 0.7 B[†]

* *The Nilson Reports*, March 1986.
[†] *Fortune*, February 4, 1985.
[‡] *Wall Street Journal*, July 4, 1985.
[§] *Consumer Reports*, January 1985.
[‖] Worldwide total.

According to Richard S. Braddock, president of Diners Club, the first goal of the card's marketing strategy was to ''unsell'' the American Express Card. By investing heavily in advertising and promotion, Diners Club was able to target the predominantly male businessperson who had been the focus of Amex's traditional marketing strategy.

The first marketing efforts utilized mailing lists purchased from major airlines' frequent flyer programs. These mailings opened with the statement: ''Frankly, Citicorp Diners Club wants your business and we're willing to work for it.'' The original offer to sign up cardholders included a credit toward the first $25 in charges, free Citicorp traveler's checks, and a round-trip ticket to anywhere in the United States for $175. These incentives appeared to be successful, at least initially, increasing Diners Club's base to almost 1.8 million cardholders by the end of 1984. By the third quarter of 1985, however, membership had risen to only approximately 2.2 million. In contrast, American Express gained approximately 1 million cardholders during that same period.

According to Braddock, the Diners Club problem was a classic chicken-and-egg dilemma. Consumers did not want the card until it was accepted by a wide array of service establishments, and the merchants were not interested in incurring the additional paperwork unless many of their customers carried the card. In May 1985, Diners Club refocused its positioning strategy, targeting executives and corporate card accounts heavily. The annual fee was raised from $45 to $55—squarely positioned between Amex's Personal and Gold Cards. The new services offered by the card included access to health clubs, office services, and other enhancements designed to appeal to the business traveler. Braddock stated that Diners Club was ''moving from a card business to a service business. We are forming a club for business travelers.'' Citicorp was reported to be planning a $35 million marketing effort in support of its newly repositioned Diners Club card.

EXHIBIT 12.6
Choice Card Test Market
Results

RANK	PRODUCT	CHARGE VOLUME (% SHARE)
1	Visa	28
2	Choice	25
3	MasterCard	23
4	Amex	16

1983 Major Retailers' Sales in DC-MD-VA Test Market

Source: Fortune, February 4, 1985, p. 22.

Choice

Citicorp was also test marketing a new credit card—Choice—in the Washington-Baltimore market and in Colorado. The Choice card featured free membership, a credit line, and a percentage rebate on charge purchases. Choice also offered Citibank savings and checking accounts, which customers could access through mail deposits and automated teller machine (ATM) cash withdrawals.

The Choice card had its origins in 1977 when Citicorp's retail banking unit purchased NAC—a Baltimore-area charge card. In 1980, Citicorp reintroduced the Choice card in two test markets. By 1983, Choice had captured 25 percent of the charge volume generated by major retailers in the Baltimore-Washington area (see Exhibit 12.6).

The key element in the Choice card's marketing strategy appeared to be establishing widespread SE acceptance for the card. Citicorp was able to do this by using its processing centers to offer SEs low discount rates. Using its Tri-Card Plan, Citicorp offered to process merchant slips for Visa, MasterCard, and Choice for 0.5 percent below the 3 percent area average, provided they agreed to accept the Choice card.

Given widespread acceptance in the local area, Choice was able to attract cardholders by offering a card with no annual fee. Purchase rebates provided an incentive for cardholders to use the card instead of whatever other cards they carried. By underpricing the competition at both the cardholder and the service establishment level, Citicorp was able to break out of the chicken-egg dilemma facing new credit cards. Nevertheless, Citicorp had not yet extended its Choice card beyond its original test market area. Industry observers noted that the Choice card had the potential to cannibalize Citicorp's existing Visa and MasterCard products, and that Citicorp would therefore need a high enough return on the deposits it gained through Choice to balance lost revenues from its MasterCard and Visa accounts.

TRS'S ENTRY INTO THE RETAIL MARKET

By the late 1970s TRS had experienced ten years of explosive growth (a 21 percent compound annual growth rate). The number of non-Amex customers who could pass the credit-worthiness test and were willing to pay the $15 enrollment charge was rapidly diminishing, however. In an effort to maintain its growth rate, TRS began to search for new ways to expand its business. One such way appeared to be adding SE industry segments beyond its traditional travel, lodging, and entertainment markets. The retail segment seemed to offer an excellent opportunity, but clearly would demand a somewhat different marketing strategy.

In 1980, TRS entered the retail market partly in response to requests from department and specialty stores (e.g., Tiffany's, the upscale New York–based jeweler). It sought to sign up retail SEs by using the argument that corporate executives away from home (the prime Amex Card segment) would be likely to do their shopping at retailers that accepted Amex Cards and that the Amex Card would thus generate incremental business. This strategy proved to be quite successful. By 1985, TRS had signed up 700,000 retail SEs, which generated $7.5 billion in Amex Card charges. A number of prestigious retailers with strong charge account programs (e.g., Bloomingdale's), which did not accept bank cards, agreed to at least test the American Express Card. With billings equal to a 3.25 percent share of total U.S. nonfood retail sales, TRS was now a major factor in the retail

EXHIBIT 12.7
Retailer Advertising

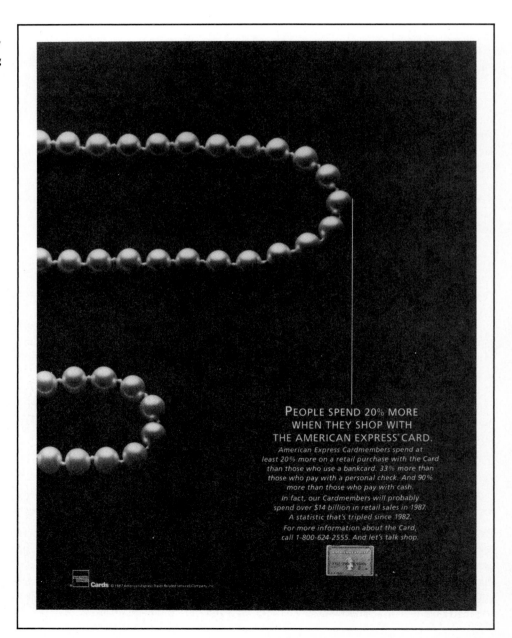

industry—in direct competition with MasterCard and Visa, as well as with the "house" cards still utilized by some retailers.

Nevertheless, the performance of the Amex Card in the retail segment was severely constrained by the unwillingness of many retail SEs to accept the card. As a "prestige" card, TRS charged the retail SE a higher discount than other cards. In 1985, it charged a maximum of 5 percent of the ticket purchase price, versus a maximum of 3 percent for competitors. (In 1984, the average fee charged by TRS to retail SEs had been 3.75 percent.) For a "rational" SE to accept the Amex Card under these conditions, it had to believe that Amex cardholders would spend more in their stores (cardholders had average household incomes of $35,000 and no preset spending limits); that traveling cardholders would bring "plus business" (e.g., large ticket purchases made on impulse when away from home); and/or that honoring the Amex Card would enhance a store's "prestige image," thus somehow leading to enough "plus" business to justify the higher credit card costs.[7]

As Amex faced increased competition, it began to reduce the discount charged to some of its more important customers. An example was the 3.25 percent discount rate offered to the Brown Group of shoe retailers. (See Exhibit 12.7 for an advertisement directed to retailers.)

The Amex SE marketing group continually monitored industry reports of retail SE sales volumes. An invitation to become an Amex Card franchisee was sent to a retailer when its reported sales reached a predetermined level, and the more attractive prospects were visited by the TRS direct sales force. While this sales volume threshold was different for each retail segment, a standardized selling approach (increased spending and plus business) was used for all potential retail accounts.

THE NONFOOD RETAIL INDUSTRY

In 1985, total U.S. nonfood[8] retail sales were divided among specialty stores ($233 billion), department stores ($185 billion), and mail order ($14 billion). Specialty stores included retailers of home furnishings, appliances, furniture, consumer electronics, apparel, and similar products. Department stores included conventional and discount department stores, the major general merchandise chains (Sears, Penney's, Ward's), and catalog showrooms. TRS's retail billings had increased by 13 percent per year between 1980 and 1985, while retail sales had grown by only about 8 percent annually during that period. Amex economists expected retail sales to grow at an 8.3 percent annual rate for the next five years, reaching $650 billion by 1990.

Retailers had recently observed increasing consumer demand for a broader range of merchandise and more product information. Specialty stores, which were, as a class, growing faster than the industry, had responded to this demand by increasing their sales staffs and becoming more focused on specific product/market segments. At the same time, traditional department stores had begun to restrict their product ranges to categories that they could "dominate" and to enhance their images through association with designer labels, exciting in-store merchandising ("retailing as theater"), and increasing use of expensive, high-quality catalogs mailed to their charge account customers. The growth of large discount stores specializing in particular product lines (e.g., off-price apparel

---

[7] One large retailer that had dropped the Amex card had done so following an internal study that showed very high usage of the Amex card among holders of the retailer's house card and relatively low usage among consumers residing in ZIP codes outside the retailer's market area.

[8] It was not customary for large supermarkets in most parts of the United States to accept credit cards as payment for merchandise, allegedly because of the low profit margins (typically less than 2 percent of sales) characteristic of this type of retailer. However, because of increasing pressure from food specialty stores, which generally did accept "plastic," and increasing consumer unwillingness to carry cash, as well as because of the high costs for check cashing, there had been a recent trend toward greater acceptance of credit cards by supermarkets.

stores, consumer electronics discount stores) and specialized superstores offering a broad range of low-price branded merchandise also reflected this trend. Competition in the industry had always been fierce and was expected to continue to put pressure on retail margins. Thus, TRS believed that some retail SEs (particularly those selling higher-priced products) would have to spend increasing amounts on promotion to maintain their existing traffic levels and build customer loyalty. In addition, deep discounting and frequent sales were likely to be required to meet competition and improve turnover.

At the industry level, TRS forecasters expected:

- Strong growth for limited-line, highly focused specialty stores, because of consumer demand for depth of merchandise selection.

- Above-average growth for superstores and off-price specialty stores, as consumers sought the lowest prices for branded merchandise.

- Above-average growth for major mall specialty stores, because of a loyal customer base, universal acceptance of credit cards, and less consumer importance placed on traditional department stores' service (e.g., house cards, delivery).

- Correspondingly slower growth for traditional department stores, discount stores, and "unfocused" specialty stores.

CONCLUSION

As Janet Frost considered the future for TRS in the retail segment, she had three recently completed studies to help her: (1) a survey that had been conducted by TRS at the National Retail Merchants Association (NRMA) annual convention; (2) a competitive analysis by external consultants; and (3) her own division's summary of the effects of changing some of the components of TRS's existing retail marketing strategy. Frost also wanted to make sure that her recommendations were consistent with Amex's overall corporate strategy. Lou Gerstner, the head of TRS since 1979, had, for example, emphasized in a recent speech to New York investment analysts:

> Amex does not see itself as a financial supermarket. Amex's strategy will be to position itself as the best-quality provider at the lowest cost in each of its preselected business lines.

The recent survey by TRS at the NRMA annual convention provided some indication of how retailers perceived the Amex Card. The objective of this research was to measure attitudes and levels of awareness of both Amex SEs and non-Amex SEs. A questionnaire was distributed requesting information on: the type and size of the SE respondent, the types of additional products and services that TRS might offer to SEs, the impact of various card products in generating "plus" or incremental business, and the levels of advertising awareness of various cards. Of the 153 survey respondents, 53 percent were affiliated with either department, specialty, or electronics stores. The fact that 82 percent of the respondents claimed that they accepted the Amex card, while the corresponding figures for Visa and MasterCard were 64 percent and 59 percent, respectively, suggested that there might have been a systematic bias of some sort in the sample.

Nevertheless, the survey found that among the various value-added products and service offerings listed on the questionnaire, marketing information (mentioned by 36 percent of all respondents) and cardholder transaction analysis reports (mentioned by 32 percent) were most popular. About 54 percent of the respondents believed that Amex generated "plus" business, as compared to 49 percent and 48 percent for Visa and MasterCard, respectively. In the area of advertising awareness, 69 percent had seen American Express advertisements relating to the retail industry, versus 60 percent and 55 percent for Visa and MasterCard. The concept of joint advertising (between Amex and retail SEs) was very enthusiastically received. Direct-mail joint marketing efforts were most highly favored (51 percent), followed by newspaper (45 percent) and television (44 percent) co-op advertising.

To help Amex better understand its competitive position, external consultants had developed perceptual maps of Amex and other cards' current and future positions along two dimensions for both SEs and consumers. The dimensions chosen for the SE map were ''value'' and ''price.'' ''Value'' was the weighted score of payment method attributes,

EXHIBIT 12.8
SE Map, 1985–1990

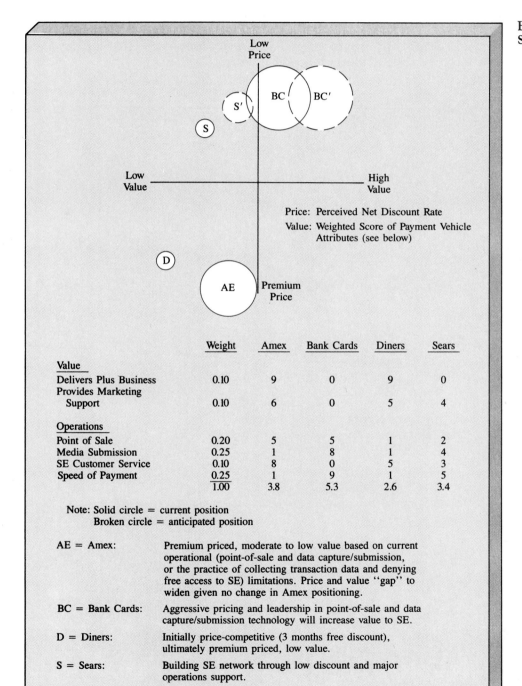

	Weight	Amex	Bank Cards	Diners	Sears
Value					
Delivers Plus Business	0.10	9	0	9	0
Provides Marketing Support	0.10	6	0	5	4
Operations					
Point of Sale	0.20	5	5	1	2
Media Submission	0.25	1	8	1	4
SE Customer Service	0.10	8	0	5	3
Speed of Payment	0.25	1	9	1	5
	1.00	3.8	5.3	2.6	3.4

Note: Solid circle = current position
Broken circle = anticipated position

AE = Amex: Premium priced, moderate to low value based on current operational (point-of-sale and data capture/submission, or the practice of collecting transaction data and denying free access to SE) limitations. Price and value ''gap'' to widen given no change in Amex positioning.

BC = Bank Cards: Aggressive pricing and leadership in point-of-sale and data capture/submission technology will increase value to SE.

D = Diners: Initially price-competitive (3 months free discount), ultimately premium priced, low value.

S = Sears: Building SE network through low discount and major operations support.

while "price" reflected the perceived net discount rate. The dimensions chosen for the consumer map were "utility" and "service." "Utility" was a measure of the extent of retail card utility (number of outlets), and "service" the extent of services offered. (See Exhibits 12.8 and 12.9 for the two maps.)

TRS's Business Development Organization had recently completed an analysis of competition in the credit card market. This study had concluded that bank cards were in a strong position to take share from Amex since they offered lower discount rates, faster payment, electronic processing, and a large and growing cardholder base. Sears was trying to gain entry into the overall SE market by extensive advertising, low/flexible pricing, and SE operational support. With a more focused strategy, Diners Club was attempting to develop a presence in department stores and upscale retail shops. CitiCorp, with its various card products, seemed to be seeking a dominant share in all aspects of the increasingly deregulated financial services industry.

EXHIBIT 12.9
Consumer Map,
1985–1990

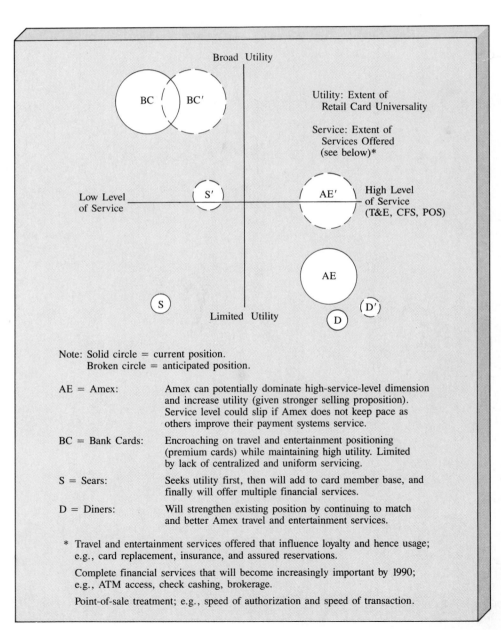

Note: Solid circle = current position.
Broken circle = anticipated position.

AE = Amex:	Amex can potentially dominate high-service-level dimension and increase utility (given stronger selling proposition). Service level could slip if Amex does not keep pace as others improve their payment systems service.
BC = Bank Cards:	Encroaching on travel and entertainment positioning (premium cards) while maintaining high utility. Limited by lack of centralized and uniform servicing.
S = Sears:	Seeks utility first, then will add to card member base, and finally will offer multiple financial services.
D = Diners:	Will strengthen existing position by continuing to match and better Amex travel and entertainment services.

* Travel and entertainment services offered that influence loyalty and hence usage; e.g., card replacement, insurance, and assured reservations.

Complete financial services that will become increasingly important by 1990; e.g., ATM access, check cashing, brokerage.

Point-of-sale treatment; e.g., speed of authorization and speed of transaction.

TRS's retail division had recently estimated the effects on TRS's position in the retail market of changing some of the components of the existing Amex Card strategy. This study was prompted by recent SE cancellations of the Amex franchise. Among the key options considered were:

1. The curtailment of country club billing (i.e., discontinuing the return of cardholder sales slips), which would immediately decrease Amex and SE operational costs. Returned sales slips (a unique Amex feature) were useful for checking billed items, however, and were believed to differentiate the Amex card from its competitors.

2. Lowering the discount rate charged to retail SEs, which would almost certainly lead to wider SE acceptance of the Amex Card. However, offering lower discount rates to retail SEs, but not to travel and entertainment SEs, might lead to considerable ill-will.

3. The introduction of a line of credit appeared to be an attractive option for Amex, as it would provide a third source of income (interest charged on the outstanding card balance), which could either be retained or used to reduce the fees charged to SEs. Taking this course might reduce the prestige image of the Amex Card, however, and increase credit losses.

4. Establishing a new card (dubbed by its proponents the Blue card) that offered a lower SE discount rate and a line of credit, but did not return sales slips. This option would largely avoid the issues associated with changing the image of the existing cards. The major drawbacks of this proposal appeared to be increased operational costs and potential confusion for SEs, who would have to separate new card transactions from existing Amex Card operations.

5. The final option was to make a major investment in a long-term program to provide all Amex retail SEs with point-of-sale equipment that would interface with a new Amex electronic funds transfer (EFT) system. While this proposal was still in the embryonic stage, a number of TRS executives felt it would be unwise to embark on a new retail strategy until further work on the EFT project had been completed.

QUESTIONS FOR DISCUSSION

1. How is the market for credit cards segmented? What are the primary needs of each consumer segment? Of each service establishment (SE) segment?

2. How is the American Express Card positioned in this market? What are American Express's major strengths and weaknesses in this market?

3. More broadly, where do credit cards fit into the overall financial services industry and market? What are American Express's major strengths and weaknesses in financial services?

4. As Janet Frost, what recommendations would you make re the American Express Card?

5. As a senior member of American Express corporate management, what would be your response to these recommendations? What changes, if any, would you make in American Express's Card strategy?

12A

CREDIT AND CHARGE CARD COMPETITIVE PROFILE (1984)

	AMERICAN EXPRESS	DINERS CLUB	PREMIUM BANK CARDS	BANK CARDS	CHOICE	DISCOVER
Cards include:	Personal, Gold, Platinum, & Corporate	Personal and Corporate	Preferred, Premium, Classic, & Gold M/C, Visa	Visa and Mastercard	Choice	Discover
Issuer:	American Express	Citicorp	Member banks (250)	Member banks (15,750)	Citicorp-owned banks in 3 test markets	Sears
Geographic availability:	Worldwide	Worldwide	Worldwide	Worldwide	Baltimore/Washington & Denver markets (tests before national expansion)	Currently in Atlanta & San Diego test markets
Annual fee:	$45, $65, $250	$55	$20–$50	No fee–$30	No fee	No fee (for 1–2 yrs.)
Finance charge:	None (except for special arrangements)	None (except for special arrangements)	18–19.8% (on unpaid balance after 30 days)	13–19.0% (on unpaid balance after 30 days)	21% (from date of purchase)	19.8% (on unpaid balance after 30 days)
Payment of charges:	Monthly in full, some exceptions	Monthly in full, some exceptions	Monthly payments or up to full balance	Monthly payments or up to full balance	Monthly payments or up to full balance	Monthly payments or up to full balance
Credit line:	Personal—none; Gold & Platinum as determined by issuing banks ($2,000 or more)	Club plus Account ($200–$25,000) line of credit for purchases of $100 or more	$3,000–$25,000	$500–$5,000	$750 & up	$500 & up
Statement form:	Signed receipts & computer summary of activity	Signed receipts & computer summary of activity	Computer summary of activity	Computer summary of activity	Computer summary of activity	Computer summary of activity
Number of card members:	16.42 million U.S.; 22 million world	2.2 million U.S.; 4.975 million world	2 million worldwide	225 million worldwide	1 million	N/A
Number of SEs worldwide:	516,726 U.S.; 1.2 million world	275,000 U.S.; 650,000 world	4 million	4 million	60,000	N/A
Discount rate:	2.4–7%	3–4%	2.5 avg. (1–5%)	2.5% avg. (1–5%)	2% avg. (1.9–2.5%)	1.89% avg. (1–4%)
Payment time to SEs:	1–30 days	1–20 days	Overnight	Overnight	Overnight	3–10 days (plan to change to overnight in early 1986)
Supplementary cards & charges:	$20–$30/card	$20/card	Free (max. 9)	$15 or N/A	N/A	N/A

	AMERICAN EXPRESS	DINERS CLUB	PREMIUM BANK CARDS	BANK CARDS	CHOICE	DISCOVER
Access to cash through checks and ATMs:	At Amex travel stores through airport dispensers & hotel/banks ($1,000 limit Personal Card, $5,000/ Gold); 5,275 in U.S., 1,414 abroad	Cash to $1,000 at designated Citibank branches & foreign offices; up to $250/stay in participating hotels/motels	Cash to $3,000 at bank & correspondent & through ATMs associated with issuing bank (charge of up to $5 for cash advances & interest charges begin at withdrawal)	Cash to credit limit or $3,000 (whichever is lower) at participating banks & ATMs (charge of up to $5 for cash advances & interest charges)	Cash to $150 monthly at Choice Financial ATMs (5) in Balt./Wash. or at Mini-bank Network (200) in Colorado	Cash to $250 monthly at Sears Financial Network Centers & participating ATM networks (currently Mellon Bank & First Bank Atlanta; 8,500 outlets)
Savings privileges:	None	None	Yes (5.5% to money market rates, depending on deposit size)	Yes (5.5% to money market rates, depending on deposit size)	Money Builder Account (9%) with matching deposits from Citibank if predetermined objective is met; Choice Res. (CDs at Citicorp Maryland— $1,000 minimum)	Family Saving Accounts at Greenwood Savings of Delaware; money market rates for total family balance of $1,000– $4,999; money market plus 1% on total family balances over $5,000
Travel-related services:	$100,00 travel insurance; baggage insurance; confirmed hotel reservations; Travelers Cheques; $500,000 insurance plus other benefits for Platinum Card	$150,000 travel insurance; no fee on Citicorp traveler's checks; confirmed hotel reservations	$100,000– $250,000 travel insurance; confirmed hotel reservations; some offer free traveler's checks	No travel insurance or up to $100,000; some offer confirmed hotel reservations; some offer free or reduced rate on traveler's checks	None	$100,000 travel insurance; 6-month membership in Allstate Motor Club; confirmed hotel reservations
Joint promotion discounts:	With numerous SE's	None on regular basis	None on regular basis	None on regular basis	None on regular basis	With American Airlines, Budget, Denny's, HCA Holiday Inn
Special benefits, incentives:	Gold & Platinum Card clubs for travel; numerous special offers on air, hotel, etc., purchases on Cards.	Club service and membership (at fee) for suites, chauffeurs, gifts, workout centers, business offices; Club Awards (point program for merchandise and travel)	May offer points for purchases toward merchandise (e.g., CitiDollars program for Citibank Preferred Visa); many also offer cash rebates on certain types of purchases for limited time (e.g., Chase MasterCard)	None	0.5% cash rebate on total purchases over $600 during 12-month periods	Bonus points equal to 1% of annual purchases applied to credit, savings, or merchandise for cardholders who charge $3,000 or more

Source: American Express Company.

239

13
GENERAL MOTORS CORPORATION
Buick Reatta

Developed in collaboration with Cheena Srinivasan[1]

In late August 1987, John Dabels, general director of divisional marketing at the Buick division of General Motors Corporation (GM), was seeking to formulate a comprehensive marketing strategy for the Buick Reatta, a two-seater luxury personal automobile scheduled for introduction the following year. Since the Reatta had first been conceived in 1981, both the U.S. automobile market and the U.S. automobile industry had undergone profound changes. During the last several years, GM had been significantly restructured, and had embarked on a new strategy, which, among other things, called for each of the company's five automobile divisions to target specific demographic and psychographic segments with distinctive products. Dabels was now faced with the task of developing a marketing strategy for what was intended to be Buick's line leader—the Reatta. This strategy would be expected to ensure the success of the new model, while simultaneously reinforcing the division's overall marketing and positioning strategies.

In carrying out his task, Dabels had commissioned what was possibly the most extensive state-of-the-art marketing research in the history of the automobile industry. As a matter of managerial philosophy, Dabels, who had been a Sloan Fellow at MIT in 1979, believed that the utilization of modern marketing tools could make a major contribution toward achieving the full potentials of GM and Buick once again. While he firmly believed that "research [was] no substitute for managerial experience and judgment," he felt strongly that the data gathered would provide a solid foundation for the development of an effective Reatta launch strategy.

BACKGROUND

Buick was one of five General Motors automobile divisions (the others were Cadillac, Oldsmobile, Pontiac, and Chevrolet). According to Alfred Sloan's legendary strategy, General Motors was to produce "a car for every purse and purpose." Each car division

[1] This case was prepared in collaboration with Cheena Srinivasan, research assistant, Sloan School of Management, Massachusetts

was to target a particular segment of the market and to operate as autonomously as possible, including having its own dealer organization and advertising agency. While some direct competition among the divisions was considered desirable, it was generally understood that Cadillac would be the company's true luxury marque, that Buick and Oldsmobile would target the middle market, that Chevrolet would stress utilitarian value, and that Pontiac would cover the gap between the mid-market divisions and Chevrolet.

Buick was one of GM's most successful units, with a wide product line, a strong dealer organization, and a large base of loyal consumers. While suffering along with the rest of the U.S. auto industry from the oil crisis, changing consumer preferences, and the onslaught of imports during the 1970s and 1980s, Buick had weathered these storms better than most, achieving record sales of almost 1 million cars and market shares exceeding 9 percent in the mid-1980s.

For the most part, Buick was perceived as a car for the middle- to upper-middle-class family. During the 1950s, for example, with its distinctive ''portholes'' styling, it had been popular among doctors (especially for house calls). Later it came to be viewed as an ''appropriate'' company car. Buick was widely known for its soft ride and creature comforts (e.g., plush velour seats), although its Buick Grand National, a modified version of the Regal coupe, had won the Manufacturers' Trophy in the 1982 NASCAR Winston Cup Grand National Series, and was said to have the fastest 0–60 mph time of any American-production car. The average Buick purchaser in 1986 was 50.1 years old, well above the industry average. According to industry research, the division was relatively weak among women and ''yuppie'' car buyers, and seemed to lack a distinct image even among its own customers.

Over the years, Buick (like other GM divisions) had gradually widened its product line in order to appeal to an increasingly broad spectrum of buyers (see Exhibit 13.1). A major reason for this product strategy was the desire of each division's dealer organization to serve the full needs of the families with which it dealt and to retain its customers through their life cycles. The result of this product strategy was considerable overlap between Buick and other General Motors divisions. This blurring of divisional boundaries had been exacerbated by GM's ''common platform'' strategy, in which comparable models from several divisions shared chassis, drive trains, and even styling. In the mid-1980s, a popular competitive advertising campaign featured buyers of high-end General Motors products mistaking lower-priced nameplates for their cars.

In 1985, General Motors had been restructured into two automobile groups: Buick-Oldsmobile-Cadillac (B-O-C) and Chevrolet-Pontiac-Canada (C-P-C). While the details had not yet been worked out, it was intended that B-O-C focus on larger, more expensive cars, and C-P-C on smaller and/or more utilitarian vehicles. Each group was to seek synergies wherever possible and minimize internal competition. Nevertheless, all five nameplates were to be retained, at least for the foreseeable future. Each division was to market through its own dealer organization and to carve out as distinct a market niche for itself as practicable. Within Buick, there was considerable disagreement between managers who wished to accentuate Buick's traditional middle-market positioning and those who felt that the division should strive for a sportier image in order to attract younger buyers. For 1988, the division's advertising copy theme was to be: ''The Great American Road belongs to Buick'' (see Exhibit 13.2).

Buick's strategy group had first put forward the idea of a two-passenger car in 1981. It had noted the growing number of one- and two-person households, the success of the Mercedes SL series, and the potential image value of a car of this type. GM Advance Design Studio had made a scaled replica of the original ''theme model'' in July 1982. The car went through a series of changes, but retained much of the original design until the final concept car, a fiberglass model, was completed in January 1983.

Institute of Technology (1987–88). All data in this case that are not publicly available (e.g., syndicated research material, marketing research data) have been disguised. Similarly, certain aspects of Buick Motor Company's decision process have been simplified.

Later in 1983, the two-seater was named Reatta (derived from the Spanish-American word for lariat). Detailed design and engineering for the new car, carried out in England, were based in part on a series of marketing research studies conducted by Buick during the previous two years.

Between 1984 and 1987, Buick conducted eight different studies to help identify the most effective position for Reatta in the highly competitive U.S. car market. Dabels suspected that the Reatta would compete most closely with Nissan's revised 300ZX, the Toyota Supra, and, above all, the Chrysler TC by Maserati, which was expected to debut a few months after the Reatta's planned introduction in January 1988. In Dabels's view, beating the TC to the market would be a real advantage in that it would permit Buick to define the "turf" on which Reatta would compete. In his opinion, Reatta's success would depend primarily on the effectiveness of its introduction strategy, especially with regard to target market selection and positioning. For this reason, he commissioned two inde-

EXHIBIT 13.1
Buick Models Offered
During the 1987 Model
Year

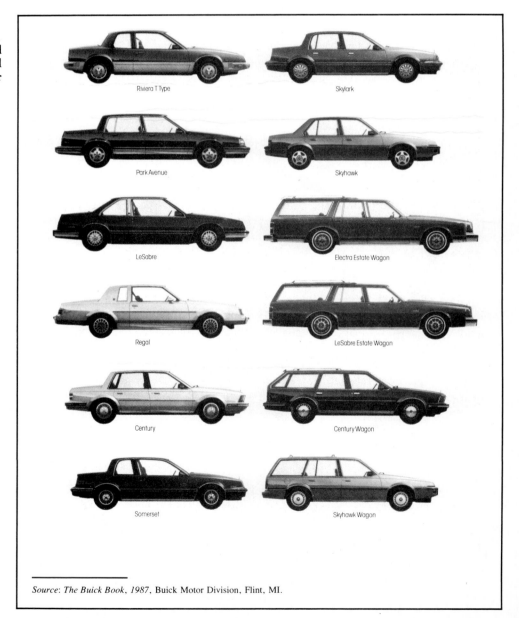

Source: The Buick Book, 1987, Buick Motor Division, Flint, MI.

pendent marketing research suppliers, Calle and Company and Information Resources Inc. (IRI), both known for their innovative approaches to marketing research, to help develop this strategy.

The two firms employed radically different research approaches and methodologies. Calle and Company, a boutique advertising agency located in Stamford, Connecticut, claimed that its methodology was unique in that it utilized ''creative stimuli that 'triggered' personally appealing qualities of the different cultural groups [target market segments].'' Though its research was highly qualitative, Calle claimed that its methodology was far more projectable than other qualitative techniques (e.g., focus groups). IRI, conversely, employed a combination of qualitative and quantitative techniques to compare ''clinic'' reactions of ''target buyers'' to the Reatta and two ''control'' vehicles (the Buick Riviera and Nissan 300ZX) whose sales histories were known.

Dabels received reports from both Calle and IRI in August 1987. The two studies,

EXHIBIT 13.2
Proposed 1988 Model Year Advertising Theme

perhaps because of their differing methodologies, had come up with totally conflicting recommendations concerning the optimal target segments and market positioning for the Reatta. Calle recommended that the Reatta be positioned as a "luxury car," primarily for professional women over thirty and men and women fifty and older. IRI, conversely, had concluded that the Reatta should be positioned as "a sports car having luxury and comfort," and that no significant differences in purchase probability across demographic groups could be inferred from its research.[2]

THE REATTA

The Reatta was Buick's proposed two-passenger, luxury sports car, based on the Buick Riviera platform, instrument panel, and 3.8-liter V-6 front-wheel-drive powertrain (see Exhibits 13.3 and 13.4). The base price for the hardtop model was expected to be approximately $25,000, and for the convertible around $30,000. Buick planned to launch the coupe version first and introduce the convertible a year later. It was not intended to be a performance car (although an advanced twenty-four-valve V-6 was targeted for as early as the 1989 model year), but was considered to belong to a new, still-undefined subspecies of "personal, luxury, prestige cars."

The Reatta was a radically styled front-wheel-drive car, an unusual configuration for the two-seater and performance car markets. In Dabels's view, it was most appropriate to view Reatta as "a new concept for Buick . . . a new product line, . . . an opportunity to establish a foothold in a future, new market."

The two-seat car market was dominated by upscale European touring cars such as the Mercedes SL series and the Jaguar XJ-S, and by "sports cars" such as the Porsche 944, 928, 924, and 911, the Alfa Romeo Spyder, the Toyota MR-2, the Nissan Z series, and the Mazda RX-7. Very sporty four-seaters, such as the Toyota Supra, Saab 900 Turbos, and Jaguar XJ-6, also appeared to compete in this market. As the "baby-boomer" population moved into their thirties, two-seaters seemed to be becoming increasingly popular, with strong market prospects for the next decade.

A part of Buick's concept for Reatta had been to make it "as European as possible." For this purpose, several well-known British-based engineering and tooling firms (e.g., Aston-Martin-Tickford) had collaborated with Buick-Cadillac-Oldsmobile designers and engineers in the development of the Reatta.

Reatta's design was quite different from those of other top-of-the-line two-seaters. As Dabels explained:

> Reatta is the only two-passenger car with adequate room. Mazda RX-7, Nissan's two-seaters, and Toyota's MR-2 are fairly cramped. What room they do have is a function of the seat configuration that slopes down and becomes uncomfortable over long distances. They are really *performance cars*, where there is a closed interaction between the driver and the car. Reatta is a two-passenger *luxurious sports* car that is truly comfortable to drive. Reatta's bench height has the feel of a regular car, and is comfortable for long trips. Another big advantage is that it has adequate luggage capacity. . . .

In designing the Reatta, Buick tried to achieve an appropriate balance between form and function. From a functional point of view, it was to be "a decent-sized, two-seat luxury car with adequate trunk room." In appearance, it was to be a "sleek, very distinctive car," which, seen from a hundred yards away, would cause the observer to say, "That is exciting—different from other two-seaters I have seen."

---

[2] IRI did suggest, however, that "directionally" Reatta seemed to appeal most to younger people with incomes below $75,000.

EXHIBIT 13.3
1988 Buick Reatta

Inner beauty.

eneath its eye-catching outer cover, Reatta has a very impressive Table of Contents. Reatta is powered by a transverse-mounted premium 3800 V6 engine with sequential-port fuel injection and balance shaft. One of the most highly advanced V6 powerplants in the world, the 3800 delivers 165 amazingly smooth, amazingly quiet horsepower. And it is coupled to a 4-speed automatic transmission with overdrive. The entire drivetrain is sparked by a virtually maintenance-free electronic ignition system.

Reatta rides and handles beautifully with a 4-wheel independent suspension system and 4-wheel power disc brakes. Its capabilities are further enhanced by computer-controlled anti-lock brakes, for controlled response on any surface, wet or dry.

Even the dual-outlet exhaust system is crafted of stainless steel, for a long and quiet life.

Reatta is designed to look at, then to look at again — very, very closely. It is an automobile of uncommon sense.

Owing to budget constraints for new-product development imposed on the division by "GM Corporate," Buick had to construct the Reatta on an existing platform. Reatta was to be built on the Riviera platform, with the same dashboard and electronic Graphic Control Center. The Riviera had experienced a major market failure after being down-sized in 1986, a cause of concern among Dabels and his colleagues.

The Reatta would be manufactured at Buick's Lansing, Michigan, plant. This plant, which had once been part of the Oldsmobile manufacturing complex, had been named the Reatta Craft Center following extensive renovations. According to J. Robert Thompson, Reatta program manager, "Since Reatta is to be a low-volume car, it will be assembled under a craft-station concept." That meant the car would be stopped on the assembly line in front of a team of workers, permitting them to pace the building of the vehicle (the usual procedure was to let the moving assembly line determine the pace). Another innovation was the planned sourcing of approximately 80 percent of Reatta parts and components with just eight suppliers, in an effort to achieve close partnerships between the components suppliers and the Reatta Craft Center.

EXHIBIT 13.4
Specification Sheet for
Buick Reatta

General	—Front-engined, front-wheel-drive coupe —2-passenger, 2-door steel and plastic body —Base price (estimated): $25,000
Engine	—OHV V-6, iron block and heads —Bore × Stroke = 3.80 × 3.40 in. (96.5 × 86.4 mm) —Displacement: 231 cu in. (3781 cc) —Compression Ratio: 8.5:1 —Fuel System: Sequential injection —Power SAE: net 165 bhp @ 4800 rpm —Torque SAE: net 210 lb-ft @ 2000 rpm
Drivetrain	—4-speed automatic transmission —Gear ratios: (I) 2.92; (II) 1.57; (III) 1.00; (IV) 0.70 —Final-drive ratio: 2.97:1
Measurements	—Wheelbase: 98.5 in. —Length: 182.8 in.; Width: 72.9 in.; Height: 51.2 in. —Curb weight: 3850 lb —Weight distribution: Front/Rear = 67/33% —Fuel Capacity: 18.2 gal.
Suspension	—Independent front Macpherson struts, coil springs, 1.22-in. anti-roll bar —Independent rear H-arm, plastic-transverse leafspring, 0.63-in. anti-roll bar
Steering	—Rack-and-pinion, power-assisted
Brakes	—10.4-in. vented discs front —10.2-in. discs rear —Anti-lock system
Wheels and Tires	—15 × 6-in. cast-aluminum wheels —P215/65R15 Goodyear GT + 4 tires
Performance	—0–60 mph in 9.75 seconds —Standing ¼-mile in 17.6 sec @ 78.8 mph —Top speed: 125 mph —EPA city driving: 19 mpg

Buick had established five major strategic objectives for the Reatta:

1. Increase consumer awareness of all Buick car lines.
2. Position Buick as a highly innovative company, especially in comparison to its current image.
3. Build floor traffic at dealers. Thus, wherever possible, the Reatta would be displayed in showroom windows to draw customers.
4. Increase Buick's sales by adding a complementary car line.
5. Obtain a high return on investment (ROI) on the Reatta.

According to Dabels, the Reatta represented a product-differentiation strategy, moving Buick away from traditional family cars toward more sporty, luxury cars. Nevertheless, in his view, the Reatta was "certainly not inconsistent with Buick's heritage as a manufacturer of mid-price and upscale luxury cars." It was intended to help Buick reposition itself in an increasingly competitive auto industry, not to make a major contribution to Buick's profits or market share. The idea was to produce an "image builder" that would, in effect, cause the market to say, "Buick is a company with great products. It introduced the Reatta right, using savvy marketing strategy. I'd like to have one of those. Yeah, Buick is doing OK these days."

KEY MARKETING ISSUES AND DECISIONS FOR THE REATTA

The major marketing elements in Buick's new-product development process were divided into four stages, the first of which was called the Technology Development phase. During this stage, the Buick marketing department:

1. Conducted strategic analysis of customer research data.
2. Analyzed competitive products.
3. Forecast sales.
4. Developed marketing specifications based on specific customer research data.

In the second stage, Vehicle Definition and Development, the marketing staff used marketing research to fine-tune the new product to its intended target customer segment and projected production volumes based on marketing research. The third stage, Design Validation: Product and Process, focusd on the development of advertising and promotional campaigns. In the fourth stage, Vehicle Production, the marketing staff helped develop merchandising programs and solicited customer feedback to be used in refining the new product further for the following model year.

Under this newly implemented process, engineering, marketing, manufacturing, finance, quality control, the strategic planning staff, and outside suppliers were to work together as a team from the outset of each new-product program. Early indications suggested that this team approach was likely to improve product reliability and customer satisfaction.

MARKETING RESEARCH

Because the Reatta represented a significant departure from Buick's traditional product/market strategy, Dabels thought it critical to define its target market segments as precisely and fully as possible. In his view, a sound definition and description of the target market would support virtually all aspects of marketing strategy formulation and provide a sound basis for long-range planning and future product enhancement.

Between July 1981 and June 1987, Buick had conducted, through various independent marketing research firms, seventeen major marketing research studies for the Reatta. The location, methodology, and purpose of each of these studies can be summarized as follows:

Buick Reatta Marketing Research History*

	DATE	DESCRIPTION OF THE STUDY
1.	1976–1979	*Buick "L" Car Analysis*: Demonstrated market potential for a new two-seat vehicle for Buick. (Conducted by Buick.)
2.	1980	*Auto Usage Trip Diaries*: Nationwide data were collected to determine: (1) who the present and future likely owners of two-seaters are; and (2) how they would use such autos. (Conducted by Transportation/ Traffic Science Department.)
3.	1981	*Study of Two-Passenger Limited-Usage Cars*: Covered issues like image, shape, body material, cargo space, manufacturer preference. (Conducted by Corporate Marketing Staff.)
4.	1981	*"Estimating the Potential Usage for Two-Passenger Automobiles"*: Identified the characteristics of the U.S. household that could substitute a two-passenger auto for one of their existing autos without changing their current travel patterns. (Conducted by GM Research Labs.)
5.	1981	*Two-Place "E" Focus Group*: Thirteen focus groups were held in Chicago and Los Angeles to learn how different owner groups would react to the Buick two-place concept. Dealer input was also gathered. (Conducted by Buick.)
6.	1981	*Two-Place Focus Group*: Four focus groups were held in Sacramento, with the same objectives as Study No. 5. (Conducted by Corporate Clinic.)
7.	1982	*Two-Place Concept Telephone Survey*: National survey to quantify the Buick two-place concept. Issues included target market, pricing, styling, and theme. (Conducted by Buick.)
8.	1982	*Two-Place Definition Telephone Survey*: Fifteen hundred interviews dealing with product definition and Buick-Cadillac interaction† were done nationwide. (Conducted by Buick.)
9.	1982	*Two-Passenger Vehicle Concept Study*: Involved eleven focus groups in Houston. The issues covered were: distinguishing the Buick luxury two-place car from the Corvette, and designing an ideal luxury two-place vehicle. This was the rudimentary framework for Cadillac-Buick differentiation. (Conducted by Buick.)
10.	1983	*Chicago Auto Show Two-Seater Research*: Buick Questor, Chrysler two-seater, and Datsun 280ZX were evaluated on several attributes. (Conducted by Corporate Marketing Staff/Buick.)
11.	1984	*GM33 Prototype Clinics*: Clinics were held in Chicago and Los Angeles to determine purchase interest, image, standard and optional equipment, content, price sensitivity, roof design, nameplate, and name. (Conducted by Buick.)
12.	1986	*Houston Reunion Focus Groups*: Houston participants involved with the Reatta at the concept stage were asked to reevaluate the actual Reatta to determine how well Buick did in translating their ideas into a car. (Conducted by Buick.)
13.	1986	*Houston Clinic*: The clinic focused on the Reatta, as well as on Buick products in general. Obtained consumer input on Reatta features (e.g., roof design, exterior colors, carpeting, door panel, interior trim, and wheels). (Conducted by Buick.)

DATE	DESCRIPTION OF THE STUDY
14. 1986	*Cleveland Clinic:* ''Strategic Planning in the 1990s'' showroom clinic reviewed image, acceptors and rejectors, interior and exterior car evaluations, cross-consideration, and psychographics, as well as defining a Reatta convertible. (Conducted by Buick.)
15. 1986	*One-Car Positioning Clinic:* Consumers in Cleveland, sitting in a classroom environment, were asked to evaluate their one-make car preference, purchase likelihood for various manufacturers, their most important car attributes, and image for selected competitive vehicles, as well as for the Reatta. This research was intended to help Buick's advertising agency focus on the most critical image issues. (Conducted by Buick/McCann-Erickson.)
16. 1987	*Regional Image:* Consumers in eight cities (Chicago, Boston, St. Louis, Denver, Baltimore, Cincinnati, Tampa, and Los Angeles) were exposed to all Buick products (including the Reatta) via videotape to determine if the image, strengths, weaknesses, purchase consideration, and vehicle fit with Buick's image, demographics, and product appeal across Buick sales areas. (Conducted by Buick.)
17. 1987	*Cincinnati Focus Groups:* Buick's advertising agency tested potential Reatta concepts with consumers to determine the most viable positioning and wording. This creative exercise was done prior to the actual ad development. (Conducted by McCann Erickson/Buick.)

* Excluding the two most recent studies conducted by Calle and Company and Information Resources Inc.
† Cadillac was scheduled to introduce a luxury 2-seater ($50,000–$60,000) in the mid-1980s.

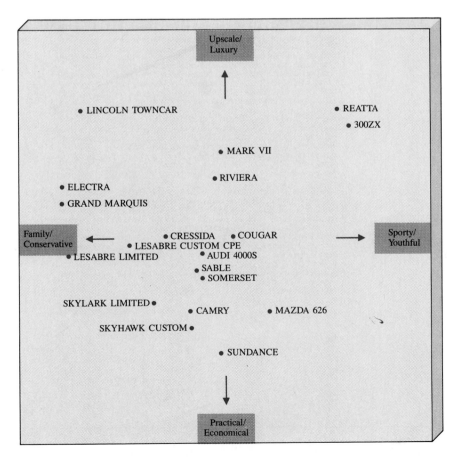

EXHIBIT 13.5
Perceptual Map Based on Product Attribute Ratings—Buick vs. Competitors

According to Paula Travenia, a senior marketing research analyst at Buick, taken together, the key findings of the studies,[3] which had been concluded through early 1987, suggested:

1. The Reatta is perceived as an upscale, distinctive-looking sporty car. (See Exhibit 13.5.)

2. The main competitor for the Reatta is expected to be the Chrysler TC by Maserati. The Maserati is expected to be competitively priced and equipped with a turbo 2.2L-4 engine. Overall, the 0–60 mph time should be equivalent; however, with the five-

---

[3] Note that none of these studies included a test drive. They either used a fiberglass model or a video exposure in their methodology.

EXHIBIT 13.6
Memorandum from Buick's Marketing Research Department Regarding Reatta's Closest Competitor

BUICK

Buick Motor Division
General Motors Corporation
Flint, Michigan 48550

January 20, 1987

To: J. W. Qualman

Subject: BUICK REATTA AND CHRYSLER TC COMPARISON

Chrysler Corporation recently announced the delay of the Chrysler TC by Maserati (official name) from Spring 1987 to Fall 1987. The vehicle will be priced in the $25,000 to $30,000 range, which places it directly in competition with the Buick Reatta, scheduled for a 1988 introduction.

Both cars will compete among 2-seater vehicles in the prestige luxury segment as high value personal luxury cars. Other two-place competitors currently in this segment include the Cadillac Allante and Mercedes 560 SL; however, the price range of these vehicles (above $50,000) all but eliminates them as direct competitors. The Chrysler TC and Reatta are expecting greater interaction with vehicles such as the Nissan 300ZX, Toyota Supra and Chevrolet Corvette. Other competitive entries may include the Jaguar XJ-SC at $42,000.

Target buyers for the vehicles are similar. The Reatta is targeting the highly educated, under 45-year-olds with incomes of $35,000 or above. The Chrysler TC is also targeting the highly educated, but with incomes in the $60,000 to $70,000 range. Chrysler's expected annual volume for these vehicles is in the range of 5,000 to 6,000 units, compared to the Reatta's 18,000 units.

The Chrysler Turbo Convertible offers buyers just two choices, at no extra cost: exterior color and drivetrain (3-speed automatic or 5-speed manual). Everything else is standard, including a hard removable roof and a soft convertible top. Other features which may strengthen this vehicle's competitive posture are the standard compact disc player, all-leather interior and turbo engine. Specifications and price information for both vehicles are summarized on attached pages.

For additional information, Chrysler has provided a toll-free number to address any questions about their upcoming vehicle (1-800-843-6636).

B. J. Moore-Pirtle

BJM:mw

Attachments

PREMIUM AMERICAN MOTORCARS

speed manual on the TC, its 0–60 mph time should be 1–2 seconds faster than the Reatta's. (See Exhibit 13.6.)

3. The Reatta is perceived to be most similar to the Porsche 924/944, Mazda RX-7, Nissan 300ZX, and the Corvette.

4. The performance ratings given to the Reatta at the Cleveland Clinic indicate that the Reatta is not perceived to be as strong a performer as the Nissan 300ZX. (The specification sheets indicated a 0–60 mph rating of 9.8 seconds for the Reatta and 7.2 seconds for the 300ZX with base engines and transmissions. (See Exhibit 13.7.)

5. The most significant purchase consideration for the Reatta was shown by prestige, luxury, and high-sport car owners. The high-sport car owners will compare the Reatta to other high-sport cars and expect it to be competitive in performance. (High-

GENERAL MOTORS CORPORATION

EQUIPMENT/PRICE		
Equipment	Chrysler TC	Reatta
EXTERIOR		
FOG LAMPS	N/A	S
CORNERING LAMPS	S	S
POWER MIRRORS—HEATED	S	S
BODY SIDE MOLDING	S	S
COLORS	6	7
TWO-TONE PAINT	N/A	OPT.—$190
INTERIOR		
AIR CONDITIONING	MANUAL	AUTO
POWER ANTENNA	S	S
CRUISE CONTROL	S	S
REAR DEFOG	S	S
ELECTRIC DOOR LOCKS	S	S
FUEL GAGES	S	S
FLOOR MATS	S	S
PASSENGER VANITY MIRROR	S	S
POWER DRIVER'S SEAT	S	S
POWER PASSENGER SEAT	S	OPT.—$240
GRAPHIC EQUALIZER RADIO	S	S
CASSETTE PLAYER	S	S
DIGITAL DISC PLAYER	S	N/A
CONCERT SOUND SPEAKERS	10	8
CLOTH SEATS	N/A	S
LEATHER SEATS	S	OPT.—$487
LEATHER INTERIOR TRIM (I/P & DOOR)	S	N/A
POWER RECLINERS	S	OPT.—$680 W/SEAT FEATURES
REAR LOCKABLE STORAGE BINS	S	S
THEFT DETERRENT SYSTEM	?	S
POWER WINDOWS	S	S
COLORS	3	4
CHASSIS		
ANTI-LOCK BRAKES	S	S
15" ALUMINUM WHEELS	S	S
EAGLE GT (TIRES)	S	S
PRICE	$30,000	$25,888 (87 ECON)

EXHIBIT 13.6 (continued) **Comparison of Reatta and Chrysler TC**

sport car owners are defined as sporty/personal car buyers who look for maximum responsiveness and high-performance engines.)

6. The Reatta is not perceived as offering very good value for the money.

EXHIBIT 13.6 (continued)
Comparison of Reatta and Chrysler TC

SPECIFICATIONS/FEATURES			
	Chrysler TC	**Reatta**	**Comments**
SIZE			
WHEELBASE	93.0 IN.	98.5 IN.	REATTA LARGER ALL-AROUND.
LENGTH	175.8 IN.	181.3 IN.	INTERIOR DIMENSIONS
WIDTH	68.5 IN.	71.7 IN.	EQUIVALENT EXCEPT
HEIGHT	51.9 IN.	51.0 IN.	CHRYSLER HAS 1″ MORE
CURB ST.	3030 LBS.	3330 LBS.	HEADROOM
POWERTRAIN			
CONFIGURATION	TFWD.	TFWD.	REATTA SHOULD HAVE
DISPLACEMENT	2.2L-4	3.8L-V6	SIGNIFICANTLY BETTER
HORSEPOWER	160 @ 5200	165 @ 5200	LAUNCH FEEL. 0–60 MAY BE
TORQUE	171 @ 3600	210 @ 2000	EQUIVALENT. PERFORMANCE
INDUCTION-			OF MASKRATT 4V HEAD WITH
FUEL	TURBO-FI	NORMAL-SFI	MANUAL 5 SPD SHOULD BE
TRANSMISSION	A3	A4	1-2 SEC. FASTER 0–60. NO
MPG-CITY/HWY.	22/35	19/27	CHARGE OPTION.
OPTIONAL	DOHC-4V M5	NONE	
FUEL TANK	14G	18.8G	
CHASSIS			
SUSPENSION—FRT	McPH. STRUT	McPH. STRUT	REATTA SHOULD BE BETTER
SUSPENSION—RR	SOLID AXLE-COIL	IND. TRANS. LEAF	HANDLING AND QUIETER
WHEELS	15″ ALUMINUM	15″ ALUMINUM	
TIRES	P205/60 EAGLE	P215/65 EAGLE	
BRAKES	4 DISC W/ABS	4 DISC W/ABS	
STEERING	RACK AND PINION	RACK AND PINION	
INTERIOR			
SEATS	LEATHER BUCKET	CLOTH/LEA. BUCKET	CHRYSLER INTERIOR HAS
STYLE	LOOSE PILLOW	TAILORED SPORT	TUFTED LA-Z-BOY
INSTRUMENTS	FULL ANALOG	FULL DIGITAL	APPEARANCE
I/P	WRAP AROUND—	FLOATING POD-VINYL	
	LEATHER		
CONTROLS	PUSHBUTTON	CRT TOUCH	
FEATURES	TRIP COMPUTER,	TRIP COMPUTER,	
	UMBRELLA,	PASS THRU	
	EMERGENCY KIT		
STEERING WHEEL	WOOD RIM TILT AND	LEATHER TILT	
	TELESCOPE		
EXTERIOR			
HEADLAMPS	COMPOSITE W/	HIDDEN	CHRYSLER HAS TRADITIONAL
	WASHERS		GRILLE. REAR ENDS ARE
TAILLAMPS	FULL WIDTH	FULL WIDTH	QUITE SIMILAR. CHRYSLER
CONSTRUCTION	STEEL INTEGRAL	STEEL INTEGRAL	HAS REMOVABLE PORTHOLE
PLATFORM	DAYTONA-LASER	RIVIERA	HARDTOP AND CONVERTIBLE
			TOP.

EXHIBIT 13.7
Comparison of Specifications: Reatta vs. Nissan 300ZX

SPECIFICATION SHEET

Buick Reatta 2 Door

Available Body Styles:	2 Door Coupe/Convertible
Base Engine:	V6, Fuel Injected, 3.8 Liter
Base Transmission:	4 Speed Automatic w/Overdrive
Fuel Economy—City/Highway m.p.g.:	18/25
(Base engine and transmission)	
Drive Configuration:	Front Wheel Drive
Acceleration 0–60 miles per hour:	9.8 seconds
(Base engine and transmission)	
Optional Engines:	None
(Additional Cost)	
Optional Transmissions:	None
(Additional Cost)	

Base Price $ N/A	**Popularly Equipped Price $ N/A**	**Price As Shown $ N/A**
Major Standard Equipment:	Major Items Included: (In addition or in place of standard equipment)	Major Items Included: (In addition to or in place of popular or standard equipment) 6-Way Power Passenger Seat Leather Seats Convertible Roof
Power Brakes		
Power Steering		
AM/FM Stereo w/Cassette		
Premium 6-Speaker Sound System		
Cruise Control		
Electronic Touch Air Conditioning		
Aluminum Wheels		
Tinted Glass		
Dual Power Exterior Mirrors		
6 Way Power Seat		
Driver's Side		
Power Windows		
Power Door Locks		
Power Antenna		
Automatic Level Control		
Tilt Steering Wheel		
Pulse Windshield Wipers		
Rear Window Defroster		

SPECIFICATION SHEET

Nissan 300ZX—2 Door

Available Body Styles: 2 Door Coupe
Base Engine: V6, Fuel Injected, 3.0 Liter
Base Transmission: 5 Speed Manual or Automatic
Fuel Economy—City/Highway MPG: 18/26
(Base Engine and Transmission)
Drive Configuration: Rear Wheel Drive
Acceleration 0–60 miles per hour: 7.2 seconds
(Base Engine and Transmission)
Optional Engines: None
(Additional Cost)
Optional Transmissions: None
(Additional Cost)

Base Price $19,310	**Popularly Equipped Price $19,310**	**Price As Shown $20,410**
Major Standard Equipment:	Major Items Included: (In addition or in place of standard equipment)	Major Items Included: (In addition to or in place of popular or standard equipment)
Removable Roof Panels		Leather Packages:
Power Brakes		Leather Seats
Power Steering		Power Driver Seat
Cruise Control		
AM/FM Stereo w/Cassette		
Air Conditioning		
Aluminum Alloy Wheels		
Tinted Glass		
Reclining Bucket Seats (w/Lumbar Support)		
Body Side Moldings		
Dual Remote Control Mirrors		
Remote Fuel Fill Door		
Power Antenna		
Power Windows		
Power Door Locks		
Tilt Wheel		
Power Antenna		
Pulse Windshield Wipers		
Rear Window Defroster		

All Prices Include Destination Charges

Calle and Company

Calle's research was based on in-depth "clinics" with "culturally influential" consumers. The study was intended to: (1) assess consumer evaluations of actual product prototypes; (2) identify Reatta's best target markets; (3) determine Reatta's consumer-perceived advantages; and (4) develop competitive sales rationales vis-à-vis other existing and potential sports and luxury cars.

Calle conducted its research in four markets: Los Angeles, Chicago, Metro–New York, and Houston. Calle described these locations as having the following market and consumer characteristics:

1. *Los Angeles Region*: Consumers have distinctive lifestyles and criteria for purchasing car.

2. *Chicago Region*: Consumers are traditional, conservative, and concerned with product value and quality.

3. *Metro–New York—Stamford, Connecticut*: This is both a trend-setting and a traditional market. Consumers are diverse in income, education, and cultural perspective. The region has both urban and suburban consumers.

4. *Houston Region*: The consumer base is transient and the economic market is volatile. There is diverse regional and ethnic positioning.

Methodology:[4] Calle selected six "diverse cultural groups" for study (see Appendix 13A.I): (1) high-status executive women; (2) high-status executive men; (3) older, "socially elite" men and women; (4) black executive men; (5) high-mileage drivers (both men and women); and (6) a "walking actor" group. A questionnaire was used to screen potential clinic participants. Approximately 20 consumers who had expressed interest in $25,000 + sports/luxury cars were recruited for each group in each market location, resulting in a total sample of almost 500. Those who were selected as participants in the study would take part in a four-hour session devoted to "Developing Better Cars."

Each clinic participant was provided with a list of creative stimuli developed by Calle. Examples of the stimuli are: Totally Uninhibited Driving, A Life Experience, Won't Waste Your Time, Congenial and Professional, For Intense Encounters, and Makes the Most of Your Instincts. At the beginning of the four-hour session, he or she was asked to circle all stimuli that would trigger a positive response to a car. Calle's methodology was based on the analysis of these responses and of the ensuing guided discussion they engendered.[5] The use of a preestablished set of stimuli in this way differentiated Calle's methodology from traditional focus group approaches. Toward the end of the session, the participants were shown fiberglass models of the Reatta hardtop and convertible models. Participants in the Calle study did not test-drive the Reatta.

Findings: Based upon its qualitative "stimuli" research, Calle concluded that consumers in the six cultural groups it had studied did not perceive Buick's car lines to be particularly stylish, sporty, luxurious, or high in performance. Rather, they considered Buicks to be "common, everyday, run-of-the-mill products that did not fit their desired requirements for either a sports or a luxury car." Calle noted that their subjects tended to describe

---

[4] See Appendix 13A for additional material on Calle's research.

[5] Calle collected information regarding consumers' tastes and preferences throughout these discussions. Clinic participants offered opinions on models that were currently available and how they differed from their expectations.

Buick automobiles as "boring and unadventurous" and generally "for older men and women."

Calle recommended that the primary target market for the Reatta be professional women over thirty. According to Calle, these women perceived Reatta as offering them the comfort, safety, smooth ride, and status of large luxury cars, along with the maneuverability and more appropriate interior capacity of smaller sporty automobiles. Calle recommended that the Reatta be positioned as a luxury car rather than as a sports car, since its clinic research had indicated that the Reatta could readily meet consumer expectations concerning luxury-related attributes, but would not be perceived as having the high-performance characteristics expected of sports cars. Based on its research, Calle recommended a number of advertising themes that it considered appropriate for targeting the Reatta at this customer group (see Appendix 13A.II).

As a secondary target market, Calle recommended older, "socially elite" men and women above age fifty. According to clinic data, this group perceived the Reatta as: (1) being the right size for two-person households; (2) being as comfortable as larger luxury cars; (3) being safer and easier to get into and out of than typical sporty cars; and (4) demonstrating that "the driver is not old-fashioned." (See Appendix 13A.III for Calle's recommended advertising themes for this group.)

Information Resources Inc. (IRI)

IRI was a rapidly growing marketing research firm well known for its innovation in the use of supermarket scanner data, electronic-based consumer panels, and pretest market forecasting techniques. From IRI's perspective, the Buick study provided an excellent opportunity to extend methodologies that had proved effective in consumer packaged goods to consumer durables. In its contract with Buick, IRI agreed to:

1. Forecast Reatta sales for the first four years after product introduction.
2. Aid in the definition of the appropriate target market for the Reatta.
3. Address the issue of product positioning: Should the Reatta be positioned as a sports car or as a personal luxury car?
4. Investigate consumers' perceptions of the Reatta's price/value relationship.
5. Assess the effect of adding a second model (a convertible) to the Reatta product family.

Methodology:[6] IRI and Buick jointly developed a screening questionnaire to identify clinic participants. The criteria for selection in the study included: current household ownership of competitive vehicles; household income greater than $45,000; willingness to pay over $20,000 for a car; and willingness to consider purchasing a two-seater car.

The 450 selected participants were invited to a clinic facility, where their first task was to sort a stack of pictures of automobiles into piles according to their perceived similarity. They were then to select their first-, second-, and third-choice cars. IRI researchers used consumer categorizations and rankings obtained in this way to analyze how consumers viewed Reatta vis-à-vis its primary competitors, and to observe whether their placement of Reatta changed after exposure to advertising, a simulated trade press article, the car itself, and/or one of two competitive models.

Each participant was assigned to one of three groups (see Appendix 13B.I). Group I, consisting of 200 participants, was, in turn, divided into two subgroups. The first of these subgroups (100 participants) was then exposed to a simulated trade press article, followed by advertising describing Reatta as "a new kind of sports car." The other subgroup (also comprising 100 participants) was not shown the article. One-half of each

---

[6] See Appendix 13B for excerpts from IRI's presentation to Buick management.

of the two subgroups was then shown a concept board, which described the Reatta as "a personal luxury car," while the other half was shown a concept board describing the Reatta as "a new kind of a sports car." After answering a series of questions concerning their perceptions of the Reatta, all 200 test-drove the vehicle. This was the first market research incorporating an actual test drive of the Reatta.

Of the remaining 250 clinic participants, Group II (150) did not view or test-drive an actual Reatta. Half of this group saw a concept board for the Buick Riviera, and then test-drove it, while the other half went through a similar procedure with the Nissan 300ZX. Finally, Group III (100 participants) test-drove the Reatta and one of the two competitive models, but was not exposed to either simulated advertising or trade press articles.

After their test drives, all participants watched one of several versions of a video simulation of word-of-mouth communication concerning the Reatta. After exposure to each level of information (concept boards, simulated advertising, simulated trade press articles, test drives, simulated word-of-mouth communication), the participants' attribute ratings and preferences were collected.

IRI analyzed the reactions of consumers to the Reatta under different information-exposure conditions. These reactions were then compared with those to the Riviera and the Nissan 300ZX under similar conditions. Since the sales histories of the Riviera and 300ZX were known, it was possible to use this analysis to produce a forecast of Reatta sales calibrated against Riviera and 300ZX actual sales results.

Findings: IRI forecast sales of approximately 10,100 Reattas between February and September 1988 (its planned introductory model year), 17,100 during the 1989 model year, and 23,900 during its third year on the market.[7] According to IRI's analysis, Reatta sales would be most sensitive to:

1. The level of consumer awareness and consideration.
2. The effectiveness of merchandising programs.
3. The competitive environment.
4. Growth in the two-seater car market.
5. Whether or not a convertible was introduced.

Appendix 13B.II describes the model and assumptions used by IRI in developing its sales forecast. It also illustrates relationships derived from the model between forecast Reatta sales and marketing variables, such as the number of consumers who could be induced to consider the new car, extended warranties, guaranteed resale programs, and more convenient routine maintenance. Appendix 13B.III contains a perceptual map for the Reatta developed by IRI.

IRI recommended that the Reatta be positioned primarily as a sports car, although advertising copy might also utilize luxury and comfort "cues" (see Appendix 13B.III). IRI did not recommend any particular target market segment for the car, however, since its research had not shown statistically significant differences in purchase probabilities across demographic groups. Overall, IRI concluded that the Reatta:

1. Met its targeted objectives:
   (a) as a conquest car that added a new dimension to the Buick line;
   (b) by expanding the Buick image with entry into a more upscale, sporty market; and
   (c) by offering key benefits through combining a sporty look with traditional Buick strengths of comfort, luxury, and roominess.

---

[7] Sales forecasts are disguised, but representative.

2. Was perceived as a car that:
   (a) had a youthful image;
   (b) was fun and exciting to drive; and
   (c) was comfortable and luxurious.

3. Received performance evaluations that were for the most part positive, although a few participants expressed concern about the car's handling and acceleration.

4. Had a relatively low perception of reliability and value.

CONCLUSION

In considering this research, Dabels recognized that a number of key decisions still had to be made. For example, he was considering a proposal to reduce the price of the Reatta, perhaps by as much as several thousand dollars. As noted, the market researchers had found that consumers did not perceive the Reatta as offering good value compared to other cars in its class. Clearly, it did not make sense to lower the price from a unit profitability point of view. Nevertheless, since the Reatta's role was to be a low-volume image leader for the division, might it not make sense to absorb a price cut in order to improve Buick's ''value'' image?

Complicating matters further, several of Dabels's colleagues had recently suggested that the introduction of the Reatta be delayed by several months in order to make certain relatively minor styling improvements (e.g., modifying the instrument panel) suggested by marketing research. (Making the Reatta more of a high-performance car could not be accomplished before late 1989, at the earliest.) Chrysler had recently announced a delay in the introduction date of the Maserati TC until the fall of 1988. Should Buick take advantage of this delay to ''ensure that the product is absolutely right,'' Dabels wondered, or would it make more sense to do everything possible to maximize the Reatta's ''first mover'' advantage?

While all of these were important issues, they were, in Dabels's view, dwarfed by the positioning dilemma. How should the Reatta be presented to the market? Was it a new kind of comfortable sports car, a personal luxury car, or what? And who should be the primary targets for the new car? What should the advertising copy focus on? Should there be an extended warranty and/or a guaranteed repurchase plan for the Reatta? Dabels knew that he needed to resolve these issues within the next several weeks so that he and his organization could get on with the task of developing the Reatta's introductory marketing strategy.

QUESTIONS FOR DISCUSSION

1. How would you characterize the consumer buying process for automobiles? What are the key factors in this decision? How do various types of consumers actually go about purchasing a car?

2. How would you characterize General Motors' situation in 1987? What role is Buick intended to play in GM's strategy?

3. How is the Buick Division ''positioned''? As a member of Buick management, how would you like to see the division positioned?

4. What appear to be Buick's objectives for the Reatta? What positioning alternatives for the Reatta are available?

5. How would you position the Reatta? What would be the other key elements in your marketing strategy for the new car?

13A

RESEARCH MATERIALS

DESCRIPTION OF CALLE'S CULTURAL GROUPS FOR BUICK DIVISION OF GENERAL MOTORS

Six diverse groups of consumers were recruited for each market investigated. Approximately 20–24 consumers contributed to the six four-hour creative development discussions in each market.

The culture groups were selected to identify lifestyle and car-purchasing trends, and to provide positioning rationale.

An overview of six major American cultures was proposed.

Status—Executive Women

Women working full-time outside the home in white-collar positions, earning $40,000 annually, individually. Interested in purchasing a sports or luxury car within the next year. Hold managerial, executive level positions. Aged 28–38. Willing and able to spend $25,000 + on car purchase.

Status—Executive Men

Criteria as above. Willing and able to spend $25,000 + on car purchase. Young, style-conscious fast-trackers. Users of vehicles for primarily short-distance, daily, around-town driving and local commuting. If not a current car owner, they lease, borrow, rent on occasion, depend on a company car or public transportation.

Older, "Socially Elite Men and Women"

Older men and women, 45 +, who are looking to purchase a sports/luxury car within the next year. Combined incomes of $60,000 +. Willing and able to spend $25,000 + on car purchase. May be a second or third car-purchase consideration.

Black Men—Executives

Black men, aged 35 +, in executive, managerial, professional occupations. Earn $40,000 + annually. Looking to purchase sports/luxury car within next year costing $25,000 +. As a culture, this group used to capture contemporary positioning language.

High-Mileage Drivers—Men and Women

Men and women who drive at least 400 miles a week or 80 miles a day. Willing and able to spend $25,000+ for a sports/luxury car within the next year.

People who for lifestyle or occupation must spend a great deal of time in an automobile. More mid-management level, these consumers face long-distance commutes or conduct business from their vehicle—i.e., real estate salespeople, manufacturer salespeople, service reps, etc. Since more than 50% of the American population is employed in service-oriented activity, we feel this to represent a very large consumer culture.

"Walking Actor" Group—Men and Women

Men and women who work full-time outside the home, and come into verbal contact with at least 10 other people during each working day. This group influences others strongly, and is very familiar with providing rationale, support for their own opinions. To provide purchase rationale for Reatta. The "articulate" culture.

All earn $40,000 in job occupations, are willing and able to spend $25,000+ for the car they purchase.

CALLE'S ADVERTISEMENT THEME LINE RECOMMENDATIONS FOR PROFESSIONAL WOMEN AGED 30+ YEARS

- Gives Women Their Own Reasons To Love A Car
- For Confident Women In Command/Control
- Working Women's Companion
- Stylish Comfort and Safety
- It Becomes You
- The Professional Way To Work
- Comfort That's Not Difficult
- For Making Business A Pleasure
- The Less Bulky Luxury Car
- The Tough And Tender Car
- Improves The Quality Of Your (Working) Life
- Stylish And Dependable

CALLE'S ADVERTISEMENT THEME LINE RECOMMENDATIONS FOR SOCIALLY ELITE MEN AND WOMEN AGED 50+ YEARS

- The Couple Of The Year
- A Life Experience
- Carefree Driving
- A Combination Of Common Sense
- The Car For Mixed Doubles
- The Intimate Passenger Car

- For Events Of Importance
- For The Way You Run Your Life
- Improves The Look And Feel Of Driving
- Street Smart!
- For Those Ahead Of Their Time ᴗ
- Watch Your Whole Life Change

13B

IRI Research Methodology:
Excerpts from IRI's Presentation to Buick Management

MEASUREMENT

Group I: Exposure to Reatta Only; Participants = 200

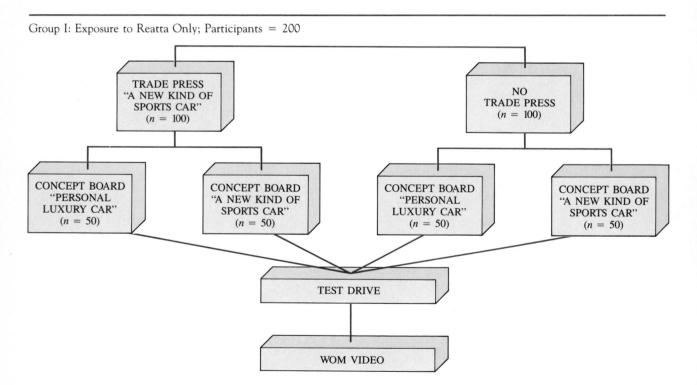

TWO DIFFERENT ADVERTISING CONCEPTS WERE TESTED

TOP DOWN

THE BUICK REATTA IS A NEW KIND OF SPORTY, PERSONAL, 2-PLACE CAR.

REATTA IS POWERED BY THE SEQUENTIAL PORT FUEL-INJECTED V-6 ENGINE WITH HANDLING AND RIDE TUNED TO MAKE YOUR DRIVING A PLEASURE RATHER THAN A WIND-BLOWN ADVENTURE.

REATTA GOES BEYOND THE MERE DESCRIPTION OF A CONVERTIBLE TO BRING LUXURY, COMFORT AND ROOMINESS YOU WOULD NEVER EXPECT FROM A SPORTY CAR LIKE THIS.

TO EXPERIENCE THIS TOTALLY NEW FEELING FROM BUICK, TAKE A TEST DRIVE AT YOUR BUICK DEALER.

THE GREAT AMERICAN ROAD BELONGS TO REATTA.

Reatta Evaluations

```
                        CAR SORT
                           │
                 TYPICAL CARS & RATINGS
                           │
              RATINGS FOR DRIVE NOW CAR
                AND CARS 1, 2, AND 3
                     ┌─────┴─────┐
         TRADE PRESS (n = 100)   NO TRADE PRESS (n = 101)
          ┌──────┴──────┐        ┌──────┴──────┐
      HERITAGE AD   TOP-DOWN AD   HERITAGE AD   TOP-DOWN AD
       (n = 50)      (n = 50)      (n = 50)      (n = 51)
          └──────┬──────┴─────┬──────┴──────┘
                 RATING FOR REATTA
                       │
                   TEST DRIVE
                       │
                RATINGS FOR REATTA
                 ┌─────┴─────┐
  POSITIVE WOM VIDEO (n = 126)   NEGATIVE WOM VIDEO (n = 75)
                 └─────┬─────┘
                RATINGS FOR REATTA
                       │
           CONVERTIBLE CONCEPTS AND RATINGS
                       │
           CAR ATTITUDES AND DEMOGRAPHICS
                       │
                REATTA OWNER PLAN
```

The REATTA:
Buick's New Sports Car

Buick is at last stepping away from their traditional image with the introduction of their surprising new sports car—the two seater Reatta. Although it is too early to tell just how successful the Reatta will be, its sleek styling and aerodynamic design is highly reminiscent of the Nissan 300ZX, the Porsche 924, and the Mazda RX-7.

Buick clearly hopes to attract a younger thinking and more upscale buyer through the Reatta's combination of sports car styling and comfort— a blend of style and common sense.

The Reatta appears to have addressed some of the complaints people have against sports cars. The car has plenty of legroom and there is ample storage space, including two covered recessed bins behind the seats and a pass-thru from the passenger compartment into the trunk.

While the early tests indicate that the handling and performance may disappoint the hard core sports car enthusiast, the Reatta's comfortable ride coupled with a quick 9.7 second 0–60 mph acceleration makes driving a real pleasure—even after hundreds of miles.

At $25,900, the Reatta is equipped with automatic transmission, air conditioning, cruise control, anti-lock brakes, AM-FM stereo with cassette, aluminum wheels, 6-way power seat, and other fine appointments. There is also an optional sunroof available.

For those who prefer to drive with the top down, a convertible is available for $31,200 and comes equipped with a manually operated top with power release and pull down, hard flush boot, and heated rear glass window.

It appears that Buick has finally designed a sports car for the American driver.

Body	Two-door coupe
Seating Capacity	Two
Engine	3.8 litre V-6 Sequential-Port Fuel Injection
Transmission	Automatic Four-speed
Length	181.3"
Width	71.7"
Height	51.0"
Luggage Capacity	12.6 cubic feet
EPA—City	19 mpg
Highway	30 mpg
Suspension	Gran Touring with front and rear stabilizer bars Independent four wheels
Brakes	Anti-lock brake system
Horsepower	165
Fuel Capacity	18.8 gallons

TWO DIFFERENT ADVERTISING CONCEPTS
WERE TESTED
(CONTINUED)

HERITAGE

THIS BUICK REATTA IS A NEW KIND OF PERSONAL, LUXURY 2-PLACE CAR WITH THE COMFORT, LUXURY AND ROOMINESS OTHER MAKERS FORGET TO INCLUDE.

REATTA IS A BUICK: SUBSTANTIAL, QUIET AND ROOMY INSIDE, RESULTING IN EASE OF ENTRY AND EXIT; SLEEK LINES AND STYLISH DESIGN THAT WON'T GET LOST IN A ROAD OF LOOK-ALIKE CARS.

REATTA HAS THE RIDE YOU SELDOM EXPECT FROM THIS TYPE OF CAR WITH THE LUXURY APPOINTMENTS ONCE THE SOLE DOMAIN OF LARGER CARS.

TEST-DRIVE REATTA, THE INTIMATE GETAWAY ANYWHERE YOU WANT TO GO.

THE GREAT AMERICAN ROAD BELONGS TO REATTA.

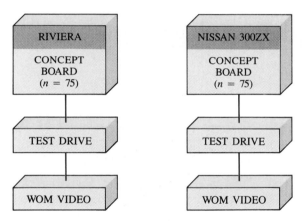

Group II: No Exposure to Reatta at All; Participants = 150

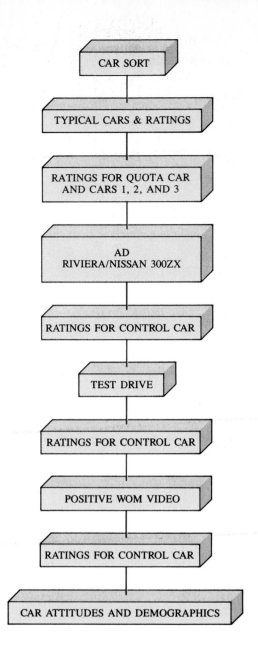

CAR SORT

TYPICAL CARS & RATINGS

RATINGS FOR QUOTA CAR
AND CARS 1, 2, AND 3

AD
RIVIERA/NISSAN 300ZX

RATINGS FOR CONTROL CAR

TEST DRIVE

RATINGS FOR CONTROL CAR

POSITIVE WOM VIDEO

RATINGS FOR CONTROL CAR

CAR ATTITUDES AND DEMOGRAPHICS

Group III: Exposure to
Reatta and to One of the
Control Vehicles;
Participants = 100

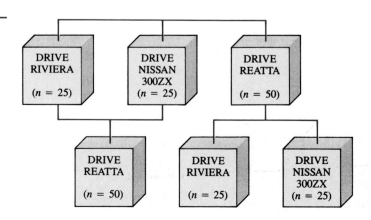

DRIVE
RIVIERA

(*n* = 25)

DRIVE
NISSAN
300ZX
(*n* = 25)

DRIVE
REATTA

(*n* = 50)

DRIVE
REATTA

(*n* = 50)

DRIVE
RIVIERA

(*n* = 25)

DRIVE
NISSAN
300ZX
(*n* = 25)

266

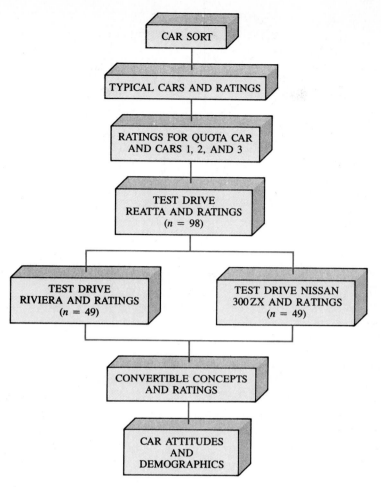

IRI FORECAST MODEL ASSUMPTIONS AND REATTA PURCHASE PROBABILITIES

INDEX MODEL USED TO CALCULATE REATTA SALES FORECAST

- FORECAST OF REATTA SALES = BASELINE SALES X
CONSIDERATION FOR REATTA/CONSIDERATION
FOR BASELINE X
PURCHASE PROBABILITY REATTA/PURCHASE PROBABILITY
BASELINE X
TWO-SEAT INDUSTRY GROWTH RATE X
MEASURE OF COMPETITION
- NISSAN 300ZX 1986 AND RIVIERA 1987 SALES ARE USED AS
BASELINE VALUES.

BASE FORECAST MODEL ASSUMPTIONS

	BASELINE SALES	*MODEL YEAR*
NISSAN 300ZX	57,187	1986
RIVIERA	15,000	1987

- RIVIERA SALES WERE REDUCED TO 9,000 (60%* OF 15,000) TO REFLECT THE PROPORTION OF OWNERS WHO WOULD CONSIDER A TWO-SEAT CAR.

* Derived from the screening interview as the percent of *Prestige Luxury* owners who would "consider purchasing a two-seat car in the next three years."

BASE FORECAST MODEL ASSUMPTIONS

- CONSIDERATION FOR THE REATTA STARTS AT 5% IN THE FIRST (PARTIAL) MODEL YEAR, GROWS TO 7% IN THE SECOND YEAR (RIVIERA LEVEL), AND LEVELS OFF AT 10% IN SUCCEEDING YEARS

MAKE & MODEL	*FAMILIAR* %	*SERIOUSLY CONSIDER* %	*CAPTURE* * *RATIO* %
CHEVROLET CORVETTE	98	30	31
NISSAN 300ZX	85	23	27
MAZDA RX-7	89	20	22
CHRYSLER LEBARON CONVERTIBLE	85	17	20
CADILLAC ALLANTE	71	12	17
CHEVROLET CAMARO	96	9	9
BUICK RIVIERA	89	7	8
BUICK SOMERSET REGAL	80	4	4
MAZDA 626	75	3	3
BUICK SKYHAWK	83	1	1

* Seriously consider as percent of familiar.

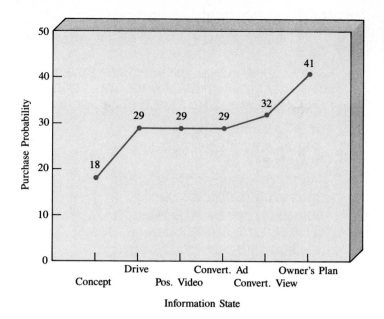

Purchase Probability for the Reatta Is Related to Information State

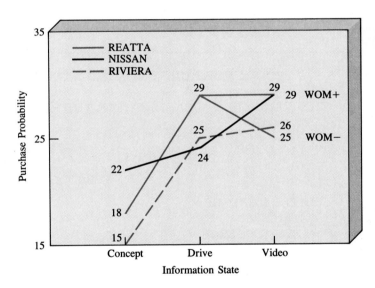

Reatta Purchase Probability Is Similar to the Riviera and the Nissan 300ZX

BASE FORECAST MODEL ASSUMPTIONS

- REATTA PURCHASE PROBABILITIES ARE ADJUSTED TO TAKE INTO ACCOUNT THE PURCHASE PROBABILITIES FOR THE FIRST-, SECOND-, AND THIRD-CHOICE CARS

    FOR EXAMPLE:

PROBABILITY OF PURCHASING A REATTA	.30
PROBABILITY OF PURCHASING THE FIRST-CHOICE CAR	.35
PROBABILITY OF PURCHASING THE SECOND-CHOICE CAR	.32
PROBABILITY OF PURCHASING THE THIRD-CHOICE CAR	.20
SUM OF FIRST + SECOND + THIRD	.87
ADJUSTED PROBABILITY OF PURCHASING A REATTA	.30/(.30 + .87) = .256

BASE FORECAST MODEL ASSUMPTIONS

- THE PURCHASE PROBABILITY FOR THE REATTA INCREASES OVER TIME

	ADJUSTED PURCHASE PROBABILITY	
	FIRST YEAR	*SECOND YEAR*
REATTA HARDTOP (ASSUMES CONVERTIBLE IS ADVERTISED)	.191	
REATTA HARDTOP AND CONVERTIBLE		.204
RIVIERA	.145	.145
NISSAN	.167	.167

- WORD OF MOUTH INCREASES THE ADJUSTED PROBABILITY OF PURCHASING A REATTA TO .22 IN THE THIRD YEAR AND .24 IN THE FOURTH YEAR.

BASE FORECAST MODEL ASSUMPTIONS

- WE ASSUME THAT THE MASERATI WILL BE INTRODUCED IN APRIL 1988 AND OTHER COMPETITIVE CARS WILL BE INTRODUCED IN THE NEXT TWO YEARS.

- THE *MEASURE OF COMPETITIVENESS* IS CALCULATED:
    —PROBABILITY THAT CONSUMER WILL CONSIDER BOTH CARS (50%), TIMES
    —PROBABILITY THAT CONSUMER WILL PURCHASE THE MASERATI, RELATIVE TO THE REATTA, AFTER HAVING SEEN BOTH .26/(.28 + .26), TIMES
    —PROPORTION OF MODEL YEAR THAT MASERATI IS AVAILABLE (6/9 IN YEAR 1; 12/12 ALL OTHER YEARS)

- WE ASSUMED THAT IN MODEL YEAR 1988 AND IN MODEL YEAR 1991, THE INTRODUCTION OF COMPETITIVE MODELS WOULD INCREASE THE COMPETITIVENESS TO:

—1988	.95
—1989	.81
—1990	.73
—1991	.73

SUMMARY OF FORECASTS

- SALES POTENTIAL COULD EXCEED 23,900* UNITS BY 1990 MODEL YEAR
- AGGRESSIVE MARKETING AND MERCHANDISING CAN HAVE A SIGNIFICANT EFFECT ON SALES BY:
    —INCREASING THE PERCEIVED VALUE OF THE REATTA
    —INCREASING THE PERCEIVED RELIABILITY OF THE REATTA

* Sales Forecast has been disguised.

POSITIONING THE REATTA

*BOTH AFTER CONCEPT AND AFTER DRIVE
THE REATTA IS CLEARLY SEEN AS A SPORTS CAR*

- BOTH ADVERTISEMENTS POSITIONED THE REATTA WITH MORE EXPENSIVE AND FOREIGN SPORTS CARS
- AD COPY WHICH STRESSES LUXURY AND COMFORT CUES CAN BE USED TO AUGMENT THIS POSITIONING
- TRADE PRESS WRITING OF REATTA AS SPORTS CAR WITH LUXURY AND COMFORT ADDS TO THIS OVERALL POSITION

271

THE REATTA WAS MOST OFTEN SORTED INTO A PILE CONTAINING SPORTS CARS

MAKE & MODEL	AFTER DRIVE %
NISSAN 300ZX	47
CHEVROLET CORVETTE	46
PORSCHE 924	45
MAZDA RX-7	44
PONTIAC FIERO	30
CHEVROLET CAMARO	26
CHRYSLER LEBARON CONVERTIBLE	19
CADILLAC ALLANTE	18
BUICK SOMERSET REGAL	5
BUICK RIVIERA	4
BUICK LESABRE	3
LINCOLN TOWNCAR	2
OLDSMOBILE 88	2
CADILLAC DEVILLE	1

READ: AFTER DRIVE 47% OF THE RESPONDENTS PLACED REATTA IN A PILE (OF A CARD SORT EXPERIMENT) OF "FAMILIAR CARS" THAT CONTAINED THE NISSAN 300ZX.

WHEN DIRECTLY ASKED AFTER DRIVE, THE REATTA IS CALLED A SPORTS CAR MORE OFTEN THAN A LUXURY CAR BY A 10—1 MARGIN

	AFTER DRIVE %
THE REATTA IS . . .	
A SPORTS CAR	91
A LUXURY CAR	9
HOW TYPICAL IS THE REATTA OF . . .	
A SPORTS CAR?	5.17*
A LUXURY CAR?	3.75

* Measured on a 1—7 scale.

THOSE WHO SAW THE *HERITAGE* AD WERE MORE LIKELY TO CLASSIFY THE REATTA WITH MORE EXPENSIVE SPORTS CARS THAN WERE THOSE WHO SAW THE *TOP DOWN* AD

MAKE & MODEL	HERITAGE %	TOP DOWN %
NISSAN 300ZX	60	50
MAZDA RX-7	57	48
CHEVROLET CORVETTE	56	42
PORSCHE 944	49	43
PORSCHE 924	49	45
PONTIAC FIERO	34	42
CHEVROLET CAMARO	25	26
PONTIAC FIREBIRD	24	31
CADILLAC ALLANTE	16	20
CHRYSLER LEBARON CONVERTIBLE	13	25

THE TRADE PRESS ARTICLE REINFORCED THE POSITION OF THE REATTA AS A HIGH-END SPORTS CAR

MAKE & MODEL	TRADE PRESS NO %	TRADE PRESS YES %
NISSAN 300ZX	49	60
MAZDA RX-7	53	52
PORSCHE 924	42	52
CHEVROLET CORVETTE	48	50
PORSCHE 944	44	48
PONTIAC FIERO	47	29
CHEVROLET CAMARO	31	19
PONTIAC FIREBIRD	36	19
CADILLAC ALLANTE	17	19
CHRYSLER LEBARON CONVERTIBLE	23	15

THE REATTA SCORES WELL ON "SPORTY" ATTRIBUTES AFTER AD EXPOSURE AND IMPROVES AFTER DRIVE, ESPECIALLY ON ACCELERATION, HANDLING AND COMFORT

ATTRIBUTE	CONCEPT RATING	DRIVE RATING	DRIVE MINUS CONCEPT
SPORTY	6.10	6.03	−0.07
APPEALS TO YOUNGER PEOPLE	5.90	5.83	−0.07
FUN TO DRIVE	5.73	5.85	0.12
ATTRACTIVE LOOKING	5.54	5.69	0.15
EXCITING	5.27	5.42	0.15
APPEALS TO WOMEN	5.25	5.44	0.19
GOOD ACCELERATION	5.10	5.73	0.64
TOUCH OF CLASS	5.02	5.47	0.46
EXPENSIVE LOOKING	5.00	5.30	0.31
HANDLES WELL	4.89	5.95	1.06
CAR I WOULD LIKE TO BE SEEN IN	4.87	5.38	0.51
HIGH QUALITY	4.82	5.17	0.35
FUNCTIONAL INSTRUMENTATION	4.73	5.26	0.52
CLASSIC STYLING	4.72	4.97	0.25
LUXURIOUS	4.72	5.25	0.53
ECONOMICAL ON FUEL	4.60	4.52	−0.08
DURABLE	4.44	4.56	0.12
QUIET RIDE	4.33	5.61	1.28
RELIABLE	4.30	4.51	0.21
COMFORTABLE	4.27	5.51	1.23
GOOD RESALE VALUE	4.22	4.30	0.08
SAFE	4.21	4.60	0.39
EASY TO MAINTAIN	4.17	4.23	0.06
GOOD VALUE FOR THE MONEY	3.99	4.21	0.22
ROOMY INTERIOR	3.91	4.91	1.00
APPEALS TO OLDER PEOPLE	3.27	4.11	0.85

AFTER DRIVE, POSITIVE COMMENTS ABOUT THE REATTA OUTNUMBERED NEGATIVES BY 2—1

	LIKES %	DISLIKES %
HANDLING/SUSPENSION/RIDE	92	25
CONTROLS/INSTRUMENT PANEL	74	53
SEATING ADJUSTMENTS/COMFORT	62	19
PERFORMANCE	51	19
ROOMINESS	39	27
LUXURY	33	7
STYLING	33	20
WOULD RECOMMEND	25	5
NOISE	20	15
VISIBILITY	16	25
BRAKES	7	5
QUALITY	5	5
PRICE	3	15
TRANSMISSION	2	10

- 58% of respondents said they would tell a friend something positive about the Reatta.

REATTA DELIVERS ITS CORE BENEFITS COMPARED TO THE NISSAN 300ZX AND THE RIVIERA

	REATTA IS	
COMPARED TO:	BETTER*	WORSE*
NISSAN 300ZX	ROOMY INTERIOR APPEALS TO OLDER PEOPLE	RELIABLE GOOD RESALE VALUE GOOD VALUE FOR THE MONEY
RIVIERA	SPORTY APPEALS TO YOUNGER PEOPLE FUN TO DRIVE EXCITING	SAFE APPEALS TO OLDER PEOPLE

* All comparisons after drive.

AFTER DRIVE, THE REATTA COMPARES FAVORABLY ON COMFORT AND LUXURY TO OTHER SPORTY CARS, WHETHER THEY ARE FOREIGN OR DOMESTIC, AND DOES LESS WELL ON SPORTINESS AND PERFORMANCE*

ATTRIBUTE	CADILLAC ALLANTE	CHEVROLET CAMARO	CHEVROLET CORVETTE	MAZDA RX-7	MERCEDES 560 SL	PONTIAC FIERO	PORSCHE 924	CELICA SUPRA
SPORTY								
APPEALS TO YOUNG PEOPLE	+							
FUN TO DRIVE		–	–	–	+	–	–	–
ATTRACTIVE LOOKING			–	–	–		–	
EXCITING			–		–		–	–
APPEALS TO WOMEN	+					+	–	+
GOOD ACCELERATION	–	+				+	–	–
TOUCH OF CLASS	–	+	–		–	+	–	+
EXPENSIVE LOOKING	+	+	–			+	–	–
HANDLES WELL	+	+				+		+
CAR WOULD LIKE TO BE SEEN IN		+	–		–	+	–	
HIGH QUALITY	+	+				+		
FUNCTIONAL							–	
INSTRUMENTATION	–		–		–	+	–	
CLASSIC STYLING		+	–			+	–	
LUXURIOUS		+	+	+		+	+	–
ECONOMICAL ON FUEL	–	+	+		+		+	–
DURABLE			+		+	+	+	
QUITE RIDE	+	+	+	+	–	+	+	
RELIABLE			+	+			+	
COMFORTABLE	–	+	+	+		+	+	+
SAFE			–			+		
GOOD RESALE VALUE								
EASY TO MAINTAIN							+	–
GOOD VALUE FOR $$$				–	–		+	
ROOMY INTERIOR		+	+	+	+	+	+	+
APPEALS TO OLDER PEOPLE	–	+	+	+	–	+	+	+
NUMBER OF RESPONDENTS	38	105	135	62	106	67	28	46

* + means Reatta rates significantly higher; – means Reatta rates significantly lower.

AFTER SEEING THE CONVERTIBLE AND DRIVING THE HARDTOP, THE CONVERTIBLE WAS SEEN AS MORE LUXURIOUS, CLASSIER AND MORE EXPENSIVE LOOKING

- CONVERTIBLE PERCEIVED BETTER THAN THE HARDTOP ON
    - LUXURIOUS
    - EXPENSIVE LOOKING
    - TOUCH OF CLASS
    - EXCITING
    - ATTRACTIVE LOOKING
    - CAR I WOULD LIKE TO BE SEEN IN
    - CLASSIC STYLING
- CONVERTIBLE PERCEIVED WORSE THAN THE HARDTOP ON
    - QUIET RIDE
    - SAFE

USING FACTOR ANALYSIS, EVALUATIONS OF CARS ON THE 26 CAR ATTRIBUTES WERE REDUCED TO THREE UNDERLYING DIMENSIONS

- "EXCITING AND SPORTY"
    - EXCITING
    - SPORTY
    - GOOD ACCELERATION
    - HANDLES WELL
    - FUNCTIONAL INSTRUMENTATION
    - FUN TO DRIVE
    - ATTRACTIVE LOOKING
    - CAR I WOULD LIKE TO BE SEEN IN
    - APPEALS TO WOMEN
    - APPEALS TO YOUNG PEOPLE
- "COMFORTABLE AND LUXURIOUS"
    - COMFORTABLE
    - APPEALS TO OLDER PEOPLE
    - LUXURIOUS
    - ROOMY INTERIOR
    - QUIET RIDE
    - SAFE
- "RELIABILITY AND VALUE"
    - ECONOMICAL ON FUEL
    - RELIABLE
    - DURABLE
    - EASY TO MAINTAIN
    - GOOD VALUE FOR THE MONEY

GROWTH IN THE TWO-SEATER MARKET

• TWO-SEATER MODEL YEAR SALES HISTORY

MODEL YEAR	SALES
1982	233,200
1983	239,400
1984	374,300
1985	403,500
1986	378,200
1987 (THRU JULY)	225,800

• MARKET SHOULD STAY IN 400,000 TO 425,000 RANGE.

Source: GM MPP Forecast Department, August 1987.

The Convertible Has Strong Appeal Based on Purchase Probabilities

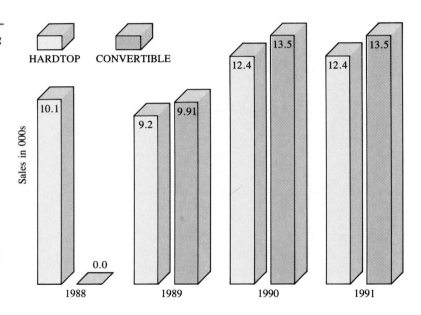

If Aggressive Marketing Can Increase the Level of Consideration for the Reatta to that of the Cadillac Allante, Demand for the Reatta Increases Dramatically

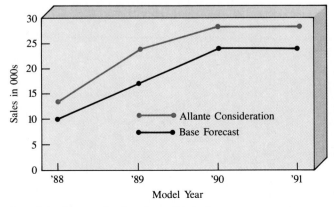

Note: Sales forecast data have been disguised.

MERCHANDISE THE REATTA THROUGH EXTRA VALUE

- WE TESTED CONSUMERS' REACTIONS TO THE *REATTA OWNER ADVANTAGE PLAN*, DESCRIBED AS HAVING:

  —EXTRA AMENITIES AND BENEFITS TO THE REATTA OWNER

  —EXCLUSIVITY

  —PLAN *COULD HAVE* THESE FEATURES:

    —FREE GENERAL MOTORS EXTENDED PROTECTION PLAN (6 YEARS/100,000 MILES)

    —FREE ROUTINE MAINTENANCE PLAN FOR THE FIRST FOUR YEARS OF OWNERSHIP

    —GUARANTEED RESALE VALUE (BUICK GUARANTEES THAT THE REATTA WILL NOT DEPRECIATE MORE THAN 10% PER YEAR)

    —FREE AUTO CLUB MEMBERSHIP FOR THE FIRST TWO YEARS OF OWNING THE REATTA

- THE FEATURES WERE SHOWN IN VARIOUS COMBINATIONS TO TEST CHANGES IN PURCHASE PROBABILITY FOR THE REATTA AS SPECIFICS OF THE ADVANTAGE PLAN WERE ADDED OR DROPPED.

Merchandising Plans Have Strong Effects: Reatta Sales Forecasts Can Increase Up to 38% Above the Base Forecast

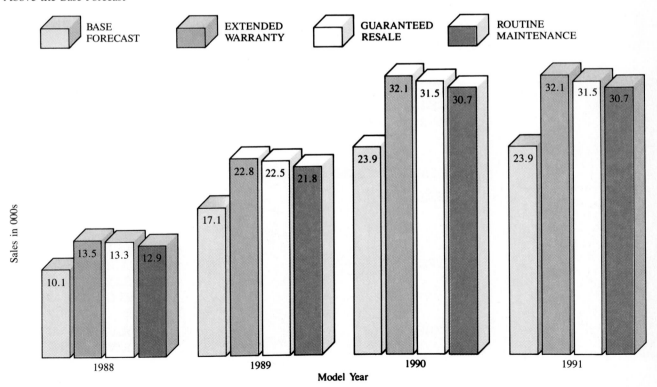

Note: Sales forecasts have been disguised.

The Reatta Is Perceived Differently Than Other Buick Cars and Improves on Comfort and Luxury After Drive

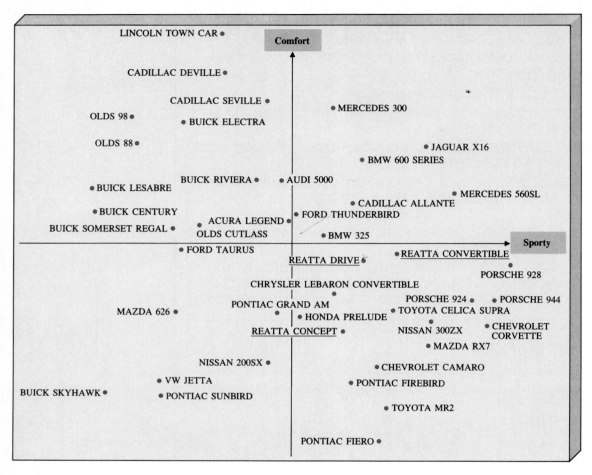

RELIABILITY AND VALUE ARE POTENTIAL AREAS OF CONCERN FOR CONSUMERS WHEN EVALUATING THE REATTA

RELIABILITY AND VALUE	CARS
HIGH	VW JETTA
	HONDA PRELUDE
	ACURA LEGEND
	TOYOTA CELICA SUPRA
AVERAGE	FORD TAURUS
	BUICK SKYHAWK
	PONTIAC GRAND AM
	OLDS 88
LOW	BUICK REATTA
	BUICK RIVIERA
	MERCEDES 560SL
	PORSCHE 924

PART THREE

STRATEGIC DECISION MAKING

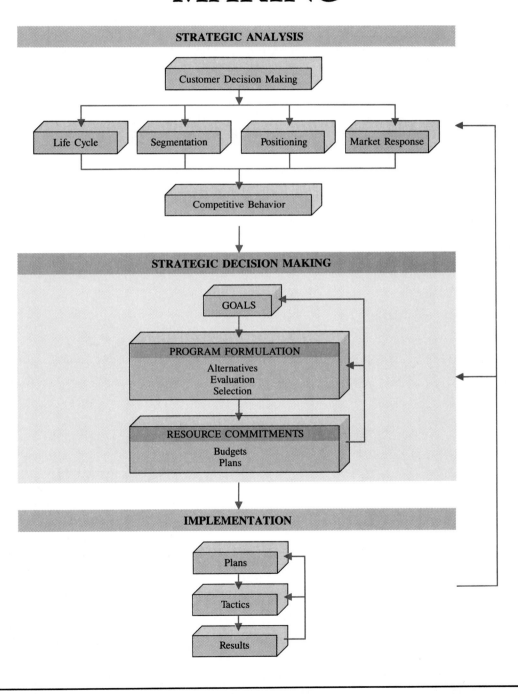

STRATEGIC ANALYSIS

Customer Decision Making

Life Cycle | Segmentation | Positioning | Market Response

Competitive Behavior

STRATEGIC DECISION MAKING

GOALS

PROGRAM FORMULATION

Alternatives
Evaluation
Selection

RESOURCE COMMITMENTS

Budgets
Plans

IMPLEMENTATION

Plans

Tactics

Results

NEW-PRODUCT DEVELOPMENT

Before we consider new-product decisions, let us review our overall strategy formulation process. The figure preceding this chapter reiterates our approach to the marketing strategy formulation process. The decision-making activities of goal setting, program formulation, and resource commitments, as well as implementation, are supported to the appropriate degree by varying levels of analysis. (See Chapter 2 for details.) In Part Two, we reviewed the foundations of marketing strategy and argued that a solid understanding of these underlying phenomena is critical to effective analysis. We emphasized the importance of Level I analysis: clear issue identification, understanding underlying factors, asking the right questions, bounding the decision appropriately, and defining the problem correctly. In many cases, moreover, we showed that it is also appropriate to employ Level II tools such as computer models, simple data analysis, and simulation methods to develop a more comprehensive analysis of underlying phenomena. We suggested that in some situations much more elaborate and complex Level III analysis will yield high benefits and should also be carried out.

In Part Three, we examine how underlying marketing phenomena relate to strategic decisions in the key areas of new products, established products, product lines, and corporate/worldwide strategy.

Relative Importance of Phenomena

Figure 14.1 portrays a matrix relationship between the underlying phenomena and the decision areas. We could argue that all the phenomena we studied are important in all areas, but some are more crucial. For emphasis, we have selected the three most critical phenomena in each decision arena and the two decisions most influenced by each phenomenon. New-product decisions are dominated by the dynamics of life cycles and design

283

activities intended to create value in a segment by physical and psychological attribute positioning. Underlying customer acceptance and competitive strategy are important, of course, but sometimes less so than the design-related phenomena.

Although the issues of managing the life cycle and positioning are also relevant to established products, managers who are formulating strategies for mature markets tend to focus on how customers make choices between alternatives offering marginal rewards as markets respond to changes in price, promotion, distribution, advertising, and/or competitive strategies. Product-line strategies are dominated by segmentation and positioning issues, and essentially depend on a trade-off between how customers react to a wide array of product-line offerings and various levels of resource productivity. Corporate and worldwide strategy is intimately related to managing the life-cycle dynamics of business units, the ROI implications of the deployment of marketing resources, and the search for competitive advantage.

In studying the chapters in Part Three, you should consider the implications of each phenomenon for each decision area. The particular situation will determine the most critical phenomena for analysis; part of the managerial task will be to identify the dominant marketing influences in each decision environment. But be careful. In certain cases, the most important phenomena may include some not highlighted in Figure 14.1.

State-of-the-Art Issues in Decision Making

Although it is tempting to try to cover all the strategic issues in each decision area, this would be impossible in a single volume. Indeed, one of the authors of this book has co-authored a text entirely devoted to the new-product management problem (Urban and Hauser, 1980). We have chosen instead to present a brief review of the basics, and then in each decision area to concentrate on a subset of current issues that draw on analysis and decision suppport tools to improve goal setting, program design, and resource allocation.

In our discussion of new products in this chapter, we will: (1) study sequential decision procedures of "reactive" and "proactive" new-product development; (2) examine the evidence on the benefits of being first in a market; and (3) explore the marketing/R&D interface and the role of "lead users" in providing a window on the future needs of customers in rapidly changing technical environments. In Chapter 15, on established products, we will focus on: (1) artificial intelligence and decision support systems; (2)

FIGURE 14.1
Strategic Decisions Versus
Phenomena

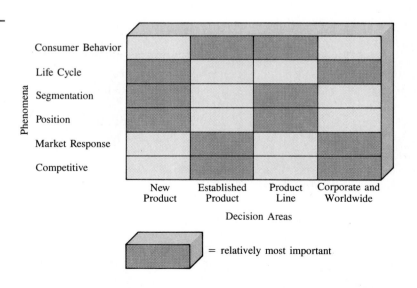

brand planning models; and (3) industrial product-marketing models. State-of-the-art issues in product-line management covered in Chapter 16 include: (1) the increasing pressures for wide lines; (2) product/market segmentation to determine how many products should be in the line; and (3) models for resource allocation across the products in the line. Our discussion of corporate marketing issues in Chapter 17 will emphasize: (1) the need to consider all corporate strategy issues as global; (2) international marketing as a wider and more complex case of segmentation; and (3) analytic models of strategic business unit portfolio strategies.

The consideration of these state-of-the-art issues should allow you to continue building a tool kit of Level I and II models. The cases presented in Chapters 18 to 21 will provide you with an opportunity to test these models' relevance in the increasingly complex environment in which strategies must be formulated.

STRATEGIC PLANNING AND NEW PRODUCTS

Often a company's portfolio of existing products seems unlikely to meet the organization's sales, profits, ROI, and/or stock price objectives. Under these circumstances, the firm should develop a strategy for adding new products to its product line.[1] At the macro level, there are five principal generic approaches to new products that might be considered:

1. Should we be innovators—pioneers in the use of technology to create or improve products to fit customer needs?

2. Should we rapidly copy competitive innovations in an effort to avoid much of the cost and risk of new-product development?

3. Should we respond to competitive introductions of new products by improving on the innovation—a "second but better" approach?

4. Should we concentrate on being a low-cost producer and use low prices as our competitive advantage, even if our products are at best "me too" relative to competitors?

5. Should we expand our product line through the acquisition of other firms or the formation of joint ventures?

Each of these generic new-product strategies has advantages and disadvantages. The General Electric/UDF case presented in Chapter 4 describes a situation where large returns may result from true innovation, but only if the firm is willing to bear a very considerable risk. The Buick Reatta case detailed in Chapter 13 describes a strategy of late entry into the sports car product category based on what is hoped will turn out to be a positioning advantage vis-à-vis a particular market segment. The Central Bell case set forth in Chapter 11 describes an organization that has not innovated, and now has to react to competitive entries stimulated by changes in the U.S. telecommunications industry. The American Express case presented in Chapter 12 describes the possible launch of a new product intended to take business away from aggressive competitors while building on the strengths of the firm's traditional product line. As may be seen in all of these examples, it is critical that management determine whether the firm should employ a proactive new-product strategy, react to market and competitive pressures as they occur, or engage in whatever generic strategy best fits the characteristics of each product/market segment in which it competes.

---

[1] The firm might, of course, also usefully consider adding new markets for existing products to its product/market strategy.

In this chapter, we consider what is known about the rewards and risks associated with new products. We then describe a sequential decision process that many firms have found helpful in maximizing incremental profit and minimizing the risk of failure. We next examine two especially critical issues in new-product development: (1) Under what circumstances does it make sense to be truly innovative? (2) How should one manage the always difficult marketing/technology interface? For each issue, we outline the key dimensions and describe the application of Level II analytic methods to its resolution. Finally, we close the chapter by considering the major directions that analytic and creative support for new-product strategy formulation are likely to take in the future.

REWARDS AND RISKS OF NEW-PRODUCT DEVELOPMENT

Importance

New products make a major contribution to corporate growth. In a survey of 700 firms (60 percent industrial, 20 percent consumer durables, and 20 percent consumer nondurables), Booz, Allen, and Hamilton (1982) found that new products accounted for 28 percent of these companies' growth between 1976 and 1981. In a similar survey primarily of industrial firms conducted in 1986, the Conference Board found that for the average firm in its sample, 35 percent of current revenue was derived from products that had not been on the market ten years earlier. New products clearly play a major role in most companies' growth strategies. In the Booz, Allen, and Hamilton study, new products produced 22 percent of the total increase in profits for the 700 firms over the previous five years.

Moreover, the contribution to sales and profits from new products seems to be increasing. According to the Booz, Allen, and Hamilton study, the fraction of sales growth due to new products was expected to increase from 28 to 37 percent, and the fraction of profit growth from 22 to 33 percent, between 1981 and 1986. Among the most commonly identified pressures for intensified new-product activity are advances in basic technology, changes in customer needs, a shortening of product life cycles, and increases in foreign competition.

Risk

While the pressures for more new-product activity are increasing, the risks associated with developing and introducing new products remain high. Booz, Allen, and Hamilton found that the failure rate of new products remained in the 33–35 percent range between 1963 and 1981. A more recent study conducted by the Association of National Advertisers (1984), which was based on responses from 138 mainly consumer products firms (74 percent packaged goods, 12 percent consumer durables, 12 percent industrial, and 9 percent services),[2] found that 27 percent of product-line extensions failed, 31 percent of new brands introduced in categories where the company was already active failed, and 46 percent of the new products introduced into categories that were new to the firm introducing them failed. While new-product failure rates obviously vary according to the firm, industry, and magnitude of innovation, it seems reasonable to conclude from the existing evidence that the *average* rate of failure for new products actually introduced into the market is in the neighborhood of 33 percent.

---

[2] Sums to more than 100 percent because some firms are active in more than one category.

The costs of such failures can be staggering. Federal Express lost over $190 million on Zap mail (*Wall Street Journal*, 1986). Polaroid wrote off $68 million on inventory alone for Polarvision instant movies, and probably incurred total losses of twice that amount on that project (*Boston Globe*, 1987). Exxon lost hundreds of millions of dollars on its ill-fated forays into office information systems and high-tech electric motors. IBM, Aetna, and Comsat collectively lost a similar amount on Satellite Business Systems (SBS), their joint venture into satellite-based telecommunications.

Failure in the marketplace is costly and painful, but represents only part of the risk. Many new products are eliminated during the development process, and the resources spent on such projects must be included in the total cost of introducing successful new products. Based on 1981 records of 48,960 ideas generated and screened for acceptability, Elrod and Kelman (1987) found that 48.2 percent of the ideas at least entered development and 38.6 percent were actually tested, but only 27 percent ultimately resulted in a commercialized product. These data imply that companies expend very considerable resources on projects that never reach the marketplace. Since approximately one-third of the products that do reach the marketplace ultimately fail, it seems reasonable to conclude that a very high percentage of corporate investment in the new-product development and introduction process does not result in successful new products.

Many studies have sought to identify the principal reasons for new-product failures. Booz, Allen, and Hamilton (1982) found that the most frequently mentioned internal obstacles to success were lack of attention to new products, emphasis on short-term profitability, inadequate market research, and delays in making decisions. The most fre-

TABLE 14.1   Reasons for New-Product Failure

1. *Market Segment Too Small*: Although a segment with differentiated needs has been identified, demand is inadequate to make the product profitable.
2. *Poor Match with Company Capabilities*: There is little synergy with the company's technical, marketing, production, and financial skills and experience. The product does not build on the organization's distinctive competence.
3. *Not Unique*: Even though the new product is technically or physically different, it is not new from the customer's point of view.
4. *Lacks Superior Quality*: The product does not reliably meet specifications that lead to high perceived quality.
5. *Little Benefit Relative to Competition*: The product does not provide significant performance advantages over alternatives already available to customers.
6. *Poor Positioning*: The product is poorly positioned because management misunderstood customers' perceptions, relative importance weights, and price trade-offs.
7. *Inadequate Support from Channel*: Channel members are not motivated to provide requisite distribution intensity or support.
8. *Forecasting Error*: Sales potential and/or rate of diffusion have been overestimated.
9. *Competitive Response*: Competition copies and/or improves product rapidly, and the firm has an inadequate strategy or insufficient resources to wage and survive a competitive battle.
10. *Changes in Consumer Tastes*: There is a shift in preferences while the product is being developed or being launched.
11. *Changes in Environment*: Tax changes, fluctuations in the prices of raw materials, and shifts in social attitudes, for example, make a product design obsolete.
12. *Ineffective Launch*: Selling, distribution, advertising, and/or delivery are not executed as planned.
13. *Insufficient Profitability*: Sales are good but margins are poor because of higher-than-anticipated costs and/or lower than expected prices.
14. *Organizational Problems*: Intraorganizational conflicts and poor management practices exist.

quently mentioned correlates of success were "product fit to market needs," "product fit with internal functional strengths," and "technological superiority." The Conference Board also studied the factors associated with success and found that "top-management support for development" and an "enthusiastic product manager" seemed to be the most important. Clearly, senior-management involvement, coupled with overall corporate strategy and policies that facilitate the development process, is the key to successful product innovation. Managers who insist that new products be technically superior, satisfy market needs, and take advantage of corporate strengths make a major contribution to the reduction of new-product failure.

In addition to such internal and strategic factors, specific errors often lead to the failure of a particular new product. Table 14.1 summarizes fourteen major pitfalls that must be avoided if a new product is to be successful.

A firm whose strategy is premised on a successful new-products program must find ways to avoid these pitfalls while creating and manufacturing quality products that meet customer needs better than competitive alternatives.

DEALING WITH RISK BY SEQUENTIAL DECISION MAKING

One way to minimize wasted resources and reduce the percentage of new-product failures is to use a sequential Go/No Go decision process in which "poor" projects are eliminated early and "good" projects are given priority. Pitfalls 1 and 2 in Table 14.1 are avoided by screening and analysis, pitfalls 3 through 8 by careful design and market testing, and pitfalls 9 through 12 by continual monitoring of the market, competitive environments, and product launch strategy. Pitfalls 13 and 14 must be addressed throughout the product development and introduction process. Figure 14.2 shows two simplified sets of decision sequences intended to minimize the risks of falling victim to one of the pitfalls. Figure 14.2A delineates a series of steps to be followed by a firm engaged in a proactive new-products strategy, while the sequence shown in Figure 14.2B would be more appropriate for a company employing a reactive strategy. Let us consider each of these two approaches in turn.

Proactive Product Development

Proactive new-product development is driven by marketing strategy. The diagnostic and strategy formulation processes described in Chapter 2 should indicate clearly how much sales and profit growth from new products the firm requires, the nature of its competitive advantage, and the product/market configurations where its distinctive competencies are likely to lead to the greatest competitive advantage. The best new-product opportunities are likely to lie in a target domain delineated by these processes.

Opportunity identification should be based on a systematic search of the target domain. New technological capabilities, when assessed vis-à-vis customer needs, may be a major source of potential advantages. Similarly, an in-depth understanding of customer requirements and buying behavior can provide insights useful for identifying appropriate new technologies.

Recent research (von Hippel, 1988) demonstrates that customers often have remarkably concrete ideas on how their needs might most effectively be satisfied, or even specific problem solutions awaiting implementation by an alert vendor. Acquisitions and joint ventures can also provide excellent opportunities by leveraging internal strengths or adding new ones that, in effect, expand the firm's target domain. While either technology or customer needs may be the prime determinant of a fruitful opportunity, we strongly believe that the most effective new-product strategies (with respect to both payoff and risk reduction) result from a balanced consideration of both technological and market inputs.

Leading firms have come to recognize how scarce a resource creativity is, and thus seek to utilize it efficiently by integrating the search for ideas as closely as possible with their overall marketing strategies. The traditional process of generating a very large number of ideas and *then* screening them is rapidly being replaced by one of identifying a few high-potential ideas in strategic areas where the firm has a competitive advantage and then evaluating them in depth.[3] If a good opportunity is found, a Go decision is made and design efforts begin. If an adequately attractive opportunity is not found, the search process recommences, generally with a modified set of targeting criteria.

---

[3] According to Booz, Allen, and Hamilton (1982), the fraction of expenditures on product development devoted to idea generation and evaluation doubled from 10 to 21 percent between 1963 and 1981.

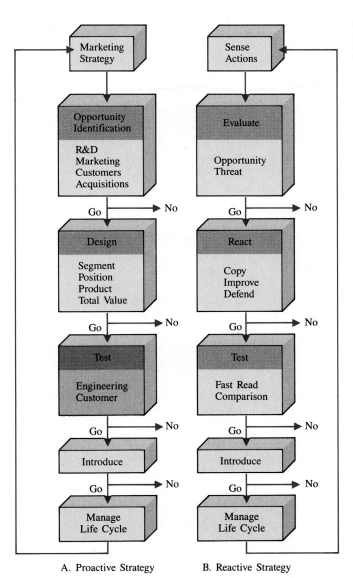

A. Proactive Strategy   B. Reactive Strategy

FIGURE 14.2
Decision Process

The first step in converting attractive opportunities into product *designs* is to define the target market segment and to specify the core benefit proposition (features, perceptual dimensions, importances, and ratings versus competition).[4] The next step is to begin the actual design process with concept specification and testing. The product features must fulfill the previously specified (and, hopefully, tested) core benefit proposition and achieve the desired "positioning" vis-à-vis the target market segments. Other elements in the "bundle" (e.g., price, advertising, promotion, selling, distribution, and service) complete the design of the product. Finally, this total bundle of utility is presented to customers for judgment. Depending on their response, the project may be aborted or there may be a Go decision for full-scale testing. A typical development process involves a series of such milestone Go/No Go decisions, after each of which the product is iteratively improved and further evaluated.

After the product design has been completed, it is essential to conduct a comprehensive *test* of customer reactions. This study should assess, *from the customer's perspective*, whether the newly designed product meets its target specifications, and then provide inputs to the development of a sales forecast for the new product. Often customer evaluation at this point in the development process leads to the discovery of new needs or criteria. The outcome of this research may be a decision to Go to introduction, to refine the product further, or to terminate the project (a No decision).

Customer testing at this stage in the process is critical. So is engineering evaluation to assure that the product is of high quality, will meet customer requirements reliably, and can be mass-produced at the desired quality and cost levels. Effective linkage among marketing, engineering, and manufacturing is increasingly important as customers become more sophisticated and markets more competitive.

Introduction can now occur on the assumption that the new product does indeed satisfy real needs and that adequate levels of profits and ROI can be earned with a minimum of risk. Actual results will, of course, depend to a considerable degree on how well the introductory strategy (production, advertising, promotion, selling, distribution, service, and pricing) is formulated and implemented and on how well the product is *managed over the life cycle*. At some point the product may be restaged (note arrow back to strategy in Figure 14.2A) or dropped from the product line.

Reactive Product Development

Although most firms seek to develop new products proactively, it may be more appropriate to adopt a reactive new-product strategy when doing so promises to reduce both costs and risks significantly. If such a strategy is to be effective, it is essential to put in place processes to *sense actions and changes* in the market rapidly and accurately. Competitive moves must be recognized quickly. New competitive products, for example, should be discovered while they are still in test market (or even earlier by watching markets, talking to customers, and interviewing suppliers). Nabisco and Keebler, for example, both read Procter and Gamble's test market for a new line of "soft" chocolate chip cookies, and were able to beat P&G to the market.

After a competitive product or activity has been identified, the next step is to *evaluate* it as a potential threat or opportunity. If it has the potential to reduce our margins or profits, we should formulate a reactive strategy to defend our product line. Even if there seems to be no direct threat to our existing product line, we might choose to emulate the new competitive entry because of the opportunity it appears to represent.

Our *reaction* might be either to copy the competitive entry as exactly as possible or to improve upon the competitor's concept or execution. If we believe we are vulnerable

---

[4] See Chapters 7 and 8 for a description of this activity.

to the new entry, we might want to reposition our existing products, add a new product to counter the threat, or vary our price, promotion, advertising, or selling tactics.

Testing of the specific elements in a reactive marketing program needs to be as rapid and "invisible" as possible to minimize the impact of a competitive response to our *reaction*. We could, for example, test our new product against the competitive entry (whose test market performance we have monitored) or we could conduct a premarket forecasting study. If the results of such studies look promising, we would move as rapidly as possible to a national launch. If not, we would recycle to the development of new reactive programs or terminate the process and wait for the next input.

Introduction and *managing the life cycle* are much the same as under a proactive strategy, except that these steps should be implemented more rapidly and less expensively. When employing a reactive strategy, it is especially necessary to modify the marketing program as soon as new competitive actions are diagnosed.

Strategy Selection

Which strategy you select will depend on the characteristics of the market concerned and on your firm's competitive advantages. If your firm has strong R&D skills and marketing power, a proactive strategy will generally be most effective, especially if the market responds to premium benefit products and rewards the pioneer in a product category with incremental sales. If, conversely, your firm is flexible and can react quickly, and the market is one where price is important and products are not perceived as widely differentiated, a reactive strategy may be appropriate. If the experience curve is not too steep, as the reactor, you may be able to charge lower prices because your lower development and introductory advertising costs outweigh whatever modest benefits your competitor may derive from being cumulatively farther out on the learning curve.

In a study of 195 industrial Canadian new products (102 successes [52 percent] and 93 failures), Calantone and Cooper (1981) found that both proactive and reactive strategies could be successful. Four proactive strategies had high success rates: (1) utilizing the firm's existing marketing and production knowledge to introduce a product with benefits to customer segments new to the firm (67 percent success); (2) developing a superior product without using synergies based on existing production and marketing knowledge (70 percent success); (3) being the first to introduce an innovative high-technology product that meets customer needs (64 percent success); and (4) reducing costs to deliver improved value to customers (70 percent success). However, all proactive strategies were not successful. "A better mousetrap" with poor marketing "succeeded" in only 36 percent of the cases, and "an innovative mousetrap that really wasn't better" failed in all cases. Judging from these data, proactive strategies generally require both demonstrably superior products *and* effective marketing to succeed.

Reactive strategies also varied considerably in degree of success. Defensive strategies that exploited technical, marketing, and production synergies within the firm to create unique product features tended to be successful. This "second but better" strategy led to market success in 72 percent of the cases. "Me too" products that were late entrants experienced less success (56 percent) than those introduced under a "second but better" strategy. Even lower success (14 percent) was achieved when the "me too" product was not synergistic with the firm's technical and production capabilities.

Clearly, both reactive and proactive strategies can lead to success. Either may be utilized exclusively, but most firms will find it beneficial to employ both types of strategy, depending on market and competitive conditions. The steps in a proactive strategy tend to be slow and methodical, while speed is essential for a successful reactive strategy. Although an effective proactive strategy continually monitors competitors' actions, response to such actions typically has to wait for the completion of design and testing. And this may be too slow in many cases. Therefore, it is best to utilize both strategies for the

✳ generation of new products: proactive strategies for major "breakthrough" innovations,
✳ and reactive strategies for defending existing businesses and responding opportunistically
✳ to major competitive initiatives.

Program Formulation, Resource Commitments, and Implementation

Whether a new product emanates from a proactive or a reactive strategy, it is necessary to formulate, evaluate, and prioritize the key elements in its introductory marketing program. The complete implementation of such a program (including appropriate decision support processes) is an exceptionally complex task, the full treatment of which exceeds the scope of this book. We shall, however, consider two major program elements, budgeting and organization design, since these topics lie at the heart of the marketing strategy process.

Budgeting: At the strategic level, it is necessary to establish an overall new-products budget that truly reflects the risks in the development process. Enough projects must be initiated that, after accounting for failure at each stage of the process (opportunity identification, design, testing, and launch), an adequate number of products (given the firm's sales and growth goals) will be introduced. If, for example, the probability of success is .5 at each of the four stages, we would have to engage in sixteen opportunity searches to identify eight attractive market/technology areas. Of eight design projects, four would meet technical and market requirements. If we then market-tested these four products, only two would meet the criteria for market introduction. If both were launched, one would succeed.

While these probabilities are only illustrative, they do demonstrate an important strategic budgeting phenomenon: significant resources must be committed early if we are to end up with enough alternatives to meet our sales and profit goals. Table 14.2 is based on more typical probability values and cost estimates of each step in the new-product process (Booz, Allen, and Hamilton, 1982). In this particular example, the total cost of obtaining a successful new product is approximately $31 million: 15 percent is spent on opportunity identification, 44 percent on design, 16 percent on testing, and 25 percent on launch. These values will, of course, vary considerably according to the firm's efficiency and the characteristics of the product and the industry. In industrial markets, for example, development costs are generally higher relative to introduction costs than in consumer products markets. In some instances (e.g., the GE and Buick cases presented in Chapters 4 and 13), the design phase alone may require expenditures of hundreds of millions of

TABLE 14.2 Typical Development Costs and Probabilities

PHASE	COST/PRODUCT IN PHASE ($000's)	PROBABILITY OF SUCCESS IN PHASE	EXPECTED COST ($000's)	PROPORTION OF TOTAL EXPECTED COST
Opportunity identification	600	.5	4,626	15
Design	3,500	.57	13,495	44
Testing	2,250	.7	4,945	16
Introduction	5,000	.65	7,690	25
Total			30,756	

Source: Adapted from Tables 1 and 2 of Terry Elrod and Alan P. Kelman, "Reliability of New Product Evaluation as of 1968 and 1981," *Working Paper* (Nashville, TN: Owen Graduate School of Management, 1987). Generation and screening are combined as "Opportunity identification"; and business analysis and development are combined as "Design."

dollars. In other industries, like gaskets or lubricants, design costs for new products may be subsumed under day-to-day operating expenses.

The simple calculation in Table 14.2 can be carried out for any firm by substituting its own specific cost and probability estimates. If the resulting total cost necessary for one successful new product is $30 million and four new products per year are required, it is necessary for a firm employing a proactive strategy to budget $120 million per year for new-product development, of which more than $50 million (44 percent) would be allocated to engineering and marketing development and design.

In practice, even this new-product budget would be insufficient. It would have to be supplemented by budgets for studying basic technology in fields selected for competitive advantage (say, $25 million) and for mounting reactive development programs to defend existing markets (say, $10 million). In this example, the total new-product development budget would be over $200 million per year!

While the appropriate budget for a particular firm will depend on *its* specific costs and probabilities, it will almost always be larger than one would intuitively expect. A proactive new-product strategy will often provide a firm with a sustainable competitive advantage, but only if the firm is willing to make major investments for the long term.

Organization: The budget and time requirements that result from these sequential probabilities lead to significant organizational challenges. The organization structure must bring about an integration of technical, production, and marketing skills, encourage creativity and entrepreneurship, facilitate a careful balancing of risks and rewards, and ensure that new-product activities are aligned with the overall corporate strategy. Numerous organization approaches to these challenges have been proposed. Among the most common are: (1) technical development laboratories; (2) new-product departments; (3) new-product committees and task forces; (4) venture groups; (5) ''skunk works''; and (6) entrepreneurial project homes. Activities of these sorts may take place at the corporate, division, and/or group level, and may report to R&D, marketing, and/or top management. No one organizational structure can be said to be the best under all circumstances. In fact, according to a recent study, over 70 percent of firms utilize multiple levels or structures for new products (The Conference Board, 1986, p. 53). We discuss this later in this chapter as we consider integrating marketing and technology.

Successful new-product strategies require large budgets and complex organizational structures. A firm's new-product strategy must be deeply embedded in its culture, organizational structure, and budgeting processes. (Readers seeking a more comprehensive treatment of these issues are referred to Urban, Hauser, and Dholakia, 1987, for a consideration of each step in the new-product development process; and to Urban and Hauser, 1980, for quantitative methods and cross-references to other sources.)

BENEFITS OF INNOVATION—ORDER OF ENTRY

Market-Generated Rewards and Strategy

One important issue in formulating new-product strategy is whether there is a significant benefit to being first in the market. Where the innovator is rewarded with a higher market share, lower costs, and/or higher prices, the attractiveness of a proactive strategy increases, since the resulting higher profits will compensate the proactive firm for its greater risks and investment in research and development. Where such benefits are insignificant, however, reactive strategies become more appealing because of the lower risk and investment inherent in following rather than leading.

A market reward for pioneering is conceptually equivalent to a patent. Because patents provide the innovator with an exclusive right to market a product for a period of time, they are very desirable. In practice, they are often difficult to obtain and costly to defend, but still, they are worth the price if they lead to a sustainable competitive advantage.

Sources of Pioneering Advantage

In addition to the protection afforded by a patent, two fundamental classes of advantage may accrue to pioneers. The first are "innate" advantages that the innovator obtains simply from having the first product available in the market. The second are "unique" advantages that only come into play when exploited effectively by the pioneering firm.

Innate advantages result from the basic behavioral phenomena that underlie choice. In Chapter 5, Customer Decision Making, we discussed memory and the concept of nodes with surrounding schema as a process for organizing information. The organization of information in long-term memory controls the accessibility and availability of that information for decision making. If the first product creates a node or subnode in a memory hierarchy, it may become the prototype or exemplar of the node. Information about competing products that is stored in the schema surrounding this node may then be referenced through comparison to the exemplar. Memory access to the node may evoke the exemplar first, producing a competitive advantage in the marketplace. Later entrants will be compared to the first product, giving the innovator the benefit of being the standard of comparison and the most distinctive product in the set. (See Carpenter and Nakamoto, 1989, for further discussion of the behavioral sources of innovation.)

The second innate advantage of being a pioneer derives from the inherent risk consumers face in adopting a new product. There is always some uncertainty about whether a new product will deliver its claimed benefits. If the first product in the market has been purchased and found to be satisfactory, subsequent entries that are objectively equivalent may still be perceived as carrying a significant amount of risk. In effect, the consumer (whose initial problem has presumably been solved satisfactorily) asks, "Why take a chance on a new product that, *at best*, is no better than the product I am currently buying?" To obtain trial under these circumstances, the second brand in the market must either charge a lower price or offer increased benefits to compensate for the perceived risk it represents. Conversely, the pioneer can charge a higher price or achieve greater sales than subsequent entries. (See Schmallensee, 1982, for an argument from economics along these lines.)

The third innate advantage of pioneering derives from the monopoly enjoyed by the innovator prior to the introduction of subsequent entries. If the innovating product is profitable during this period, it will have produced profits that will never be available to followers.

Unique advantages are available to pioneers from two sources. First, pioneers are in a position to exploit the experience curve. Because of their time lead in the market, they can build cumulative volume faster than competitors. This is a unique advantage, but only if programs are put in place to build dominant volume. An aggressive second entrant that buys market share through heavy marketing expenditures may catch and surpass the pioneer in cumulative volume, and become the low-cost producer.

Positioning can also be an advantage. If the pioneer positions its new product optimally with regard to claimed product benefits, competitive game theory suggests that it can sustain its first-mover advantage even after competitors enter the market. Although later entrants could copy the innovator's positioning exactly, simulations employing game theory suggest that over a wide range of competitive responses a "copycat" strategy would not maximize the follower's profitability. It is better for followers to differentiate their products even though in doing so, they will never be as successful as the innovator—*provided the innovator has selected the best initial position.*

Empirical Evidence of Pioneering Advantage

According to PIMS data on forty industrial product markets, firms that claimed to be pioneers on the average obtained a dominant market share of 40 percent. Four years after one new competitor entered each market, these shares declined to 28 percent, but nevertheless remained higher than the 15 percent average share of the new entrants (Biggadike, 1976).

Similar PIMS data for 371 consumer products also indicated that pioneers retained an advantage. Respondent firms were asked to classify each of their strategic business units (SBUs) as pioneers, early followers, or late adopters. On the average, pioneers had 29 percent market share, early followers 17 percent, and late entrants 12 percent (Robinson and Fornell, 1985). Analogous industrial product data for 1209 SBUs showed 29 percent share for pioneers, 21 percent for early followers, and 15 percent for late entrants (Robinson, 1988b).

An in-depth study of eighty-two brands in twenty-four categories of frequently purchased consumer products suggests that early entrants do indeed obtain innate rewards, but also that positioning and advertising are important moderators of the order-of-entry effect (Urban, Carter, Gaskin, and Mucha, 1986). Market share of later entrants relative to the first entrant was regressed against the order of entry (2, 3, 4, . . .), relative positioning advantage as measured by the preference for the entrant relative to the pioneer, and relative expenditures on advertising. High levels of statistical significance were found, and predictive testing on forty-seven new brands in twelve categories confirmed the results. The innate effects shown in Table 14.3 indicate that the first brand's share will drop as subsequent identical brands enter: from 100 to 58.5 percent following a second entry, to 43.6 percent following a third entry, and so forth, until the pioneering brand's share has fallen to 27.3 percent in a six-brand market.

Note that while the pioneering brand does retain a share advantage regardless of the number of subsequent entrants, a late entrant can, under certain circumstances, overcome this advantage. In several of the observations in this study, a later entrant achieved a greater share than the pioneer through improved product positioning and more aggressive marketing.

In an examination of time series and cross-sectional data in consumer packaged goods, the order-of-entry effects were found not only in share data but also in trial and repeat behavior (Kalyanaram and Urban, 1990). This analysis also indicated that although late entrants will achieve lower share levels, they will reach these levels faster than early entrants. The penalty in the long run was present, but the later entrants were partially compensated by gaining their reduced share faster than pioneers.

In theory, all the firms in a given market can use advertising to increase market share. Although pioneers have no innate or unique advantage in this regard, they often seem better able to obtain benefits from aggressive spending on advertising than later

TABLE 14.3   Market Shares and Order of Entry

ENTRY ORDER	1ST	2ND	3RD	4TH	5TH	6TH
1st	100					
2nd	58.5	41.5				
3rd	43.6	31.0	25.4			
4th	35.7	25.4	20.8	18.1		
5th	30.8	21.9	17.9	15.5	13.9	
6th	27.3	19.4	15.9	13.8	12.4	11.2

entrants. We call this a "moderating" advantage because it can be used to modify the underlying innate and unique advantages. In consumer and industrial markets, product quality and breadth of product line can similarly be used to moderate advantage (Robinson and Fornell, 1985, and Robinson, 1988b). Empirically, pioneers seem to have better quality and wider product lines, and to spend more on advertising.

Strategic Implications

These theoretical and empirical arguments suggest that a proactive strategy may be rewarding even when formal patent protection is not available. In most cases, a substantial market share advantage will accrue to the first entrant in a market. If there are significant experience curve effects, the first entrant should be able to translate its lead in cumulative production into a meaningful cost advantage, and its lead in market share into a secure market franchise. The pioneer must be careful, though, to ensure that later entrants are not able to use improved positioning or heavier expenditures on advertising and promotion to catch up and take the lead. In today's highly competitive markets, a pioneer that rests on its laurels is unlikely to sustain its competitive advantage.

These studies also have implications for firms employing reactive strategies. While a "me too" strategy based on a parity product is unlikely to achieve as high a market share as that of the first entrant, it may nevertheless be profitable if the industry and market are basically healthy. Moreover, it may be possible for the later entrant to come into the market with an improved product that is backed by aggressive marketing. In the absence of effective competitive response, this "second but better" strategy may overcome the innate advantage of the pioneer and result in market leadership.

MARKETING/TECHNOLOGY INTERFACE

Critical Success Factor

The success of a proactive new-product strategy is highly dependent on a firm's effectiveness in linking technology and customer needs. Since customers only buy products that they perceive as filling their needs, it is critical that customer input be brought to bear early in the new-product design process. "Marketing" in its broadest sense (the total fulfillment of customer requirements) must be closely integrated with technology at every step in the design and engineering of new products if risks are to be reduced and innovation is to be successful.

The challenge is how to combine these very different inputs. Leading firms have commonly employed two basic approaches. The first is to develop a technological advantage, then find a market for the products that result from the technological innovation, and finally, sell the product to that market. The second is to identify a market need, develop a product to satisfy it, and then sell that product to the targeted market segment. Both approaches have been successful, and each has strong advocates. The first has been termed the *R&D approach*, and the second the *marketing approach*.

Polarization between these two basic approaches was common in the 1960s and 1970s, and led to much organizational conflict and debate. Upon reflection, it now seems obvious that each approach has its advantages, and that what is required is their integration, rather than the selection of one or the other. Empirical studies indicate the importance of both technological and user inputs. According to one major study covering a wide variety of industries, between 60 and 80 percent of successful technologically based products were developed in direct response to market needs and demands (Utterbach, 1974).

In today's rapidly moving and highly competitive markets, most firms find it necessary to employ integrated strategies combining marketing and technology in the design of new products. Some of the best "marketers" we know are heads of R&D who have comprehensive perspectives on customer needs. We can also cite marketing vice presidents with in-depth knowledge of the technologies underlying their businesses. Unfortunately, however, it is far more common for marketing managers, with inadequate understanding of technology, to have little choice but to emphasize short-term promotional and sales efforts; and for R&D managers, with limited customer contact (at best), to merely pay lip service to satisfying customer needs. Our experience suggests that true integration between technology and marketing only occurs when strategic programs "to make it happen" have been put in place.

Integration Mechanisms

Three mechanisms have typically been used by firms to support strategies requiring the integration of marketing and technology: (1) formal organizational structures; (2) interpersonal relations; and (3) analytical support.

A variety of formal organizational structures can be utilized to facilitate the integration of marketing and technology. Table 14.4 enumerates a number of alternatives. Empirical studies suggest that no one form is dominant and that most firms use multiple structures. A single organization might, for example, have a growth and development group with a charter to develop new business areas (reporting to a vice president); a new-products department charged with designing product-line extensions (located in the marketing department); a marketing research function to assess customer needs for new technologies (in the R&D group); and a separate entrepreneurial division intended to provide a home for innovators with new ideas.

One reason why no one formal integrating mechanism is dominant is that the problem is often fundamentally an interpersonal one. Marketing managers are usually not technically trained, tend to have short-run perspectives, prefer structured tasks, and often are outgoing. Engineers and scientists generally lack training in marketing and management, tend to focus on long-term results, are comfortable working on unstructured tasks, and are frequently reserved. Obviously, the potential for conflict is high.

In his study of 289 new-product development projects across fifty-six firms, Souder (1987) classified firms as having "harmonious" or "disharmonious" relations between marketing and R&D. He found disharmony in 59.2 percent of the projects: "severe disharmony" (lack of appreciation and distrust) in 38.7 percent of cases, and "mild disharmony" (lack of interaction and communication, reluctance to criticize friends) in 20.5 percent. Harmonious relations were observed in only 40.8 percent of the projects. In 29.1 percent of these cases, either marketing or R&D was dominant, while in only 11.7 percent did the two functions appear to be engaged in equal partnerships. Perhaps the most important finding of this study, however, was the clear relationship Souder found

TABLE 14.4 Formal Organizational Structures to Integrate Marketing and R&D

1. R&D reports to V.P. marketing
2. Marketing reports to R&D
3. Growth and development department with assigned R&D and marketing staff
4. Matrix of R&D and marketing efforts assigned to new-product development projects
5. Venture teams including R&D and marketing
6. R&D representative assigned to each SBU
7. Dedicated marketing research group in R&D
8. Integrated design group consisting of marketing, R&D, engineering, and manufacturing
9. SBUs with budgets to buy internal (or external) R&D or marketing skills from corporate staff groups
10. Division to house entrepreneurs with access to corporate R&D and marketing resources

between organizational harmony and success in new-product development. Of the projects characterized by severe disharmony, 68 percent failed, in contrast to a failure rate of 23 percent for those experiencing mild disharmony and only 13 percent for those enjoying harmonious relations between marketing and R&D.

Our opinion is that it is far too limiting to view the problem as merely one of integrating the marketing and R&D departments. In order for the two functions to work together rather than at cross-purposes, marketing and R&D personnel must be sensitized to the requirements and processes of each other's disciplines. In many leading companies, engineers attend formal marketing education programs and marketers study technology, and managers are transferred between engineering management and marketing management positions. Some companies have also found it effective to form "dyads" in which a marketer and an engineer work together to accomplish a common set of tasks. In Japan, it is common for an engineer to serve as a salesman before being placed in an R&D group. More and more business schools are teaching technology to their students, while engineering students frequently take at least some "marketing" electives. Clearly, the manager in the twenty-first century will have to be well versed in both marketing and technology if he or she is to play a major role in strategic management.

The third component in a program to integrate technology and marketing is analytic support of the process. "Quality functional deployment,"[5] for example, represents the formalization of good marketing, engineering, industrial relations, and manufacturing theory. First, customers define "quality" in *their* terms through techniques such as perceptual semantics and attribute/price/value trade-offs. These customer requirements are then transformed into detailed engineering specifications through an "integrated design" effort that evaluates alternative product designs and production processes simultaneously. The product is designed to meet both functional specifications and manufacturing constraints and efficiencies. If trade-offs in design are made, they reflect all three aspects of customer preference: engineering requirements, production reliability, and cost. The product is manufactured with strict quality control and active worker participation. A strong customer service function is charged with ensuring that the customer ultimately receives the benefits originally identified as the "purpose" of the new product. This and similar processes are intended to *force* integration of customer needs, responsive product design, manufacturing quality control, and service.

Analytic market research methods can help measure and quantify customer perceptions and trade-offs (see Chapter 6 of this book; and Urban and Hauser, 1980). There are two common objections to the use of customer input early in the design process: "Customers do not know what they want until they see it" and "The technology is changing so fast that marketing research will soon be out of date." Many times these concerns are valid, but firms have found it possible to overcome them by employing the "lead users" concept. This concept is based on the premise that there are some users who are far ahead of the majority of the market in understanding technology, and who are grappling today with needs that the remainder of the market will only face well into the future. To the degree that this is a valid supposition, lead users (if identified and willing to cooperate) can provide a "window" through which future customer needs and buying behavior can be observed.

Research indicates that such users not only have *needs* but may also have developed *solutions* to the problems resulting from their needs. Such solutions range from insights into how a problem might be solved to a working and tested prototype. Users are often active in generating products—in some fields, they invent the majority of successful new products. Two seminal studies of this phenomenon found that users rather than vendors designed and developed 82 percent of all commercialized scientific instruments and 63

---

[5] This approach evolved out of statistical quality control systems developed by Americans, but implemented as "total quality control" by Japanese firms (Feigenbaum, 1956; Cusumano, 1985). (See Hauser and Clausing, 1988, for more detail.)

percent of all semiconductor and electronic subassembly manufacturing equipment innovations studied (von Hippel, 1976 and 1977).

Lead Users and Product Innovation: A Case Study

The lead user concept is illustrated by a recent study of computer-aided design (CAD) systems (Urban and von Hippel, 1988). This study focused on the submarket for CAD software employed in the design of printed circuit boards.[6] These PC-CAD systems play important roles in placing chips on the board, routing the solder wires called "vias," testing, and manufacturing. The objective of the study was to determine, first, whether lead users could be identified, and then, whether their proposed "solutions" to a given problem could provide the basis for a product concept that would appeal to the remainder of the market. "Traditional wisdom," as expressed by a leading CAD supplier, held that it was unlikely that users would develop their own software, partly because the algorithms required were very sophisticated and the graphical interfaces very complex, and partly because such an effort required major resources.

The study attempted to identify lead users by specifying a series of indicators that reflected being at the leading edge of an important technological trend and the customers' propensity to create solutions to enable them to benefit from the trend. Consultation with experts in the field led to the identification of a significant trend toward greater density of integrated chips on a board (more chips per square inch). Higher density could be accomplished by using multiple layers in the board, making the vias narrower, or by using surface-mounted chips.[7] It was hypothesized that users who employed these technical methods, were innovative, felt dissatisfied with commercially available systems, and had adopted CAD early would be most likely to build their own PC-CAD systems.

It would be possible to utilize these indicators by informally calling on customers and potential customers, talking to sales and service personnel, interviewing industry experts, and/or contacting user groups. The Urban and von Hippel study used a more formal approach rooted in market research procedures. A questionnaire based on the indicators was developed and administered to 136 electronic engineers and engineering managers. Contrary to industry expectations, CAD users were found to be very active in developing their own solutions: 25 percent had built their own PC-CAD systems, while 45 percent had modified commercial systems. A subset of lead users was identified through cluster analysis. Lead users in this cluster used more surface mounting (87 percent versus 56 percent), narrower vias (11 mills versus 15 mills), and more layers (7.1 versus 4.0). They were more likely to have built their own systems (87 percent versus only 1 percent), to be innovative (3.3 versus 2.4 on a 4-point innovativeness scale),[8] to be dissatisfied with existing commercial systems (4.1 versus 5.3 on a 7-point satisfaction scale), and to have adopted CAD earlier (1973 versus 1980).

Five of the lead users who had developed their own systems were invited to attend a group session where specs would be established for a new PC-CAD system based on the solutions they had developed. Under the concept they came up with, the new CAD system would have direct links to numerically controlled machine tools, easier computer interfaces, central data storage, and functional simulation capabilities (electrical, mechanical, and thermal), and would be capable of designing boards of up to forty layers, routed with thinner vias, which utilized surface-mounted devices.

---

[6] Printed circuit boards hold integrated circuit chips and other electronic components and interconnect these into functioning circuits.

[7] In surface mounting, chips and other components are soldered to the board instead of being mounted on legs that fit into drilled holes.

[8] This scale ranged from 1, "adopt a new technology only when it is established," to 4, "always on the leading edge of technology."

The customers originally identified in the screening phase of the study were then resurveyed to test the new concept versus each respondent's current system, and also what each respondent considered to be the best available commercial system. Each respondent's first-choice selection, preference (constant sum judgments), and probability of purchase were assessed. It turned out that 78.6 percent of the respondents preferred the new concept; their constant sum preference value was 40 percent higher than for their current system, and 25 percent higher than for the best commercially available system. In fact, the concept developed by the five lead users in the group session was preferred to the best available commercial system *even at twice the price*.

ANALYTIC SUPPORT AND THE FUTURE OF NEW-PRODUCT STRATEGY

Lead user studies and order-of-entry analyses are only two examples of the many techniques available to support the sequential steps in new-product development shown in Figure 14.2. Perceptual mapping, conjoint analysis, and premarket forecasting are proven techniques that help reduce risk and improve products. Many more Level II and III techniques are being developed. Nevertheless, it is essential to remember not to begin Level II or III analysis before having satisfactorily completed Level I. Poor marketing analysis and forecasting is worse than none! A myopic forecast may cause a firm to reject a technology with major potential, while a forecast that does not adequately take into account the possibility of competitive retaliation could lead a firm into dangerous marketing territory.

Before embarking on a new-product strategy, make sure that you: (1) have developed a sound overall marketing strategy and decided whether to be proactive or reactive in product innovation; (2) have systematically and adequately budgeted for your new-product program; (3) have maximized creativity in finding market and technical opportunities; (4) have involved lead users in the design effort as much as possible; (5) understand the core benefit that your new product or service is intended to offer; (6) know who will be competing with you and what their competitive strategies are likely to entail; and (7) have blended qualitative and quantitative inputs in an overall assessment of the risks and rewards of your chosen strategy.

The future will be increasingly challenging for managers charged with responsibility for new products. There will be more competition, both domestically and internationally, in design and marketing. Success will depend on getting to the right markets fast with the right products, and then aggressively defending whatever advantage has been achieved through innovation. Level II and III analytical methods will be increasingly utilized to indicate when testing can be compressed or curtailed and to balance the increased risk of failure versus the potential gain of being an early entrant (see Urban and Katz, 1983, for a consumer packaged goods example).

Efforts to get to market faster will encompass engineering and production as well as marketing. Careful, early market research will minimize expensive and time-consuming "re-engineering." Overlapping development and careful coordination will reduce total development time (see Clark and Fujimoto, 1987). In increasingly saturated markets, it will be necessary to supplement creativity with analysis and to evaluate technological advances early in the design process. While there will be substantial opportunities for firms that make full use of the growing powerful array of tools available to them, the world will become increasingly threatening to organizations that are locked into traditional ways of thinking and doing things.

QUESTIONS FOR DISCUSSION

1. Figure 14.1 shows the relative importance of phenomena in each decision area. Assume that each cell not indicated is the most important and discuss why it might be more important than indicated.

2. If new-product innovation is so risky, why undertake it?

3. What are the causes of new-product failure? List them in decreasing order of importance and describe how a manager could minimize the risk presented by the top five causes.

4. When is a reactive new-product strategy better than a proactive one?

5. Why include customers early in the opportunity identification and design process? Is it not better to push the technology and use engineering judgment to create real product innovations, since customers probably will not be able to judge them accurately?

6. Table 14.2 indicates that more money is spent on product design than on product introduction. How can this be when we know that for any single product taken to market the introduction costs will be larger than the design cost for that product?

7. Our new brand of tartar-control toothpaste is just as good as P&G's Crest according to blind product test comparisons, our advertising copy tests show we will be at parity with Crest, and we intend to spend as much on advertising and promotion as P&G; therefore, we will get the same market share as they have after two years. What is wrong with this argument? What would be necessary to obtain a share equal to Crest's if our brand is the fourth entrant into the market?

8. In your opinion, what are the three most important reasons why marketing and R&D engineering do not work well together? What actions can be taken to overcome the problem?

9. Lead user studies can take place at Levels I and II of analytic support. What activities would go on in a Level I study? In a Level II study? When would Level II be appropriate?

REFERENCES

ASSOCIATION OF NATIONAL ADVERTISERS. 1984. *Prescription for New Product Success.* New York: Association of National Advertisers.

BIGGADIKE, RALPH E. 1976. *Entry Strategy and Performance.* Cambridge, MA: Harvard University Press.

BOOZ, ALLEN, AND HAMILTON. 1982. *New Product Management for the 1980's.* New York: Booz, Allen & Hamilton.

BOSTON GLOBE. 1987. ''Jury Says Polaroid Should Pay $80m.'' July 11, p. 33.

CALANTONE, ROGER, AND ROBERT G. COOPER. 1981. ''New Product Scenarios: Prospects for Success.'' *Journal of Marketing* 45: 48–60.

CARPENTER, GREGORY S., AND KENT NAKAMOTO. 1989. ''Consumer Preference Formation and Pioneering Advantage. *Journal of Marketing Research* 26: 285–298.

CLARK, KIM B., AND TAKAHIRO FUJIMOTO. 1987. ''Overlapping Problem Solving in Product Development.'' Working Paper. Boston, MA: Harvard Business School.

THE CONFERENCE BOARD. 1986. *The Commercial Development of New Products.* New York: The Conference Board.

CUSUMANO, MICHAEL A. 1985. *The Japanese Automobile Industry.* Cambridge, MA: Harvard University Press.

ELROD, TERRY, AND ALAN P. KELMAN. 1987. ''Reliability of New Product Evaluation as of 1968 and 1981.'' Working Paper. Nashville, TN: Owen Graduate School of Management, Vanderbilt University, p. 23.

FEIGENBAUM, A. V. 1956. ''Total Quality Control.'' *Harvard Business Review* 34: 93–101.

GATIGNON, HUBERT, ERIN ANDERSON, AND KRISTIAAN HELSEN. 1989. "Competitive Reactions to Market Entry: Explaining Interfirm Differences." *Journal of Marketing Research* 26: 44–55.

GUPTA, ASHOK K., S. P. RAJ, AND DAVID WILEMON. 1986. "A Model for Studying R&D–Marketing Interface in the Product Innovation Process." *Journal of Marketing* 50: 7–17.

HAUSER, JOHN R., AND DON CLAUSING. 1988. "The House of Quality." *Harvard Business Review* 66: 63–73.

KALYANARAM, GURUMURTHY, AND GLEN L. URBAN. 1990. "Dynamic Effects of the Order of Entry on Market Share, Trial Penetration, and Repeat Purchase for Frequently Purchased Consumer Goods." Working Paper. Cambridge, MA: MIT Sloan School of Management.

MANSFIELD, EDWIN. 1988. "The Speed and Cost of Industrial Innovation in Japan and the United States: External vs. Internal Technology." *Management Science* 34: 1157–1168.

ROBERTS, EDWARD B. 1988. "Managing Invention and Innovation." *Technology Management* 31: 11–29.

ROBINSON, WILLIAM T. 1988a. "Marketing Mix Reactions to Entry." *Marketing Science* 7: 368–385.

———. 1988b. "Sources of Pioneer Advantages: A Replication Applied to Industrial Goods Industries." *Journal of Marketing Research* 25: 87–94.

ROBINSON, WILLIAM T., AND C. FORNELL. 1985. "The Sources of Market Pioneer Advantages in Consumer Goods Industries." *Journal of Marketing Research* 22: 297–304.

ROSENBLOOM, RICHARD S., AND MICHAEL A. CUSUMANO. 1987. "Technological Pioneering and Competitive Advantage: The Birth of the VCR Industry." *California Management Review* 29: 51–75.

SCHMALLENSEE, RICHARD. 1982. "Product Differentiation Advantages of Pioneering Brands." *American Economic Review* 72: 159–180.

SOUDER, W. 1987. *Managing New Product Innovations*. Lexington, MA: Lexington Books, pp. 161–178.

TAKEUCHI, HIROTAKA, AND IKUJIRO NONAKA. 1986. "The New Product Development Game." *Harvard Business Review*, January/February: 137–146.

URBAN, GLEN L., THERESA CARTER, STEVEN GASKIN, AND ZOFIA MUCHA. 1986. "Market Share Rewards to Pioneering Brands: An Empirical Analysis and Strategic Implications." *Management Science* 32: 645–659.

URBAN, GLEN L., AND GERALD M. KATZ. 1983. "Pretest Market Models: Validation and Managerial Implications." *Journal of Marketing Research* 20: 221–234.

URBAN, GLEN L., AND JOHN R. HAUSER. 1980. *Design and Marketing New Products*. Englewood Cliffs, NJ: Prentice Hall.

URBAN, GLEN L., JOHN R. HAUSER, AND N. DHOLAKIA. 1987. *Essentials of New Product Management*. Englewood Cliffs, NJ: Prentice Hall.

URBAN, GLEN L., AND ERIC VON HIPPEL. 1988. "Lead User Analyses for the Development of New Industrial Products." *Management Science* 34: 569–582.

UTTERBACH, JAMES M. 1974. "Innovation in Industry and the Diffusion of Technology." *Science* 183: 620–626.

VON HIPPEL, ERIC. 1976. "The Dominant Role of Users in the Scientific Instrument Innovation Process." *Research Policy* 5: 212–239.

———. 1977. "The Dominant Role of the User in Semiconductor and Electronic Subassembly Process Innovation.'' *IEEE Trans. Engineering Management*, EM-24: 60–71.

———. 1986. ''Lead Users: A Source of Novel Product Concepts.'' *Management Science* 32: 791–805.

———. 1988. *The Sources of Innovation*. Oxford: Oxford University Press.

WALL STREET JOURNAL. 1986. ''Federal Express Will Scuttle Zap Mail, Take $190 Million Write-off, Stock Soars.'' September 30, p. 2.

15
MANAGEMENT OF ESTABLISHED PRODUCTS

TRANSITION FROM NEW TO ESTABLISHED PRODUCT

Both proactive and reactive strategies are intended to lead to one or more new products that then must be managed over the course of their product life cycles (see Figure 14.2). After introduction, the new product advances through the stages of growth, maturity, and decline. The degree of success it achieves will depend on how well each of these stages is managed. As we have seen, many pioneering new products fail to sustain their initial competitive advantage, and thus fail to maximize their long-term contributions to profits.

In recent years, it has become common for firms in a wide range of industries to employ the product or brand manager system to manage their product marketing over the life cycle. Under this approach, a particular product is assigned to a specific product or brand manager, who is supposed to manage it much as if it were a free-standing business. He or she is expected to develop an annual plan for the brand, obtain approval for that plan, and then monitor the plan's execution, making whatever revisions are necessary. Generally, the product manager has very little direct authority, but rather is expected to manage the brand through leadership and persuasion, calling on resources from other organizations (e.g., manufacturing, the brand's advertising agency) as appropriate. Although matrix organizations of this type are not without problems, they have generally been found to be an effective means of ensuring adequate focus on individual brands without incurring the high costs of resource duplication. (See Corey and Star, 1970, for an in-depth treatment of this subject.)

While product managers tend to be most significant during the postintroductory stages of the life cycle, many firms employing product management systems assign a product manager to a new product prior to its introduction. Whenever possible, this individual should have worked on the project during its preintroduction phases, in order to have obtained both expertise and a sense of authorship. In the case of a line extension or ''flanker,'' the product manager's role might not be very different from what it would be for an established brand. If the new product represents a major introduction, however, its launch should be managed by the new-product team that developed the product to ensure that its core benefit strategy is implemented effectively. Only if the product manager has extensive experience and is committed to the strategy used in development and testing should he or she be in exclusive control of the introduction.

ROLE OF THE PRODUCT MANAGER

The primary task of product management is to manage the life cycle of a product in such a way as to achieve profit levels that make both the risks taken in development and the commitment of assets during the life cycle worthwhile. In a wider sense, it is product management's responsibility to ensure that the product continues to offer a superior bundle of utility to its target segment in the light of changing customer needs and competitive alternatives.

In this role, the product manager is the customer's voice in establishing a product's marketing strategy. This strategy is usually described in a marketing plan encompassing the product's (1) target markets, (2) competitive positioning, (3) communications program (e.g., advertising, promotion, personal selling, telemarketing, direct mail), (4) distribution channels and physical distribution, (5) customer fulfillment (e.g., product warranties and service), and (6) price. This strategic document reflects many of the fundamentals covered in the first ten chapters of this book. Customer decision-making processes and response analysis, for example, are critical inputs to establishing communications programs, distribution policies, and price levels. Effective targeting depends on market segmentation and the astute selection of the appropriate subsegment(s) for attention. The market share that results from a plan is a critical output of strategy formulation; after costs are modeled, it is the link between marketing strategy and ultimate profits, return on investment, and stockholders' interests. (We will address the translation of the strategy into an annual plan in depth in Chapter 23.)

In addition to being the primary architect of the product's marketing strategy, the product manager is responsible for monitoring changing customer needs and competitive offerings. In carrying out these tasks, the product manager will generally work with the firm's own marketing research and competitive analysis units, as well as with outside sources such as consulting firms, marketing research firms, and advertising agencies. Using the information gathered in these ways, the product manager is expected to assess the long-term competitive strength of the product and to recommend whatever modifications or replacements seem to be desirable.

Just as important as the formulation of a product strategy is the product manager's designation of the specific tactics to be employed. Assume that the brand manager for a brand of toothpaste has decided to use consumer and trade promotions to build share and profits. In support of this strategy, tactical considerations might include: the specific weeks the promotions will be run; the nature of the trade incentive (e.g., one free pack with the purchase of twelve, a larger pack at the same price, a higher advertising allowance, and/ or a cash rebate to the retailer); the consumer promotion elements (e.g., direct-mail coupons, coupons within print ads, in-pack coupons, two-for-one specials, the size of the price discount); and the regions where the promotion is to be run. Similarly, the product manager for a new industrial product whose strategy calls for a "heavy" communications program would need to: establish personal selling call norms for each product and each customer; design selling incentives and training programs; specify the communications mix (e.g., direct mail, telemarketing, advertising, video conferences, brochures, video tapes); arrange for the assembly of account teams (e.g., sales, systems engineering, technical service, and management representatives); determine and disseminate price and discount schedules; and promulgate decision rules to deal with competitive price actions. In cases such as these, the translation of strategy into specific tactics is greatly complicated by the number of variables (and combinations of variables) involved, as well as by the vast number of options possible for each variable.

While the product manager is not responsible for the direct implementation of the specified tactics, he or she is responsible for ensuring that they are carried out. This paradox stems from the nature of matrix organizations. The product manager has no direct authority over personnel in the resource departments (e.g., sales, the advertising department or agency), who report to the heads of their respective functions or organizations. Conceptually, in the act of approving the product manager's annual plan, top management instructs the resource departments to carry out its mandates, and the product manager then acts as the delegate of top management in monitoring fulfillment of the specifications laid out in the plan. In practice, effective product managers generally rely on persuasion and persistence to do their job, and make every effort not to appeal for support from higher-ups in the organization (e.g., the vice president/marketing).

The most challenging dimension of a product manager's job may be the formulation of the annual brand plan, but all too often the bulk of his or her time is spent in "fighting fires" as unexpected problems develop in the execution of tactics. Why is the trade promotion being resisted in Denver? What do we do about price cuts by private brand suppliers in San Francisco? Why are inventories low in New Jersey? Issues such as these must be diagnosed, corrected, and monitored. Doing so effectively requires adequate data, good problem recognition skills, meaningful measures and controls, fast reaction time, and a commitment to get things back on track.

Perhaps the most important of the product manager's tasks is to report upward in the organization to the product group manager ("grouper"), the marketing director, and top management. Such reporting includes the presentation and justification of plans, regular updates, and urgent situation reports. In a matrix organization, the product manager's plans and inputs are important influences on the decisions that are taken by higher management and then passed down to the resource departments. Initiatives come from the product manager, but actual decisions are made at higher levels. Often the grouper or marketing director sets budgets and gets involved in tactical decisions (e.g., copy decisions, price cuts). In many instances, such higher-level managers are able to integrate (or at least coordinate) the plans of several brands (e.g., to avoid asking the sales force to support two major promotions at the same time) and/or to bring to bear on a given decision much greater depth and breadth of experience than that of the product manager. In extreme cases, product managers must adopt a "do as you are told" posture, and recognize that the CEO is the ultimate product manager.

Despite these problems, the product manager/resource department matrix organization has proved effective in achieving focus on disparate brands and market segments without unduly diluting or duplicating effort. Over the past fifty years, high rewards have been earned by firms ranging from aerospace companies to packaged goods manufacturers that use product managers as integrators for strategy formulation, implementation, and control. Today this form of organization is common in virtually every industry.

Nevertheless, during the past five years, some leading packaged goods manufacturers have begun to ask if the brand manager concept has outlived its usefulness. Two major factors have contributed to this questioning. First, differentiating marketing strategies and programs for individual regions within a given national market has become much more important. Different promotions are utilized in New York, Los Angeles, and Des Moines, or in the French-speaking and Flemish-speaking regions of Belgium, on the grounds that customer tastes and competition vary from one part of a country to another. Ironically, at the same time as they are seeking to "globalize" their international marketing strategies, some leading packaged goods firms are seeking to disaggregate marketing strategies *within* their larger national markets.

Second, in many packaged goods markets, increasingly concentrated retail structures have greatly augmented the power of supermarket and drug chains. "Deals" are often demanded for purchase commitments, shelf facings, end-aisle displays, and local newspaper advertising. Retailers have become so powerful in some packaged goods markets that they can command cash payments (e.g., $2,000 per store as a "slotting allowance" to take on a new product or $1,000 per store for an end-aisle display). The deal may be made through the chain central office or at the local store. Often it spans several products, so the controlling dimension is not brand but distribution outlet. The appropriate strategic focus may thus be at the regional level across brands, rather than at the brand level across regions.

The "regional grouper" may replace the product manager in planning and implementing communications and promotion strategies. The product manager would still exist, but would become essentially a specialist in product design and positioning. Overall planning and implementation would be performed by regional managers responsible for several product lines. In effect, the matrix organization would now be three-dimensional: geography/product/resource.

ANALYTIC SUPPORT FOR LIFE-CYCLE MANAGEMENT

The complexity of life-cycle management has increased because of the growing emphasis on "micromarketing," the expanding power of distribution channels, the saturation of many markets (e.g., there are more than 300 car models available in the world), intensifying competition from both domestic and international rivals, and, in many markets, more knowledgeable and sophisticated customers. Fortunately, these trends are being matched by much richer data bases and much more powerful analytic techniques. The ability of today's packaged goods product manager to access weekly UPC data at the store and item levels exemplifies both the positive and the negative dimensions of this trend. While more data can help managers make better decisions, the sheer size of the new data bases raises questions about how this resource can be effectively harnessed to support life-cycle management. There is a growing need for powerful models of the product management function that lead to improved strategies, tactics, and control procedures.

Many of the analytic components cited earlier in this book support effective life-cycle management. Preparation of a good product plan requires an understanding of: the basic behavioral decision processes used by customers (Chapter 5), product life cycles (Chapter 6), market segmentation (Chapter 7), product positioning (Chapter 8), market response to marketing variables (Chapter 9), and competitive behavior (Chapter 10). All the analytic support models, measurement methods, and computer systems discussed earlier are relevant to the development of product strategies and plans. Product-positioning maps for various segments of the market, for example, are invaluable tools when defining the scope of a market and trying to identify possible dimensions for competitive advantage. Life-cycle analysis may be used to ascertain the appropriateness of adding flankers to an established product versus rejuvenating it through major innovation or even replacing it with a new entry. Market response models are very helpful when seeking to allocate the communications budget between advertising and promotion. All of these decision areas are supported by an in-depth understanding of customer information processing, product-evaluation processes, and purchasing decision making.

It is not necessary to review at this point the analytic methods outlined earlier. Rather, we will concentrate on two state-of-the-art topics—artificial intelligence and product-planning models.

ARTIFICIAL INTELLIGENCE AND DECISION SUPPORT SYSTEMS

One of the most significant technological advances of the last twenty-five years is the development of low-cost computer capacity that can be used with powerful software to access, manipulate, and analyze data. Rapid computation speeds and advances in marketing science have led to increasingly sophisticated decision support models. Personal computers networked to large data bases and employing high-resolution color graphics have simplified and humanized the manager/computer interface. The age of the user-friendly decision support system is here.

The concept of decision support is not new in marketing. It was first proposed in 1969 (Montgomery and Urban) as a four-box system (see Figure 15.1). The boxes represent the data, the model, and statistical and interface capabilities. This paradigm has stood up well over time. In the early days, models utilizing time-shared computers and desktop terminals were developed to support major decisions in advertising, pricing, distribution, personal selling, and new products (see Montgomery and Urban, 1969, for a summary). The data were based on personal audits of retail stores, consumer panels, and market research surveys. Today the technology is based on PC workstations connected to large mainframe data servers with user-friendly software; the data are UPC- and electronic panel–based; and models have grown in power, relevance, and usefulness. Single-source data suppliers offer increasingly accurate comprehensive data at reasonable cost in an ever-expanding number of industries and product categories, while faster and more complete data access and analysis are now possible through decision support systems (Little, 1979; McCann, 1986).

The capabilities of a modern decision-support system are outlined in Table 15.1. Systems of this type allow users to: access data at their desks from both company and external data bases; utilize statistics to forecast sales and understand data; use exception reports to identify problems; perform analyses and run models to find solutions; and carry out a wide range of analytic procedures to improve strategic decision making.

A second major technology that emerged in the 1970s was artificial intelligence (AI). Initially, the objective was to use computers to replicate medical decision making. With respect to infectious diseases, for example, early AI applications attempted to simulate a doctor's diagnosis and treatment protocols with a computer-based set of logical hierarchies and decision rules (Davis et al., 1977). AI technology advanced in the 1980s to produce generic software packages ("inference engines") that employed interactive PCs to capture practitioners' decision rules. Today PC-based software systems called "shells" allow easy implementation of AI concepts through "expert systems" (see Michie, 1979).

These concepts have become increasingly relevant to marketing in recent years. Researchers are seeking to capture the expert intelligence of the best marketers and analysts to improve marketing decision making. Three types of marketing experts appear to be

FIGURE 15.1
The Four Components of a
Management Decision
Support System (MDSS)
Source: Adapted from David B.
Montgomery and Glen L.
Urban, *Management Science in
Marketing* (Englewood Cliffs,
N.J.: Prentice Hall, 1969), p.
18.

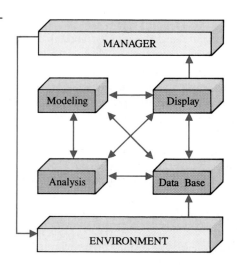

TABLE 15.1 Decision Support System Capabilities

	FUNCTIONS
Data Bases	*Consumer Markets:* UPC, warehouse and factory shipments, scanner panels, surveys, TV meters and media audits, promotions, test markets, controlled experiments. *Industrial Markets:* Customer order files, potential customers, SIC and demographics, sales call records, competitors' sales and key customers, surveys comparing competitors and our firm, efficient updating and data maintenance, high dimensionality (product SKU, time, area, customer, retailer, distributor), integrated common access data, timely data (e.g., daily, weekly).
Interface	Desktop workstations networked to mainframes and other users, menu-driven commands, windows, report generation, exception reports, rank orders by user criteria, color graphs (user specified), spreadsheets and word processing and electronic mail integration to data, easy to use and understand, multiple users (market research, product manager, regional manager, sales managers, group product manager, marketing director, V.P./marketing, CEO, retailers, and distribution firms).
Statistics	Exploratory data analysis procedures, cross-tabs and significance tests, time series analysis and forecasting, regression and Logit analysis, multidimensional scaling and conjoint analysis, event analysis, model-fitting procedures.
Models	User-modeling capability, positioning and market definition, competitive gaming and market response, new-product premarket and test market forecasting and profit maximization, perception-preference-choice models, communication mix (advertising, selling, telemarketing), brand planning, and resource allocation.

especially important: (1) the statistician who generates forecasts and estimates response to marketing variables; (2) the analyst who digs through the data to find trends, diagnose problems, and alert management to situations that demand attention; and (3) the product manager. Expert systems currently under development attempt to describe the data and decision protocols used by a given type of expert, and then to replicate them in the computer. In theory, both the quality and speed of marketing analysis and decision making should improve as such systems become widely available.

Applications of AI to marketing are still in the preliminary phase. The lack of structure in most marketing problems, the absence of consumer response laws, and the scarcity of expertise have constrained the power of early AI systems. Nevertheless, the work done by the statistician is generally reasonably well structured and utilizes procedures that are definable and consistent over time. Based on more than twenty years of marketing science experience, we are confident that demand forecasting and market response analysis can be usefully modeled (McCann, 1986).

The analyst who identifies and diagnoses marketing problems uses more complex cognitive processes, but the procedures employed can also be defined in computer terms. For example, bimonthly retail sales data help an analyst determine where problems (e.g., loss of share or margin) exist and why they seem to have occurred (e.g., ineffective promotion, competitive actions, category trends). Using conventional analytic methods, such analysis may require four hours for one brand in one geographic region. (Today's comprehensive data suppliers offer detailed UPC-derived data on 20,000 items in 2,000 stores each week!) If a good analyst could be replicated by an expert system, it would be possible to carry out appropriate analysis at a very detailed level and to report the results only in cases where action is required. Figure 15.2 is an example of a report written by an AI system that does just this for a frozen pizza. The system, called CoverStory, generates a report to management automatically based on the protocols in the system that

FIGURE 15.2
AI System Output Based on UPC Analysis
Source: John D. C. Little.

To: **VP of Marketing**

From: **CoverStory**

Date: 01/03/90

Subject: **Maxwell House Grnd Caff Summary for Four Weeks Ending January 29, 1989**

Maxwell House Grnd Caff's share points in Total United States was 12.1 in the Total Coffee category for the four weeks ending 1/29/89. This is an increase of .2 points from a year earlier but down .2 from last period (4 Week Ending Jan 1, 89). This reflects volume sales of 9.2 million equiv pounds - up 5.7 percent since last year. Category volume (currently 108.8 million equiv pounds) rose 1.4% from a year earlier.

Maxwell House Grnd Caff's share points is 12.1 - up .2 from the same period last year.

Display activity, featuring and unsupported price cuts rose over the past year - unsupported price cuts from 16 points to 32. Price (2.20 dollars) and distribution (99 percent of acv) remained at about the same level as a year earlier.

Components of Maxwell House Grnd Caff Volume

Among components of Maxwell House Grnd Caff, the principal gainers are:

Maxwell House Grnd Caf 13oz: up 5.1 points from last year to 5.1 (but down .1 since last period)

Maxwell House Grnd Caf 39oz: +3.7 to 3.7

The major loser:

Maxwell House Grnd Caf 16oz: -6.1 to .5

Maxwell House Grnd Caf 13oz's share points increase is partly due to 75.1 pts of ACV rise in ACV Wtd Dist vs yr ago.

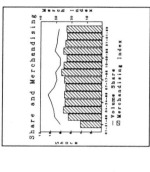

Share and Merchandising

    — Volume Share
    ▨ Merchandising Index

1

Competitor Summary

Among Maxwell House Grnd Caff's major competitors, the principal gainer is:

Community Grnd Caff: up .7 points from last year to 1.5

The major losers:

Folgers Grnd Caff: -2.5 to 23.7 (but up .8 since last period)

Chock Full O Nuts Grnd Caff: -1.0 to 2.4

Chock Full O Nuts Grnd Caff's share points decrease is associated with 10.4% rise in price versus a year ago.

Market Highlights

Maxwell House Grnd Caff showed significant gains relative to a year ago in:

Denver, Co: up 4.6 points from last year to 9.4. This is partly due to 20.2% fall in price since last year but was counterindicated by 21.5 ACV points rise in display activity versus a year ago.

but posted declines in:

Chicago, Il: -3.1 to 10.9. This follows 19.8 ACV points increase in display activity since last year but occurred in spite of 7.3% decrease in price versus a year ago.

Boston, Ma: -2.1 to 16.4. This occurred in the face of 10.0% decrease in price versus a year ago.

Among competitors to Maxwell House

Grnd Caff, major regional changes occurred as follows:

Baltimore, Md: **Folgers Grnd Caff** is up 8.3 points since last year. This follows 17.7% fall in price since last year.

Dallas, Tx: **Maryland Club Grnd Caff** fell 8.1 points. This follows 6.2% increase in price versus a year ago. **Hills Brothers Grnd Caff** is up 14.1 points. This follows 75.1 pts of ACV increase in ACV Wtd Dist versus a year ago and 32.4% fall in price vs yr ago. **Folgers Grnd Caff** fell 9.3 points.

San Francisco, Ca: **Mjb Grnd Caff** fell 8.3 points. This is partly due to 11.6% increase in price since last year.

2

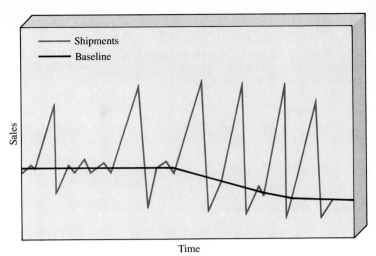

FIGURE 15.3
Sales and Baseline
Source: Reprinted with permission from Magid M. Abraham and Leonard M. Lodish, "Promoter: An Automated Evaluation System," *Marketing Science,* Spring 1987, p. 110. Copyright © 1987 by the Marketing Science Institute, Cambridge, MA.

replicate an outstanding analyst who has spent considerable time digging through and analyzing UPC data for the product.

Developing an expert system that emulates the planning function of the product manager is likely to prove especially challenging, if only because of lack of expertise concerning market response functions and uncertainty about competitive actions and responses. While judgment will clearly continue to play a major role in the product-planning process, expert systems will increasingly be able to provide meaningful inputs to that process.

The PROMOTER model, which is used to evaluate promotions for frequently purchased consumer brands, is an early example of an expert system capable of being employed in this way (Abraham and Lodish, 1987). In this model, an expert system emulates an analyst who is trying to estimate a brand's baseline sales (i.e., the sales that would occur in the absence of promotion). (Figure 15.3 shows actual sales and baseline sales for a particular brand.) If a true baseline could be established, incremental unit sales and profits

TABLE 15.2 Profit Summary of Promotions

TOTAL UNITED STATES			
Promotion*	**Incremental Cases**	**Incremental Weeks†**	**Profit**
OI 1.50$, BB .60$ (06.01.82)	850,848	4.2	$ 4,835,654
OI 1.00$, BB 1.10$ (09.01.83)	941,084	4.3	$ 1,775,566
PP .30$ (08.01.81)	684,281	3.4	$ −448,301
OI 1.10$, BB 1.80$ (08.03.82)	1.29138M	6.0	$ 6,106,978
PP .30$ (03.01.84)	376,578	1.9	$−3,112,433
OI 1.80$, BB 1.00$ (04.28.83)	734,710	3.3	$ 1,591,344
OI 1.10$, BB 1.90$ (09.01.83)	666,810	3.0	$ −144,781
BB .90$, PP .30$ (12.19.83)	431,453	2.1	$−4,464,380
OI 2.10$, BB 1.50$ (05.03.84)	884,509	4.0	$ 480,964
OI 2.10$ (08.30.84)	1.0511M	4.7	$ 3,442,260

* OI is Off Invoice. BB is Bill Pack. PP is Price Pack. (The number next to the promotion type is the dollars per unit, and the date is in parentheses.)
† Incremental sales expressed as a number of weeks of base business.
Source: Reprinted with permission from "Promoter: An Automated Evaluation System," *Marketing Science,* Spring 1987, p. 119. Copyright © 1987 by the Marketing Science Institute, Cambridge, MA.

FIGURE 15.4
Overview of Baseline Estimation Procedure

Source: Reprinted with permission from Magid M. Abraham and Leonard M. Lodish, "Promoter: An Automated Evaluation System," *Marketing Science,* Spring 1987, p. 112. Copyright © 1987 by the Marketing Science Institute, Cambridge, MA.

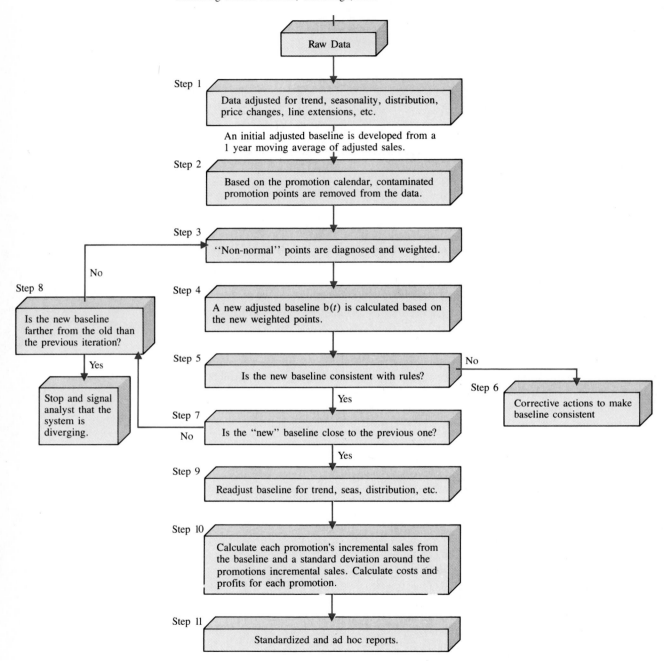

attributable to promotion could then be calculated as the difference between the baseline and the actual results. Unfortunately, however, determination of a true baseline is not a simple task because weaknesses in the available data (e.g., multiple, inconsistent data sets, missing data, promotions absent from the promotion calendar, statistical outliers) make judgment and additional analysis necessary. Such analysis is currently performed by a skilled, experienced individual who *senses* that something is missing or doesn't fit.

As anyone who has tried to work on this problem knows, this is painstakingly detailed work. Separate promotions may have been run for each SKU (e.g., size, flavor) and micromarket (e.g., metro area or region), and it may be necessary to utilize multiple sources of data (e.g., shipments, warehouse withdrawals, retail UPC sales). If, for example, 5 SKUs were promoted in 30 markets and 3 data sources were available, 450 analyses would be required. If store-level data from, say, 500 retail outlets were also to be examined (see discussion in Chapter 8 on response analysis and UPC data), it would be infeasible to perform the requisite number of analyses.

In order to address this problem, PROMOTER uses an expert system that replicates what an experienced analyst would do if he or she had the time to attack the problem. Figure 15.4 shows the steps carried out by the expert system, noting those points where human intervention is necessary. Table 15.2 shows the output of such a system. Since there is wide variation in the degree to which individual promotions meet their marketing objectives, knowledge obtained from expert systems such as PROMOTER can play a critical role in formulating brand strategies and plans.

BRAND PLANNING MODELS

As discussed in the last section, it is increasingly possible to substitute expert systems for statisticians and analysts under some conditions; but has the state of the art advanced to the point where it is feasible to use such methods in planning tasks that require managerial judgment of ill-structured events? In this section, we consider models that use decision support systems to help product managers for both consumer and industrial products with the planning task, and then discuss the extension of expert systems into this domain.

Planning Models for Packaged Goods

Many models have been built to help brand managers. Some are based on statistics, others on judgment (see Lilien and Kotler, 1983, for a summary). BRANDAID (Little, 1975) is a good example of the state of the art. It is a generalization and extension of the ADBUDG advertising response model described in Chapter 9. Recall that in ADBUDG advertising had a direct effect on current share and a carryover effect on subsequent sales; in BRANDAID, the current-period effect is generalized over several marketing resources by a set of response indices, and the carryover effects by "response templates." A response index represents the proportional change in the sales in a period due to a change in the resources devoted to a marketing variable. (You may find it useful to review Figures 9.1 and 9.2 on pages 154 and 155 at this point.) The response template describes the effects of changes in a variable in one time period on sales in future periods through the use of a multiplicative index that reflects the proportional change in sales in period $t + 1$, $t + 2$, etc., for a change in the variable in period t (review Figure 9.4 on page 157).

Let's consider a simple example of this type of brand planning model. Figure 15.5 describes response functions for advertising and promotion. Index values representing trend, seasonal, and the response templates are shown in Table 15.3. Assume that our current base of sales is $10 million per month, and that we currently plan to spend $1 million per month on advertising and another $1 million per month on promotion to maintain the base level as well as its trend and seasonal pattern. Our forecast would then be that shown in the first column of Table 15.4. The values are $10 million, multiplied by the trend index, multiplied by the seasonal index in Table 15.3.

What would happen if we increased advertising to $1.5 million per month in period t only? We can calculate the result by multiplying $10 million by 1.2, resulting in an increase of sales in period t of 20 percent, as shown in Figure 15.5 ($1.5 million corresponds to 1.2 index value). Sales in period t would be forecast as $12 million. According to

FIGURE 15.5
Response Functions

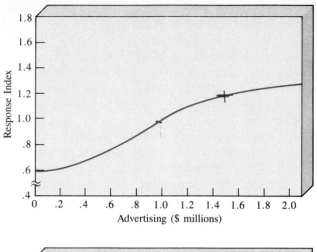

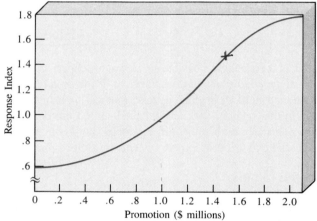

Table 15.3, .8 of the sales gain would carry over to $t + 1$. Sales in $t + 1$ would be the base case values of period t, plus .8 of the 2 million sales gain ($8.8 + .8 \times 2$), or $10.4 million. Sales in $t + 2$ would be $13.2 million ($12 + .6 \times 2$), and in $t + 3$, $16.6 million ($15.6 + .5 \times 2$). With these values and cost data, we could then calculate profits for each period and assess the profitability of increasing advertising in period t.

Similarly we could use the promotion response function to determine the effect of spending $1.5 million on promotion in period t. The response function indicates that sales would increase 50 percent to $15 million in period t, but that negative carryover effects would reduce sales in future periods. In $t + 1$, sales would be base case sales, less .3 of the increase in period t, or $7.3 million ($8.8 - .3 \times 5$), while the period $t + 2$ value would be $11.5 million ($12 - .1 \times 5$). Although the effect of promotion is greater than

TABLE 15.3 **Example Value of Indices**

	RESPONSE TEMPLATES			
	Trend	**Seasonal**	**Ad Template**	**Promotion Template**
t	1.0	1.0	1.0	1.0
$t + 1$	1.1	.8	.8	$-.3$
$t + 2$	1.2	1.0	.6	$-.1$
$t + 3$	1.3	1.2	.5	1.0

	Base Case Sales	Increased Advertising	Increased Promotion	Increased Advertising and Promotion
t	10.0	12.0	15.0	18.0
$t + 1$	8.8	10.4	7.3	8.6
$t + 2$	12.0	13.2	11.5	12.6
$t + 3$	15.6	16.6	15.6	16.6
Total	46.4	52.2	49.4	55.8

that of advertising in the first period, the total effect over four periods turns out to be less for promotion than for advertising ($49.4 million versus $52.2 million).

The combined effect can be calculated as the proportionate change due to advertising times the proportionate change due to promotion. In period t, this is 1.8 (1.2 × 1.5), while sales would be equal to the base case value multiplied by the combined index (10 × 1.8) or $18 million. Similarly, $t + 1$ and $t + 2$ can be calculated as shown in Table 15.3 (e.g., in $t + 1$: 8.6 = 8.8 × (10.4/8.8) × (7.3/8.8)). The resulting total sales for the combined strategy (i.e., spending $1.5 million *each* on advertising and promotion in period t) would be $55.3 million.

We have just created a very simple brand planning model. We can convert the sales numbers derived from this model to profit estimates easily through the use of PC software such as Lotus 1–2–3 or Excel if we have appropriate cost data. The resulting simple spreadsheet, which would reflect direct-response, carryover, and interaction effects, could then be used to forecast the sales and profit impact of alternative marketing strategies.

The model could be extended for more periods, variables, competitive effects, channels of distribution, and packaging alternatives (see Little, 1975). The model would be more complex, but still it would be relatively easy to use, especially if supported by a PC balance sheet interface backed by report-generation and graphical capabilities. Using such a model, product managers would be able to simulate a large number of alternative brand plans in considerable detail, thereby (hopefully) improving brand performance in both the short and the long run.

Can We Replace the Brand Manager with Expert Systems? As models become more powerful, will it be possible to take the next step—to replace the product manager with an expert system? Why not, for example, program the computer to generate a wide range of alternative strategies (within "reasonable" constraints), and then "recommend" the one or two strategies that appear to best meet prespecified criteria (e.g., profits, ROI, market share)? For this to be possible, it would be necessary for the expert system to employ accurate response functions and response templates. PROMOTER suggests that this capability may not be far off. In fact, PROMOTER-type models have been extended using Logit and UPC data to obtain improved baselines that can be used to identify the incremental impact of specific marketing variables on sales (see Blattberg and Levin, 1987; Little, 1988; and Lodish, 1988). Using such models, data suppliers will be able to report response analysis coefficients routinely, much as they now do share and switching data. These coefficients will be of considerable help to product managers seeking to assess the effects of past promotion and advertising strategies, and in the longer run, they will provide critical inputs to the development of brand manager–oriented expert systems.

Nevertheless expert systems are not likely to replace product managers for two primary reasons. First, it would be very difficult, if not impossible, for such a system to incorporate adequately the competitive context in which a brand is marketed. While game theory (review Chapter 10) clearly has a contribution to make in this respect, it is unlikely to become powerful enough to encompass the complexity of the real competitive environment (e.g., many competitors, multiple variables, extended time periods, and unknown decision rules). A good brand planning model could help assess the impact of competitive reactions and initiatives, but a brand manager would still be required to decide what competitive moves to make.

The second reason it would be difficult to replace a product manager with an expert system is that a large part of the brand manager's job is to create *new* marketing strategies. New promotions, advertising campaigns, packages, flankers, and/or channels may produce totally new scenarios, greatly limiting the value of response effects derived from past data. The best brand managers have as their goal not merely to maximize profit within the existing rules of the competitive game, but also to break through competitive constraints with innovations that will be valued by customers and form the basis for a sustainable competitive advantage.

Brand planning models and their attendant response analyses will be increasingly critical ingredients in successful product management. Better computers, data, models, and expert systems will enable brand managers to delegate many of their routine planning tasks to automated systems so they can concentrate on maximizing profits through creative innovation.

Planning Models for Industrial Products

Response function concepts such as those discussed above can be modified for use with industrial and high-technology products. In this section, we describe a planning model that has been employed successfully in industrial markets. In developing this model, the first step is to segment the firm's customer base according to sales records. Next, the new customer-generation process and historical patterns of sales over time are modeled. Response functions are then linked to these flows, utilizing the methodology developed for the life-cycle modeling of durables (see Chapter 6 and the Buick Reatta case in Chapter 13). Finally, the resulting model is used to forecast sales and to evaluate alternative sales force and pricing strategies.

Case Example: The subject of this case is a rapidly growing software and consulting company that currently has 225 clients who generate $15 million in sales. Clients either buy the software on a timesharing basis or implement it on their own computer systems. The company sells (but does not manufacture) mainframe and PC computers to clients who want to buy a complete, dedicated system. It has three SBUs that service the (1) market research, (2) marketing, and (3) financial planning and analysis markets. The firm earns 25 percent after tax on sales, and both sales and earnings are growing by 35 percent per year. The product manager for the software system was asked to forecast the next three years of sales and to develop an annual plan.

Sales Profiles: The first step in the product manager's planning effort was to segment the market by sales levels and sales patterns over time. Individual client sales records were cluster-analyzed to specify three segments (see Figure 15.6). These "sales profiles" depicted each client's purchase level, given the number of quarters it had been a client. Segment A represents clients that grew steadily to purchases of $200,000 per quarter; in segment B, purchases grew initially, then leveled off at $40,000 per quarter, and ultimately weakened; while clients in segment C grew to $10,000, but then decayed to almost zero. The 5 percent of clients in segment A were responsible for most of the firm's success. Segment B clients were also contributors, but the 63 percent of clients in segment C essentially tried and then rejected the service. This finding raised concerns and suggested the need for new strategies. A base case forecast was generated and used to evaluate a number of alternative strategy simulations.

FIGURE 15.6
Sales Profiles

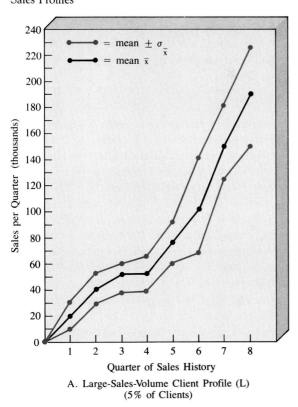

A. Large-Sales-Volume Client Profile (L)
(5% of Clients)

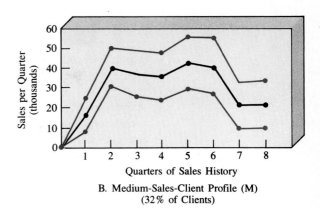

B. Medium-Sales-Client Profile (M)
(32% of Clients)

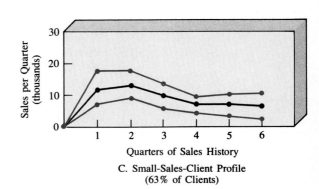

C. Small-Sales-Client Profile
(63% of Clients)

Base Case Forecast: A simple customer flow model was developed to represent the inflow of new clients and the progression of their purchases over time (see Figure 15.7). Sales efforts led to new clients, who flowed into the three segments according to the historical proportions (5, 32, and 63 percent). Given the size of the current sales force and its historical effectiveness in converting sales calls into new clients, the model calculated the number of new customers of each type that would be generated by a specified level of sales calls. Call quantity was based on the currently planned number of sales

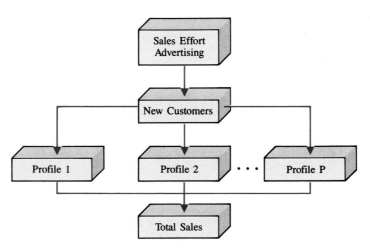

FIGURE 15.7
Customer Flow

317

representatives and estimates of the time they could allocate to calling on potential new accounts after servicing their old accounts and fulfilling their training and administrative responsibilities. According to this base case analysis, sales would grow from $3 million per quarter to $6.5 million per quarter over three years. Even though 63 percent of the clients were subject to extreme decay in segment C, enough segment A and B clients would be acquired to maintain growth. Sensitivity analysis indicated that sales would be static if sales efforts were reduced by one-third.

Planning Scenarios: Competition was increasing, however, which made it likely that prices would come under pressure. Consequently, the base case forecast was probably unduly optimistic. The product manager was asked to determine whether it would be a good idea to employ a more aggressive product plan than that assumed in the base case. She then considered two scenarios. Scenario 1 called for an increase in the size of the sales force; Scenario 2 assumed a preemptive price cut of 50 percent.

Under Scenario 1, five new salespersons would be hired. The forecast in this scenario was for *no* sales increase in the first year, and for a 16 percent increase during the second year. This lag effect occurred because the model assumed that the number of sales calls conducted by the experienced sales representatives would be a function of the time available after serving existing clients and training the new salespeople. In the first year, training would take up a considerable amount of their time, which would not be fully compensated for by the efforts of the new salespersons. The net effect would be a profit decrease in the first year, but a net increase over the three years (see Figure 15.8).

Simulations of the price-cut strategy (Scenario 2) reflected assumptions concerning the response functions of prospective clients, and took into account the fact that any price reductions for consulting and software upgrades would also have to apply to existing clients. It was deemed likely, moreover, that price reductions of the magnitude being considered would delay entry by several potential competitors. These effects were modeled by modifying the response function for the increased productivity of sales calls at lower prices, reducing the profit margin on sales, and increasing the inflow of new clients. The response function estimates were based on a regression of past sales and prices in the industry, a consumer survey, and delphi opinions of sales managers. The simulation indicated that a price cut of the magnitude under consideration would increase sales and market share, but would not improve profits.

FIGURE 15.8
Profit Impact of One More
Salesperson

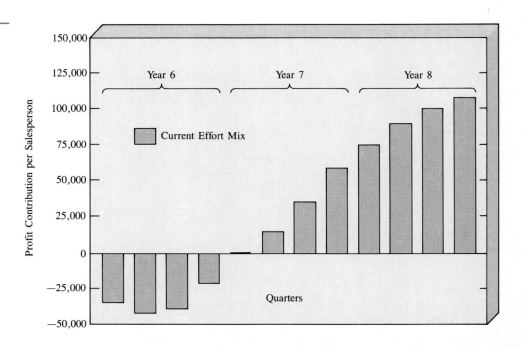

Consequences: Armed with these analyses, the product manager proposed hiring the five sales representatives, cutting prices to preempt competition, and initiating a program of product improvement intended to increase the perceived value of the service to clients in segments B and C. Simulations of this total strategy indicated no increase in sales or profit over the base case in the first year, but a 75 percent increase in sales and profits over three years as sales calls increased, the productivity of sales calls improved with lower prices, and a higher proportion of clients ended up in segments A (10 percent) and B (50 percent). Even with this plan, introduction of a major new product would be required if growth of 30 percent per year in sales and profits was to be achieved. Consequently, the product manager also recommended a $500,000 budget to develop a new PC/work-station–based product.

The product manager in this case was in the uncomfortable position of proposing a strategy that would result in a decrease in short-term earnings. If higher management had employed short-term criteria, her strategy would not have been approved. Fortunately, corporate management was convinced by the product manager's multiyear analysis that it would be best to forgo short-term earnings in order to achieve stronger long-term market position and profits, and therefore approved her proposed strategy with only minor mod-ifications. (It turned out that her forecasts were within 3 percent of actual results.) In situations like this, it is critical that plans be extended beyond the one-year financial planning horizon, and that the evaluation and reward system for the product manager take into account the inherent lags in the marketing system.

PRODUCT MANAGEMENT IN THE INFORMATION AGE

Summary and Future

Product management over the life cycle will continue to be critical to the success of most organizations. Matching marketing bundles to customer needs and behavior will become more challenging as competition grows, tastes change, and a wider array of marketing tactics becomes available. Analytic support will become more important and feasible as data bases, computers, and expert systems improve, and it will become increasingly difficult for a product manager to be effective without the ability and willingness to use such analytical tools.

Nevertheless, successful product managers will continue to rely heavily on qualitative analyses and creativity. They will have to be able to create and evaluate a wide variety of potential strategies and tactics, and to generate new competitive frameworks.

The product manager of the future will have to be both a strategist and a tactician, skilled in qualitative and quantitative analysis, and able to exercise sound managerial judgment. These are tough "job specs" that will only be met through a combination of talent, education, and managerial leadership.

QUESTIONS FOR DISCUSSION

1. If product managers have no direct authority to order changes, how can they ef-fectively plan the strategy for a product and implement it?

2. Should a product or brand manager be assigned to a product before or after it is designed and launched? How would the role of the product manager differ before and after launch of the product?

3. What are the advantages of a regional product group management over a national product management organization? The disadvantages?

4. What new capabilities do UPC data give consumer packaged goods manufacturers?

Will other industries acquire this kind of customer transaction data? How could they use it?

5. What do you think will be the role of AI systems in marketing strategy development in the 1990s?

6. With the increasing availability of data, models, and AI systems, how will the product manager's job change?

7. Why are industrial product management problems more difficult to model and estimate than those for packaged goods?

8. What is the role of the product manager in the service industry? How is it similar to or different from the role of consumer goods brand managers?

9. Should we have global product managers? Why or why not?

10. Does it make sense to develop annual plans if many of the effects of our marketing actions have longer-term effects?

11. If it is the third quarter and we are achieving our sales objectives but are lagging on profit contribution, should we cut advertising expenditure in the fourth quarter to make the annual profit goal?

REFERENCES

ABRAHAM, MAGID M., AND LEONARD M. LODISH. 1987. "PROMOTER: An Automated Promotion Evaluation System." *Marketing Science* 6: 101–123.

BLATTBERG, ROBERT C., AND ALAN LEVIN. 1987. "Modeling the Effectiveness and Profitability of Trade Promotions." *Marketing Science* 6: 124–146.

COREY, E. R., AND STAR, S. H. 1970. *Organization Strategy: A Marketing Approach.* Boston, MA: Harvard University Press.

DAVIS, R., B. BUCHANAN, AND E. SHORTLIFFE. 1977. "Production Rules as a Representation in a Knowledge-Based Consultation System." *Artificial Intelligence* 18: 15–45.

GUADAGNI, PETER M., AND JOHN D. C. LITTLE. 1983. "A Logit Model for Brand Choice Calibrated on Scanner Data." *Marketing Science* 2: 203–239.

LILIEN, GARY L., AND PHILIP KOTLER. 1983. *Marketing Decision Making: A Model Building Approach.* New York: Harper and Row.

LITTLE, JOHN D. C. 1979. "Decision Support Systems for Marketing Managers." *Journal of Marketing* 43: 9–27.

———. 1975. "BRANDAID: A Marketing Mix Model, Structure, Implementation, Calibration and Case Study." *Operations Research* 23: 628–673.

MCCANN, JOHN M. 1986. *The Marketing Workbench: An Information and Knowledge Support Environment.* Homewood, IL: Dow Jones–Irwin.

MICHIE, D., Ed. 1979. *Expert Systems in the Microelectronic Age.* New York: Columbia University Press.

MONTGOMERY, DAVID B., AND GLEN L. URBAN. 1969. *Management Science in Marketing.* Englewood Cliffs, NJ: Prentice Hall.

ROCKART, JOHN F., AND DAVID DELONG. 1988. *Executive Support Systems.* Homewood, IL: Dow Jones–Irwin.

ROCKART, JOHN F., AND JAMES E. SHORT. 1989. "IT in the 1990s: Managing Organizational Interdependence." *Sloan Management Review* 30: 7–18.

SHAPIRO, BENSON P. 1985. "Rejuvenating the Marketing Mix." *Harvard Business Review* 63: 28–34.

PRODUCT-LINE MANAGEMENT

NEW AND ESTABLISHED PRODUCTS WITHIN A PRODUCT LINE

In the last two chapters, we traced the life cycle of the product from inception and testing to market launch, growth, and maturity. In our discussion thus far, we have dealt primarily with a single product, usually treating it as independent of other products in the company's product lines. In most instances, however, it is not appropriate to look at individual products in isolation. The Buick Reatta is only one of Buick's car lines sold through a single dealer organization (the others are Century, Electra, La Sabre, Regal, Rivera, Skylark, and Skyhawk). GE's UDF engine is part of a family of commercial jet engines spanning the range of airline needs. The American Express Platinum Card is part of a comprehensive product line that also includes the Personal (Green), Gold, Corporate, and Optima Cards. Indeed, virtually every product today functions as part of an interrelated set of product offerings to meet a variety of customer needs.

In formulating product-line strategy, managers need to address a number of critical strategic issues:

1. How many products should be in the line?
2. How should the products in the line be targeted and differentiated?
3. How should resources (financial, production, distribution, and sales force) be allocated across the product line to maximize its long-run profitability?

In this chapter, we examine these questions and describe the analytic support apparatus available for dealing with them. First we look at the forces that drive firms to market multiproduct product lines. Then we link product-line issues to market-segmentation concepts presented earlier in this book, and propose a framework for analyzing the coverage and duplication of the line. Next we discuss product interdependencies within the contexts of profit planning for the line and allocating resources across products. After describing the use of all three levels of analytic support tools, we conclude the chapter with a discussion of the implications of increasing pressures for even more product proliferation.

Manufacturing costs are generally minimized through large-volume production runs of standard products. (Recall our discussion in Chapter 10, Competitive Behavior, of the dramatic cost decline achieved by Henry Ford with the Model T.) Similarly, distribution costs tend to be lower if only one product must be sold, stocked, and serviced. At a given level of sales, profits usually will be highest if those sales have been achieved with a single product. If this is true, why are so many product variants offered by so many firms?

Customer Preferences and Competition

The primary answer lies in a combination of the heterogeneity of customer preferences and the nature of competitive dynamics. Potential customers rarely agree on a single set of specifications for their "ideal" product; indeed, they often differ markedly on the importance and value they assign to specific attributes. If these differences are large enough, customers will pay a premium price to obtain a product that fits their needs closely. A somewhat bizarre example of this phenomenon occurred in the early 1970s, when a manufacturer repackaged standard heavy-duty liquid detergent as a specialized product for classic cars, yachts, and other specialty uses. The various versions of this product (each with its own brand name and packaging) were then sold successfully at prices approximately three times the price for the same detergent sold with general purpose positioning. Similarly, in the 1920s, when General Motors offered new features and options (e.g., colors, enclosed body, electric starting, hydraulic brakes), customers switched from the lower-cost Model T to the more expensive GM models. As a result, profits for General Motors and customer satisfaction both increased.

Although heterogeneity in customer preferences alone would often lead to multiproduct product lines, the dynamics of competition often drive marketers to offer more products than they would otherwise prefer. Over time, as competitors seek to increase their market shares, they frequently find it advantageous to introduce new products that, in effect, subsegment an existing market segment by offering benefits more precisely calibrated to the specific needs of a portion of that segment. Other firms selling to that segment come under pressure to follow suit to avoid losing share, with adverse consequences for both sales revenues and unit manufacturing costs.

Butler Manufacturing, for example, had to offer a lower-priced version of their highly successful pre-engineered metal buildings after Dixie Steel Buildings and other firms introduced lesser-featured, lower-priced buildings to the market. Alternative premium and economy offerings are common in industrial markets. When customers differ in their quality/price trade-offs, there is generally an opportunity for more than one product in the line. Alternatively, the same customer might prefer different quality/price combinations for different purposes. A customer for pre-engineered buildings, for example, may have a different set of preferences for office, factory, and storage applications. Once one firm adds a new product, competitors seek to defend their positions by also adding new products to their lines.

It is surprising how many products are added to a line to meet customer subgroup preferences as competition develops. Each General Motors car division manufactures and markets five or more car lines (Chevrolet offers at least sixteen: Nova, Celebrity, Corvette, Caprice, Corsica, Beretta, Cavalier, Spectrum, Monte Carlo, Sprint, Camaro, Blazer, Astro, Van, Pick up, and Suburban). For each car line, there are several basic models (Buick, for example, offers standard, luxury, and sports packages) and numerous options (e.g., colors, transmissions, engine sizes, air conditioning, radio, phone). Now that more than 300 different models are being marketed in the United States (Honda, Toyota, and Nissan each added a new, upscale car line with several models in 1988 and 1989), and more than 400 worldwide, one cannot help but be skeptical about the logical basis for so much product proliferation in an industry where the design and manufacturing costs for each new model are so high.

Similar phenomena can be observed in virtually all types of businesses. Industrial products manufacturers frequently offer complex product lines that subdivide functional requirements into many increments. IBM, for example, offers more than twenty numbered computer models, ranging in performance from the PS2/25 personal computer to super-computers. In consumer packaged goods, product-line extensions called "flankers" are added in new flavors, fragrances, or packages (e.g., Crest mint and wintergreen flavors, jell and paste forms, and tube and pump packages). In energy products SUNOCO offers five grades of unleaded gasoline (from Economy to Ultra) as well as two grades of "regular." HARTMARX manufactures multiple brands of men's suits, ranging from Kuppenheimer at the low end through Hickey-Freeman in the luxury category.

Desire for Variety

Customer preference for variety also leads to product-line extensions. In foods, customers generally prefer to vary their menus from meal to meal. They demand alternatives largely because they value change in and of itself. One behavioral basis leading to this consumption pattern is the satiation of a particular sensory attribute, with the result that consumers give higher importance to another variety (McAlister, 1982). If, for example, you value variety highly and have just had a Choco-Chocolate Chip Häagen Dazs ice cream cone, you will probably choose another flavor for your next cone. In cereals, consumers commonly keep three or four variants on the shelf and switch among them. In cases of this sort, extending the product line increases market share, not because of preference differences across consumers, but because of the desire for variety among individual customers.

Life-Cycle and Multiproduct Pressures

Differences in preferences across customers, desire for variety by individual customers, and competitive dynamics thus work together to foster multiple product offerings. This tendency toward product proliferation is especially pronounced during the latter stages of the product life cycle. Early in the life cycle, product lines typically are narrow (perhaps only a single item), but then tend to widen as competition increases and subgroups are targeted with products customized to satisfy their specific needs.

As products are added, some duplication between product offerings is almost inevitable. It is virtually impossible to market a complex product line in which each product is independent of every other. In mature product categories excess proliferation is all too common. Low-cost flankers have often been added as much to generate excitement for the line as to tap meaningful segment desires. These extensions may help sustain market share and delay product decline, but managers need to consider dropping (as well as adding) products to the line. Indeed, during the decline phase of the life cycle, when efficiency and cost leadership become especially critical, it is common for manufacturers to pare back their product lines in an effort to cut costs.

HOW MANY PRODUCTS SHOULD BE IN THE LINE?

Assuming that we will offer multiple products in our line, we need to decide how many and how to target them. Our overall task is to maximize long-term return on investment, which turns out to be a very complex goal when products and segments are interdependent.

Let's consider first the problem of whether or not to add a product to the line. We need to estimate *incremental* sales attributable to the new product. In Figure 16.1, case A is an example of a new product added to the line when there is no overlap between customers for the new product and customers for our existing product. The new product sells 100,000 units, all of which are incremental. In case B, however, the products are interdependent, with the result that total sales increase only 20,000 units, even though 100,000 units of the new product are sold. In effect, 80,000 of the new product's sales have been cannibalized from our existing product.

The dynamics of life cycles make the incremental analysis more complex. Consider case B from Figure 16.1 as extended in Figure 16.2. Here the total sales of the line grow each year, but products 1 and 2 are in the decline phases of their life cycles. The new product's incremental sales contribution is 20,000 units in 1991, but grows to 50,000 units by 1993—considerably more than in case B in Figure 16.1. In estimating incremental sales effects, it is essential to make the comparison with what sales otherwise would be during the period in question, rather than with what they are now.

Dropping a product also requires incremental thinking. In Figure 16.3, Case B illustrates a situation where dropping product Z would result in almost no change in sales for the total product line. This type of pattern is frequently observed when there has been excessive proliferation. While the sales force might well argue that all product Z's sales would be lost to the firm, the impact may be negligible if the products overlap significantly. Product-line strategy requires a clear understanding of the market and cost interdependencies between products. If we are to maximize profitability, we must be able to specify the correct number of products in the line and to allocate resources appropriately among them.

An effective approach to formulating product-line strategy is to begin by describing the competitive structure in the market and segmenting products that compete with one another into separate groups. The objective is to minimize through segmentation the kind of overlaps portrayed in Figures 16.1 and 16.3. Once we have segmented the products

FIGURE 16.1
Adding a Product in 1991

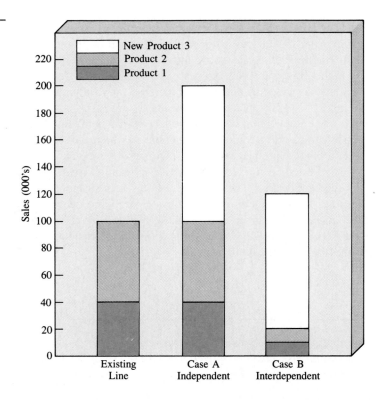

in the market into separate groups, we are in a position to consider a variety of product-line strategy options. If, for example, it appears that the products appeal to mutually exclusive segments, it may be best to offer only one product to each segment, thereby minimizing the number of products offered and their overlap, while covering all market opportunities. This strategy *under these conditions* could lead to a highly desirable combination of low costs and high sales. Conversely, we might choose to target one or some

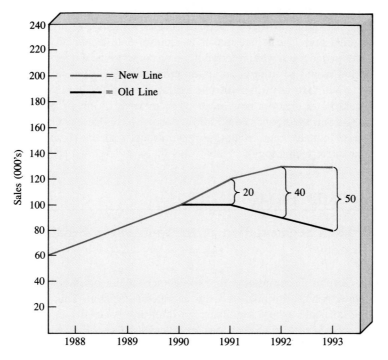

FIGURE 16.2
Incremental Sales Dynamics

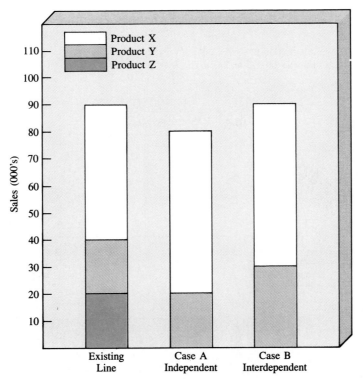

FIGURE 16.3
Dropping a Product

(but not all) segments, explicitly forgoing some sales opportunities in order to minimize costs, focus organizational attention, or establish as clear an identity as possible. A third option might be to create a new-product segment rather than compete in the existing product-market structure.

Recall the heart pacemaker example in Chapter 7, Market Segmentation. In that instance, we found that four segments defined the market: a "sophisticated" segment subdivided into (1) dual chamber and (2) advanced programmable pacers; and a "simple segment" divided into (3) preset and (4) basic programmable pacers. Offering a product line that spans all four of these segments would cover all opportunities. (Although the original preset heart pacemaker was out-of-date technically, it continued to be used for older patients and was preferred by some doctors who did relatively few implants.) Another option would be to target only the programmable segments, the sole segments in which we could take advantage of our unique capabilities in micrologic chips. A third option would be to create a new segment by means of a major product innovation. Perhaps a radio-controlled pacer could allow doctors to revise pacer characteristics without doing a new implant, thus creating a new product segment (assuming that doctors accept the innovative technology).

PRODUCT-MARKET SEGMENTATION

Product Segmentation as an Approach to Product-Line Strategy

In Chapter 7, we argued that the choice of the primary basis for segmentation (e.g., demographics, attitude, use) was a strategic decision. This is especially true for product-line decisions where segments can often most usefully be defined by the products that compete with one another for consumer purchases. Figure 16.4, for example, illustrates

FIGURE 16.4
Illustrative Product Segmentation of Camera Market Based on Film Type
Note: For simplicity's sake only a subset of cameras offered on the market is shown here.

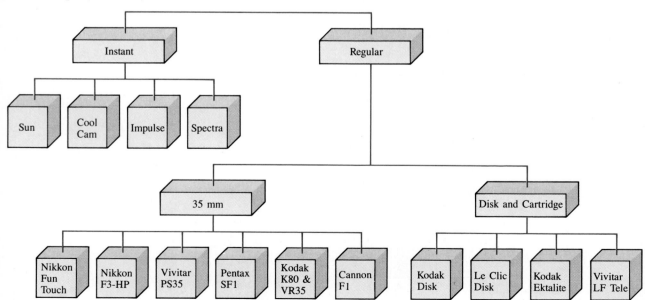

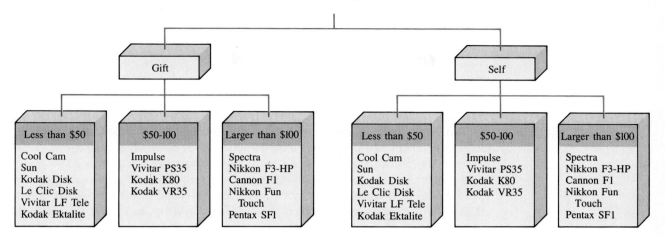

the segmentation of the still-camera market on a product basis, with instant and regular cameras viewed as distinct product-market segments. The implication of this structure is that instant cameras compete with one another, but not with regular cameras, and vice versa. Regular cameras are subdivided into 35mm and other (cartridge and disk), while instant cameras are subdivided according to Polaroid's range of models. If this segmentation scheme is valid, Polaroid does not have to worry greatly about competition from the new low-price automatic 35mm cameras, since they would be competing primarily with other 35mm cameras. Indeed, under this scenario, Polaroid can introduce its own 35mm camera without significantly impacting sales of its existing line of instant cameras.

Consider, however, Figure 16.5, which suggests a fundamentally different product-market segmentation structure. In this schema, the market is segmented on the basis of motivation for purchase rather than by product type. First it is divided between purchases for one's own use and purchases for gifts; then it is further divided into several price classes. Under these conditions, instant and 35mm cameras compete directly with each other in some segments, so it would be appropriate for Polaroid to view the new, simple-to-use, low-priced 35mm cameras as a direct threat to its Spectra and Impulse instant camera business.

A third possibility is shown in Figure 16.6, where occasion for use is the primary segmentation dimension. In this schema, cameras used on vacations, in "serious" photography, by children, and at parties and social occasions would each comprise a separate segment, and many families would own and use several different types of cameras. Under these conditions, the competitive structure would be more complex: Polaroid would compete against "disk and instamatic" cameras with its low-priced Coolcam cameras for kids; and against low-priced 35mm automatic cameras with its Impulse and Spectra models.

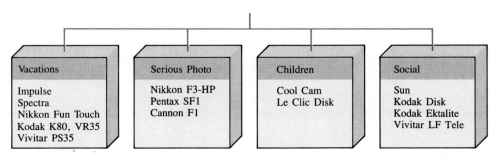

FIGURE 16.6
Illustrative Product
Segmentation Based on Use

Except for several special purpose models (not shown in Figure 16.6), Polaroid would not be competing directly in the ''serious photographer'' market segment.

Thus, product-line and competitive strategy issues are shaped significantly by one's view of the operative product-market structure. But which structure *is* most valid? It is marketing's responsibility to answer this question, thereby greatly influencing the strategy formulation process.

Defining Product-Market Structures

Three approaches have proved especially useful in defining product-market structures. The first is judgment. Experienced managers, observing shifts in market share following the introduction of new products or changes in pricing or advertising, can often infer the pattern of competitive interaction in a market. If rapid growth in automatic and low-priced 35mm camera sales coincided with a flattening in instant-camera sales, for example, that would be a fairly strong indication that these two camera types do not represent independent markets, but compete with each other. (Figure 16.4 would then be incorrect.) Inferences can also be drawn from focus groups where customers are asked to talk about the alternatives they consider when making a purchase and why they view those alternatives as competitive choices. Similarly, retailers may be able to provide information concerning which cameras consumers consider to be alternatives.

Two market research methods are frequently used to refine such judgments. Both are based on customers' assessments of how products compete. The first asks customers to group products according to how similarly they perceive them. Consumers might, for example, be given cards bearing descriptions of, say, seventy-five cameras (pictures, specifications, and prices). After eliminating the cards for those camera models with which they are not familiar, they would be asked to group the cards into piles based on how similar they perceive them to be. While some customers may form many piles, and others only two or three, the resulting clusters often provide powerful insights into the ''true'' competitive segmentation of a market. (See the discussion of the Buick Reatta case below for a fuller description of this methodology.)

The second research method is to ask customers for their first-choice product, and then inquire what product they would choose if that product were not available. In the camera market, consider those whose first choice is a Polaroid Spectra. If the preponderance of this group say that they would choose a Nikon Fun Touch if the Spectra were unavailable, this would be a strong indication that the product-market structure is consistent with Figures 16.5 or 16.6, but not with Figure 16.4. If this sentiment appeared to be widely shared, it would lend support to the hypothesis that the observed leveling off of instant camera sales was a function of competition from automatic 35mm cameras, whose sales were known to be growing rapidly. Conversely, if those whose first choice was a Polaroid Spectra expressed a second choice for the Polaroid Impulse, and those with a first preference for the Nikon Fun Touch would select the Minolta Freedom as their second choice, Figure 16.4 would appear to be a more accurate depiction of market dynamics. Under these circumstances, the observed leveling off of sales of instant cameras might be due to the maturing of the life cycle for instant photography (perhaps the feature has grown stale or there has simply been a decline in the percentage of households with small children), rather than substitution by the new 35mm cameras.

Product Segmentation in the Buick Reatta Case

Recall in the Reatta case presented in Chapter 13 that one of the most important issues was whether the Reatta would be viewed as a ''sports'' or ''luxury'' car. If it came to be positioned as a luxury car, it would be directly competitive with the Buick Riviera.

If it were seen as a sports car, however, it would cover a new market opportunity with little potential for the cannibalization of other Buick models.

Both market research methods described above were used to address this issue. First, consumers who would consider a two-seat auto and were willing to spend more than $20,000 for a car were shown 120 car descriptions (pictures and specifications on a 3-by-5 card). They selected the cards for the cars they were familiar with (sixty, on average), and then formed piles based on perceived similarity. The Reatta, after concept and test-drive exposure, most often shared a pile with the Nissan 300ZX (47 percent), Chevrolet Corvette (46 percent), Porsche 924 (45 percent), and Mazda RX-7 (44 percent). The Reatta was placed in the pile with the Buick Riviera only 9 percent of the time, which would suggest that customers view the car as similar to sports cars and dissimilar to the Riviera. More sophisticated analysis would allow us to describe this classification structure more completely.

The similarity data obtained from the piles can be converted into a product-segmentation structure by the use of a modification of the *cluster analysis* statistical technique we described in Chapter 7. In this case, data first are arrayed in a matrix in which both the rows and columns are labeled (in this case, by car names). A value of 1 is placed in a cell whenever a customer places two cars in the same pile. If the first interviewee placed the 300-ZX and the Reatta in the same pile, a 1 would be entered in the cell defined by the row for Reatta and the column for the 300-ZX, as well as in the row for the 300ZX and the column for the Reatta. When the matrix has been completed, cells with high scores will represent pairs that were viewed as similar by a large number of customers (see Table 16.1).

Cluster analysis combines into groups the cars labeled by the rows that have similar values across the columns. For example, if Toyota Supra is commonly placed in a pile with the 300-ZX (a high value in the Supra and 300-ZX cell), and the 300-ZX with the Mazda RX-7, and the Toyota Supra with the Mazda RX-7, the row values for these cars will be similar. If two cars have the same values for all entries along the rows, we would say they have an identical pattern of similarity with other cars and we would assign them to the same group. If the rows are completely different, we would assign them to different groups.

In practice, of course, the rows will not be exactly the same, so we measure how closely they resemble each other by calculating the differences in the row values. The formal criterion most commonly used in cluster analysis is to assign the variable of interest (in this instance, car models) to clusters, so that the variance (i.e., the sum of the squared differences between the row values divided by the number of cars in the group) within groups is small and the variance between groups is large, thus maximizing the separation

TABLE 16.1 Similarity Matrix

	REATTA	RIVIERA	300ZX	SKYHAWK	TOYOTA SUPRA	VW SIROCCO	BMW 300	RX-7
Reatta	x	3	150	20	140	70	80	140
Riviera	3	x	10	70	30	40	80	20
300 ZX	150	10	x	4	200	60	70	150
Skyhawk	20	70	4	x	10	75	50	40
Toyota Supra	140	30	200	10	x	85	100	175
VW Sirocco	70	40	60	75	85	x	60	125
BMW 3W	80	80	70	50	100	60	x	110
RX-7	140	20	150	40	175	125	110	x

between groups and the homogeneity within groups. The end result in the Reatta case is the grouping of cars shown in Figure 16.7.

In the study on which this figure is based, nine product segments were defined and then labeled judgmentally. The Reatta was assigned most often to cluster 5 (28.2 percent of the respondents), which was labeled "Lower-Priced Sports Sedans," and cluster 6 (15 percent), "Performance Sports Cars." It was placed in the "U.S. Luxury Cars" segment (cluster 8) with the Riviera by only 9 percent of the respondents, and least often in the

FIGURE 16.7
Product Segmentation for Reatta Data

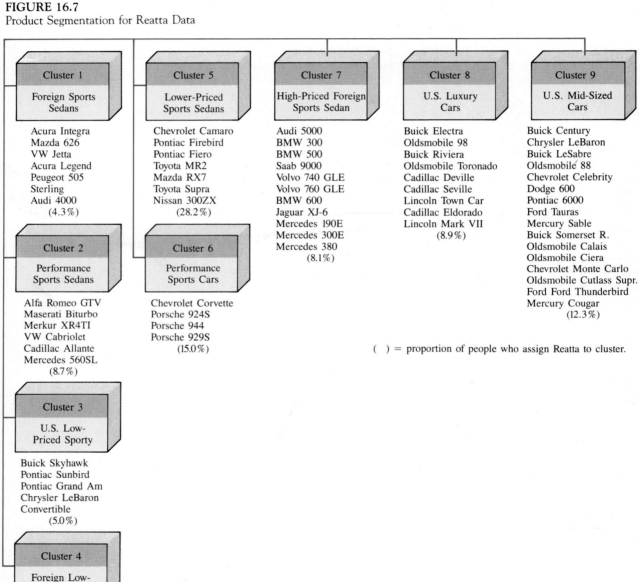

( ) = proportion of people who assign Reatta to cluster.

"Foreign Sports Sedans" segment (cluster 1). These data suggest that the Reatta can be targeted at a new segment, and is unlikely to cannibalize other Buick models to a significant extent.

    The fact that products are viewed as similar does not necessarily mean that they are competing directly with each other in the consumer choice process. To test this possibility, the researchers determined in which cluster each customer's most preferred car resided, and then calculated the probability that he or she would buy another car in that segment if the most preferred car were not available. This "forced switching" measure was calculated from respondents' stated probabilities of purchase, as obtained from the market research. The forced switching probabilities indicated there was a strong segmentation structure to the market (see Urban, Johnson, and Hauser, 1984 for details). In the case of the nine-cluster solution, all segments were significant at the 10 percent level when the observed forced switching was compared to the random structure switching probabilities. This analysis confirmed the hypothesis that the addition of the Reatta to the line would generate incremental business, and not significantly reduce the sales of other Buick models.

Product-Segmentation and Product-Line Composition

Once we have constructed a product-segmentation structure for a market, we can estimate coverage and duplication. Do we have a product competing in each segment? If not, do we want to? Do we have a competitive advantage to bring to that segment? If we do, or if we can develop one, there may be an opportunity to obtain significant incremental business.

    If we have more than one product in a product segment, we should ask if we have too much overlap and whether we should consolidate the line by eliminating one or more products. If our products do not have different product positions (i.e., appeal to different benefit segments, groups with different attribute importances), there is a good chance that our product line is too broad.

POSITIONING PRODUCTS WITHIN A PRODUCT LINE

Once a target segment has been defined, it is necessary to position our product within that segment. To do this analytically, we construct a perceptual map for each segment in which we propose to compete, and then consider the advantages and disadvantages of alternative positionings for each segment. Would it, for example, be better for each of our entries to stand alone, or should we market to multiple segments using an umbrella branding strategy?

Positioning Within Product Segments

Assume, for example, that Figure 16.5 is the correct description of the market for cameras. Let's consider the "self" purchase branch of the hierarchical market structure and construct a map for each of the three subbranches defined by price ranges. Assume that the dimensions are quality of picture (color realism, sharpness, skin tone reproduction, correct shading); ease of use (automatic exposure and focus, speed to print, easy-to-understand operation, compact size); and cost (of camera, film, development). On each branch, the cameras that appear on the maps and the importance of the three dimensions may vary.

    Figure 16.8 shows three different maps, indicating the ideal vectors given the assumed importances of the dimensions (recall that the slope of the vector reflects the importance of the dimension). In this illustration, consumers in the low-price segment (less than $50) consider ease of use and cost to be most important in selecting a camera, while camera

FIGURE 16.8
Positioning of Cameras in
"Self" Purchase Segments

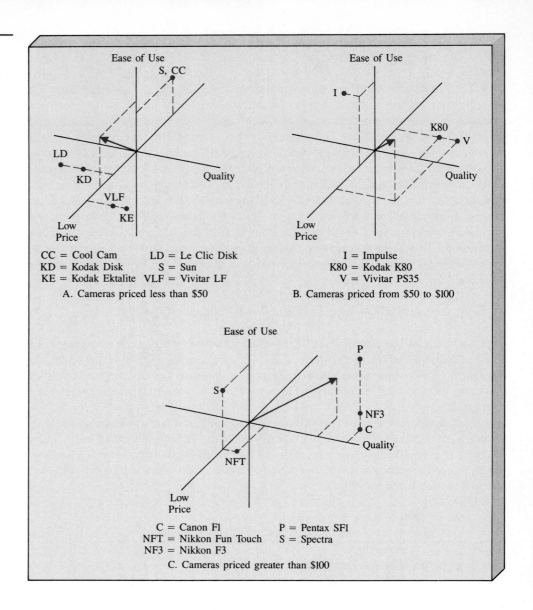

CC = Cool Cam   LD = Le Clic Disk
KD = Kodak Disk   S = Sun
KE = Kodak Ektalite   VLF = Vivitar LF

A. Cameras priced less than $50

I = Impulse
K80 = Kodak K80
V = Vivitar PS35

B. Cameras priced from $50 to $100

C = Canon Fl   P = Pentax SFl
NFT = Nikkon Fun Touch   S = Spectra
NF3 = Nikkon F3

C. Cameras priced greater than $100

buyers in the high-price segment (greater than $100) see quality as most important and price as least important. Members of the mid-price ($51–$100) segment view all three dimensions as equally important.

It is not necessarily true that all segments will be defined by the same dimensions. The high-price segment, for example, may be strongly influenced by an additional dimension—let's call it "professional"—which is characterized by advanced features (e.g., zoom lens, filters, manual f-stop and focus), and full-sized professional appearance. It is critical to have a good sense of the perceptual map for each market segment, so that each model in the product line can be positioned in its segment as effectively as possible.

Umbrella Positioning

In Chapter 8, Product Positioning, we noted that when a common dimension exists across the maps of the various segments served by a line of products, it might be desirable to establish an umbrella position for the entire line. In the automobile market, for example, the "quality" dimension (e.g., reliable, durable, good fit and finish, high level of featuring, and low maintenance cost) crosses all segments. Honda has established an overall reputation for marketing cars of the highest quality. As a result, it can take advantage of an effective umbrella position when advertising to all segments. Many consumers also perceive Honda as a producer of rather utilitarian cars with ordinary performance, so when Honda wanted to tap the sports sedan segments of the market, it decided to launch a new brand, Acura, and to sell it through a separate dealer organization. They sought to position the Acura as a better BMW, but kept some Honda identification ("Acura, a Division of Honda") in order to take advantage of the company's umbrella image for quality. The Sterling, which is similar to the Acura, but produced in Britain by British Leyland (in a strategic alliance with Honda), has not fared as well, presumably in part because it lacks the advantage of the Honda umbrella.

When using umbrella positioning, it is important not to seek to establish an overall position on a dimension that some segments view as negative. In the Honda case, one advantage of the Acura name is that it does not suggest to the classic Honda segments, which presumably value efficiency and utility highly, that Honda has abandoned them in its pursuit of a new, sporty upscale image.

If umbrella positioning is feasible, it can significantly increase advertising efficiency. Generally, the cost per thousand of reaching a mass market is considerably lower than for a specific customer segment, and threshold levels of reach and frequency against the target market can be attained at considerably lower levels of expenditure. Under ideal circumstances, umbrella positioning allows the overall line to be positioned against competition, while retaining flexibility to promote individual products "under the umbrella."

Creating a New-Product Segment

We have seen how the *existing* segmentation of a market has profound implications for product-line strategy. An even bolder strategy, with even higher potential payoff, is *not* to compete in the currently defined segment, but rather to redefine the structure of the competition. Generally, this is hard to accomplish, and requires a major product innovation and a large investment in marketing communications, but the impact can be extraordinary. With its introduction of instant photography in the 1950s, for example, Polaroid revolutionized the structure of the photography market and established itself as an important player in the photographic industry.

Today it is conceivable that electronic still cameras will provide another such opportunity, perhaps also for a new entrant. (Such cameras take photos digitally and store the resulting information on reusable magnetic media either for later playback on a television set or printing by means of a separate printer.) This technology, by replacing chemical technology, could revolutionize photography—in effect, adding a new branch for electronic cameras to the segment structure of the market. Some or all of the older branches might then disappear, or they might persist as subsegments that prefer the older approach. (Phonograph records and cassettes continue to be purchased by some consumers, despite the advent of compact discs.)

Alternatively, electronic cameras may compete with other cameras on the traditional dimensions of quality, ease of use, and cost. If the market is divided by use, as in Figure 16.5, we would expect electronic cameras to compete at premium prices, by offering better-quality and ease-of-use alternatives to chemical film technologies. In this case, there would probably not be a new set of branches, but a new (presumably strong) competitor in some or all of the existing branches.

In this type of situation, it is crucial to continually monitor changes in the segment structure of the market and to ascertain the dimensions on which the new technology is compared *by potential customers* (not product planners) with existing products. Even before actual new products based on the new technology are introduced, the approaches to segmentation analysis described earlier can be applied to concepts, prototypes, and display models.

An interesting example of an attempt to create a new market structure is the introduction of the Video Writer by Magnavox. The Video Writer is essentially a PC dedicated to word processing in the home. It has a video screen, built-in printer, and menu-driven instructions. The price ($500) is not far below that of a fully featured low-end PC, but its target market and positioning are very different.

The Video Writer is intended to be a plug-in-and-use system. Even those who are afraid of computers can learn to use the extended typing features in a few minutes. It is not necessary to load DOS or to call up applications software. All the user has to do is read the menu and start typing.

Video Writer appears to have created a new product segment in the PC market. People who consider this product are looking for a typewriter, and do not think of themselves as being in the market for a PC. They do not use spreadsheets or data bases, nor do they require the ability to write programs or interface with other compatible computers. They do not even consider IBM, Apple, or the so-called clones as purchase alternatives.

This product segment was pioneered by Magnavox, but now Brother has introduced an almost identical product called the Word Processor 55 and Smith-Corona has launched the PWP-6 portable word processor. A new product segment, located between electronic typewriters and PCs, seems to be emerging. Magnavox, a new entrant into the typewriter and PC industries, seems to have obtained a foothold in the market as a result of its innovative approach to product segmentation. (See Chapter 23 where we use this market in a case illustration of marketing planning.)

As a final example, consider the beer market. In the late 1970s, "light" beers (low-calorie, less filling beers) created a new segment in a market previously defined by premium, import, and domestic regular beer. Miller earned a long-run competitive advantage by opening this new segment.[1] In 1988, a similar revolutionary strategy was followed in Japan by Asahi, which introduced "dry" beer, a stronger beer with more alcohol (owing to longer fermenting), a less sweet taste, and macho positioning (Gene Hackman and Mike Tyson were used in the introductory advertising campaign in Japan). Dry beer increased Asahi's sales by 33 percent, largely at the expense of Japan's two largest brewers, Kirin and Sapporo. All three firms are now marketing this new type of beer worldwide. Indeed, Kirin has responded to Asahi's attack by introducing eight new beers in an attempt to preempt future market opportunities and fill any gaps in its product lines. Many U.S. brewers now offer "dry" beers in response to the Japanese threat.

RESOURCE ALLOCATION AND THE PRODUCT LINE

After we have defined the product segments that characterize a market, chosen which segments to target, and decided how to position our products within them, our next tasks are to decide what the marketing budget for the overall product line should be and how to allocate that budget among the products in the line. The answers to three critical questions will strongly influence these decisions: (1) How responsive are the sales and profits of each product to incremental expenditures on marketing? (2) How much demand interdependency is there among the individual products in the line? (3) How interrelated are the cost structures that underlie the product line?

---

[1] Miller's innovation was not in developing a new product (several previous light beers had failed), but in positioning it as a beer for macho, heavy beer drinkers, who would now be able to drink more beer, rather than for "two-beer-a-week" types who were worried about their waistlines.

Usually the executive responsible for a line of products gets requests from his or her product managers for *more* funds (almost never will a product manager ask for fewer resources). There are always reasonable arguments for more money: If the brand is declining, increased marketing expenditures are necessary to regain share and compete aggressively. If share is growing, now is the time to capitalize on the market opportunity.

How do we sort out these issues? We could simply add up the requests and submit the total, but corporate guidelines generally suggest an ''acceptable'' budget level that is considerably lower than that sum. We could reduce the initial product budget requests proportionally to fit the overall limit, but this approach, while organizationally palatable, would almost certainly result in less-than-optimal profits for the total product line. Moreover, the product managers in the organization would soon learn ''how the game is played,'' and inflate their budget requests accordingly.

The critical question we must answer is how alternative allocations of advertising, selling, promotion, distribution, and new-product resources will affect overall product-line sales, operating profits, and ROI. Either explicitly or implicitly, the total product-line market response function must be estimated. This function is, in practice, largely a summation of individual brand responses. In our experience, the best approach to this very challenging problem is to model the market response of each existing and new product, and then simulate the overall product-line effects of alternate allocations. With a sales forecast based on each allocation, we can calculate the profitability of that particular allocation, taking into account whatever shared costs may be present. We would then compare the alternatives and select the most profitable one.

This would be a relatively simple procedure if each product were completely independent and we could simply add up the individual results. We would then use the response models and life-cycle models described in Chapters 9 and 6 to estimate the response functions for each of the existing and new products in the line, sum the responses to get an estimate of the overall consequences of each alternative allocation scheme, and compare the results. In practice, however, the various products in a line usually share resources (e.g., production facilities, pooled sales forces, marketing channels) and may compete in the same market segments, resulting in significant interdependencies. Consequently, it would often be misleading to treat each product as independent in modeling the profit consequences of alternative allocation schemes. Perhaps for this reason, Procter & Gamble recently announced a significant restructuring of its legendary product management system to give more authority to group or category managers.

Demand Interdependencies

As we noted earlier, it is a rare market that can be divided into mutually exclusive segments. Generally, the segments overlap to at least some degree, and a significant number of customers will consider products in more than one segment. Under these circumstances, the price, advertising and promotion, and selling efforts for one product will affect the sales of others in the line. This is especially true when an umbrella positioning is being employed *and* there is significant overlap among the segments being served. If, for example, a flanker is added, its advertising can generally be expected to benefit the rest of the line.

Another form of interdependency occurs when multiple products in the line have a common channel. In marketing frozen foods, for example, one is confronted with limited freezer space at the retail level. Major supermarket chains typically allocate this space (at least initially) by supplier rather than by product. Similarly, industrial products distributors typically limit the total funds and space they are willing to devote to stocking the inventory and spare parts of a particular manufacturer. Given these circumstances, if you wish to add a new item to your line, it will almost inevitably take shelf space away

FIGURE 16.9
Cross-Price Response
Function

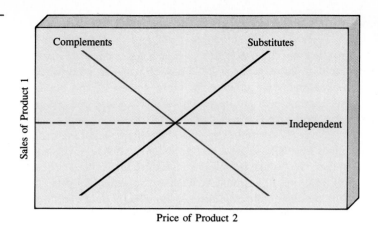

from your other products. Sometimes you can "buy" additional shelf space by promoting to the retailer, but the cost of doing so may negate the benefits of introducing the new item.

One should begin to address the interdependency issue by estimating judgmentally the effects of marketing actions in support of one product on the sales of other products in the line. Then one can draw cross-product response function graphs that show this relationship. Consider Figure 16.9, which illustrates how the price of product 2 affects the sales of product 1. If the slope is horizontal, the price of product 2 does not affect the sales of product 1 (i.e., they are independent). If, however, the slope is not horizontal, the sales of the two products are interdependent. If sales of product 1 increase when the price of product 2 is raised, the products are viewed as interchangeable by at least some customers, who switch from one to the other as their price relationship changes. Conversely, if the sales of product 1 *increase* as product 2's price is decreased, the two products may be said to be complementary: as sales of product 2 increase, so do sales of product 1, perhaps because of joint usage or increased traffic drawn to their shared distribution channel by the price decrease.

Figure 16.10 shows the cross-response price function for a new industrial chemical with respect to two existing products. The graphs indicate that the sales of the new product will come in part from the old products; the degree of cannibalization will depend on the relative prices of the new chemical and the old products. In this case (which will be

FIGURE 16.10
Sales of Two Existing
Products as a Function of
New-Product Price

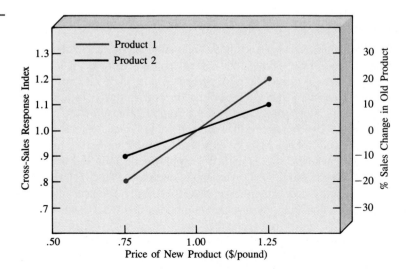

discussed more fully below), the problem is further complicated by the fact that all three products are sold by the same sales force, creating the need to allocate a fixed resource among them. Such marketing interdependencies must be understood fully and taken into account when allocating marketing budgets to the individual products in an interdependent product line.

Cost Interdependencies

Cost interdependencies are often as important as demand interdependencies. Recall that in Chapter 10, Competitive Behavior, we discussed the need to understand the relationship between cumulative sales volume and unit costs. At the product-line level, we must consider, in addition to individual product experience curves, the effects of combined experience and scale on the cost structures of the individual products in the line.

One approach to this problem would be to sum the volumes of the individual products in the line and use the cumulative total in an experience equation (see equation [10.1]). This would be appropriate only if all the cost elements were uniformly shared across all the products. A better approach would be to disaggregate the value-added components of each product and estimate the scale economies and experience effects that could be obtained by sharing them across the line. Figure 16.11 shows the value-added components for a line of paper products (Porter, 1985). In this example, the technology costs (R&D) are shared by multiple products, all products benefit from economies in procurement, inbound and outbound logistics are subject to economies of scale, and marketing efficiency increases with volume.

Note that while most value components in this case gain from increased volume and experience, the operations and service components do not. In this instance, the production operations for the various products are totally independent. If, however, two or more products shared a single production line or plant facility (or service organization), we would expect them to benefit from shared scale and experience.

The economic consequences of such sharing are best estimated through the use of models that permit us to analyze the impact of changes in the volume of individual products on unit costs across the product line. We can then use the output of such models (costs, prices, *and* resource allocations at various volumes) to forecast profits and select the alternative that promises the most favorable long-run profits.

Product-Line Profit Modeling

The profits of a product line can be viewed as being generated by a set of products at various points in their life cycles. If we forecast sales for each product based on the current composition of the product line and the allocation of resources to individual products, and then sum the estimated sales at various points in time, we will have an initial sales forecast for the line. If we calculate costs for the line by summing the value-added components after adjusting for shared costs and economies, we will have an estimate of total costs. Combining the two, we can forecast profits for each year up to the planning horizon.

Using these forecasts (volume, costs, and profit) as the baseline, we will be able to estimate the effects of adding products to the line by developing a life-cycle sales curve for each new product (as part of the line), and then reducing (increasing) the sales forecasts for established products if there is substitution (complementarity). After we recalculate costs and profits, we can determine the incremental sales and profits as shown in Figure 16.2.

An Industrial Chemicals Case: Given this general approach to the profit evaluation, consider the example of a new polyethelenelatex compound that is to be added to an

FIGURE 16.11

Illustrative Interrelationships Between Value Chains in Paper Products

Source: Reprinted with permission of The Free Press, a Division of Macmillan, Inc., from *Competitive Advantage: Creating and Sustaining Superior Performance* by Michael E. Porter. Copyright © 1985 by Michael E. Porter.

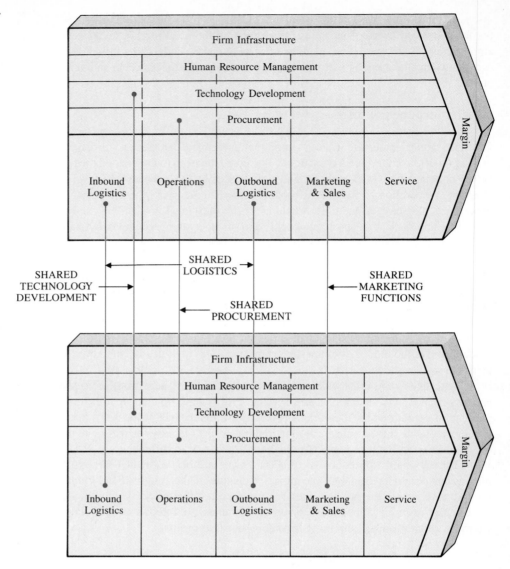

existing line of two plastic compounds. Figure 16.12 shows the forecast of new and established products over six years. It also shows (the dotted line) the reduction in sales of the two old products that is expected to result from the introduction of the new product. Sales of the new product, and the degree of substitution with the established products, are a function of the new product's pricing level, advertising spending, and sales force allocation. As the price of the new product is lowered, its volume increases according to a price response function and its life cycle shifts forward in time. While this increases the sales advantage of the new product prior to competitive entry, it also increases cannibalization of existing product sales (see Figure 16.10 for the cross–price response function).

The unit costs for the three products are independent, but the new product is subject to substantial experience effects, particularly when there is enough volume to move from pilot to full plant production. The sales force sells all three products, with its time being allocated on the basis of preestablished norms that can be modified as necessary.

We would first use a spreadsheet model to calculate the incremental discounted cash flow of adding the new product to the line under various pricing and resource-allocation scenarios. Would the entire line be more profitable, for example, if we priced the new

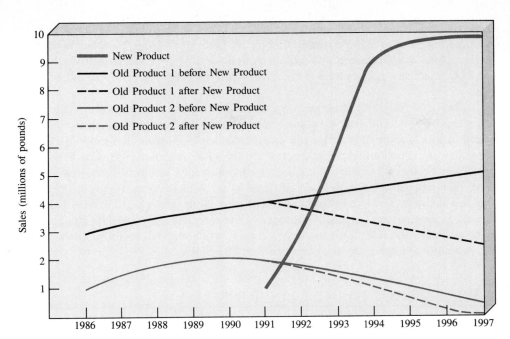

FIGURE 16.12
New- and Old-Product Sales

product high and gave it extensive sales force support, or would it be better to price it lower with less sales force support? Or might we be still better off using a combination of low price and heavy sales force support?

Because of uncertainty in the forecasts of volumes and costs on which this analysis would be based, we would also want to use Monte Carlo simulation methods to estimate the variance on the incremental profit (see Urban, 1968). Under a particular scenario, what would be the probability of achieving the firm's target ROI level? Column 1 of Table 16.2 shows the results of such a simulation under the base case pricing and sales strategy

TABLE 16.2 Chemical Case Study Results

	REFERENCE PROGRAM	LOWER PRICES	LARGER PLANT	LARGER SALES FORCE
Discounted differential profit	$6,000,000	$10,833,000	$11,561,000	$12,219,000
Investment	$8,000,000	$ 8,000,000	$ 8,300,000	$ 8,400,000
Probability of achieving target rate of return	Less than 50%	86%	88%	91%
Advertising level per year	$10,000	$10,000	$10,000	$10,000
Percent of sales effort per year	1.0	1.0	1.0	1.3
Price in Year				
1	$350	$250	$250	$250
2	$350	$250	$250	$250
3	$350	$250	$250	$250
4	$250	$180	$170	$190
5	$250	$200	$160	$200
6	$250	$210	$170	$210
7	$250	$170	$170	$180
8	$250	$180	$180	$180
9	$250	$180	$180	$190
10	$250	$190	$190	$200

Source: Glen L. Urban, "A New Product Analysis and Decision Model," *Management Science*, Vol. 14, No. 8 (April 1968), p. 514.

scenario. The discounted incremental profit is estimated at $6 million, but the probability of achieving the firm's 15 percent ROI objective is less than 50 percent. While the new product alone would generate $8.5 million in profit (with a 75 percent chance of achieving the ROI objective), performance at this level would probably not justify adding it to the line.

But other marketing strategies were also simulated. As may be seen in Table 16.2, lower prices build cumulative volume more rapidly, thus utilizing the full-scale plant added in Year 4 more efficiently, and justifying an enlarged plant in Year 7. Under this scenario, total product-line profits increase by almost $5 million compared with the base case. While sales of the old products decrease more rapidly, profits from the new product more than compensate for these cannibalized sales. A larger plant (twice the capacity) and an increased sales force allocation further increase the profit performance. Based on numerous simulations of alternative strategies, it appears that this aggressive strategy (low price *and* increased sales force support) will maximize both product-line profitability and the probability of achieving the corporate ROI objective.

ANALYTIC SUPPORT FOR PRODUCT-LINE DECISIONS

The complexity of the product-line problem requires moving beyond Level I analysis (clear strategic problem and issue identification) to higher levels of quantification and analysis. The industrial chemicals example we have just considered emphasizes how important it is to quantify *incremental product-line* (versus single-product) profits before deciding whether to add a new product to an existing product line. Product-segmentation and interdependency analysis, as described above, represent effective Level II inputs to the product-line decision process. At a minimum, managers should draw product-segmentation structures based on a clear understanding of competitive market boundaries, and use spreadsheet models to analyze the implications of demand and cost interdependencies.

A number of Level III analytic support tools are also available. Various statistical techniques are useful in estimating cross-elasticities among products (see Urban, 1969; and Naert and Leeflang, 1978, for examples). These econometric approaches require careful application because such cross-elasticities are second-order effects, which are notoriously difficult to estimate accurately.

There have been numerous advances in product segmentation based on advanced clustering and other algorithms (Day, Shocker, and Srivastava, 1979; Kalwani and Morrison, 1977; Rao and Sabavala, 1981; and Srivastava, Leone, and Shocker, 1981); and variety phenomena (Lattin and McAlister, 1985). A most promising Level III technique is based on conjoint analysis and choice modeling. In this approach, each individual is modeled as having a utility for each product attribute. Through simulation, each can then choose from a line of product options (see Green, 1984). By repeated simulation across a sample of customers, one can evaluate different product-line compositions and pricing strategies vis-à-vis competition. When a cost model based on shared cost economies is appended, incremental profits can be calculated (see Green et al., 1981; and Kohli and Krishnamurti, 1987). More recently, efforts have centered on the use of optimization procedures in comprehensive product-line models (Dobson and Kalish, 1988; McBride and Zufryden, 1988; Shugan, 1989).

The relatively new field of information processing, which attempts to understand the role of memory structure, categorization, elimination, and consideration in an individual's formulation of and choice among an evoked set of alternatives (see Sujan, 1985; and Bettman and Sujan, 1987, for examples), has great promise for Level III analysis. In the future, we expect the integration of such processes with conjoint choice models to significantly improve our ability to identify the "correct" product segmentation in a market.

Product-line strategies are becoming more and more important in overall marketing strategy formulation. Intensifying global competition, in combination with maturing life cycles and increasing market saturation for many product categories, leads to attempts at finer and finer segmentation. As a result, products proliferate, overlap increases, and the complexity of selling, production, inventory, and service mounts steadily.

Moreover, flexible manufacturing promises to make even finer segmentation possible in the near future. In automobiles, once automated machines, robots, and modular design concepts are fully utilized, the same production line will be able to produce a full range of vehicles, from four-wheel-drive utility trucks to limousines. In the telecommunications industry, software is already being used to customize basic electronic hardware to meet end-user requirements precisely. Under these circumstances, the cost premiums associated with multiple products or customizaton will decrease.

Similarly, improved information technology may bring down certain distribution, inventory, and service costs associated with complex product lines, although other costs in these spheres are likely to rise. Given this increasing complexity, rational product-line decisions will require improved value-added models and methods for estimating demand and cost interdependencies.

With companies coming under greater pressure to add products to their lines, the need to systematically prune existing products is becoming ever more critical. Top management must insist that managers at all levels consider whether they should drop an existing product at least as often as they consider whether they should introduce a new one. To ignore this necessity is to invite unwise proliferation, consumer confusion, and rising inventory and logistics costs.

As more and more markets are served by multiple competitors with wide product lines, it will be harder to earn better-than-average profits through conventional means. One way to seek a competitive advantage under these circumstances is to strive for cost leadership or greater marketing efficiency through the use of Level II and Level III analytical methods to establish a product line that fully meets the needs of divergent customer segments with a minimum of overlap. But greater returns are likely to accrue to those firms that create new product segments, or even whole new markets. In either case, there will be an enormous need for managers who are able to integrate new and established product strategies at the business unit level to create product lines that satisfy customers' needs better than their competitors.

QUESTIONS FOR DISCUSSION

1. Why are there so many items in the product lines of today's firms? What will limit the number of products offered in a single company's line?

2. The product manager says, "We have to add this new product to our line so that we can increase sales," and the sales manager says, "We cannot afford to drop any product from our line because we will lose sales that we may never regain." What are the possible strategic fallacies in these statements?

3. Why is product segmentation rather than demographic or psychographic segmentation the best approach for product-line decisions?

4. Consider the beer market. Describe the product segments you suspect are present and the brands in each. Use judgment to draw a perceptual map for each segment. What are the managerial implications for the brewers? How would you create a new product segment in this market?

341

5. What is the difference between a "cross-response function" and a "response template"?

6. If products in your product line overlap, how do you as product-line manager set the overall line budget when faced with independent requests from each product manager?

7. How do production cost structures influence the marketing strategy for a product line?

8. When should you prune the product line? What analytic methods can help you make this decision?

REFERENCES

BETTMAN, JAMES R., AND MITA SUJAN. 1987. "Effects of Framing on Evaluation of Comparable and Noncomparable Alternatives by Expert and Novice Consumers." *Journal of Consumer Research* 14: 141–154.

DAY, GEORGE S., ALLAN D. SHOCKER, AND K. SRIVASTAVA. 1979. "Consumer Oriented Approaches to Identifying Product Markets." *Journal of Marketing* 43: 8–20.

DOBSON, GREGORY, AND SHOLOMO KALISH. 1988. "Positioning and Pricing a Product Line." *Marketing Science* 5: 107–125.

GREEN, PAUL E. 1984. "Hybred Models for Conjoint Analysis: An Expository Review." *Journal of Marketing Research* 21: 155–169.

———, J. DOUGLAS CARROLL, STEPHEN M. GOLDBERG, AND PRADEEP K. KEDIA. 1981. "Product Design Optimization—A Technical Description of the POSSE Methodology." Working Paper. Philadelphia, PA: The Wharton School, University of Pennsylvania.

KALWANI, MANU, AND DONALD MORRISON. 1977. "A Parsimonious Description of the Hendry System." *Management Science* 23: 467–477.

KOHLI, RAJEEV, AND RAMESH KRISHNAMURTI. 1987. "A Heuristic Approach to Product Design." *Management Science* 33: 1123–34.

LATTIN, JAMES M., AND LEIGH MCALISTER. 1985. "Using a Variety-Seeking Model to Identify Substitute and Complementary Relationships Among Competing Products." *Journal of Marketing Research* 22: 330–339.

MCALISTER, LEIGH. 1982. "A Dynamic Attribute Satiation Model of Variety Seeking Behavior." *Journal of Consumer Research* 9: 141–150.

MCBRIDE, RICHARD D., AND FRED S. ZUFRYDEN. 1988. "An Integer Programming Approach to the Optimal Product Line Selection Problem." *Marketing Science* 5: 126–140.

NAERT, P. A., AND P. S. M. LEEFLANG. 1978. *Building Implementable Models*. Boston, MA: Martinus Nijhoff/Leiden.

PORTER, MICHAEL E. 1985. *Competitive Advantage*. New York: The Free Press.

RAO, R. VITHALA, AND D. J. SABAVALA. 1981. "Inferences of Hierarchical Choice Processes from Panel Data." *Journal of Consumer Research* 8: 85–96.

SHUGAN, STEVEN J. 1989. "Product Assortment in a Triopoly." *Management Science* 34: 304–320.

SUJAN, MITA. 1985. "Consumer Knowledge: Effects on Evaluation Strategies Mediating Consumer Judgments." *Journal of Consumer Research* 12: 16–31.

SRIVASTAVA, R. K., R. P. LEONE, AND A. D. SHOCKER. 1981). "Market Structure

Analysis: Hierarchical Clustering of Products Based on Substitution in Use.'' *Journal of Marketing* 45: 38–48.

URBAN, GLEN L. 1968. ''A New Product Analysis and Decision Model.'' *Management Science* 14: 490–517.

_____. 1969. ''A Mathematical Modeling Approach to Product Line Decisions.'' *Journal of Marketing Research* 6: 40–47.

_____, PHILIP L. JOHNSON, AND JOHN R. HAUSER. 1984. ''Testing Competitive Market Structures.'' *Marketing Science* 3: 83–112.

WILSON, LYNN O., AND JOHN A. NORTON. 1989. ''Optimal Entry Timing for a Product Line Extension.'' *Marketing Science* 8: 1–17.

17
WORLDWIDE CORPORATE STRATEGY

THE PRODUCT LINE, SBU, AND WORLDWIDE CORPORATE HIERARCHY

In the last chapter, we considered a number of managerial issues resulting from the aggregation of individual products into product lines. Such product lines can be further combined into strategic business units (SBUs), which, in turn, can be brought together to form an overall corporate strategy. In this chapter, we appraise marketing's role at various levels in the corporate planning hierarchy, with particular emphasis on the representation of customer requirements in the corporate strategic planning process.

In our discussion of strategy, we do not treat international or global strategy as a distinct topic because we firmly believe that it is unsound to consider corporate and international strategy separately in today's global business environment. Virtually every business has at least some international content (if only the sourcing of some of its raw materials). Larger corporations almost always both manufacture and market at least some of their products in a number of countries. Manufacturers in Japan, the United States, and Europe often produce and assemble their products in the same low-labor-cost countries (e.g., Taiwan, Korea, Mexico), and then compete fiercely with one another in both their own and third-country markets.

Services, similarly, face growing global competition. To cite a few well-known examples, McDonald's fast-foods restaurants (U.S.) and Holiday Inn hotels (U.S.), as well as Benetton (Italy) and Cartier (France) retail outlets, can be found throughout much of the world. Today financial services are typically provided on a twenty-four–hour basis through computer systems and telecommunications networks that are largely independent of the home country of the financial institution providing the service.

Even if a firm sells products and services only in its home country, it is likely to face "foreign" competition of one sort or another. Toyota imports automobiles to the United States as well as building cars here. Honda (Japan) and British Leyland (U.K.) have formed a strategic alliance to produce the Sterling, which they then export to third countries such as the United States, where its primary competitor appears to be the Honda Acura. In the United States, Honda is developing the capacity to produce 590,000 cars (worth $6 billion), and plans to export 50,000 of those American-built cars to Japan and 25,000 to other parts of the world by 1990. Honda is likely to become the third-largest *American* producer of cars in the 1990s, building and selling more cars in the United States than in Japan. At that point, would Honda be a Japanese or an American company? Or something else altogether?

Strategic alliances, joint ventures, and formal mergers are blurring traditional distinctions between domestic and foreign competitors. Ford owns 25 percent of Mazda and produces the Ford Probe and Mazda 626 on the same line in the United States. General Motors and Toyota jointly produce cars (the Nova, GEO Prism, and Corolla) in the United States, even though GM has a substantial stake in Isuzu, one of Toyota's Japanese competitors. Alcatel (France) has purchased ITT's international telephone business, thus becoming one of the biggest providers of telecommunication services in the world. AT&T's former operating companies are also becoming increasingly global: US West has installed automated teller machines (ATMs) in London, while Bell South (in a joint venture) is establishing a financial communications network in Buenos Aires and Southwestern Bell has won the contract to market the yellow pages in Australia.

Experts differ as to whether the world in the 1990s will become increasingly global or split into major trading blocks (e.g., the European Economic Community [especially after the 1992 agreements and the removal of the Berlin Wall], the Pacific Rim, the Americas). Whichever scenario one prefers, it seems virtually certain that in most industries competition will increasingly be carried out by a set of multinational firms that take a global perspective in making R&D, marketing, production, and finance decisions. The objective will be to maximize worldwide market position and profitability, rather than to optimize for subsystems such as nations or (even) regions.

International marketing strategy should be integral to corporate strategy—part of the strategic perspective from the beginning, not an ''add-on'' after domestic strategy has been formulated.

In our view, the much-discussed globalization-versus-nationalization dilemma in marketing is in fact a special case of the standardization-differentiation dichotomy that pervades any discussion of marketing strategy. As we shall see, the question is essentially: what is the appropriate basis for market segmentation? A given market can, for example, be segmented on a demographic, attitudinal, behavioral, or product attribute basis, or some combination of these dimensions. In some cases (e.g., school textbooks, flags), it obviously makes the most sense for the primary basis of segmentation to be geographic or national. In other cases (e.g., certain fashion products and high-technology capital goods), other bases for segmentation are almost certainly more appropriate.

The use of customer segmentation as the basis for worldwide marketing strategy highlights marketing's critical role in the corporate strategy formulation process. In this chapter, we describe our approach to segmentation in some detail, address a number of especially important SBU definition and resource allocation issues, and consider the implications of these issues for the organization and management of a firm that has a truly global perspective. We then discuss the role of leadership in a global firm's marketing effort, and examine some of the Level I and Level II analytic models that are becoming increasingly useful—indeed, essential—in formulating strategies for complex global enterprises. Finally, we consider some of the most important challenges likely to confront the strategic management process in the next decade.

MARKETING'S ROLE IN CORPORATE STRATEGY

Marketing Phenomena

The success of any enterprise is ultimately a function of individual decisions made by individual customers. In developing strategies at the SBU and corporate levels, it is imperative not to lose sight of the fact that *sales are earned one customer at a time*. Thus, strategies must be translated into core benefit propositions for every product or service in every target market segment. No matter how advanced the technology, sophisticated the production facilities, or creative the financing, if customers do not perceive the value offered by your product to be superior to that offered by your competitors, your strategy will fail. It is marketing's responsibility to contribute insights, knowledge, forecasts, and programs that lead to superior perceived value, and thus maximize corporate profitability.

The market phenomena studied in earlier chapters of this book are critical inputs to worldwide corporate strategy development. If one is to make the appropriate technology, production, and financing decisions, one must understand the customer decision process in each SBU's markets and how alternative benefits are evaluated by various segments of consumers. Life-cycle, positioning, and segmentation phenomena can play key roles at the SBU and corporate levels, and should be taken into account in the strategy formulation process. Market response graphs and equations may be used at the corporate level to simulate resource allocations across SBUs, while segmentation plays a major role in establishing worldwide strategies. Integrating these phenomena within a corporate competitive strategy is a challenging task that largely depends on effective marketing analysis and strategic thinking.

Integrating Marketing Inputs with Research and Development, Production, and Finance

Although marketing is critical, it is only one of several major inputs that must be integrated. Technological, production, and financial factors must be blended with marketing considerations within a global perspective, as shown in Figure 17.1.

Marketing and R&D must be closely linked because the effective and efficient use of technology requires a comprehensive understanding of current and potential customer needs. A competitive advantage in technology often leads to unique value at the customer level, but only if there is a good fit between the benefits made possible by that technology and customer needs. Polaroid, for example, is still taking advantage of its forty-year-old technological lead (and strong patent protection) in the field of instant photography. Initially, this advantage was exploited primarily in consumer markets ("Quick, get a picture of the baby in the bathtub, Harry!"), but today a major proportion of the company's revenues is derived from industrial, government, and professional markets. It is worth noting, however, that technological advances in a distinct but related industry (one-hour

FIGURE 17.1
Functional Integration for
Worldwide Strategy

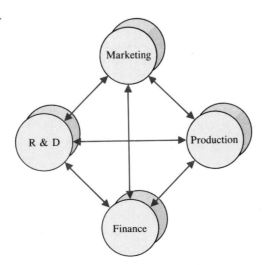

automatic film developing and finishing) have recently significantly lessened the competitive advantage derived by Polaroid from its monopoly on *in-camera* instant developing. The value to the consumer of Polaroid's technology was fast pictures, not one particular way of achieving that benefit.

Even a great technical innovation that meets a real market need is unlikely to succeed if it does not result in products that can be produced at high-quality levels and low costs. The U.S. auto industry learned by painful experience that style and market position were not enough to sell cars if consumers believed that they were in quality inferior to competitive alternatives. Many consumers were willing to pay premium prices for Hondas in the early 1980s, while in the computer industry many customers elect to stay with IBM (which has a reputation for high product quality and responsive service), even though competitors may offer more advanced features and lower prices.

Consumer trade-offs between perceived quality and price play a major role in determining who wins and who loses in the marketplace. Market response to perceived quality must be integrated with R&D and production cost functions to define a value point that represents the strategic optimum. Today "total quality" and QFD (quality/function/deployment) seek to achieve the integration of design, production, delivery, and service in pursuit of optimum quality. For these processes to work, there has to be a clear understanding of the specific benefits and costs associated with the thousands of decisions that must be made in the product-development process. A change in product design, for example, may improve consumer perceptions of quality, but complicate the manufacturing, distribution, or service processes to the degree that "real" (i.e., long-term perceived) quality is jeopardized.

Marketing is responsible for first obtaining and then communicating a clear understanding of how various segments of customers would respond to alternative variations in quality and price. Using these response functions, marketing can generate forecasts for product planning and production. Alternative forecasts for distinct product strategies (i.e., different targeting, positioning, levels of price, promotion, advertising, sales, and distribution) contribute to the cross-functional integration of production and marketing by providing critical inputs for reaching optimal capacity, scheduling, and distribution decisions.

Financial capabilities are critical at both the SBU and the corporate level. If we do not have the resources to adequately fund research and development, production, start-up, and product launch and marketing costs, we stand little chance of achieving our objectives. Similarly, it is essential that our resources be adequate vis-à-vis the resource capabilities of our strategic competitors. If we do not have sufficient resources to sustain our position in the face of intensified competition—whether in advertising, selling, channel incentives, and/or price—it is unlikely that we will be able to survive in the long run, even if we have the best product design and production processes.

In global markets, fluctuations in foreign exchange values often make pricing and marketing more difficult. If foreign exchange rates change, should prices in the local currency of the market country fully reflect the change? Or should we reduce our profit margins (to maintain competitive price levels) when the relative value of our currency rises and, conversely, maintain our price (thus raising our profit margin) when the relative value of our currency falls? In 1987–1988, for example, Porsche increased its prices in the United States by over 40 percent, reflecting a drop of that magnitude in the value of the U.S. dollar vis-à-vis the deutsche mark. Largely for this reason, Porsche's sales in the United States, which had accounted for 50 percent of its revenues, dropped 30 percent, leading to large losses and subsequent layoffs in Germany. Might it have been more profitable, in both the short run and the long run, for Porsche to have absorbed some of the currency value change, thus reducing its margins, but presumably maintaining a larger proportion of its volume? Or might Porsche have hedged more fully against a decline in the value of the dollar, thus maintaining both margins and volume? As you can see, what appears on the surface to be technical financial decisions can have extremely important impacts on marketing effectiveness.

To reiterate: A successful global strategy requires the comprehensive integration of marketing, financial, production, and technology decisions and policies. Marketing, however brilliant, is only one part of the equation.

Obtaining Global Competitive Advantage Through Marketing

In the 1960s and 1970s, much of the United States' economic success could be attributed to the strength of its technology. In computers, plain-paper copiers, and photographic film, for example, U.S. companies had a clear lead over their foreign rivals. By the late 1980s, however, the Japanese and Europeans had achieved worldwide competitive advantage in many product classes through a combination of higher product quality and/or lower costs. In the 1990s, according to many observers, it will be difficult to sustain a competitive advantage in technology, product quality, or production costs.

Under such circumstances, how will firms strive for competitive advantage? There are a number of options, but one important possibility is through superior marketing. A firm with superior skills in segmenting markets, identifying inadequately satisfied customer needs, and positioning, advertising, promoting, selling, and providing after-sale service to satisfy those needs is a probable candidate for market leadership, even if it holds only a parity position in technology and manufacturing.

The essential argument of this book is that powerful analytic tools are increasingly available in marketing, and that corporations that hope to prosper in the years ahead had better learn to use them effectively. These tools should be viewed as analogous to the production quality control methods that were developed in the 1960s, but were largely ignored in the United States and Europe. Japanese industry has now demonstrated to the world that statistical quality control techniques do work and, more importantly, that firms that use them effectively can achieve significant competitive advantages. What will it take to convince management that scientific and analytic marketing methods can be the source of similar advantage? We hope this book will do its part, but strongly suspect that the decisive factor will be innovative firms utilizing such methodologies to humble their more traditional competitors.

WORLDWIDE MARKET SEGMENTATION

Bases of Segmentation

Traditionally, most firms operating internationally treated each country as a separate market—in effect, a distinct market segment defined by geographic and political parameters. In many cases, this is, in fact, the best primary dimension for market segmentation. Currencies, customs, lifestyles, languages, needs, tastes, and marketing infrastructures (e.g., distribution channels, advertising media) do vary significantly among countries, while segmentation on the basis of national boundaries is often practical because of the market insulation created by import restrictions and duties and regulations.

But "geographics" is only one of a set of possible demographic characteristics for defining segments. Porsche, for example, targets the affluent (over $100,000 income) and younger (ages thirty-five to fifty) segment of the automobile market. Its $50,000 cars compete as much with boats and second homes as with other cars. Although Porsche does modify its core strategy for individual countries, its primary segmentation scheme is based on income and age, and it has found that there is a marked similarity in the needs and buying behavior of consumers in its target segment whether in Mexico, Sweden, or the United States (or Germany, for that matter).

Moreover, demographics are only one potential basis for segmentation. As outlined earlier in this book, attitudes, importances, uses, and competitive products are often valuable alternatives. This is true in worldwide as well as in domestic markets. Porsche might, for example, define its target market on the basis of the cars it views as its major competitors (Ferrari, Maserati, Jaguar XJ-12, BMW 635i, Lotus). Or it might use correlates of product attribute importance. (Porsche owners, for example, place very high importance on *ultimate performance* in cornering and acceleration, and are relatively unconcerned with space and fuel efficiency). Or it might choose psychological bases for segmentation. Porsche buyers are looking for the best *appropriate* car *for them*, and consider ownership of, say, a Black Porsche 928 or red Porsche Cabriolet to be symbolic of success in a fast-action professional career (e.g., as a successful entrepreneur).

Hierarchical Segmentation of World Markets

A critical step in the formulation of an effective strategy is the selection of the most appropriate basis for segmentation. Often it is useful to employ a segmentation hierarchy to specify the relative importance of multiple segmentation dimensions (review Figures 7.1 and 7.2 on pages 122 and 123).

Take, for example, the worldwide market for office copiers. It is clearly segmented by both geographics and copying speed and capacity. Figure 17.2 illustrates a segmentation hierarchy in which the primary basis for segmentation is geographic,[1] with speed and capacity as a secondary dimension. Figure 17.3, conversely, uses product speed and capacity as its primary dimension for segmentation, and geographic regions as a secondary dimension. The high-speed segment consists of high-capacity, expensive machines, the primary market for which is large insurance and financial services firms and large government and industrial organizations seeking improved productivity. The low-speed segment includes low-priced, low-capacity copiers intended for small businesses and organizational units primarily concerned with low acquisition costs and/or dedicated resources for small work groups. The mid-speed segment is intermediate in terms of product, use, and attitude attributes.

The implications for product design and marketing differ according to what view of the market one takes. Consider the hypothetical market potential values in Table 17.1. Under a geographically based segmentation scheme, each region would place the highest

---

[1] In this example, the "Far East" consists of Japan, Australia, and the rest of Asia; the "Americas" comprise North, Central, and South America; while "Europe" includes Western Europe, Eastern Europe, and Africa.

FIGURE 17.2
Segmentation by Region

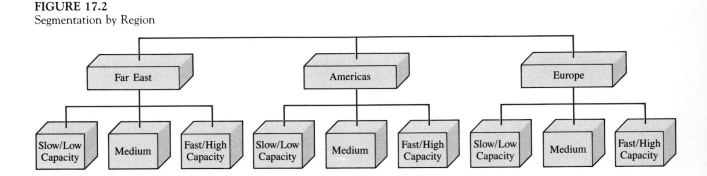

FIGURE 17.3
Segmentation by Product Speed and Capacity

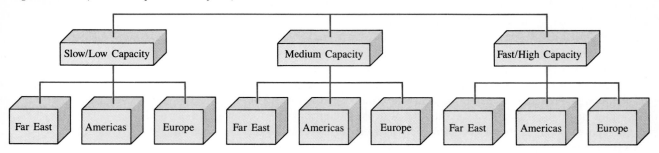

priority on the machine with the largest potential in its region. This would be the fastest machine in the Americas and Europe, and the slower machine in the Far East (see asterisks in the column entires). If design priorities were based on the votes of market segment managers, a large, fast, expensive machine would be built (the Americas and Europe would vote against Asia). Conversely, if segmentation was by machine capability rather than by region, the medium-speed machine would have design priority because of its market segment potential (see dagger in row totals). In practice, the firm would generally not need to restrict itself to one product or market segment. As emphasized in Chapter 7, Market Segmentation, the decision to cover all segments or to target one or a selected set is a critical strategic decision that should not be made until a basis for segmentation has been selected and a hierarchy of segmentation attributes established.

Worldwide Segmentation versus a Single-Product Global Market Perspective

It is tempting to segment the world by countries or regions and market differently to each of them, but many times this is not the appropriate course to follow. First, as mentioned earlier, some method of segmentation other than geographic may be preferable. Second, it is often far more costly to differentiate products for disparate market segments than to offer standard marketing bundles across market segments. Economies of scale and experience effects may reduce costs to the extent that the firm can offer prices so much lower than it could if it used a differentiated marketing strategy that customers are willing to forgo a certain amount of customization to their specific needs and preferences.

Levitt (1983a and 1983b) argues that (1) price/value sensitivity is increasing in a world of scarcity, (2) tastes are growing more homogeneous across national boundaries,

TABLE 17.1 Hypothetical Office Copier Market Potential
($ millions)

	FAR EAST	AMERICAS	EUROPE	TOTAL
Slow/low capacity	450*	300	300	1050
Medium capacity	375	450	375	1200†
Fast/high capacity	150	525*	450*	1125
Total	975	1275	1125	3375

* Indicates which machine has the greatest potential in each region.
† Indicates which machine has the greatest market segment potential overall.
Source: Adapted from H. Blitzer, Lecture at MIT, April 24, 1989.

and (3) the marketing infrastructure (e.g., advertising agencies, marketing research firms) is becoming increasingly global. As a result, he posits that worldwide, standardized global products and brands will grow in importance. He notes, for example, that McDonald's has largely standardized its marketing approach from the Champs Elysées in Paris to the Ginza in Tokyo; and that Kentucky Fried Chicken, which has over 1,000 successful outlets in Japan alone, uses the legendary Colonel Sanders as its advertising symbol throughout the world. IBM sells the same line of computers in much the same way everywhere. FAX machines are virtually identical throughout the world, the vast majority being made in Japan, where economies of scale lead to low production costs and high reliability.

Under a global standardization strategy, costs are reduced and individual preference differences are deemphasized. Use of a standardized global strategy is essentially a decision not to segment the world market on the basis of geography, but instead to treat it as one homogeneous opportunity. This strategy assumes that the price or product quality advantages emanating from standardization will outweigh specific customer preferences in enough cases to make it the appropriate choice.

Levitt's critics argue that the differences between countries are so great that even lower prices will not induce customers to buy standard products; that a competitive product customized to local tastes can defeat a low-cost standardized global product even though its price is higher; and that advances in "flexible" manufacturing are counteracting the cost advantages of standardized products. In this view, cultural differences often require marketing programs uniquely designed for a country or, at a minimum, heavily modified to meet local needs.

An interesting example of this point of view is provided by Kao, a leading Japanese consumer products company, which recently introduced BUB, a new bath product, in Japan. BUB is an effervescent CO_2 tablet that releases bubbles when it comes into contact with water. This "new therapeutic bath tablet warms the body to the core" and "reduces early morning lethargy due to low blood pressure." The CO_2 "permeates the skin to stimulate the muscle cells and facilitate blood circulation."

A product with these characteristics and this positioning fits well with the Japanese bathing regimen. Soap is never used in the bath although a shower with soap is taken before the bath. The bath is viewed primarily as a relaxing and meditative experience. Would this product have a global market? Probably not. The role played by the hot bath in Japan is probably unique, at least at present. The recent rapid growth of hot tubs and whirlpool baths in North American and Western Europe may change this, however.

Many product categories are characterized by strong differences among countries in cultural attitudes and practices (see Fields, 1984, for a fascinating compilation of additional examples from Japan). In these cases, segmenting the world by country and offering a custom-designed marketing plan for each market is probably the optimum strategy. Conversely, there are some products that lend themselves better to global strategies. Technical products and luxury consumer goods tend to fall into this category.

There is clearly no single "right" answer to the global-versus-national controversy. What is required is an in-depth analysis of the market for a particular product to determine which side of the trade-off should carry more weight.

Country Differences in a Worldwide Segmentation Strategy

A standardized global product and marketing program on the one hand, and a unique marketing program for each country on the other hand, are extreme alternative strategies. In most situations, there will be at least some potential for obtaining lower costs through greater scale and experience effects, and some potential for satisfying differences in customer needs and preferences across countries. The resolution of the trade-off of these effects is represented by the segmentation hierarchy. If country differences are at the top, marketing programs should be differentiated for individual markets. If demographic, attitudinal, attribute importance, or use are at the top of the hierarchy, marketing programs should generally be standardized globally for that particular segment. Even under these circumstances, however, some modification of the marketing program to fit local conditions is generally desirable. While the physical product may be standardized, for example, it might make sense to customize local advertising, selling, and distribution strategies, inasmuch as there are few economies of scale in these areas and local differences in media, channels, and customer ''hot buttons'' may be important.

In cases of this sort, the objective is to achieve maximum customization to meet local conditions while minimizing lost cost savings from understandardization. While IBM markets a relatively standard product line worldwide, for example, products (especially software) are modified to meet language requirements and differences in business (e.g., accounting) practices. Similarly, IBM Japan has developed a unique set of selling techniques that fit the buying processes of Japanese businesses better than those that have proved so successful in North America and Europe.

Coca-Cola markets essentially the same product throughout the world, although its sweetness (the sweetening agent is added by the local bottler) does vary somewhat among markets, even (reputedly) in the United States. In Japan, however, Coca-Cola's product line includes hot ready-to-drink Georgia Blend Coffee in cans, which is sold through the hot and cold vending machines that are located on virtually every busy street.

Successful global firms are not inappropriately constrained by their strategies. They do not hesitate to take advantage of differences among national markets when the benefits of doing so outweigh the costs.

In our view, the first step in formulating a worldwide strategy is to define the primary basis of segmentation, and the second is to specify the optimal subsegmentation hierarchy. Given this description of the market, the marketing strategist then decides which segments to compete in and how far to go in modifying all or part of the marketing program to meet the heterogeneous preferences of individual segments. Such trade-offs, in practice, can be quite complex, as illustrated by the following minicase.

Corning Glass's Corelle dinnerware has numerous advantages (e.g., better durability and appearance) over the plastic dishes it was intended to replace. In the United States, it has been extremely successful, totally dominating the category. In France, however, Corelle achieved scant success, despite low prices (fixed costs had been covered by North American sales), very heavy advertising, widescale distribution (Corning ovenware was very popular in France), and new patterns targeted for French tastes (see Figure 17.4). The core of the problem turned out to be the simple fact that in France Corelle competed with lower-cost pottery and glassware rather than with plastic dishes, which the French had never accepted. Corning France then developed a line of stove-top cookware called Vision (see Figure 17.5). Although not technically advanced—in fact, the heavy glass slowed heat transfer—the new product was valued highly by French customers for its transparency, which permitted observation of the food as it cooked. Vision achieved very considerable success in France, and subsequently was introduced in a large number of other countries. French advertising for Vision emphasized cooking quality and visibility, while American ads stressed durability (showing an aluminum pan being melted in a Vision pot). Thus, the same product was positioned differently in the two countries, reflecting differences in the importance French and American consumers placed on key product attributes. Utilizing this type of positioning differentiation, Vision has been extremely successful worldwide, and is now being given new life through modification for microwave cooking.

This minicase illustrates the complexity of balancing cost economies and technological advantages in a worldwide market where preferences and uses vary. Although Corelle met customer needs in some countries, it provided very little incremental benefit in others. As a physical product, Vision was standardized globally, but its core benefit proposition and advertising were differentiated according to national conditions. The

FIGURE 17.4
Corelle Trade Promotion

Corelle®

la première vaisselle fine garantie 2 ans

DECOR BLEU

ARTICLE				COLISAGE					
Désignation	Vaisselle Corelle	Référence	Dimensions Capacité	Quantité par colis	Dimension cm L x l x h	Poids kg			
Assiette plate		8.305.36	ø 25 cm	12/36	25,8 x 17,4 x 25,8	14,8			
Assiette creuse		8.306.36	ø 21,5 cm	12/36	27,9 x 22,5 x 20	9,9			
Assiette dessert		8.307.36	ø 21,5 cm	12/36	22,2 x 18,9 x 21,9	9,5			
Coupe (étui de 4)		8.318.36	ø 16 cm	1/6	33,6 x 23,3 x 16,8	5,1			
Paire tasse à café (coffret de 4)		8.945.36	10 cl	1/6	46,8 x 37,2 x 19,2	6,5			
Saladier		8.606.36	ø 21,5 cm	3/12	37,2 x 22,6 x 22	3,5			
Saladier		8.607.36	ø 26 cm	3/12	41,6 x 27 x 26,3	6,4			
Plat de service ovale		8.625.36	31 x 25 cm	3/12	32 x 17,2 x 25,6	4,5			

353

FIGURE 17.5
Vision Advertising

primary segmentation dimension for Corelle was geographic; for Vision, it was specific product characteristics. Each situation must be thoroughly analyzed in its own terms, and addressed accordingly.

STRATEGIC BUSINESS UNIT RESOURCE ALLOCATION

In many cases, the segmentation hierarchy helps to determine the appropriate corporate organizational structure. If national differences are paramount, it is generally appropriate to organize on a geographic basis, with strategic business units (SBUs) corresponding to countries or groupings of countries. Conversely, if the top level of the segmentation hierarchy is product or industry related, it may be more appropriate to organize on a worldwide product division basis.

The SBU structure should divide the overall business into distinct components appropriate for intelligent resource allocation. If the SBUs are countries, budgets and targets are set by country; if the SBUs are based on products, resources are allocated by product group. Whatever the basis for segmentation, it will provide the top level of strategic conceptualization and the primary structure for resource allocation.

In allocating resources, we need to take into consideration many of the marketing phenomena cited earlier in this book. The life-cycle concept, for example, is often invaluable. SBUs early in their life cycles typically need large infusions of cash to finance growth in production capacity, inventories, and marketing expenses. Those in the mature phase, conversely, are likely to generate cash for investment in other SBUs. If a SBU is entering the decline phase, it is necessary to decide whether to milk the business (essentially an exit strategy) or to attempt to slow the decline so that the business will provide a continuing positive cash flow.

Share of market is a critical phenomenon in those businesses where profitability is highly dependent on market volume (typically those characterized by large R&D expenditures, steep experience curves, or considerable scale economies in manufacturing, marketing, or distribution). Under these conditions, it is generally wise to concentrate resources in a relatively small number of business units where share is high or can be increased, rather than to spread resources across a large number of SBUs with low potential market shares.

In Chapter 2, we discussed the use of matrices combining competitive advantage and market attractiveness as frameworks for diagnosis (see Figure 2.3 on page 20). When competitive advantage is treated as equivalent to market share (i.e., as largely a function of market share) and market attractiveness is defined on the basis of rate of market growth, the resulting matrix takes the form popularized by the Boston Consulting Group (BCG) in the 1970s. In this matrix, ''Star'' SBUs are characterized by high market share and high market growth, ''Dogs'' by low share and growth, ''Cows'' by high share and low growth, and ''Question Marks'' by low share and high growth. BCG's strategic prescription was to allocate cash generated by Cows to fuel the growth of the Stars in the portfolio, and to strengthen the Question Marks, which would thus be transformed into Stars, which would ultimately mature into new Cows. Dogs were to be terminated as painlessly as possible and the resources generated by their elimination invested in Stars, Question Marks, or new businesses.

Though this and similar matrices developed by General Electric, McKinsey, and others proved overly simplistic in practice, they did make an important contribution to strategic management by highlighting the value of looking at a corporation as a portfolio of businesses, and then allocating resources to those businesses in accordance with an explicit conceptual structure. In the absence of such a framework, inertia tends to result in resources being overallocated to mature businesses. The matrix as generalized in Figure

2.3 remains a useful Level I analysis tool. Later in this chapter, we will outline a Level III SBU market response model that formally considers stages of the life cycle and market response curves, as well as market attractiveness (growth) and market share.

MARKET-BASED ORGANIZATION

As we have seen, it generally makes the most sense to define SBUs on the basis of the segmentation hierarchy and to build up the corporate organizational structure from the SBU structure. Today functional organizational structures (i.e., R&D, production, marketing, finance, and control) are employed much less frequently than even twenty years ago, largely because of the increased product and market diversity faced by most businesses. Similarly, the traditional way of organizing for international business—making a primary distinction between the home country and the "international" division—is rapidly becoming obsolete. A worldwide view of markets is now the dominant force shaping organization structure.

It is more and more common for corporations that operate on a global scale to be organized on a worldwide product division or group basis. Within each worldwide business unit, functional areas or product lines serve as the primary organizing dimensions. Corporate central staffs such as R&D, legal, human resources, public relations, new-product development, and strategic planning may supply services to the divisions, supplementing divisional capabilities in these areas. Kodak, for example, structures its major SBUs on a product basis: Film, Chemicals, Information Systems (copiers and microfilm), Pharmaceuticals (Sterling Drugs), Life Sciences, and Diversified Technical Products (e.g., X-ray, optical disks). Worldwide business responsibility is assigned to each product division, while a wide array of corporate technical, legal, human relations, and planning functions support divisional capabilities.

Under certain circumstances, companies choose to organize at the highest level on a geographic rather than a product basis. During the early 1980s, for example, Kodak defined its SBUs on the basis of four large geographic regions. Each region, in turn, was organized on a product basis. By the mid-1980s, however, Kodak had reverted to the product-based structure, with global responsibility for a particular product range assigned to each SBU. After trying it both ways, Kodak management apparently decided that, for strategic management purposes, differences between technologies and products were more significant than differences between geographical regions.

Increasingly, customer segments rather than products or regions are used to define the top level of the organizational hierarchy. Major international banks, for example, typically operate their corporate and consumer businesses as separate units. Polaroid's first organizational cut is between its consumer and industrial markets.

The organizational structure should be aligned with the product or user market characteristics (demographics, geographics, uses, or importances) employed for worldwide segmentation. The highest level in the segmentation hierarchy should define both the SBU structure and the first cut in the organizational structure. Within each SBU, either secondary segmentation dimensions or functional dimensions can then be used as bases for organizing subunits. Corning's worldwide Customer Products group, for example, could be organized by types of cookware (Figure 17.6A), by geographic region (Figure 17.6B), or by function (Figure 17.6C).

The complexity of global business demands similarly complex organizational designs. Enterprises of this type have little choice but to operate through matrix structures, whether they choose to describe their organizations in this way or not. Whatever the primary dimension selected for organizing the company, it is necessary that formal or informal integration mechanisms cross the solid lines on the organization chart.

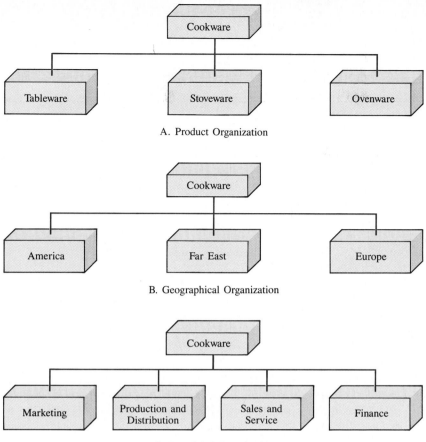

A. Product Organization

B. Geographical Organization

C. Functional Organization

FIGURE 17.6
Organization Alternatives

Early forms of integration were the brand manager structure in packaged goods companies and the program manager structure characteristic of aerospace companies. In both cases, an individual brand, product, or program manager was given responsibility for a specific product or closely related group of products, and was expected to ensure that the various functional departments (e.g., R&D, manufacturing, marketing, logistics) and subdepartments (e.g., marketing research, advertising, sales, and promotion in the marketing department) worked together to implement the ''product plan.'' Today there is even greater need for close integration at all stages of the product cycle, and firms have devised extremely complex processes to facilitate *lateral relations* among organizational units.

Consider Figure 17.7, a partial organization chart of Digital Equipment Corporation (DEC). Separate Engineering, Industry Marketing, Product Marketing, Sales, Distribution, and Service groups interact to generate DEC's offerings to customers. Ten groups in Engineering develop the basic architectures and computer platforms for system components. The Industry Marketing groups define the product specifications necessary for success in specific market segments. Product Marketing designates the package of components that will fit market needs (i.e., meet the specifications laid out by Industry Marketing). The Sales group, which is organized first into geographical regions and then into customer segments, seeks to solve customer problems with DEC systems and products. The Service and Distribution groups handle logistics, installation, and maintenance.

All of these groups are actually ''marketing'' groups—that is, each is responsible for a portion of the task of understanding and satisfying customer needs. In the Engineering

357

FIGURE 17.7
Digital Equipment Corporation (1988)

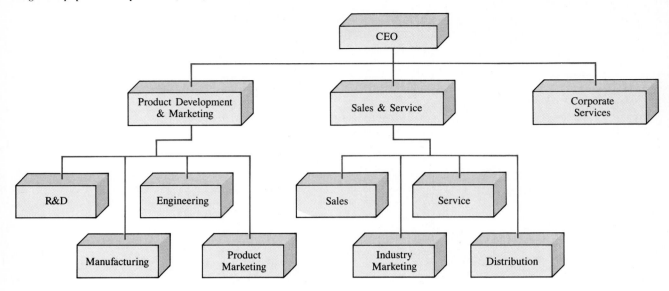

group, for example, Base Marketing Managers strive to get key customer input into the design process early. In addition, each engineering project has a Product Management Group, with explicit responsibility for the needs/technology interface. These are clearly "marketing" functions, even though they are located in the Engineering groups.

DEC has chosen to locate marketing activity centers throughout its organization, but they must work closely together if they are to be effective. Lateral relations are achieved through committees, project groups, task forces, and interpersonal relations. A network that builds consensus has been established (see Rufkin and Harar, 1988, for more detail on DEC organizational processes). The formal organization chart is a mere shadow of the informal organization that really runs DEC.

The importance of geographic layout in facilitating interactions among groups has long been recognized (see Allen, 1977). Today electronic mail, facsimile transmission, and continually updated computer data bases are enhancing communication and integration even when physical proximity is not practical. At DEC, electronic links such as these play a critical role in the lateral integration process, permitting worldwide collaboration on the development of products and marketing programs.

There is no single "best" formula for the design of an effective organization, but marketing inputs and activities must permeate all functions. Achieving customer satisfaction through an intense customer benefit orientation should be the primary goal in product design, production, selling, service, and distribution. Whether formally or informally (and generally through a combination of the two), processes must be in place to ensure strong lateral coordination of marketing activities.

CORPORATE MARKETING LEADERSHIP

Strategy and organization are necessary but not sufficient ingredients for success in today's global competitive environment. Organizational leadership is at least as essential. While it is difficult to define this critical factor precisely, experience suggests that the following ingredients are especially important.

Vision

An effective leader has a clear vision of how his or her firm is going to create competitive advantage by offering customers superior benefits and value. This vision includes a view of which products will be offered to which market segments, and what positioning advantages will be sought in each segment. It is translated into a mission statement, essentially a goal-oriented derivative of the vision, which is used as the operational lever to drive the strategic planning process. While there are many approaches to strategic planning, most take the form of sequential goal specification; program generation, evaluation, and selection; and resource commitment through planning and budgeting. During this process, the leader's most important role is to inspire the organization to establish an ambitious mission and achieve it. Leaders are passionate about their visions, and energize their organizations to achieve them.

Technical and Cultural Expertise

Effective leaders know what they are talking about. They understand both the marketing requirements and the technical foundations of their products. Though they may not be scientifically trained in each discipline relevant to their product range, they are technically literate. They are not intimidated by technical descriptions, feel confident in asking questions, and know when to rely on experts for answers. No matter how technical the product, an effective leader must comprehend fully how it is intended to generate benefits for customers. He or she must be comfortable with marketing technology—data, models, statistics, and computers. The leader is not expected to be a statistician or model builder, but should know when to request Level II or III analyses.

Marketing leadership also requires broad cultural awareness and perspective, an acute sensitivity to the global issues that generate both opportunities and threats. An effective leader is not required to speak many languages and be an expert on all countries (any more than he or she can be an expert in all relevant technical disciplines), but must possess and display a strong respect for the diversity of beliefs, attitudes, and practices present in the firm's markets. In the cultural arena as in the technical, the effective leader knows how to ask the right questions of the right people at the right time and (most important of all) how to listen carefully and critically to their answers.

Simplification and Bias Toward Action

Senior managers of diversified global businesses need to make decisions of almost overwhelming complexity. The effective leader has the insight necessary to simplify such problems and to make the appropriate choice among disparate alternatives. Depending on cognitive style, he or she may reduce the complexities of the problem early or late in the decision process, but in the end, the essential issues are identified and the essential questions are answered.

Establishing priorities and keeping the organization focused on them is a critical leadership task. Often the leader must streamline organizational structures and processes to minimize bureaucracy and maximize the amount of organizational energy devoted to the enterprise's strategic priorities. Organizational agility is a prerequisite to timely responses to major threats and opportunities.

In most cases, such responsiveness should take place within the context of the leader's vision. While it will sometimes be necessary to modify that vision in the face of markedly changed circumstances (e.g., the crude oil supply moving from surplus to shortage to surplus), an effective leader exhibits tenacity and courage in the face of unexpected changes in the firm's environment and performance. It is the leader's role to push his or her organization through difficult times—to ensure that it "stays the course."

Delegation

An effective leader works through other people to achieve results. He or she delegates responsibilities and trusts colleagues, gaining, in turn, their trust. They respect their leader for his or her values, expertise, and commitment. The true leader invites dissent, listens hard, and doesn't reach a final decision until hearing and considering all points of view. Once a decision has been taken, however, he or she insists on uncompromising support for that decision, whatever people's previous views. Obtaining this type of consensus and support is perhaps the most challenging of all of the leader's tasks.

Innovation

A leader recognizes when there is a need for change and inspires the organization to respond creatively. In his or her organization, new opportunities are identified and targeted; taking reasonable risks is encouraged; constructive "failure" is accepted; and creative attitudes are fostered. The leader demands that the organization be innovative in basic technology, product design, production, distribution, selling, advertising, promotion, and service—all with the view of satisfying the customer better than competitors.

Engendering change is one of the most challenging tasks in any organization. The marketing concept argues that the successful organization must satisfy the needs of a target market segment better than its competitors. If those needs change, or if competitive alternatives change, it follows that the successful firm must also change if it is to retain its position. Effective leaders understand this marketing dynamic, and recognize that they must be the primary change agents in their organizations because often subordinate managers are understandably reluctant to leave their "comfort zones." Effective leaders utilize open communication and participatory management to build a consensus for change that pervades their organizations.

ANALYTIC SUPPORT

As we have noted, one important attribute of the effective leader in today's world is familiarity with relevant marketing technology in order to call on Level II and Level III decision support tools when appropriate. In this section, we review Level II tools and Level III models that are useful in allocating resources among SBUs, planning the global introduction of new products, and gaining insights into the complex systems dynamics that have such profound effects on long-run profitability.

Level II Analysis

A number of Level II analytical tools are especially useful in formulating SBU and corporate strategies. Models of marketing phenomena, for example, support the strategy formulation process in a number of ways. Life-cycle models (Chapter 6) can help assess the attractiveness of various markets by predicting their growth rates. Perceptual maps (Chapter 8) for each country in which a firm competes can provide a basis for ascertaining competitive advantage. Game theory (Chapter 10) can be used to delineate the bounds of likely competitive responses and to suggest alternative strategic options. Response analysis (Chapter 9) is often invaluable in estimating the marginal impact of allocating additional resources to a particular business.

Cluster analysis can be extremely helpful in defining the appropriate strategic customer hierarchy for a company. In using this technique, it is critical that all important attributes be represented, and that the sensitivity of alternative clustering solutions to the inclusion or omission of individual variables be assessed (preferably by a professional statistician).

The goal of the clustering algorithms is to group customers so that they are homogeneous within and heterogeneous across clusters. Statistical discriminant analysis is used to determine which variable is most important in defining cluster membership. This variable becomes the primary descriptor of the strategic segmentation hierarchy, while the other variables are used to describe the profile of the segment (see Figures 7.1 and 7.2 on pages 122 and 123 for a review of segment profiling).

In this technique, data are placed in a matrix, with rows representing customers or buying units (e.g., divisions of companies) and columns representing attributes such as national idiosyncrasies, product preferences, uses, and demographics. Table 17.2 illustrates the use of this methodology to develop a segmentation hierarchy for the office copier market. If the resulting clusters represent groups based on machine size, the segmentation scheme shown in Figure 17.3 would be appropriate. If the clusters turn out to be by region, the scheme shown in Figure 17.2 would be a preferable choice. But some other cluster solution might be even better. Perhaps the needs and behavioral characteristics of individual industries (e.g., finance, manufacturing, education) would provide a better basis for segmentation. An inspection of the data in Table 17.2 suggests that there is greater homogeneity within industries and machine attributes than there is within countries. A complete data matrix, evaluated through formal cluster analysis, would be necessary to assess the validity of this assertion.

Spreadsheet analysis is a good tool for calculating the financial impact of alternative allocations of resources, given a particular segmentation scheme and definition of SBUs, as well as specific parameters in the life-cycle and response models. Alternative schemes, definitions, and parameters can also be evaluated in this way. If we are thinking of allocating resources to a growing market segment, for example, and the response and competitive reaction models suggest that we would thus increase our share in that market, we could use spreadsheet analysis to estimate the implications of these events for revenue, cash flow, and profits at both the SBU and corporate levels. If this analysis were done for each allocation, a combination of such analyses would provide the basis for a comprehensive

TABLE 17.2   Hypothetical Data Matrix for Global Segmentation of the Office Copier Market

		IMPORTANCE (1–10)				REGION (0, 1)				INDUSTRY (0, 1)		
Buying Unit	Copies per hr. (000s)	Cost	Quality	Speed	Reliability	Far East	America	Europe	Finance	Manufactur- ing, Actuarial	Govern- ment	Other
Citibank	1000	6	9	10	10	0	1	0	1	0	0	0
AIG Insurance	900	5	10	8	9	0	1	0	1	0	0	0
Nomura	500	6	9	10	10	1	0	0	1	0	0	0
Credit Suisse	300	4	10	9	10	0	0	1	1	0	0	0
GM	1500	10	6	6	7	0	1	0	0	1	0	0
Dexter Corp.	20	9	8	4	8	0	1	0	0	1	0	0
Peugot	100	9	7	6	8	0	0	1	0	1	0	0
GE Jet Eng.	30	8	10	6	6	0	1	0	0	1	0	0
Sony	300	8	9	8	9	1	0	0	0	1	0	0
Phillips	600	10	8	8	8	0	0	1	0	1	0	0
Noxell	10	9	8	4	8	0	1	0	0	1	0	0
IRS	2000	10	5	5	7	0	1	0	0	0	1	0
Gov. of Korea	75	8	6	6	8	0	1	0	0	0	1	0
Novotel	20	8	9	5	7	0	0	1	0	0	0	1

corporate resource allocation model. A proposed set of allocations might, for example, lead to considerable growth in market share in a good many high-growth businesses. Under these circumstances, we might have to raise additional funds on the capital markets to fuel the proposed growth strategy. If this is impractical (e.g., they won't lend us the money) or deemed undesirable (e.g., additional debt might make us vulnerable to an unfriendly takeover), we would then have to devise a somewhat less ambitious strategy.

Level III Analysis

The spreadsheet-based SBU resource allocation model described above can be extended to Level III capabilities by elaborating its market response component and incorporating a resource-optimization function. Larreche and Srinivasan (1981, 1982) have built such a model, which they call STRATPORT. It explicitly designates response functions and specific cost inputs for each business or project, and then uses a math programming algorithm to maximize long-run profit subject to resource constraints. Conceptually, the model combines externally available funds (and the cost of obtaining them) and internally generated cash into a pool that is allocated to the firm's SBUs in such a way as to maximize profit. It thus formalizes the matrix of competitive advantage and market attractiveness we outlined in Chapter 2 (Figure 2.3), and specifically deals with the effects of applying marketing resources to change market share and the impact of share on economies of scale and therefore on cost.

Figure 17.8 illustrates the application of STRATPORT at the SBU level for a five-year planning period. It is assumed that market share is a function of marketing investment, as specified in the following market response equation:

(17.1) $\quad M_t = L + (U - L) E^a/(B + E^a)$

where:

$$M_t = \text{market share at time } t$$
$$E = \text{marketing investment in SBU planning period}$$
$$L, U = \text{lower and upper limits on market share}$$
$$B, a = \text{response parameters}$$

According to this equation, market share can be increased from the lower limit (L) to the upper limit (U) in an S-shaped curve by investing funds in marketing (e.g., advertising, selling, promotion). The M_t value is not achieved in a single period, but is modeled as an asymptotic curve that approaches the ultimate share over the course of the planning period. The shape of this curve is similar to that used to describe the advertising response function in the ADBUG model (see Chapter 9), but in this case is used to estimate the effect of total marketing investment rather than just advertising expenditures.

In an effort to capture the longer-run consequences of marketing investment, STRATPORT models the postplanning period effects of various levels of marketing investment during the planning period, taking into account the level of marketing investment necessary to maintain share. In this model, the firm's cumulative production leads to experience effects that impact the firm's unit costs, and cumulative industry sales lead to an industry experience function that determines industry costs. A market price curve is then used in conjunction with these cost functions to forecast competitive practices and, ultimately, industry price levels. Taking the resulting estimate of unit volumes from the first model, and considering unit costs, unit prices, and necessary nonmarketing investments (e.g., additional plant capacity), it is possible to forecast the cash flow and profitability that will be achieved over time by a particular SBU, given a specified level of investment in marketing. If this is done for each SBU, the total model can be used to optimize the

FIGURE 17.8
Structure of STRATPORT for a Single Business Unit
Source: Reprinted from *Journal of Marketing,* published by the American Marketing Association. From "STRATPORT: A Decision Support System for Strategic Planning" by Jean Claude Larreche and V. Srinivasan, Vol. 45, No. 4 (Fall 1985).

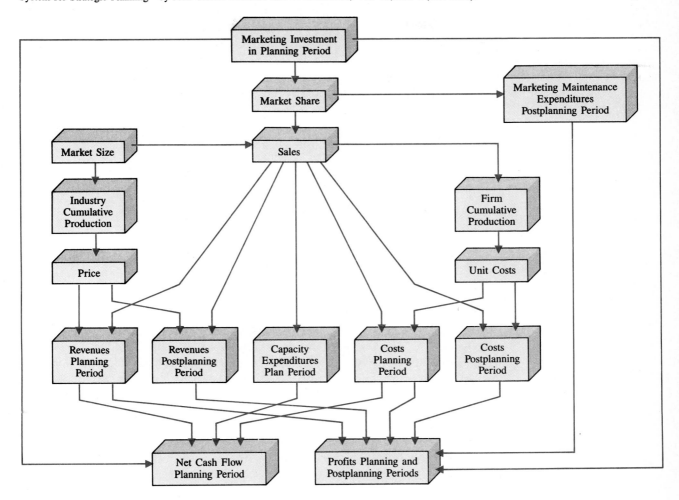

allocation of resources among SBUs, given a specified level of total investment (i.e., available resources).

Once these parameters have been established, the model can be used to simulate the effects of various levels of total investment at various costs of external financing as well as alternative allocations of resources to the SBUs. The model contains an optimization routine that, in effect, continues to evaluate the process until it finds the allocation that maximizes profit given a particular set of model assumptions and resource constraints.

Figure 17.9 shows the outcomes of applying the model to six hypothetical SBUs, with an assumed set of model parameters (e.g., *L, U, B,* and *a* in equation [17.1]) for each SBU. Two SBUs are new businesses; the third has a high market share in a low-growth industry (a Cow); the fourth has a high market share in a growing industry (a Star); the fifth has a low share in a high-growth industry (a Question Mark); and the final SBU has a low share and is in a low-growth market (a Dog). In the base case (assumed to be the status quo), the total firm (i.e., the six SBUs taken together) generates $297 million in net cash flow and a profit of $1.4 billion in the planning and postplanning

363

FIGURE 17.9
Optimum Profit/Cash Flow
Envelope
Source: Reprinted from *Journal of Marketing,* published by the American Marketing Association. From ''STRATPORT: A Decision Support System for Strategic Planning'' by Jean Claude Larreche and V. Srinivasan, Vol. 45, No. 4 (Fall 1985).

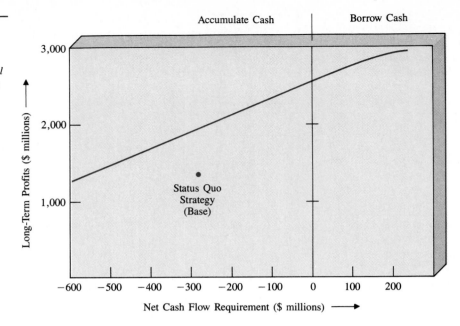

periods. Using the model to reallocate the same level of funds among the SBUs, it is possible to increase profits to almost $2 billion by allocating additional funds to the Star, Question Mark, and one of the new businesses, while reducing allocations to the Cow and the Dog. As may be seen on the graph of the model outcomes, additional investment in the firm would be likely to be extremely profitable. If an additional $200 million could be raised on the capital markets, for example, and allocated optimally to the firm's SBUs, total profits would increase from $2 billion to approximately $3 billion. In calculating the return on investment of the additional $200 million, one would, of course, employ discounted cash flow analysis to take into account the time value of money.

A model of this type has great potential as a strategic management tool. While it is often difficult to estimate the required parameters (e.g., response effects, experience curves), sensitivity analysis can determine the range of outcomes resulting from reasonable values for critical inputs. Given the increasing complexity of the product-market (SBU) portfolios in large-scale global enterprises, companies that become comfortable with such models—knowing how *not* to use them as well as how to use them—are likely to have a significant competitive advantage over their less sophisticated counterparts.

More specialized Level III models have also proven to be valuable inputs to the strategic planning process. The new-product premarket forecasting models discussed in Chapters 6 and 14, for example, are being used by some leading-edge companies to establish the timing for the global rollout of new products. Primary market research is conducted in each prospective country as the rollout proceeds. These data are then integrated by the model with past parameters to forecast the sales results of alternative marketing strategies. In some cases, such research suggests that the same products, advertising approach, and pricing should be used worldwide (or throughout a particular region); in other cases, that advertising and/or pricing should be differentiated for individual national markets; and in still other cases, that there is inadequate potential to introduce the product at all in some countries.

As global opportunities, competition, and strategies become even more complex, models such as those cited in this chapter, while helpful, will not be powerful enough to incorporate the range of phenomena and considerations essential for effective strategic management. Instead, models that encompass the cross-functional and cross-segment effects of corporate strategy (see Figure 17.1) will be required. Such models do not yet exist, but some promising work employing systems dynamics methodologies is currently under way in this area (see Forester, 1961; and Sterman, 1988).

365
WORLDWIDE CORPORATE
STRATEGY

FUTURE OF STRATEGIC DECISION MAKING

We have now come to the end of the text portion of the strategic decision-making part of this book. The following four chapters are cases that challenge us to test the concepts developed in this part of the book. We have argued that an effective strategic manager will undertake a thorough analysis of the threats and opportunities facing his or her firm, the firm's strengths and weaknesses, and the underlying marketing phenomena that drive the firm's businesses *before* attempting to make strategic decisions. We have highlighted key decision issues in the new-product, product, product-line, and corporate strategy areas, and have selectively described innovative concepts, models, and methodologies available to support effective strategic decision making.[2]

Looking forward, we believe that the trend toward the utilization of increasingly comprehensive and powerful models will continue, as will the growing requirement for cross-functional integration. These trends, taken together, are likely to place an ever-increasing premium on leadership capabilities and ''people'' skills.

As suggested earlier in this chapter, we expect that North America, Japan, and Europe will be essentially at parity with respect to technology, product quality, and manufacturing costs in many industries in the 1990s. Under these conditions, we believe that marketing will be an even more important basis for sustainable competitive advantage than it is currently. Nevertheless, we expect leading firms in all three regions to achieve similar skill levels and to have access to equivalent marketing technologies by the middle of the decade.

As the playing field becomes more level, organizational effectiveness and managerial competence will become the factors most critical to success. In such a parity world, the rewards will go to the firms that play the game smarter. They will be smarter than their competitors both in formulating strategies and in implementing them. They will be better at using analytical support tools, more creative, more innovative, and capable of more quickly converting their innovations into profits. Intellectual capital will become the scarce corporate resource, the primary basis for separating the winners from the losers.

QUESTIONS FOR DISCUSSION

1. Why is it unwise to separate corporate strategy into domestic and international components?

2. ''International marketing is no different from segmentation of a domestic market.'' Do you agree or disagree? Why or why not?

3. What are the similarities and differences in domestic segmentation and global segmentation?

4. How does marketing relate to corporate strategy formulation? Explain the most important linkages to the overall organization's functional areas and their integration into a comprehensive strategy.

---

[2] This chapter has treated only a subset of the most important corporate strategy issues, especially those where the interface between the marketing process and global strategic management are particularly critical. Readers seeking a more comprehensive treatment of corporate strategic planning should refer to Hax and Majluf (1984), Drucker (1974), Lorange and Vancil (1977), Mason and Mitroff (1981), and Steiner (1979).

✳5. What product or market attributes would lead to global segmentation by country rather than by psychographics or product type?

6. Is it possible to have global segmentation across countries and still vary other marketing-mix elements by country? Which marketing tactics might be varied by country?

7. How does the formal organization of the firm relate to marketing strategy? Should all marketing activities be located in one unit?

8. What is the most important attribute of a global business leader? Why? How does one learn the needed leadership skills?

9. Should all managers speak at least one foreign language? Why or why not?

10. What are the advantages and limitations of the STRATPORT model in resource allocation across SBUs?

11. In the future, will nations or multinational companies be the dominant determinant of competition? Will regions protect their markets through regulation and political action, or will multinational companies be free to establish trade practices on a global basis with few constraints from governments? How will the answer to this question affect marketing strategies?

REFERENCES

ALLEN, THOMAS J. 1977. *Managing the Flow of Technology*. Cambridge, MA: The MIT Press.

BARTLETT, C. A., AND S. GHOSBAL. 1987. "Managing Across Borders: New Organizational Responses." *Sloan Management Review*, Fall: 43–53.

CUSUMANO, MICHAEL A. 1988. "Manufacturing Innovation: Lessons from the Japanese Auto Industry." *Sloan Management Review* 30: 11–18.

DRUCKER, PETER. 1974. *Management: Tasks, Responsibilities, Practices*. New York: Harper and Row.

FIELDS, GEORGE. 1984. *From Bonsai to Levi's*. New York: Macmillan.

FORESTER, JAY. 1961. *Industrial Dynamics*. Cambridge, MA: The MIT Press.

HAX, ARNOLDO C., AND NICOLAS S. MAJLUF. 1984. *Strategic Management*. Englewood Cliffs, NJ: Prentice Hall.

KASHANI, KAMRAN. 1989. "Beware the Pitfalls of Global Marketing." *Harvard Business Review* 67: 91–98.

LARRECHE, JEAN CLAUDE, AND V. SRINIVASAN. 1981. "STRATPORT: A Decision Support System for Strategic Planning." *Journal of Marketing* 45: 39–52.

———. 1982. "STRATPORT: A Model for the Evaluation and Formulation of Business Portfolio Strategies." *Management Science* 28: 979–1001.

LEVITT, THEODORE. 1983a. "Globalization of Marketing." In *Marketing Imagination*. New York: The Free Press. pp. 20–49.

———. 1983b. "The Globalization of Marketing." *Harvard Business Review*, May/June: 92–102.

LORANGE, PETER, AND RICHARD F. VANCIL. 1977. *Strategic Planning Systems*. Englewood Cliffs, NJ: Prentice Hall.

MAGAZINER, IRA C., AND MARK PATINKIN. 1989. "Fast Heat: How Korea Won the Microwave War." *Harvard Business Review* 67: 83–93.

MASON, RICHARD O., AND IAN I. MITROFF. 1981. *Challenging Strategic Planning Assumptions*. New York: John Wiley.

RUFKIN, GLENN, AND GEORGE HARAR. 1988. *The Ultimate Entrepreneur*. Chicago: Contemporary Books.

QUELCH, J. A., AND E. J. HOFF. 1986. "Customizing Global Marketing." *Harvard Business Review*, May/June: 59–68.

STEINER, GEORGE A. 1979. *Strategic Planning*. New York: The Free Press.

STERMAN, JOHN D. 1988. "Deterministic Chaos in Models of Human Behavior: Methodological Issues and Experimental Results." *Systems Dynamics Review* 4: 148–178.

WIECHMANN, ULRICH, AND LEWIS G. PRINGLE. 1979. "Problems That Plague Multinational Marketers." *Harvard Business Review*, July/August: 118–124.

CABOT CORPORATION
E-A-R® Division Consumer Marketing Strategy

Developed in collaboration with David W. Charpie[1]

Robin Brumwell, general manager of Cabot Corporation's E-A-R® Division, listened critically as Stan Osweiler, E-A-R's® marketing manager, outlined his presentation for the following Tuesday's Executive Committee meeting. In particular, Brumwell focused on Osweiler's recommendation that the division enter the consumer noise-reducing earplug market. As he listened to Osweiler's presentation, Brumwell could not help but wonder whether entering this market would be a sound move. Consumer earplug sales for the first year were now projected to be no more than $750,000, compared to E-A-R® Division industrial sales of $47 million. He wondered aloud whether E-A-R® had selected an inappropriate entry strategy, or if the consumer market had less potential than he had thought.

Since taking over as E-A-R® general manager in 1986, one of Brumwell's main objectives had been to explore the possibility of E-A-R® developing an earplug for the U.S. consumer market. This proposal was driven by two important considerations. First, Cabot was about to lose the patent umbrella that had established it as a leader in industrial noise reduction. As a result, E-A-R® expected powerful competitors to try to build a business in this market. The present size of this market (about $50 million a year) suggested that it would be difficult for two large competitors to coexist; unless the total market were expanded, one of them would probably fail. Second, pilot consumer campaigns for the earplug in Japan and Europe had met with enough success to suggest that a significant potential market existed in the United States.

Brumwell firmly believed that the potential was there. Friends often requested samples of the product to help them sleep at home or on long plane flights. Industrial firms supplied by E-A-R® were always ordering more plugs than needed because "employees like to use them at home or give them to their friends." Moreover, published

---

[1] This case is largely based and incorporates considerable material from Mr. Charpie's M.I.T. M.S. thesis (1988), which should be consulted for references and further detail. Selected proprietary data have been disguised.

data suggested that sleeplessness was a significant problem for almost one in ten American female adults and one in eight males.

Brumwell listened as Osweiler reported the results of the division's recent extensive marketing research. It was a story Brumwell had heard many times before, yet the inferences drawn from it still disturbed him. When Osweiler completed his dry run, Brumwell thanked him for his time, complimented him on his preparation, and turned to look out his office window. As Osweiler prepared to leave, Brumwell asked him to bring in the market research data. "I want to look at it one more time before we head up to Waltham."

COMPANY HISTORY

Cabot Corporation was founded in 1882 as a proprietary partnership by Godfrey Cabot and his older brother, Samuel. Each contributed $5,000 to form two jointly owned companies. One company made paints and stains; the other produced carbon black, which was used in the paints and stains.

The carbon black company initially operated in West Virginia, where it drilled and operated natural gas wells that provided the raw material for carbon black manufacturing. To monitor this business, it was necessary for one of the partners to travel monthly to Pittsburgh by train, from Pittsburgh to Charleston, West Virginia, by stagecoach, and then by horseback into the hills where the natural gas wells and carbon black plants were located. Godfrey Cabot, who had been trained in Europe as a chemist, was fascinated by the carbon black part of the business. However, Samuel, who was a city person, was more interested in marketing paints. After two years, Samuel proposed to Godfrey that they divide the businesses between them—Godfrey taking 100 percent of the pigment business, and Samuel 100 percent of the paint business. In 1988, the paint company was still family owned, with headquarters in East Boston; the carbon black company, which had become the modern Cabot Corporation, was publicly owned and headquartered in Waltham, Massachusetts.

Cabot flourished in West Virginia, growing rapidly after natural gas was discovered. In the late 1800s, carbon black was used as a pigment for coloring paints, stains, shoe polish, and stove polish. In the first decade of the twentieth century, the business was given an enormous boost when Charles Goodyear discovered that carbon black reinforced rubber. If a rubber compound was mixed with approximately one-third carbon black content, the rubber acquired greater strength and resistance to wear—characteristics that were particularly important in the rapidly expanding tire market.

At the same time, it was discovered that natural gas was a better low-cost fuel to burn for residential heating than city gas (the synthetic product produced by a water-gas reaction that was then used throughout the northeastern United States). As a result, when Cabot discovered natural gas in northern Pennsylvania, it bought land, drilled wells, laid pipeline, and supplied the city of Rochester, New York, with natural gas as a residential fuel.

The early Cabot Corporation grew on the basis of two businesses: natural gas and carbon black. When sources of natural gas diminished in Appalachia and large quantities were discovered in the Southwest—notably in East Texas and in the Texas Panhandle—the Cabot Corporation moved its carbon black manufacturing operations to the Southwest. This occurred in the 1920s, under the leadership of Tom Cabot, the oldest living son of Godfrey. Tom supplied new dynamism to the company's management force and led the expansion into the southwestern United States.

Tom Cabot served as chief executive from 1955 to 1961, and was followed by his oldest son, Louis Cabot (Godfrey's grandson), who was CEO from 1961 until 1969. Only then, nearly a century after its founding, did Cabot turn to an outsider—Robert Charpie, who was still serving as CEO.

Cabot went public in 1962, following the death of the founder at the age of a hundred and one (he had stopped walking to work at ninety-eight). By that time, Cabot had expanded into other specialty chemicals—notably fumed silica and plastic dispersions of carbon black in polyethylene and vinyl. Cabot also tried other businesses, including titanium dioxide, molded and extruded plastics, self-propelled drilling rigs, and workover rigs for the domestic oil fields. During World War II, Cabot even became the principal supplier of small- and medium-sized cannons to the United States and its allies. In the 1970s, Cabot expanded into the specialty metals business, notably nickel- and cobalt-based super alloys.

ORGANIZATION

Cabot was organized into three substantial business groups. One, a mixture of businesses dependent on natural gas, was referred to as the Energy Group. This group was responsible for domestic oil and natural gas exploration and production, natural gas pipelines and supply, the production of natural gas liquids, and the importation of liquefied natural gas from Algeria to the East Coast of the United States. The Energy Group represented approximately 45 percent of Cabot's revenues and assets.

The Carbon Black Group represented about 35 percent of Cabot's revenues and assets. In contrast to the Energy Group, which was completely domestic, the carbon black business was mostly international, although Cabot remained the largest manufacturer of carbon black in North America. Cabot had twenty-one carbon black plants in eighteen countries making every kind of carbon black in every important industrial market outside the Eastern Bloc. The great success of the international part of this business had set Cabot apart from its competitors, reflecting an important element of Cabot's culture—the ability to successfully adapt to the widely varying operating requirements of a diverse set of countries.

R&D was critical to Cabot's carbon black strategy; the company spent more on both process and product development than the rest of the industry combined. The major rubber companies tended to turn to Cabot first when they needed a new grade of carbon black. As a result, Cabot-originated carbon blacks constituted more than 80 percent of the world market. While others quickly copied Cabot developments, Cabot had been able to retain its lead in proprietary production technology.

The third group of businesses consisted of specialty chemicals and materials (fumed silica, E-A-R®, plastic dispersions) and a series of smaller businesses serving a variety of specialty markets. In the smaller, emerging specialty chemical businesses, Cabot's strategy was to enter niches that it could dominate, and where technical excellence was rewarded with high price and high market share.

THE E-A-R® DIVISION

Cabot had purchased the National Research Corporation (NRC) from the Norton Company in 1972. NRC's assets had included a staff of scientists and engineers, a patent portfolio, and an ongoing research program. One major NRC project had been to develop a treated polyvinyl-chloride (PVC) polymer that could be used to suppress vibration and noise in industrial settings. The resulting product, named E-A-R® (energy-absorbing resin), was a blue-calendered sheet used as an underlay for motor mounts or between pieces of clanging metal in paper machines and foundries. Prior to NRC's purchase by Cabot, this product had not proved to be commercially successful.

Shortly after the acquisition, however, a NRC scientist, Ross Gardner, made a doctored PVC compound in foam form. He noticed that after the foam was compressed, it slowly recovered its original shape. A cube one inch on a side, when squeezed in a person's hand, would take more than a minute to return completely to its initial shape, but it always recovered that shape.

When the energy-absorbing characteristics of the foam product were measured, it was determined that the foam had maximum attenuation in the audible range. Further, over the entire audible frequency range, the foam produced significant sound absorption. This led to the suggestion, by Gardner, that it might be possible to manufacture a foam earplug that would be comfortable to wear, disposable, and effective as a sound absorber. When the first earplugs were made, these hopes were immediately realized. When correctly rolled up and inserted into the ear, the earplug conformed to the individual's ear as it expanded toward its original shape. The tight fit in the individual's ear canal served to maximize noise reduction.

This combination of properties, and the concept of a form-fitting foam earplug made from doctored vinyl, were patented by Cabot throughout the industrial world during the mid and late 1970s.

Cabot began production of the earplugs in a converted research facility in Billerica, Massachusetts, in 1974. The manufacturing process utilized very simple equipment, with the completed product being packaged by hand in daily meetings by the wives of the technical staff.

The plug was introduced to a number of industrial markets in 1974. Bright yellow in color, it was easily recognizable. Sales grew rapidly, and the earplug business achieved a profitable status almost immediately.

At that time, there was no other foam earplug on the market. The principal competitors made rigid, high-priced earplugs or earmuffs, or used simple, low-cost waxed string— a pliable, wax-permeated cotton string that could be molded to fit the ear. (Bilsom-Sweden, the leading manufacturer of waxed string earplugs, was the largest supplier in the world of throwaway noise-suppression products in the mid-1970s.) In this environment, the E-A-R® plug sold on the basis of superior performance, cost, and convenience. Sales grew at a very high compound rate. By the early 1980s, E-A-R® had become the market leader in disposable plugs in almost every major geographical location. Worldwide, the product's market share exceeded 50 percent.

Since Cabot defended its E-A-R® patents aggressively in every jurisdiction, there had been no serious threats to its strong proprietary position. In anticipation of the expiration of its initial patents in the early 1990s, Cabot began to aggressively reduce costs and prices to secure its market position on nonproprietary grounds. Every six months from January 1976 to July 1983, for example, Cabot had lowered the wholesale price of its earplugs roughly 5 cents per pair (i.e., to 7.5 cents per pair in late 1983).

Cabot had also attempted to strengthen its earplug franchise through the development of new products employing E-A-R® technology. Among the most notable of such endeavors were: earplugs with cords to be worn in industrial environments where an earplug falling into the product would be disastrous (e.g., food processing); molded earplugs for users who preferred a solid earplug to the foam product; earmuffs for high-noise environments like airplane ramps or the headbox operation of a paper machine; and a sound-activated earmuff, which permitted the wearer to engage in normal conversation without loss of audio acuity until a loud noise occurred, at which point the earmuff would react, blocking the noise instantly so that there would be no hearing damage even from very high level, abrupt close-up noises such as explosions.

At the same time, Cabot began to seek nonearplug applications for its noise-reduction technology. After several unsuccessful forays into markets requiring extensive customization and installation, Cabot decided to focus its noise-reduction strategy on a narrow

EXHIBIT 18.1
Competitive Pricing
Analysis

	SERENE® 3 PAIRS	FLENT'S EAR STOPPLES 6 PAIRS	FLENT'S QUIET PLEASE FOAM 5 PAIRS	MACK'S 2 PAIRS
Manufacturer's list price	$0.95	$1.70	$1.70	$0.85
C.O.G.	$0.35	N/A	N/A	N/A
% C.O.G.	37	—	—	—
Gross margin	$0.60	—	—	—
% gross margin	63	—	—	—
Retail price	$2.09	$2.99	$3.19	$1.69
Consumer cost per pair	$0.70	$0.50	$0.64	$0.85
Retail gross margin	$1.14	$1.29	$1.49	$0.84
% retail gross margin	54.5	43.1	46.7	49.7

set of target markets: executive aircraft, electronics, and defense. Within these areas, Cabot concentrated on higher-priced executive aircraft, on computer printers, and on defense applications such as shell racks in battle tanks[2] and sound and vibration suppression in deep-running submarines. In each of these applications, E-A-R® technology offered sufficient value added to command a significant price premium. These businesses represented almost 10 percent of E-A-R® Division sales in 1987, and made a significant contribution to divisional profits.

While these results were gratifying, the potential for applications of this type was considered to be small relative to the earplug market. Over the years, Cabot had made a number of efforts to extend its success in earplugs for industrial applications into consumer markets, but with limited results. It had, for example, sought to convince manufacturers of products such as shotguns and chain saws to include samples in their packages, and had made arrangements with about a dozen airlines to include E-A-R® plugs in their giveaway kits on long flights. It had also sought to sell earplugs directly to consumers in Japan, the United Kingdom, and the United States. While such efforts had proved to be quite successful in Japan and to have considerable promise in the U.K., the company had met with virtually no success to date in the United States. Indeed, a recent study suggested that no more than 1 percent of U.S. consumers had ever bought earplugs, and that no more than about 2 percent had ever used them at home (the discrepancy was presumably attributable to "migration" of earplugs from the workplace to the home).

In recent years, a number of companies had sought to develop a consumer market for noise-reducing earplugs: Bilsom (with both the old waxed string plug and a new foam plug), 3M (with a recently released foam plug called Attenutech), Cabot (with flesh-colored E-A-R® plugs), Siebe-North (with white private-label earplugs made by E-A-R®), and several small competitors who were not major players in the industrial market. The most notable among the latter were Flent's and Mack's. Flent's consumer product line consisted of waxed string and foam earplugs, as well as swimmers' earplugs. Through superior trade deals, Flent's was currently the market leader. Mack's Pillow Soft earplugs were made of moldable silicone, which the user rolled into a ball and pressed against the ear canal opening. Mack's strategy was to convince doctors to recommend

---

[2] If an enemy shell penetrated a tank and hit the ammunition racks, causing one shell to explode, a chain reaction would cause other shells to explode, totally destroying the tank and its crew. The appropriate deployment of E-A-R® material was able to prevent this chain reaction in many instances.

its plugs to patients for swimming, sleeping, and ear injuries. While still trailing Flent's, Mack's was currently the fastest-growing brand of consumer earplugs. (See Exhibit 18.1 for competitive pricing data).

E-A-R® marketing executives believed that Cabot would have significant competitive advantages in the consumer earplug market if that market could be developed to a meaningful size. Cabot's foam plugs were believed to be superior to competitive products from a performance perspective (i.e., effectiveness, comfort, and ease of use). Except for the color and shape of the earplugs, however, there was little difference among the competing foam products. While E-A-R®'s material provided the best noise-reduction rating (NRR), the difference was probably imperceptible to the customer. Cabot's high-volume manufacturing (more than 1 million pairs per day in the United States alone) gave it a significant cost advantage, while its highly automated packaging operations could probably be adapted to the consumer market.

MARKETING RESEARCH

Beginning in the fall of 1985, the E-A-R® Division undertook an extensive series of research activities to determine: (1) whether there was sufficient potential in the consumer earplug market to make it worthwhile for Cabot; and (2) if there was such potential, what would be the best way to realize it. Recognizing that the division lacked consumer marketing experience, management engaged Smith/Greenland, a well-known marketing research and consulting firm, to help it develop a strategy to promote E-A-R® plugs to consumers and to assist it in evaluating its market entry efforts.

As a first step, a qualitative study was conducted to learn more about consumers' perceptions of noise and to obtain their reactions to eleven potential product concepts. This study resulted in a reduction in the number of concepts from eleven to two: "noise reduction" and "sleep aid." The noise-reduction concept contended that effective earplugs would quiet disturbing noises dangerous to nerves and hearing; let the wearer control surrounding noise; be soft and comfortable, and mold to fit the user's ears; and reduce annoying noise without blocking out important and wanted sounds. The sleep aid concept argued that effective earplugs would quiet disturbing noises so that the user would be able to fall asleep naturally and quickly; would be more natural than sleep medication; would be soft, comfortable, and mold to fit the wearer's ears; and would reduce annoying noise, but not block out important and wanted sounds.

Smith/Greenland's research program consisted of five major studies:

1. *E-A-R® Concept Refinement*: Exploratory Focus Group Research (conducted February 1986).

2. *E-A-R® Plug Concept Test and In-Home Congruence Test* (conducted March–May 1986).

3. *Serene®[3] Soft Foam Earplugs*: Advertising/Promotion Tracking Study—Wave One (conducted February–March 1987).

4. *Serene® Early MarketCast*: Interim Analysis (conducted February 1987).

5. *Serene® Soft Foam Earplugs*: Advertising/Promotion Tracking Study—Wave Two (conducted June 1987).

---

[3] The Serene brand name had been selected for research purposes in order to avoid confusion with E-A-R®–branded plugs that were available in a limited number of retail outlets as a result either of previous efforts in the consumer market or of migration from industrial channels.

E-A-R® Concept Refinement: Exploratory Focus Group Research

Six focus groups were conducted among target consumers in New York (Westchester County), Chicago, and Los Angeles on February 12, 13, and 17, 1986. Each group was composed of approximately ten men and women, ages thirty to sixty years old, who met screening qualifications (e.g., reported trouble sleeping, problems resulting from noise). Six alternative product positionings were evaluated using eleven concept boards (see Exhibit 18.2), and E-A-R® plugs were given to each respondent to elicit spontaneous reactions to the products.

The purpose of this initial qualitative research was to: (1) explore how consumers felt about hearing, and what they knew about hearing; (2) find out how consumers reacted to noise in their daily lives; (3) evoke reactions to the use of ear protection in general and E-A-R® plugs in particular; (4) obtain feedback on alternative concepts; and (5) explore reactions to the actual E-A-R® plug product relative to expectations created by the concepts.

Based on this research, it appeared that consumers tended to misperceive the nature and performance of foam earplugs. They assumed, for example, that the plugs would block out all sounds, while E-A-R® plugs actually muffled and reduced noise while allowing some sound to come through. Similarly, consumers said that E-A-R® plugs looked hard, uncomfortable, and too big and difficult to use, whereas E-A-R® plugs in reality were soft, comfortable, and easy to use.

Despite these perceptual drawbacks, consumers expressed a willingness to consider using E-A-R® plugs to control, reduce, or quiet irritating and/or dangerous noise while sleeping; while trying to concentrate, read, or relax; while working with power tools; and/or while attending a rock concert.

The concepts with the strongest consumer appeal were "sleep aid" and "performance improver." The sleep-aid concept focused on the notion that "A good night's sleep shouldn't require a chemical reaction." The performance improver concept suggested you could "Improve your concentration with a little peace and quiet."

The connection to sleeping pills (i.e., "chemical reaction") turned out to be of secondary importance to the respondents because most who had transient sleep problems did not take pills. The washability of the E-A-R® plugs also seemed to be perceived as a minor benefit; indeed, it generated some doubts concerning hygiene. Focus group members strongly preferred flesh color to the bright yellow used in E-A-R®'s industrial plugs.

E-A-R® Plug Concept Test and In-Home Congruence Test

A two-cell concept test was conducted using personal interviews at shopping malls. The target group consisted of 557 men and women, between the ages of twenty-five and sixty, who claimed to be bothered by noise. In the concept test, conducted between March 13 and April 9, 1986, the product was presented to target consumers in a manner close to a fully developed advertising campaign. Those who passed the screen for the sleep-aid concept said they were bothered by noises that interfered with sleeping, while those who qualified for the noise-reduction concept claimed to be bothered by noises other than those that interfered with sleeping.

The target groups were exposed to a description of the product and an explanation of its appropriateness for their needs. The concepts were presented on audiotape, as "concept recordings" or simulated radio commercials (see Exhibit 18.3). After listening to the "commercials," consumer's interest in purchasing the product was measured. Additional diagnostic questioning was intended to indicate whether a given concept com-

EXHIBIT 18.2
Concept Boards
Concept 1A

A GOOD NIGHT'S SLEEP SHOULDN'T REQUIRE A CHEMICAL REACTION

For some people, sleeping pills are necessary. But for others, a good night's sleep may only depend on shutting out the noise.

E-A-R plugs can be a more natural way to get the rest you need without having to take sleeping pills. By using E-A-R plugs, you'll quiet the noise that's bothering you. In fact, E-A-R plugs have been rated the very best at doing just that. Quieting noise.

E-A-R is not only the most effect-ive earplug, it's also very comfortable. For years E-A-R has been the number one earplug used in industry, and no one appreciates comfort in an earplug more than someone who wears them all day long. What's more, E-A-R plugs last a long time. They can be washed and worn again up to ten times and still maintain their original quality.

So why swallow pills when you don't have to? When the safest, most natural way is to put something in your ear.

SLEEP PLUGS
BY E-A-R

Concept 1B

THE SLEEPING AID THAT'S THE EASIEST TO SWALLOW GOES IN YOUR EAR.

A lot of people have trouble sleeping at night. And while some will require a sleeping pill, there are others who would sleep better if they just shut out the noise.

E-A-R plugs can be a more natural way to get the rest you need without having to take sleeping pills. By using E-A-R plugs, you'll quiet the noise that's bothering you. In fact, E-A-R plugs have been rated the very best at doing just that. Quieting noise.

E-A-R is not only the most effective earplug, it's also very comfortable. For years E-A-R has been the number one earplug used in industry, and no one appreciates comfort in an earplug more than someone who wears them all day long.

What's more, E-A-R plugs last a long time. They can be washed and worn again up to ten times and still maintain their original quality.

So why depend on a chemical reaction to fall asleep? Wouldn't you prefer a little peace and quiet?

SLEEP PLUGS
BY E-A-R

HEARING LOSS CAN BEGIN AT AN EARLIER AGE THAN MOST PEOPLE THINK.

Recent studies have shown that noise can affect hearing at a very young age. Research also shows that if measures aren't taken to reduce excessive noise, hearing loss can result. And often, the hearing loss that does occur can't even be corrected by a hearing aid.

With E-A-R plugs, you can reduce the effects of noise. In fact, E-A-R plugs have been rated the very best plug for doing just that. Reducing noise.

E-A-R is not only the most effective earplug, it's also very comfortable. For years E-A-R has been the number one earplug used in industry, and no one appreciates comfort in an earplug more than someone who wears them all day long. What's more, E-A-R plugs last a long time. They can be washed and worn again up to ten times and still maintain their original quality.

All you have to do is open your ears and you'll know when to wear E-A-R plugs. It could be when you're walking a city street, while you're mowing the lawn or perhaps when you use power tools around the house.

When it comes to your hearing, you should do all you can to protect it. Unlike many other things, once you lose part of your hearing, you may never get it back.

E-A-R® PLUGS

IT'S NOT JUST AGING THAT ROBS YOU OF YOUR HEARING IT'S NOISE.

Some things may get better with age, but unfortunately, hearing isn't one of them. Research has shown that noise, over the years, can have a cumulative effect. And it's not until you get older that hearing loss becomes apparent. Oftentimes, the hearing loss that does occur can't even be corrected by a hearing aid.

However, there are measures you can take to ward off hearing loss. E-A-R plugs can protect you, not only from noise that's a nuisance, but from noise that can be damaging. In fact, E-A-R plugs have been rated the best plug for doing just that. Protecting you from noise.

E-A-R is not only the most effective earplug, it's also very comfortable. For years E-A-R has been the number one earplug in industry, and no one appreciates comfort in an earplug more than someone who wears them all day long. What's more, E-A-R plugs last a long time. They can be washed and worn again up to ten times and still maintain their original quality.

You know, when you think about it, it's a crime that noise can rob us of our hearing. But isn't it an even bigger crime when we don't do anything about it?

E-A-R® PLUGS

WHILE POWER TOOLS DO A LOT FOR YOUR HOME, THEY DON'T DO MUCH FOR YOUR HEARING.

Home improvement has its costs. And one thing it can cost you is your hearing.

But now you can turn the volume down because E-A-R plugs help to block out the irritating noise. In fact, E-A-R plugs have been rated the very best earplug at doing just that. Reducing noise. And, fortunately, when you reduce the noise, you reduce your chances of hearing loss.

E-A-R is not only the most effective earplug, it's also very comfortable.

For years E-A-R has been the number one earplug used in industry, and no one appreciates comfort in an earplug more than someone who wears them all day long. What's more, E-A-R plugs last a long time. They can be washed and worn again up to ten times and still maintain their original quality.

So while power tools can be a big help when doing repairs around the house, you should keep one thing in mind. They can also do a lot of damage.

E-A-R® PLUGS

NOISE IS BAD FOR YOUR EARS. IT'S EVEN WORSE FOR YOUR STOMACH, YOUR HEART AND YOUR CIRCULATION.

Loud noise is more than a nuisance. It's a hazard to your health.

You see, researchers have linked excessive noise with heart trouble, circulation problems and digestive disorders.

But now you can use E-A-R plugs to block out dangerous noise. In fact, E-A-R plugs have been rated the very best earplug for doing just that. Reducing noise.

E-A-R is not only the most effective earplug, it's also very comfortable. For years E-A-R has been the number one earplug used in industry, and no one appreciates comfort in an earplug more than someone who wears them all day long. What's more, E-A-R plugs last a long time. They can be washed and worn again up to ten times and still maintain their original quality.

That's important because you'll want to wear E-A-R plugs in a number of different situations. It could be when you're walking down a city street. Or while you're mowing the lawn or using power tools around the house. E-A-R plugs can even shut out those disturbing noises that keep you from sleeping at night. Or from reading your favorite book.

With all you do to take care of your health, you should also be wearing E-A-R plugs.

After all, you won't be protecting just your ears, you'll be protecting your whole body.

E-A-R® PLUGS

Concept 4B

THERE ARE SOME SOUNDS OF THE GREAT OUTDOORS YOU CAN DO WITHOUT

Unfortunately, along with crickets, robins and owls, there are lawnmowers, chainsaws and power tools. And instead of music to your ears, your ears are left ringing long after the noises have gone away.

But now you can turn the volume down because E-A-R plugs help to block out the irritating noise. In fact, E-A-R plugs have been rated the very best earplug at doing just that. Reducing noise. And, fortunately, when you reduce the noise, you reduce your chances of hearing loss.

E-A-R is not only the most effective earplug, it's also very comfortable. For years E-A-R has been the number one earplug used in industry, and no one appreciates comfort in an earplug more than someone who wears them all day long. What's more, E-A-R plugs last a long time. They can be washed and worn again up to ten times and still maintain their original quality.

So next time you plan to do it yourself, be more careful with your tools. They may do a lot for your home, but they don't do much for your hearing.

E-A-R® PLUGS

Concept 5A

THE ABILITY TO CONCENTRATE ISN'T JUST SELF CONTROL. IT'S ALSO NOISE CONTROL

When you're trying to think, distractions may come in many forms. There are stereos. There's office chatter. And then there are those loud voices that come from behind you on a plane or bus.

Now there's a better way to deal with loud distractions than just sitting there gritting your teeth. Now you can turn the volume down because E-A-R plugs help to block out the irritating noise. In fact, E-A-R plugs have been rated the very best earplug at doing just that. Reducing noise. Which means your concentration level is no longer left at the mercy of others.

E-A-R is not only the most effective earplug, it's also very comfortable. For years E-A-R has been the number one earplug used in industry, and no one appreciates comfort in an earplug more than someone who wears them all day long. What's more, E-A-R plugs last a long time. They can be washed and worn again up to ten times and still maintain their original quality.

With all that's going on around you, it's difficult not to be distracted. But now finally, you can get a little peace and quiet.

E-A-R® PLUGS

ESCAPE THE NOISE WITHOUT LEAVING THE CITY.

There's no doubt the city has many things to offer. Unfortunately, noise is one of them. Which is no small wonder, when you think of all the trains, cars and buses. Not to mention the jackhammers and the bulldozers.

But now you can turn the volume down because E-A-R® plugs help to block out the irritating noise. In fact, E-A-R® plugs have been rated the very best earplug at doing just that. Reducing noise. And, fortunately, when you reduce the noise, you reduce your chances of hearing loss.

E-A-R is not only the most effective earplug, it's also very comfortable. For years E-A-R has been the number one earplug used in industry, and no one appreciates comfort in an earplug more than someone who wears them all day long. What's more, E-A-R plugs last a long time. They can be washed and worn again up to ten times and still maintain their original quality.

There's no doubt you can find many things in the city. But who would've thought you'd be able to find peace and quiet.

E-A-R® PLUGS

IMPROVE YOUR CONCENTRATION WITH A LITTLE PEACE & QUIET

It's not easy reading War and Peace when Bruce Springsteen's blaring in the next room. But there's a better way to deal with loud distractions than just sitting there gritting your teeth. Now you can turn the volume down because E-A-R® plugs help to block out the irritating noise. In fact, E-A-R® plugs have been rated the very best earplug at doing just that. Reducing noise. Which means your concentration level is no longer left at the mercy of others.

E-A-R is not only the most effective earplug, it's also very comfortable. For years E-A-R has been the number one earplug used in industry, and no one appreciates comfort in an earplug more than someone who wears them all day long. What's more, E-A-R plugs last a long time. They can be washed and worn again up to ten times and still maintain their original quality.

So while we can't always be by ourselves when we want to read or when there's work to be done, at least now it'll sound that way.

E-A-R® PLUGS

EXHIBIT 18.2
(continued)
Concept 6B

NEW YORK CITY
SUBWAYS
ARE NOW
15 TIMES
QUIETER.

But it wasn't the City of New York that took care of the problem. It was E-A-R plugs that turned the noise down.

In fact, E-A-R plugs have been rated the very best earplug for doing just that. Turning down noise. And, fortunately, when you reduce the noise, you reduce your chances of hearing loss.

E-A-R is not only the most effective earplug, it's also very comfortable.

For years E-A-R has been the number one earplug used in industry, and no one appreciates comfort in an earplug more than someone who wears them all day long. What's more, E-A-R plugs last a long time. They can be washed and worn again up to ten times and still maintain their original quality.

If E-A-R plugs can do this for New York City subways, imagine what they can do for the noises that bother you.

E-A-R PLUGS

municated relevant product benefits and to suggest why consumers accepted or rejected the concept.

Interviewing was conducted in five geographically dispersed markets: Baltimore, Washington, D.C., Chicago, Dallas, and Los Angeles. To ensure that all potential consumer groups were appropriately represented, quotas for age and sex, based on U.S. census data, were employed. The completed interviews were then weighted to make them conform to the known age/sex profile of those eligible for each concept.

Following each interview, the respondents were asked to take the product home for two weeks. Those who agreed were given four pairs of earplugs, and were reinterviewed at the end of the two weeks. The objective of these interviews was to measure how well product expectations were met by actual experience with the product. All users were given an instruction card, and those who had questions about product safety received a page of safety assurances.

Based on this study, the researchers concluded that almost half (47 percent) of the population in the twenty-five to sixty age group who lived in cities or suburban areas

SFX:	STARTING UP OF BUS AND SOUND OF IT PULLING AWAY; JACKHAMMER POUNDING; CARS HONKING; THE ROAR OF AN ELEVATED TRAIN; AN AIRPLANE; A STEREO BLARING; CHAIN SAW.
V.O.:	Along with the beautiful sounds in the world are some that aren't so beautiful. They're the noises we have to deal with every day— whether we're in the city, at home, or traveling.
	These are noises that are not just irritating—but dangerous. For it's not only our nerves that suffer from excessive noise. Noise can also do permanent damage to our hearing.
	But there is an answer. A way to *quiet* the noise. It's a new soft foam earplug that helps you *control* the noise around you.
	And because it's made of soft foam, it molds to your ear, so it's very comfortable.
	Which, when you're choosing an earplug, can be as important as reducing the noise.
	So the next time you're subjected to irritating noise . . .
SFX:	BUS, THEN JACKHAMMER . . . (AS BEFORE)
V.O.:	Put in soft foam earplugs, and listen to how *differently* noise can sound.
SFX:	(NOW MUFFLED) CARS HONKING; THE ROAR OF THE ELEVATED TRAIN; AIRPLANE; STEREO, CHAIN SAW . . .
V.O.: (MUFFLED)	Soft foam earplugs. They turn the volume *down*, not *off*. Because there are some sounds you don't want to miss . . .
WIFE:	(CALLING TO HUSBAND) Honey, dinner's ready . . .

EXHIBIT 18.3
Scripts for Radio Commercials
Script for Simulated Radio Commercial: Reducing Irritating Noise/Hearing Loss

SFX:	RADIO PLAYS ". . . Hit radio . . ."
D.J.:	(ON RADIO) It's 11 P.M. in the big City, I'll be with you till . . ."
SFX:	CLICK FROM RADIO BEING TURNED OFF. A BIG YAWN AND PROLONGED STRETCH IS HEARD FROM PERSON WHO IS IN BED READY TO GO TO SLEEP. (PAUSE) ALL OF A SUDDEN, TWO CATS ARE HEARD FIGHTING OUTSIDE WINDOW. THEN METAL GARBAGE CAN IS TIPPED OVER AS CATS SCREAM. NEIGHBORHOOD DOGS THEN START BARKING. NEXT THE SOUND OF A SPORTS CAR ROARING DOWN STREET IS HEARD AND IT COMES TO SCREECHING HALT NEXT DOOR. TEENAGERS ARE LAUGHING AND PARTYING LOUDLY AS THEY MAKE THEIR WAY INSIDE. DOOR IS HEARD SLAMMING SHUT, THEN THE STEREO BEGINS BLASTING AS COMMOTION INSIDE CONTINUES.
V.O.:	Just because you're ready to go to sleep, it doesn't mean everyone else is.

EXHIBIT 18.3
(continued)
Script for Simulated Radio Commercial: Sleep Aid

were bothered by noise; that one out of five (18 percent) was bothered by noises that interfered with sleep; and that 29 percent were bothered by other types of noises. A demographic breakdown of these groups suggested that a higher proportion of women (52 percent) were bothered by noise than men (42 percent). Although both concepts appealed to all demographic groups, younger women had the highest levels of positive purchase interest (i.e., the sum of ''definitely,'' ''probably,'' and ''might'' buy). The total probability of trial was estimated at .22 for the noise-reduction positioning and .24

EXHIBIT 18.4
Positive Purchase Interest

	FEMALE		MALE	
	25–39	**40–60**	**25–39**	**40–60**
Noise reduction	41%	29%	29%	25%
Sleep aid	46%	39%	30%	25%

EXHIBIT 18.5
Total Positive Repurchase
Intention After Product
Use

	CONCEPT ACCEPTORS	CONCEPT REJECTORS
Noise reduction	77%	40%
Sleep aid	82%	40%

for the sleep-aid positioning ("definite," "probable," and "might" scores were multiplied by .9, .4, and .1, respectively, in calculating the total). (See Exhibit 18.4.)

The noise-reduction idea was generally well accepted. However, the comfort claim, not emphasized in the concept, was rejected by those who did not feel a need for noise reduction. (The comfort attribute was rated higher after product use.) Those favorable to the noise-reduction concept also liked the product's ease of insertion/removal, safety benefits, and "calms your nerves" claims, which were not explicit in the concept statement. Conversely, protection against hearing loss, which was emphasized in the concept, was not frequently volunteered as a reason for considering future purchases.

The sleep-aid concept was also well received, with "noise reduction," "soft/comfortable," and "natural/take the place of medication" being positively perceived. "Safety," "can be worn for long periods of time," and "calms your nerves," which were not explicit in the concept, were perceived by those favorable to the concept but not by those opposed to it.

After concept testing, respondents were given samples of the product. A majority (60 percent) noted the product looked different from what they expected. Respondents found the product larger, softer, and more comfortable-looking than anticipated.

After respondents had used the product for two weeks, purchase interest was even more favorable among those with positive purchase interest at the concept stage (see Exhibit 18.5). The overall repurchase probability among concept acceptors was estimated at about 50 percent after weighing definite and probable intent to repurchase responses.

Among the noise-reduction group, all concept claims were fulfilled by product use. Sleep-aid concept acceptors' expectations were also met for the most part, but their initial strong impression that the earplugs "help you sleep" was dampened somewhat. Most participants did not use up or throw away any of the earplugs they were given. This was equally true for respondents attracted by both concepts. Although the product was used an average of four times during the two-week use period, the test did not run long enough to estimate the use-up or replacement rate.

Serene® Soft Foam Earplugs: Advertising /Promotion Tracking Study—Wave One

The purpose of Wave One of the Serene® Advertising/Promotion Tracking Study was to establish a benchmark of awareness and usage of Serene® and major competitive brands. Screening for target market respondents was accomplished through determining their agreement or disagreement with three noise-related questions: (1) "Do you sometimes have difficulty concentrating on what you want to do because of an aggravating noise you can't control?'' (2) ''Are you sometimes exposed to loud or annoying noise that bothers your ears or aggravates your nerves?'' (3) ''Do you sometimes have difficulty sleeping because of annoying noises to the extent that it bothers you and you would like to do something about it?'' Qualification required at least one affirmative response.

Four hundred telephone interviews, conducted by Central Marketing, New York, under Smith/Greenland's supervision, were completed by February 22, 1987, with target segment respondents in four cities that were to be used as test markets: Albany, New York; Bakersfield, California; Quad Cities, Illinois and Iowa; and Savannah, Georgia. Equal quotas were established for men and women; half of each group were to receive the Serene® sample (50 out of 100 subjects in each market).

Negligible levels of brand awareness, advertising recall, and sampling awareness existed in the four test markets for any brand of earplug (including Serene®) prior to the test market. While nearly one-third (31 percent) of the total sample had used noise-reducing earplugs previously, relatively few (4.5 percent) had used them outside the workplace, and fewer still (1.75 percent) had used plugs purchased at retail. Based on the incidence rates and usage data generated in the study, Savannah was characterized as high in potential and the Quad Cities as low. Albany and Bakersfield were considered average in potential.

Serene® Early MarketCast: Interim Analysis

A forced-awareness market test experiment was conducted on Serene® earplugs, Wednesday through Saturday, February 18–21, 1987. The primary objectives of this test were to provide an estimate of the in-market repeat rate and the purchase cycle for the new product, and to identify the product's strengths and weaknesses.

On Monday and Tuesday, February 16 and 17, Serene® was placed in distribution in fifteen drugstores in each of the test market cities. Consumers age eighteen and over who demonstrated an intent to shop (by selecting a shopping cart) were given a four-color advertisement for the product that contained two coupons: one good for 50 cents off any purchase in the store that day, and one good for 40 cents off a single $1.89 package of Serene® earplugs purchased that day. Following a usage period of approximately two weeks, Serene® buyers were contacted by telephone and interviewed. At the completion of this interview, triers were recruited into a limited diary panel for the purpose of monitoring their purchases of earplugs over the next twenty-four weeks. These panelists were contacted by telephone every four weeks to determine if they had purchased additional Serene® earplugs.

For purposes of analysis, the researchers assumed 30 percent awareness and 65 percent net effective distribution, based on expected advertising and promotion spending levels and their experience in similar product categories. They then sought to estimate the repeat rate from the telephone callback responses. The estimated first measured repeat rate was 50 percent, which was higher than the norm for successful new-product lines in similar categories. This estimate was based on reported future purchase intent, average price/value as perceived by the user, and each user's like/dislike rating. The researchers estimated further that the average time between purchases would be about thirteen weeks (90 days), and that the mean number of units a customer would purchase would be 1.0 at trial and 1.1 at repeat.

Serene® Soft Foam Earplugs: Advertising/Promotion Tracking Study—Wave Two

The purpose of Wave Two of the Serene® Advertising/Promotion Tracking Study was to measure changes in awareness and usage of Serene® and competitive brands in the four test markets after advertising and sampling programs had been in force for three months. (In the test markets, television advertising equivalent to a $2 million introductory national budget [utilizing either sleep improvement or noise reduction as the copy theme] was employed, while samples were sent to half of the households that had been preselected for later interviewing.) This study was intended to measure the target market's awareness of Serene®, its advertising, and its sampling programs on an unaided and aided basis; its claimed purchases of Serene®, and reasons for and frequency of use; and its purchase intentions for earplugs in general and Serene® in particular.

Based on the three screening questions used in Wave One, almost 44 percent of the potential respondents qualified as members of Serene®'s target market segment. Four hundred telephone interviews, conducted by Central Marketing, New York, were completed with target respondents in the test markets on May 22, 1987. Equal quotas were established for males and females, and for recipients and nonrecipients of the Serene® sample. One hundred interviews were completed per market.

Potential respondents, whether qualified for the interviews or not, were tested on unaided and aided awareness of Serene®. For the qualified respondents, total brand awareness of Serene® after three months was 21 percent among those who had received a Serene® sample and 11 percent among those who had not. For nonqualified respondents, 20 percent of sample recipients and 15 percent of nonrecipients were aware of Serene® when prompted.

The sampling program, although generating significant increases in brand awareness, did not trigger product trial, purchase, or future purchase intentions. As a consequence,

EXHIBIT 18.6
Flow Model and Rough
Estimate of First-Year Sales
for Bothered-by-Noise
Market
(in millions)

Total population		238*
Fraction in urban areas	×	0.74
Fraction in target age bracket (25–60)	×	0.46
Fraction bothered by noise	×	0.47
Population eligible for noise reduction product		38
Fraction aware first year (average)	×	0.30
Fraction in market	×	0.30†
Fractional availability (average)	×	0.65
Fraction likely to purchase	×	0.22
Population that will try product		0.49
Fractional repeat purchase rate	×	0.58‡
Units repurchased in first year		0.28
Total units purchased in first year		0.77

* Population data from U.S. Bureau of Census.

† Based on Early MarketCast results. Coupon distribution forced in-store awareness on 17,451 potential customers. Assuming a random sample of the potential target market:

$$541 = (17{,}451 \times 0.47) \times (M \times 0.22)$$

where 541 = Population purchasing E-A-R® earplugs

M = Fraction of population in market

‡ Assumes uniform trial rate of $T/4$ per quarter (where T is yearly trial rate), repeat purchase rate of 50 percent, and 1.1 units bought per repurchase:

Quarter	Trial	1 Repeat	2 Repeat	3 Repeat	Total
1st	$T/4$	$T/8$	$T/16$	$T/32$	$7T/32$
2nd	$T/4$	$T/8$	$T/16$	—	$3T/16$
3rd	$T/4$	$T/8$	—	—	$T/8$
4th	$T/4$	—	—	—	—
Total	T				$17T/32$

Total units purchased at repeat = $(7T/32) \times 1.1 = 187T/320$
$$= 0.584T$$

unaided and total recall of the Serene® sample among sample recipients was low (6 percent and 14 percent, respectively). (Note that this is awareness of receiving a sample, not overall advertising awareness.) The correlation between media weight and brand awareness was also low; overall brand awareness of Serene® among the target market was marginally higher where advertising expenditures were lower. However, these results were considered insignificant given the low overall recall of Serene® advertising. The researchers noted, however, that those respondents who reported that they were ''bothered by noise'' when sleeping were 50 percent more likely to be aware of Serene® and its advertising. While they were not more likely to have used plugs to correct their sleep problem, they claimed a higher purchase intent. The average overall awareness was estimated to be in the range of 30 percent over the first twelve months.

Sales Forecast Based on Macro-Flow Model

At this point, a consultant was retained to develop a sales forecast for the E-A-R® plug based on the market research that had been conducted to date. This consultant employed a widely used simulation technique known as macro-flow modeling. In this approach, each consumer is represented by a behavioral state describing his or her level of information about his or her potential purchase. For example, a consumer might be aware of the

EXHIBIT 18.7
Macro-Flow Model and Rough Estimate of First-Year Sales for Sleep-Aid Market
(in millions)

Target adult population	81*
Fraction female	× 0.51
Fraction bothered by noise while trying to sleep	× 0.20
Population eligible for sleep-aid product	8.26
Fraction aware first year (average)	× 0.45
Fraction in market	× 0.30†
Fractional availability (average)	× 0.65
Fraction likely to purchase	× 0.32‡
Population that will try product	0.23
Fractional repeat purchase rate	× 0.58§
Units repurchased in first year	0.13
Total units purchased in first year	0.36

---

* Population data from U.S. Bureau of Census for ages 25–39.

† Based on Early MarketCast results. Coupon distribution forced in-store awareness on 17,451 potential customers. Assuming a random sample of the potential target market:

$$541 = (17,451 \times 0.47) \times (M \times 0.22)$$

where 541 = population purchasing E-A-R® earplugs

M = fraction of population in market

‡ Intent to try for women 25–39. The 46 percent from Exhibit 18.4, the sum of might, probable, and definite intent, becomes .32 when weighted by .9, .4, and .1, respectively.

§ Assumes uniform trial rate of $T/4$ per quarter (where T is yearly trial rate), repeat purchase rate of 50 percent, and 1.1 units bought per repurchase:

Quarter	Trial	1 Repeat	2 Repeat	3 Repeat	Total
1st	$T/4$	$T/8$	$T/16$	$T/32$	$7T/32$
2nd	$T/4$	$T/8$	$T/16$	—	$3T/16$
3rd	$T/4$	$T/8$	—	—	$T/8$
4th	$T/4$	—	—	—	—
Total	T				$17T/32$

Total units purchased at repeat = $(7T/32) \times 1.1 = 187T/320$
$$= 0.584T$$

product as a result of advertising only, or that consumer might be unaware of the product in question. A consumer who was aware of the product (by whatever means) might or might not have tried it. Of those who had tried the product, some might have repurchased it, while others would not have done so. The phenomena necessary to interrelate key events of this type are connected in a flow diagram in which consumers "flow" from one state to the next. Given estimates of the rates of flow between states, we can calculate dynamic sales patterns.

The consultant's macro-flow model, employing inputs derived from Serene® marketing research data, estimated first-year consumer sales of 770,000 three-pair units and second-year volume of slightly over one million units for the "bothered by noise" positioning, and 360,000 packages sold in the first year and 467,000 units for the second year with sleep-aid positioning. (See Exhibits 18.6 and 18.7 for the computer flow model for the detailed period-by-period results). He attributed the increase in second-year volume to additional trials in year 2, the apparent long purchase cycle for earplugs, and the delayed impact of the sampling. He pointed out, however, that his forecast would change substantially if the inputs to the model were modified. Accelerating the timing of the proposed sample drop and newspaper coupons, for example, would increase forecast year 1 volume by approximately 170,000 units for the bothered-by-noise position.

CONCLUSION

After reviewing these data, Brumwell found himself more unsure than ever concerning what Cabot should do about the consumer earplug market. The research seemed to suggest that E-A-R's® sales level in this market would fall short of the level that the corporation generally required for entry into truly new businesses. But Brumwell felt that there must be something wrong either with the data or with the introductory marketing programs that had been tested. "There are roughly 240 million people in the United States," he mused. "If only 1 percent of them bought just six pairs (two packages) a year—at, say, a 95 cents manufacturer's selling price per three-pair package (equivalent to approximately $2.09 at retail)—we would have $5 million in revenue and enough profit at this level of sales to go ahead.

QUESTIONS FOR DISCUSSION

1. From a strategic point of view, why is Cabot interested in consumer earplugs?

2. What has been Cabot's experience in this market to date? Why?

3. How would you evaluate Cabot's recent marketing research in the consumer earplug market? What were the major findings? How much confidence do you have in these findings?

4. Specifically, how would you interpret the results of the "flow model" cited in the case?

5. As general manager of the E-A-R® division, what would be your strategy for the marketing of consumer earplugs?

Developed in collaboration with Jeanne Stanton[1]

In September 1988, top management of *USA Today* was evaluating the paper's recent performance and seeking to formulate a marketing strategy for the next several years. Launched in 1982 as the nation's first national general interest daily newspaper,[2] *USA Today* was now second in circulation to the *Wall Street Journal*, and an acknowledged presence in all major metropolitan markets. Circulation was currently running at a record 1.8 million, while advertising revenue for the year was expected to exceed $150 million.

These accomplishments were especially impressive given the lackluster performance of the daily newspaper industry during the 1980s. Daily circulation and, especially, penetration (circulation per household) and readership were down,[3] as was the newspaper industry's share of total advertising expenditures. (On a more positive note, Sunday circulation and readership and classified advertising were doing very well in most markets, and most newspapers' profitability remained high.) The causes of these adverse trends were complex, but seemed to be closely related to strong competition from both television and other print media, especially "targeted" magazines, free shoppers' guides, and weekly community newspapers; less frequent readership by women, and by young people, who typically read only a Sunday paper and (perhaps) one or two other issues per week;[4] and an increasing tendency by major retail advertisers to split their expenditures among several

---

[1] Assistant Professor, Simmons College, Graduate School of Management.

[2] National newspapers had long predominated in many foreign countries, but had never been considered feasible in the United States because of the nation's immense size and multiple political jurisdictions. In recent years, satellite transmission and automated platemaking had made a true national paper feasible for the first time. The first paper to use the new technology in a concerted way was the *Wall Street Journal*, which printed in multiple sites in order to achieve timely delivery of its specialized financial and business newspaper. The *New York Times* had been rolling out a "national edition" for many years, but had not yet achieved true national distribution when *USA Today* was launched in 1982.

[3] In most markets, fewer than 60 percent of adults eighteen and over reported that they had "read a newspaper yesterday," compared with 80 percent or more fifteen years previously. Among young adults (eighteen to twenty-five), the figure was below 40 percent.

[4] Some media analysts believed that the cognitive style of a high proportion of people born after (say) 1950 was different from that of their predecessors, largely because of intensive early exposure to television. In particular, these analysts pointed to an apparent reduction in attention span and a strong preference that information be provided in concise "bites."

media, including direct mail. Some analysts alleged that much of the problem stemmed from the near-monopoly status, and resulting blandness, of most local papers, and the continuing demise of afternoon papers, which had been especially appealing to housewives and blue-collar workers.

Against *USA Today*'s circulation success, detractors frequently cited the paper's continuing financial deficits. ''*USA Today* Produces Readers But Not Profits,'' the title of a July 1988 article in the *Wall Street Journal*, was a typical commentary. The Gannett Corporation had already invested nearly $650 million in pretax dollars in the new paper, which was expected to lose another almost $25 million in 1988.

Tom Curley, president of *USA Today*, was faced with the challenge of maintaining circulation growth while controlling costs. This would be increasingly difficult, he believed, since the new paper was now distributed in all major metropolitan areas, and would thus have to obtain additional circulation largely through deeper penetration of existing markets. While the rallying cry to ''sell more papers with less money'' was heard in all *USA Today* offices, Curley wondered how he could further the corporate objective to ''get profitable,'' while simultaneously achieving the goal of 2 million circulation by 1991.

In Curley's view, *USA Today*'s ''launch mentality'' had fostered a tolerance for high distribution costs, costs that now needed trimming. Profits would continue to be adversely affected by the rising cost of newsprint, while advertising could not be depended upon to produce offsetting revenue in the near future.

USA Today's television show, introduced in 118 cities in September 1988, had been expected to stimulate significant circulation increases. Unfortunately, it had received extremely low ratings in its first week, and its future was uncertain.

Curley wondered whether changes in the content of the newspaper might contribute to sustained circulation growth. Despite the fact that *USA Today* readers had relatively high educational levels, for example, a number of observers had commented on what they considered the paper's lack of depth. The sports section continued to be popular, but Curley thought that other sections could be revamped to bring in more women readers, and that the offerings in the lifestyle and news sections could be made more substantial.

HISTORY

USA Today, the first national daily newspaper aimed at a general audience, was launched on September 15, 1982, in the Washington-Baltimore market. There had been a great deal of prepublication promotional activity, and the first edition sold out promptly. As described in *The Making of McPaper*, ''The Nation's Newspaper [debuted] in the nation's capital, flanked by the nation's two greatest monuments, surrounded by the nation's leaders, all of it wrapped up in red, white, and blue.''[5]

Behind this impressive launch was the considerable expertise and financial strength of the Gannett Corporation, owner of eighty-eight daily and thirty-five weekly newspapers in forty-two states. In 1988, total daily circulation for the Gannett Group was about 6.2 million, or 10 percent of the U.S. total. Gannett newspapers (other than *USA Today*) ranged in circulation from 685,000 for the *Detroit News* to 5,900 for the Port Clinton, Ohio, *News Herald*.

Before the first issue appeared, members of the Gannett corporate staff had spent months researching the market, testing prototypes, and analyzing how to establish a nationwide newspaper distribution system.

The paper itself represented the journalistic philosophy of its creator, Allen H. Neuharth, then CEO of Gannett. As a nationally distributed publication, the paper was,

---

[5] Peter Prichard, *The Making of McPaper: The Inside Story of USA Today*, copyright 1987 by Gannett News Media Services. Quotations from Prichard's account of the history and development of *USA Today* are used throughout this chapter.

in Neuharth's words, "to serve as a forum for better understanding among the country's diverse readership." More specifically, the paper would be "user friendly," with a clear format, bright colors, lively writing, and content both relevant and interesting.

Early issues of the paper emphasized domestic over international news. The paper's editorial style was embodied in the front page, which, according to *The Making of McPaper*, was planned "to have the right mix of hard news, features of wide interest, and promotional items." Graphics and photos were both colorful and arresting; pictures of women, minorities, and ordinary citizens replaced the traditional front-page photographs of middle-aged men in business suits. The left column offered an easy-to-read guide to all sections of the paper. In the lower left corner, "USA Snapshots" provided useful, and often surprising, statistical data about life in the United States.

Creating the paper had required a massive investment of money and people. Although initially most printing was done on equipment owned by other Gannett newspapers, substantial investments in presses and other physical facilities had been required. The project had been heavily staffed with "loaners" from other Gannett newspapers; these editors and reporters represented 65 percent of the *USA Today* staff at the beginning. Even Neuharth acted as a "loaner," spending weeks in the newsroom until late at night, rewriting leads, polishing headlines, and reading proofs. During this period, Neuharth insisted that he be supplied with the latest front-page "dummy" and other material nightly, and kept the editorial staff continually apprised of his response to their efforts via memos such as the following:

> . . . We absolutely must not allow ourselves to be satisfied with any Page 1 headlines . . . until they have been rewritten and massaged to perfection. Too often we accept something that is far less than the best. We must view every word in every headline from the point of view of the potential reader, totally unfamiliar with the content of that day's newspaper, walking up to the vending machine and wanting to be grabbed by what is seen in the top half of Page 1.

Critics had from the first commented unfavorably on *USA Today*'s concise editorial content and upbeat style. The most damning criticism came from those who, while predicting imminent failure, dubbed the publication "McPaper" (a pun on the highly successful fast-food chain McDonald's).

USA Today staff members, who worked long and late hours to produce the paper, were dismayed at the vitriolic nature of much of the early criticism. Prominent figures in journalism denounced the editorial product as superficial. The paper was called "Neuharth's ego trip" and "junk-food journalism." According to *The Making of McPaper*, many members of the newspaper establishment, offended by Neuharth's ambition, "distrusted Gannett, disliked Neuharth, and despised *USA Today*."

USA Today circulation passed 1 million in April 1983, slightly later than had been expected. This feat had been accomplished by a virtual invasion of major cities (Atlanta, Minneapolis, Houston, Los Angeles, Chicago, and New York) by squads of workers installing hundreds of distinctive vending boxes. Although the 1 million number had been deemed a critical milestone for attracting advertising to the paper, experience suggested that generating substantial advertising revenue would remain a challenge for some time.

USA TODAY INNOVATIONS

Despite the widespread criticism of its style and content, certain features of the *USA Today* format soon began to appear in other newspapers. The paper was generally credited with stimulating an almost universal recognition of the need to upgrade printing quality, as well as with prompting a broader and more creative use of color. Its weather page—a full-page, color-coded analysis of weather and temperatures in all parts of the United

States (with detailed forecasts for twenty-eight major cities)—led to greatly increased emphasis on the weather by many other publications. "Factoids," graphics that encapsulated information for easy reading, were being used increasingly, even by papers as prestigious as the *New York Times*. Many daily newspapers also sought to emulate *USA Today*'s succinct and upbeat editorial style.

Al Neuharth, quoted in *The Making of McPaper*, had his own opinion as to why the paper was so widely imitated:

> *USA Today*'s secret is very simple. It communicates with the reader on a personal level, very quickly, clearly, and directly in an upbeat, exciting, positive environment. It's giving readers information that they want and need in order to form their own opinions. *USA Today* had made reading a newspaper an enjoyable experience again.

EDITORIAL CONTENT AND APPEARANCE

USA Today was published Monday through Friday in four sections, with a fifth "bonus section" added an average of four times per month. From its inception, it had been distinguished by its use of color and graphic design. Other hallmarks were concise coverage of national and international news stories, its color-coded weather map, a wealth of statistical information communicated via graphics and "factoids," and extensive coverage of sports events.

The four sections—News, Money, Life, and Sports—were color-coded for easy reader identification. Each section functioned almost like a discrete newspaper, with front-page "ears,"[6] an index column, a "USA Snapshots" box, a daily page 1 cover story, and separate pagination. This format was strictly adhered to every day to make it easier for the reader to find his or her favorite features. The visual appearance of the top half of the front page of the News section was considered especially important, as this was the part of the paper visible in vending boxes. Front-page story photos and graphics were chosen as much for consumer appeal as for illustration of a feature story.

USA Today generally ran twenty-five pages of news and twelve to thirty pages of advertising, including classified. Content of the four sections was as follows:

- *News (color-coded blue)*: This section contained national and international news stories. "Across the USA," a daily feature, provided several news items from each of the fifty states. An "Opinion" page aired diverse points of view on a single topic (e.g., nutrition labeling, gun laws, use of drugs by athletes). The weather page was always the back page of the first section.

- *Money (color-coded green)*: Companies and industries were covered in this section. A stock market summary included "Marketline—An Investor's Guide to What's Happening in the Markets"; "Company Spotlight," two-plus pages of stock prices; and "Moneytalk—A Quick Read on Your Personal Finances." (On August 6, 1988, Money covered financial institutions offering the highest-yielding CDs; new automated teller machines in Pittsburgh subways; a University of Iowa system to pay tuition by computer; and new developments in credit cards. It also included a "factoid" illustrating the fact that older people are more likely to have wills.)

- *Life (color-coded royal)*: Stories in the entertainment and lifestyle section ranged from coverage of serious health-care topics (e.g., angioplasty) to profiles of movie and rock stars. The daily "Jeannie Williams" column carried Hollywood gossip,

---

[6] A newspaper term for editorial content in the upper corners of a page. In many papers, for example, the right "ear" of the front page contained a brief weather forecast.

VIA SATELLITE THE NATION'S NEWSPAPER 50 CENTS

USA TODAY

NO. 1 IN THE USA...5.3 MILLION READERS EVERY DAY

AL's CY YOUNG
TWINS' VIOLA, 24-7 IN '88 1C

HOW GRID COACHES TACKLE STRESS 3C
▶ JOHN MADDEN TALKS ABOUT THE GRIND

SPEEEED BOAT RACING POWERS UP
By Acey Harper
DON JOHNSON: Catch the new ponytail, 1D ▶ DON JOHNSON IS IN RUNNING TODAY, 1C

THURSDAY

MAXISERIES 'WAR' NEARS
18-HOUR DRAMA LONGEST, BIGGEST, MOST COSTLY 1D
▶ OLD ROLES, NEW CAST, 7D

'LABOR' DAY FOR THE HUXTABLES
▶ COS IS GRANDDAD, 3D

ALZHEIMER'S: SIGNS, WHERE TO GET HELP 4D

JANE SEYMOUR: Steps in for Ali MacGraw, 1,7D ABC

EXCLUSIVE PROFILE

THE WHIZ WHO STOPPED THE USA'S COMPUTERS

Robert T. Morris was reared in New Jersey, in a home where they kept sheep to trim the front lawn. They vacationed in Iceland, and on a canal boat in Britain. Be active, not passive, his parents taught him. He's shy. Super bright. Plays the violin. Would fit naturally into Silicon Valley. And some say that one day last week he shut down 6,000 USA computers.
FULL REPORT 1B, 5B

Election wins 'sinking in now'

Bush taps Baker for State Dept.

By Johanna Neuman and Jessica Lee
USA TODAY

WASHINGTON — George Bush made his first moves as president-elect Wednesday — naming top aides and meeting with President Reagan.

"I can hardly believe it. It's beginning to sink in now," Bush told a welcoming rally.

Less than 12 hours after claiming victory — in which about half the eligible voters cast ballots — Bush:

▶ Tapped James Baker — longtime friend, campaign chief and former Treasury secretary — to be secretary of State in his new administration.

▶ Named chief of staff Craig Fuller and strategist Bob Teeter as transition team captains.

"I will for the most part bring in a brand-new team of people from across the country," he said.

▶ Promised to take "keen personal interest in the Cabinet and a lot of other appointments." Recalling that "the Nixon Cabinet was all announced in one dramatic announcement ceremony," Bush said, "I'm not going to do that."

▶ Lavished praise on his running mate, Dan Quayle, predicting: "He's going to be one of the great vice presidents. You watch him closely."

▶ Held out the prospect of an early summit with Soviet leader Mikhail Gorbachev, but not before he's inaugurated.

Bush, saying he received a "thoughtful communication" from Gorbachev, pledged "my determination to keep this new bilateral relationship moving forward."

▶ Said more Cabinet announcements will come "fairly soon but not before I come back" from a Florida vacation.

Familiar face, new phase

By H. Darr Beiser, USA TODAY
WINNERS: Reagans greet the Bushes at White House after 426-112 electoral win.

Bush's things to do
In the 72 hours before he takes office, the next president must:

Source: U.S. Census Bureau
By Jeff Dionise, USA TODAY

COVER STORY

Bush's oil days core of friendships

'We'd take turns having each other over' to drink beer, barbecue in the backyard

By Jean Becker
USA TODAY

Back in 1980, when George Bush first ran for president, it was James Baker who told him it was time to give up.

"George, you've got to know when to hold 'em and know when to fold 'em," Baker told his old friend, explaining that Ronald Reagan was pounding them. "The campaign is finished. You're the only one who doesn't seem to know it."

Now it's 1988, and Bush is the man on top. He made it official Wednesday that he wants James Baker to be his secretary of State. It was no big surprise; Baker's name had been pinned to that job for months.

But Bush's first Cabinet nomination — along with several other appointments he made — gives a first clue to the man who'll be the 41st president.

At the core of Bush's existence is his commitment and loyalty to family and friends — people who have been with him through the long haul. They come before all else.

And it will be from that well that he'll draw the support and talent he'll need to get through the next four years.

"You are going to see George Bush friends," says Bobby Holt, an old friend from Midland, Texas, whom Bush appointed co-chair of his inaugural committee.

"But it's because George has so many friends — great friends — with a broad scope of talent. That's how he's positioned himself."

But longtime friend Hugh Liedtke, head of Pennzoil, says, "That doesn't mean he'll engage in cronyism. He's not going

Please see COVER STORY next page ▶

Princeton bonds helped free Marcos

By Wayne Beissert
USA TODAY

Princeton University — where Albert Einstein taught, George Shultz was tattooed and Brooke Shields studied — now has a new distinction.

The Ivy League school's construction bonds were the collateral that freed Imelda Marcos.

"Oh my god. People will be just horrified," sniffs Suju Vijayan, leader of Princeton Students for Social Responsibility.

The bonds — $125 million to repair buildings — were sold through a state agency. Tobacco heiress Doris Duke bought some and used them for Imelda's $5 million bail. Duke loses if Imelda skips, not Princeton.

Imelda and husband Ferdinand are accused of looting $100 million from the Philippines treasury.

Students are "not very supportive of the Marcoses," student leader Dwight McBride says. "They'll be very upset."

Insurance revolt in making

By Catherine Hedgecock
USA TODAY

Watch for an auto insurance revolt to roll across the USA now that California voters have passed a controversial plan to slash runaway rates.

In fact, insurance companies are so concerned about fallout from the ballot initiative approved Tuesday that four lawsuits immediately were filed in the California Supreme Court. Charge: The new law is unconstitutional because it will force insurers to operate at a loss.

One of the firms filing suit, Fireman's Fund Insurance Cos., said it will stop selling auto insurance in California.

Under the California plan, which takes effect immediately, insurers must lower almost all insurance rates, including auto, home and business coverage, by 20 percent below November 1987 rates — and can't raise them again for two years.

A key provision would require an additional 20 percent cut in auto insurance rates for good drivers. Now, rates can top $2,000 a year even for drivers with clean records.

"It's going to reverberate through the other 49 states," said Jubilant consumer advocate Ralph Nader, who backed the plan — one of five insurance initiatives on the ballot. The other four failed.

Legislatures, bolstered by the California victory, are likely to move quickly to rein in rates in their states.

"It's going to be a bold legislator indeed who ignores the rights of consumers," said Nader. He expects consumers in the 23 other states that allow ballot initiatives to push insurance plans like California's.

Several states already have been affected by the California movement:

▶ In New Jersey, which has the highest average auto insurance rates, laws set to take effect in January will increase rates for bad drivers, limit lawsuit awards and cut insurance industry profits.

▶ Massachusetts last week passed a law cutting car insurance rates by 16 percent. Fear that a California-style initiative would be launched sped the bill through the legislature.

Voters turned off, turnout turns down

Special for USA TODAY

The 50 percent voter turnout Tuesday was the lowest in 64 years, officials said.

About 91 million ballots were cast, roughly half the number of eligible voters, said Curtis Gans, director of the Committee for the Study of the American Electorate.

"We had an unprecedented number of voters who said they didn't like either candidate," said Gans. Not voting "became a rational act."

The 1924 race between Calvin Coolidge and John W. Davis drew slightly more than 48 percent of the electorate.

Turnout was low except in New Hampshire and Nevada.

THURSDAY, NOVEMBER 10, 1988

NEWSLINE
A QUICK READ ON THE NEWS

WEATHER: Chilly, windy, wet Northeast, Southeast, Midwest, North Central; cool South Central with showers likely; wet Rockies, West, except Calif. Full color page. 14A.

WALL STREET DOWN: Dow loses 8.25 points to 2118.24. Highlights. 3B. Tokyo Nikkei index closed down 46.36 points today at 28,156.42.

TAKEOVERS: Pillsbury wins more time in fight against takeover; Borden, Quaker Oats covet pieces of RJR Nabisco; anti-takeover sentiment growing. 1B.

MITCHELL DIES: Former Attorney General John Mitchell, 75, suffered an apparent heart attack Wednesday on a Washington sidewalk; career as bond lawyer, confidant of President Nixon clouded by 19 months in prison served for part in Watergate cover-up. 10A.
UPI
MITCHELL: 'Never any bitterness'

LEROY, TEXAS: A fundraising concert Monday — starring Willie Nelson — hopes to raise $30,000 to help townspeople hurt when uninsured bank failed; 200 residents wonder where $6M in deposits went; Nelson grew up in nearby Abbott. 11A.

NATION: Florida has another startling trial that looks at the divide between mercy killing and murder. 10A.
▶ Rayon plant reopens; cheers Virginia town, NASA. 10A.
▶ Reynolds, Herrington resigning from government. 10A.

WASHINGTON: Air Force grounds B-1 bombers pending inspections; one crashed Tuesday. 4A.

ABROAD: Pakistani court aids chances of Benazir Bhutto's party in Nov. 16 vote. 10A.

TODAY'S DEBATE: Guns and laws. In USA TODAY's opinion, gun laws work. 12A.
▶ "It's time to lock up violent criminals, not our constitutional gun rights," counters Alan Gottlieb, author of *Gun Rights Factbook*. 12A.

MONEY: 1990 cars already unveiled — Plymouth's Laser, Mitsubishi's Eclipse. Both are sports coupes. 1B.
▶ Exodus starts from *Atlanta Journal, Constitution*. 2B.
▶ Plastic parts — sound advice for long-term growth. 3B.
▶ Here's Dulux EI, the longer-lasting light bulb. 5B.
▶ Fascinating *Maxwell*, book on British publisher. 9B.

SPORTS: Larry Bird's bad foot: Therapy, then will try to ward off "last alternative" of surgery. 10C.
▶ Golf's biggest bonanza starts today. 1C,10C.

LIFE: If you're tired of always being tired, you may have chronic fatigue syndrome; how to tell. 4D.
▶ Gel used in breast implants could raise cancer risk. 1D.
▶ Linda Kelsey kicks stage fright *Day By Day*. 3D.
▶ Eddie Murphy really can sing, says Cameo's leader. 2D.
▶ Tonight's *Knightwatch* debut dubbed provocative. 3D.

COMING THURSDAY: A look at Barbara Bush's brand of understatement as first lady.

Compiled by Tim McQuay

© COPYRIGHT 1988 USA TODAY, a division of Gannett Co., Inc.

USA SNAPSHOTS
A look at statistics that shape the nation

Crime and the superpowers
Daily crime rates in the USA and Soviet Union, based on government reports.

Crime	USA	Soviet Union
Theft	20,547	2,180
Rape	250	24
Murder	55	16

Source: U.S. Justice Department, Soviet Interior Ministry
By Elys McLean-Ibrahim, USA TODAY

ELECTION COVERAGE

3A: Key races from across the USA	13A: Excerpts from Bush and Dukakis news conferences
4A: What to expect in next administration	2B: Jellybeans out, fried pork skins in, banking committee
6A: Results in Senate, governor races	1C: Quayle's favorite: Here comes golf!
7A: House results	1D: ABC wins election night ratings
8A, 9A: Results in state, local races	
12A: Gun debate	

EXHIBIT 19.1
(continued)

12A · THURSDAY, NOVEMBER 10, 1988 · USA TODAY

USA TODAY

"USA TODAY hopes to serve as a forum for better understanding and unity to help make the USA truly one nation."

—**Allen H. Neuharth**
Chairman and Founder
Sept. 15, 1982

John C. Quinn
Editor-in-Chief

John Seigenthaler
Editorial Director

DEBATE

GUNS & LAWS

Today's debate includes our opinion that gun laws work, an opposing view from Washington, another view from North Carolina, and voices from across the USA. Also, guest columnists from Massachusetts and Virginia debate controls on dial-a-porn services.

We need more laws to control handguns

People in Miami are getting the message. Handguns kill.

Last year, Florida made it easier to get handguns; this year in Miami's Dade County, gun murders are up 17%.

People in Seattle and nearby Vancouver, British Columbia, are getting the message, too.

A study published today finds that Seattle residents are five times as likely to be killed by handguns, even though the cities are virtually identical. The conclusion: Vancouver's strict handgun laws work.

People in Maryland not only are getting the message; they're sending one to the rest of the USA. Tuesday, they ignored a $5 million lobbying effort by gun interests and voted overwhelmingly to end sale of some handguns.

That's a victory for common sense.

The simple truth is that making handguns cheap and easy to obtain makes life cheap and easy to lose.

This year, guns will be involved in 11,000 murders, 15,000 suicides, 175,000 assaults, 221,000 robberies and 90,000 rapes. Just statistics, you say? Look again.

At that rate, there's a good chance that you'll be one of those statistics some time during your life.

Then there are gunshot accidents. This year they'll kill 1,900 people and injure 200,000 more.

There's no quick cure for that crime and carnage. Guns are part of our society. They're used for sport and self-protection. The Constitution guarantees the right to keep them.

For all those reasons, a scatter-gun approach seeking to confiscate everyone's guns would be wrong.

But the shots fired in Maryland and Vancouver and communities across the USA are another matter.

They're right on the mark.

They seek to take guns — particularly cheap Saturday Night Specials — out of the hands of criminals while keeping the guns of honest citizens right where they are.

They are not the proposals of wild-eyed gun grabbers — contrary to the scare stories spread by the gun lobby and the claims of one columnist writing on this page.

Maryland's law creates a nine-member commission that can ban the sale of some handguns. The commission will include two representatives of the gun industry.

Vancouver bans concealed weapons, requires a permit to transport a pistol, and allows pistols to be fired only at licensed ranges — hardly a radical idea in an urban area.

This nation's police chiefs favor a federal law that would impose a mandatory waiting period before a gun could be purchased, verification of the purchaser's identity, a mandatory criminal-records check, and a requirement for training in use of firearms.

Those are cautious, common-sense solutions to a deadly problem. We need them.

We needn't choose between protecting ourselves with guns or with laws. We can do both.

That's the message from Miami and Maryland — a message that echoes with every gunshot across the nation.

IT'S SATURDAY NIGHT, AND YOU'RE SOMETHING SPECIAL!
WANNA' GO OUT AND PAINT THE TOWN RED?

By David Seavey, USA TODAY

SHERRY ROBERTS
Guest columnist

Our gun fantasies are no joke

GREENSBORO, N.C. — Each year, my father went hunting — until the cold day he shot a deer.

Then he didn't have to go anymore.

The dead deer, a trophy of years of beer drinking, card playing, gun-toting on wintry mornings, hangs on the wall of the den and remains an integral part of our lives.

In every family picture, including my wedding photos, it is there, its antlers sticking out of someone's head.

It is a visual reminder that the consequences of guns stay with us forever.

Nothing comes back from the dead: not deer, not a child shot for his jean jacket in a school hall, not a shopkeeper killed for a six-pack of beer and $12 in change.

We have watched so many movies and so much television that we have forgotten how final things can be.

The U.S. Department of Justice estimated 27,000 children between ages 12 and 15 were handgun victims in 1985.

Children are running around this nation with black-market Uzi submachine guns and killing each other.

They are sneaking firearms from dad's closet and taking them to school in order to "protect" themselves from other gun-toting youths.

Where did they learn these lessons? Who were their examples? Their role models?

Mothers, fathers, aunts and uncles who continue to believe that the answer to rising violence is to take up generators of more violence.

These people are so intelligent, it scares me.

Law enforcement officials say about 200 people a year successfully use handguns to defend themselves, while another 22,000 die from guns as a result of homicides, suicides or accidents.

Sherry Roberts is a free-lance writer.

On Election Day, some smart people in Maryland said they'd had enough: of violence, of killing, of handgun terrorism. The use of handguns, they said, had gotten out of hand.

If we are lucky, this wave of intelligence will sweep across the nation and public safety will come to mean more than the safety on a gun.

When I was a child, the goofy thing to do, the way to make someone look foolish, was to hold up two fingers behind his head, like antlers or rabbit's ears.

It was supposed to be funny, a joke.

The victim would swat you away and everyone would laugh.

Today, they'd blow your fingers off with a .357 Magnum.

And that's no joke.

ALAN GOTTLIEB
An opposing view

Protect us from laws curbing handgun rights

SEATTLE — This week we saw the nation's No. 1 gun-grabber, Michael Dukakis, go down to defeat.

And saw the people of Nebraska overwhelmingly pass an amendment to their state constitution to guarantee the right to keep and bear arms — the 43rd state to do so.

In Maryland, gun owners nearly overturned that state's handgun ban law despite editorial support from media elitists and the political establishment's wrongful use of state employees' and taxpayers' funds that negated the money raised and spent by the National Rifle Association and others to defend freedom.

On this, the 20th anniversary of the passage of the USA's first major gun-control bill, the issue is hot again. Unfortunately, due to the anti-gun hysteria whipped up by the media and politicians who have failed to control violent drug crime, the main issue of this controversy is overlooked: Does gun control work? Can it reduce crime?

In the 20 years since Congress passed the 1968 gun control act and numerous restrictive gun laws have been put on the books by state legislatures and county and city councils, one thing has become clear: Gun control has failed.

The studies and statistics that prove the failure of gun control don't come from the offices of the "gun lobby." They come from the Social and Demographic Research Institute of the University of Massachusetts, the National Institute of Justice, and the School of Criminology at Florida State University, among others.

The University of Massachusetts study concluded, "There is little evidence to show that gun ownership among the population as a whole is an important cause of criminal violence." It added that evaluations of the 20,000 gun laws on the books generally show their effect to be "modest or non-existent."

Alan Gottlieb, author of Gun Rights Factbook, *is chairman of the Citizens Committee for the Right to Keep and Bear Arms and founder of the Second Amendment Foundation.*

> "Private ownership of firearms serves as a deterrent to crime."

A second study concluded that a ban on small, inexpensive handguns would result in criminals using more powerful handguns or sawed-off shotguns, resulting in a higher fatality rate, the exact opposite of the intent of gun control.

The Florida State University study concluded private ownership of firearms serves as a deterrent to crime. It found, "Evidence indicates that private gun use against violent criminals and burglars is common and about as frequent as legal actions like arrests."

Politicians impose handgun bans because they are a cheap way to create the impression that they are doing something about crime. It's time to lock up violent criminals, not our constitutional gun rights.

QUOTELINES

"We're going to take out some politicans and I wouldn't be surprised if he was one."
— *Neal Cox, Firearms Coalition, on Maryland Gov. William Donald Schaefer, leader of gun control forces*

"We don't want these lousy, no-good guns in our streets. We are not giving up on drugs and crime. Get the drugs out; get the guns out."
— *Gov. William Donald Schaefer*

Schaefer

"Don't ban guns, ban Schaefer."
— *Maryland campaign sign*

"The people of Maryland have dealt the NRA a major blow; their actions serve as a catalyst for gun control."
— *New Jersey Senate Senate President John Russo*

VOICES FROM ACROSS THE USA/Do you think we need stronger handgun laws?

LARRY FARRIS, *24*
Business owner
Springfield, Ore.

No. Handgun laws only restrict those who are willing to abide by those laws. There is a standard of freedom that handguns allow, and there is a price for that. The price could be the unintelligent use of handguns. But if someone wants a weapon, there won't be too much difficulty getting it, no matter what the laws say.

MARY BETH BENJAMIN, *61*
Association secretary
Houston, Texas

Yes, we do. I come from a family of hunters, and they don't agree with me on this. But we need better control of them. It's too easy for people to get guns and then go out and shoot someone who looks at them cross-eyed. My biggest concern is the accidental killing of children who find them around the house.

CATHERINE NOLAN, *30*
Assemblywoman
Queens, N.Y.

This is a state issue, and I'm pretty satisfied with New York's law. One of the challenges is balancing people's right to bear arms with the fact that someone can cross state lines with an illegal gun and kill a cop. I understand why the nation is split on the issue. Maybe that's something that President-elect Bush could address.

JOHN MARSCHALK, *60*
Sales consultant
Lake St. Louis, Mo.

Yes. I'm a former Marylander, and I think there is a critical need for improved control over handguns. I'm certainly in favor of people having gun hobbies and hunting privileges, but I don't consider this an issue of taking away something that's reasonable. It's a matter of identifying ways to control harming people.

BRENDA HUMPRHEY, *41*
Journalist
Portland, Maine

Talk of handgun control means nothing in Maine because we haven't had the problems of big, urban cities. Maine has such a strong sportsmen alliance that hunters go berserk at the idea of gun control. Having lived in crime-ridden cities, however, I understand people who feel they need guns to protect themselves.

H. BRUCE KENNEDY, *42*
Controller
Dunedin, Fla.

Yes. Florida's new gun law has been scrutinized and is being revised to include a longer waiting period. There needs to be more education on handguns through the National Rifle Association. More education on the usage of handguns or any type of weapons would be beneficial to everyone. It would cut down on quick sales.

MARYNELL REECE, *68*
Volunteer
Scandia, Kan.

There should be some control on handguns, but not absolute control. I still believe in individual rights of determining certain things. With the crime rate as high as it is in most cities, people have become uneasy and nervous and have a need for self-protection. It's important, though, that they learn safety precautions for guns.

FACE-OFF: Cracking down on dial-a-porn

Say no to this telephone trash

By Jim Moore
Guest columnist

ALEXANDRIA, Va. — So a Washington official of the American Civil Liberties Union calls the shutdown of a California dial-a-porn service by the Federal Communications Commission a "chilling effect." Well, grab a parka, 'cause it's gonna get a lot colder.

The purpose of the law is not, as the ACLU fears, to "scare people into submission." It is to stop the proliferation of telephone pornography.

It is to draw a line — a line beyond which those who seek to profit in this particularly invasive form of pornography may no longer go.

Pornography is not the issue. Responsibility is the issue. Or, more accurately, the abrogation of responsibility by groups such as the ACLU and national voices who encouraged an entire generation to slough off responsibility.

"Tune in, turn on and drop out," said Timothy Leary, and, while libertarians and liberal leaders vouchsafed the message, a generation of young Americans did just that. Today, that generation's children either idolize drugs or are terrorized by them, they are either defeated by school or disabled by it, they either lack a moral base entirely or see daily what little base they have disintegrating beneath their feet. By plugging the moral gap into which telephone pornography flowed, the FCC shored up that base.

Jim Moore is a free-lance writer.

The issue is responsibility. Responsibility for the lawmakers to make the tough choices, responsibility for the chief executive to act out of both personal and national indignation on behalf of our children and our grandchildren to follow, and responsibility of parents to choose family over careers, to choose loving discipline over day care, to choose the future of their children over the present for themselves.

Don't bleed on the Constitution, friends. The rights you imagine it to contain are not rights to offend, are not rights to traumatize, are not rights to shock with pornographic zeal. They are rights to enjoy life unfettered of the detritus of society; they are the rights to lift this nation up, not bring it down; they are the rights to lead a responsible and principled life.

Hang up the phone; the porn line is dead.

Say no to government sex patrols

By Roger Libby
Guest columnist

AMHERST, Mass. — To Congress and the FCC regulators: Stay out of my sexual fantasies, my erotic adventures. Why must government decide what's good for my sex life? I demand my constitutional rights to freedom of expression, privacy, the pursuit of happiness.

A cowardly Congress banned "obscene" and "indecent" commercial telephone messages. Constitutional challenges have prevented enforcement of the law, but this didn't stop the Federal Communications Commission from forcing a California service to terminate "obscene" messages on interstate lines and to keep "indecent" messages from those under 18.

The edict: be less explicit; use a children's standard for all. Never mind that we can use technology to stop children from hearing phone sex. Parents deserve the right to block access to phone lines, but I object to the government censoring my sexual stimulation.

Thanks to FCC bully tactics, we will now hear censored messages. The goal is to stamp out explicit sex. The chilling effect on those who produce and enjoy arousing media is terrifying and nauseating.

Even though the Supreme Court has wrongly declared that sex can be obscene (violence is never mentioned) it wisely ruled that a state could not tell citizens what they may read or view in their homes.

Roger Libby is a sociologist and lecturer on human sexuality.

Adult telephone lines aren't public. We have private conversations and we choose to hear taped messages. Government must stay out of our sexual imaginations. Hasn't Prohibition taught us anything?

Sex doesn't cause violence. Sex enhances pleasure and intimacy. Whatever augments delicious sex should be encouraged — not made illegal. Sex isn't a substance to be abused; it's a celebration of our uniqueness.

Sexually explicit communication leads to self-fulfillment and increased sexual awareness. It's only when sex is combined with force that it's negative. Most dial-a-fantasy is mutual lust, not forced sex. Sexual pleasure is essential to healthy living.

Sexual enthusiasts and civil libertarians: We must counter this pleasure-phobic purity crusade. It's censorship — not sex — that's obscene.

EXHIBIT 19.1
(continued)

complemented by "People—Behind the Scenes with the Famous and the Fascinating." The "Television" page included industry news, a prime time schedule, and program highlights, as well as a "Nutrition" feature. Classified advertising was anchored at the back of Life.

Sports (color-coded red): In addition to a daily cover story and conventional sports reporting, this section (which typically ran ten pages) offered two pages of major sports scores and one page of team statistics. "Across the USA in Sports" contained at least one sports news item from each of the fifty states. "Update" summarized sports industry news, including personnel changes in major sports and scores for tennis, golf, bowling, and other sports.

The weekend paper, published on Friday, was the week's best-seller; it routinely sold more than 2 million copies. Editors planned the issue to give three days' worth of news and information. Beginning with the March 1989 ABC[7] audit statement, *USA Today* would show its Friday (weekend) circulation and its Monday–Thursday (weekday) circulation separately. Current estimates were that the weekday circulation average would exceed 1,635,000 copies per day (of which more than 900,000 would be single-copy sales) and that the weekend average would be above 2,025,000 copies.

As noted, the format for each section was identical every day of the week, providing easy access for readers interested in one topic or category of news. An index to each section appeared on the left side of the front page, under "Newsline," "Sportsline," "Lifeline," or "Moneyline," and each section featured a "USA Snapshots" statistics box on the lower-left-hand corner of its section front. On one day, for example, "Snapshots" featured per capita consumption of water by state (News), sources of income for the elderly (Money), common concerns of adults (Life), and golf trophy winners (Sports).

Bonus sections (color-coded gold) were increasingly frequent (fifty-four were planned for 1988). During the 1988 Summer Olympics, *USA Today* included a bonus section every day. On a typical day, the Olympics bonus section carried six and one-half pages of advertising and nine and one-half pages of Olympics news, feature stories, scores, and statistics. The section provided useful information ranging from "Today on TV" to how to convert to Korean time from each of the U.S. continental time zones, as well as Alaska and Hawaii. As with all *USA Today* sections, stories were illustrated with high-quality color and black-and-white photos and graphics. (See Exhibit 19.1 for sample pages from *USA Today*.)

EDITORIAL PHILOSOPHY

The stated policy of *USA Today* was to serve the nation's readers, as opposed to its editors, reporters, and advertisers. In practice, this meant that editors at the new publication were forced to rethink not only what news to cover but also how to present it. Neuharth's editorial ground rules demanded journalism that focused on the positive aspects of events—even disasters—and that evaluated content on the basis of reader interest. *The Making of McPaper* described Neuharth's journalistic philosophy as a "new journalism of hope . . . [:] to cover all of the news, with accuracy, but without anguish, with detail but without despair." Neuharth backed up this philosophy with a minimum newshole of twenty-five pages each day, regardless of the amount of advertising in that edition, and insisted that advertising space be allocated so as not to interfere with the paper's format.

A staff guide included the following stylistic guidelines:

---

[7] The Audit Bureau of Circulations (ABC), an organization run by a board consisting of representatives from both media and advertisers, was the primary source of credible circulation data. Advertisers generally viewed circulation claims that had not been audited by the ABC as highly suspect.

Tell the Story Quickly and Clearly. Don't Waste Words.

Because *USA Today* has a different mission than most newspapers, so do the reporters and editors. Our readers are upscale, well-informed and looking for a supplement to—not a replacement for—their regular newspaper. So our stories may contain less background on events, more emphasis on what's new. Our paper has less space. So every story, every word, counts.

Keep It Tight.

Propel the story with punctuation. Colons, semicolons, bullets and dashes can replace some words. . . . Condense background information. Don't prattle on for several grafts explaining what happened at Love Canal, or spend an entire graf telling who Phyllis Schlafley is. Our readers are well-informed.

John Quinn, editor of *USA Today*, was also an executive vice president of Gannett and a Pulitzer Prize juror. When asked what being a "general interest paper" really meant, Quinn replied as follows:

General interest means that the paper appeals to a broad cross-section of readers. We deliver conventional content in an unconventional way. We are looking for "news junkies"—people who look to more than one source of news; people who are active, ambitious, well-off, trendy. People from somewhere else, who root for a team other than the home team. It is more a state of mind than a demographic category.

The challenge of a general interest newspaper is to be *general interest*—both to the elderly and the young taking care of them, to teenagers as well as to adults. The news staff reflects the characteristics of our readership: they are relatively young, and include single parents and working mothers.

Quinn pointed out that the paper had changed somewhat in six years, primarily in its news presentation, which had evolved from an early "spot news" orientation to harder, more sophisticated news stories. In looking ahead, he noted:

The newspaper has to be consistent. We can't jerk readers around just because editors get bored with a particular format. Our journalistic philosophy is the "forward spin," i.e., what is the future significance of a particular event?

Evolution has to focus on doing our kind of reporting better and on doing more original reporting. We won't ever do "secretary of state"–type news because others already do it well. We listen to Rather and Brokaw so we won't report the news the same way.

We did a feature on truck safety. We documented every truck accident in the USA in a 24-hour period, a minute-by-minute listing. We should do more across-the-USA collections of comparative information—for example, SAT scores by state.

At the beginning we wanted the newspaper to develop a personality of its own, not be a vehicle for columnists. Also, many were already tied to other publications. Now we have Jeannie Williams in Life, and Dan Dorfman is starting in Money. But I don't think we'll ever get heavily into conventional newspaper features. We get requests for things like a food column. We don't want to duplicate local efforts, so what we will do is look at price, availability, and quality of food across the U.S.

Circulation is gaining more slowly now. Single-copy newspapers depend on *news*, and we haven't had the stories this year. So the editors need to be enterprising. We do have a broader range of topics and we can break one long story into several smaller ones. That way the reader can pick and choose.

We are becoming a first rather than a second read for many people. We are never the *only* read. We don't think our purpose is to replace, but we can provide a service.

Ron Martin, executive editor, had been managing editor of the *Miami Herald* and the pre-Murdoch *New York Post* prior to becoming *USA Today* planning editor in 1980.

Martin said that the initial strategy for the News section was to be different, but that the early front page had been "too different."

> We have moved a lot closer to a mix of conventional stories and special *USA Today* stories. We put a special focus on these stories. We try to push the story ahead. What does it *mean*? What will happen? This is "personal impact" journalism.

Similarly, the "Opinion" page sought to be different by covering only one topic daily, but presenting a number of viewpoints. Martin believed that readers responded favorably to the "fairness" of this approach. A "Debate Page" exploring other aspects of the day's "Opinion" topic had been added. According to Martin, "Right now we are tinkering with it." (See Exhibit 19.2 for an article on the opinion page published in the corporate magazine *Gannetteer*.)

EXHIBIT 19.2
Article on the Opinion Page from "Gannetteer," August 1988

Copyright 1988, Gannett Co., Inc. Reprinted with permission.

It's no debate: Opinion page seeks balance

By Molly Badgett
Gannetteer

They bicker, argue, nitpick, laugh and sometimes shout, but all in the name of fairness, accuracy and balance of opinion.

They are the members of the USA TODAY editorial board, and their job is to produce, five days a week, an interesting and comprehensive package of opinions on the day's news for readers.

Unlike most other editorial pages, USA TODAY's Opinion page — except for a small, gray window offering "One Line on the News" — covers a single topic from right to left, from subtle insight to extreme argument, on the same day.

During the planning stages for USA TODAY, it was decided the editorial page would focus on the diversity of a single issue.

"The idea was to inspire, provoke a debate, a dialogue, and give our readers enough perspectives on the page that day to engage in an intelligent dialogue about the topic under discussion," Deputy Editorial Director Paul McMasters says.

The Inquiry page, which records topical interviews with newsmakers, also emerged from this idea.

John Seigenthaler, editorial director, set the standards for the editorial board — that its 10 members would represent diversity in gender, geography, race, political philosophy and other factors — and for the editorial page:

• that the issues in debate would not only be timely, but would be of high reader interest.

• that the board would reach a consensus on each topic. Issues that aren't debatable or on which the board can't come to a consensus viewpoint often are presented on the facing Inquiry page.

• that columnists from all over the U.S. would contribute concurring or opposing opinions.

"We feel that we're writing for the entire audience out there, not just specific parts of it. And the people that appear on our page should be reflective of that audience," McMasters says.

One of the board's biggest fears: being short a column. It almost happened once.

On the night of the Chicago mayoral election of 1983 when Harold Washington was elected, the editorial board had scheduled columns by Washington and by Chicago politician Edward Vrdolyak for the next day.

The deadline was 6:30 p.m. By 7 p.m., neither had called.

The board had one column as a

David Seavey, illustrator/cartoonist for the Opinion page, takes on his own in this cartoon.

backup; they never counted on having to find a second. Everyone called everywhere searching for someone to write a comprehensible column in less than an hour, McMasters says.

Then, the telephone rang: Bill Cosby was calling to see if USA TODAY wanted an opinion on the election. Dictation was taken, the column was written and there was "no dreaded white space" in the newspaper that day.

In its own 55-line editorial, USA TODAY frames an issue, expresses the board's viewpoint, sums up opposing views, then counters them and proposes possible solutions.

Finding a skilled writer with good credentials and expertise to oppose that

editorial is not an easy task, McMasters says. What helps occasionally is that in reaching a general consensus, the board's opinion falls in the middle of an issue; guest columnists and opposing writers then fall to either side. The result: at least three vigorous arguments on a topic.

The Opinion page also relies on a "stable" of regular contributors for opposing viewpoints or simply other perspectives.

McMasters says these regulars give readers someone with whom to identify and provide well-written, solid arguments under tight deadlines.

McMasters says USA TODAY's Opinion page prides itself on presenting all points of view on a subject.

"One of the main things that we find, and we are gratified by, is that there is a perception of fairness on the part of the reader, obviously, because they're seeing all the views, including an opposing view, on the same page on the same day," McMaster says.

"And we're getting that same sense of fairness perceived by those we oppose. Because they're not having to write a letter to the editor that may or may not get in two weeks later when the reader has forgotten what the issue was."

People all over Gannett work toward this goal:

• The editorial board members spend about two hours each morning debating the issues and deciding who's the best person to call on for other perspectives;

• Regional editors and staff members at other Gannett newspapers contribute by adding perspectives from places other than Washington, D.C.;

• Photographers at Gannett newspapers provide the names and faces for the "Voices Across the USA" section;

• Editorial director Seigenthaler always reviews the page's content before giving final approval.

"We don't think we ignore anything; we try our best not to," McMasters says.

"We do try our best to keep looking out there rather than into Washington for the source of all of our debates. Obviously in some aspects everything leads back to Washington . . . but we try our best every day to put our editorial in terms of our readers — the man and woman on the street. And every topic, even foreign topics, we try to put in terms of our readers. Because that's what USA TODAY does," he said. ∎

Martin evaluated the four sections as follows:

All the sections have their constituencies. Sports initially was a big draw. Money now has a strong identity and does a terrific job with personal finance. Life has become the Bible for the entertainment industry. Talk show hosts all use it. It outdoes *Variety* at getting stuff together quickly. News is the most difficult to define.

Martin noted that the culture pervading *USA Today* was "special" in a number of important respects:

Early on we were attacked, so we turned our backs and united in an effort to succeed at what we were doing. Adversity created camaraderie. We became a team.

We tend to get younger people whom we can mold—not veteran journalists set in their ways. You have to think about where you *fit* in the paper—*if* you fit. I tell people it is a tremendous opportunity to communicate. But if what you really love is your writing style, maybe this is not the place for you.

The message coming down is that there will be no turf wars. We must have the best *paper*, not the best section. The rewards here are for the spirit of cooperation.

READERSHIP

USA Today's circulation had been running at an average of approximately 1.65 million during the third quarter of 1988. (See Exhibit 19.3 for 1983–1988 circulation data.) According to Simmons[8] studies, the paper's typical reader was male, a frequent traveler, and had a relatively high level of education and income. (See Exhibit 19.4 for additional readership data.) In 1984, Simmons had reported that an average copy of *USA Today* was read by three to four readers, whose incomes and educational levels tended to be higher than those of readers of *Time*, *Newsweek*, and *U.S. News World Report*.

According to Larry Lindquist, senior vice president for circulation, *USA Today*'s circulation during the third quarter of 1988 had consisted approximately of 840,000 single copies; 473,000 subscription copies; 25,000 Classline copies (discounted bulk sales to

---

[8] A supplier of syndicated readership data to many magazines, newspapers, and their advertisers.

	TOTAL AVERAGE PAID*	BULK SALES†
December 30, 1983	1,138,030	41,804
March 30, 1984	1,284,613	48,361
September 30, 1984	1,162,668	84,656
March 30, 1985	1,162,606	113,728
September 29, 1985	1,170,559	182,338
March 30, 1986	1,168,222	248,855
March 30, 1987	1,311,792	232,755
March 30, 1988	1,345,721	285,614

* Excludes bulk sales.
† Represents copies sold at a discount to airlines, hotels, motels, car rental agencies, railroads, and other business concerns.

EXHIBIT 19.3
ABC Circulation Data for 1983–1988

EXHIBIT 19.4
Simmons Data on USA
Today Readership

USA TODAY READERSHIP

	1988	1987
Adults	5,253,000	5,541,000
Male	59%	61%
Female	41%	39%
Median age	40 yrs.	38 yrs.
Median household income	$40,067	$35,904
Median personal income	$24,699	$24,084
Readers per copy	3.19	3.44

GENERAL PROFILE OF USA TODAY ADULT READER
(% Composition)

	1988	1987	Change
Men	59	61	−2
18–24	14	16	−2
25–34	24	26	−2
35–44	22	25	−3
45–54	18	15	+3
55–64	12	12	—
65+	10	7	+3
Women			
25–54	64	66	−2
25–49	57	60	−3
18–34	37	42	−5
18–49	71	76	−5
Baby boomers	36	39	−3
Marital Status			
Married	63	61	+2
Not married	37	39	−2
No. of People in Household			
1	10	12	−2
1–2	41	43	−2
3–4	44	41	+3
5+	14	16	−2
Any Child in Household	41	43	−2
Under 2 yrs. old	7	7	—
2–5 yrs. old	13	14	−1
6–11 yrs. old	19	20	−1
12–17 yrs. old	21	22	−1
Education			
Attended college+	62	57	+5
Graduated college+	34	30	+4
Working Status			
Employed	76	75	+1
Full-time	67	69	−2
Part-time	8	6	+2
Dual-Income Households	35	31	+4
Home Ownership	73	74	−1
Census Geographic Regions			
Northeast	18	23	−5
South	34	33	+1
North Central	32	29	+3
West	16	15	+1

	1988	1987	Change
Live in Top 10 ADIs	19	23	−4
25	50	46	+4
50	68	67	+1
100	86	85	+1
County Size			
A	40	37	+3
B	34	38	−4
C	17	17	—
D	9	8	+1
A & B	74	75	−1

BUSINESS PROFILE OF *USA TODAY* READER
(% Composition)

	1988	1987	Change
Household Income			
$30,000+	67	61	+6
35,000+	58	52	+6
40,000+	50	41	+9
50,000+	35	26	+9
Personal Income			
$25,000+	37	36	+1
30,000+	30	25	+5
35,000+	23	17	+6
Occupation			
Professional/managerial	28	29	−1
Professional/managerial/ technical	31	31	—
Top management	13	14	−1
Top and middle management*	38	34	+4
Involved in business purchases in past year	25	22	+3

CHANGE SHEETS: ADULT READERSHIP COMPARISONS

	1988 Simmons (thousands)	1987 Simmons (thousands)	Change (thousands)	Change (%)
USA Today	5,253	5,541	−288	−5.2
Business Week	6,201	5,608	+593	+10.6
Forbes	3,348	3,376	−28	−.8
Fortune	3,583	3,385	+198	+5.8
Money	5,514	5,849	−335	−5.7
Wall Street Journal	4,603	4,478	+125	+2.8
Newsweek	17,254	17,278	−24	−.1
Sports Illustrated	19,029	17,263	+1766	+10.2
Time	23,476	23,236	+240	+1.0
U.S. News & World Report	10,831	11,760	−929	−7.9

* The ''top and middle management'' figures are based on titles of people who are professional/ managerial/technical or self-employed (10 percent).

EXHIBIT 19.4
(continued)

EXHIBIT 19.5
Data on Readership by
Section and Number of
Issues Read per Publishing
Week

READER PROFILE BY SECTION

This chart reflects section readership by demographics. It reads as follows: 99% of male readers read News.

	News	**Money**	**Sports**	**Life**
Male	99%	90%	89%	90%
Female	96%	81%	61%	95%
Age 25–49	98%	89%	79%	92%
HHI $35,000 +	98%	90%	80%	93%
HHI $50,000	100%	91%	80%	92%
Attended college +	98%	88%	79%	93%
Graduated college +	98%	92%	82%	92%
Professional/ managerial	97%	90%	82%	92%
Top management	98%	92%	81%	91%

Source: ICR Reader Profile Study, April 1986.

ADI*	TOTAL HOUSEHOLDS*	TOTAL SALES (% PENETRATION)		
		1985	**1986**	**1987†**
1. New York	6,870,400	81,258 (1.18)	82,185 (1.20)	87,154 (1.26)
2. Los Angeles	4,611,800	74,225 (1.61)	61,333 (1.33)	62,862 (1.32)
3. Chicago	3,090,100	54,157 (1.75)	56,187 (1.82)	49,269 (1.58)
4. Philadelphia	2,654,600	70,452 (2.65)	65,160 (2.45)	67,716 (2.55)
5. San Francisco	2,104,500	31,866 (1.51)	31,576 (1.50)	30,756 (1.43)
6. Boston	2,047,900	26,464 (1.29)	43,794 (2.14)	43,456 (2.11)
7. Detroit	1,694,800	34,082 (2.01)	30,954 (1.83)	30,006 (1.76)
8. Dallas	1,572,100	23,620 (1.50)	25,128 (1.60)	25,552 (1.58)
9. Washington, D.C.	1,551,300	52,818 (3.40)	69,781 (4.50)	68,269 (4.32)
10. Houston	1,431,600	28,845 (2.01)	20,401 (1.43)	20,599 (1.43)
11. Cleveland	1,428,100	34,012 (2.38)	39,337 (2.75)	37,366 (2.62)
12. Pittsburgh	1,223,500	39,830 (3.26)	45,872 (3.75)	44,630 (3.70)
13. Seattle	1,212,500	27,322 (2.25)	28,876 (2.38)	27,961 (2.25)
14. Atlanta	1,203,000	33,643 (2.80)	41,008 (3.41)	52,299 (4.16)
15. Minneapolis	1,199,300	34,760 (2.90)	38,132 (3.18)	33,939 (2.75)
16. Miami	1,188,600	16,077 (1.35)	18,141 (1.53)	22,182 (1.85)
17. Tampa/St. Petersburg	1,069,800	12,683 (1.19)	13,348 (1.25)	16,634 (1.37)
18. St. Louis	1,059,400	14,124 (1.33)	14,138 (1.33)	19,682 (1.80)
19. Denver	1,203,400	22,954 (2.24)	22,295 (2.18)	20,899 (2.04)
20. Sacramento	967,500	16,573 (1.71)	6,613 (0.68)	4,826 (0.48)

* ADI ranking from *Circulation 87/88*; household figures from *Circulation 87/88*.
† Penetration percent is based on household figures from *Circulation 87/88*, which are not included in the exhibit; therefore, the penetration percentages given for 1987 are based on household figures that vary slightly from the 86/87 ones.

educational institutions); and 318,000 Blue Chip copies (discounted bulk sales to hotels, car rental companies, and airlines, which then distributed them, usually free, to their customers.[9] A 1986 in-house research study of 300 subscribers and 500 single-copy readers found that 98 percent read the News section, 92 percent read Life, 87 percent read Money,

[9] Blue Chip circulation was counted by the ABC, but was shown in a separate category as "bulk sales." Such circulation

MONTH	1984	1985	1986	1987
1	870,099	795,356	736,519	772,061
2	858,347	802,725	733,543	772,568
3	892,113	848,225	772,856	808,926
4	913,878	856,302	782,760	829,937
5	878,189	849,266	757,395	822,678
6	839,866	862,470	732,463	—
7	882,581	851,661	754,533	—
8	910,373	853,662	798,595	—
9	814,483	837,114	816,297	—
10	836,650	822,119	800,068	—
11	861,925	753,812	793,393	—
12	787,548	697,783	757,234	—

Source: Company records.

EXHIBIT 19.7
Average Daily Single-Copy Sales of *USA Today* by Month, 1984–1987

and 80 percent read Sports. The lower readership for Sports was attributed to the fact that a relatively low percentage of women readers (61 percent) read that section. (See Exhibit 19.5 for reader profiles for each section.)

The mid-1988 Simmons figures showed that the newspaper's readership was down slightly, but that current readers had somewhat higher income and occupation levels. Specific areas of increase were in older age groups; three- to four-person households and dual-income households; and college-educated readers. *USA Today* subscribers tended to be older and more affluent than single-copy readers. Readership in the Northeast, as well as in the top ten ADIs,[10] was *down* by 5 percent, while the next fifteen ADIs were *up* over 4 percent. (See Exhibit 19.6 for more detailed readership data for the top twenty ADIs.)

An issue of continuing concern was the "loyalty" of *USA Today*'s readers, given the predominance of single copies in its circulation mix. According to a fall 1987 MRI study, the average number of issues read per publishing week was 3.2; 40 percent of readers claimed to read five out of five issues per week. Moreover, the circulation staff noted that, according to a recent article in *Editor and Publisher*, the majority of all newspapers sold in the United States, especially in central cities, were single copies; single copies were preferred by persons leaving for work early in the morning, before a paper could be delivered to their home; and people who purchased single copies did so because they intended to actually read the paper. (See Exhibit 19.7 for single-copy sales data.)

ORGANIZATION

The *USA Today* organization was headed by Neuharth, who, although seldom physically present in the newspaper's offices during the past several years, continued to oversee editorial policy and to contribute news features.[11] John Quinn, who had been recruited to Gannett's Rochester, New York, papers by Neuharth in 1966, had become chief of

---

tended to be discounted by advertisers, a position with which *USA Today* disagreed strenuously. Advertising sales personnel pointed out that the primary recipients of Blue Chip circulation had excellent demographics, and were a captive audience for the paper in their hotel rooms or airline seats.

[10] *Area of Dominant Influence*—the geographical area covered by a VHF television signal. Because of television's dominance as an advertising medium in many categories, the ADI was increasingly being used as the standard for market definition.

[11] Most notably, "BusCapade," in which he and a team of writers reported from each of the fifty states, and—more recently—"JetCapade," in which similar reports were filed from thirty foreign countries.

the Gannett news division in 1979, and editor-in-chief of *USA Today* in 1983.[12] Noneditorial functions were divided among a managerial triumvirate consisting of Cathie Black, Tom Curley, and Tom Farrell. As publisher, Black was responsible for advertising. Curley, president of *USA Today* since 1986, headed circulation. Tom Farrell, a former banker and member of the Gannett treasury department, was general manager, with responsibility for finance, systems, production, and personnel.

The circulation organization under Curley was structured to provide for both local autonomy and corporate supervision. Twenty-eight *USA Today* general managers (GMs) were located across the United States. In addition to the usual circulation functions of sales, distribution, and collection, they were responsible for financial reporting, systems, and personnel. According to Lindquist:

[12] *USA Today*'s first editor, John Curley, succeeded Neuharth as Gannett CEO in 1986.

Volume II, Number 41
95,257

A NEWSLETTER FOR THE USA TODAY CIRCULATION SALES TEAM.

SUMMER SALES: GO WITH THE READERS . . .

The 1988 tourist season got off to a slow start in June. Delayed school closings and more cautious spending patterns got some of the blame. But recent efforts to turn up new fishing holes are encouraging and show what can be done despite obstacles. Some examples are:

--in Minneapolis, 26 racks were placed at interstate rest stops, selling 805 copies over July 4th; Ben Sahr says that haulers are servicing most of the locations;

--in Oklahoma, Bill Windsor reports selling more than 700 copies at newly opened Grand Lake in northern Oklahoma; Leo Kelly urges everyone to check every lake and campsite;

--in Maryland, the Washington cluster got 19 rack locations adjacent to the Ocean City boardwalk with sales averaging 10 a day from each rack; the cluster compromised with the city and did not put racks on the boardwalk;

--in Maine, Brad Blake got vending machines at Bar Harbor for the first time and is nudging other summer communities for locations; Bob Alcorn added 120 racks in New Hampshire;

--in Colorado, Bill Jones reports earlier delivery times in the southern part of the state due to a press window created by the opening of Salt Lake print site will increase sales by more than 1,000;

--in northern California, San Francisco is aiming to triple sales at Yosemite, which has been restrictive and difficult in the past;

--in southern California, Breakfast Builder sales average more than 1,000 a day for the Los Angeles cluster; the cluster recently sold four new Marriott cafeterias, five Guckenheimer cafeterias and its first Morrison's.

Those breakthroughs are contrasted with this reader report from one other summer area:

"Forty miles to the southwest, USA TODAY is supposed to arrive by noon but often isn't available until 1 p.m. or later, the stores said. And most of the racks are in tough shape -- rusting, dirty, marred face plates . . . . Given the number of big please boats and the high volume of traffic, the area may have some summer potential."

With single copy sales lagging, a little extra summer sweat can make up for a lot. Don't stay in the city wishing. Find a good fishing hole.

The difference between a GM and a circulation manager at a traditional paper is that the GM is the boss, more like the publisher of a local paper. The GM is on the firing line. We can't take a bright editor or advertising manager and just put them into the GM job. They need to know about finance and systems, and have an aptitude for sales. They have to know what works, because they make a lot of decisions.

A typical GM's staff included a controller, a regional marketing manager, three or four circulation managers, a wholesale manager, and up to seven sales representatives. Circulation managers were compensated with both salary and commission. The GMs reported to one of four regional vice presidents, who in turn reported to Lindquist. Lindquist reported to Tom Curley.

USA Today headquarters supplied the local offices with specialists who served as consultants in the areas of marketing, sales, and systems. Carolyn Vesper, vice president

---

TEAM USA PEOPLE . . .

Debbie Lublin to mail/customer service representative/Seattle.

Paul London to circulation director/New Jersey from wholesale manager/Pittsburgh.

Dennis Mountney to circulation manager/Western New York from West Virginia manager/Pittsburgh.

Len Narewski to New Jersey manager/Philadelphia from circulation manager/Western New York.

Eric Snyder to home delivery manager/Philadelphia from the Baltimore Business Journal.

Dick Borghi to telemarketing manager/Phoenix from telemarketing rep.

Tonya Hubbard to accounting supervisor/Los Angeles from receptionist.

Thomas Curley
President
USA TODAY

EXHIBIT 19.8
(continued)

national circulation sales, for example, provided sales support for national accounts. According to Lindquist:

> Carolyn makes calls [for Blue Chip sales] on the corporate headquarters of the airlines, hotels, and car rental companies. But in most cases headquarters can only bless the idea. Local officials make the decisions, so our local people make the sales.

Curley visited each GM office annually for a review session, during which all department managers made presentations. "There is tremendous pressure and it busts the weak ones out in a hurry, but it also develops tremendous managers," Lindquist commented. Lindquist believed that these review meetings were very positive, but he worried about "keeping morale at the current level." (See Exhibit 19.8 for a copy of *Team USA*, the weekly newsletter sent to all members of the circulation staff.)

EDITORIAL

The newsroom was headed by Ron Martin, executive editor, and a staff of six senior editors and seven department editors. The department coordinated its efforts through a series of daily and weekly meetings. "Budget meetings" were attended by the editors of all departments three times daily: at 7:30 A.M., 3.00 P.M., and 5:00 P.M. At each meeting the content and front page for each section were reviewed. According to Martin, "We plan in more detail and further ahead than any other paper. To avoid overlap and duplication we must compare notes." Martin described the planning process at *USA Today* as follows:

> The research staff puts together a "universal calendar," which includes all annual events we may want to cover, i.e., everything we know will happen in the future. Each department develops a week-by-week plan for coverage and what the mix should be. At the weekly editors' lunch we preview the next week in detail. Will we change the cover story for next Wednesday's Money section? What color material will we need—a photo or graphics?

At the 9:30 A.M. daily budget meeting all stories were reviewed and major adjustments were made. By the 3:00 P.M. meeting, that day's content was relatively fixed and the discussion served primarily to share information and to keep all editors apprised of what would be featured in other parts of the paper. At one three o'clock budget meeting, for example, each editor summarized the content of his or her section. Then Martin asked questions about a page 1 story on "Back to School" and another story in the Life section. He also questioned the extensive coverage of a recent accident at a European air show (to which another editor responded that air shows were "a big way of life in Europe, and also in parts of the U.S., like around Cleveland").

These meetings also gave the editors an opportunity to share in-house news, such as that the previous Friday's paper was the third highest ever in single-copy sales; that the Yellowstone fires were costing $1,200 per day in lost sales; and that advertising for the eighth period was over budget.

Despite the extensive planning,[13] Martin noted:

> We can try to plan, but we are still in the news business. News is what sells. We have a Page 1 cover story ready, but if a terrific news story breaks, we throw it out or move it. Then we really scramble.

---

[13] According to Martin, transmission via satellites (which processed one page at a time), thirty-three print sites, and heavy use of color made it necessary to have unusually elaborate and formalized planning processes.

EXHIBIT 19.9
A Day in the Life of *USA Today*
Reprinted with permission of USA Today.

405

Martin added that the communication process extended to all levels and areas of the organization, with a resulting benefit to team effort:

> At traditional papers, [noneditorial] executives don't come to news budget meetings. Here we talk to each other all the time. We all are committed 100% to making this work. We have a lot invested. *I* know how tough it is to sell an ad, to have single copy be the bulk of your circulation. So I want to help any way I can.

An institutionalized means of striving for editorial excellence was the monthly "McNugget Awards" ceremony. Prompted by the "McPaper" criticism, one of the senior editors instituted a contest for concise, fact-filled articles. Monthly awards of $100 were given to copy and graphics staff who, in Tom Curley's words, "do little things well." In addition, larger annual awards (thirty-four staff members shared $23,000 in 1988) were given for especially noteworthy accomplishments.

Gary Hook, news operations manager, served as a liaison between the news departments, production operations, circulation, and marketing. He attended all news meetings and maintained continual communication with personnel in the field. When he started his current job, Hook undertook to educate himself about the production process, visiting numerous print sites. He then studied marketing and circulation. According to Hook, "I am one of the few people who understands how the whole operation works, what pieces fit together, who the people are with the information." (See Exhibit 19.9 for a schematic rendering of "A Day in the Life of *USA Today.*")

Hook went on to describe his role in the production process:

> If the news side has a special need, I work out the logistics with production. The sports department has tremendous needs for the Summer Olympics, for example. We broke the whole [Olympics] schedule down day-by-day and put it together with our schedule. Next we took the entire Olympics roster and broke it down by state, so marketing can tailor their efforts to certain areas. South Dakota, for example, is sending two wrestlers. You can be sure that we will promote that locally!
>
> *USA Today* is a captive of time. It takes an average of five minutes to transmit a page. The presses begin at 11:45 P.M. We work back from there. Money is first off the floor, then Life, News, Sports.
>
> We know where we stand at any point in time, with respect to print sites and truck routes. Although we seldom do (we like to have the paper be the same all over the country), if some major news breaks in Macon, Georgia, we can get the event into the papers for that area.
>
> After each news meeting I send a hot line to the field, telling them about special features and what the front page will look like above the fold. One day we had a picture of Hugh Hefner and his financée—we knew that would sell papers. A story in Money on local ad agencies sold 500 extra copies in the Minneapolis market. . . .
>
> One of the best things about this paper is that it ploughs new ground. Change has been the only constant. Now I fear that a complacency may set in, that people will begin to say, "This is how we do things."

ADVERTISING

Cathie Black, *USA Today*'s publisher, had been recruited by Neuharth in 1983 to establish the newspaper as a medium for national advertisers. A former publisher of *MS.* and *New York* magazines, Black was experienced both with start-up publications and the New York advertising community.

Black said that advertising sales would total over $150 million in 1988. "We have carved out quite a niche in five years," she commented.

We have positioned *USA Today* as a unique medium. It is like a daily newsweekly, so we target those who advertise in *Business Week*, *Time*, and *Fortune*. We have stressed the vitality and the excitement of the format, umbrella coverage, and national penetration. We believe that we have the best of both worlds—the immediacy of a daily paper and the color of a weekly.

The top categories of advertisers included automobile manufacturers, airlines, hotel chains, computers, and financial services:

GM is our number one advertiser, with over 250 pages per year. Every car manufacturer in the country uses *USA Today*—they like the size of the audience, the reader profile, and the dynamic 4-color reproductions. IBM is the third or fourth largest advertiser. It sets a high-quality tone. In retailing we get Sears, K-Mart, and a surprise, Toys-R-Us. They will do over 70 pages in 1988. They like the prestige of the publication, and the fact that we have an audience comprised of both men and women. They track the audience very carefully and they find that it works.

Key criticisms from media buyers were that *USA Today* had become stale and that it had a much shorter shelf life than the newsweeklies with which it compared itself. A media director from DDB Needham commented, ''Advertisers use it as an overlay. You would never buy *USA Today* to supplant your more targeted media buys.'' Another agency executive claimed to find nothing unique about the publication, no ''niche.'' There was a general tendency among media buyers to discount the Blue Chip portion of circulation— the nearly 318,000 readers who received the paper free each day.

Media buyers were frequently skeptical of the paper's comparison of itself to magazines, claiming that paid circulation was much larger for newsweeklies and that magazines were read more thoroughly. Black disagreed:

We believe that's old thinking, but it will take time to counter that impression. Some people think it's expensive for one day—we say it's high quality exposure. During meetings with advertisers we try to create an open environment where they will at least spend some time listening. We say, ''Don't drop *Time* and *Fortune*, just give us a little piece of that.''

We have *size* going for us. One technique we use is to blow up magazine ads and show them what they look like *USA Today*-size.

Black explained that *USA Today* had not been successful in selling packaged-goods advertisers like Gillette and General Mills because they didn't need an upscale audience. Bonus sections, such as the twenty-four special sections during the 1988 Summer Olympics, offered a custom-made vehicle for certain advertisers. Apparel was a developing category, and *USA Today* carried a lot of sport shoe advertising. Black claimed that New York– based advertisers were especially hard to sell!

They think if a publication isn't the *Times* or the *Journal*, it isn't any good. If a company is in another city, people have no trouble with *USA Today*.

Black questioned the conventional wisdom concerning ''magic numbers'':

What happens when we reach 2 million circulation? Nothing. There is no magic number at which a Madison Avenue agency will buy. It is more important to show steady growth. We still have a lot of room to raise ad rates. The flags are all pointing in the right direction. There are no real trouble spots. The question is, can we grow enough to support costs? *USA Today* didn't start out as an advertising vehicle—it has always been for the reader.

General Manager Tom Farrell emphasized the importance of advertising to *USA Today* profitability:

We have two sources of revenue: advertising and circulation. With circulation revenue our goal is to cover distribution, marketing, and administrative expenses. And we do. We would also like to cover as much of printing and newsprint costs as we can. But with 25 pages of news and 12 to 30 pages of advertising, advertising must bear its share of the burden. We must keep the circulation base growing so we can raise the rates. Right now, the mix is 50/50; in traditional daily newspapers, advertising is at least 70% of revenue.

Why is *USA Today* so out of whack? Because we are in a bind that will take time to get out of. We started out with package deals, and that's a tough habit to break. As we have grown in circulation, we have jumped the price, but we are limited by what the traffic will bear.

There is a delicate balance between closing the gap and pricing ourselves so high that we lose volume. And there is the issue of shelf life. The weeklies are around longer, and they make deals that we don't. We can't make deals because we have to make money.

In the beginning, *USA Today* advertising had been consciously priced lower than the newsweeklies and the *Wall Street Journal*. During the past six years, the new paper's advertising rates had risen, both as a function of growing circulation and through a series of eight increases in CPMs (cost per thousand readers). By 1988, *USA Today*'s CPMs were higher than *Time*'s (on a page-for-page basis), but still lower than the *Wall Street Journal*'s.

Advertising revenue had increased only slightly during the first quarter of 1988 because of downturns in financial services and classified advertising. In the first six months of 1988, overall ad pages were down 4 percent, broken down by category as follows: travel—up 29 percent; computers—up 10 percent; tobacco—up 119 percent; automotive—down 2 percent; financial services—down 67 percent; classified—down 35 percent; and retail—down 18 percent.

According to a Wall Street source, "the disappointing [financial services] advertising results are mainly due to lost commitments from Shearson, Fidelity, and American Express." Newspapers throughout the United States were experiencing "soft" retail advertising in 1988, while the newsweeklies, which depended largely on national packaged goods, automotive, and travel advertising, were having, at best, a "flat" year.

Black attributed the loss of classified revenue to the disruption caused by the relocation of the department from New York to *USA Today* headquarters in Rosslyn, Virginia:

We should have been in Rosslyn from the start, rather than at 54th and Madison at $55 per square foot. When we moved we had 100% staff turnover.

EXHIBIT 19.10
Circulation, Subscription
Cost, and Advertising Rates
for *USA Today*, *Wall Street
Journal*, and Competing
Newsweeklies

PUBLICATION	CIRCULATION*	SUBSCRIPTION COST/YEAR	ADVERTISING RATE†	CIRCULATION CPM‡
USA Today	1,650,000	$130.00	$ 54,000	$32.73
Time	4,600,000	58.24	120,130	26.12
U.S. News	2,360,000	39.95	71,080	30.12
Business Week	870,000	39.95	52,980	60.90
Fortune	750,000	47.97	43,380	57.84
Newsweek	3,300,000	41.08	91,945	27.86
Wall Street Journal	2,000,000	119.00	89,740§	44.87

* 1988; approximate.
† Per four-color page.
‡ Advertising cost per thousand circulation.
§ Black-and-white page.
Source: Company records.

	USA TODAY	TIME	NEWSWEEK	U.S. NEWS & WORLD REPORT	BUSINESS WEEK	TOTAL	USA TODAY AS % OF TOTAL
Advertising Pages							
1987	4,068	2,360	2,564	1,700	4,708	15,247	25.7%
1986	3,485	2,575	2,544	1,666	3,894	14,054	24.0
1985	3,375	2,696	2,713	1,770	4,216	14,770	22.0
1984	2,344E	2,817	3,003	1,758	4,972	14,894	15.7
1983	1,411E	2,699	2,958	1,785	4,644	13,497	10.5
Year-to-Year Changes							
1987	+16.7%	−8.3%	+0.8%	+2.0%	+20.9%		
1986	+3.3	−4.5	−6.2	−5.9	−7.6		
1985	+44.0	−4.3	−9.7	+0.7	−15.2		
1984	+66.1	+4.4	+1.5	−1.5	+7.1		
1983	NM	+2.2	+3.3	+2.6	+7.4		
Advertising Revenue							
1987	$120	$328.8	$239.3	$106.1	$217.5	$1,011.7	11.9%
1986	89	344.8	238.9	101.1	166.6	940.4	9.5
1985	64	346.6	247.1	102.6	169.1	929.4	6.9
1984	38	335.6	247.1	101.5	184.8	907.0	4.2
1983	16	298.6	218.7	93.9	156.5	783.7	2.0
Year-to-Year Changes							
1987	+34.8%	−4.6%	+0.2%	+4.9%	+30.6%		
1986	+39.1	−0.5	−3.3	−1.5	−1.5		
1985	+68.4	+3.3	Unch	+1.1	−8.5		
1984	+137.5	+12.4	+13.0	+8.1	+18.1		
1983	NM	+16.5	+12.0	+12.0	+16.8		

Note: E = estimate; NM = not material.
Source: Wall Street research.

★ **PROFILE**

USA TODAY . . .
The Nation's Newspaper

Launched on September 15, 1982 by Gannett Co., Inc., USA TODAY is the fastest-growing new newspaper ever. Average daily paid circulation has reached 1.65 million, and syndicated research shows that USA TODAY now delivers an audience of more than 5.5 million*, making it the No. 1 newspaper in the USA.

Distributed nationally . . .
Through home and office subscriptions . . . at newsstands and vending machines . . . plus Blue Chip sales to airlines, hotels, rental car and other hospitality companies.

And internationally . . .
To readers in Europe, the Middle East, Asia and the Pacific. Transmitted via satellite and printed in Switzerland, Hong Kong and Singapore, USA TODAY International provides overseas readers with colorful news of the USA as only USA TODAY can.

Four full-color sections . . .
News, Money, Sports and Life . . . each with four-color editorial and four-color advertising availabilities for spreads, half-spreads and full pages.

Unique discounts . . .
Volume discounts starting at 10% for 6 pages . . . plus a special Multiple Insertion Discount program.

An affluent, educated audience . . .
Measured by Simmons, MRI and Monroe Mendelsohn . . . comparable to or better than the best of the newsweeklies.

*Source: SMRB 1987

Age 25-49	% Comp
USA TODAY	60%
Time	58
Sports Illustrated	57
Newsweek	56
U.S. Population	50

HHI $50,000+	% Comp
USA TODAY	26%
Newsweek	28
Time	26
Sports Illustrated	22
U.S. Population	15

Attended/Graduated College+	% Comp
USA TODAY	57%
Newsweek	60
Time	56
Sports Illustrated	50
U.S. Population	36

Professional/Managerial	% Comp
USA TODAY	29%
Newsweek	30
Time	26
Sports Illustrated	22
U.S. Population	16

Source: SMRB 1987

EXHIBIT 19.12
(continued)

RATES

- USA TODAY's Domestic edition is distributed primarily in the 50 states and Canada.

- USA TODAY International publishes a European edition and an Asian edition, each of which can be purchased separately. For International edition rates for Domestic edition advertisers and further information, see pages 28–30.

- USA TODAY Worldwide combines the Domestic edition and International editions at a special rate savings.

To qualify for Worldwide rates, advertisements must be the same size and coloration in both the Domestic and International editions, but need not be scheduled for the same day.

NOTE: For Domestic and Worldwide advertisements, four-color and spot-color are available only in spreads, horizontal half-spreads and full pages.

Due to overseas holidays and publishing schedules, advertisements placed in USA TODAY Worldwide may occasionally run on different days in the Domestic and International editions. USA TODAY cannot accommodate bleed advertising or advertising using metallic inks.

Spreads
26⅝ x 20¾ in.

	Circulation	Four-Color	Spot-Color	Black & White
Domestic	1,650,000	$103,276	$95,330	$79,442
Worldwide	1,685,000	$112,683	$103,192	$85,184

Horizontal Half-Spreads
26⅝ x 10½ in.

	Circulation	Four-Color	Spot-Color	Black & White
Domestic	1,650,000	$75,258	$62,715	$50,172
Worldwide	1,685,000	81,103	67,907	54,070

Full Pages
13 x 20¾ in.

	Circulation	Four-Color	Spot-Color	Black & White
Domestic	1,650,000	$54,356	$50,175	$41,812
Worldwide	1,685,000	59,644	54,604	45,059

CIRCULATION DISTRIBUTION

For a guide to the coverage of USA TODAY's 26 domestic markets for copy splits and dealer listings, please refer to the map inside.

ADI DISTRIBUTION

USA TODAY circulates domestically in all of the Top 100 ADI markets. 95% of USA TODAY's total circulation is distributed in the Top 100 ADI's.

COPY SPLITS

A. USA TODAY's Domestic edition can accommodate up to 26 copy splits for national advertisements. These must be the same size, on the same page, and in the same color (all four-color, all spot-color, all black & white). For copy-split market availabilities, please refer to the list on page 18.

B. USA TODAY International offers copy splitting for its European and Asian editions. Contact your advertising sales representative for full details.

C. Copy splits are available on all USA TODAY ad sizes (ROP), Bonus Sections and Special Advertising Sections.

D. Charges (applied to first insertion only):
   1. Four- and Spot-Color: $300 per change
   2. Black & White: $250 per change
   with no additional charges for repeated materials, provided there are no changes in copy.

DEALER LISTINGS

A. Material for dealer listings can be supplied camera-ready or can be typeset by USA TODAY.

B. Copy changes are available from the printing sites serving these markets:

Atlanta	Nashville
Boston	New Orleans
Charlotte	New York Metro Area
Chicago	North Central Florida
Cincinnati	Philadelphia
Cleveland	Phoenix
Dallas	Pittsburgh
Denver	San Francisco
Detroit	Seattle
Houston	Southern Florida
Kansas City	St. Louis
Los Angeles	Washington/Baltimore
Minneapolis	Western New York

C. For deadlines on copy-split and dealer-listing advertising materials, please refer to page 12.

D. Charges for typesetting will be based on volume and complexity.

BONUS SECTIONS

USA TODAY Bonus Sections are freestanding fifth sections of the newspaper written by USA TODAY editors on a single topic of appeal to readers.

Rates

Circulation	Unit	Cost
1,650,000	Center Spread	$119,583
	Back Page	68,760
	Page 4/C	59,792
	Page 2/C	55,193
	Page B/W	45,993
	⅔ Page	36,795
	½ Page	27,595
	⅓ Page	21,461
	¼ Page	17,667
	⅙ Page	11,779
	⅛ Page	9,717

For information on Worldwide Bonus Section rates, please contact your advertising sales representative.

Discounts

A. Volume
Advertisers who run volume in Bonus Sections within a contract year earn the following discounts:
- 3-4 Bonus Section pages = 10%
- 5-7 Bonus Section pages = 15%
- 8+ Bonus Section pages = 25%

B. Frequency/Small Space (⅓-page or smaller)
- 4-5 Insertions = 5%
- 6-7 Insertions = 7%
- 8+ Insertions = 9%

> **NOTE:** Bonus Section advertising contributes to but does not earn USA TODAY volume discounts.

Deadlines

Bonus Section deadlines differ from ROP deadlines. Contact your advertising sales representative for details.

For more information, please contact:
Manager, Bonus Sections
USA TODAY
535 Madison Avenue, 29th Floor
New York, NY 10022
(212) 715-5573

1988 CALENDAR

Titles	Issue dates	Closing dates
Stock Market Round-Up	January 4	Closed
NFL Playoffs	January 8	Closed
Super Bowl XXII	January 29	Closed
Tax Guide	February 1	Closed
Autos '88	February 8	Closed
Winter Games Preview	February 12	Closed
10 Winter Games Sections	February 15-26	Closed
Winter Games Wrap-Up	February 29	Closed
Business Travel	March 7	February 22
NCAA Playoffs	March 14	March 3
European Travel	March 21	March 7
NCAA Final Four	April 1 (Friday)	March 17
Baseball '88	April 4	March 21
Golf	April 7 (Thursday)	March 24
Camera & Video	May 2	April 18
Small Business	May 9	April 25
Summer Travel	May 16	May 2
Motor Racing	May 27 (Friday)	May 18
New Office	June 6	May 20
Weekend Getaway	June 13	May 27
Baseball All-Star Game	July 11	June 30
Democratic National Convention	July 15 (Friday)	June 29
Republican National Convention	August 12 (Friday)	July 28
College Football	August 26 (Friday)	August 17
NFL Preview	September 2 (Friday)	August 24
Summer Games Preview	September 16	August 30
Summer Games	September 19	September 2
Summer Games	September 20	September 6
Summer Games	September 21	September 7
Summer Games	September 22	September 8
Summer Games	September 23	September 9
Summer Games	September 26	September 12
Summer Games	September 27	September 13
Summer Games	September 28	September 14
Summer Games	September 29	September 15
Summer Games	September 30	September 16
Summer Games Wrap Up	October 3	September 19
Baseball Playoffs	October 4	September 23
World Series	October 14 (Friday)	October 4
Personal Finance	October 17	September 30
Business Travel	October 24	October 7
Election Preview	November 4	October 17
College Basketball	November 11 (Friday)	November 2
Winter Travel	November 14	October 31
Bowl Games	December 30 (Friday)	December 12
NFL Playoffs (1989)	January 6 (Friday)	December 27
Super Bowl XXIII (1989)	January 20 (Friday)	January 11

> **NOTE:** All dates subject to change. All Bonus Sections run on Mondays except the Summer Games sections or where indicated.

EXHIBIT 19.13
Page from *USA Today* 1988 Rate Brochure on Bonus Sections

Our biggest classified users are real estate; mail order; condo rental; franchises; and ads for adoption and missing children. Classified could account for 12% to 20% of our business.

(See Exhibit 19.10 for circulation, subscription prices, and advertising rates for competing publications; Exhibit 19.11 for advertising pages and market share for *USA Today* and competing publications for the years 1983–1987; Exhibit 19.12 for *USA Today* rates and copy specifications; and Exhibit 19.13 for promotional material on the 1988 bonus sections.)

CIRCULATION

With daily volume now running at above 1.8 million papers, more than 900,000 single-copy sales on the average day, and nationwide distribution, the circulation function at *USA Today* was far more complex—and expensive—than at most traditional newspapers. Despite extensive prelaunch planning, there had been a number of major operational problems. Early launches in large eastern cities (e.g., New York and Philadelphia) were met by violent opposition to the appearance of hundreds of *USA Today* boxes; in Philadelphia, for example, members of the Teamsters Union blew up racks and barricaded delivery trucks. Original distribution plans had assumed there would be only single-copy

411

sales. When this decision was reversed and home delivery was begun in 1983, an inadequate computer system resulted in extensive billing and delivery errors. As distribution expanded to include hotels, airlines, offices, and educational institutions, circulation systems began to ''come unglued.'' Subsequent problems included a lack of sales records, ''turf wars'' between *USA Today* and other Gannett newspapers, theft, unclear sales goals, and a high rate of returns.

Phil Gialanella, *USA Today*'s first president (and head of circulation), was quoted in *The Making of McPaper* as explaining that ''fourteen launches in twenty-nine weeks,'' late press times, and irregular deliveries had ''a devastating effect on sales and costs.'' Tom Curley, who became president in March 1986, was the sixth head of the circulation function in the first four years of the newspaper's existence.

In the third quarter of 1988, *USA Today*'s circulation had been broken down approximately as follows:

	COPIES	%
Single copy	840,000	50.7
Home delivery		
Carrier	232,000	14.0
Mail	241,000	14.6
Blue Chip	318,000	19.2
Classline	25,000	1.5
	1,656,000	

The primary promotional tools for single-copy sales were the 130,000 *USA Today* blue-and-white vending boxes and each day's front page ''above the fold.'' Both home delivery and single-copy sales were supported by a media advertising budget of $2.25 million (including traded space, but not in-paper promotions) in 1988.

Approximately 900,000 subscription orders were processed annually, including new orders and renewals. Of these, approximately one-third were ''agency orders,'' received through a clearing house;[14] one-third resulted from telemarketing campaigns; and one-third were generated by various local and national promotions. In the annual ''All Star Game'' promotion, for example, subscription coupons were distributed with ballots at major sports events, and fans used the *USA Today* ballots to vote for an ''All Star'' team. This promotion, which generated 22,000 orders in 1988, was essentially a barter arrangement with major league baseball, *USA Today* taking responsibility for distribution of ballots in return for an outstanding promotional opportunity.

According to Curley, ''cost per order'' and retention rates varied markedly among sources of new subscriptions:

	COST PER ORDER	RETENTION RATE (after 85 days)
Agency orders	$20	22%
Telemarketing	$12	42%
Promotions	$22	48%

[14] Clearing houses solicited subscriptions for many types of publications through a variety of methods, most notably direct-mail sweepstakes. Under ABC regulations, prices could be discounted up to 50 percent without the resulting sale losing ''paid'' status.

Farrell pointed out that subscription sales represented the newspaper's largest cost after newsprint and distribution. Early problems had included duplication of selling efforts and unpaid-for subscriptions, but experience had improved efficiency:

> As we have become more prominent we have been able to work barter deals. We run subscription offers on Cable TV in exchange for a page of advertising, for example, and the "All Star" subscription offer costs us next to nothing. We are also reducing the number of reminder notices we send out, and the grace period for renewals.

The cost of distribution varied from city to city. With the current pressing need to cut costs, *USA Today* management was carefully evaluating marketing strategy, distribution systems, and customer service. According to Farrell:

> In the early days we spent so much time launching new markets we didn't look back. Our hope in selecting major markets was to gain greater penetration in a smaller geographic area. But that hasn't proved to be the case.

Lindquist summarized the uniqueness of the *USA Today* circulation effort as follows:

> We must cover a staggering amount of territory: 130,000 racks, 70,000 stands, 500,000 subscribers. In most traditional papers the circulation mission is to increase volume. Here we must do that *and* cut expenses. Can we charge more in Alaska and Hawaii because it costs more to freight it? Is there a way to reduce pilferage from rack sales?

USA Today's distinctive blue-and-white TV-shaped newsracks required $1.25 million for maintenance and refurbishing per year. Single-copy sales were by far the most profitable (two copies per day paid for a box), while home delivery was the most expensive method of distribution. Bulk-mailed newspapers (51 percent of subscriptions) cost 16 cents per copy in postage, and had to be presorted, bundled, and delivered to the post office by 2:00 A.M. for same-day delivery. Home delivery was accomplished either by an adult carrier, with billing by mail, or by wholesalers who performed both distribution and billing.

Lindquist explained why home delivery was often poorly executed: "A normal paper has 30 to 50 subscribers per 100 homes, but with *USA Today* we may have only 3 or 4 out of the same 100. This makes it awfully tough (and expensive) to deliver."

Farrell said that the nature of the distribution system often depended on the local labor situation and on consumer preferences. "The South is more of a rack environment," he noted, "while Western cities tend to be 'drive cities' where people commute long distances and have different purchase patterns. We take it market by market."

> We have never advocated replacing the local daily, so we must find people who need a second paper. Our ideal reader is someone who is mobile. If there were fifty more airports in this country we'd have it made.
>
> Our best markets have a highly concentrated population of transient people; a strong economy; and a relatively high income and education level. The *worst* market would be Denver: the population is very spread out, they have a strong allegiance to the local papers, and distribution is primarily home delivery—which is very difficult, due to distance and climate. On the other hand, Washington is an ideal market, except for the traffic.

Farrell explained that considerable effort had been spent "trying to refine rack distribution":

> The highest yielding copy is the rack copy. Forty-five cents comes back to us, compared to an average yield of thirty-eight cents on subscription copies and twenty-six cents on Blue

Chip copies.[15] So how many copies do we put in a rack? Our goal is to get our returns from racks, newsstands, and retail outlets down to 27%, but we don't want to miss sales.

(By way of comparison, one industry observer estimated return rates in Southern California of 40 percent for *USA Today*, 15 percent for the *Los Angeles Times*, and 8 percent for typical local papers.)

Curley was adamant about the need to improve the effectiveness and efficiency of the circulation function. In the draft of a speech he intended to deliver at an upcoming management meeting, he noted that newsprint and printing costs would have increased by about $25 million (or 25 percent) between 1986 and 1989, and went on to ask:

> Can we cut returns by 1% below budget, saving $500,000? Can we cut $1 off [our cost per start] and save $400,000? Can we increase voluntary [i.e., unsolicited] starts by 10%, generating $500,000? Can we automate office functions, reducing one person in each office, and moving toward a paper-less circulation department, saving $1 million? Do we need 28 repetitive financial staffs? Do we have the ability to hire, supervise and train 29 independent customer service centers, let alone afford them?

CONCLUSION

To become profitable, or even to just break even, Curley and his staff believed that *USA Today* would have to achieve greater market penetration without a proportional increase in sales and distribution costs.

Curley had established the goal of 2 million circulation by 1991. He expected to achieve this goal through major increases in home- and office-delivered subscriptions and modest growth in single-copy sales. Over time, he expected the proportion of Blue Chip sales to decrease slightly.

One Wall Street analyst argued that for *USA Today* to go very far beyond the break-even point would require substantial additional investment, which he believed would be slow in coming. *USA Today* supporters countered that successful weekly magazines had taken much longer to become profitable—ten years for *Sports Illustrated* and eight for *Money*, for example.

Advertising agency executives, accustomed to the newsweeklies, continued to stress the publication's "limited shelf life" and to wonder whether the *USA Today* audience was either consistent or desirable for advertisers.

As he considered his mandate to "sell more papers with less money," Curley couldn't help but muse, "What got us where we are won't get us where we need to be."

QUESTIONS FOR DISCUSSION

1. How would you characterize the market for editorial and advertising information in the United States? How is this market segmented? How are various media (including "typical" daily and Sunday newspapers) positioned in this market?

2. What are the essential elements in *USA Today*'s marketing strategy? Who are the target customers (readers and advertisers) for this product? What is its intended

---

[15] *USA Today* had been launched at a price of 25 cents, which was typical for a metropolitan newspaper at that time. Its single-copy price had been raised to 50 cents in August 1985. (Most metropolitan papers continued to be priced at 25 to 35 cents in late 1988.) With 10 percent "shrinkage" (i.e., missing copies), the maximum permitted by ABC, the average yield from single-copy sales was 45 cents per copy.

positioning? What is the core benefit proposition? Specifically, what are the strategic roles of the product (editorial and advertising content), communications (advertising, display, and promotion), distribution, customer service, and pricing? How have these strategic dimensions evolved over time?

3. What do you consider to be *USA Today*'s primary strategic challenges at the time of the case? How should the paper go about meeting these challenges?

4. As the new CEO of Gannett, John Curley (not the *Tom* Curley who figures so prominently in the case), what would be your long-term strategy for *USA Today*? What level of additional resources over what time period would you be willing to commit to this product? What strategic goals would you set?

20
SUN MICROSYSTEMS

Developed in Collaboration with Kathy L. Kessel-Hunter[1]

In late April 1988, Ed Zander, vice president corporate marketing of Sun Microsystems, was trying to decide what his position should be on several critical strategic issues currently facing the corporation. Since its founding in 1982, Sun had experienced considerable success, achieving sales of $537 million and earnings of $36 million in fiscal 1987 (see Exhibit 20.1). Its success had largely come about as a result of the explosive growth of the ''workstation'' market, where the overwhelming bulk of Sun's business was concentrated. The attractiveness of this industry, in combination with massive strides in technology, had recently led to a significant blurring of boundaries between segments of the computer market, with important implications for Sun. Most significantly, it meant that Sun's ''turf'' would now be increasingly vulnerable to attacks from vendors traditionally focused above (e.g., DEC, moving down from minicomputers) and below (e.g., IBM and Apple moving up from personal computers); and that Sun would increasingly have to market its products to new segments of customers through new marketing approaches and channels.

As a member of senior management, Zander had been asked to provide ''Marketing's'' input into the resolution of Sun's strategic dilemma. From a technology point of view, it seemed probable that Sun would have the capability to develop products targeted at any of the product/market segments under consideration. While it seemed unlikely that Sun would be able to match the manufacturing cost economies of larger competitors such as DEC and IBM, it was not expected that this deficiency would make a crucial difference in the marketplace. The critical issue, management believed, was whether Sun had, or could acquire, the image, skills, infrastructure, and resources necessary to compete with companies such as Apple, DEC, and IBM, either on its own turf or in their traditional markets. What, in fact, were Sun's real alternatives? And how should it select among them?

---

[1] This case is largely based on and incorporates considerable material from Ms. Kessel-Hunter's M.I.T. M.S. thesis (1988), which should be consulted for specific sources and references. Certain information in this case has been disguised or simplified.

EXHIBIT 20.1
Sun Financial Statements

	1987	1986	1985	1984	1983
YEAR ENDED JUNE 30					
		(Dollars in 000's except per share)			
Net Revenues	$537,537	$210,126	$115,249	$38,860	$8,657
Costs and expenses:					
Cost of sales	$272,722	$101,983	$ 61,697	$21,309	$4,486
R&D	$ 69,578	$ 31,041	$ 15,193	$ 4,813	$1,868
Selling, general and admin.	$126,933	$ 57,257	$ 24,103	$ 9,022	$1,715
Total costs & exp.	$469,233	$190,281	$100,993	$35,144	$8,069
Operating income	$ 68,304	$ 19,845	$ 14,256	$ 3,716	$ 588
Interest income	$ 834	$ 369	($14)	$ 286	$ 136
Income before taxes	$ 69,138	$ 20,214	$ 14,242	$ 4,002	$ 724
Provision for taxes	$ 32,840	$ 9,025	$ 5,709	$ 1,344	$ 70
Net income	$ 36,298	$ 11,189	$ 8,533	$ 2,658	$ 654
Net income/share	$ 1.11	$ 0.42	$ 0.36	$ 0.13	$ 0.04
ASSETS					
Current Assets:					
Cash & temporary investments	$216,494	$ 49,681	$ 29,552	$ 3,513	$1,579
Accounts receivable	$ 98,277	$ 40,380	$ 16,464	$11,653	$2,515
Inventories	$ 66,145	$ 33,611	$ 15,726	$ 8,051	$1,205
Other current assets	$ 15,848	$ 3,835	$ 1,269	$ 511	$ 59
Total current assets	$396,764	$127,507	$ 63,011	$23,728	$5,358
Net property & equip.	$ 99,870	$ 45,546	$ 16,434	$ 5,644	$2,014
Spare parts and other assets	$ 27,328	$ 9,329	$ 4,724	$ 1,820	$ 381
	$523,962	$182,382	$ 84,169	$31,192	$7,733
LIABILITIES AND STOCKHOLDERS' EQUITY					
Current liabilities:					
Notes payable	$ 36,212	$ 14,960	$ 4,362	$ 900	
Accounts payable	$ 62,995	$ 29,761	$ 8,619	$ 5,112	$1,571
Accrued liabilities	$ 31,183	$ 9,129	$ 3,928	$ 997	$ 383
Other current liabilities	$ 25,003	$ 13,545	$ 10,753	$ 1,852	$ 181
Total current liab.	$155,393	$ 67,395	$ 27,662	$ 8,861	$2,135
Long-term debt	$127,444	$ 4,481	$ 6,514	$ 3,421	$ 749
Other liabilities	$ 391	$ 2,159	$ 1,615		
Stockholders' equity	$240,734	$108,347	$ 48,378	$18,910	$4,849
	$523,962	$182,382	$ 84,169	$31,192	$7,733

Source: 1987 Annual Report.

SUN MICROSYSTEMS

Sun had been a classic Silicon Valley start-up in 1982, when its twenty-seven-year-old co-founders, Andy Bechtolscheim and Vin Kholsa, recruited Stanford Business School classmate Scott McNealy and Berkeley University UNIX[2] guru Bill Joy to form the

---

[2] The UNIX operating system had initially been developed at AT&T's Bell Labs, which had received an overwhelming response when it offered inexpensive licensing agreements to universities and research laboratories (i.e., $300, rather than thousands of

EXHIBIT 20.2
**Sun's Workstation Installed
Base**
Source: Sun's VAR Program Bulletin.

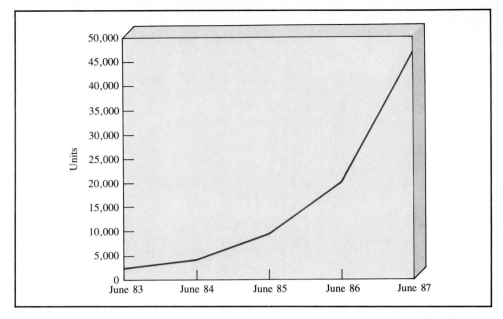

company. Sun's goal was to stake out a position in the emerging engineering workstation market, which had been pioneered by Massachusetts-based Apollo Computer in 1980.[3] (An engineering workstation was a medium-sized computer system designed specifically for engineering functions such as product design and software development.) Apollo had been highly successful, but Sun's founders believed that they had a better approach. In particular, they intended to develop and market systems characterized by "open architecture" and adherence to industry standards. In essence, Sun's founders believed that the engineering market would prefer high-function systems capable of utilizing both proprietary and off-the-shelf software created by third-party developers to "closed" architecture, proprietary systems such as those marketed by Apollo.

As an early entrant into the burgeoning workstation market, Sun had experienced enormous success. Between 1982 and the end of 1987, Sun's shipments had increased by at least 50 percent every six months (see Exhibit 20.2). With calendar 1987 sales of $754 million, Sun had surpassed Apollo (it had already passed Apollo in earnings in 1985) and appeared to be the clear U.S. workstation leader in both shipments and installed base. (DEC, however, was expected to surpass Sun in worldwide installed base by the end of 1988.) During the first quarter of 1988, Sun had reported an 81 percent gain in revenue over the same period a year earlier, but earnings (held down by rising prices for scarce memory chips) had grown only 40 percent.

THE WORKSTATION INDUSTRY

The workstation industry began to take off in 1980 when Apollo introduced its so-called engineering workstation. Over time, the prefix "engineering" was dropped from the product's name, as the category came to be defined by functionality rather than by ap-

---

dollars for competitive operating systems such as DEC's VMS). A second major version of UNIX emerged when Bill Joy, then a graduate student at Berkeley, rewrote Bell Lab's UNIX software to run on the department's DEC VAX computer. When word of Joy's version spread, the school was swamped with requests from VAX customers. Soon afterward, Joy left Berkeley to join Sun, where he led the effort to develop a new version of UNIX (known as SunOS), which combined the AT&T and Berkeley versions. According to industry analysts, being the first workstation vendor to offer UNIX had given Sun an advantage with scientist and engineer opinion leaders, who had developed a strong preference for that operating system.

[3] The workstation had actually been first developed by Xerox's Palo Alto Research Center (PARC) in 1973, and first commercialized by Three River's Corporation in Pittsburgh in about 1979.

plication. According to one recent industry study, a workstation in the late 1980s could best be defined as a high-performance, single-user, multitasking computer with extensive networking and graphics capabilities. Workstations were usually characterized by a 32-bit computer with a large high-resolution display, virtual memory, a multitasking operating system such as UNIX or VMS,[4] and considerable RAM memory and disk storage. In the full line of computers, workstations were bracketed on the low end by personal computers (PCs), and on the high end by multiuser minicomputers. (See Exhibit 20.3 for a comparison of workstations and personal computers.) Workstation prices ranged from approximately $5,000 to $200,000 in early 1988.

Around the time Apollo introduced its first workstation, many engineers had become frustrated with the waits and other constraints of timesharing and batch processing, and were eager to obtain control of their own computing resources. These engineers provided a natural constituency for engineering workstations, especially as their capabilities grew. At first, workstations had been purchased primarily for new engineering groups, where their purchase could easily be justified by the fact that they sold at prices considerably below those of minicomputer-based systems with similar capabilities. Over time, however, they were increasingly replacing existing minicomputers, especially older systems and those that were leased rather than owned. According to some analysts, by the mid-1990s, virtually all design engineers would have their own workstations, rather than working on dumb terminals "tethered" to minicomputers or sharing a computer (or terminal) with other members of their work group.

Product Categories

Workstations could be grouped into low-end, mid-range, and high-end classifications. *Low-end* systems, which were priced from just under $5,000 to $20,000, were typically offered in a desktop configuration, with 2–32 MBytes of physical RAM memory, and

---

[4] VMS was a DEC operating system that ran on most current DEC computers, regardless of size, and was compatible with all DEC operating systems. This "compatibility" advantage was believed to have contributed significantly to DEC's increase in market share in the mid-1980s, especially vis-à-vis IBM, which was then marketing three distinct, essentially incompatible operating systems.

TYPE OF SINGLE-USER SYSTEM

Feature	Personal Computer	Workstation
Primary operating system	DOS, OS/2, Mac OS	UNIX, VMS, Aegis
Distribution channel	Primarily retail	Direct, OEM, VAR
Primary market focus	Commercial	Technical

Distinguishing Product Characteristics

Primary application	Text	Graphics
Integer performance (MIPS)	5.0 maximum	40 maximum
Typical display resolution	480 × 640	1024 × 1024
Graphics capability	2D only	3D available
Operating system	Single tasking	Multitasking
Examples	Compaq, HP Vectra, Apple with Mac OS	Apollo, Sun, Apple with A/UX OS

EXHIBIT 20.3
Key Differences Between Workstations and Personal Computers

Source: International Data Corporation, 1988.

40–600 MBytes of disk storage. They were used primarily for two-dimensional design and drafting, software development, computer-aided publishing, and commercial applications. Sun, DEC, Hewlett-Packard, and Apollo offered competing products in this range. Critical success factors appeared to be the availability of third-party applications software, perceived reliability, manufacturing capability, and distribution channels. By early 1988, several personal computer manufacturers, including IBM, Apple, and Compaq, had introduced new products that had capabilities similar to those of low-end workstations.

Low-end workstations were increasingly competing in traditional personal computer markets by offering users more power, better graphics, and networking capabilities. During 1987, this trend intensified, as major workstation companies reduced the prices of their low-end systems to match those of the high-end PCs; added co-processors that gave workstation users access to the huge base of IBM-compatible software; and signed up commercial value-added resellers (VARs) in an effort to penetrate commercial markets. In particular, low-end workstations had received a favorable response from financial services companies (especially portfolio managers and brokers), who valued highly the multiwindowing capability of UNIX-based systems.

Mid-range systems offered more power to handle both two-dimensional and three-dimensional graphics applications. Prices ranged from $20,000 to $80,000. Typically offered in a deskside mode, mid-range systems were configured with between 2 and 32 MBytes of physical RAM memory, and disk storage varying from 40 MBytes to 5.6 GBytes. Common applications included finite element analysis, electrical and mechanical design and drafting, and computer-integrated manufacturing. DEC, Sun, Hewlett-Packard, and Apollo were the major competitors in this product category.

High-end platforms, sometimes referred to as "desktop graphics supercomputers," coupled high-performance computing (generally based on RISC[5] processor technology) and three-dimensional graphics, operating at speeds up to 10 MIPS.[6] New entries from Stellar and Ardent were expected to reach speeds as high as 30 MIPS by the end of 1988. Prices ranged from less than $40,000 to approximately $200,000.

Workstations in this class were typically used in applications that required sophisticated graphics and were computation-intensive, such as solids modeling, electronics design, visual simulation, scientific modeling, animation, geophysical science, medical imaging, defense, and artificial intelligence. According to a number of observers, demand for additional graphics and speed in such applications was virtually insatiable. Silicon Graphics, Sun, Apollo, and Hewlett-Packard were the primary competitors in this market segment, but new entries from start-up firms such as Stellar and Ardent were receiving considerable attention in the marketplace. Manufacturer margins were currently about 10 percent higher on high-end systems than on low-to-mid-range systems.

A key dimension in the evolving workstation industry was the importance of open architecture and adherence to industry standards. From its beginning, Sun had adopted and promoted the use of standard components and the easy "portability" of software among multiple-vendor environments. (Apollo, in contrast, initially relied heavily on proprietary hardware and software.) By building its early workstations around readily available modules, Sun had been able to reduce its start-up costs, and more importantly, as one industry analyst explained, "to grasp onto a credible 'hook' which it promoted mercilessly." "Freedom" had been a key rallying cry in early Sun marketing efforts. Sun co-founder (and head of R&D) Bill Joy was frequently quoted by the trade press to

---

[5] *Reduced Instruction Set Computing* worked in simple, brief steps, eliminating extraneous instructions so that the computer could execute common instructions faster than computers using traditional CISC (complex instruction set computing).

[6] *Millions of Instructions Per Second*, a standard measure of computational speed. The IBM PC operated at approximately 1 MIP, while the IBM AT ran at up to 1.8 MIPs. It should be noted, however, that the speed at which a particular type of applications software runs is not necessarily proportional to the theoretical speed (in MIPs) of its host machine.

the effect that, since no single vendor (even Sun) was likely to develop and produce the best version of every product type, users should maximize their freedom to pick and choose. Other workstation companies resisted initially, but by early 1988, virtually all had adopted (however reluctantly) the UNIX multitasking operating system and Motorola's 32-bit MC680X0 family of processors, as well as basic standards for networking, windowing, and graphics.

Standard hardware, operating systems, networking protocols, and user interfaces were especially important in their ability to attract third-party software and hardware suppliers to develop products to run on such standard systems. Software developers, for example, were eager to create software products for the UNIX operating system environment because they knew there was a large installed base of UNIX users, whether on minicomputers, PCs, or workstations. Sun's readiness to license its proprietary SPARC (RISC-type) chip design to outside manufacturers, for example, represented a major effort on its part to promote industry standards and open architecture. By early 1988, some type of RISC-based workstation was offered by every workstation vendor with the exception of DEC, which seemed, as one observer put it, ''to be straining awfully hard to protect its huge installed base of VAX-oriented users.''

''X-Windows,'' which had been developed at MIT in project ATHENA (supported by DEC and IBM, among others), had been adopted by all major workstation vendors as their standard user interface by early 1988. Sun had been one of the last vendors to adopt X-Windows, since it had been trying to promote its own Network/extensible Window System (NeWS) as the industry's standard. Finally, it capitulated, and unified NeWS with the X-Window system into X.11/NeWS—in effect, adopting the emerging industry standard, which facilitated the transfer of graphics across a heterogeneous network.

Relations with third-party software suppliers was an increasingly critical competitive variable. Workstation companies sought to induce software developers to supply products for their platforms by offering equipment discounts, training, and marketing assistance. The leading workstation companies offered as many as 1,000 applications software products from third-party vendors. The fact that Mentor Graphics software was designed for Apollo systems, for example, was considered a major factor in Apollo's continuing success in the electronics design market.

THE WORKSTATION MARKET

Definitions of workstations varied among suppliers of research information to the industry, especially with regard to whether a UNIX or equivalent operating system had to be included for a unit to be counted as a workstation. On the grounds that units without such operating systems were typically used as process controllers, some research suppliers excluded them from their estimates of market size. Using this more restrictive definition of the market, industry sales had reached $2.5 billion in 1987, and were expected to reach $2.9 billion in 1988 (see Exhibit 20.4).

In 1987, the two leading application areas for workstations were design automation (38 percent) and computer-aided software engineering (CASE) (25 percent). (See Exhibit 20.5.) Design automation included computer-aided design (CAD), computer-aided drafting, and computer-aided engineering (CAE). Key CAD applications were mechanical, electrical, electronic, architectural, and civil computer-aided design. These applications required graphics capabilities, but were less computer-intensive than CAE. Users were primarily designers and drafters in manufacturing industries such as automobiles, aerospace, heavy machinery, and consumer goods.

CAE was typically used for such analytical tasks as finite element modeling and analysis, solid modeling, structural analysis, mechanical computer-aided engineering,

EXHIBIT 20.4
**Workstation Market
Forecast by Type of
Processor**
Worldwide Revenues of
U.S. Vendors, 1987–1992
($ million)

Processor Category	1987	1988	1989	1990	1991	1992	% Growth 1987–1992
Traditional*	2320	2400	2700	2900	3000	3100	6.0
Mac II†	55	200	336	450	520	640	63.4
80386-based‡	98	275	400	540	620	570	42.4
Total	$2473	2875	3436	3890	4140	4310	11.8

* Includes Motorola 680X0-based, proprietary (e.g., VAX) and RISC-based systems. Excludes Intel 386-based system from Sun.

† This category also includes the Mac II follow-on product(s).

‡ Estimates of shipments of Sun's 386-based product are included in this category.

Source: International Data Corporation, December 1987.

EXHIBIT 20.5
1987 Workstation Market

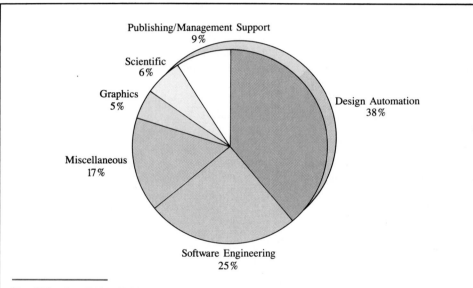

Note: Differs from Exhibit 20.6 because of different sources and methodology.

Source: Michael R. Leibowitz, ''Workstation Wars: The Battle of the Big 7,'' *High Technology Business*, November 1987, pp. 22–29. Copyright © 1987, Infotechnology Publishing Corporation. All rights reserved.

circuit simulation, and civil engineering. Because this class of applications required more computer power than straight drafting, near-supercomputer capabilities were often necessary.

CASE applications ranged from simple file management and documentation control to code generators and optimizers. Important requirements for software developers were windowing, to view the compilation and testing of several programs simultaneously; and networking, to facilitate the sharing of computer resources.

Other markets included new compute- and graphics-intensive applications, as well as applications within the commercial sector. Among the most important newer applications were artificial intelligence, geophysical science, scientific modeling, and defense research (e.g., the Strategic Defense Initiative); the visual simulation of such phenomena as flight aerodynamics, medical imaging, and radar display; and molecular modeling, industrial design, VLSI (chip) design, manufacturing simulation, and robotics planning. (See Exhibit 20.6.) Such simulation required real-time response, and was typically carried out on high-end workstations, such as those manufactured by Silicon Graphics.

The commercial sector was projected to be one of the highest-growth segments for workstations in the future. Some analysts forecast that by 1991, 85 percent of all workstation revenues would come from the commercial sector, a segment presently accounting for less than 5 percent of industry sales. The commercial sector currently included investment banks, brokerage houses, insurance companies, real estate agencies, banks, hospitals, and the like. Generally, end users in the commercial sector were not as technically oriented as engineering users, and relied more heavily on value-added resellers (VARs) and dealers to provide the technical assistance and support they required. Typically, they sought to purchase commercially available software packages rather than to develop their own software.

Workstation vendors typically sold their products to three classes of customers: (1) large users, who bought direct; (2) original equipment manufacturers (OEMs), which incorporated the workstations in systems that they then sold to end users; and (3) value-added resellers (VARs).

Large Users

Large-volume end users represented approximately 40–50 percent of industry sales. These accounts (e.g., Ford Motor Company, McDonnell Douglas) typically purchased hundreds of workstations at one time, often for an entire department or an entire plant. Workstation

Primary Application	Total 1986 Market ($ million)	% of 1986 Revenues
Software engineering (CASE)	363.0	30.6
Design and drafting (CAD)	300.9	25.4
Design engineering & analysis (CAE)	158.5	13.4
Technical management/support	97.1	8.2
Scientific research & R&D	68.1	5.7
Subtotal	987.6	83.3
Measurement and control	53.8	4.5
Economic & financial modeling	27.3	2.3
Geoscience & Geoengineering (graphics)*	23.3	2.0
Simulation (graphics)	19.1	1.6
Defense (graphics)	13.1	1.1
Animation (graphics)	13.1	1.1
Biological & chemical engineering (graphics)	11.2	0.9
Industrial process analysis (graphics)	1.5	0.0
Imaging (graphics)	0.2	0.0
Other	34.7	2.9
Total	1185.0	100.0

EXHIBIT 20.6
Technical Workstation Market by Primary Application Area

Note: Differs from Exhibit 20.5 because of different sources and methodology.

* Includes some graphics-intensive operations.

Source: International Data Corporation, 1987.

vendors served these accounts with their direct sales forces, assigning account representatives to potential large-volume customers. In making their buying decisions, these customers were influenced by the overall package being offered, including availability of third-party hardware and software, networking capability, technical advice, service warranties, and price/performance specifications ratios. Because investments in applications software were typically very high relative to the cost of the workstations, customers tended to stay with their current vendor unless there was a good reason to switch.

Third-party software and hardware suppliers frequently made the initial meaningful contact with the customer, and then brought the workstation vendor in for a joint sales effort. In such circumstances, the third party was not an OEM or a VAR, since it did not actually take title to the equipment being sold.

Original Equipment Manufacturers

Original equipment manufacturers (OEMs) accounted for approximately 40 percent of shipments, with 10 percent of OEMs representing nearly 90 percent of sales. Most OEMs configured systems incorporating a workstation vendor's hardware and (perhaps) operating system with their own proprietary software, but a minority (representing perhaps 5 percent of OEM sales) actually embedded the workstation into their own hardware products. Some OEMs took responsibility for servicing the workstations included in their systems, while others passed on the ninety-day warranty supplied by the workstation vendor to the end user, who would then purchase a standard service contract from the workstation vendor.

OEMs provided systems integration and technical assistance for the end user, often arranging for other third-party hardware and software suppliers to provide additional features. Workstation vendors gave OEMs discounts from list price, which varied from 0 to 40 percent, depending on the vendor, the type and amount of value to be added, and the quantity of systems to be purchased over a specified time frame. Sun and Apollo assigned dedicated account managers to their major OEMs, and sold to all OEMs directly. DEC, in contrast, served smaller OEMs (less than $500,000 in orders per year) through industrial distributors.

Value-Added Resellers

Value-added resellers (VARs) fell into two broad categories: regional VARs and larger systems integrators. Regional VARs focused on small- to medium-sized end users that typically purchased only a few systems at a time and had annual revenues of less than $100 million. Generally, these VARs specialized in a particular application niche, such as architecture or design automation. They "added value" by: (1) opening new market segments; (2) servicing a geographical area or customer that could not be economically covered with a direct sales force; (3) adding software; and (4) providing technical assistance, systems integration, and installation. One successful regional VAR was Boston CAD, which might, for example, acquire an AutoCad software package from AUTODESK, add a plotter, write the interface software to allow this printer to run on a particular type of workstation, and then resell it to an end user. While VAR discounts from the workstation vendors were typically 25–30 percent, VAR profitability depended primarily on fees for training, technical advice, and systems integration services, rather than on margins on workstations.

The second type of VAR, large systems integrators, such as EDS (a subsidiary of General Motors), were dedicated to assisting (even managing the computer resources of) a small number of high-volume buyers. These systems integrators acted as the prime contractors to provide a full-scale computing environment. Depending on the situation, they received discounts of 0–40 percent, and varying amounts of direct support. In many cases, they were assigned a full-time account representative and treated preferentially, since these accounts represented large amounts of potential business and typically required systems integration efforts beyond the resources of most workstation vendors.

425

SUN MICROSYSTEMS

SUN'S MARKETING STRATEGY

From the first, the essence of Sun's marketing strategy had been to seek price/performance leadership while using standard components and promoting open architecture. Key to Sun's open-systems product-design philosophy was the use of standard technologies such as the UNIX operating system, VMS system bus, Ethernet local area network, and Motorola 680X0 microprocessors. Wherever standards were not available, Sun created them, publishing the interface specifications and offering attractive licensing agreements to encourage others to adopt the same approach. Sun sought to integrate these multiple technologies in an open-system architecture to provide a high-performance computing environment for technical professionals. By basing systems on standards, Sun made it easier for software and hardware developers to port products to Sun workstations, and for computer users to integrate Sun's workstations with a variety of other computer products. As co-founder and CEO Scott McNealy explained, Sun's strategy was ''just a fast ball down the middle; nothing fancy, nothing tricky.''

Sun's open-systems approach appealed to computer buyers, who increasingly resented having to lock themselves into proprietary technologies. Leading customers began demanding ''open'' systems, which used industry standards to incorporate products from different manufacturers. Companies such as Apollo, DEC, and Hewlett-Packard, which marketed systems based on proprietary technologies, initially resisted the call for standards and open architecture, but by 1988, all had given in to at least some degree. As McNealy explained, ''In the past, computer companies have been able to charge a premium for proprietary technology. In the future, they will have to offer a discount.''

Sun argued that the technical computing world was heterogeneous, since machines from different vendors excelled at specific tasks. To facilitate the integration of disparate machines and operating systems, Sun developed the Network File System (NFS) within its Open Systems Network (OSN). In accordance with its commitment to encourage the development of industry standards, Sun published specifications of the NFS protocols, placed implementations of the underlying communications protocol in the public domain, and licensed relevant source codes at a low price to over 130 commercial and university users.

By adopting industry standards, Sun encouraged hundreds of third-party software and hardware vendors to develop more than 1,000 applications that ran on Sun workstations. Sun's CATALYST program provided incentives to these developers, such as equipment loans, special discounts, the listing of their products in a CATALYST reference catalog, and the demonstration and sales of their products by Sun marketing and sales personnel.

Sun invested a large proportion of its revenues (13 percent in 1987) in R&D, and was known for rapidly introducing new products with markedly improved price/performance, even when doing so obsoleted existing products that still appeared to be in the growth phases of their life cycles. During the five years since its founding, Sun had introduced a new workstation every twelve to eighteen months, in comparison with typical computer life cycles of two to five years. According to Zander, aggressive product development and introduction had been Sun's best defense against competitors seeking to ''clone'' its products, a process that, in theory, ought to have been relatively simple given Sun's use of off-the-shelf standard components. Carol Bartz, president of Sun's Federal Systems Division, emphasized that ''We wouldn't hesitate to bring out a new product at a price and performance level that absolutely destroyed an existing line. Why should we wait for the competition to do it? That's a brand new concept in this business, and we've proved you can make money doing it.''

Sun's first workstations were mid-range in functionality, and were targeted primarily at computer-aided-software engineering and the simpler design-automation applications. Over time, Sun had expanded its product line both upward (notably the Sun-4 range of workstations, which were based on its new SPARC chip and operated at speeds of up to 10 MIPs) and downward (its 3/50 entry-level system, which was based on the Motorola 68020 processor, had a monochrome display and operated at speeds of up to 1.5 MIPs; and its 386i_ high-performance PC, introduced in early 1988). Sun's products ranged in price from under $5,000 for the 3/50 to $100,000 for a fully configured Sun-4 workstation environment. Low-end systems accounted for about 25 percent of Sun's revenues in 1987, while high-end systems represented a growing proportion of shipments. As of January 1988, Sun had shipped over 50,000 workstations, about 70 percent of which were the low-to-mid-range Sun-3 systems.

As shown in Exhibit 20.7, Sun's biggest market in 1987 was design automation; it accounted for 33 percent of sales (versus 24 percent in 1986). The next biggest markets were computer-aided software engineering, at 23 percent (down from 86 percent in 1986), and ''emerging markets'' (e.g., government, financial services, artificial intelligence, earth resources, oil exploration, simulation, and medical imaging).

Sun's introduction of its model 3/50 in 1987 at a price below $5,000 had startled the industry. Apollo workstations with similar capabilities had been selling for almost twice as much. Instead of matching Apollo's prices and going for high margins, Sun management had decided to use this product to build market share. According to McNealy, ''Clearly the market would bear a higher price, but we think there's an elasticity of [demand] greater than one in the marketplace.'' In the view of one noted industry observer, it was unlikely that Sun would be able to make much (if any) profit on the 3/50 per se; but in a classic case of ''giving away the razors to sell razor blades,'' the company was expected to come out ahead by upgrading the systems through the addition of servers and more disk capacity, by making future sales of higher-level systems to the same customers, and by obtaining maintenance and service revenues.

EXHIBIT 20.7
Sun's 1987 Workstation Sales

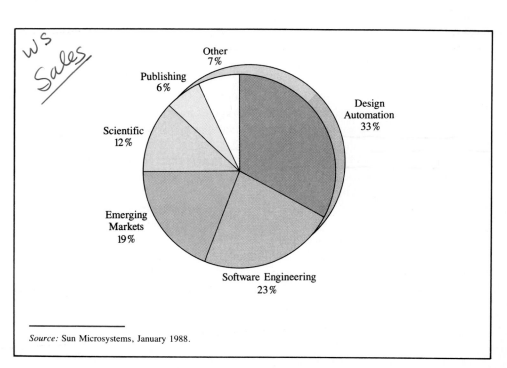

Source: Sun Microsystems, January 1988.

Sun formed a key technology-sharing alliance with AT&T in October 1987, when AT&T announced that it would license Sun's SPARC chip design to develop a family of high-performance minicomputers and workstations. In addition, Sun and AT&T would jointly develop a standardized version of UNIX, combining the features of AT&T's version 5.2 and SunOS. A major goal of this alliance was the development of a true alternative to IBM as the "mainstream" computing environment for the 1990s. To further cement these agreements, AT&T agreed in January 1988 to acquire up to 20 percent of Sun's stock over a three-year period, providing Sun with approximately $300 million. In April 1988, Sun and AT&T announced a prototype version of a new product called Open Look, which was intended to transform the forbidding UNIX operating system into one that would be user friendly toward nontechnical users. The graphical user interface, designed by Sun with the help of Xerox, would provide on-screen images and an ease-of-use rivaling Apple's Macintosh and IBM's PS/2 personal computers. Sun and AT&T invited dozens of software companies, chip makers, and other computer makers to take advantage of Open Look and the new refined version of UNIX.

Other workstation vendors appeared to be less than delighted by the Sun-AT&T alliance. According to *Business Week*, the chairman of Apollo claimed that AT&T and Sun "were giving themselves as much as an 18-month advantage in bringing Open Look products to market ahead of other suppliers of Unix computers. Within a month . . . , DEC, IBM, HP and several other computer makers had banded together to announce the Open Software Foundation (OSF), a consortium dedicated to producing an alternative to the AT&T-Sun version of Unix."

Sun's communications strategy included an aggressive public relations program, advertising in technical computer publications, periodic direct mailing to customers and prospects, and attendance at trade shows, as well as a series of seminars for specific OEM, university, commercial, and government customers and prospects. An active user-group program included sponsorship of an annual nationwide meeting, quarterly newsletters, and regular exchange of information (in both directions) between Sun and its customers.

Sun employed a large direct sales force, which called on OEMs, large-volume end users, and VARs. The average Sun salesperson brought in nearly $3 million in revenue in 1987, more than twice the industry average. While sales in the early 1980s had been primarily to OEMs, they were now more evenly distributed among OEMs, large-volume end users, and (increasingly) VARs.

In November 1987, Sun launched a major new effort intended to greatly increase its presence in VAR channels. According to Scott McNealy:

> The VAR marketplace represents a significant opportunity for Sun to diversify its distribution base worldwide. The program will enable Sun to capitalize on the vertical marketing clout of VARs, and penetrate new markets with value-added systems solutions.

VARs were to be selectively authorized to sell certain Sun products with specific value-added applications in restricted geographic areas. In administering its VAR program, Sun would seek to minimize conflict between the VARs and the direct sales force and OEMs. As part of its VAR program, Sun would provide:

- A lead referral program, in which Sun's field sales force would distribute quality end-user leads to VARs.

- A cooperative marketing program, which would cover advertising, direct-mail campaigns, product literature, education, trade shows, and special events.

- A representatives program, through which Sun would assign a field sales representative and an account manager to act as liaisons between the VAR and Sun (answering questions about prices, programs, products, terms, and conditions) and to assist directly in critical sales situations.

- Extensive sales tools: Sun would supply VARs with videos, slide presentations, proposal materials, competitive analyses, and extensive product literature.
- Product training and intensive technical courses, as well as ongoing in-the-field sales development training.
- A corporate hotline with assigned technical support engineers.
- A hardware maintenance program to enable the VAR to utilize Sun's service organization to complement its own capabilities.

According to Sun executives, the new VAR program was a critical strategic move designed to extend Sun's presence in key vertical markets, such as computer-aided design, software engineering, manufacturing, and publishing, and to open channels to newer markets, especially mainstream commercial applications. Discounts available to the VARs differed depending on circumstances, but were said by Sun executives to be "fully competitive" with industry practices.

In April 1988, Sun introduced a new desktop system, the Sun 386i_, based on the Intel 80386 microprocessor, with suggested retail prices ranging from $8,000 to $14,000. This new system offered both MS-DOS—the standard operating system for IBM-compatible PCs—and UNIX—the standard operating system for technical users. The top of the line was expected to operate at 5 MIPs, compared to a maximum of 2 MIPs for most high-end PCs (e.g., the newly introduced IBM PS-2/80), and to have twice the memory of other 80386-based machines. According to McNealy, "[The 386i_ is] going to give us the edge. No other high-performance machine out there today can run UNIX and DOS like this one." Some analysts noted, however, that with this introduction, Sun had to support three distinct architectures: SPARC (RISC) for its high-end systems, the Motorola 68000 for its 3/50 series, and now the Intel 80386. While Sun argued that it would be able to sustain a common user interface across the three architectures ("three architectures, one look"), skeptics doubted that this would be possible without sacrificing many of the advantages of each of the three approaches. One commentator noted that Sun did not seem to have yet made up its mind whether to position the 386i_ as a low-end workstation or as a high-end PC. Would Sun, he wondered, seek distribution for its new product through major computer retailers such as Computerland, or would distribution largely be limited to VARs and OEMs?

COMPETITION

Almost a dozen competitors had entered the workstation industry by 1988, most seeking to establish positions in relatively small niches. Many of these companies had not yet shipped their first product, and some would never move beyond the concept stage. Like other major participants in the industry, Sun subscribed to a number of proprietary research services and otherwise monitored competitive developments. In early 1988, several competitors appeared to be especially significant from Sun's point of view. (See Exhibits 20.8, 20.9, and 20.10 for market share and financial data on the leading competitors.)

Apollo

Apollo, which had created the workstation industry when it launched its first workstation in 1980, had experienced extraordinary growth and profitability until 1985, when the semiconductor and electronics industries suffered a severe slump. In concentrating its sales on a few large OEM customers in the design-automation area, Apollo had, according to one observer, "put far too many of its eggs in one basket—the wrong basket."

EXHIBIT 20.8
End-of-Year Revenue Growth of Leading Workstation Vendors

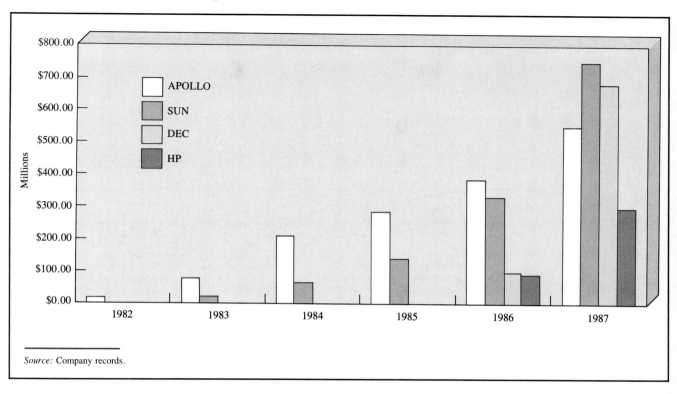

Source: Company records.

RANK	VENDOR	1986 SHIPMENTS	% OF 1986 MARKET SHARE	1987 SHIPMENTS	% OF 1987 MARKET SHARE	1987 RANK
1.	Apollo Computer	16,000	35.3	24,000	18.5	3
2.	Sun Microsystems	14,000	30.9	34,100	26.3	2
3.	HP (9000 Mod 300)*	7,125	15.7	15,000	11.6	4
4.	Digital (VAXstation)	3,700	8.2	40,100	31.0	1
5.	Symbolics	1,444	3.2	1,125	0.9	8
6.	IBM (RT PC)	1,200	2.1	3,400	2.6	7
7.	Silicon Graphics	930	2.1	5,750	4.4	5
	Intergraph			4,058	3.1	6
	Subtotal	44,399	97.9	127,533	98.4	
	Other†	948	2.1	1,958	1.6	
	Total	45,347	100.0	129,491	100.0	

EXHIBIT 20.9
1986 and 1987 Worldwide Workstation Shipments and Market Share of U.S.–Based Vendors

* These HP systems include only those shipped with an operating system. HP shipped a total of 28,500 Model 300s during the calendar year 1986, but 75 percent of those offered Basic or Pascal in lieu of an operating system.

† In 1986, no other company had a greater than .8 percent market share.

Source: International Data Corporation, 1987, 1988.

429

1986 RANK	VENDOR	1986 REVENUES ($ million)	% OF 1986 MARKET SHARE	1987 REVENUES ($ million)	% OF 1987 MARKET SHARE	1987 RANK
1.	Apollo Computer	391.7	33.1	553.6	20.0	3
2.	Sun Microsystems	341.2	28.8	754.4	27.3	1
3.	Symbolics	112.5	9.5	101.6	3.7	7
4.	Digital (VAXstation)	102.7	8.7	689.0	24.9	2
5.	HP (9000 Mod 300)†	99.5	8.4	300.0	10.9	4
6.	Silicon Graphics	59.4	5.0	116.0	4.2	5
7.	IBM (RT PC)	59.4	4.1	102.0	3.7	6
	Intergraph			98.7	3.6	8
	Subtotal	1155.0	97.5	2715.3	98.4	
	Other‡	30.0	2.5	46.6	1.6	
	Total	1185.0	100.0	2761.9	100.0	

* Revenues for the workstation market include the sale of workstations, servers, software tools and utilities, peripherals such as PC coprocessor boards and laser printers, service, and custom consulting fees.

† These HP systems include only those shipped with an operating system. HP shipped a total of 28,500 Model 300s during the calendar year 1986, but 75 percent of those offered Basic or Pascal in lieu of an operating system.

‡ In 1986, no other company had a greater than .8 percent market share.

Source: International Data Corporation, 1987, 1988.

Apollo responded swiftly to its loss in 1985 by investing heavily in converting to open architecture and industry standards.[7] It adopted major communications standards, such as Ethernet and IBM's token ring, made available an IBM PC-AT bus in its low-end workstations, and planned to introduce a new operating system in June 1988, which would combine Berkeley's Version 4.3 and AT&T's System 5.0 UNIX. Nevertheless, according to Sun analysts, Apollo's networking approach was optimized to link large numbers of Apollo computers, while Sun's was more suitable for a truly heterogeneous environment.

Apollo offered a full line of workstations, with emphasis on medium-to-high-end markets where graphics performance was especially important. It had traditionally stressed performance rather than price in its marketing approach, matching Sun's price cuts when necessary, but rarely initiating a price reduction on its own. In line with this strategy, Apollo announced in March 1988 that it would introduce a new high-end workstation with near-supercomputer capabilities in late 1988. The DN10000 would embrace a number of new technologies, including parallel processing, RISC architecture, and 64-bit addressing (double the 32-bit design of most minicomputers and workstations). It would have four parallel processing chips, each with a performance range of 15–25 MIPS, and was expected to be priced from $70,000 to $130,000.

Digital Equipment Corporation

Digital (DEC) had long been a dominant force in technical markets, where a large proportion of design engineers used DEC VAX timesharing systems. However, many of the

---

[7] Following a loss in 1985, Apollo turned a small profit (2.3 percent of sales) in 1986, and continued to improve its profitability (to 4 percent of sales) in 1987.

tasks performed by these engineers could increasingly be carried out more effectively and economically by workstations. DEC had introduced its own line of workstations (VAXstations) in the mid-1980s, and by 1987 led the industry in worldwide shipments, accounting for almost one-third of the units sold that year. DEC's strategy apparently was to sell its workstations mainly to its existing VAX customers, many as replacements for its VT-100 dumb terminals.

DEC offered a broad line of VAXstation workstations, ranging from its entry-level model, priced at approximately $5,000, to a high-end offering, priced at approximately $40,000. VAXstation architecture was consistent with the rest of DEC's VAX minicomputer line, allowing easy integration into an all-DEC-networked environment. DEC stressed the compatibility of software across its entire product line, but had been slow to support UNIX (DEC called its version Ultrix). At the end of 1987, the Ultrix catalog listed only sixteen CAD/CAE graphics packages.

DEC's historical emphasis on proprietary operating systems and software had limited its ability to win new customers for its workstations, and had apparently caused defections among VAX users. (UNIX had been shipped with only 20 percent of VAXstations, versus 70 percent for Apollo and 90 percent for Sun.) According to Dataquest, 75 percent of Apollo and Sun workstations installed in 1987 had been installed in DEC VAX shops. DEC had counterattacked by reducing the price of its low-end workstation below $5,000 in June 1987 and introducing two new models (the 3200 and 3500) in September of that year. These two models offered significantly improved performance and were said to be competitively priced. In January 1988, DEC announced an agreement with Apple to jointly develop the networking interface between VAX and Apple's personal computers. If successful, this alliance would permit DEC to penetrate low-end distribution channels and markets, and would give Apple access to DEC's large customer base.

Hewlett-Packard

Hewlett-Packard (HP) had entered the computer industry in the 1970s with a broad line of multiuser minicomputer products, diversifying from its traditional business of scientific calculators and industrial test and measurement instruments. In the early 1980s, it had expanded into the more office-oriented personal computer market when it introduced its IBM-compatible Intel 80286-based personal computer, and into the workstation market with a line of products targeted at its existing scientific and technical customer base.

HP's workstation entries included two series of products, one family (HP 9000 Model 300 workstations) based on the Motorola 680X0 family of microprocessors, and the higher-end family (HP 9000 Model 800 systems) based on HP's own proprietary RISC processors. More than half of HP's low-end workstations were installed as dedicated processors, and had been shipped with only Basic or Pascal rather than an operating system. HP had, however, shipped UNIX with over 75 percent of its 800 series systems during 1987.

HP's workstation strategy apparently was to leverage the loyalty of its existing account base by maintaining its excellent reputation for service and support and offering competitive price/performance ratios. According to some analysts, HP's ability to grow with the industry was likely to be hindered by the fact that its commercial-oriented computer business and technical workstation business were assigned to highly autonomous, geographically separate organizational units.

Silicon Graphics

Silicon Graphics (SGI) targeted its workstations at applications requiring high-speed graphics, where it had several product advantages. Currently, SGI was especially strong in animation, mechanical design automation, scientific modeling, visual simulation (including applications such as flight, medical imaging, and radar display), industrial design, VLSI design, and manufacturing simulation. SGI offered both 68020 and RISC-based models, with prices ranging from approximately $20,000 to $80,000.

While SGI adhered to three important industry standards (UNIX, Ethernet, and Network File System), it utilized its own proprietary set of VLSI chips for graphics and geometry processing. Contrary to Sun's approach, SGI chose to build these chips in-house rather than rely on outside chip manufacturers. In late 1987, partly because of its Geometry Partners Program, SGI had more three-dimensional graphics applications running on its high-end workstations than any other vendor. Its strategy appeared to be to maintain superior graphics performance and to expand its product line downward into the low-end and mid-range segments.

Symbolics

Symbolics focused on the artificial intelligence market with its symbolic processing architecture, tailored for rapid execution of LISP (List Processing Language), the most commonly used computer language for artificial intelligence and other advanced symbolic processing applications. Its target markets included research institutions, the government, and, recently, the financial sector. American Express, for example, planned to use Symbolics systems for instant customer credit checks. However, 1987 had been a disastrous year for Symbolics; revenues dropped from $114 million to $103 million, and it incurred a $25 million loss. According to some analysts, Symbolics' customers were increasingly reluctant to pay a premium price for nonstandard proprietary technology.

Two new entrants at the high-end were *Stellar* and *Ardent*, both of which had announced new products in early 1988. Their products were targeted between the high-end existing workstations and minisupercomputers. With performances exceeding 20 MIPS, these "graphics supercomputing workstations," were expected to be priced between $100,000 and $150,000. Key applications were expected to be molecular modeling, computational fluid dynamics, and computer animation. At present, scientists working in these fields were generally forced to use batch processing on large mainframe computers. Industry analysts estimated that graphics supercomputing workstations would account for 10 percent of the technical workstation market by 1990.

IBM

IBM had entered the low end of the workstation industry in early 1986 when it introduced the RT-PC, which was based on a proprietary RISC microprocessor. The RT-PC was not much of a success, achieving less than a 4 percent market share during 1986 and 1987, with two-thirds of its shipments configured as multiuser commercial systems. While IBM offered its own version of UNIX (called AIX) and had adopted industry windowing standards, the RT-PC's price/performance apparently had not been viewed as "competitive."

During 1987, IBM introduced an entire new line of PCs, which included the PS/2 Model 80, based on Intel's 80386 32-bit microprocessor. While the PS/2 Model 80 was considered inferior to the RT-PC in a number of technical respects, it was generally felt that it was only a matter of time before the RT-PC was phased out in favor of the more recent "untarnished" model. As of early 1988, the PS/2 was still waiting for the full implementation of the OS/2 operating system from Microsoft, and did not yet fully support UNIX. In the view of some observers, IBM's biggest challenge would be to encourage development of third-party software for the PS/2 series.

Compaq's Deskpro 386 was similar to the IBM PS/2 Model 80, and was believed to have potential as a low-end workstation. Similarly, Apple's new Macintosh II was regarded as a good entry-level workstation and a strong alternative to the Sun-3/50 and Sun-3/60 low-end systems. The Mac II and the Sun-3/60 offered similar performance, but the Mac II was easier to use and more responsive to user input. In March 1988, Apple and Texas Instruments announced that they would jointly develop a new low-priced workstation based on Apple's Macintosh II, to be used for artificial intelligence applications.

NEC, Sony, and Hitachi

While not currently significant factors in the market, NEC, Sony, and Hitachi, had all recently announced or introduced new low-end workstations. Sun management claimed that it was not very worried about their entry because ''the twelve- to eighteen-month life cycles of our products are just too short for the Japanese to copy.''

CONCLUSION

As Zander reviewed the market and competitive data available to him, he wondered what recommendations he should make concerning Sun's future course. He knew that the company's culture was almost evangelical—to convert as much of the computer industry as possible to Sun's concept of ''computer freedom.'' But how much of this mission should one rapidly growing company take on? Was it really wise for Sun to seek to become a broad-based computer company (some analysts were touting Sun as ''another DEC''), or would it make more sense for Sun to plow more deeply in fields where it was already established? In particular, Zander wondered what changes in Sun's marketing approaches and channels would be necessary to achieve success with its new 386i_, and what programs should be undertaken to compete effectively with IBM, DEC, and Compaq in low-end markets.

QUESTIONS FOR DISCUSSION

1. How would you characterize the ''workstation'' market? How is the market segmented? What are the primary needs and buying behavior of customers in each major segment?

2. What are the critical factors for success in each segment? How have these factors changed over time? How are they likely to change in the next several years?

3. How would you explain the success that Sun had achieved at the time of the case?

4. How would you assess Sun's current position? What do you consider to be Sun's most significant threats and opportunities?

5. As Ed Zander, speaking from a marketing perspective, what changes (if any) in Sun's strategy would you recommend?

21

CITIBANK INDONESIA
Developing a Market for Electronic Banking

Developed in collaboration with Myrtha Waworuntu[1]

> There are conditions in America that necessitate the use of [telephones] more than here. Here, we have a superabundance of messengers. The absence of servants has compelled Americans to adopt communications systems.
>
> *Sir William Preece,*
> *Chief Engineer, British Post Office,*
> *Testimony in the House of Commons (1879)*

In midsummer 1987, R. Hartanto, vice president of electronic banking of Citibank Indonesia, wondered what steps, if any, he should take to rejuvenate Citikilat,[2] his bank's faltering electronic banking product. Citikilat had been launched five years previously as the first in a series of new electronic services for Citibank Indonesia's customers. Initially, Citikilat had met with an enthusiastic response from both the bank's marketing officers and their clientele. At the end of its first year, a high percentage of the bank's major customers had signed up for the service, and Citibank was well established as the leading provider of electronic banking in Indonesia. By mid-1987, however, the program was clearly in trouble. In recent months, more customers had terminated the service than had signed on, while average usage per customer was low and did not seem to be increasing. Moreover, a shift in leadership and strategy at Citicorp headquarters in New York had increased pressure for products aimed at the corporate market to meet strict profitability criteria. Citikilat clearly did not meet these standards.

---

[1] This case is largely based on and incorporates considerable material from Ms. Waworuntu's M.I.T. M.S. thesis (1988), which should be consulted for specific sources and references. Historical material has been largely drawn from H. van B. Cleveland and T. F. Huertas, *Citibank 1812–1970* (Harvard, 1985). Names of Citibank personnel in Indonesia and financial data have been disguised.

[2] *Kilat* in Indonesian means lightning, and conveys a sense of speed. It was customary, for example, to stamp urgent letters "KILAT."

Citibank was the largest bank in the United States and one of the largest financial institutions in the world. Founded in 1812, its long history had been characterized by an unusual degree of innovation and risk taking, and a willingness to stake out positions that put it at odds with much of the banking community. It had, for example, from the first maintained reserves greater than those required by the government in order to be able to offer "ready money" to its clientele. It had been the first major bank to segment the corporate market by industry and to assign specialized "marketing officers" to each segment. When the 1913 Federal Reserve Act empowered national banks to establish branches overseas, National City Bank (as it was then called)[3] opened its first international branch in Buenos Aires. By 1915, additional branches had been opened in the leading commercial cities of South America, and a controlling interest in the International Banking Corporation, an American overseas bank with a network of Far Eastern branches, had been acquired.

Over the years, Citibank had consolidated its position as the leading bank in New York through a series of mergers and an aggressive building program, all the while continuing to expand in international markets. In pursuit of its strategy to become a truly worldwide financial institution, it established a branch in virtually every commercially important country in the world. During the 1960s, new branches were opened in Taiwan and in Dubai on the Arabian Gulf, while the bank deepened its existing network in India by adding branches in Madras and New Delhi and second offices in Calcutta and Bombay. Additional offices were also opened in Hong Kong, Singapore, Indonesia, and other Asian countries. In Latin America and the Caribbean, offices were established in Bolivia, Ecuador, El Salvador, Honduras, Jamaica, Trinidad, Tobago, and many other countries.

In New York, the bank's branch network continued to expand. In 1957, Citi had seventy-three branches, considerably fewer than Manufacturers Hanover and the Chemical Bank. Eleven years later, having more than doubled the number of its branches, Citibank had the largest branch network of any New York bank. It was not until 1967, however, that Walter Wriston (soon to become president, and then chairman) found a way to break through the regulatory barriers that were constraining Citi's domestic growth outside of New York. Chief among these was the Bank Holding Company Act of 1956, which restricted a bank's operations outside its home state. Wriston discovered that a memorandum of the Bank Holding Company Act pointed out that the act applied only to holding companies that owned two or more banks. This meant that a holding company that owned a single bank—a "one-bank holding company"—would not be subject to the Bank Holding Company Act, and, not being itself a bank, could enter lines of business prohibited to banks. Citibank thus gave birth to its own parent, Citicorp: the first one-bank holding company.

Between 1971 and 1986, Citibank grew to an asset base of $196 billion and became securely established as the largest bank in the United States. (The second-largest bank, Bank of America, had only $95 billion in assets.) During the previous twenty years, Citi had used the new freedom it had attained as a one-bank holding company to take advantage of a number of profound changes taking place in its environment. In particular, it had responded strategically to major shifts in information technology, the regulatory environment, and economic conditions.

Information Technology

Information Technology (IT) comprised a family of related technologies for data processing, telecommunications, office and professional support systems, decision support,

[3] The bank went through a number of name changes in its long history. For purposes of simplicity, it will be referred to throughout this case as "Citibank" or "Citi."

and production control. In a 1982 study, the Hudson Institute concluded that ''technological change has become an even more important force than inflation in driving change in the financial services industry. . . . Technology has achieved such momentum that even if interest rates were low for some time, rapid change in financial services would continue.''

The so-called paper explosion has been one of the main causes of increased usage of IT by financial institutions. Between 1940 and 1970, for example, the number of checks written and processed in the United States increased over 1,100 percent, to 40 billion. If handled manually, the processing of these checks would have required the efforts of over half the entire U.S. work force. Even with significant automation, the cost of check processing had risen to $20 billion in 1983; and this cost was expected to increase at an accelerating rate, at least through 1990. Growth in other types of financial transactions (e.g., 10 billion charge card transactions per year) was further exacerbating the paper explosion.

The decreasing cost of computer hardware and telecommunications, especially in comparison to escalating wages and salaries, also fueled the trend toward more automated offices. Automated teller machines (ATMs), for example, considerably reduced the labor component of delivering consumer banking services. The cost of an ATM (including its enclosure) had fallen to about $30,000 and was expected to decline further. The cost of a bank teller was $25,000 per year and rising.

The paper explosion plus the availability of smarter, more flexible, and more powerful machines led to a race among financial institutions to use technology as a competitive weapon in the war against time, spatial distance, and sheer volume. In addition, IT made possible new forms of service differentiation. While service had traditionally been defined by the (hopefully) pleasant voice and friendly smile of a human teller, it had increasingly come to mean the timely provision of multiple options and choices.

Regulation

The regulatory environment during this period was characterized by: (1) deregulation of interest rates for deposits and loans; (2) removal of most geographic constraints; (3) fewer restrictions on mergers and acquisitions; and (4) increased acceptability of innovative product offerings. The Depository Institutions Deregulation and Monetary Control Act of 1980 (DIDMCA) abolished interest rate ceilings on the grounds that they ''discourage persons from saving money, create inequities for depositors, [and] impede the ability of depository institutions to compete for funds.'' The McFadden Act of 1927 had prohibited branch banking outside of a bank's home state, but by the late 1960s, bank holding companies were increasingly being allowed to conduct business across state lines through subsidiaries. In 1978, the International Banking Act amended Regulation K (which governed the organization, regulation, and capitalization of U.S. banks doing business overseas) to permit the development of a national branch network (in up to ten cities) for the purpose of conducting international banking.

At the same time, the rapid diffusion of ATMs was blurring geographic market boundaries. Many local and regional banks were establishing networks of shared ATMs, which allowed customers access to their accounts to withdraw cash, make deposits, and transfer funds from anywhere in the United States. By 1987, one-fifth of the nation's 14,000 banks belonged to at least one of roughly 100 regional and national ATM networks.

Mergers and Alliances

Intraindustry mergers and strategic alliances were also becoming more prevalent. To the surprise of many observers, the Justice Department offered no opposition to the regional ATM networks, while the comptroller of the currency asserted that out-of-state banks that entered into ATM sharing arrangements did not violate the McFadden Act. Many of the nation's leading banks anticipated that geographic constraints would essentially be eliminated in the next two or three years, and were jockeying to be in the best starting position when the regulations were actually lifted.

Products

The products that could be offered by various types of financial institutions were also being freed from most regulatory constraints. Commercial banks were increasingly being permitted to offer consumer investment services such as buying and selling stocks, commodities, and bonds, as well as investment advisory services. Bank America Corporation, for example, had recently acquired the Charles Schwab discount investment brokerage, and commercial banks could now underwrite equity and bond issues. In addition, banks were increasingly being allowed to compete in a broader range of nonbanking activities such as data processing and insurance. At the same time, it should be noted, large diversified financial institutions such as American Express and the big brokerage houses and insurance companies were increasingly offering products that competed directly with traditional commercial bank services.

Economic Conditions

The prevailing economic conditions during the late 1970s and 1980s greatly influenced the strategies of financial institutions. Volatile inflation rates, stock and bond markets, foreign exchange rates, and interest rates forced both consumers and corporate treasurers to become more sophisticated and less risk-averse in their investment behavior. Corporate treasurers became increasingly preoccupied with cash management and the development of creative and innovative methods of obtaining outside funds. Many large firms, for example, now bypassed financial intermediaries and went directly to the market with a wide range of commercial paper, significantly impacting the loan portfolios of large money center banks such as Citibank.

Japan's very large balance of payments surpluses in the 1980s had greatly strengthened the assets and reserves of its major banks. Like Citibank, the Japanese banks were investing heavily in worldwide telecommunications and data-processing capability and seeking to become truly global in scope.

CITIBANK MANAGEMENT AND CULTURE

After Wriston's retirement in 1984 and a series of ensuing management changes, Citi was directed by a relatively young management team. Although Citi's new chairman, John Reed,[4] and the heads of the Institutional Bank and the Individual Bank, Lawrence Small and Richard Braddock, had each been with Citi more than twenty years, they were all still less than 50 years of age and came from nonbanking backgrounds. Reed's degrees were in American literature, metallurgy, and management; Small, a one-time classical guitarist, had been so serious about the flamenco guitar that he once spent a year living with Spanish gypsies; Braddock had been a product manager for consumer products such as Tang at General Foods. (Braddock's chief lieutenants were also General Foods alumni;

---

[4] Reed went to work at Citi in 1964, after obtaining his master's degree in management from the Sloan School of Management at M.I.T. He first joined the International Banking Group (IBG) planning staff, where he was so successful that only five years later he was promoted to senior vice president, becoming the youngest man ever given that title at Citibank. Reed then joined the Operations Group (OPG), where he introduced the "paper factory" concept and ran the division as a high-speed, continuous-process production operation. Later he took charge of the "consumer bank," where he made heavy use of information technology to greatly increase Citibank's position in retail banking. In 1984, after twenty years at the bank, Reed was picked by his predecessor, Walter Wriston, to be Citicorp's new chairman.

Pei Yuan Chia, who ran Citicorp's card division, for example, had at one time been brand manager for Brim decaffeinated coffee.)

The new team had worked together in the Citibank operating group in the late 1960s and early 1970s. At that time, the "whiz kids" had concluded that 85 percent of that group's management was obsolete, and had made major personnel changes. According to those who know Citicorp well, there was an unwritten but explicit understanding among its top managers that they were paid to be risk takers. For example, the Citicorp credit card group periodically approved several thousand applications at random, performing no credit evaluation beyond verifying that the applicant was not bankrupt. According to Chia, it was known that some of these cardholders were obviously bad risks, but Citi decided to let them use their cards freely for a year in order "to get a better statistical fix on how deadbeats behave." "A banker," Chia continued, "would have a heart attack watching us do this." Similarly, Citi's consumer banking group was currently engaged in an admittedly high-risk venture to establish free-standing Citistations throughout suburban America. Only one out of ten Citistations would be manned; the remainder would be equipped with automated teller machines (ATMs) that rose and fell to the height of the customer's car window. In pointing out that Citistations might not turn out to be a successful business, Braddock noted, "Failures are part of the landscape if you're trying to change things and grow."

Decentralization represented another key dimension of Citi's management philosophy. Citi's strategy was to enter many different markets and to delegate as much power as feasible to the people closest to the customer. Individuals had considerable freedom to run their own shows with very little interference from headquarters. As Jack Carvier, country head for Indonesia, explained, "I can approve credits up to levels that other foreign banks here have to get headquarters approval for."

Citi's decentralization was supported by a new, unusually comprehensive reporting and control system. McKinsey and Company, a leading management consulting firm, had been asked to specify what data should be gathered and reported, and to recommend a system for collecting, organizing, analyzing, and reporting that information. One McKinsey consultant involved in the project recalled:

> We found, in the first place, that the management . . . didn't even have a good profile of its markets and its customers. It didn't really know in summary form what [its position was] with respect to discrete market segments. And without that sort of information it is pretty difficult to manage the business. . . . There was very little account profitability and not even market-segment profitability information.

As a result of this study, Citi adopted a very tight reporting and control system. The profitability of each business was reported in detail down to the product level. Reporting schedules were rigorous, and organizational units that failed to meet deadlines were reprimanded severely.

It was Citibank policy to frequently transfer senior managers geographically. The average assignment of an expatriate manager in Indonesia, for example, was about three years. In combination with a tight reporting and control system, this policy was intended to make it possible for Citi to operate through very decentralized operations without diluting its overall direction and strategy.

STRATEGY AND ORGANIZATION

Reed had recently restructured the corporation into what he called "the Five I's": the Individual Bank, the Institutional Bank, the Investment Bank, the Insurance Business, and the Information Business. Each organization was responsible for selling a specific range of products to a specific group of customers. Although the groups were separate and directed by individual management teams, they all shared Citicorp's overall direction and strategy.

The Individual Bank

The Individual Bank provided a full range of financial services to individual consumers throughout the world. In the United States, it had a business relationship with one out of every five households. Its financial services could be divided into three major categories: (1) transactional services, such as checking accounts, money orders, traveler's checks, charge cards, and brokerage services; (2) savings services, such as passbook accounts, certificates of deposit, and investment accounts; and (3) loan services, such as personal loans, lines of credit, and mortgages.

In recent years, Citi had placed increasing emphasis on the Individual Bank, which had surpassed the Institutional Bank as the corporation's largest business in 1986. In Reed's view, consumer banking was especially attractive because its risks were more statistically predictable than those in either commercial or investment banking. In 1986, consumer loans had been equal to 51 percent of Citi's total portfolio, up from 45 percent the previous year. The Individual Bank's revenue had grown at an annual rate of 29 percent for the last five years, and it was expected to earn more than $1 billion per year within the next several years.

The Institutional Bank

The Institutional Bank was responsible for worldwide business with corporations, governments, nonprofit organizations, and financial institutions. It was organized into seven groups, four of which were *geographic* (the North American Finance Group; the Asia/Pacific Banking Group; the Caribbean, Central, and South American Banking Group; and the Europe, Middle East, and Africa Banking Group), two of which were based on *customer segments* (the Financial Institutions Group, which was responsible for Citicorp's relationships with financial institutions in nearly 100 countries, and the World Corporate Group [WCG], which served Citicorp's major multinational corporate customers worldwide), and one of which was *functional* (the recently established Global Electronic Markets Group).

The Institutional Bank's revenues and earnings had been relatively stagnant in recent years because the large corporations on which it had traditionally focused were increasingly issuing commercial paper rather than borrowing from banks. Consequently, Citi's strategy was to downsize the Institutional Bank through significant personnel cuts in North America, Europe, and Asia. The North American commercial banking staff was to be reduced from 22,000 to 17,000 by 1990, while cutbacks in West Germany had resulted in the closing of Citi's offices in Hanover, Cologne, and Nuremberg. In Asia, where the culture led employees to expect to stay with their companies for their entire careers, the cutbacks were expected to have severe effects on employee morale.

The Investment Bank

The Investment Bank offered investment banking and securities-related products and services to Citi's customers throughout the world. Its activities encompassed investment and merchant banking, securities trading and brokerage, foreign exchange and money market activities, investment management, venture capital, and securities trust and custodial services. Its primary dealings were with corporations, governments, and financial institutions, for whom it managed debt and equity issues (outside the United States), municipal underwritings, private placements, and project finance, and also assisted in mergers, acquisitions, and divestitures.

Citibank had recently increased its emphasis on investment banking, partly because of deregulation in the United States, and partly because of the need to recapture its large corporate customers' capital financing business. Looking forward, Citi envisioned worldwide electronic marketplaces for stocks, bonds, and foreign exchange. It planned to be a major player in these markets by: (1) hiring top investment banking talent;[5] (2) acquiring existing brokerage houses; (3) acquiring existing financial information providers such as Quotron; (4) introducing computer-based trading systems for brokers and money managers; and (5) linking institutional customers' personal computers to trading desks via a global electronic network. As Reed explained to *Forbes*:

> There is no one—and I mean no one—who is building a global investment bank in the sense that we are. Other investment banks operate in one or two maybe three markets; we are in fifty. That is not generally accepted or understood.

The Insurance Business

The Insurance Business was not yet truly active in the United States, where efforts were under way to eliminate regulations that prohibited chartered banks from providing insurance products. Citicorp had, however, begun to develop an insurance business abroad, largely through acquisitions. The purchase of a brokerage firm in the United Kingdom, for example, enabled Citicorp to distribute and underwrite insurance in both Asian and European markets.

The Information Business

The Information Business, which was Citicorp's newest major venture, was expected to undergo rapid expansion during the next decade. Citicorp management believed that the ability to deliver prompt, accurate information electronically would provide the bank with an important competitive advantage. At the end of 1986, Citicorp had more than 200 data centers, operating within a worldwide communications network comprising over 125,000 terminals—85,000 of which were located in customers' offices or homes.

CITIBANK'S TECHNOLOGY STRATEGY

According to one industry observer, "On a scale of 1 to 10, when it comes to willingness to invest in technology-based business ventures, Citi is a 10—and few others score higher than a 7." Citi's emphasis on technology began in the mid-1960s, when it hired a group of fifty-four employees away from Los Angeles–based Scantlin Electronics to form Transaction Technology Inc. (TTI), which was to become its internal computer vendor. TTI's first products were proprietary ATMs and the sophisticated communications network that supported them. During the four years when it had a virtual ATM monopoly in New York (1969–1973), Citibank had increased its share of the retail banking market from 4 to 13 percent.

More recently, Citi had invested over $500 million in an advanced worldwide data communications network using technology developed for the U.S. Defense Department. According to leading industry analysts, only Chase Manhattan Bank and Bank of America

---

[5] Doing so would create severe strains on Citicorp's salary schedules, since investment bankers, at least during the "hot" years of the mid-1980s, earned substantially more than their commercial banking counterparts. Commercial banks wishing to attract experienced investment bankers would have to pay them much more than they did their mainstream commercial bankers. According to Reed, Citibank was willing to do this, at least in the short run.

had networks that even approached Citi's. Citi's network was unique, however, both in scope (ninety-three countries in 1987) and in the fact that it was "truly global from all points to all points."

Citicorp operated the world's largest nongovernment information-processing operation outside the data-processing industry. According to internal sources, annual expenditures on information technology were almost $900 million. A Salomon Brothers 1985 study of the banking industry noted that Citi's investment in technology exceeded the equity capital of all but two of the nation's largest banks. As one Citicorp manager explained:

> We're convinced that tomorrow's success depends on the investment we make today in technology. It's clearly the future and we are betting on it.

There were a number of reasons for Citi's emphasis on electronic banking. First, as a very large, decentralized organization, Citi had a great deal to gain from establishing a low-cost delivery system. As Peter Bleyleben, manager of the Boston office of the Boston Consulting Group, noted:

> Scale was never a factor in banking before automation. . . . Automation has made scale important. Since required investments in data-processing systems are large, the greater the volume, the faster the payback and the lower the ongoing operating costs per transaction.

Second, Citi already had a global electronic network in place, while its primary competitors were still scrambling to get theirs established. Bringing electronic banking power closer to the customer would enable Citi to take fuller advantage of its network, and provide it with a competitive advantage. Citi had, for example, established a global network of brokerage firms that were members of seventeen different exchanges. Putting linked dealing stations into the hands of major investors would allow them to take advantage of cross-border opportunities that were possible only because of the global network.

The third reason for Citi's aggressiveness in electronic banking was related to its efforts to penetrate the investment banking market. Despite its late entry, Citi had the scale and resources to make it a contender in this industry, provided that it could find a unique basis for competitive advantage. In the opinion of senior Citicorp executives, the newly emerging electronic marketplaces were likely to provide such a basis. As Reed told a meeting of senior Citi executives:

> It seems to me that there is no organization other than our own that has a better right to try to foster, develop, and make available to the world's customers these types of electronic marketplaces.

In the Individual Bank, the thrust of electronic banking was on ATMs, point-of-sales (POS) systems, and home banking. ATMs offering simple cash withdrawals were expected to be progressively complemented by a new generation of customer-operated terminals that provided more sophisticated services, such as deposit taking, statement reporting, and bill paying. POS terminals were usually located in high-activity retail outlets. Shoppers with POS cards could pay for goods with their cards instead of cash. As the cashier passed the card through a card reader, the customer entered a personal code. If the card was valid and the account balance sufficient, the funds would be debited from the customer's account and credited to the retailer. Home banking made it possible for consumers to check their account balances, transfer funds among accounts, make investments, and pay bills through the use of a PC (or, for simple transactions, a Touch-tone telephone). In a recent *American Banker* survey, 39 percent of the respondents said they would be happy to do all of their banking without ever having to go into a branch office.

In the Investment Bank, Citi had introduced a computerized trading system called Street Sense for brokers, dealers, and money managers. Street Sense compressed the securities trading process so that it could be accomplished faster and with fewer people. According to one executive:

> Investors don't want to look at the screen, see numbers, do an analysis, and then call somebody up on the phone and place an order. They just want to push one button.

In the Institutional Bank, office banking products had been developed to respond to the changing needs of corporate clients. Until the late 1950s, affiliates of multinational firms had managed their cash positions country by country, since many currencies were not convertible and the movement of funds was frequently blocked by exchange controls. By the 1970s and 1980s, however, the long-awaited "global treasury" had become a reality. Multinational corporations now insisted on being able to transfer funds from countries with cash surpluses to countries with cash deficits—instantly! Citi's corporate electronic banking products were intended to improve service to its multinational customers by providing up-to-the-minute reports on their worldwide cash positions and by greatly speeding up the transfer of funds from one country to another.

CITIBANK IN INDONESIA

When Suharto succeeded Sukarno as president of Indonesia in March 1968, he quickly moved to restore stability to a country that had battled for its independence for more than two decades. One of his first major moves was to set in motion an ambitious program of economic development. Citibank established a branch in Jakarta shortly thereafter (in June 1968), considerably later than it had entered most ASEAN[6] countries, but at the right time to take advantage of the sustained, oil-driven economic growth that Indonesia would experience over the next two decades.

In 1987, Citibank Indonesia was the largest foreign bank in the country, with an asset base of $578 million (U.S.)[7] and a substantial commercial and retail clientele. It had grown from a one-office operation of 16 employees in 1968 to two buildings and 450 employees in the southern and northern sections of Jakarta. Pretax income for 1986 had been $16 million, up from $11 million in 1985.

The relationship between Citibank Indonesia and its parent corporation was complex. While the Indonesian subsidiary was headed by a country CEO who reported to the Asia/Pacific Region, in reality, Citibank Indonesia consisted of four separate banks (the Investment Bank, the Institutional Bank, the Individual Bank, and the Private Bank), as shown in Exhibit 21.1. The country CEO's primary role was to act as the bank's official representative—cutting ribbons, giving speeches, and meeting government officials.

Each of the four "Banks" had its own chief, who reported to his "Bank's" Asia/Pacific regional headquarters in Singapore, Tokyo, or Hong Kong. Each "Bank" was operated separately from the others, but was expected to advise the country CEO (who himself headed one of the "Banks") on the strategy of its individual business. Resource allocation was negotiated among the "Banks." The Individual Bank, for example, charged the Private Bank for the premises it utilized, while the Technology Management Area, a component of the Institutional Bank, charged the other three "Banks" for data processing and related technical services.[8]

---

[6] The Association of Southeast Asian Nations (ASEAN) included Brunei, Indonesia, Malaysia, the Philippines, Singapore, and Thailand.

[7] All Indonesian financial data have been converted to U.S. dollars at the July 1987 rate of exchange.

[8] The Individual Bank Indonesia had recently decided to develop its own technology management group so it would have fuller control over this dimension of its business.

EXHIBIT 21.1
Citibank Indonesia Reporting Structure

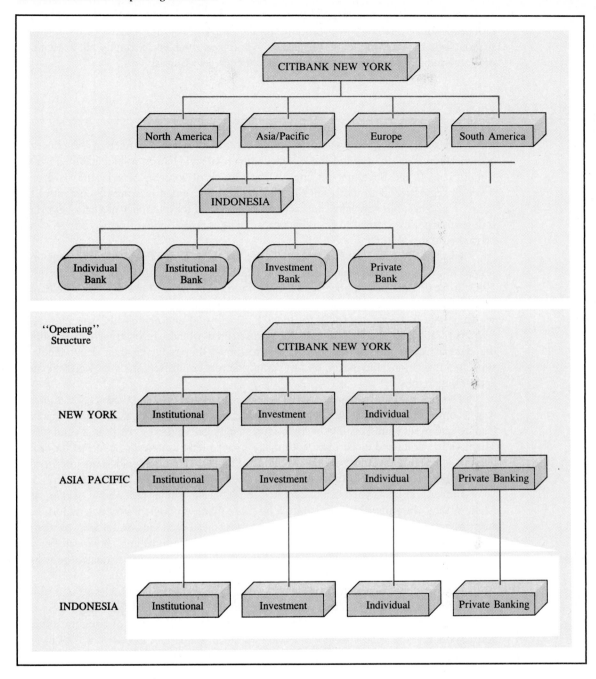

Citibank Indonesia reported to headquarters through a system utilized throughout the corporation—the Management Profitability Report (MPR). The MPR analyzed the country's business by individual product/market segments and highlighted those segments that met profitability criteria and those that did not. The performance of each business segment was evaluated against the country plan, which had previously been approved by senior management. Each business segment was more or less left to its own devices in determining how best to meet its objectives.

443

Citibank employed a higher percentage of graduates of foreign universities than any other corporation in Indonesia.[9] The vast majority of the bank's marketing officers, for example, had studied in the United States. In contrast to other firms in Indonesia, Citibank Indonesia had a distinctly Western culture and employed a high degree of automation. Although there were only eight expatriates working at the bank, virtually all written and oral communication among managers was conducted in English.

THE INDONESIAN BANKING SYSTEM

Indonesia's banking system was very tightly controlled by the Central Bank. It consisted of Bank Indonesia (the Central Bank), the commercial state banks, private national banks, foreign banks, and development banks. The growth of foreign-owned banks had been severely regulated, with the result that this sector represented less than 5 percent of the industry in 1987. No new bank licenses had been issued for a number of years, and Bank Indonesia's policy seemed to be to encourage bank mergers in an effort to strengthen the private banking sector.

Historically, the state banks and the private (both national and foreign) banks had served relatively distinct markets, but since the passage of a series of bank reforms in 1983, these distinctions had been gradually eroding. The reforms allowed the state banks, which accounted for roughly 80 percent of the country's commercial banking assets, to set their own interest rates (both for loans and deposits) and abolished restrictive credit ceilings for the entire banking sector. The primary goals of these reforms were to encourage the state banks to actively mobilize domestic funds, thus reducing their dependency on subsidies from Bank Indonesia, and to shrink interest rate differentials between the state and private banks.

The Indonesian financial sector also included several nonbank financial institutions (e.g., joint venture investment banks), leasing companies, and insurance companies. Capital and money markets had become increasingly active during the past several years. The nation maintained close links with many major international financial institutions; it was a member of the International Monetary Fund, the International Bank for Reconstruction and Development (the World Bank), and the Asian Development Bank.

Eleven foreign-owned banks operated in Indonesia. Under Indonesian banking legislation, they were permitted to maintain no more than two branches (which had to be in Jakarta) and were prohibited from lending to companies based outside Jakarta, except for loan syndications with local banks. (Under recent export credit rulings, however, foreign banks would be allowed to finance export transactions for customers located anywhere in Indonesia.)

Citibank, the largest foreign bank operating in Indonesia, had a substantial local and multinational clientele, comprising more than 800 Institutional Bank customers and more than 3,000 Individual Bank customers. It offered a wide range of banking services and provided ready access to global capital markets. While its business was still largely commercial, its Individual Bank, which served the expanding middle class, had recently been growing considerably faster than the bank as a whole.

The Indonesian government exercised very strong controls on the dissemination of information, including financial market data. Its news agency, ANTARA, had a monopoly on the distribution of public information and was a participant in all contractual agreements between information users and providers (including foreign information services such as

---

[9] The large number of foreign graduates in Citibank Indonesia was largely the result of a program at Citibank headquarters in New York to recruit foreign students studying at top U.S. schools. Citibank Indonesia also had a policy of training as many as possible of its staff abroad, in order to expose Indonesian managers to employees from other countries and the United States.

Reuters and Telerate). Telecommunications costs were high. A leased telephone line within Jakarta cost $600 per month, and a line to Singapore between $7,000 and $25,000 per month. Leased lines were classified as either "common carriers" or "noncommon carriers." A common carrier (i.e., one that permitted data input) cost 200–300 percent more than a noncommon carrier.

Reliable local trade, finance, and business information was scarce, and government figures were often not considered credible. Under these circumstances, many companies operating in Indonesia had learned to do business in what was essentially an information-deficient environment. According to an expatriate manager for Procter & Gamble—a company well known throughout the world for its heavy reliance on marketing research—the Indonesian market offered P&G the highest growth potential in Southeast Asia, despite the fact that P&G could not "determine that the average Indonesian Folgers coffee drinker has a mean age of 30.56, and 1.42 cars and 2.01 kids in his or her household."

CITIBANK INDONESIA

ELECTRONIC BANKING

Citibank Indonesia's electronic banking venture had been instigated by Jack Carvier, who had been head of Citi's Institutional Bank in Indonesia in the early to mid-1980s. Carvier had received his first foreign assignment, as senior country operating officer in Greece, thirteen years after joining the bank. After five successful years in Greece, he had been transferred to Indonesia.

At that time, the Institutional Bank was coming under considerable pressure in many countries. Large corporations were increasingly bypassing banks and raising funds directly in the capital markets. Loans had become less profitable, with write-offs running at more than two times the normal rate. Citi's Institutional Banks around the world were instructed to seek new sources of revenue. Carvier himself believed that the future lay in fee-based transactional banking.

Within the Institutional Bank, the World Corporate Group (WCG) served major multinational corporations and (at that time) had responsibility for global electronic banking. Steve Korach, head of the WCG in Indonesia, was asked by Carvier to generate new products and services. Initially, he investigated the possibility of selling computer training services to Institutional Bank customers (e.g., for a fee, Citibank Indonesia would train local managers to use computer software such as Lotus 1-2-3). After considerable research and discussion, this project had been terminated on the grounds that the potential market was too small; not enough companies had computers or planned to buy them in the near future.

Korach then looked into offering innovative electronic banking (EB) products to customers. The proposal he developed recommended that terminals (later, PCs) be leased to Citibank customers for a nominal fee and linked to Citibank's EB system. Korach believed that the convenience of EB would encourage customers to increase their transaction banking activities with Citibank, and that EB would make it possible to get around the restrictions on branch banking outside of Jakarta. At present, for example, companies in Surabaya, the second largest city in Indonesia, were unlikely to do business with Citi unless they were heavily involved in foreign trade. In Korach's view, such companies would be likely to be attracted by a direct computer link with a major international bank in Jakarta.

At this time, Citibank Indonesia was already a full-fledged participant in Citi's global electronic banking network, including CitiMail, electronic trading, and the Global Communication Network (GCN) (see Exhibit 21.2). Citibank Indonesia was generally considered to be the most technologically advanced company in the country.[10] With the bank's

---

[10] The bank's IBM 308 mainframe computer was the only one of its kind in Indonesia, for example. IBM had stationed a maintenance team in Indonesia that was totally dedicated to serving Citibank.

EXHIBIT 21.2
Citibank Indonesia Network

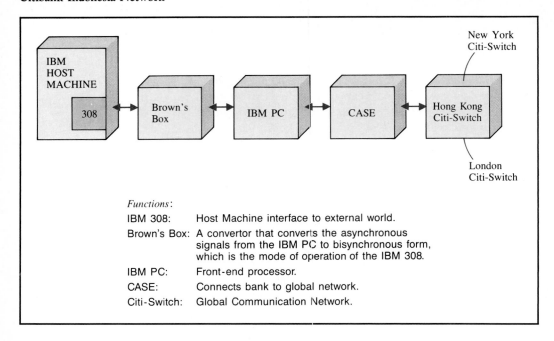

Functions:

IBM 308: Host Machine interface to external world.

Brown's Box: A convertor that converts the asynchronous signals from the IBM PC to bisynchronous form, which is the mode of operation of the IBM 308.

IBM PC: Front-end processor.

CASE: Connects bank to global network.

Citi-Switch: Global Communication Network.

computer network, marketing officers could access their clients' account status through terminals on their desks. As they became aware of this procedure, some customers literally remarked; "I wish your computer terminal was on my desk so that I could make the inquiry myself without bothering you."

The idea of putting EB power into the hands of customers was thus already in the air when Korach made his proposal. Citi's Hong Kong[11] branch had already begun offering customers EB services, and—at least initially—seemed to be doing quite well. With blessings from the Institutional Bank regional headquarters in Hong Kong, EB was launched in Indonesia in early 1982.

Citibank Indonesia's first EB product was called Citikilat ("Citi-Lightning"). With Citikilat, users could execute most banking activities without leaving their offices. The technology, which had been developed elsewhere in Citicorp, involved connecting a personal computer in each customer's office directly to the bank's mainframe computer via the public telephone network. (See Exhibit 21.3 for a depiction of the functional components of the EB system.)

Citikilat comprised three distinct services: (1) Account Inquiry; (2) Business Information Inquiry; and (3) Transaction Initiation. Account Inquiry allowed customers to access their account balances, daily statements, and incoming and outgoing cash flows, as well as to obtain various other types of information concerning their personal or corporate accounts. Business Information Inquiry included up-to-the-minute foreign exchange rates, money market rates, market indication rates, industry news, stock prices, and other business information. Finally, Transaction Initiation allowed the user to send funds transfers, initiate letters of credit, and transfer funds between accounts.

Citibank provided each customer with a modem, a Delta Box (a security device), and (in some cases) one or more PCs. It installed the service in the customer's offices

---

[11] Hong Kong, which was the financial capital of Southeast Asia and a common regional headquarters for Western companies, had a much more fully developed financial and information infrastructure than Indonesia. In the view of Citibank managers, Hong Kong tended to have much more sophisticated companies and managers than any other country in Southeast Asia.

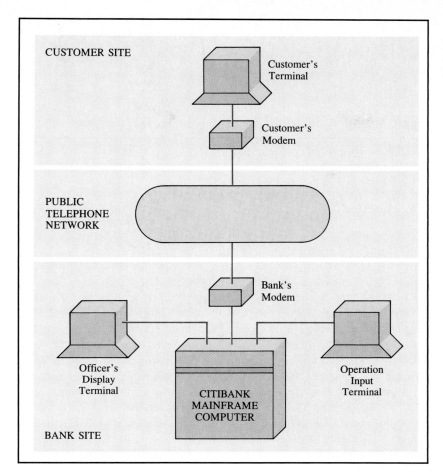

EXHIBIT 21.3
Components of an
Electronic Banking System

and trained customer personnel in the use of the system. For this service, customers were charged a one-time installation fee of $150 and a subscription fee of $150 per month.

All Institutional Bank marketing officers were given the goal of selling three EB subscriptions a year. As a further incentive, the marketing officer with the highest Citikilat subscriptions sales was to receive a cash award. The fact that EB seemed to be a "pet project" of top management also boosted the marketing officers' enthusiasm for the product.

The EB unit supported the marketing officers' efforts with a series of seminars at expensive hotels in Bali, an Indonesian island known for its beauty and amenities. Prospective clients were to attend a multimedia presentation on the potential of EB and how it related to their business, and then take part in a hands-on EB workshop.

Citibank, which was known throughout Asia as "a great school of banking," had a reputation for giving high-quality educational seminars that featured interactive workshops, dynamic speakers, and hearty feasts. The response to the Citikilat seminars was excellent, with 80 percent of those invited sending their senior finance managers or MIS personnel, and a large percentage of those who attended expressing interest in trying the system.

Following the Bali seminars, the bank's marketing officers began offering a free trial period and signing up Citikilat customers. The initial customers received strong support from EB training and maintenance teams, and there were frequent user group sessions and newsletters. Based on this feedback, modifications were made in screen format, the number of passwords for each account, authorization levels, the frequency

447

of foreign exchange updates, and the specific content of the "news reports" provided by the system.

Over the next several years, additional EB products that had been developed at Citicorp were offered:

EB SERVICE	YEAR INTRODUCED	INSTALLATION	MONTHLY FEE
CitiPhone	Late 1982	$150	$ 150
Global Report	1984	$150	$ 250 + $100/hr.
CitiWriter	1984	$ 75	$ 50
CitiPDC	1985	$150	$ 100
CitiMarket	1985	$150	$1500

Citiphone directly connected individual households and small businesses to the bank's mainframe computers via pushbutton telephones. The computer, responding with an electronically simulated voice, provided information on the status of the customer's accounts in response to the codes entered on the telephone's keypad. Global Report integrated news and data from international information services such as Dow Jones, Quotron, Comtex, the Knight-Ridder Commodity News Service, and Standard & Poor's. CitiMarket provided currency rates and other money market indicators. CitiPDC was an EB service offered to companies whose businesses involved large volumes of postdated checks. CitiWriter was a stand-alone, automated check-writing, record-keeping, and reconciliation system. (See Exhibit 21.4 for examples of product brochures.)

In the view of Citibank managers, the introduction of EB in Indonesia had been "fairly successful." By the end of 1984, Citibank had 300 EB connections, 248 of which were for Citikilat. At this time, Citibank's two major competitors in Indonesia, Bank of America and the Chase Manhattan Bank, began offering EB services. Chase offered a global EB and information service to a select group of major multinational customers. In 1987, the service had approximately forty corporate users in Indonesia. Bank of America's Asian group, based in Hong Kong, had developed a product called MICRO-WORLD especially for Asian markets. MICRO-WORLD was a microcomputer, MS-DOS, DBASE II system that sought to minimize communications with the host computer, and thus reduce communications costs. Marketed in Indonesia with the slogan "The Next Generation Electronic Product Is Here," it had a user base of twenty companies as of mid-1987.

Meanwhile, back in the United States, John Reed was directing the bank toward giving more priority to consumer and investment banking, and placing less emphasis on the Institutional Bank. Throughout the organization, more attention was being paid to the profitability of individual businesses. A McKinsey study had shown that transactional banking was not as profitable as it had seemed, so fees for transactional services were increased in most markets, including Indonesia. A considerable proportion of Citibank Indonesia's transaction-oriented customers soon migrated to banks that charged more competitive prices.

At the same time, Citibank Indonesia adopted a new profitability management concept called "profitability management by product," a significant departure from its earlier focus on departmental profitability. According to the new system, EB had a very poor bottom line, since its heavy processing and maintenance costs far outweighed the revenues it generated through installation and subscription fees. Whereas EB had previously been viewed largely as a "sweetener" for the bank's transaction customers, it was now considered a profit center and was expected to carry its own weight.

By late 1986, the marketing officers were being pressured by top management to focus on selling Investment Banking products and the cash rewards and other incentives

EXHIBIT 21.4
Examples of EB Product Brochures

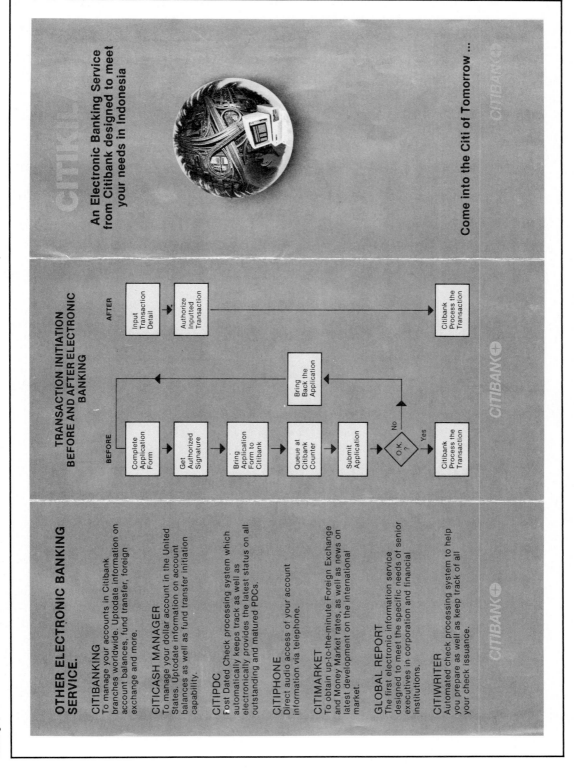

OTHER ELECTRONIC BANKING SERVICE.

CITIBANKING
To manage your accounts in Citibank branches worldwide. Uptodate information on account balances, fund transfer, foreign exchange and more.

CITICASH MANAGER
To manage your dollar account in the United States. Uptodate information on account balances as well as fund transfer initiation capability.

CITIPDC
Post Dated Check processing system which automatically keeps track as well as electronically provides the latest status on all outstanding and matured PDCs.

CITIPHONE
Direct audio access of your account information via telephone.

CITIMARKET
To obtain up-to-the-minute Foreign Exchange and Money Market rates, as well as news on latest development on the international market.

GLOBAL REPORT
The first electronic information service designed to meet the specific needs of senior executives in corporation and financial institutions.

CITIWRITER
Automated check processing system to help you prepare as well as keep track of all your check issuance.

TRANSACTION INITIATION BEFORE AND AFTER ELECTRONIC BANKING

BEFORE

Complete Application Form → Get Authorized Signature → Bring Application Form to Citibank → Queue at Citibank Counter → Submit Application → O.K.? — No → Bring Back the Application

O.K.? — Yes → Citibank Process the Transaction

AFTER

Input Transaction Detail → Authorize Inputted Transaction → Citibank Process the Transaction

CITIKU

An Electronic Banking Service from Citibank designed to meet your needs in Indonesia

Come into the Citi of Tomorrow ...

CITIBANK

449

EXHIBIT 21.4
(continued)

CITIBANK+

CITIKILAT
Basic Reports and Other Key Features

INTRODUCING CITIKILAT

We at Citibank understand how time consuming monitoring your banking transaction can be. Now with Citikilat, you can overcome those cumbersome chores, easily.

Citikilat is another innovative electronic banking service of Citibank Jakarta. It allows our customers to communicate to our computer via a terminal located at their own offices. Through this connection, Citibank can then provide you with the essential information on your transactions, international financial information; and capability to initiate banking transaction.

CITIKILAT BENEFITS

IMPROVED CASH MANAGEMENT
By subscribing to Citikilat, you save valuable man-hours in reconciling your banking transactions with the availability of a more timely, accurate, and easier access to key information on your banking transaction.

BETTER SECURITY
To ensure the information confidentiality, the system is password protected. This means that only authorized users who have been assigned their own unique access code, can retrieve information from the system.

MORE CONVENIENT
Through the transaction initiation feature of Citikilat, you can initiate banking transaction from your own office with convenience.

CITIBANK+

CURRENT ACCOUNT REPORTS

Reports balances, transaction details and 30 day history of your accounts. Supports easy, daily reconcilement of accounts as well as providing information for efficient funds management.

TREASURY REPORT

Daily detailed reports on Foreign Exchange and Money Market rates. Also available are updates on major stock exchange, precious metal prices and a commentary on money market developments.

OTHER REPORTS

Provides summaries as well as detailed information of all currently outstanding Letter of Credit, Loans, Time Deposits and Foreign Exchange contracts.

TRANSACTION INITIATION

Permits initiation from your office of Fund Transfer, L/C opening/amendment, and Time Deposit opening; all are protected by our advanced security system and comprehensive audit trail.

for selling EB products were being eliminated.[12] Under considerable pressure to reduce expenses and headcount, the EB division began to phase out many of its more ambitious programs, to monitor service quality less frequently, to shorten training sessions for users, and to reduce its maintenance force. If it had not been for the bank's commitment to loyal EB users who had come to rely on the system, EB would probably have been eliminated altogether at this time.

In seeking to reduce costs, the EB staff conducted a study of customer EB activity level. According to this study, a number of the ''pioneers'' who had received free ''trials'' had not used the system for six months or more. This finding led to the ''Great Sweep,'' in which the EB maintenance crew visited such accounts, terminated their service, and removed the bank's personal computers and modems. A considerable number of the companies affected by the Great Sweep seemed not to mind, as one put it, ''getting rid of those paperweights.'' According to one EB staff member, at least some of these customers had only agreed to install Citikilat out of politeness to their marketing officers.[13]

THE FUTURE

''Robbie'' Hartanto, Citibank Indonesia's vice president in charge of EB, observed that at the rate things were going, he would soon need to start looking for a new assignment. There was no chance of transferring to other Citibank EB groups in the neighboring ASEAN countries, since they had been eliminated a year previously. In fact, Indonesia was the only ASEAN country still actively offering EB, although the service was said to be still thriving in Hong Kong.

Hartanto brought in a team of management consultants to investigate: (1) the perceptions of users regarding the EB system and service; (2) current usage of the various components of the system; and (3) future enhancements that might be made to the EB system. The team conducted personal interviews with approximately twenty-five ex-users, and twenty-four Citikilat users over a two-week period. Bank personnel (the EB staff as well as the marketing officers) selected the interview sample and arranged all appointments. The user sample consisted primarily of heavy Citikilat users who regarded Citibank as their primary bank.

Hartanto also assigned an internal task force to interview the marketing officers in the bank, to assess the financial performance of the unit as a whole, and to investigate the high attrition rate of EB users.

After completing their studies, the two teams identified four specific problem areas. First was the diminishing customer base. Over the past twelve months, the bank had lost sixteen more EB customers than it had signed up, resulting in a reduction of the Citikilat customer base from 222 in June 1986 to 206 in June 1987(see Exhibit 21.5). According to the interviews, ex-users did not perceive that Citikilat, and electronic banking in general, added value to current banking services. None of the ex-users claimed to have obtained significant cost savings as a result of using the system. Clerical wages were low, and messenger delivery was essential for so many other functions that EB customers would not have been able to dispense with their ''M-boys''[14] even had they wanted to.

---

[12] This did not displease the EB staff, which felt that it had been doing a large portion of the ''real work'' (e.g., presentations, training, and customer service), but had not received special rewards for doing so.

[13] Indonesian culture valued civility and politeness very highly.

[14] There was nothing in Western countries that was directly equivalent to the ubiquitous messenger boy (M-boy) in Indonesia. The M-boy wiped the windowpanes, swept and mopped the office, unclogged the water basins, and the like. While it was the secretaries' job to fluff up the pillows in the executive lounge, it was the faithful M-boy who prepared and served coffee for the staff and guests, photocopied documents, distributed office notices, and sorted and distributed incoming mail. Part of his job was to act as the company's private postman for hand-delivering important documents (e.g., between a bank and the office). In 1987, an M-boy was typically paid the equivalent of $15 a month.

EXHIBIT 21.5
Recent EB Sales Experience

MONTH	NEW CONNECTIONS	TERMINATIONS	PRODUCT	NET SALES BY PRODUCT		
				Kilat	Phone	Market
Jul '86	1	2	Kilat	−1		
	1	1	Phone		0	
	1		Market			1
Aug '86	2		Kilat	2		
		1	Phone		−1	
			Market			0
Sep '86	1		Kilat	1		
			Phone		0	
		2	Market			−2
Oct '86		1	Kilat	−1		
		1	Phone		−1	
			Market			0
Nov '86	1	1	Kilat	0		
			Phone		0	
		1	Market			−1
Dec '86	1	4	Kilat	−3		
	2	1	Phone		1	
			Market			0
Jan '87		3	Kilat	−3		
	2		Phone		2	
	1		Market			1
Feb '87	1	2	Kilat	−1		
	2	1	Phone		1	
		1	Market			−1
Mar '87	1	3	Kilat	−2		
	2		Phone		2	
			Market			0
Apr '87		6	Kilat	−6		
	1	1	Phone		0	
	1	1	Market			0
May '87	1	1	Kilat	0		
	2		Phone		2	
			Market			0
Jun '87	1	3	Kilat	−2		
			Phone		0	
	1	1	Market			0
			Total (net)	−16	6	−2
				Kilat	Phone	Market

In discussing their experience in making payments through Citikilat, the ex-users noted that they favored the widespread practice of suppliers personally collecting checks, since they got to use the funds if the supplier was late in collecting and there was no possibility of the payment going astray. Several respondents pointed out that it was common practice in Indonesia to maintain multiple banking relationships,[15] and that since Citikilat did not allow consolidation of other banks' information, the system had not proved to be as useful for cash management as they had hoped.

---

[15] In Indonesia, a company typically had a relationship with a government local bank in order to maintain good relations with government bureaus, and a relationship with two or three foreign banks to obtain loans. The share of the company's business received by a given bank was not solely a function of its rates or service levels. Johnson & Johnson Indonesia, for example, split its business more or less equally between its main banks, Chase and Citibank, because it considered doing so to be "fair."

Of the twenty-four current Citikilat users interviewed, only three were using the transaction initiation module on a regular basis. Inquiries about current balances and transactions were the most frequently used features of the system. The reasons most commonly given by respondents for not using a wider range of functions included concerns about security, having relationships with more than one bank, and preferring hand delivery of payments.

The consultants noted that several other factors might have been contributing to relatively low Citikilat usage levels. Some ex-users claimed that high telephone rates prevented them from using the service frequently enough to justify the monthly subscription fee. (A company that used the service thirty to forty minutes per day would incur incremental telephone charges equivalent to $15 per month, enough to hire an M-boy.) A more subtle problem concerned Indonesian attitudes toward seniority. In most companies, high-level executives did not mingle with lower-level managers, with the exception of their direct subordinates, or *anak-buah* (''little nymphs''). To use Citikilat, the boss had to walk over to the terminal of one of his little nymphs to authorize a transaction, and then wait while the transaction was being transmitted. Citibank Indonesia, where everyone from the country CEO to the janitor was on a first-name basis, had apparently not anticipated the discomfort this aspect of the system would cause more traditional managers.

Many of the Indonesian managers interviewed in the study seemed to be extremely concerned about the possibility of electronic fraud. The consultants hypothesized that this concern might have been related to the special significance of a person's signature in Indonesia, where signatures tended to be as artistic, intricate, and illegible as possible (and therefore extremely difficult to forge). When an Indonesian manager used Citikilat, the consultants noted, he was forced to replace this artistic inscription with an impersonal authorization code and the touch of a button.

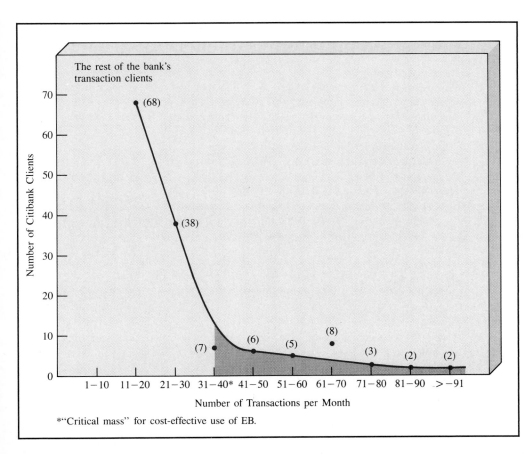

EXHIBIT 21.6
Potential EB Clients
(Current EB clients not included)

The rest of the bank's transaction clients

*''Critical mass'' for cost-effective use of EB.

The consultants thought that it might be significant that all EB brochures and instruction manuals were printed in English. Although Citibank's contacts with local companies were virtually always conducted in the local Indonesian language, no Indonesian EB promotional materials were available. According to the consultants, a non–English-speaking local manager, when confronted with this foreign-language material, would either have to "lose face" and ask the marketing officer to translate the brochures, or say "Thank you for the brochures" and put them away in his drawer.

The studies also pointed to the diminishing prospect pool for Citikilat. At $150 a month, Citikilat would only be cost effective for a customer above a "critical mass" of transactions. As the bank's emphasis had shifted away from the Institutional Bank, and price increases had reduced the number transaction-oriented customers, the pool of Citikilat prospects had shrunk significantly. (See Exhibit 21.6.)

Both teams were concerned about how to rejuvenate interest in EB among the marketing officers. The personal interviews (see Exhibit 21.7) conducted by the internal team suggested that most marketing officers felt that EB did not add enough value to their clients' business to justify the cost of the service. Several of the marketing officers' complaints about Citikilat seemed to refer to earlier versions of the system, however. One officer, for example, grumbled for fifteen minutes about his client's complaints concerning stale data, apparently believing that the Citikilat data base was updated by batch processing at the end of the day. In fact, the data were now updated on a continuous real-time basis, as they had been for more than a year.

The consultants noted that as many as one-third of user complaints could be traced to a particular component of the system—Protocol Converter Interface, called in Indonesia

---

EXHIBIT 21.7
Exerpt from Electronic Banking Survey of Marketing Officers, June 1987

(*11 out of 24 marketing officers returned survey*)
Response is in bold italic.

0. When was the last time you recommended an EB product to your client and what product was it?
   Average: 8 months
1. We at EB regard the marketing officers as an important and valuable link between EB and our prospective customers. What do you perceive as the reasons your fellow marketing officers are not more aggressively recommending EB products to their clients?
   Please cross boxes for top THREE or LESS reasons:

Are not aware of the available EB products and their prices.	*0*
Are not aware of how EB can benefit the clients	*3*
Received negative feedbacks from clients using EB	*9*
There are too many operational problems with the product	*7*
The commission for selling EB is too low compared to other products.	*5*

2. I have recommended or sold this product before:

Citikilat	*11*
Citiphone	*6*
Global Report	*2*
CitiPDC	*1*
Citimarket	*2*
Citiwriter	*2*

3. What is the most common main objective(s) raised by prospective clients for not subscribing to EB?

• Price	*8*
• Nothing lacking with current traditional system	*4*
• Concerned about security	*2*
• Others	*2*

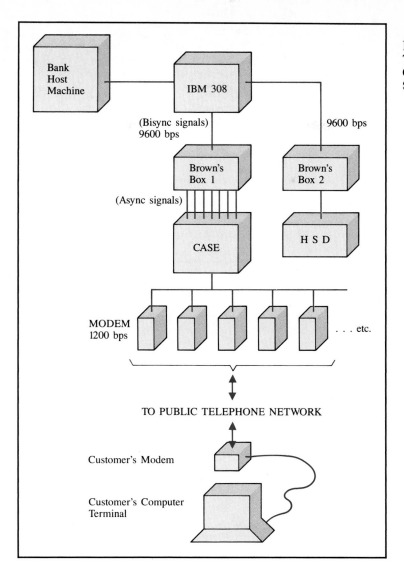

EXHIBIT 21.8
Technical Components or Citibank Indonesia EB System

the Brown's Box. (Exhibit 21.8 shows a block diagram of the system that supported EB. The HSD shown in this diagram was a security device that processed the client's password.) The two Brown's Boxes converted incoming asynchronous signals to the bisynchronous signals necessary for the IBM 308, a mainframe computer that had been designed primarily for batch processing. Users had complained most frequently about busy lines and the slowness of the system when logging in. This speed was controlled by the Brown's Box that processed messages at 9600 bps (bits per second). Since a connection could only be established after the HSD approved the password, and since this required passing through the Brown's Box twice, the wait for password approval on busy mornings could be as long as twenty minutes.

Hartanto was convinced that he could solve this problem by replacing the Brown's Box with an IBM 7071, such as was used for this purpose by Citibank Hong Kong. He doubted, however, that he would be able to get authorization for a $200,000 investment to support a business that might be on its last legs. What steps, he wondered, might he take to restore the EB business to good health? Should he advertise EB[16] for the first

---

[16] See Exhibit 20.9 for the proposed copy. The objective of this copy execution was to make EB seem "friendlier" to the target audience.

EXHIBIT 21.9
Draft of Proposed Citikilat
Advertisement

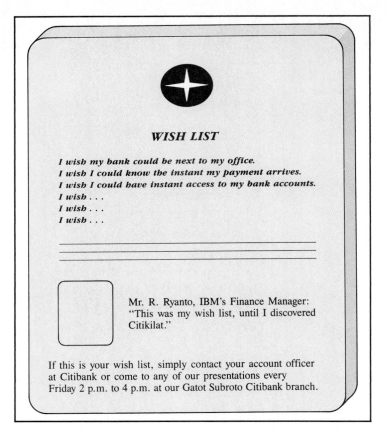

time, for example, or should he repackage Citibank's EB offerings? Or would it make more sense to admit that Indonesia wasn't ready for electronic banking and look for a new assignment?

QUESTIONS FOR DISCUSSION

1. How would you characterize Citibank's overall corporate strategy?
2. How would you characterize the market and competitive environments for banking services in Indonesia?
3. What seem to have been Citibank's objectives for Citikilat?
4. What seems to have gone wrong?
5. As Robbie Hartanto, what would you do now?
6. As a member of Citicorp senior management in New York, what would you make of this episode?

PART FOUR

IMPLEMENTATION

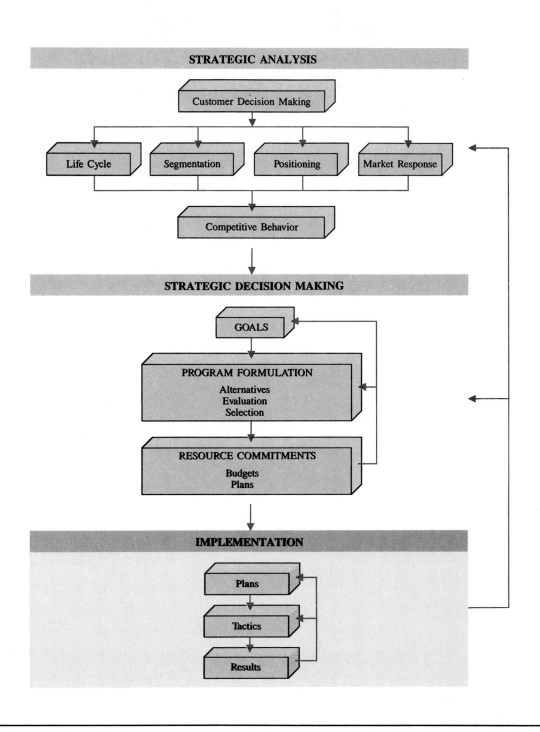

STRATEGIC ANALYSIS

Customer Decision Making

Life Cycle

Segmentation

Positioning

Market Response

Competitive Behavior

STRATEGIC DECISION MAKING

GOALS

PROGRAM FORMULATION

Alternatives
Evaluation
Selection

RESOURCE COMMITMENTS

Budgets
Plans

IMPLEMENTATION

Plans

Tactics

Results

TACTICS AND CONTROL

CONVERTING STRATEGIC PLANS INTO ACTION AND RESULTS

Effective strategy formulation is based on a comprehensive analysis of customer decision making, life-cycle characteristics, segmentation, positioning, market response, and competitive behavior. A fundamental understanding of these phenomena is essential if we are to develop intelligent marketing programs, set meaningful budgets, and make productive plans. These basic marketing phenomena are key inputs in developing new products, in managing established products and product lines, and in shaping worldwide product-market portfolios.

But all of this analysis is only worthwhile if it leads to the *execution* of a winning strategy. As in football, you cannot win, even if you have a great game plan, unless you can kick, pass, run, and tackle better than the other team. The battle is fought in the trenches, and it is there that superiority must be achieved.

In Chapter 2, we described the translation of programs into resource commitments and plans, while in Chapter 17, we discussed resource allocations to strategic business units. (You may find it useful to review these chapters at this point.) These allocations were based on overall judgments regarding how various markets would respond to alternative levels of resources, given assumptions concerning cost structures, competitive actions, and market growth. Marketing strategies drawn from analysis at this level would necessarily be highly aggregated and general. Effective *implementation*, conversely, requires describing such resource allocations in very specific terms and associating explicit time lines with them.

The strategic *core benefit proposition* (i.e., how our marketing program proposes to create value for customers and to establish competitive advantage) is the single most important output from the strategic planning process. It is based on decisions concerning target segmentation and positioning, as well as on broad commitments of resources to advertising, selling, promotion, distribution, pricing, and service, These overall commitments subsequently need to be translated into specific programs and plans, and then

459

into detailed tactics. It is essential that the essence of the strategy not be lost or diluted during this process.

All tactical decisions must be measured against a clearly defined strategy to achieve what we call *strategic coherence*. Each element of the tactical plan must be consistent with the overall strategy; together, the tactical commitments should generate synergy in establishing the desired core benefit proposition. When creating advertising copy, for example, care should be taken not to lose sight of the basic strategic thrust in an effort to be "exciting" or "original." The final advertising seen by the target customer must support the overall strategy, if strategic coherence is to be achieved.

We cannot discuss all of the many tactical issues associated with various strategies in this chapter. Indeed, complete books are written on such topics as advertising (Aaker and Meyers, 1975), pricing (Monroe, 1979), promotion (Lodish, 1986; Blattberg and Neslin, 1990), distribution (Stern and El Ansary, 1977), and selling (Churchill, 1981). Our focus here is on *strategic coherence*. We delineate the tactical variables, but our primary focus is on ensuring that these variables work together to achieve strategic goals.

Once a tactical plan has been developed and approved, it is then necessary to *monitor* and *control* its implementation. One should always begin by ascertaining whether the approved marketing program was, in fact, implemented as planned. Very often, for example, it may prove difficult to hire the planned sales force or open the planned distribution channels on schedule, or even to deliver the planned product in adequate quantities. Assuming that the program was implemented more or less as planned, our next step is to compare actual and predicted results. If the results we are achieving do not match our expectations, we will need to revise our tactics or reexamine the underlying strategic planning assumptions.

Analytic support can be extremely valuable in the implementation and monitoring and control processes. Later in this chapter, we present a short case to illustrate the use of analytic support for these purposes. The chapter closes with a consideration of the strategic planning process itself and a discussion of those factors that appear to impact greatly the effectiveness of that process.

TRANSITION FROM STRATEGY TO TACTICS

Pitfalls likely to impede strategic coherence exist in each major decision area. Let us now consider some of the most important ones.

Product Design

The core benefit needs to be fulfilled with respect to both product features and manufacturing quality. Moving from an overall positioning statement to a product that delivers the benefits in the core benefit proposition is not an easy task. Creative engineering talent must be recruited, motivated, and organized. Product design problems must be resolved. If, for example, the positioning for a new software product is based on "ease of use," it is more desirable to opt for a technical solution that is capable of satisfying 90 percent of customer needs in a user-friendly way than to adopt a state-of-the-art solution that meets 99 percent of their needs at the cost of increasing learning difficulties and maintenance problems. Alternatively, it might be appropriate to target a technical breakthrough that achieves both sophistication (at, say, the 95 percent level) and a high degree of user friendliness. Channeling R&D efforts toward achievement of the core benefit proposition is critical to the design of superior products. Design trade-offs should reflect the agreed-upon strategy and culminate in products that deliver the sought-after benefits to customers.

Another critical success factor in new-product strategy implementation is the ability to manufacture the product at high-quality standards. Product design must be translatable into a product that can be manufactured consistently to meet design specifications. A twenty-layer printed circuit board, for example, may appear to provide the ideal means of providing users with high-density integrated circuit components on a board, but if specifying so many layers leads to a high manufacturing defect rate, the design is not a good one. In tactics as well as in strategy, the interactions of marketing, R&D, and production must be carefully considered (review Figure 17.1 on page 341).

Time-to-market is increasingly important as market and competitive conditions change ever more rapidly. When we are racing to meet tight deadlines, we often take inappropriate risks. Should we do additional technical or customer testing to make sure we have made the optimal feature trade-offs and have developed an effective introduction strategy? Should we refine our volume estimates more precisely, or should we risk going by rough estimates in order to reach the market sooner? Although there are long-run benefits to being first in the market (review Chapter 14), these can be negated if we lose product quality or strategic coherence. We may find ourselves risking heavy expenditures to pioneer a new market, only to have competitors establish dominance with a superior product. The balancing of product features, manufacturing quality, and time-to-market is an exceptionally difficult area of tactical decision making. In seeking the appropriate balance, it is essential to continue to focus on delivering benefits to customers. We should not "Go" with the new-product launch unless we are confident that it substantiates its core benefit proposition from the customer's perspective.

It is essential that the product itself support the objective of strategic coherence. The core benefit proposition must be translated into a set of design specifications, manufacturing procedures, and introductory decisions that bolster its basic premises. In designing, manufacturing, and delivering the product, we must constantly remember that our goal is to provide value to a target set of customers that is superior, from their point of view, to the value offered by competitive alternatives.

Advertising

The effectiveness of a communications program depends on the relationship between the characteristics of the target audience and the budget, media, and copy used. Overall spending must be set at a level sufficient to achieve desired reach and frequency against the target audience. Response models (review Chapters 9 and 15) are useful in setting budget levels, but spending productivity will depend greatly on the specific media selected. Television may have a lower cost per thousand impressions than newspapers, for example, but be less efficient in reaching the target audience. Still, a television impression, buttressed by sight, sound, and motion, may have more impact than a print impression.

Media buying decisions can be very complex, but must be consistent with the target audience, positioning, and copy called for by the strategy. In seeking low-cost media buys, it is all too easy to forget the basic premises of the strategy. Many advertisers and agencies have found it helpful to utilize simple tactical media models to maximize reach and/or frequency against the target market within the constraints of a preestablished media budget (see Little and Lodish, 1969; and Little, 1979). But no model can substitute for managerial judgment concerning the effectiveness of particular types of impressions.

Selection of copy is also critical to the achievement of strategic coherence. A television commercial showing a popular punk rock group performing as a new two-seat sports car drives through a disco would almost certainly attract attention and convey a youthful image, but it might be inappropriate for a $35,000 automobile targeted at managers and professionals. Moreover, such a commercial might have an impact (positive or negative) on the images of other cars offered by the company.

Advertising copy should be new, fresh, exciting, original; it must capture attention, develop comprehension, generate awareness, and produce attitude changes that lead to purchase. But if it is to support rather than work against the overall marketing objectives, it must be consistent with the strategy for the product (and, often, the firm).

One must also guard carefully against the tendency to overpromise. In an effort to obtain trial for a new packaged good or to generate shopping interest in a consumer durable, advertising agencies may come up with overly enthusiastic copy claims. While advertisements featuring such claims may be successful in achieving trial or shopping interest, they often lead to customer ill-will (even anger) because the product's actual benefits do not match the expectations aroused. In most cases, it is far sounder to employ realistic claims, even though this means that trial will build more slowly since trial obtained in this way is more likely to lead to repeat purchases and positive word-of-mouth communication.

Sales Force Management

Strategic coherence is as critical in sales force management as it is in advertising. Sales training, sales support materials, and reward systems must be consistent with the overall strategy. Personal communication, while often expensive, has many advantages in establishing key selling points that effectively portray the product and in custom tailoring the message to the needs and concerns of the target customer. The core benefit proposition should be central to the salesperson's presentation. The salesperson should elicit customer objections and points of resistance, and use the promised benefits of the marketing program to deal with them. If, for example, the core benefit proposition is to help customers solve a specific set of problems in using a particular plastic compound through better engineering and technical service, a consultative, problem-oriented selling process, directed at establishing a partnership with the customer, would probably be the best approach. If, however, the strategy is to be the lowest-cost producer and sell on the basis of price and availability, the sales presentation should emphasize price and delivery. In the latter instance, the sell would be "harder" than the "soft sell" of the partnership proposition.

Recruiting criteria, training, and reward systems would also be different for the two strategies. In implementing the first strategy, a highly educated salesperson (e.g., a graduate engineer) who has completed a fairly elaborate training program (including on-the-job training under a seasoned, consultative salesperson) and is compensated with salary plus bonus would probably be the best choice. For the second, low-price strategy, a less educated (e.g., junior college graduate) and less elaborately trained salesperson compensated largely by commission would probably be more appropriate. Both approaches could be successful in their respective strategy frameworks; the critical task is to match the correct sales management policies with the proper strategy.

As tactical communications programs become more complex (review Chapter 9), maintaining consistency among advertising copy, telemarketing scripts, promotional pieces, and personal selling will be a significant challenge. If media advertising and direct mail are both to be used to establish perceptual positioning, for example, each must persuasively establish a core selling proposition. This selling proposition is a selected subset of the core benefit promises that can be effectively communicated in a particular medium (i.e., it might be different for direct mail and media advertising; or even for various media—say, television versus newspapers). In our plastics case, for example, advertisements in the trade press might be used to establish the technical engineering breakthroughs of our product (e.g., heat and chemical resistance, strength, and color), while advertisements in more general media (e.g., the *Wall Street Journal*, *Business Week*, even television) might be used to reinforce our overall corporate image for integrity, product quality, and customer service. The prior successful communication of these messages through media advertising would facilitate the personal selling task by demonstrating how our engineering capabilities brought to bear at the customer's plant justify a premium price for our product line.

Price and Promotion

In the language of economics, prices should be set to maximize profits given a particular cost structure and estimate of elasticity of demand. An important marketing corollary of this principle is that long-term profits are most likely to be maximized if the price selected is consistent with the overall strategy for the product and, especially, its desired positioning. If a premium-quality positioning is sought, a premium price is likely to enhance the positioning. Actually, the higher costs associated with a product seeking a positioning based on premium quality would require a premium price in most cases. Even when this is not so (e.g., following a technological breakthrough leading to superior quality *and* lower costs), it will almost always be preferable to charge a premium price and maximize margin than to charge a ''bargain'' price and maximize volume. The latter tactic would be inconsistent with the intended positioning and work against strategic coherence.

If a superior-quality positioning is being sought, pricing tactics should emphasize benefits and value and discourage price competition. Strategic coherence demands that prices be held firm at the point of purchase. Management must train sales people to handle customer pressures for lower prices and to say ''no'' to price concessions. If the product, in fact, delivers superior benefits, it should be able to obtain a premium price as long as it provides incremental value per dollar to customers.

If the strategy is not based on a unique benefit proposition, the firm must be capable of competing on a price basis. In this instance, the firm should be prepared to engage in aggressive price-cutting where necessary to achieve a stable competitive pricing situation. Recall from Chapter 10 our discussion of the dangers of a price war and the need to examine ''nice'' strategies as well as aggressive ones. In such a scenario, manufacturing costs and marketing tactics must be carefully coordinated to balance incremental marketing expenditures against expected scale economies and experience effects.

Promotion can usefully be viewed as a short-term price reduction, even if the form of the promotion adds value (e.g., a premium offer) rather than reduces price per se. The specifics of the promotion must, of course, be consistent with the overall marketing strategy, especially since effective promotions are generally supported with advertising and incentives to the trade. In most cases, it would be inappropriate to support a premium-positioned product with a lottery sweepstakes or game, although the *Times* of London (an elite newspaper) did just that successfully by tying its contest to the management of a hypothetical investment portfolio.

Even for a premium-positioned product, skillful promotion can be an effective tactic if the lower price or higher value results in tapping a new segment of the market or achieving gains against competitors. Under ideal circumstances, these efforts achieve incremental sampling of the product without upsetting the existing price structure. If the product indeed delivers superior benefits, a substantial proportion of those induced to sample it should be willing to pay the regular (premium) price after the promotion has run its course.

A successful promotion may precipitate competitive retaliation, thereby resulting in a competitive ''game'' similar to that engendered by a pure price cut. A firm should not undertake aggressive promotion unless it has thought through how competitors are likely to respond and is prepared to enter into a ''promotion war'' that may lead to lower profits with no increase in sales, at least in the short run. Conversely, if a competitor is capable of promoting aggressively, it is essential that we have plans and mechanisms in place to defend our market share. Effective promotional tactics must be consistent with a realistic competitive strategy based on a comprehensive analysis of the capabilities and probable intentions of both current and potential competitors (review Chapter 10). If we cannot win in a promotion war, it is essential that we recognize that fact and act accordingly. Under such circumstances, we may wish to seek a more differentiated product position or utilize ''nice'' tactics to encourage a cooperative competitive equilibrium.

Distribution Channels

Distributors, wholesalers, and retailers are often utilized to increase convenience by bringing the product or point of purchase closer to the customer than would otherwise be practical. While the decision to use such channels is generally motivated by their physical distribution function, it is important to realize that they often also carry out functions such as merchandising (presentation, display), personal selling, advertising, pricing, and after-sales service. The total package of functions performed by the channel should be consistent with the overall strategy for a product or product line. A distributor that lists your product along with those of five other manufacturers (some of which may have dubious reputations) as well as its own private label would probably not significantly enhance a premium positioning. For a premium-positioned product, exclusive (or, at least, selective) sales agents and distribution channels are generally more appropriate, even though more costly.

Conversely, a product whose core benefit proposition is based on price and availability will generally find it most effective to use nonexclusive mass distribution to maximize convenience and sales volume, and thus drive down costs. Possible permutations are endless, and far beyond the scope of this book (see Stern and El Ansary, 1977, for a complete treatment). At the strategic level, the material thing to remember is that channel composition is critical to providing the desired ''bundle of utility'' to the end customer, and that the choice of channel(s) must be consistent with the rest of the marketing strategy.

One very important function that is often assigned to channel members is customer service. Generally, the delivery of a product's benefits doesn't begin until after the sale has been consummated. In many instances, delivery, installation, customer training, and maintenance are key determinants of whether the utility and value promised in the design, advertising, selling, and pricing of the product will be experienced by customers.

If available channels have (or are capable of obtaining) high levels of skill in these areas, it is almost always more cost effective to use them for these functions than to perform them oneself. Xerox was slow to respond to competitive attack by Savin and other Japanese small copiers in part because it believed that copiers were too ''high tech'' to be sold and serviced effectively by independent office equipment and supplies dealers. Later Xerox recognized its error and moved to establish its own network of such dealers. Similarly, IBM ultimately shifted the sales and service of its typewriter product line from a direct sales and maintenance force to authorized independent typewriter dealers (see Chapter 24), and used independent dealers for its personal computer and related product lines almost from the outset.

In many product categories (e.g., high tech, consumer appliances), however, leading manufacturers have concluded that these functions are so important (or so difficult to perform well) that they must carry them out themselves. It is noteworthy that IBM considers product service so crucial to its long-term success that it continues to operate an extensive parallel PC service organization, even though many of its dealers are fully capable of carrying out most service tasks. Xerox also continues to deliver, install, and service many of its own products, largely because continuous error-free operation is so central to its strategy. Doing so is expensive, but warranted by the requirements of strategic coherence.

Marketing Mix

Upon deeper examination we find it useful to distinguish between two types of coherence that must be present if strategic coherence is to be achieved. On the one hand is *vertical coherence*, the need for consistency between tactics and the strategy they support that we have been emphasizing thus far in this chapter. On the other hand is what we might refer to as *horizontal coherence*: the need for internal consistency among the various elements in the marketing mix. Product quality, advertising and promotional campaigns, sales force tactics, distribution methods, customer service programs, and pricing policies must both be consistent with the core benefit proposition and blend synergistically into the ''bundle of utility'' that the customer experiences when making a purchase decision or using the product.

Let us consider this issue in the context of a supplier of ABS plastic materials to parts molders in the automotive industry. Such a supplier might elect to utilize the full-service materials distributors currently serving that market, thereby achieving vertical coherence with a strategy premised on ''full service.'' If, however, its product-development program calls for building a problem-solving relationship with the molders, horizontal coherence may require direct sales and distribution. This might also be true if the communications program included targeted advertising and sales calls on the automotive manufacturers themselves to achieve differentiation on the basis of a premier technical reputation and ''pull.''

Strategic coherence demands that all tactical decisions be scrutinized for both vertical and horizontal coherence. Measurement and incentive systems must be designed to encourage such scrutiny and identify potential inconsistencies early in the process. Without such systems, and a coherent perspective, the benefits of good strategic analysis and decision making are likely to be lost before the customer even sees the core benefit proposition.

CONTROL

No matter how much care has been taken in developing a marketing plan, reality rarely conforms to expectations. Environmental conditions (e.g., the economic environment, customer preferences, technological possibilities, and/or competitive actions) change; tactics are not executed precisely as planned; unavoidable delays are experienced; certain key planning assumptions turn out to be wrong. While it is impossible to foresee all contingencies, one can build a control system that provides early warning, diagnoses why planning assumptions are not being met, and takes corrective actions. (See Figure 22.1 for a schematic depiction of such a control system.)

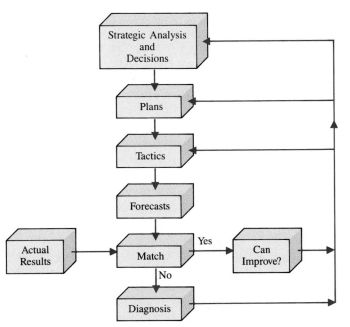

FIGURE 22.1
Tactical and Strategic Control

Even when actual results (e.g., sales volume, market share) match the forecasts, it is important to guard against complacency. Underlying phenomena should be analyzed to determine whether the results are occurring for the reasons set forth in the plan. Are sales, for example, coming from the market segment(s) we had targeted? At the expense of the competitors we had predicted? If not, it may be necessary to revise our plan, even though results are on target. If we find we are gaining market share at the expense of a strong rather than a weak competitor, for example, we may need a completely different competitive scenario than we originally envisioned.

Marketers must continually monitor the changing environment and not hesitate to modify even the most carefully drawn and currently successful plan when significant changes occur. No matter how well we are doing, we should continually ask: (1) How can we do better? (2) What changes must we make to ensure continued success?

Tactical Control

Tactical plans should always include detailed forecasts of results. These should encompass conventional financial measures (e.g., sales by product SKU by market area by week, or market share by reporting period by sales territory) as well as expectations concerning underlying phenomena (e.g., in consumer packaged goods, trial and repurchase rates). When actual and forecast results do not match, it is important to carry out a timely diagnosis as to *why* the shortfall (or surplus) is occurring. All that may be required is a Level I analysis (e.g., getting on an airplane and visiting salespeople and customers), but there are times when a Level II analysis (e.g., making use of a computer-based decision support system with artificial intelligence capabilities) will provide a richer explanation of the discrepancy. A comprehensive and detailed analysis of all available data might, for example, suggest that the problem is essentially due to a delay in order by one key customer and the loss of another major order as a result of aggressive pricing by a particular competitor. Following this diagnosis, the organization concerned would probably wish to revise its marketing tactics (e.g., selling aggressiveness, pricing), its internal procedures (e.g., monitoring orders), its forecasts, or all three.

A control system of this type should be viewed as adaptive. When initial forecasts turn out to have been too high or too low, the system, in effect, learns from experience and becomes more and more adept at calibrating reality. In many instances, small experiments that generate knowledge concerning underlying responses prove to be a useful supplement to direct learning from the marketplace.

Especially interesting in this regard are situations where results exceed expectations. A forecasting error of this type may indicate that a planning assumption is wrong. If an in-pack coupon promotion produces more sales than expected, for example, the original response assumption may have been too conservative. If so, inserting a more correct response function into a Level II model, and then using the model to evaluate alternative promotional programs, may lead to the conclusion that incremental expenditures on promotion would result in significantly increased profits. Similarly, in the automobile industry, if particular models or options appear to be selling better than anticipated, it might be appropriate to shift the model mix toward configurations preferred by consumers and/or increase prices and margins, thereby improving the initial marketing plan.

When actual results match forecasted values, there are strong grounds for presuming the models are working well, although, as noted above, they may be doing so for the wrong reasons. It is essential to remember, however, that successful organizations strive constantly to learn and to achieve ever-improving performance. One manager we know describes her job as "continually seeking to invalidate the model we use by creating radically new tactics."

A promotion linking our shampoo and conditioner with a hot-air styling wand sold exclusively through department stores may open up a new channel and market segment, for example. Because this approach has never been tried before (at least, not to our knowledge), we would not be able to forecast results on the basis of previous experience. Rather than relying on historical data, we would have to use judgment (perhaps based partly on limited testing or experimentation) to estimate the response functions that the model requires. Under these circumstances, continual modification of these estimates on the basis of actual experience would, of course, be especially important.

Strategic Control

An effective control system is essential if we are to react quickly to problems, seek new opportunities when things work out well, and engage in continual experimentation and learning. Viewed in this way, the control system clearly functions as both a tactical and a strategic tool. Analysis of a significant deviation between actual and predicted results may indicate that the underlying cause lies in tactics, in strategy, or in a combination of the two.

Let us return for a moment to the manufacturer of ABS plastics described above. Six months after launching its new marketing approach, it finds that its strategy of using consultative problem solving to link itself to parts molders and OEMs in the auto industry is failing because of margin erosion. Deeper analysis may suggest that the cause is tactical (e.g., sales managers may be giving price concessions too freely) or strategic (i.e., the basic strategy is wrong in some fundamental respect). Perhaps significant subsets of the target market segment strongly prefer low price to premium service, and are unlikely to be converted from this position. If so, this manufacturer needs either to exclude these customers from its target market and sales forecasts or to revise its strategy. It might, for example, want to consider using market segmentation to offer two different ''bundles of utility'': one on a commodity basis and the other supported by full service. The lower-priced limited-service product would require a highly efficient, low-cost manufacturing operation and would be sold through distributors; while the full-service product (presumably utilizing the same low-cost manufacturing facility, but—perhaps—100 percent inspection and higher-quality packaging) would be sold by a direct sales force and supported by a technical service account team.

Modification of the plan to this degree would represent a fundamental shift in strategy and, as such, require the involvement of top management. It is the responsibility of tactical managers to alert top management at the first clear signs of strategic problems. When actual and predicted results are compared, one should continually ask, ''Is the strategy working?'' and ''Are the assumptions underlying our strategic analysis being confirmed by market results?''

Top managers may wish to use an executive information system (EIS) to provide analytical support for this task (see Rockart and De Long, 1987). In such a system, executives work with information systems specialists to define a data base that emphasizes the factors they consider important, and then access that data, either directly through a personal computer or terminal or indirectly through specialized staff support personnel.

One approach that has proved especially useful in developing such systems is to begin by identifying the critical success factors for the range of strategies that are being employed or that are likely to be considered (see Rockart, 1979). Critical success factors are defined as the *limited* number of factors upon which the competitive performance of the organization ultimately depends. An EIS focuses on the differences between actual results and forecasts for critical success factors only, thus providing top management with an easy-to-use query system that can help diagnose strategic problems.

Consider the strategic history of Polaroid Corporation in the late 1980s, when sales performance fell well below expectations. Although promotion was used to boost sales, the fundamental problem was that new products were not rejuvenating the life cycle as hoped, in part because of competition from 35 mm ''point-and-shoot'' cameras and ''one-hour'' photo finishers. Top management had recognized that instant photography was in the mature phase of its life cycle, but thought that new products (e.g., the Sun and Impulse lines) could restore growth—a critical success factor if Polaroid was to retain its independence. When it became clear that this strategy could not generate enough growth, management focused its attention on alternative means of achieving growth. First, they embarked on a program of diversification into industrial products and markets, but critical success factor analysis showed that such forays, even if successful, would not be sufficient. In management's view, Polaroid's future viability would largely depend on its ability to develop new ''photographic'' products that would be superior to their competitors in a world in which electronics had replaced chemistry as the primary means of ''imaging.'' Given this critical success analysis, management embarked on a massive $400 million R&D effort to achieve such technological superiority. While switching from chemistry to electronics as the basis for technological superiority is certainly a major undertaking, what Polaroid is really doing is continuing to rely on heavy investment in R&D to provide it with demonstrable product differentiation. Even if it succeeds in its present course, however, it will probably not achieve the ''monopoly'' position it held for so long in instant photography. The loss of the monopoly advantage will clearly require Polaroid to make major shifts in its marketing and manufacturing strategy. It is still too early to evaluate the effectiveness of Polaroid's efforts, but they do provide us with an excellent example of critical success factor analysis leading to a major change in a major firm's strategy.

IMPLEMENTING ANALYTIC SUPPORT TOOLS

A major premise of this book is that analytic support tools can make significant contributions to the strategy formulation process. In practice, the effective implementation of such analytic support tools often turns out to be a challenging undertaking. Let us now consider some of the key issues in this area.

As we have noted throughout, Level I analysis should always precede strategic decisions. The strategic problem must be clearly defined, the key issues must be delineated, and the fundamental questions must be addressed. After these tasks have been completed, it is usually sound practice to generate and systematically evaluate at least several alternatives for accomplishing organizational goals before deciding on a strategic course.

Usually, Level II analysis, formalizing Level I analysis with simple mathematical models, market research, and computer simulations, will make an incremental contribution that justifies the additional time, effort, and expenditure involved. But again, in no case should you attempt Level II analysis without having completed a systematic Level I analysis. While Level II analysis based on data and simple models will generally be sufficient, more elaborate Level III models will sometimes prove worthwhile. Such modeling should not be attempted, however, until you have gleaned as much information as practical from Levels I and II. Indeed, the output from these levels often provides critical input to Level III.

Even when the levels are executed sequentially, implementation problems are often encountered. One common error is failure to use the analysis in decision making, or even worse, misusing the output of the analysis. Level I analysis may be ignored because of time and emotional pressures, or because no one wants to question a program that is supported by key players. At Levels II and III, the analysis may appear to be a ''black box,'' and consequently not be understood or believed by many of the key participants in the strategic decision.

Information derived from analysis often takes on a power role in organizational politics, leading to extreme sensitivity among some managers regarding its use. An executive may understand the results and implications of a particular analysis all too well, but choose to ignore or even discredit the analysis for organizational reasons. Since much of strategy is essentially resource allocation, it is virtually inevitable that organizational units from which resources are being diverted will question and resist the analysis on which such decisions are based. In implementing analytic support, therefore, it is essential to recognize the many ''irrational'' dimensions of organizational reality and be prepared to deal with them as they manifest themselves.

Effective implementation requires that managers be *able* and *willing* to use the results of the analysis. Managers must understand the assumptions and structure that underlie the analysis, and not view it as a ''black box'' that is properly the province of staff analysts. Such specialists will almost always be required to carry out the actual analysis, but they should consider it one of their primary tasks to educate the managers who are to use the analysis. They should never treat analytic methodologies as mysterious secrets that are comprehensible only to an elite. For the decision support system to be effective, managers must feel in psychological control (see Little, 1970, for more discussion of this point).

Given adequate training, most managers can readily understand Level II models, but even so, they may resist using the output of the analysis. Willingness to use a model, once understood, is dependent on the personal objectives of the user, which may not be fully consistent with corporate goals. To minimize this problem, it is critical that individual incentives and rewards be as congruent as possible with the organization's long-term goals.

Level III models by their nature are complex. Managers are not likely to use them unless they have reasonable confidence in their comprehension of the assumptions that are built into the model and how the model works. Sequential movement from Level I to Level II to Level III helps somewhat, by lessening the incremental learning required at each stage, but even under ideal circumstances, quite a few Level III models are too complex for many managers to understand adequately. Often they are acutely sensitive to inputs, structural assumptions, and modeling errors, which really should be dealt with only by a skilled specialist. Under these conditions, the best approach is to build a long-term relationship between a manager or group of managers and a particular specialist who is an effective teacher able to engender confidence and trust based on demonstrated performance rather than jargon and promises.

Let us now consider these issues in the context of a ''case'' derived from the authors' experience. You should read this case from a managerial perspective, asking yourself what decisions need to be made, what decisions you would make, and how you would go about implementing those decisions in this particular organization.

At the same time, you should consider the specifics of how analytic support tools were implemented in this situation. What level of analytic support was used? Was it the correct level for this problem and organization? Was Level I analysis done before Level II and III analysis? Was the analysis implemented properly? Was it communicated effectively and understood by the decision hierarchy? Were the real decision makers able and willing to use the results?

What would you have done if you were the new-product brand manager? What analysis would you have conducted? How would you have communicated its results?

What was the role of top management in the use of analytic support? What changes, if any, would you make in the firm's organizational structure and/or decision processes?

There is a clear relationship between strategic issues and the role of analytical support. State-of-the-art modeling provides a treasure trove of exceptionally rich data, which can be mined for critical inputs to the strategy formulation process. Whether it is or not is probably as much a function of organizational skills as of technical competency.

PARADISE FOODS CASE

Bill Horton sat alone in his office late Friday afternoon anxiously leafing through computer printouts, even though he could recite their contents from memory. Horton was waiting for his boss, Bob Murphy, to report back the decision on a subject the marketing committee had been debating for more than four hours. The issue—whether Paradise Foods should authorize national rollout of a new product, Sweet Dream, to complement its established frozen specialty dessert, LaTreat. Horton was product manager for Sweet Dream, and Murphy was the group manager responsible for all new products in Paradise's dessert line.

"I'm glad you're sitting," Bob quipped uncomfortably as he entered Bill's office. "The news isn't good. The committee decided not to go ahead."

"I don't believe it," Bill protested. "I started to worry when the meeting dragged on, but I never thought they'd say no. Damn. Eighteen months down the drain."

"I know how you feel, but you have to understand where the committee was coming from. It was a real close call—as close as I can remember since I've had this job. But the more carefully they considered your test results, the more it looked like the returns just weren't there."

"Not there? All they had to look at was Appendix B in my report—the data from Midland and Pittsfield. Sweet Dream got a 3% share after 26 weeks. A trial rate of 15%. A repurchase rate of 45%. If national performance were anywhere close to that, we'd have our launch costs back in 14 months. Who can argue with that?"

"I'm on your side here, but I only had one vote," Bob said defensively "We both knew what Barbara's position was going to be—and you know how much weight she carries around here these days." Barbara Mayer was the Paradise group manager responsible for established dessert products. She became a "grouper" in 1985, after two enormously successful years as LaTreat's first product manager.

"And to be honest, it was tough to take issue with her," Bob continued. "What's the point of introducing Sweet Dream if you end up stealing share from LaTreat? In fact, Barbara used some of *your* data against us. She kept waving around Appendix C, griping that 75% of the people who tried Sweet Dream had bought LaTreat in the previous four weeks. And repurchase rates were highest among LaTreat heavy users. You know how the fourteenth floor feels about LaTreat. Barbara claims that adjusting for lost LaTreat sales means Sweet Dream doesn't recover its up-front costs for three years."

Launched in 1983, LaTreat was the first "super premium" frozen dessert to enter national distribution. It consisted of 3.5 ounces of vanilla ice cream dipped in penuche fudge and covered with almonds. An individual bar sold for just under $2 and a package of four was $7. Unlike LaTreat, which came on a stick, Sweet Dream resembled an ice cream sandwich. It consisted of sweet-cream ice cream between two oversized chocolate chip cookies and coated with dark Belgian chocolate. Its price was comparable to LaTreat's.

Under Barbara Mayer, annual sales of LaTreat soon reached $40 million, and it began making a significant contribution to dessert group profits. It accounted for almost 5% of the market despite a price about 50% higher than standard frozen specialties. Lately, however, competition had stiffened. LaTreat faced tough challenges from three direct competitors as well as several parallel concepts (like Sweet Dream) at various stages of test marketing. The total frozen specialties market had grown fast enough to absorb these new entrants without reducing LaTreat sales, but revenues had been essentially flat through 1986 and 1987.

Bill understood the importance of LaTreat, but he was not the type to mince words. "You and I both know things are more complicated than Barbara would have people believe," he told Bob. "There wasn't the same cannibalization effect in Marion and Corvallis. And we never did a test in Midland and Pittsfield where Barbara's people were free to defend LaTreat. We might be able to have it both ways . . ."

Bob interrupted. "Bill, we could stay here all night on this. But what's the point? The committee's made its decision. You don't like it, I don't like it. But these aren't stupid people. It's hard to argue with the dessert group's batting average over the last five years. This may ring hollow right now, but you can't take this personally."

"That's easy for you to say," Bill sighed.

"You know how this company works," Bob reminded him. "We don't hold withdrawal of a new product against the manager if withdrawal is the right decision. Hell, it happened to me ten years ago with that dumb strawberry topping. It made sense to kill that product. And I was better off at the company for it. The fact is, the committee was impressed as hell with the research you did—although to be honest, you may have overwhelmed them. A 40-page report with 30 pages of appendixes. I had trouble wading through it all. But that doesn't matter. You did a great job, and the people who count know that."

"I appreciate the sentiment, but that's not why I think this is the wrong decision. Sweet Dream is a GO on the merits."

"Go home, play some golf this weekend," Bob counseled. "Things won't seem so bleak on Monday."

Bill never made it to the country club. Instead, he spent the weekend worrying about his future at Paradise and puzzling over how the marketing committee could have reached its no-launch decision.

Paradise Foods was a large, successful manufacturer of packaged foods and household products whose markets were becoming increasingly competitive. Bill believed that Paradise was vulnerable in this treacherous environment because of its failure to keep pace with technological change—in particular, the increasing sophistication of marketing research based on computer modeling, supermarket scanner data, and targetable cable television. Paradise certainly used these tools, but to Bill's way of thinking, top management didn't embrace them with the same enthusiasm as other companies.

When Bill became product manager for Sweet Dream, he promised himself he would do a state-of-the-art research job. The plan was to compare the performance of Sweet Dream in two test markets exposed to different advertising and promotion strategies. The campaign in Midland, Texas and Pittsfield, Massachusetts struck an overtly self-indulgent tone—"Go

FIGURE 22.2
Sweet Dreams Taste Position

FIGURE 22.3
Sweet Dreams Indulgence Position

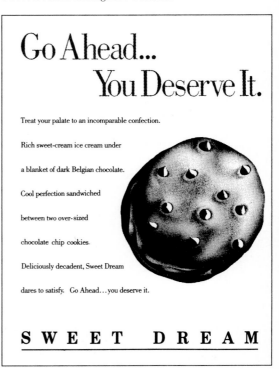

Ahead, You Deserve It''—and used limited price promotion to induce trial. The campaign in Marion, Indiana and Corvallis, Oregon emphasized superior quality—''Taste the Goodness''—and used promotion aggressively. Sunday newspapers in the two cities frequently carried 50-cents-off coupons, and Sweet Dream boxes included a 75-cent rebate voucher.

Bill used two computer-based research services—InfoScan and BehaviorScan—to evaluate Sweet Dream's performance and long-term potential.[1] InfoScan tracks product purchases on a national and local basis for the packaged-goods industry. It collects point-of-sale information on all bar-coded products sold in a representative sample of supermarkets and drugstores. It generates weekly data on volume, price, market share, the relationship between sales and promotional offers, and merchandising conditions. Bill subscribed to InfoScan to monitor competitive trends in the frozen specialties segment.

BehaviorScan is used in marketing tests to measure the effect of marketing strategies on product purchases. In a typical BehaviorScan test, one group of consumer panelists is exposed to certain variables (i.e., print or television advertisements, coupons, free samples, in-store displays), while other participating consumers serve as a control group. Company analysts use supermarket scanner data on both groups of consumers (who present identification cards to store checkout clerks) to evaluate purchasing responses to marketing campaigns. A typical BehaviorScan test lasts about one year.

Bill Horton's research program had generated a stack of computer printouts several feet high. He had spent much of the spring trying to unravel the complex interactions between different advertising and promotion strategies for Sweet Dream, the various promotion deals Paradise was running on LaTreat, and the proliferation of other frozen specialties. Despite Bob's advice to relax, Bill spent Sunday afternoon in front of his home computer, massaging the data one last time.

On Monday, Bill arrived at his office a few minutes late. He was surprised to find Barbara Mayer waiting for him.

''Sorry to drop in on you first thing,'' she said, ''but I wanted to let you know what a fantastic job you did on the Sweet Dream test. I'm sure you were disappointed with the committee's decision, and in a way I was too. It would have been great to work together on the rollout. But the data were pretty clear. We didn't have a choice.''

''Well, I thought the data were clear too—but in the opposite direction.''

''Come on, Bill, you can understand the logic of the decision. The Midland and Pittsfield numbers were fine, but they were coming at the expense of LaTreat. There wasn't so much cannibalization in Marion and Corvallis, but the Sweet Dream numbers weren't as good either. Trial was acceptable, but repurchase was low. We might make money, but we'd never meet the hurdle rate. Every so often a product just falls between two stools.''

''So we'll do more tests,'' Bill countered. ''We can play with the positioning in Marion and Corvallis. Or we can start from scratch somewhere else. I can have us wired to go in three weeks.''

''We've already taken 18 months on Sweet Dream,'' Barbara said. ''The committee felt it was time to try new concepts. I don't think that's so unreasonable.''

''You're forgetting two things,'' Bill replied. ''First, with freezer space as tight as it is, the longer it takes to come up with another product, the harder the stores are going to squeeze us. Second, other people are going to find out how well Sweet Dream did in Midland and Pittsfield. We're the only ones who get the BehaviorScan numbers, but you know the competition is monitoring our tests. What do you think Weston & Williams is going to do when it sees the results? It'll have a Sweet Dream clone out in a few months if we don't launch.''

Weston & Williams (W&W) was a leading supplier of household products that was diversifying into foods, including desserts. It had a reputation as a conservative company that insisted on exhaustive prelaunch research. But the trade press recently had reported on W&W's decision to rush Pounce—a combination detergent, colorfast bleach, and fabric softener—to the market on the basis of very preliminary tests and data from a competitor's test markets. W&W had thus become the first national entrant in the ''maxiwash'' category.

---

[1] InfoScan® and BehaviorScan® are actual services offered by Information Resources, Inc.

"Bob made that argument Friday," Barbara said. "But you can guess how far he got. The guys upstairs have a tough enough time taking our own computer data seriously. They don't buy the idea that someone else is going to jump into the market based on *our* tests. Plus, that would be a huge risk. Pounce may have given Weston & Williams all the gray hair they can stand for a few years."

"From what I can tell, Barbara, the only issue that counted was cannibalization." Bill's voice betrayed a rekindled sense of frustration. "I understand you want to protect LaTreat. I understand the company wants to protect LaTreat. But it seems to me we're protecting a product that's getting tired."

"What are you talking about?" Barbara objected. "Profits aren't growing as fast as they used to, but they're not dropping either. LaTreat is solid."

"Come on, Barbara. Your people have really been promoting it in the last two quarters—shifting money out of print and TV and into coupons and rebates. Total spending hasn't changed, so profits are OK. But LaTreat has gotten hooked on promotion. And all the wrong kinds of promotion. You've got people accelerating future purchases and price-sensitive types jumping in whenever LaTreat goes on sale. Who needs that?"

"Where are you getting this stuff?" Barbara demanded. "I didn't see it in your report."

"I spent the weekend running some more numbers," Bill replied. "Take a look at this."

Bill punched a few buttons on his computer keyboard and called up a series of graphs. The first documented the growing percentage of LaTreat sales connected with promotional offers. A second graph disaggregated LaTreat's promotion-related sales by four buyer categories Bill had created from BehaviorScan data. "Loyalists" were longtime customers who increased their purchases in response to a deal. "Trial users" bought LaTreat for the first time because of the promotion and seemed to be turning into loyal customers. "Accelerators" were longtime customers who used coupons or rebates to stock up on products they would have bought anyway. "Switch-on-deal" customers were nonusers who bought LaTreat when there were promotions but demonstrated little long-term loyalty. Bill's graph documented that a majority of LaTreat's coupon redeemers fell into the last two categories, with "loyalists" accounting for a shrinking percentage of sales.

Finally, Bill called up his ultimate evidence—a graph that adjusted LaTreat sales to eliminate the effect of promotions. (See Figure 22.4.)

"I'm amazed you spent your weekend doing this," Barbara said, "but I'm glad you did. It'll help us think through future marketing strategies for LaTreat. But it doesn't change what the committee decided. It's time to move on."

FIGURE 22.4

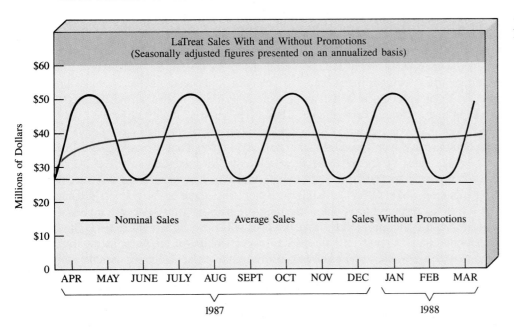

"I'm not so sure," Bill replied. "I hope you don't mind, but I think I should show these data to Bob. Maybe he can convince the committee to reconsider. After all, if LaTreat is weakening, it's going to show up in your profit figures sooner or later."

"Data don't make decisions, Bill, people do. And the people on the marketing committee have been in the industry a lot longer than you. Their gut tells them things your computer can't. Besides, you and I both know that when you collect this much data, you can make it show just about anything. Go ahead and talk to Bob, but I'm sure he'll see things the same way I do."

IMPLEMENTING THE STRATEGIC PLANNING PROCESS

Many approaches to the strategic planning process have been proposed (please review Figure 1.1 on page 6 for the authors' preferred paradigm). While varying in detail, all essentially lay out an orderly, sequential process with ample provision for feedback and revision. In practice, however, many organizations find it difficult to carry out meaningful strategic planning. Sometimes the process itself bogs down or becomes trivialized. At other times, impressive planning documents are completed and then filed away, never to be consulted again.

Clearly, there are significant impediments to effective strategic planning. Managers must recognize and understand these barriers so they can take purposeful steps to overcome them.

Why Strategic Planning Does Not Work

Most managers labor under a myriad of short-term pressures. Daily schedules are full to the bursting point; crises of various magnitudes have to be handled; customers demand action; fires must be fought. In some companies, daily (even hourly) fluctuations in stock prices are monitored closely, and action taken accordingly. Not surprisingly, as much as nine-tenths of a typical organization's energy is devoted to managing day-to-day operations. As more than one manager has ruefully observed, "If we don't get through today, there ain't going to be no tomorrow!" Because of their natural tendency to focus on the short term, managers must often be forced to pay attention to the long run if it is not to be lost in the shuffle.

Strategic planning can be a shallow exercise. It is all too usual for a slick report with beautiful graphics to be produced, filed, and forgotten. This phenomenon seems to be especially common when the plan was drawn up by the strategic planning department or (even worse) when an outside consulting group has done most of the work. There are important roles for consultants and staff planning specialists in the strategic planning process. Their specialized skills can be extremely useful in structuring the process and obtaining and analyzing critical data. They often serve as highly effective catalysts, in effect, forcing the organization to expand its horizons beyond the day-to-day. But it is bad policy to have such specialists take the lead in developing the strategy or writing the plan. While many managers would be delighted to have them do so ("Get the strategic plan off my back so that I can fight today's fires!"), an organization that succumbs to this temptation would almost certainly be better off without a plan. Unless the managers who are to be responsible for implementing the plan have been deeply involved in its preparation, it is highly unlikely that the plan will have significant impact. Successful implementation of strategy requires shared understanding of the phenomena driving the firm's business, as well as consensus concerning the organization's mission, goals, key programs, and resource allocations.

Even when managers are involved in the planning process, however, the resulting plans and tactics may be inconsistent with the organization's measurement processes and/

or incentive structures. In the newspaper industry, for example, it is common for strategic plans to call for increases in circulation and readership, but for bonuses to be paid almost solely on the basis of annual profits. Since increasing circulation generally requires marketing investment that is unlikely to pay off until subsequent years, it is not surprising that many newspaper publishers put far less emphasis on building circulation than is called for in their strategic plans.

Managers must be able *and* willing to carry out the actions called for in their strategic plan, or it simply will not happen. If they feel threatened by the planning process (e.g., if it requires that their organizational unit be compared with ''best of breed'' or if it seems likely to lead to a loss of resources), they are likely to deliberately impede it. (This was one of the key dimensions of the Paradise Foods case presented earlier in this chapter.) For the strategic planning process to be effective, managers at all levels must ''buy into'' the plan. Operational managers (salespeople, brand managers, market research managers), middle managers (group brand managers, sales managers, advertising directors), and top managers (the senior vice presidents responsible for marketing, R&D, and manufacturing, the sales and advertising vice presidents, and even the chief operating officer and chief executive officer or managing director) must all understand the planning process fully, feel they have had a real opportunity to contribute to the plan, and agree, at least in broad outline, with its conclusions.

Another major impediment to effective strategic planning is the lack of sufficient data. In these circumstances, it is necessary to decide whether to use those data that are available, and supplement them with managerial judgment, or to operate without strategic direction. We feel it is better to identify critical phenomena and success factors, obtain the best information available, and formulate at least a draft strategic plan. One outcome of this process is likely to be a clearer recognition of what additional data are required and, hopefully, a plan to acquire such data. Clearly, timely monitoring, control, and revision are especially important when implementing a strategy developed with less than adequate data.

Strategic Planning Process Aids

An increasingly popular and apparently effective approach to implementing the strategic planning process is to conduct a strategic planning retreat, attended by key managers, to build consensus and develop interpersonal relationships. Typically, such a meeting is held off-site, and runs for three to five days (with time off for golf, wine tastings, and other group-oriented recreation). If all goes well, the meeting ends with a consensus on the firm's mission and how it can be carried forward in the next year.

A range of techniques can be used to facilitate such meetings. In the authors' experience, it is usually beneficial to begin with a situation review and strategic analysis (see Figure 2.1 on page 12); proceed to an analysis of the organization's strengths and weaknesses in light of its mission; and then consider major changes in the environment and whether they represent threats or opportunities. This process generally leads to a recognition of the potential need for revision of the organization's strategy and the formulation of program priorities. At the completion of the meeting, it is usual for the next steps in the planning process to be described and assigned. In some cases, specific strategic actions are approved right at the meeting (e.g., to undertake a major study of competitors, to develop an R&D proposal for a new technology, to investigate a specific acquisition).

Organization change consultants are often engaged to assist in running such meetings. If skillful, they are sensitive to a variety of human motivations and know how to accommodate them in the planning process. As outsiders, they may be able to get the retreat participants to focus on the forest rather than the trees, and may be more willing than managers caught up in the hierarchy to elicit comments critical of the organization's position and strategy.

Any meaningful strategy formulation process has to change the organization. This should be recognized explicitly, and provisions should be made for planned organizational change. Sometimes the strategy will call for deep-rooted change in the values and norms that constitute the culture of the organization (see Schien, 1984). In such cases, the words and charts in the strategic plan will have little effect until a process of culture change has at least been begun. While such transformations are extremely difficult to achieve—and take years, if not decades, to permeate the organization—it is folly to set forth on a new strategic course without first fully thinking through the cultural barriers to its implementation.

The strategic retreat is only the start of the strategy formulation process. There must be appropriate and adequate follow-up if the consensus that has been reached is not soon to be forgotten in the crush of short-term activities.

It is usually a good idea to lay out a formal process to convert an agreed-upon mission and set of program priorities into operational budgets and plans. It is useful to represent key tasks as milestones that must be reached by a particular time and to associate specific names or titles with the accomplishment of each task. Ideally, the process captures both the top-down vision of senior management and the bottom-up sense of realism of the troops in the trenches.

Figure 22.5 depicts a process designed to realize this ideal. The process begins by asking managers at all levels to carry out a careful analysis of their realms. The objective is to produce a shared diagnostic view of the phenomena underlying the business, the strengths and weaknesses of the organization and its products, and the major environmental threats and opportunities it faces. Goals are set and modified iteratively through dialogue—both across functions and across managerial levels—to generate a shared organizational mission and a process for translating that mission into specific goals. Programs are developed, resource commitments are made, and tactical plans intended to achieve the organization's goals are devised.

At each point in the process, decisions are iterated and revised at every managerial level in order to combine the best attributes of the top-down and bottom-up styles of management and to engender broad psychological commitment. The wide variety of strategic planning schema that have been developed (see Hax and Majluf, 1984, or Lorange and Vancil, 1977, for a review) are, with few exceptions, similar in broad outline to the process depicted here.

One promising advanced strategic planning technique is Strategic Assumption Surfacing and Testing or SAST (see Mason and Mitroff, 1981), which has been used effectively

FIGURE 22.5
Strategic Planning Process

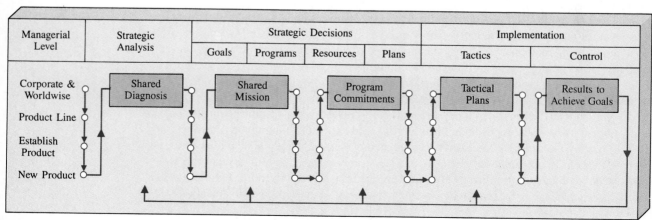

by a number of organizations faced with a high degree of complexity and/or uncertainty. A key feature of this methodology is the clear designation of the assumptions upon which the strategy will ultimately rest. These assumptions are derived from debate among groups of stakeholders who may have different views of the world. Key assumptions are tested for plausibility and judgment and, where possible, evaluated by scientific research. An adversarial debate process is then employed to synthesize the assumptions, generate policy and action alternatives, and select among them. There may be disagreement, for example, as to where a particular product or business is in its life cycle. Some may feel that although growth has slowed, it can be rejuvenated; while others are just as convinced that maturity has set in, and imminent decline is inevitable. The debate to resolve this disagreement would be based on both managerial judgment and ''science'' (e.g., models such as those discussed in Chapter 6). Consensus on the life-cycle stage would be sought and, hopefully, achieved, and then used as the basis for formulating an effective strategy for the future.

CONCLUSION

In our view, there is no one best approach to strategic planning. Each organization should familiarize itself with the major approaches, and then develop and follow a process that has been customized to maximize congruence with its own culture and managerial style.

Whatever methodology is ultimately employed, adequate attention must be given to the implementation process. Without effective implementation, even the most brilliant and elegant strategic plan is essentially worthless.

Organizational success requires both appropriate strategies and specific plans that follow from them. There must be an effective process for monitoring, control, and revision. Analytic support tools often have a major role to play here. Where significant organizational or cultural change is required, it must be thought through carefully and implemented in a sensitive and timely manner.

QUESTIONS FOR DISCUSSION

1. Define ''strategic coherence.'' Why is it difficult to obtain? Give three examples of inappropriate transfer of strategy into tactics.

2. What, in your opinion, is the greatest pitfall organizations encounter in striving for strategic coherence?

3. Compare and contrast vertical and horizontal coherence. Give an example that shows them in conflict.

4. If our sales and profits match our forecast, we do not need to worry about taking control actions. True or false?

5. What is the difference between strategic and tactical control? Which is more difficult to diagnose and execute?

6. What are the barriers to effective implementation analysis at Level I? At Level II? At Level III? How would you overcome them if you were the vice president of marketing?

7. What is the most important impediment to implementation of the strategic planning process itself? How would you overcome it?

8. How does corporate culture affect strategic planning?

9. Should strategic planning be a ''top-down'' or ''bottom-up'' process?

10. What proportion of an organization's time should be spent on strategic planning

versus tactical implementation? Is it possible to do too much planning? Why or why not?

REFERENCES

AAKER, DAVID A., AND JOHN MEYERS. 1975. *Advertising Management*. Englewood Cliffs, NJ: Prentice Hall.

BLATTBERG, ROBERT C., AND SCOTT A. NESLIN. 1990. *Sales Promotion: Concepts, Methods, and Strategies*. Englewood Cliffs, NJ: Prentice Hall.

BONOMA, THOMAS V., AND VICTORIA L. CRITTENDON. 1988. "Managing Marketing Implementation." *Sloan Management Review*, Winter: 7–14.

BUTANEY, GUL, AND LAWRENCE H. WORTZELL. 1988. "Distributor Power Versus Manufacturer Power: The Customer Role." *Journal of Marketing* 52: 52–63.

CHURCHILL, GILBERT A. 1981. *Sales Force Management: Planning Implementation and Control*. Homewood, Il: Richard D. Irwin.

COLLINS, JULIA M. 1989. "Image and Advertising." *Harvard Business Review*, January/February: 94–99.

COUGHLAN, ANNE T., AND BIRGER WERNERFELT. 1989. "On Credible Delegation by Oligopolists: A Discussion of Distribution Channel Management." *Management Science* 35: 226–239.

DE BRUICKER, E. S., AND G. L. SUMME. 1985. "Make Sure Your Customers Keep Coming Back." *Harvard Business Review*, January/February: 92–98.

ELIASHBERG, JEHOSHUA, AND DONALD A. MICHIE. 1984. "Multiple Business Goals Sets as Determinants of Marketing Channel Conflict: An Empirical Study." *Journal of Marketing Research* 21: 75–88.

HAX, ARNOLDO C., AND NICHOLAS S. MAJLUF. 1984. *Strategic Management: An Integrated Perspective*. Englewood Cliffs, NJ: Prentice Hall.

HUGHES, G. DAVID. 1983. "Computerized Sales Management." *Harvard Business Review*, March/April: 102–112.

HUTT, MICHAEL D., PETER H. REINGEN, AND JOHN R. RONCHETTS, JR. 1988. "Tracing Emergent Processes in Marketing Strategy Formation." *Journal of Marketing* 52: 4–19.

LEWIS, W. STERN, AND FREDERICK D. STURDIVANT. 1987. "Customer-Driven Distribution Systems." *Harvard Business Review*, July/August: 34–41.

LITTLE, JOHN D. C. 1979. "Aggregate Advertising Models: The State of the Art." *Operations Research* 27: 629–667.

———. 1970. "Models, Managers, and the Concept of a Decision Calculus." *Management Science* 16: 466–485.

——— AND LEONARD M. LODISH. 1969. "A Media Planning Calculus." *Operations Research* 17: 1–35.

LODISH, LEONARD M. 1986. *Advertising and Promotion Challenge*. New York: Oxford University Press.

LORANGE, PETER, AND RICHARD F. VANCIL. 1977. *Strategic Planning Systems*. Englewood Cliffs, NJ: Prentice Hall.

MASON, RICHARD O., AND IAN I. MITROFF. 1981. *Challenging Strategic Planning Assumptions*. New York: John Wiley.

MONROE, KENT B. 1979. *Pricing: Making Profitable Decisions*. New York: McGraw-Hill.

ROCKART, JOHN F. 1979. "Chief Executives Define Their Own Data Needs." *Harvard Business Review* 57: 81–93.

ROCKART, JOHN F., AND DAVID W. DE LONG. 1987. *Executive Support Systems*. Homewood, Il: Dow Jones–Irwin.

SCHEIN, EDGAR H. 1984. "Coming to a New Awareness of Organizational Culture." *Sloan Management Review* 25: 3–16.

———. 1985. *Organizational Culture and Leadership*. San Francisco: Jossey-Bass Publishers.

STERN, L. W., AND A. I. EL ANSARY. 1977. *Marketing Channels*. Englewood Cliffs, NJ: Prentice Hall.

23
THE MARKETING PLAN: AN EXAMPLE AND REVIEW OF MARKETING STRATEGY

INTRODUCTION

So far in this book we have considered the subject of marketing strategy from a variety of perspectives. Regardless of the perspective, however, our approach insists that the marketing strategist must obtain a clear understanding of broad corporate strategy and underlying marketing phenomena (customer decision making, life cycle, segmentation, positioning, market response, and competitive behavior) before attempting to develop a comprehensive marketing strategy for an individual business or product line. We have suggested the sequential utilization of Level I, II, and III analysis to gain this understanding, and have considered a number of key implementation issues that arise when carrying out a complex strategy. Throughout, we have emphasized the importance of coherence among the corporate strategy, the underlying phenomena, and the marketing strategy, as well as between the marketing strategy and the implementation or action plan.

In this chapter, we use the development of a comprehensive, annual marketing plan to review many of these points. This seems a suitable method of summarizing the key teaching points of this book, since many young managers will be asked to develop a marketing strategy for the first time as part of their firm's annual planning process. In carrying out this task, it soon becomes clear that the annual marketing plan is where the long-term strategy "hits the pavement," where long-run programs are translated into specific, short-term objectives and action plans. Consequently, the annual marketing plan should be rich in analysis and strategic understanding, not a mere mechanical projection of sales trends and financial impacts. An annual marketing plan that focuses on "fire-fighting" or little more than the attainment of earnings-per-share goals for the next four quarters is, in our view, of very little value.

PREPARING THE MARKETING PLAN

480

Most professionally managed organizations require some sort of marketing plan as part of their overall management planning process. Such plans can be relatively simple, or very major undertakings. In almost all cases, however, the marketing plan will describe: (1) the current business situation and overall market being addressed (historical perspective, market size, growth and segments, product offerings, new-product activity, competitors, market shares, channel participants); (2) the mission of the organization and its financial goals; (3) the major opportunities and threats the firm faces (including an honest diagnosis of its strengths and weaknesses relative to competition); (4) the key underlying marketing factors (e.g., customer information processing, product life cycle, segmentation, competitive product positioning, and competitive behavior); and (5) the market's response sensitivity to marketing actions (e.g., levels of price, promotion, advertising, and personal selling). Based on this diagnosis and analysis, the plan would next lay out in detail (6) the proposed marketing program (e.g., target market segments, positioning, product technology and features, product-line composition, pricing and margins, channels, advertising, sales, service), and explain why it is expected to succeed and why it is better than alternative programs. It would then (7) identify critical linkages to other functions (e.g., production, engineering) and global corporate strategy and their implications; and (8) establish objectives for unit and dollar sales, market share, and various measures of financial return (e.g., return on investment [ROI], return on assets [ROA]) for both the coming year and, at least on a rough basis, the next three to five years. Finally, a comprehensive marketing plan would include (9) specific action plans (who is to do what by when) for the next year; and (10) a process to monitor performance vis-à-vis the plan and to respond to changing conditions.

In effect, the marketing plan ties the whole thing together. It provides managers, in a single document, with descriptions of the environment, the marketing strategy and tactics, and the specific goals to be achieved. It delineates a standard against which actual performance can be measured, serves as a baseline when planning for subsequent periods, and lays out specific marketing actions intended to support the accomplishment of long-term corporate strategy.

A variety of marketing planning formats are employed by different organizations. In some organizations, these are standardized across all business units, while in others, managers are urged to develop formats and approaches appropriate to the business they manage. In almost all cases, however, each business is expected to present relatively standardized financial forecasts and budgets, generally in considerable detail for the first year covered by the plan and in broader strokes for the subsequent three to five years.

In this chapter, we use a fairly typical planning format to present a hypothetical marketing plan for a Japanese firm entering the North American and European markets for home word processors. Our format is to devote the top of each page to the text of the plan, and the bottom to commentary that relates that portion of the plan to key learning points that have been covered in this text. The data in the plan are hypothetical, but representative and useful for pedagogical purposes. This plan does not contain all the concepts and techniques you should remember from this book, but it is a summary of some of the most critical ones.

A MARKETING PLANNING EXAMPLE: MASAMOTO'S ENTRY INTO THE NORTH AMERICAN AND EUROPEAN MARKETS FOR HOME WORD PROCESSING[1]

Background

Assume that you are a product manager working in the U.S. subsidiary of the Masamoto Corporation, a large Japanese manufacturer of telecommunications equipment, computers, consumer electronics products, and office equipment. Already well established in the

---

[1] This example, including the name of the firm, the situation described, and specific data, is purely hypothetical, but reflects the authors' planning experiences with a number of firms in related markets.

North American and European markets for personal computers, copiers, FAX, VCRs, and large-screen color-projection television sets, Masamoto in 1985 introduced a line of three electronic typewriters in those markets. These typewriters, which utilized daisywheel print technology, ranged in price from $150 for the basic model to $475 for the top-of-the-line Suprema, which featured automatic lift-off correction, a twenty-four–character display, and (as an option) up to five pages of memory. Masamoto achieved considerable success with this product line, which was state of the art at the time and was sold at a very competitive price, primarily through department stores, appliance and electronics "superstores," and, to a limited extent, typewriter dealers. As the product manager for these products, you received considerable credit for their success.

In late 1988, you were called to Japan, where you were shown the prototype of a new Masamoto product. This product, known as the Yamakura Word Processor or YWP, had capabilities comparable to an IBM PC/AT in running word-processing software (e.g., Word Perfect, Multimate), but resembled a typewriter in ease of use (see Figure 23.1). The YWP had a full 30-line screen, a built-in inkjet letter-quality printer with three fonts, and elaborate text-editing features (e.g., moving, adding, deleting, automatic footnotes, bold and underline, and internal spell check). The product weighed 12 pounds, had 512K RAM, a 1M hard disc, and a $3\frac{1}{2}$-inch floppy disc drive, which produced discs that could be read by most major brands of computers. The YWP was operated by dedicated keys clearly labeled with specific commands (e.g., print, save, spell check, backspace, tab, etc.), and required no loading of software. Essentially, all that was necessary was to plug it in, turn it on, and begin typing. In contrast to a "real" PC, however, the YWP could not carry out functions such as programming, spreadsheets, graphics, or games. Masamoto hoped to establish a price for the YWP only modestly lower than the lower-priced IBM PC clones currently on the market.

The Assignment

At corporate headquarters in Tokyo you are congratulated on your successes with the typewriter line and informed that you have been nominated for promotion to worldwide home word processor marketing manager with responsibility for introduction of the YWP in the North American and European markets. These markets have been selected because of their level of economic development and computer literacy. Your responsibilities for the electronic typewriter line will be turned over to an associate who will, for the foreseeable

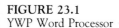

FIGURE 23.1
YWP Word Processor

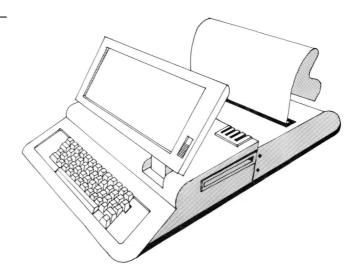

future, report to you. As your first task, you are to develop a comprehensive marketing plan for the YWP. Because of the importance of the YWP, the plan will be reviewed and, hopefully, approved by the Masamoto/North America and the Masamoto/Europe organizations, as well as by the Masamoto Electronics Product Group in Japan.

It is now January 1989. You are to have a plan ready in six months for the aggressive launch in the fall 1990 selling season in Canada, the United States, and Europe. At the Masamoto research laboratories in Japan, work is under way on a home word processor that will support the large, complex character sets necessary for languages such as Japanese and Chinese. If this R&D program is fruitful, and your launch in North America and Europe is successful, Masamoto would like ultimately to market the YWP on a truly global basis.

The Masamoto Plan

In the following pages, we present your plan document as you submitted it to the directors of marketing of Masamoto/North America and Europe. At the bottom of each page of this text we highlight the important concepts demonstrated in your plan and cross-reference portions of this book relevant to the concepts and analytical support tools used in the plan. Recall that all the numbers in this case are hypothetical and should not be used for research.

MARKETING PLAN FOR THE YWP HOME WORD PROCESSOR

MARKET OPPORTUNITY

The number of personal computers for home use is increasing at 30 percent per year worldwide (see Exhibit 1); the most common use of home computers is word processing (see Exhibit 2). Typewriter sales, which were relatively flat at about 3 million units per year, recently began to decline as consumers adopt computers for home use. Typewriter sales largely represent replacement of old machines (on average, every seven to ten years), although a significant number of "new" purchases occur as students enter high school and college. In recent years, the replacement process has generally resulted in the substitution of an electronic typewriter or a PC for an existing manual or electric typewriter. New purchases have similarly been split between the two product configurations. In both instances, PCs have been gaining market share at the expense of electronic typewriters. Masamoto has obtained a 15 percent market share in the electronic typewriter market with its product line, but this is now a declining market.

A new segment, known as the "home word processor,"[1] seems to be emerging. A home word processor has the power of advanced word-processing software running on a personal computer, but is easier to use because it is dedicated solely to word processing. This market was pioneered in 1987 by the Magnavox Videowriter produced by Philips Electronics (see Exhibit 3). The Videowriter

EXHIBIT 1
Writing Instrument Sales, 1980–1988

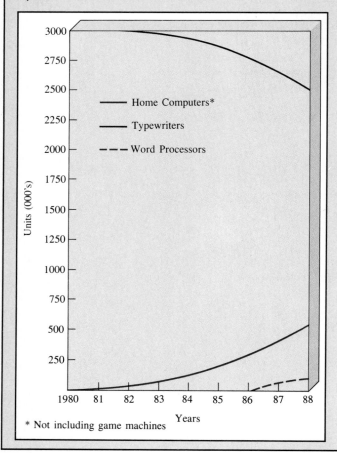

Units (000's)

Home Computers*
Typewriters
Word Processors

1980 81 82 83 84 85 86 87 88

Years

* Not including game machines

EXHIBIT 2
Home-Use Patterns*

Word processing	95%
Spreadsheets	40%
Games	25%
Education	20%
Programming (e.g., Basic)	10%
Other	5%†

* Fraction of owners of personal computers who say they use home computers for designated function.
† E.g., graphics, data base management.

1. Markets become more segmented as they evolve and technology changes.

EXHIBIT 3
Magnavox Videowriter

Just how simple do word processors have to get before you begin using one?

Even simpler than your old typewriter?

No problem. Because we've made one that eliminates all the intimidating things you've always associated with word processors.

And we call it the Magnavox Videowriter.®

The Videowriter is easier to set up than other word processors.

The average word processor has three separate pieces to hook together. A keyboard, a monitor and a printer. And that can be somewhat complicated.

Take the Videowriter home and you have a complete, portable unit. Virtually no set-up is necessary.

The instructions are easier to follow.

Unlike our competition, you don't need an instruction manual to use it.

All the instructions you need appear on the right side of the screen. So you can learn as you go.

The keys are easier to understand.

Most word processors have keys marked "ESC," "function" and "local command."

The Videowriter has keys marked "spell," "delete" and "help."

In fact, all our keys tell you exactly what they do. We think it's a lot easier to learn a keyboard when you can understand the keys.

And the price is easier to afford.

Surprised? We sell the Videowriter® Word Processor for around the price of a good electronic typewriter.

And, unlike most word processors, that price includes everything you need.

So go to your local Magnavox dealer and try one for yourself.

Chances are, you'll find the only hard part about working with the Videowriter is deciding what to write.

MAGNAVOX
Smart. Very smart.

has a full keyboard, an 18-line screen, and a built-in dot-matrix letter-quality printer. It is distributed through both computer stores and department/mass merchandiser outlets, at retail prices ranging from $549 to $699.

Within less than a year of Videowriter's introduction, Brother introduced its directly competitive model WP-55 (see Exhibit 4).[2] Soon thereafter, Smith-Corona introduced its PWP-14, with a 24-line display and 64k RAM, at $799 retail list price. Although Magnavox pioneered in this market, Brother soon took the lead, apparently because of its strong position in the typewriter market, aggressive advertising and pricing, and the superiority of its daisywheel printing technology, which produced higher print quality than Magnavox's dot-matrix approach.

The home word processor market segment is small, but growing rapidly as it captures buyers who resist the complexity of personal computers but want more functionality than a typewriter provides.[3] In 1987, 76,000 units were sold; in 1988, 114,000 were shipped. Projections are for the market to grow to 166,000 units in 1989, and 240,000 in 1990. Currently, approximately 60 percent of sales are occurring in North America, 35 percent in Europe, and 5 percent in other markets.

This plan outlines a marketing strategy to capture the market opportunity represented by the rapid growth in the home word processor segment of the typewriter/computer market.

MATCH TO MASAMOTO'S STRENGTHS

Exploiting the market opportunity in home word processing requires technical, marketing, and production expertise. Masamoto has great strength in producing high-quality electronic products at low cost. The *Consumer Electronics Reports*'s "highest quality" and "best value" ratings for the Suprema electronic typewriter attest to this fact, as do our internal records, which show that we have been able to reduce costs (and real prices) by 10 percent per year

2. Although pioneers have innate advantages, these can be overcome by improved product quality, lower price, and increased marketing expenditure.

3. Forecasting life cycles is often critical to quantifying the market opportunity for a new product.

4. Strengths that match the market are critical to creating a competitive advantage that can be sustained over time. Ideally, such strengths are corporate and cross-functional.

5. A candid assessment of relative weaknesses and possible threats is essential to planning a strategy. Weaknesses must be overcome, while threats must be monitored closely.

6. Competitive reactions are important in determining share and profit potential. We should not assume competitors will be passive.

since the Suprema's launch in 1985. Our experience in LCD (liquid crystal display) screens and access to advanced and low-cost chips will be advantages for us in creating hardware features that allow full functions in a small package. Our marketing experience with the electronic typewriter line will help us greatly as we enter the word processor market. We know the department store and mass merchandise channels well and have good trade relations.[4]

Our strengths match the market well; but there are several threats to our full realization of our potential in this market, and several weaknesses that we must avoid or overcome.[5] First, it is critical to remember that we are not the pioneers in this category. We will, in fact, be introducing the YWP four years after Magnavox's entry. Magnavox has been challenged by Brother for market leadership, and it is likely that both firms will react strongly to a new entrant that tries to take a substantial share of the market.[6] They have the advantage of being in the market early with successful products. We propose a strategy that offers the consumer more value than existing products, with considerable margin for response to competitive reactions by Magnavox or Brother.

Brother is particularly strong in marketing, and has considerably more experience and proven capability than we do in channel relationships, dedicated sales force management, and effective advertising and promotion.[7]

In addition to potential responses from Brother and Magnavox, we face substantial threats from new entrants and potential new entrants. The most recent entrant is Panasonic with its KX-W1500 (similar in design to the Brother machine, with a daisywheel printer). The cost of entry is not very high, so we can expect additional new competition from personal computer manufacturers (e.g., Apple, IBM, Compaq), typewriter manufacturers (e.g., Olivetti, Olympia, Sharp), and retailers (e.g., Radio Shack). Such competitive activity, at least in the short run, would be likely to increase the power of distributors and retailers and put severe pressures on manufacturer margins. Since exit costs, although likely to be high, would not be prohibitive, we would expect an industry shakeout (such as recently oc-

curred in electronic typewriters) within three to five years, with resulting competition split among four or five key players.[8] Our goal is to be one of these survivors. We must view this as a long-run opportunity, and invest to create a superior product at a lower price that gains and holds a strong market position. We will need continuing R&D to keep ahead of the competition as they imitate our new features and capabilities.[9]

Another threat if we enter the home word processor market emanates from the further evolution of the capabilities of typewriters and personal computers. Typewriters are becoming more and more powerful (more lines in memory that can be edited, spell check capabilities). Personal computers are becoming easier to use. Atari and other game producers are widening their views of the home market, and may apply their mouse, joy stick, and graphics capabilities to word processing. In general, computer literacy is increasing, which should lead to a reduction in resistance to PC-based word-processing packages.[10]

In this plan, we outline a strategy based on a superior product, low price, and aggressive advertising, distribution, and promotion. The idea is to use creative marketing to build on our traditional skills in technology and production.[11]

GOALS AND OBJECTIVES

Masamoto's overall corporate philosophy is to seek market leadership by creating value for our customers by supplying high-quality products at a low cost. It is through serving customers with a total quality program that we will grow in sales, earn reasonable profits, increase stockholder value, and provide continued satisfaction to our employees and partners.[12] Translating this overall strategy to the YWP, our objectives should be to develop the best product in the market, become the number one or two producer in terms of market share (i.e., grow factory sales to approximately $125 million in five years in real terms), break even by the end of the fourth year, earn a 15 percent before-tax

7. One needs a program to overcome structural disadvantage relative to competition.

8. Entry and exit analysis is important in forecasting the share and margin potential of the segment.

9. The initial plan should reflect long-run investment strategies and not be based on assumed continuation of existing technology.

10. Be alert to the rapid changes that characterize markets as they develop.

11. Analytics *and* creativity are both needed for strategic success.

12. Success in marketing is based on supplying value to customers (benefits/price). This generates the resources to reward the other stakeholders in the firm (stockholders, employees, dealers).

profit on sales by the end of five years, and return 7 percent in real terms (3 percent real cost of capital plus 4 percent risk premium) on the $50 million to be invested in the venture.[13]

MARKETING ANALYSIS

Before making a sales forecast and laying out our proposed marketing program, let us briefly review the analysis of key marketing phenomena on which our proposal is based.[14]

Customer Decision Making

We must clearly understand how customers make choices in the word processor market.[15] We envision two very different decision processes: (1) the replacement of an old typewriter when it breaks; and (2) a new purchase to satisfy a new need (e.g., a person goes to college) or to upgrade by taking advantage of new technology. Exhibit 5 shows the information-gathering and decision steps we believe characterize the decision process. We see three precipitating events: (1) the household's existing typewriter breaks; (2) a child or relative reaches the point where he or she requires typing or computer capability; and/or (3) awareness of new word-processing technologies leads to a desire for potential new benefits.[16]

In the first instance (an existing typewriter breaks down), observation suggests that most customers will return to the place of purchase (or a similar outlet) to investigate alternatives, especially repair.[17] In most cases, the repair will be relatively expensive, and displays of the new electronic typewriters (and possibly word processors) and salesperson interaction will suggest that replacement makes more sense than repair.[18] If an attractive alternative is found (product attribute utilities and price), and if the perceived chances of finding a better alternative are low relative to the effort necessary, the customer is likely to buy.[19] If the first alternative is not satisfactory, or if the customer feels there may be a better alternative elsewhere, he or she may engage in further search. Such search might expand to include computer stores, if the consumer has been stimulated to consider this channel by friends, ads, press articles, or consumer guides.

In a second scenario, awareness of new technology through exposure at work to personal computers, media advertising, articles or TV shows, or friends, can trigger shopping.[20] In this case, we feel that the customer will typically visit a computer store, where he or she will learn about PC word-processing capabilities, as well as the wide array of other functions a PC can perform. Computer store sales personnel are generally well trained, aggressive (in comparison with those at mass merchandisers), and very willing to demonstrate their products. If the customer is convinced in the store that he or she has now found the best alternative in terms of power, ease of use, and price, the search will be over and the purchase consummated. In most cases, however, we expect that the customer will still be experiencing considerable uncertainty, and will therefore postpone purchase. He or she will then seek additional information from friends and the media (perhaps buying and at least skimming one or more PC magazines), and additional store visits.[21] This process may be repeated several times. At the point where it is felt that a good alternative has been found and that it is not worth shopping further, a decision to buy will be made.

Buying for a child going off to college may take the form of a combination of the typewriter replacement and computer buying processes. If the parent is a computer owner and the student is accustomed to using the parent's computer at home, the choice will probably be a PC, and the search process will be confined to computer stores. On the other hand, if the parent is computer illiterate and uses a typewriter, it is likely that the replacement process will be followed. In some cases, the child may jointly make the purchase with the adult.[22] In buying for another party (the child, in this case), the customer is, in effect, acting as a purchasing agent for the ultimate user, whose attribute weightings may or may not be taken into account.

---

13. Overall goals must be converted to measurable criteria to enable forecasting, decisions, and control.

14. Never write a plan without carefully analyzing the key marketing phenomena. You must understand them well if you are to make intelligent choices in creating your marketing strategy.

15. Good marketing begins by understanding customers' information processing. Generally, they will not consider all information and will use heuristics to simplify the complex decision environment.

16. Purchasing is usually precipitated by some event. You may be able to influence this event or expose customers to information that will influence their next purchase process steps in a positive way regarding your product.

17. Retrieving information from memory is often one of the first steps. In this case, the consumer has to remember the type of outlet where the product was purchased, and perhaps even the specific store.

EXHIBIT 5
Customer Decision Making

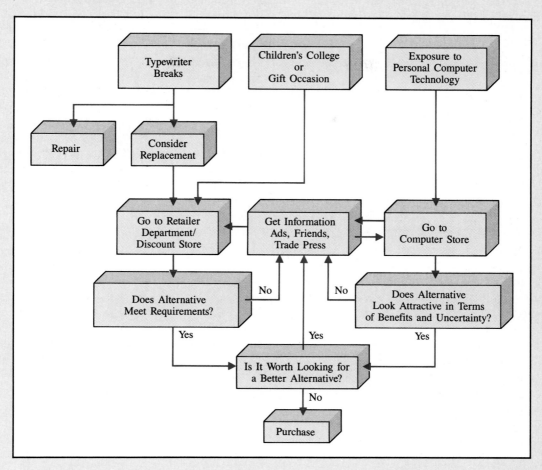

We find that the basic decision-making process is similar in North America and Europe, although in certain European markets, the substitution of low-end PCs for typewriters seems to be taking place more slowly than in the United States. Channels of distribution vary by country, but the critical distinction between replacement and initial purchase processes is equally relevant to an understanding of consumer behavior in both markets.

The important implications of these consumer behavior scenarios for our marketing plan are: (1) we need to communicate effectively with consumers in the replacement segment; (2) it is important to generate awareness of the technology through both paid advertising and public relations; (3) we need to obtain support from the computer stores as well as from our traditional typewriter outlets; (4) it is critical to have effective display and demonstration

18. Be sure to understand the relative influence of the store and other information sources, such as friends and media, and when these information sources are triggered.

19. The value of information will be compared to the cost of obtaining that information to see if additional active searching for information is likely to be worthwhile.

20. Innovators will be more aware of external information. A diffusion-of-innovation process will take place in which others observe the early purchasers' (opinion leaders') experience with the product.

21. Such information is valuable in identifying which product had preferred attributes and in reducing the perceived risk associated with the purchase decision.

22. Modeling of multiperson buying requires careful attention so that the purchase influences of each participant are described and the joint decision making is understood. Such joint decisions are common in purchases of consumer durables and industrial products.

489

in the retail outlet; and (5) we need to reduce uncertainty so that the customer will consummate the purchase rather than continue his or her search for information and reassurance.

Life Cycle

We have considered three separate life cycles (typewriters, home PCs, and word processors) in some detail. The first is the typewriter sales pattern, which is clearly in a mature phase with some decline owing to competitive technologies. Although improved electronic typewriters now dominate the market, the life cycle has not been rejuvenated and sales are mostly replacement. The second life cycle we considered is the sales pattern for personal computers used in the home (see Exhibit 1). A Level I view of these data indicates this product is in the growth phase.[23] A fitting of the Bass model to these data points to substantial growth potential in the next five years, but with a reduction of the growth rate in each year ($P(0) = .002$, $Q = .4$, $M =$

EXHIBIT 6
Life-Cycle Forecasts for 1989–1999

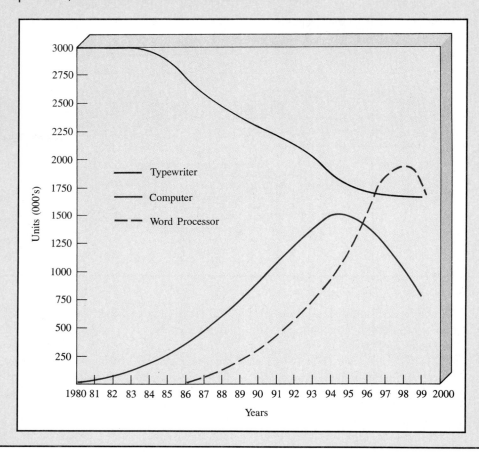

23. Level I analysis should always be done before Level II analysis.

24. Statistical fitting of the Bass model can be useful when there are enough data (at least 6 years) or the ultimate potential (M) can be estimated judgmentally.

490

25,000,000).[24] Exhibit 6 shows the projections for the period 1990–1999 for both the typewriter and home personal computer markets, as well as the actual sales of home word processors for 1986–1988. Although there are not enough data to fit the three years of sales statistically, it is clear that word processors are in their birth phase. The implications of these life cycles for our forecasts are evident. We must consider both the typewriter and the PC industries, and estimate how much sales of home word processors will come from each source. Our market research indicates that 85 percent of typewriter owners would consider a personal computer or word processor when it is necessary to replace their typewriter, which suggests that the segment of typewriter replacers who will trade up to the new word processor is likely to grow. The segment of personal computer purchasers who will trade down to the word processor is smaller, but when added to the replacers should accentuate word processor sales growth.

We envision that our new product will enter a market in its growth phase. We will have to concentrate on building the category with advertising, promotion, and dealer training. We should focus on one or two models, and only add others to capture major segments as the market develops. We do not expect price competition to be severe because all viable manufacturers will be experiencing growth in absolute sales. We will have to adopt an entrepreneurial stance in this market, seeking to stimulate its overall growth while aiming at becoming number one or two in market share.[25]

In forecasting the life cycle for home word processors, we use our standard life-cycle model, with $P(0) = .035$, $M = 25,000,000$, and $Q = .55$, parameters that are consistent with what initial data are available. We expect initial sales to be higher than they were for the home PC market, because the home market is now more developed than when PCs first came on the market, and that Q will be larger as a result of higher current diffusion rates. Our final sales forecast was derived by normalizing the total market size to the sum of existing typewriter sales (3 million units) plus 25 percent of combined potential PC and word processor sales. This 25 percent incremental category growth is based on our premarket forecasting model research of the overall home writing machine market. As may be seen in Exhibit 6, this forecast anticipates that sales of home electronic typewriters will decline over the next ten years as home word processors and PCs increasingly dominate the market. Our flow model estimate of overall sales was consistent with the life-cycle model forecasts.

Segmentation and Targeting

There are two primary ways to look at segmentation in this market.[26] Product segmentation allows us to see the overall competitive structure and dynamics, while psychographic segmentation provides guidance in designing advertising and sales strategies. These two views of the market are compatible, and differ largely in which dimensions are at the top of their respective segmentation hierarchies.[27]

Our product-segmentation structure was derived from an analysis of recent customer shopping behavior. If customers shopped for two types of products, we consider them to be alternatives in the purchase decision, and therefore competitive. We also examined customer preferences, asking consumers what product they would choose if their most preferred product were not available. We then used Level II analysis to group products so that the probability of switching to another product was high within the product class and low across product segments.[28]

There are currently three product segments: typewriters, personal computers, and home word processors, each of which is attractive to customers with distinct economic and psychological profiles. This segmentation structure applies to both the North American and most European markets, but typewriters continue to represent a larger proportion of consumer preferences in Europe.

This product-segmentation structure supports the emergence of the new word processor market. The dynamics of this structure strongly suggest a marked reduction of the size of the typewriter market, since we found that when people are aware of home word processors, they are

---

25. Remember the generic life-cycle strategies, but recall that ''dynamic sales patterns'' is a better name for the life cycle because many actions we or our competitors take can influence the sales level of our brand and the product class.

26. There is not one best way to segment the market. It depends on how the segmentation is to be used to support decisions.

27. Although there is no one universally best segmentation structure, the alternatives should be consistent and reflect alternative views of the same multidimensional customer data on attitudes, demographics, uses, and product competitiveness.

28. The Level II techniques for segmentation include clustering and hierarchical models (see Chapter 7).

willing to switch from their traditional preferences for type-writers. Similarly, consumers who preferred personal computers had a strong preference for a dedicated word processor as a second computer in the home or for a college-bound young adult.

The psychographic segmentation structure also consists of three segments: computer literates, computer rejecters, and functional adopters (see Exhibit 7). The computer literates feel comfortable with computers; have many uses for computers at home and work (spreadsheet modeling, programming, and data analysis, as well as word processing); have an average of three and one-half years of college education and an income of $40,000; shop at computer stores for word processing; and prefer brand-name computers. Computer rejecters are fearful of computers, with which they have had little experience; feel uncomfortable with change; have less education; earn an average of $25,000; shop primarily at discount or department stores; and tend to consider only traditional type-writers. The functional adopter is concerned about the difficulty of learning to use computers; needs only word-processing capability; has an average of two years of college-level education and $32,500 in income; evokes type-writers as a decision alternative, but would consider a computer; and shops at department or discount electronic stores.[29] Our study found differences across countries in

EXHIBIT 7
Psychological Segmentation and Profiles

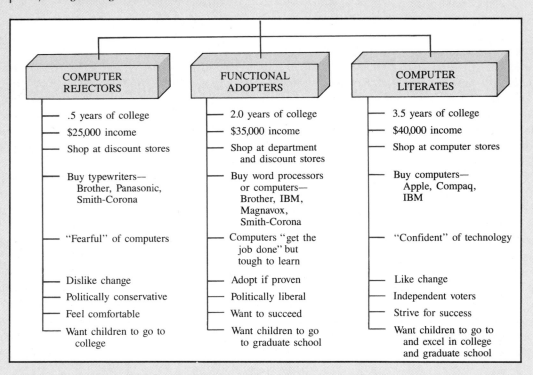

COMPUTER REJECTORS	FUNCTIONAL ADOPTERS	COMPUTER LITERATES
.5 years of college	2.0 years of college	3.5 years of college
$25,000 income	$35,000 income	$40,000 income
Shop at discount stores	Shop at department and discount stores	Shop at computer stores
Buy typewriters—Brother, Panasonic, Smith-Corona	Buy word processors or computers—Brother, IBM, Magnavox, Smith-Corona	Buy computers—Apple, Compaq, IBM
"Fearful" of computers	Computers "get the job done" but tough to learn	"Confident" of technology
Dislike change	Adopt if proven	Like change
Politically conservative	Politically liberal	Independent voters
Feel comfortable	Want to succeed	Strive for success
Want children to go to college	Want children to go to graduate school	Want children to go to and excel in college and graduate school

29. Profiling the attributes that are best in discriminating between segments helps define differences.

30. We want there to be large differences between segments, and small differences within them.

31. One must either compete in a single segment, offer differentiated products to several segments, or ignore the segmentation differences.

32. Factor analysis links the measures of perception recorded in attribute rating to underlying dimensions.

33. Positioning is based on understanding the number and nature of the dimensions customers use to differentiate between purchase alternatives.

34. A perceptual map allows a manager to see how his or her product compares to competitors on the perceptual dimensions customers use in evaluation.

35. One way to capture price in a perceptual map is to define it as a separate dimension. Another is to divide the scores on each dimension by price.

36. Positioning can vary across segments or strive for an overall umbrella effect.

the incidence of the major psychological segments, but these were smaller than the differences across psychological segments.[30]

This segmentation structure suggests that we will want to consider distinct advertising approaches, distribution channels, and salesperson incentive and training programs for each psychographic segment.[31] The three implicit consumer decision models emphasize the need to be sensitive to differences in motivation and information processing.

Positioning

Our research found that the two primary perceptual dimensions were power and ease of use. In our perceptual maps (based on factor analysis[32]), "power" was related to positive attribute ratings on: ability to do more than word processing, memory capacity, screen size, speed, spreadsheet analysis, use by whole family, printing quality, printing speed, professional quality of printing, and correction of spelling mistakes. "Ease of use" was related to positive ratings on: easy to learn, easy to operate, easy to set up, easy to maintain, convenient size, and portability. A third dimension was overall "quality," which was associated with: built to last, reliable, made by a reputable manufacturer, attractive design, fast service, good warranty, free of defects at delivery, and the availability of "hot line" assistance.[33]

A perceptual map for the overall market is shown in Exhibit 8.[34] The coordinates of the points were scaled by dividing by price.[35] The perceptions of products were similar across the three product segments shown in Exhibit 7, but the importance of the dimensions varied.[36] The consumers who were in the computer rejector segment place greater importance on the ease-of-use dimension and less on the power dimension than those in the computer literate segment (see vectors labeled *CL* for computer literates, *CR* for computer rejecters, and *FA* for functional adopters.)[37]

One implication of this map for our product strategy is that if we have one product, it should reflect a balance between power and ease of use: more power than typewriters, but less than computers; more ease of use than computers, but less than typewriters. We show one positioning possibility as YWP in Exhibit 8. Here we have advantages versus typewriters and computers, and are equal to, or better than, our word processor competitors on all three dimensions. Another possibility is to have two models in our line: one with minimal functionality and a low price, and the other with greater power selling for a higher price.[38] In the first positioning, we need to have more power than typewriters without sacrificing ease of use. In the second positioning, we need greater ease of use than personal computers, while matching their power in the functions most relevant to the home environment. In both cases, we need very high quality products, distinctive features to substantiate the positioning, and relatively low prices.[39]

Market Response

We know from our experience in typewriters that the market is very sensitive to promotion.[40] Over 60 percent of typewriter purchases are made at Christmas, for June graduation, and during the back-to-school season. Promotions during these periods can dramatically increase trade presence and sales. We have found that a 10 percent price cut, special in-store displays (obtained by an additional dealer incentive of $25 per machine sold), and cooperative feature advertising in local papers (we pay 50 percent of the cost) can increase sales significantly. In recent experiments between matched markets, we found that promotion at this level generated a 20 percent increase over unpromoted levels, without a detectable subsequent decline in sales due to advancing the buying cycle.[41] We estimate the cost of such promotions at $3 million and the incremental profit generated as $5.5 million.[42] We would expect similar response in the new home word processor market. Promotion response depends on the details of the promotion and the market (e.g., Belgian consumers appear to be more responsive to price cuts than Swedish consumers), but our experience suggests that well-conceived promotions in this

37. Benefit segmentation consists of grouping customers who can be represented by vectors whose slopes reflect the relative importance of each dimension.

38. If the market has two different segments, positioning one product equally on both dimensions of a map can lead to lower sales than if two products are used to span the opportunities. In this case, two unique benefit propositions are presented to the market.

39. The product must be built to substantiate the positioning with valued features, quality, and price.

40. Market response analysis is based on identifying the marketing variables that generate the greatest sales change for the lowest cost.

41. Market experiments are one way to determine market response. Others are judgment and statistical analysis of past data. The dynamics of response must also be considered. In promotion, there may be a dip after a promotion owing to inventorying by the channel or the customer.

42. Market response should be evaluated in terms of profits generated, not just sales results.

EXHIBIT 8
Perceptual Map for Overall Home Writing Machine Market

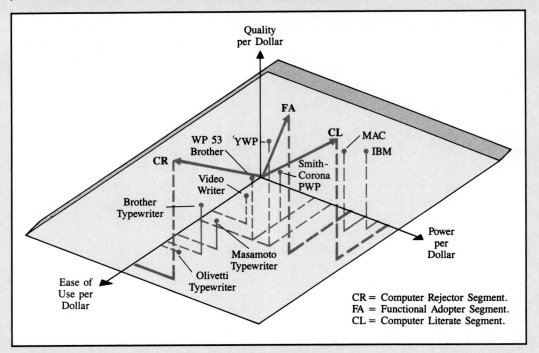

market have a high probability of generating extra sales and profits.

Since customers are sensitive to price, it is essential that we establish a base price that delivers value. As analyzed with our perceptual map, the perceptions of our products divided by their prices must put us in a competitive position with respect to the utility-per-dollar coordinates.[43]

Advertising response is important in all segments. We need to reach 75 percent of the market with an average frequency of three exposures in the first six months of the launch to gain a minimal awareness level to support our dealership and promotional programs. In the United States, according to simulations employing our premarket forecasting model, an advertising budget of $10 million would produce 50 percent awareness in our target markets the first year. We estimate that increasing the advertising to $15 million would increase awareness to 65 percent.[44] Advertising costs and response to specific copy approaches vary significantly among countries, as do media availability and regulations. Our models suggest that a $7.5 million investment in media advertising would generate 30 percent awareness in our primary European target markets (the U.K., France, Germany, Benelux, and Scandinavia).

Distribution is increasingly difficult to obtain, and channel members are becoming increasingly powerful. This is particularly true in Europe, but is also becoming evident in the United States and Canada. We need to emphasize dealer satisfaction if we wish to achieve our sales

43. Base prices should be linked to positioning and promotion used for short-term price reductions and competitive reaction.

44. We should think of advertising response in terms of reach and frequency and sales. The goal is to estimate the marginal response in sales and profits to changes in advertising expenditure.

45. Distributors and retailers must be considered as customers as well. We need to position, price, and promote to the channel members if we want them to buy our proposition and sell, stock, and service our product.

EXHIBIT 9
Technology Trends

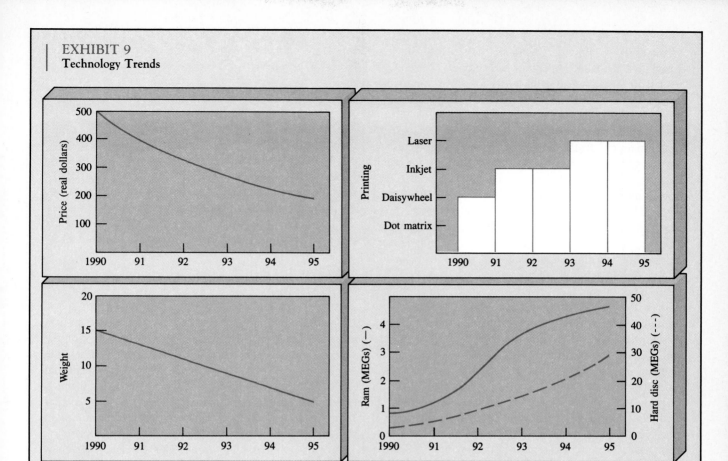

and market share goals. We should have a program to compensate the dealers for the risk of handling new products, and make sure that our heavy media advertising explicitly draws customers to *our* dealers' stores. We must offer ''better-than-competitive'' real margins to the trade; perhaps we need to include rebate programs where they would be helpful in maintaining retail prices. Training and incentives for dealers sales personnel and superior display and point-of-sale materials will also be critical.[45]

Understanding market response will be critical as we seek to make trade-offs among spending on promotion, advertising, and trade support and profitability. We are currently developing a comprehensive model to assist us in making such choices.[46]

Competitive Response

As discussed above, we anticipate entry of new competitors and defensive actions by Brother and Magnavox. Since the home word-processing market is in the growth phase, however, we expect such firms to concentrate on adding product features, reducing costs, and exploiting advances in technology. Competition will be intense, but a price war can probably be avoided.[47] Promotions and price cuts will fuel

46. Market response analysis is the basis for forecasting sales and maximizing the profit potential of a product.

47. The risk of a price war should be investigated through a payoff matrix. If a war is likely, cooperative strategies should be considered and actions should not be taken before carefully predicting how competitors will react and where a set of reactions will lead.

product category growth rather than lead to significant market share changes. Competitors will certainly strive to defend their market shares, but will focus on stimulating category growth and gaining dominance through product innovation.[48]

Competition for channel support will require high dealer margins, dealer support and training, and the maintenance of good relations (e.g., attractive billing and credit policies, acceptance of product returns, fast order processing and delivery, quality service capability).[49] This competition for retailer support will be as important as direct competition for consumer preference. The effect of promotions will be positive because we will be giving dealers more profit contribution and encouraging earlier adoption through lower actual retail prices.

While promotion, advertising, and channel competition will be important, in the long run, competitors who are able to achieve cost leadership by moving most quickly down the cumulative volume curve are most likely to prevail.[50] The life cycle of the overall home word-processing segment will extend over many years, but individual models will have life cycles of twenty-four and thirty-six months. We must be willing to obsolete our own line as well as competitors' products through technological changes that enhance print quality, increase screen sharpness, reduce weight, and improve functionality.[51] (See Exhibit 9 for a depiction of the major price and product attribute trends we expect over the next five years.)

Competing successfully in this market will require superiority in product, price, promotion, and channel attributes. These elements of our strategy must be fully congruent with our understanding of customer decision making, life cycles, segmentation, positioning, and market response.[52]

MARKETING PROGRAMS

Based on in-depth analysis of the emerging home word-processing market and industry, we have developed the following marketing programs and sales and profit forecasts.

Target Market Segments

We plan to aim at both the "replacement" and the "new" markets (review Exhibit 5).[53] Within these broad markets, our primary targets can be defined from two points of view. From the perspective of product features and competitive set, we will focus on the "home word processor" segment. From the perspective of communications strategy, we will segment the market further by targeting the psychologically defined "functional adopter" segment (see Exhibit 7).[54]

Positioning—Core Benefit Proposition

Our core benefit proposition is to have the easiest-to-use, most powerful, and highest-quality word processor on the market, and have it be perceived as offering the best value to customers. For the "functional adopter" segment that we have targeted, this means we will have to develop specific features to establish superiority relative to other home word processors on all three of the most important dimensions on our perceptual map (see Exhibit 8).[55]

Our products will offer neither as much power as computers nor as much ease of use as typewriters, but we will deliver superior utility to our target customers. Our goal is to deliver the most perceived value within our segment, not the lowest price.[56]

Features, Pricing, and Product Fulfillment

We must consider the evolution of our product line over time as we establish features to substantiate our positioning. Exhibit 10 outlines our specifications based on a conjoint analysis of the features and their trade-off by customers in terms of costs. In 1993, we plan to widen the product line to two models,[57] the YWP 1000 and the YWP 2000, which

---

48. Market share is a possible correlate to ROI, but take care to understand the mechanisms of how share creates profits before committing to a share strategy.

49. Competition exists at the channel level as well as at the consumer level. Channel competition can also produce "wars" that destroy profitability. Payoff matrices and co-operative strategies should be examined.

50. Building cumulative volume and a dominant share is important when there are significant experience effects in manufacturing and other activities in the value chain. In this case, the firm with the dominant share will have the lowest costs and therefore the highest profits and/or greatest ability to survive price competition.

51. The creation of a unique competitive advantage is the best way to obtain market leadership. This may be in product innovation, cost, positioning, or marketing tactics such as selling, advertising, distribution, or service. Successful long-run product-line strategy depends not on maintaining a single product but rather a line that generates the maximum incremental contribution.

EXHIBIT 10
Product Features and Prices

	1991 MODEL	1994 MODELS	
	YWP	YWP 2000	YWP 1000
Printer	Inkjet	Color laser	Laser
Storage RAM	512K	4meg	1meg
DISK	1meg	20meg	10meg
Screen	30-line CRT	30-line plasma	30-line
Weight (including printer)	12 pounds	6 pounds	6 pounds
Software	3 fonts	12 fonts Graphics	6 fonts
Price (retail)	$499	$499	$399

will have more storage and software capability than our initial entry.[58] With two products we will be well positioned to compete effectively in what we expect to be relatively distinct price-sensitive and premium-feature-sensitive segments.[59]

We clearly anticipate very rapid technological progress (see Exhibit 9). We propose a dedicated five-person engineering and marketing team with a budget of $1,250,000 per year for product engineering and market research with lead users.[60] Although we will not be developing new chips and screens ourselves,[61] we will aim to be superior in system integration based on partnerships inside Masamoto as well as external strategic alliances. The price declines we forecast follow historic norms for electronic products of this type, and assume both reductions in components costs and experience curve effects in assembly, distribution, and marketing. We expect some softening of prices as a result of competition, with our initial $499 price point falling to $399 by early 1992. We will launch our 1994 models in the fall of 1993 at $399 for the YWP 1000 and $499 for the YWP 2000.

As we reach the 1996–1999 period, the distinction between the home word processor and typewriter will disappear at the high end of the market. We anticipate that the market will settle into a "writing machine" market made up of two product segments: word processors and computers. The distinction will be that the computers will offer a wide array of functions, while the word processors (which will have largely replaced electronic typewriters) will be dedicated to typing and simple home software (e.g., spreadsheet and checkbook balancing). As the product category evolves, it is imperative that we maintain our traditional reputation for superior product innovation and quality.[62]

Channels of Distribution

We will utilize two channels of distribution to reach our market. Department and discount stores will be used to serve the "functional adopter" segment, while computer stores will be used to reach: (1) customers who are aware of the new computer technology, but are not inclined to learn how to use a full-function personal computer; (2) "computer literates" who want a word processor as a supplement to their PC (e.g., for a student living at home). In both types of outlets, demonstration capability is likely to be critical.

We will set up self-demonstrators in discount stores, and we will train sales personnel in computer and department stores to demonstrate the YWP. Our premarket research indicates that the probability of purchase doubles after a demonstration in which the customer spends ten minutes using the unit to type a letter.[63] Even a computer illiterate should feel comfortable with the YWP word processor after a brief hands-on demonstration. We will grant a $25-per-machine allowance to outlets that install a demonstration unit and train 90 percent of their sales staff to demonstrate the YWP.[64]

52. Competitive strategy is the integrator of the market analysis effort.

53. A consideration of the customer decision process should drive strategy formulation and the planning process.

54. Looking at the market from two points of view is perfectly legitimate if the two representations are consistent views of the same market data. The profile of variables in each segmentation structure should provide a complete view of the customers.

55. Sometimes it is not possible to establish superiority on all dimensions and one is selected for competitive advantage. But some type of perceived overall superiority must be achieved if the results are not to be inferior sales or margins.

56. If you have created a superior product, do not give it away by pricing it too low. Premium products earn premium prices and profits, but be careful that the value customers perceive is higher than competitive alternatives.

57. Level III analytical support is often appropriate in new-product design.

EXHIBIT 11
TV Storyboard

58. It is often wise as the life cycle matures to widen the line so that all subsegment opportunities are covered.

59. Such price sensitivity is a benefit segmentation. Positioning based on price is usually linked to alternative features. When segments exist, a product line offers the potential to cover all opportunities and be viewed as superior in each segment.

60. Be sure to integrate technology and market inputs. Organize formally and informally to do so and continually involve lead users in the requirements process.

61. Overcoming the NIH (''not invented here'') syndrome is critical to success in high-tech markets.

62. Quality consists of reliability, performance, and the matching of product features and pricing to customers' expectations of appropriate quality.

EXHIBIT 12
Print Copy for Computer Literates

63. Premarket forecasting is a valuable tool in reducing the risk of failure and finding the sensitive marketing variables that must be used to improve profitability.

64. Strategic coherence is critical. For example, if we claim ''easy to learn'' as a product attribute, we must communicate this in both our channel and our advertising tactics.

Advertising

Our primary copy platform, aimed at the functional adopter segment, is: "Join the new world of home word processing." The message is that there is now a new way to type documents and it is time to replace your old typewriter[65] (see Exhibit 11 for TV storyboard). During May-June and August-September, we will supplement this primary television campaign with a print campaign stressing that giving a word processor to your child will help him or her to become a better student. We will allocate 50 percent of our $10 million advertising budget to TV; 25 percent to broadly based print media (e.g., *Time*, *Newsweek*); and 25 percent of a separate print campaign in consumer computer media (e.g., *PC World*) directed at PC owners who are potential buyers of a second, dedicated word processor (see Exhibit 12). In addition, we plan to allocate $1 million to cooperative advertising (50 percent paid) with our retailers.

Service and Warranties

Because of the key role quality plays in our positioning, we will offer the best warranty in the field—five years on parts and labor. We will maintain our own repair service offices in England, Germany, Canada, and two locations in the United States (New York and Denver). Dealers will be trained to make very simple repairs (e.g., replace cords), but all major work will be done in Masamoto-controlled service facilities. Postage will be paid by Masamoto from and to the dealer or the customer (if it is sent directly to Masamoto). Phone confirmation of customer satisfaction will be carried out for all units serviced.[66]

A direct-dial no-cost telephone service for customers will be maintained in each country (e.g., 800 service in North America, FreeFone in the U.K.). This "hot line" will answer customer and dealer questions and ensure that buyers get adequate training. A video training tape will be sent to dealers and customers who request it.

Global Coordination

Our segmentation analysis indicates that the differences among countries are not dominant in terms of targeting, positioning, and product design.[67] However, many local differences exist in regulations, language, channels of distribution, and competition. While we will have a global strategy, our local subsidiaries will have authority to make distribution, promotion, and advertising decisions. Brand managers will be responsible for modifying fonts, advertising copy, channel selection and incentives, and service policies to maximize profits in each country.[68] Brand managers will be assigned in Canada, the United States, Great Britain, Benelux, Ireland, France, Germany, Scandinavia, and Southern Europe. These brand managers will operate in a matrix organizational structure, reporting both to the Masamoto country manager and to the worldwide home word processor (YWP) marketing manager.

SALES AND PROFIT FORECAST

Our sales and profit forecast is shown in Exhibit 13 (all values are in real terms—before any increases due to inflation). Factory sales revenues grow to $128 million by the end of the fifth year; we break even in the fourth year; and ultimately earn more than 7 percent on our $50 million investment.[69]

Sales Forecasting

Our sales forecast is based on independently derived category sales and market share estimates. We use the forecasts of industry sales from Exhibit 6. Based on our premarket clinic flow model, we estimate our share to grow from an initial 15 percent in 1991 to 35 percent in 1994, and 40 percent thereafter. This forecast reflects a leadership position based on superior product design, quality, and marketing and sales. We expect average suggested retail

---

65. Be sure that the advertising copy developed for a product is consistent with the overall strategy. Good copy is important, but it must always support the strategy.

66. We do not sell products but rather the benefits they produce for users. Be sure your customers continue to obtain these benefits over time.

67. Country-based geographic segmentation is not always the best way to address the worldwide market.

68. Even when a global product strategy is adopted, the ability to adapt to local-country differences may improve profits substantially.

69. Think of new products as a long-term investment. Do not expect major innovations to pay off in the short term.

prices to soften from $499 to $399 by 1993.[70] When we introduce our two new models, we expect our average price to increase to $425 (25 percent YWP 2000 at $499 and 75 percent YWP 1000 at $399), and then subsequently decline under competitive pressure as the life cycle matures. We calculate factory revenue as 65 percent of suggested retail prices.

Cost Assumptions

In estimating our cost curve, we assume a 10 percent annual cost reduction because of decreases in component costs that do not depend upon our volume of production (i.e., shared experience curves). In addition, we estimate that we will benefit from a 90 percent experience curve (costs drop to .9 of previous levels with each doubling of *cumulative* production) as our volume increases (initial unit cost is $300 at the 1991 production level).[71] In 1994 $61 and in 1997 $85 is added to the then-existing base cost to pay for improved product features.

Profit and ROI

Profits for the venture are shown in Exhibit 13. We show a loss ($13.2 million) in the first year, after deducting from

EXHIBIT 13
Financial Projections

	FISCAL YEARS (SEPTEMBER TO SEPTEMBER)								
	1991	**1992**	**1993**	**1994**	**1995**	**1996**	**1997**	**1998**	**1999**
Sales units	51,000	119,300	197,000	309,900	463,500	579,800	679,600	728,100	696,300
Retail price (real)	499	450	400	425	425	400	375	350	325
Average factory price (65%)	$324.35	$292.50	$260.00	$276.25	$276.25	$260.00	$243.75	$227.50	$211.25
Factory sales revenue (000's)	16,580	34,900	51,220	85,610	128,040	150,750	165,650	165,640	147,090
Unit costs ($)	300	225	180	178	148	125	132	114	100
Advertising ($000's)	10,000	7,500	5,000	10,000	9,000	8,000	7,500	7,500	7,500
Promotion ($)	1,278	2,982	4,926	500	500	500	500	500	500
R&D (000's)	1,250	1,250	1,250	1,250	1,250	1,250	1,250	1,250	1,250
Service (000's)	260	850	1,840	3,390	5,800	8,600	12,000	15,642	19,123
G&A (000's)	1,660	3,490	5,120	8,560	12,800	15,080	16,560	16,560	14,710
Profit before tax ($000's)	−13,200	−8,000	−2,380	6,850	30,300	44,900	38,100	41,080	34,630

70. When you make long-run forecasts, be sure to consider the possibility that your competition is as smart and aggressive as you are.

71. Cost reductions can be as a function of time as well as of cumulative volume. Be sure to separate the two phenomena in forecasting.

$16.6 million in sales revenue production costs of $15.3 million, a $10 million advertising budget, $1.3 million in promotion incentives for dealers to demonstrate the product, $260,000 for warranty service, the $1.25 million R&D budget, and $1.66 million in general and administrative expenses. Advertising is reduced after the launch (until the new models are introduced in 1994), but promotion is increased. We expect to lose money for the first three years, but to earn very high returns in the years 1995 to 1999. On a discounted cash flow basis (using the corporate real discount rate of 7%), we expect to earn $73 million in discounted after-tax profits, compared to an investment of $50 million. The resulting ratio of return to investment is 1.46, which is quite favorable given our firm's risk profile and the fact that we have only estimated cash flows for ten years.

The YWP program is demanding: substantial investment is required, continual innovation is necessary, time-to-market is critical, and prices will decline. But we can earn a good return in this market.[72]

Control

Our market, technology, and competitors are moving rapidly, which will require state-of-the-art monitoring and control procedures on our part. We will review our strategy every six months, and support this review with: (1) market research to ensure that we are competitive and leading the market; (2) a technology review to ensure that we are not "blindsided" by new developments; (3) customer follow-ups to make sure that our products and service are perceived as the very best; and (4) distributor and dealer surveys to verify that demonstrations are being carried out effectively and that our channel partners are satisfied with our service and support. We will review the execution of our positioning, targeting, product, and communication strategies.[73]

We will implement a decision support system based on our factory shipments and UPC scanner data on our retail sales in a sample of 250 stores. Our data bank will include market research studies (e.g., telephone interviews to determine brand awareness, attitudes, and usage, as well as market share and competitive standing), quality surveys, and competitive intelligence on media spending, channel programs, pricing, and new-product programs. We will use the models and statistical procedures developed in this plan to compare actual to expected results, make corrections, and continually search for improvements in our marketing strategy and tactics.[74]

ACTIONS

The specific actions to be undertaken in the next sixteen months are shown in Exhibit 14. We will coordinate production and distribution, dealer recruitment, advertising development, market research, warranty service, and public relations to achieve an effective launch in the fall of 1990. Very detailed PERT charts are available upon request.

RECOMMENDATIONS

We recommend full implementation of our plan to market the YWP word processor in 1990. There is a market opportunity, it matches our strengths, and we can convert it into profitable results. We will create a quality product that will be the technological leader in the field. It will generate value for customers by being easier to use than a computer and more powerful than a typewriter. We will be superior to our competitors in the home word-processing market in power, ease of use, and reliability and durability, and approximately equivalent in price. We will aggressively market the YWP with advertising, dealer training and demonstrations, competitive pricing, and superior service. We can become the leader in this market (40 percent share),

---

72. If the strategic analysis is done carefully and completely, then profit forecasting and "bottom line" results can be generated quickly and supported by marketing analysis.

73. Control should include strategic issues. Are our longer-term strategic assumptions reasonable? Is our strategy working? Are short-term problems the result of failures in execution, or is our strategy wrong?

74. Control includes diagnosing problems, correcting them, and searching for improvement in all elements of the marketing program.

EXHIBIT 14
Short-Term Activities

ACTIVITIES	1989					1990										
	Sept Oct Nov Dec	Jan	Feb Mar Apr May		Jun Jul Aug			Sept Oct Nov		Dec
Production	Set up line and suppliers		Production test		Ship product					
Distribution	Recruit retailers and distributors			Train retail sales staff/ Promotion plan		Point-of-purchase Install				Monitor demo results
Sales	Sell channel			Aid in training and dealer advertising				Support dealers		
Advertising	Final TV copy and print ads		Test ads and buy media			Revise and final copy		National advertising and promotion		
Service	Write service manual		Train dealers		Stock parts		Correct any defects			
Market research	Monitor market		Ad copy test		Set up UPC sample		Telephone survey			
R&D	Work on YWP 2000		Monitor technology							
Global	Global strategy meeting	Tactical plans by country	Review tactics		Coordinate ad/training materials			Share learning		Strategy review

reach $128 million in factory sales revenue, and be profitable on a cumulative basis within five years. We forecast $30 million net profit before tax in the fifth year and over $40 million in the sixth year. We expect to return more than our target rate of return on our $50 million investment within seven years.

The Masamoto Plan demonstrates many of the key teaching points of this book. It represents a combination of Levels I, II, and III analysis, as well as a good blend of creative and analytical skills. Its assumptions are supported with careful analysis and based on a fundamental understanding of customer decision making, life cycles, segmentation, positioning, market response, and competitive behavior. It stresses the basic marketing concept of technical innovation to create customer benefit on a global basis, and represents the coherent implementation of the stated marketing strategy through advertising, promotion, distribution, pricing, and service tactics. The firm earns profits for its stockholders, pays salaries to its employees, and compensates its channel partners based on the creation of utility for society.

QUESTIONS FOR DISCUSSION

1. What is the difference between a marketing plan and a marketing strategy? Between a marketing plan and tactical implementation?

2. Should all business units, product lines, and products use the same format for their plan? Why or why not?

3. What do you like about the Masamoto Marketing Plan?

4. What do you dislike about the Masamoto Plan? Give specific suggestions for improvement.

5. What levels of analysis were used in the plan? Was the level (I, II, or III) appropriate? Did the level always follow our recommended sequence?

6. How would you rank the Masamoto strategy in terms of creativity?

7. Did the Masamoto plan correctly link the strategy to the tactics? Is the plan feasible to implement?

8. List what you think are the five most important teaching points highlighted throughout the Masamoto Plan. Why did you select them?

9. What key concepts taught in this book were *not* highlighted in the Masamoto Plan?

CHAPTER

24

INTERNATIONAL BUSINESS MACHINES CORPORATION
Marketing Strategy for Typewriters and PC Printers

Developed in collaboration with Mr. Gregory C. Adams[1]

In late March 1989, IBM officials in Lexington, Kentucky, were seeking to take stock of the worldwide typewriter and PC printer businesses that they managed and to chart a course for the future. These businesses had undergone profound shifts during the past decade, leading to significant changes in IBM strategy and, recently, a major improvement in IBM's market position. According to senior IBM officials in Lexington, the key questions that now had to be addressed were: (1) How strong are our overall business and market positions? (2) What key developments in customer needs, technology, and competitive capabilities and behavior are most critical to our future? (3) What should be our strategic goals for this business three, five, and ten years out? (4) How should we manage our product line, our channels, and our customer relationships in the shorter term?

COMPANY BACKGROUND

IBM had for the previous thirty years been the world's largest manufacturer of computers and office automation products. With sales of $59.6 billion, IBM ranked fifth in *Fortune's* annual listing of the world's fifty largest corporations. Its operations were primarily in the field of information-handling systems, equipment, and services, especially computers, software, communications systems, workstations, typewriters, and related supplies and services. Most products were sold through its worldwide direct marketing organizations, which were characterized by highly trained sales forces that were considered "the best in the world" in intensive, "value-added" systems selling and in achieving account

---

[1] This case is largely based on and incorporates considerable material from Mr. Adams's M.I.T. M.S. thesis (1989), which should be consulted for specific sources and references. While believed to be a realistic description of the situation described, the specific managerial processes described in the case, and certain confidential data have been disguised. "Selectric," "Wheelwriter," "Proprinter," "Quickwriter," "Quietwriter," "Personal Typing System," "Personal System/2," and "Personal Page Printer" are trademarks of IBM, and should only be used accordingly.

control.[2] In recent years, IBM had begun to distribute selected products, such as personal computers (PCs), PC software and printers, and typewriters, through authorized dealers and remarketers. In most of the fields in which IBM did business, analysts estimated that its manufacturing costs were at least as low, and probably lower, than those of its primary competitors. Research and development expenses of 7.5–10 percent of sales were believed to be among the highest (on a total dollar basis) in the world.

While IBM clearly had made its mark in the data-processing business, it had, in fact, been historically at least as successful in the worldwide market for office typewriters. As of 1989, there were more IBM typewriters, including over 15 million Selectrics®, in homes and offices around the world than any other IBM product.

INDUSTRY HISTORY

The history of the typewriter began in 1714 when a "writing machine" was patented in England. The next 150 years saw many variations, but it was not until 1867 that a typewriter was first marketed by E. Remington and Sons, a firearms manufacturer. The basic design of the typewriter changed little over the next century. It was a keyboard-equipped machine that produced printed characters by impressing type upon paper through an inked ribbon. An operator would press the desired key, which would then mechanically work a series of levers and springs that would flip a bar bearing the desired letter against an inked ribbon, which impressed the letter on the paper. This simple machine allowed individuals, businesses, and organizations to produce neat, easy-to-read documents with speed and convenience.

This rapidly growing market, which had reached 120,000 units in the United States alone by the end of the 1920s, attracted new entrants such as Underwood, which soon became the industry leader, and was observed closely by major business machine companies such as Burroughs Adding Machine, National Cash Register, and IBM, an aggressive young company best known for its unit record (punch card) tabulating equipment.

THE IBM ELECTRIC TYPEWRITER DIVISION

IBM's entry into the typewriter market was based on a strategy of providing new technology, quality, and reliability. In the early 1930s, Underwood was the leading U.S. typewriter manufacturer, with a wide line of manual models. Since the turn of the century, however, several smaller firms had begun experimenting with the use of electricity to drive the typewriter. In what were coming to be called "electric typewriters," a motor was used to flip the type bars, causing each to strike with equal force, resulting in a smooth, printed effect. At twice the price of manual models, however, electric typewriters seemed to have a very limited market, especially during the depression of the 1930s.

Electromatic Typewriters was one of the companies struggling to introduce the new technology in the United States. In 1933, IBM acquired the company's tools, patents, and production facilities, and invested more than $1 million to redesign the Electromatic typewriter, improve research facilities, and establish service centers. The results were seen in 1935, when the company introduced the IBM Electric Typewriter, Model 01.

---

[2] "Account control" was achieved when a customer concluded that its interests would be best served by, in effect, delegating a significant portion of its information systems procurement process to its IBM account team. As the CEO of one large bank in the southeastern United States commented, "We let IBM focus on our data-processing requirements so that we can focus on being the best bankers in the regions."

"Operated by motor and controlled by a feather-light touch," the Model 01 improved the typist's productivity by as much as 50 percent. It quickly became the first successful electric typewriter in the United States.

In 1941, IBM announced another radical breakthrough in typewriter technology: proportional letter spacing. Since its invention, the typewriter had used a single-spacing principle that provided the same width for all characters, regardless of size. This gave typewritten material an uneven appearance, with too much space around thin letters such as *I*'s and *J*'s and not enough around wide letters such as *M*'s and *W*'s. IBM typewriter engineers had developed a mechanism that would measure each alphabetical character in units, thus allowing a typewriter to closely simulate type-set material.[3]

By the end of the war, IBM electric typewriters had a firm grip on the expanding office typewriter market. A generation of secretaries had used nothing but the IBM Electric 01, and apparently saw no reason to switch brands since IBM continued to lead the industry in advanced features and functions.

In Europe, however, a number of strong firms, such as Triumph-Adler (later Adler Royal) and Olympia in Germany, Hermes in Switzerland, Olivetti in Italy, Imperial and Wellington in England, and Contin in France, had established strong positions in their home markets, and were increasingly exporting to other European countries and even to North America. Industry observers estimated the European market as about two-thirds the size of the U.S. market. Competition was characterized by a strong national company in each country that held more than 50 percent of the market in that country, with the remaining market distributed among many companies, including IBM.[4]

In 1955, IBM established the Electric Typewriter Division as an autonomous division with its own development, manufacturing, and sales and service force. The next year, Lexington, Kentucky, was chosen as the site for the new division's first dedicated plant. The plant would eventually comprise nearly 400 acres and 4 million square feet of owned and leased space. The new facility contained the world's most modern typewriter assembly operation, as well as the only engineering laboratory in the world devoted primarily to electric typewriter development.

In 1961, IBM introduced its newly developed Selectric® Typewriter. The IBM Selectric® was based on a unique and highly innovative design that replaced type bars and the moving carriage with a "golfball" printing element. The different letters and characters were fixed on the element, which spun and tilted to press the appropriate symbol against the ribbon and the paper. According to IBM advertising, the printing element was capable of skimming across the page so quickly that even the fastest typist could not jam it.

The IBM Selectric® was the most successful typewriter in history, solidifying IBM's leadership in the U.S. typewriter market and significantly increasing IBM's market share worldwide. During the 1960s and 1970s, IBM continually upgraded its features and capabilities (e.g., introduction of the very successful Correcting Selectric® II, with its IBM Lift-Off Tape, in 1973), maintaining its product superiority and improving its market position. By the end of the 1970s, IBM was estimated to have captured approximately 70 percent of the U.S. office typewriter market.[5]

---

[3] The war effort delayed product introduction until 1944.

[4] The other major population center in the world, the Far East, did not develop as a typewriter market until the 1980s, largely because it was not economically feasible to adapt the ideograph-based languages of this region to existing typewriter technology. By the 1980s, however, the use of European languages (especially English) for business purposes, the romanization of the national languages of countries such as the Philippines, Malaysia, and Indonesia, and the development of an alphabet-based version of Japanese had led to a modest growth in this market.

[5] The company's position was so dominant that the Federal Trade Commission began a study in 1976 to determine if IBM had unfairly monopolized the office typewriter market. The investigation was dropped in February 1978, with the FTC concluding that IBM had not violated the law and that no further action was required.

In 1964, the Typewriter Division's name was changed to the Office Products Division (OPD) to reflect a strategy of diversification into related office automation products such as dictating equipment and (later) copiers. IBM sold its typewriters and other office products directly to customers through the OPD field force. While the average transaction value and revenue per account were much smaller in office products than in computers, the OPD field force employed account analysis and systems selling techniques similar to those used by IBM's computer sales force. The OPD field force was professional, aggressive, and articulate, and took pride in its account knowledge and ability to achieve account control. Both sales and service personnel wore the traditional IBM dark business suits, white shirts, and wingtip shoes.[6]

The field force operated through branch offices in every major city in the United States. In the mid-1960s, there were 120 OPD branches employing approximately 3,800 marketing representatives. An average branch consisted of 25 marketing representatives, 2 marketing managers, 10 administrators to handle customer orders, 2 administration managers, and a branch manager, and served approximately 7,000 customers. (The IBM Data Processing Division branch responsible for mainframe computing in the same territory would have had approximately 50 customers.) A branch this size had a sales quota of roughly 450 typewriters per month. Supporting the branch were 50 service representatives and 4 service managers, as well as, on average, 2 marketing support representatives, who assisted customers in setting up their machines and installing new applications.

IBM recruited top people from colleges and universities across the country to become its marketing representatives. Grades, student activities, campus involvement, and communication skills, rather than a specific major, were the primary criteria for hiring. In selecting candidates, branch managers relied heavily on personal interviews, looking, as one veteran explained, for "peddlers, people who were excited about selling." Those candidates who were selected were then put through an intensive three-month training program. The first two months were spent in the local office studying the IBM product line and learning to give a quality demonstration. It was not uncommon at a local branch meeting for a new trainee to be called upon to demonstrate an IBM typewriter in front of the entire office.

After this two-month period, the trainee spent one month at OPD's advanced training center in Dallas, Texas. The instructors in the center were top marketing representatives who used this assignment to prepare themselves for careers in marketing management. They taught the trainees about marketing, selling, and the IBM culture. Emphasis was placed on "needs satisfaction," a technique that taught the trainee how to discover a customer's need, help that customer understand his or her need, and then present the IBM product that would satisfy the need.

OPD had extensive records on all IBM typewriters installed in the United States, including the typewriter model, installation date, and the customer's name and location. The local branch office also kept files that included historical data and key contacts for all customers. Territories, based on the number of typewriters in a particular geographic area, were developed from these data. The number of typewriters installed was considered to be a prime indicator of the opportunity in a given territory, and was used as a basis for assigning an appropriate sales quota.

The OPD marketing representative compensation plan was designed to encourage high levels of sales performance. At 100 percent quota fulfillment, approximately 50

---

[6] IBM founder Thomas J. Watson, Sr., had observed that other companies' service people were not treated with the same respect as sales representatives. Watson wanted his service people respected and wanted them to have self-esteem. The white shirts and business suits, along with their comprehensive training, were intended to promote those goals.

percent of a representative's income came from commissions, with greater-than-proportional increments above quota. OPD marketing representatives typically received healthy quota increases each January, but generally recognized that such quotas had been "rationally arrived at" and that they would be well compensated when they achieved admittedly "stretch" objectives. OPD's philosophy was to pay its successful marketing representatives considerably more than they could earn at any other firm in the industry.

Once in the territory, marketing representatives made between ten and twelve calls a day. (A frequently quoted formula for success was: "Calls plus demos equals sales.") OPD's systems selling approach differed from the selling tactics employed by most of its competitors. Instead of calling on purchasing agents, OPD representatives focused their efforts on the actual decision makers. They used various questioning techniques learned in their "needs satisfaction training" to enhance their understanding of a customer's business, applications, and problems. One effective program was the Typing Station Analysis Study, a free study of each typing station's productivity and effectiveness. Representatives would use this study to learn about the customer's business, to discover needs, and to create an opportunity to present their findings along with IBM solutions. IBM representatives wanted to be perceived by the customer as solutions salespeople, not typewriter salespeople.

OPD also focused on providing value-added support. Training on IBM typewriters was available at the branch office in seminars and small hands-on sessions. Although the IBM representatives would provide such training at customer locations if requested, it was often a special event for the secretary to get the morning off to go to the IBM office for training. Because of the importance it assigned to the role of the secretary in the customer decision-making process, the OPD branch made sure that such sessions were first-class events. And on National Secretary's Day, a secretary could count on a rose from the IBM representative.

The Selectric® Typewriter, which had more than 2,500 parts, averaged two repair actions and one maintenance action per year.[7] OPD had developed an organization of almost 7,000 service representatives that operated parallel to the marketing organization. The quality image of the IBM typewriter was reinforced by the fact that if it did go down, someone would come there quickly to fix it, twenty-four hours a day, seven days a week. The service representatives went through the same IBM culture training as the marketing representatives, and were encouraged (and compensated) to know their accounts intimately and to pass on information and leads to the marketing representatives.

By the late 1970s, IBM was firmly established as the worldwide leader in office typewriters. Its evolving Selectric® family represented the standard for both reliability and product features. Its large, loyal customer base, supported by an aggressive and professional sales and service organization, was the envy of its competitors throughout the world.

Moreover, the office typewriter market was growing rapidly. The number of U.S. administrative support and clerical workers, for example, grew from 7.6 million in 1950 to 18.1 million in 1980. If a clerical worker was paid a $10,000 per year (plus social security and benefits), an investment of $1,000 (spread over four years) in a world-class typewriter to maximize his or her productivity could be easily justified.

Similar growth was taking place in Europe. Strong national manufacturers tended to dominate the major countries, but IBM was a significant competitor in virtually every important market. Thomas Watson, Sr.'s vision of "world peace through world trade" had led him to establish agencies in Europe during the early 1900s (IBM had provided unit record [punch card] machines primarily for census purposes), and to enter into licensing arrangements throughout Europe with local companies, which received exclusive rights

---

[7] By 1983, this had been reduced to one repair action per year.

to manufacture and sell IBM equipment in their own countries. After World War I, IBM erected small plants in Germany, France, and Great Britain, and established additional agencies in Europe, Latin America, and parts of Asia.

In 1950, Watson split IBM into two parts. The parent company, IBM, would conduct business only in the United States and would be run by his son, Tom Watson, Jr. Business in the rest of the world would be managed by IBM World Trade Corporation and would be run by his other son, Dick Watson. By 1989, IBM World Trade operated in 132 countries, employed 150,000 people, and generated about half of IBM's revenues and profits. It prided itself on its long-term policy of employing nationals of the countries where it did business and ensuring that they could run their own full-fledged business units. In the view of many observers, IBM, more than any other company, had truly positioned itself as a global enterprise, whose operations were considered virtually local companies in many of the countries where it did business. Heavy investment in R&D laboratories and state-of-the-art manufacturing outside the United States and employment of foreign nationals in high-level executive positions at headquarters were believed to contribute significantly to this image. (In a well-received advertising campaign of the mid-1980s, IBM had been able to claim that there was more local content [R&D and manufacturing] in an IBM computer sold in the United Kingdom or in France than in a comparable computer sold by the leading "national" computer manufacturer in either country.)

The Office Products Division had worldwide responsibility for its product line, working through IBM World Trade local branch offices and its marketing representatives. In Europe, the wide use of the Roman alphabet, a strong marketing organization, and world-class products such as the Selectric® Typewriter provided IBM with the opportunity to become the overall market leader. While it could not achieve the 70+ percent market share it had in the United States during the 1970s, industry observers estimated that IBM's share of the total Western European office typewriter market was approximately 33 percent—greater than that of any competitor. Market share in individual countries varied, depending on the strength of local competitors and national preferences. In Italy, for example, where both factors were significant, IBM might have only a 25 percent market share, while Olivetti (which stressed aesthetic design as much as technology) had 65 percent. In Sweden, Hermes had the dominant position, while in Germany, it shifted back and forth between Olympia and Triumph-Adler.

THE ELECTRONIC TYPEWRITER

Electronic typewriters, often referred to as ETs, were first introduced in 1978. Using new, cost-effective microchip technology, the ET differed from the electric typewriter similarly to the way in which a pocket calculator differed from a traditional adding machine. Instead of the roughly 2,500 levers, springs, gears, and screws inside the case of a Selectric® Typewriter, an ET contained only a small number of electronic circuit boards and a printing element that glided across the paper. When the keys on the typewriter were depressed, a handful of microprocessor chips told the machine what to do.

ETs performed all the standard functions of advanced electric typewriters. In addition, they offered powerful editing and revision features, and automated many manual functions, such as centering and underscoring. They were also much more reliable than electrics, and had very few moving parts.

The heart of the ET was its memory. The early models, for example, could "remember" the last ten characters typed. If a word was spelled incorrectly or another mistake was made, the typist pressed an "edit" key. The ET then erased the last ten characters by either typing over them with a special white ribbon or using a clear ribbon with a sticky surface that pulled the ink off the paper.

Other exciting functions were also made possible by the typewriter's memory. Typists often typed faster than a machine could print, for example, thus jamming the keys. To cope with this, internal memory kept track of each key pressed, and the ET continued typing even after the fingers were lifted from the keyboard. The problem of skipped letters or jammed typebars was for all practical purposes eliminated.

While initially much more expensive than traditional electrics, the ETs' added functionality and increased reliability made them attractive to many customers. More importantly, the fact that ETs were based on microchip architecture meant that subsequent models would be cheaper and have more function as microchip technology continued to develop.

The first ET was introduced in 1978 by QYX, a start-up venture that had been acquired by Exxon Enterprises, an organization established by the large oil company to diversify into the booming office automation market. More than 12,000 QYX machines were sold that first year. IBM soon followed with the Electronic Typewriter models 50 and 60, which achieved combined sales of 50,000 units and captured nearly 80 percent of the 1978 ET market. This market, however, still represented only 6 percent of the overall U.S. office typing workstation market (see Exhibit 24.1). Indeed, it took almost five years for ETs to attract serious attention from secretaries and office workers. By this time, they had become dazzling devices, available in a wide range of feature-specific models.

By the mid-1980s, industry analysts tended to divide electronic typewriters into four major categories. First was the basic machine, which ranged in price from $400 to $700, and incorporated automatic features and line-correction capabilities that were well suited for the intermediate typing loads typical of small businesses. Second was the mid-range machine, which was designed for heavy-duty office work, and priced from $700 to $1,200. These machines boasted print speeds of 15 to 20 characters per second, and

EXHIBIT 24.1
U.S. Office Typewriter Sales (Units in Thousands)

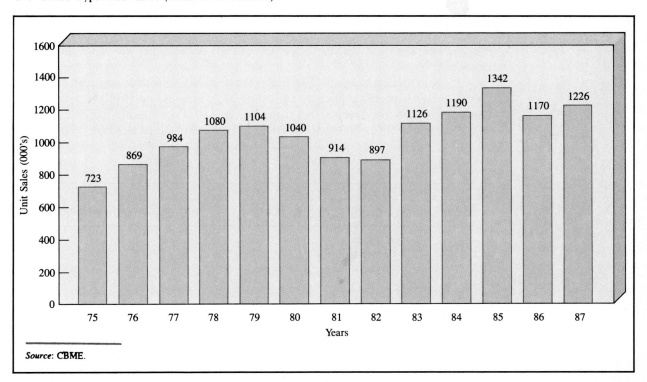

Source: CBME.

memories of 1,000 to 5,000 characters that could be used for storage of commonly used phrases, formats, and short letters. In addition, one- or two-line correction memory was provided through a high-resolution 80-character liquid crystal display.

The third, or high-end, category offered all the mid-range features plus a memory of up to 30,000 characters that provided for significantly expanded text-editing capabilities. High-end machines usually had a dictionary that detected misspelled words, provided alternatives, and facilitated correction. Approaching the function of a dedicated word processor, these ETs were priced between $1,500 and $2,500.

The fourth version, incorporating a full 25-line-by-80-character CRT screen, was introduced in 1983. Machines in this category offered memory up to 80,000 characters, and disk drives for storage on floppy diskettes. They were designed to be used as dedicated word processors to prepare lengthy reports and other documents that required extensive revision, but they could also be used in a ''direct type'' mode to handle routine tasks such as typing memos, envelopes, labels, and forms. Depending on the specific features, machines in this category cost between $2,500 and $4,000.

This wide range of capabilities made ETs attractive to virtually all types of organizations and offices. In small organizations, they were usually the most advanced text-processing equipment, and were therefore relied on very heavily. Larger organizations were more likely to utilize dedicated word-processing systems (e.g., Wang) for large text-creation tasks, and to use ETs on secretaries' desks throughout the organization for smaller jobs and traditional tasks such as typing letters or envelopes.

Surveys demonstrated that ET users were using the machine as an office workhorse. More than 50 percent of companies that owned ETs said that they produced over 100 pages of documents a day (see Exhibit 24.2). While between 1978 and 1980, almost 70 percent of the ETs shipped were basic machines, as more features and functions were added, heavy users did not find it difficult to justify the added expense of a higher category, especially since prices continued to drop. By 1983, only 28 percent of the ETs shipped were basic machines, and this trend continued in 1984 and 1985 (see Exhibit 24.3).

Technological advances in the print element on typewriters were also contributing to the success of ETs. Most ETs used a daisywheel printer, a disc-shaped print element with a central hub and flat petal-like spokes. It produced executive-quality documents in a wide variety of type styles, including multiple languages and scientific notations. It matched the print quality of the Selectric® golfball element, but was much quieter and faster.

It soon became clear that electric typewriters were on their way out. The only advantage they had left was price, and that was rapidly diminishing. (In 1983, for example, Canon introduced a mid-range machine for around $800, significantly less than the 1983 IBM electric model, the Selectric® III.) While ETs had obtained less than 20 percent of

EXHIBIT 24.2
Average Daily Typed-Page
Volume at ET Owners'
Company Site

NUMBER OF PAGES TYPED DAILY	PERCENTAGE OF OWNERS
1–10 pages	12.5%
11–25 pages	9.7%
26–50 pages	16.7%
51–99 pages	8.3%
100 pages or more	52.8%

Source: Venture Development Corporation.

	1978	1979	1980	1981	1982	1983	1984	1985	1986
Basic	46	65	73	85	94	140	200	340	260
Mid-range	9	17	30	65	157	290	400	690	762
High-end	5	8	22	45	63	50	70	120	181
CRT	—	—	—	—	—	20	35	124	136
Total	60	90	125	195	314	500	705	1274	1329

Source: Venture Development Corporation.

EXHIBIT 24.3
U.S. Sales of Basic, Mid-Range, High-End, and CRT Display Office ETs (units in thousands)

the U.S. market as late as 1981–1982, by 1983, they accounted for nearly 50 percent of new office typewriter shipments. Thereafter, sales of electric typewriters declined by 20 percent a year, with ETs constituting more than 80 percent of shipments in 1986 (see Exhibit 24.4).

OPD management soon concluded that ET technology was so revolutionary that it was likely to impact not only the typewriter itself but also the way it was developed, manufactured, sold, and serviced. It appeared that many of IBM's advantages in the office typewriter market, developed painstakingly over the past fifty years, would be significantly devalued by the new technology, which threatened not just IBM product superiority but IBM's large and expensive direct marketing and service organizations as well. Moreover, the new technology eliminated many significant barriers to entry, which made the office typewriter market attractive to a host of new entrants, especially from the consumer electronics industry.

In 1979, OPD had nine major competitors in office typewriters; in 1981, seven additional foreign manufacturers entered the market: Brother, Canon, and Silver-Reed from Japan; Adler-Royal from West Germany; Facit of Sweden; and Hermes of Switzerland. The seventh, Remington-Rand, a U.S. company, sourced its ETs from Olympia in West Germany. Seven more firms entered in 1982–1983, including Xerox and 3M from the United States, and Sharp and Panasonic from Japan (see Exhibit 24.5).

As each competitor came into the market, IBM lost a little more share. The company watched its ET market share drop 10 percent a year from 1979 to 1981, even before Japanese producers became a significant factor (see Exhibit 24.6). By 1989, there were approximately thirty-five ET manufacturers, predominantly based in the Far East.

Japanese producers seemed to be in an ideal position to take advantage of the shift in demand from electric to electronic models, given their easy access to low-priced, high-quality parts and superior mass-production technology. With falling prices and average transaction values, however, their margins were unlikely to be sufficient to hire, train,

	1983	1984	1985	1986	CATEGORY GROWTH RATE
Electric	500	400	320	260	– 19%
Electronic	500	705	1210	1327	38%
Totals	1000	1105	1530	1587	16%

Source: Venture Development Corporation.

EXHIBIT 24.4
U.S. Sales of Electric and Electronic Office Typewriters (units in thousands)

1978	1979	1980	1981	1982	1983
Qyx	Olivetti	Syntrex	Brother	Xerox	Sharp
IBM	Olympia	Contitronix	Facit	3M	Panasonic
		SCM	Adler-Royal	Teal	
			Hermes	Swintex	
			Canon	TEC-America	
			Silver-Reed		
			Remington-Rand		

	1978	1979	1980	1981
IBM	80%	70%	60%	50%
Qyx	20%	17%	12%	10%
Olivetti	—	10%	10%	12%
Olympia	—	—	10%	15%
Adler-Royal	—	—	—	7%
Other	—	3%	8%	6%

Source: Venture Developoment Corporation.

and support direct sales organizations, the traditional method of marketing office type-writers. Instead, they broke new ground by using office equipment dealers for sales and service.

ET manufacturers could sell feature-rich office typewriters to dealers at such a low cost that the resulting margins justified considerable training and incentives for the dealers' relatively unsophisticated and unaggressive sales personnel. Moreover, the new ETs were so reliable (averaging less than one repair action every two years) and so easy to service[8] that product maintenance capability soon came to have relatively minor salience for many customers.

PERSONAL COMPUTERS

On August 12, 1981, the IBM Personal Computer (PC) was announced. This announcement received extensive press coverage, and was to radically transform the information-processing industry. IBM, by announcing its PC, had endorsed the personal computer as a viable product. Between August and December, the company shipped 13,000 PCs. Over the next two years, more than 500,000 IBM PCs would be sold.

IBM quickly established itself as the leader of the new industry, which was soon growing at 20–30 percent per year. By the end of 1988, more than 66 million IBM and competitive PCs had been installed, with an additional 16 million new or replacement PCs being sold each year.

By 1982, IBM officials were considering the implications of the personal computer for the office typewriter market. The company was committed to the PC, and was expanding

---

[8] The ET's design consisted primarily of microchip cards. In most cases, a problem could be remedied by replacing one of the cards.

plant capacity to meet projected high levels of demand. A personal computer with a powerful word-processing package was a strong alternative to an electronic typewriter. Although more expensive and not as easy to use, it offered extensive text-processing capabilities, as well as the capability of being used for other applications such as spreadsheets and electronic mail. There were many who argued that it was only a matter of time before personal computers totally replaced electronic typewriters and ushered in the paperless office.

Other analysts and managers argued that there would be a market for both for many years to come. They contended that the personal computer was a professional tool, while the typewriter was a clerical tool; and that the typewriter was an efficient paper-handling device, while a PC, with its printer, was not. Secretaries whose major tasks were the production of invoices, short letters, envelopes, and forms found it cumbersome to power up a software package, coordinate the peripherals, make sure the right printer was hooked up, and insert the right paper into the paper feeder before they began typing. Moreover, continuing advances in ET technology (e.g., menu-driven software, more memory for large text-editing jobs, CRT displays), combined with ETs' low cost, ease of use, and flexibility, were likely, in these observers' view, to maintain the ET's competitiveness.

PC PRINTERS

IBM officials also noted a number of intrinsic relationships between the typewriter industry and the burgeoning market for the small, inexpensive printers that were used with PCs (see Exhibit 24.7). While IBM did not produce a PC printer (it marketed a dot-matrix printer produced by Epson, a Japanese manufacturer, under the IBM logo), there appeared to be a natural technology transfer between printers and typewriters. Indeed, a case could be made that a printer was essentially a typewriter without a keyboard. Costs would be

EXHIBIT 24.7
Worldwide Shipments of Low-End Printers (left) and Average Selling Price of Low-End Printers (right)

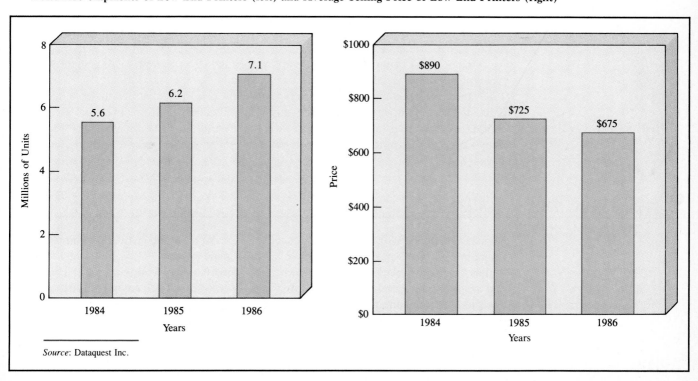

Source: Dataquest Inc.

EXHIBIT 24.8
IBM Worldwide Office
Typewriter Sales (% of
Total Sales)

	1982	1983	1984	1985	1986	1987	1988
U.S.	62.8	69.3	71.6	72.6	60.6	64.5	60.5
Europe	17.4	15.5	15.0	18.2	25.1	23.5	27.2
Latin America	7.2	5.6	5.4	3.4	8.2	6.8	6.2
Canada	4.7	3.8	3.2	1.9	1.8	1.7	1.9
Asia/Pacific	4.9	3.6	2.8	2.1	2.8	2.1	2.5
Middle East/Africa	2.7	1.9	1.8	1.5	1.3	1.2	1.4
Caribbean	.3	.3	.2	.2	.3	.2	.4

Source: IBM.

greatly reduced if these two complementary products were designed so that they had common parts, assembly procedures, and experience curves; while technological progress in printing methodology or quality would clearly benefit both product lines.

There were two basic categories of PC printers: impact and nonimpact. Impact printers employed either a daisywheel element or dot-matrix technology to transfer ink to paper. Dot-matrix impact printers used a printhead made up of wire bristles or pins arranged in a block to strike a ribbon against paper, creating the image. While the daisywheel currently produced higher resolution, it was slower and more expensive than the dot-matrix printer, and was expected to be largely displaced by advances in dot-matrix and nonimpact technology.

Nonimpact printers employed laser, inkjet, thermal, and thermal-transfer technologies. Laser printers, which were considered most likely to dominate this category, used a laser beam that projected an image onto a photoconductive drum, which then picked up toner particles and transferred them to paper. At present, they achieved the highest resolution and speed, and were less noisy than impact printers, but at $1,500 to $5,000, they cost two to three times as much as daisywheel printers and four to five times as much as dot-matrix printers.

While OPD had a presence in every major market in the world, 80 percent of its typewriter volume came from the United States and Europe (see Exhibit 24.8). As of 1983, the worldwide market for office typewriters was estimated at just under 4 million units. Industry observers, along with many OPD officials, were, however, projecting a continuous decrease in this market as a result of the substitution of PCs for office typewriters. They expected that office typewriter volumes would shrink to under 3 million units by 1990.

STRATEGIC TRANSFORMATION

Beginning around 1980, IBM officials engaged in considerable debate over the company's future in the office typewriter business. While ETs made up only 20 percent of the market at that time, IBM analysts had concluded that typewriters based on the new technology had the potential to totally replace electric typewriters. Although the company had quickly risen to a number one position in the rapidly growing ET market, some IBM officials questioned its ability to remain a major player, considering the apparently diminished advantages of its superior R&D, marketing, and service capabilities.

OPD faced intensifying competition, especially from Japanese manufacturers such as Canon and Panasonic. The Japanese companies, with their superior mass-production

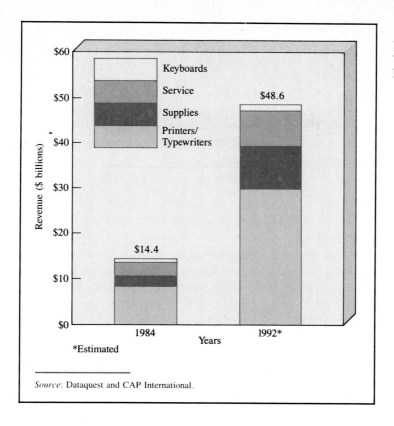

EXHIBIT 24.9
Worldwide Industry
Revenue

Source: Dataquest and CAP International.

technology and low-cost labor, were able to introduce improved products at lower prices each year, marketing through extensive networks of office equipment and supplies dealers. They provided aggressive margins, motivating their dealers to give high priority to ET sales and to offer large commissions to their sales forces. The dealer representatives were aggressive, usually well known in the community, and willing to give incentives such as free trials, aggressive trade-ins, and free service for a year.

After IBM's introduction of its PC in 1981, some IBM officials concluded that the market for even advanced ETs was likely to decline rapidly over the next decade. These officials tended to favor a staged withdrawal from the typewriter business. Others, however, cited proprietary studies that concluded that there would be a significant worldwide market for typing workstations, PC printers, supplies,[9] and service for many years to come (see Exhibit 24.9), and argued that IBM would be foolish to abandon an attractive market where its position was so strong. The PC would have some impact, but these officials believed that the typewriter had its own market and could be properly positioned. Combining manufacturing of PC printers and typewriters would likely have a favorable effect on design and manufacturing costs for both product lines, they believed, while the follow-on revenue from supplies would increase the attractiveness of the business further.

At this point, several alternative strategies were considered and analyzed from both a strategic and a financial perspective. The first alternative was to get out of the business.

[9] Supplies (e.g., ribbons, printwheels, printheads, correction tapes, electronic fonts, and typing elements) for both typewriters and printers contributed significantly to the attractiveness of those businesses and provided excellent margins to their manufacturers. In a recent study, the Buyer's Laboratory had analyzed the total life-cycle cost of electronic typewriters. In one case, an electronic typewriter that sold for $995 had cumulative costs of $4,450 for five-year maintenance charges, ribbons, and printhead supplies. Another ET, that sold for $1,280, had five-year ribbon costs of $1,892. The cost of consumable supplies alone over a five-year period averaged almost twice as much as the initial cost of an electronic typewriter. The cost of a maintenance contract was generally 10 percent of the retail price per year. In the parts and supplies business, a typewriter or printer manufacturer that introduced a new printing technology had an early lead, before other market suppliers copied the technology and began introducing competitive products.

With seventeen aggressive competitors cutting prices and constantly bringing out new products, and overall demand likely to decline in favor of the PC, the office typewriter seemed unlikely to generate satisfactory margins in the future. By withdrawing from the business in a timely manner, IBM could shift R&D, manufacturing, and marketing resources to its core and strategic business, computers, which was expected to grow at a 15 percent annual rate for the next decade.

The second alternative was based on the premise that the typewriter franchise that had been built over the years was too valuable to give up, but did not represent sufficient opportunity to warrant major new investment. If, however, costs and prices could be reduced sharply through productivity improvements in current manufacturing processes, higher volumes being pushed through the sales force (assuming that a direct sales force would continue to be used), and considerable reduction in the size of the service organization, it was likely that the business would generate positive cash flow for many years to come.

The third option would be to remain in the business and take advantage of the IBM typewriter franchise and marketing organization, but to modify some of the business processes that hampered IBM's profitability and competitiveness. One approach might be for IBM to source its ETs from efficient, low-cost foreign manufacturers, providing the IBM sales and service organizations with competitively priced and featured products. Alternatively, IBM might set up its own plant in Taiwan or Singapore to manufacture low-cost typewriters.

The fourth possibility was to retain R&D and manufacturing at Lexington, but to modify OPD's marketing process by switching to independent dealers (who were clearly eager to carry the IBM line), company-owned stores, or some combination of the two. This option would clearly require a major investment in production processes and technology to reduce costs. A number of OPD officials were concerned about selling through independent dealers, however, wondering how they could monitor and control dealer loyalty and dealer practices that might be contrary to the way IBM chose to do business. There was also concern within OPD as to whether it possessed the skills necessary to run its own retail organization.

The New Strategy

Having identified the major options, IBM established a series of task forces that were to analyze every aspect of the industry. They took trips throughout the world to study markets, technology, and, in particular, foreign manufacturing operations. They analyzed the role of the typewriter in IBM's long-range strategy, and concluded that the company would have to become both the lowest-cost manufacturer and the most efficient marketer if it was to stay in the business. To the surprise of many, the task forces concluded that the optimum location to accomplish these objectives was Lexington, Kentucky.

After almost three years of study and internal debate, in July 1982, the Corporate Management Committee, comprising IBM's highest officials, including the chief executive officer, approved what was essentially Option Four and authorized investment to begin in January 1983. The new strategy called for a true transformation, on a global basis, of IBM's typewriter business, including product development, manufacturing, and marketing. An investment of $350 million would be made to convert the Lexington plant into one of the most automated manufacturing facilities in the world. Workers needed new skills to cope with the change from a metal-based, electromechanical, labor-intensive product line to an electronics- and plastics-based automated product line. Ultimately, a $10 million education program retrained more than 2,000 Lexington employees to operate a totally transformed manufacturing facility.

The primary goals in product development were to design products that could be built by automation, to shorten their development cycles, and to maximize the use of common parts in multiple products and even generations of products. In the past, development engineers had come up with new-product designs and given them to manufacturing for production. Now development and manufacturing would be combined under a single product manager, and manufacturing engineers would participate beginning with the product-definition phase, helping to determine whether the proposed parts could be manufactured efficiently and then developing automated processes to manufacture them. "Design for automation" became the rule. New products were based on layered designs, which meant they could be assembled sequentially from the bottom, facilitating use of robots. Common fasteners were used and nearly all screws were eliminated.

Each product manager had worldwide responsibility for his or her product. The new generation of typewriters was designed to support twenty-two different languages with minimal modifications of keyboards and typefaces. Initially, an IBM manufacturing facility in Amsterdam handled European manufacturing, but by 1986, all worldwide development and manufacturing had been moved to Lexington.

A major element in the new strategy was the recognition of the potential commonality in components and modules between ETs and PC printers. Product development was based on the premise that a printer was essentially a typewriter without a keyboard. The two could therefore be broken down into modules with significant structural and manufacturing similarities. IBM's strategy was to build a mixture of typewriters and printers side by side on the same assembly lines, maximizing the use of common components and subassemblies.

In 1984, Lexington began producing the new typewriter models. The first, the Wheelwriter 3®, required 100 percent new parts. The next, the Wheelwriter 5®, required only 11 percent new parts. The following new model, the Quietwriter 7®, which used nonimpact printing technology rather than the Wheelwriter's® impact printing wheel, required 63 percent new parts, but the subsequent nonimpact product required only 13 percent new parts. Then, in late 1985, IBM introduced a whole new family of typewriters and printers, which required only 23 percent and 6 percent new parts, respectively.

Computer-integrated manufacturing (CIM) was the heart of IBM's $350 million investment. The key objective was to achieve a combination of maximum flexibility (with regard to both current and future products) and minimum manufacturing costs. The automated systems were designed so that they could produce any product that fit within a 26-by-22-by-18-inch work envelope.[10] An IBM automation manager summed it up when he said, "We could make toasters and VCRs, too, if they fit the envelope."

There were five major subassembly areas—motors, keyboards, electronic cards, paperfeed, and covers—as well as final assembly and test areas. Each subassembly area was fully automated and connected by conveyors and automated guided vehicles to final assembly and test, as well as automated packing and shipping areas. The processes, subprocesses, and workstations of every subassembly area were computer-integrated to ensure a smooth and continuous flow. IBM computers, robots, and proprietary software were used in the majority of operations.

The marketing changes were equally fundamental. As ETs evolved rapidly in function, many customers became more dependent on their IBM sales representative for cost/benefit analysis and training. At the same time, however, falling prices for a given level of functionality led to reduced dollar margins per unit and a lesser ability to support an expensive direct sales organization. After elaborate analysis, IBM concluded (as it had previously for PCs) that it would be more cost effective and efficient, and result in better market coverage, to utilize a marketing strategy in which most of the Lexington products were sold by independent dealers rather than by a direct IBM sales force.

---

[10] The IBM Proprinter was an example of such flexibility. Developed and intended for manufacture at an IBM plant in Charlotte, North Carolina, the printer was transferred to Lexington, where it was manufactured with Lexington-designed products.

The process actually had begun in 1982, when the three IBM marketing divisions, organized along product lines, had been reorganized along customer lines into two new divisions. The National Accounts Division (NAD) now had responsibility for IBM's 1,000 largest U.S. customers, while the National Marketing Division (NMD) was to sell to everyone else. The idea was to have one IBM marketing representative or account team calling on the customer to sell everything from a typewriter to a mainframe computer.[11]

In addition, IBM began opening its own stores, called IBM Product Centers. These retail outlets sold the newly announced IBM PC, low-end printers, PC software, type-writers, and supplies. The stores were IBM's first attempt at low-cost marketing coverage. While the bulk of the U.S. typewriter volume was still sold by the IBM direct sales organizations, the Product Centers generated 10 percent of sales in 1982.

Even as Lexington was implementing CIM in 1983, IBM was aggressively evolving the independent dealer marketing channel for PCs and typewriters through its new National Distribution Division (NDD). Total shipments of typewriters increased in 1983, but only 50 percent of those sales were generated by the two direct IBM sales forces. The other half came from the Product Centers and newly announced channels, including direct mail to American Express cardholders, sales through several upscale retail department stores, a telemarketing facility, and a small group of authorized typewriter dealers (ATDs).

IBM's experiment with American Express and prestigious retail stores produced only 1 percent of typewriter volumes; ATDs, in contrast, were generating large volumes per outlet. Given these results, the company moved rapidly to sign up independent dealers. In 1984, 600 dealers produced 28 percent of typewriter sales; by the end of 1985, 856 dealers were producing 56 percent, while the direct sales forces were producing 21 percent and the Product Centers 12 percent.

In 1986, IBM completed the changeover of typewriter marketing from the direct channel to the ATDs. The company sold its Product Centers to NYNEX in July, and in September withdrew typewriters from its direct marketing force. Except for sales to the U.S. government, a typewriter could no longer be purchased directly from IBM. U.S. dealer ranks swelled temporarily to over 1,000 (accounting for 84 percent of typewriter volume) for the year.

Beginning in 1982, similar changes in marketing organization strategy were carried out in Europe and the Far East. The roles of the direct marketing divisions in those parts of the world were reduced as IBM country managers began to sign up dealers aggressively. By the end of 1986, all IBM typewriter marketing worldwide, except for some minor unique situations, was handled through ATDs.

In most cases, the ATD was an established independent office equipment or office supplies dealer covering a limited geographic area. Before becoming an IBM ATD, it probably had carried some other vendor's ET line and/or used IBM Selectric® Typewriters. An ATD's product line typically included typewriters and supplies, desktop copiers, personal computers and printers, office furniture, and FAX machines, purchased from multiple vendors in each product category. Typewriters were its single largest product line, with half of its outbound sales force of fifteen specializing in that product. An ATD's premises typically consisted of limited desk space for its sales force, a demonstration and service area, and a store front to conduct other business. Service revenue had a major impact on profitability.

An IBM ATD bought IBM typewriters at a discount for resale and carried out warranty service. IBM provided the ATD with marketing support through advertising,

---

[11] The three marketing divisions had been the Data Processing Division, responsible primarily for large mainframe based systems; the General Systems Division, responsible for mid-sized systems; and the Office Products Division, whose product scope included typewriters, copiers, dictating equipment, and supplies. In announcing the organizational change, IBM spokespeople stressed the desire of customers for a single point of contact with the company. According to press accounts, there had been numerous instances of two or more ''competing'' IBM sales forces making conflicting proposals for a particular application to a particular customer.

promotion and sales kits, direct-mail campaigns, and dealer education. IBM tried to select and position its dealers so as to give them a degree of territorial exclusivity.

In 1982, when IBM launched its highly successful PC, NDD had moved to establish an extensive network of personal computer dealers (PCDs). When IBM entered the under-$1,000 PC printer market in 1986 with the Proprinter®, it was marketed through NDD's PCD network, as well as the IBM direct sales forces, which also sold PCs, but not through the ATD channel.

While the ATDs were for the most part one- or two-store family businesses, the PCDs were usually members of large chains such as Computerland and Businessland. Printers were not the PCD's major product category, but had a significant impact on dealer profitability. In the opinion of some observers, dealers had the ability to "steer" a customer to any of a number of "known" brands with more or less equivalent features. As a result, manufacturers competed to offer the best margins and dealer incentives in the hope of obtaining disproportionate "push" at the point of sale, often borrowing approaches (e.g., dealer contests, dealer rebates tied to volume thresholds) from industries such as home appliances, consumer electronics, and automobiles.

Lexington and NDD worked together to develop programs designed to help dealers increase their sales of IBM products. There was a consistent flow of new products and enhancements, pricing actions based on feedback from the dealers, incentive programs and support, and dealer education. Wherever possible, such programs were designed to make it clear that IBM expected its ATDs and PCDs to emphasize IBM products in their merchandising strategies.

Nevertheless, it took IBM some time to learn how to market effectively through independent dealers. Most ATDs sold both IBM and competitive products, and sought to maximize their short-term profitability by influencing the mix of brands and models that they sold. While most were initially highly enthusiastic about becoming authorized IBM dealers, it was soon apparent that IBM would have to be fully competitive in product features, terms and conditions, and retail margins. A large number of ATDs, for example, seemed to be steering customers aways from IBM typewriters when they found that they were not producing actual margins as high as other vendors' products. IBM had initially believed that the more dealers (assuming they met IBM quality standards) carrying IBM products, the better. But by 1985, with almost 900 ATDs signed up in the United States, saturation was occurring. Most customers had at least two—and in many cases, more than two—conveniently located dealers available to them. Dealers began cutting prices, which lowered their actual margins on IBM products and increased their motivation to sell other brands that were less subject to price competition.

In June 1986, IBM held meetings with the ATDs to announce a number of significant changes. New products were introduced; revised prices, terms and conditions, and enhanced dealer programs were presented. Over the next eighteen months, through attrition and nonrenewal of individual dealer agreements, the number of dealers was reduced to approximately 700.

More recently, IBM had made a major commitment to a co-op advertising program under which it would provide its dealers with advertising materials and return to them a percentage of the revenue they generated on IBM products, to be used for local advertising (see Exhibit 24.10).[12] Another well-received program was one in which each ATD dealer sales representative was assigned an IBM-MasterCard account. Each time the representative sold a new IBM typewriter, he or she would earn bonus points, which could be converted into dollars available to pay for personal purchases charged to the MasterCard.

IBM had greatly increased its typewriter and PC printer advertising as it shifted from direct marketing to independent dealers. This increase had been intended to ensure

---

[12] Dealers would actually be reimbursed at a level 1.15 times this revenue amount to cover their time and efforts in carrying out their dealer advertising campaigns.

EXHIBIT 24.10
Dealer Co-op Ads

One for all.

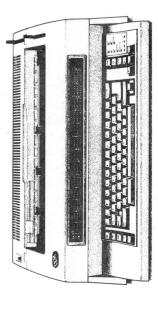

The IBM® Wheelwriter® Series II Typewriters

Whatever kind of typing you do, IBM Wheelwriter Series II Typewriters can help you do it faster, better and easier.

Need a typewriter that has Spell Check, automatic centering and error correction? It's yours in the Wheelwriter 10. Need a typewriter that also has a memory revision and one-line display? It's the Wheelwriter 30. Need a typewriter with advanced functions like word processing and a full-page display? You've got it in the Wheelwriter 50 or 70.

Of course, every Wheelwriter gives you the classic IBM touch. And high-quality IBM supplies make any Wheelwriter you buy an even better value.

So, call or come in and get the feel of IBM Wheelwriters. They're made for the work you do.

DEALER NAME

® IBM and Wheelwriter are registered trademarks of International Business Machines Corporation.

The "most outstanding entry level electronic typewriter."
—Buyers Laboratory, Inc.

The IBM® Wheelwriter® 10 Series II Typewriter

A leading independent testing laboratory found the IBM Wheelwriter 10 good news.

But it wasn't loaded up with top-of-the-line features just for the lab. IBM packed it with features you use, like Spell Check—make a mistake and a soft beep alerts you. The full-page memory and express cursor keys allow you to make corrections anywhere on the page—fast. And the economical, high-quality IBM supplies it uses make it an even bigger value.

IBM dependability with the classic IBM touch. It's no wonder the Wheelwriter 10 is making news.

So, call or come in and get the feel of the IBM Wheelwriter 10. It's made for the work you do.

DEALER NAME

® IBM and Wheelwriter are registered trademarks of International Business Machines Corporation.

EXHIBIT 24.10 (continued)

Memory on display.

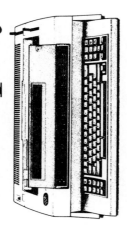

The IBM® Wheelwriter® 30 Series II Typewriter

The IBM Wheelwriter 30 with memory display can help you with all the typing you do.

You can store a lot of memorables, and the 80-character display will quickly locate them for you. If your spelling's a little rusty, the built-in Spell Check II helps catch mistakes, re-spell and retype words. And, because it can be upgraded, the Wheelwriter 30 will adapt to meet your future typing needs.

Of course, it's got IBM dependability and the classic IBM touch. And the economical, high-quality IBM supplies it uses assure you of ongoing value.

So, call or come in and get the feel of the Wheelwriter 30. It's made for the work you do.

Authorized
Typewriter
Dealer

DEALER NAME

® IBM and Wheelwriter are registered trademarks of
International Business Machines Corporation.

The Ideal Tool for Word Processing and Statistical Typing.

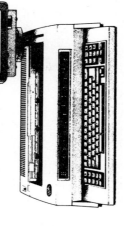

The IBM® Wheelwriter® 50 Series II Typewriter

What makes the IBM Wheelwriter 50 ideal? It depends on what you do. Editing? Reports? Charts? Word processing? Labels? Filling in forms? It does it all. Fast. Easily. And dependably, too.

You can switch back and forth between word processing and typing at the touch of a key. It's also upgradeable. So, when your typing needs change, the Wheelwriter 50 can change along with them.

Of course, it's got IBM dependability and the classic IBM touch. And the economical, high-quality IBM supplies it uses assure you of ongoing value.

So, call or come in and get the feel of the Wheelwriter 50. It's made for the work you do.

Authorized
Typewriter
Dealer

DEALER NAME

® IBM and Wheelwriter are registered trademarks of
International Business Machines Corporation.

Courtesy of IBM.

EXHIBIT 24.10 (continued)

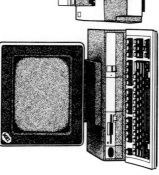

EXHIBIT 24.10 (continued)

For Typewriters
For PCs
For Systems

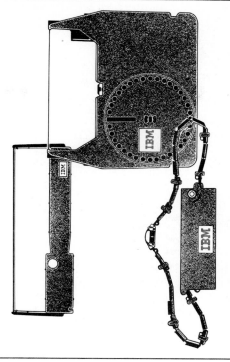

Your IBM® typewriters, word processors, PCs and Systems printers are only as good as the supplies you use. IBM Supplies—your work deserves nothing less.

DEALER NAME

Authorized Supplies Dealer

® IBM is a registered trademark of International Business Machines Corporation.

Two great names in office supplies:

IBM and your IBM Authorized Supplies Dealer

Nothing performs on your office equipment like genuine IBM® supplies. And nobody performs better for IBM customers than your IBM Authorized Supplies Dealer.

To earn that title we have to be the best.

We have to meet IBM's strict standards for fast, reliable, effective service.

Most important, we have to prove that we have a history of satisfying you, our customers.

And once we earn the title "IBM Authorized Supplies Dealer," we have to work hard to keep it by strictly adhering to IBM's high standards of quality, service and reliability.

So, whether you're buying supplies for IBM typewriters, word processors, printers or computers, you can depend on us for the best. Call us today to place your order for IBM supplies.

DEALER NAME

® IBM is a registered trademark of International Business Machines Corporation.

Authorized Supplies Dealer

EXHIBIT 24.11
1989 ET Advertising

526

What do you do after you make the best-selling office typewriters?

Make them even better.

Introducing the IBM Wheelwriter Series II typewriters.

From the people who brought you the typewriters that secretaries prefer most—a new line of typewriters that offers even more.

Corrections are faster. Spelling is checked automatically. Displays are adjustable. And dozens of pages can be stored in memory.

Yet these new typewriters are remarkably easy to use, especially for frequent revisions. In just a stroke or two, you can erase words, move entire blocks of text, zip around the page, boldly emphasize a point and reprint unlimited originals. It's a whole new class of typewriters with the classic IBM touch.

If your needs change after you buy, so can these typewriters. They can be upgraded easily to other models that offer additional functions and displays.

And they come with new state-of-the-art ribbons that give you superior print quality.

See this new family of typewriters at your Authorized IBM Typewriter Dealer. Just call 1 800 IBM-2468, ext. 55 for a dealer near you.

The IBM Wheelwriter® Series II typewriters. Everything you always loved about IBM typewriters. And then some.

"Now that's a typewriter."

The Bigger Picture

adequate exposure of decision makers in key target customer segments to IBM's core benefit propositions; to minimize the effect of dealer salespeople who either were incapable of disseminating the IBM product story or chose not to; and to stimulate customer traffic to IBM ATDs and PCDs, thus improving sales opportunities and (presumably) motivating grateful dealers to push IBM products.

IBM advertising was controlled by corporate headquarters in Armonk, New York, which worked with IBM's advertising agencies on copy strategy and media selection. An overall advertising budget was established each year and then allocated to the various product lines. Typewriters averaged 9 percent of the total U.S. budget ($11 million in 1988), printers about 5 percent. Lexington and NDD provided the product and industry input. NDD had to give its approval before a campaign could begin.

The primary advertising objective for typewriters from 1983 until recently had been to achieve high customer awareness. With the gradual deemphasis on typewriters by the direct sales organization, IBM wanted to make sure customers knew it was still in the business. (An example was the ''We're Your Type'' campaign, which featured a catchy song and scenes of IBM typewriters being used in all kinds of offices and professions.) IBM officials had recently concluded that this initial strategy had accomplished its objectives. A new advertising strategy, directed at communicating why a customer should buy an IBM typewriter and why that decision should be made now, was currently being implemented (see Exhibit 24.11).

Results

It was apparent almost immediately that the new strategy was working. The new line of typewriters had greatly enhanced features (which placed them well ahead of most competitors) and significantly reduced costs, and met with an excellent response from both dealers and customers. A comparison of a mainstream product built in 1984, the IBM Selectric® III, with a comparable product built on the new line in 1988, the IBM Wheelwriter

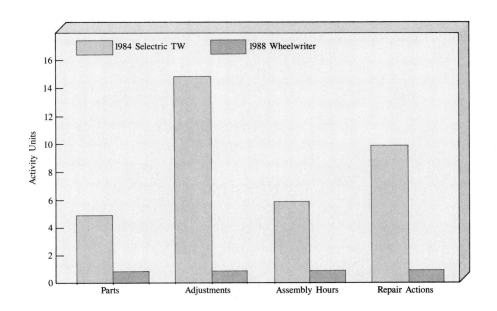

EXHIBIT 24.12
Gains from "Design for Automation" Program

10® Series II, was striking. While the suggested retail price of the Wheelwriter® was $60 less, its electronic capabilities, such as a 4,000-character correction memory and a 50,000-word spell check dictionary, provided added benefits that were estimated at double the value of the 1984 model. This marked improvement in price/performance was made possible by the gains derived from design innovation and manufacturing automation. The Selectric® had required five times as many parts, needed fifteen times as many adjustments, and utilized six times as many assembly hours as the Wheelwriter®; the number of warranty repair activities decreased by a factor of 10 (see Exhibit 24.12). In aggregate, Lexington

EXHIBIT 24.13
1986 Sales of ETs by Industry Participants (% of dollars)

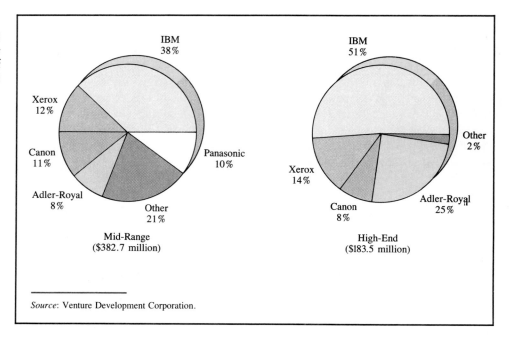

Source: Venture Development Corporation.

EXHIBIT 24.14
1988 Sales of ETs by Industry Participants (% of dollars)

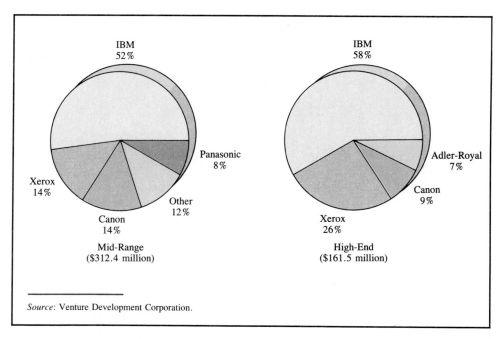

Source: Venture Development Corporation.

achieved year-to-year productivity gains of well over 10 percent (measured in both physical and dollar output terms) each year (with one exception) between 1984 and 1989.

The marketplace reaction was quite favorable. As noted earlier, IBM's typewriter market share had been eroding steadily since 1978, when ETs were first introduced, reaching a low point of 38 percent (mid-range) and 51 percent (high-end) of U.S. office typewriter revenues in 1986 (see Exhibit 24.13). By 1988, however, after the new product lines had been established and the dealer channel developed and stabilized, mid-range market share had increased from 38 to 52 percent, and high-end share from 51 to 58.4 percent (see Exhibit 24.14). In mid-1988, IBM announced two new models in the CRT display category (see Exhibit 24.15), which were expected to result in a strong position

EXHIBIT 24.15
1988 CRT Advertising

A new class of typewriters with the classic touch

IBM Wheelwriter 50 Series II Typewriter

Advances in typing at your command

With the IBM Wheelwriter® 50 Series II Typewriter, you can see what you type before it shows up on paper. You'll have a 25-line CRT screen to plan and lay out your page before it's ever typed out. So you can be sure your work will turn out exactly the way you want it all the time.

The new Wheelwriter 50 Typewriter brings you some of the most powerful typing features available. In addition to the display, you'll get 60,000 bytes of memory; the ability to copy, move or delete a block of text; and a global search/replace feature.

What's more, as part of the new IBM Wheelwriter Series II Typewriter family, it's based on the same 8088 micro-processor technology found in IBM personal computers. And it uses IBM's new Easystrike® Ribbons—High Yield and Superior Write—designed to bring out the best in Wheelwriter Typewriters.

All of this is combined with the classic touch that makes IBM typewriters the favorite of secretaries. And you can count on the Wheelwriter 50 Typewriter to be your favorite in the future, too. It can be upgraded to the IBM Wheelwriter 70 Series II Typewriter when you're ready for more advanced features.

IBM

The Bigger Picture

Use the latest typing technology with ease. Not only does the Wheelwriter 50 Typewriter give you greater typing capabilities, it gives you greater typing flexibility. Whether you're preparing letters, reports or statistical charts, you'll be able to do your work more smoothly. Instead of making corrections on paper, for example, you can check facts and figures, margins and spacing on the screen—and set things straight right then and there.

And you can view everything on screen with ease. Your work will always look crisp and clear, thanks to the Wheelwriter 50 Typewriter's high-resolution display. For even more viewing comfort, the Shade feature lets you choose white characters on a black background, or black on white—whichever is best in your environment. And with the optional CRT arm Series II, you can even look at your screen from different angles or move it to the left or right side of the typewriter.

Keep the best of what you type at hand. Once your letters, charts and tables are finished the way you like, you can save the ones you want for future use. Because the Wheelwriter 50 Typewriter has 60,000 bytes of memory, you can store up to 30 pages of material. When you take advantage of an optional 3.5-inch diskette unit, you can save just about everything you need to use more than once.

Find last month's typing with a few quick keystrokes. Stored material is as easy to find as it is to save on the Wheelwriter 50 Typewriter. All you have to do is press the Menu key and select Directory. You'll get a display of all jobs in storage, their length, margin settings and the space left for new jobs. From there, you can call up any job you need. And if you want a printed copy of what's in storage, the menu lets you get that, too.

Do two things at once. With the Wheelwriter 50 Typewriter, you'll be able to switch from storage to typing in a flash with the Type/Screen key. So when

Courtesy of IBM.

EXHIBIT 24.15
(continued)

IBM Wheelwriter 70 Series II Typewriter

A new class of typewriters with the classic touch

Word processing and typing combined in one package

Now you can switch from word processing to typing without changing machines. That's because the new IBM Wheelwriter® 70 Series II Typewriter is essentially two machines in one. Use it as a word processor to prepare lengthy reports and other documents that require extensive revision. Or use it as a typewriter to handle such routine tasks as typing memos, labels and forms.

You can move back and forth between the two whenever your work demands. One minute you can be making additions and deletions to a document. And the next you can be addressing an envelope—just by using the Type/Screen key.

Part of the new Wheelwriter Series II Typewriter family, the Wheelwriter 70 Typewriter combines advanced electronic features with the best of the basics. And it offers the ease of use and classic touch that have made IBM typewriters the first choice of secretaries everywhere.

Like the Wheelwriter 10, 30 and 50 Series II Typewriters, this typewriter is driven by powerful 8088 microprocessor technology. And it works with IBM's new Easystrike® Ribbons—High Yield and Superior Write—designed to bring out the best in all Wheelwriter Typewriters.

Use word processing to full advantage. With the Wheelwriter 70 Typewriter, you'll have a 25-line CRT screen to plan and position your page before it's ever typed out. And you'll have 80,000 bytes of memory to store the work you want to keep. That's enough memory to hold up to 40 pages of memos, tables and reports. And it can be expanded to unlimited storage with the 3.5-inch Diskette Option Series II.

The Wheelwriter 70 Typewriter's menu-driven word processing features can be applied to all your ordinary tasks—and some out-of-the-ordinary tasks as well. Take the compiling and storing of mailing lists, for example. The Wheelwriter 70 Typewriter's mail and phone list features save you from typing frequently used names and addresses over and over. You only have to input them once, and the Wheelwriter 70 Typewriter does the rest. It lets you select addresses by Zip Code or other category, then combine them with documents in memory. So you can produce mailing labels, mailing lists and perfectly addressed form letters right at your desk.

Tap the resources of personal computers. Not only can you store documents and files on your Wheelwriter 70 Typewriter, you can combine them with information from IBM and IBM-compatible personal computers as well as the IBM Personal Typing System.™ So you won't have to recreate work already done by another department, for example. Just borrow its 3.5-inch diskettes, merge the material you need with your own, and print out letter-quality work on your Wheelwriter 70 Typewriter.

Press a few keys for a variety of functions. The Wheelwriter 70 Typewriter's clear and simple keyboard makes it easy for you to get your work done. Just by hitting the Type/Screen key, for example, you can shift from typing to word processing in an instant—and just as quickly return to your work on the screen. And with a touch of the Help key, you can get assistance every step of the way.

Highlights

Here are just some of the advanced features and functions that give the IBM Wheelwriter 70 Typewriter the flexibility to handle simple and sophisticated jobs alike.

IBM

Courtesy of IBM.

in that rapidly growing market—one in which IBM had not previously competed (see Exhibit 24.16).

Similar results were experienced outside the United States, particularly in Europe, where officials at IBM's European headquarters in Paris declared 1988 their strongest year in typewriters in the past decade.

The move into the PC printer business by IBM also appeared to have been successful. While market shares and dealer support were still considerably less than for typewriters, Dataquest, Inc., a highly respected source of industry data, reported that by October 1985, IBM was selling more low-end printers through retail channels than any other supplier—despite the fact that the company had not produced its first PC printer until the fourth quarter of 1984.

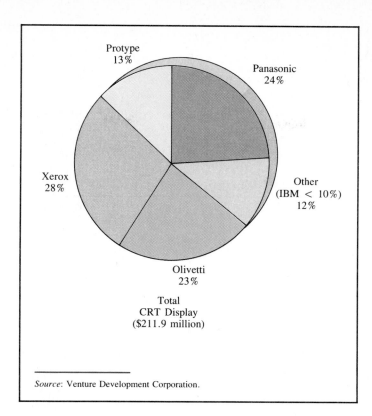

Protype
13%

Panasonic
24%

Xerox
28%

Other
(IBM < 10%)
12%

Olivetti
23%

Total
CRT Display
($211.9 million)

Source: Venture Development Corporation.

EVOLVING COMPETITION

While IBM was carrying out its "transformation," the electronic typewriter industry was also undergoing significant change. By 1987, it was apparent that the industry had become overcrowded. Low barriers to entry, combined with growth in the market, had attracted many new entrants, while most traditional participants had found ways to retain pieces of the growing action. Much of the market growth, however, reflected the accelerated replacement of electric typewriters by businesses seeking the advanced features of ETs. When a high proportion of such replacement had been completed, demand leveled out. At the same time, the value of the dollar relative to the yen and the major European currencies decreased, reducing many of the cost advantages of non–U.S.-based vendors. By 1988, firms such as Ricoh, Epson, Minolta, Sanyo, and Ericcson had exited the business, apparently because they were unwilling or unable to invest in the research and development necessary to keep up with increased functionality and improved price/performance, or in the promotion and channel support required to establish a well-recognized brand name in this mature and crowded market. While many competitors remained, a small group of manufacturers with strong brand names began to dominate the market.

IBM faced a different competitive situation in the personal computer printer industry, which in 1988 supported 50 major players[13] and nearly 200 manufacturers. The projected

---

[13] Most notable competitors were: (1) Apple, Epson, Panasonic, and Xerox in impact printers, and (2) Canon, Hewlett-Packard, Apple, and Xerox in nonimpact printers. Canon provided on an OEM basis the "engine" for Hewlett-Packard, Apple, and a score of other laser printers. Xerox, which had recently announced that it would exit all but the very high end of the ET market, was considered to have a strong lineup of daisywheel, dot-matrix, and inkjet printers.

531

EXHIBIT 24.17
Office ET Marketing (1988
Estimates)

DEALERS		MARKET SHARE*	
IBM	700	IBM	32.0%
Canon	750	Canon	8.7%
Olivetti	500	Olivetti	5.0%
Panasonic	650	Panasonic	9.8%
SCM	1200	SCM	0%†
Xerox	350	Xerox	16.8%
DISCOUNTS		**ADVERTISING**	
IBM	33–40%	IBM	$11 M
Canon	NA	Canon	$ 4 M
Olivetti	36–41%	Olivetti	NA
Panasonic	39–50%	Panasonic	$3.4 M
SCM	34–42%	SCM	NA
Xerox	34–40%	Xerox	$15 M

* VDC—Total office ET revenue (all categories).

† SCM did have 50% of consumer market, but none of industrial market.

growth of personal computers and workstations implied healthy growth in printers as well. As a product manager for a Japanese printer manufacturer marveled:

> This market is truly amazing; we've had a few plateaus but basically it's been nothing but up-up-up, and it's still charging hard. Just as one technology matures, onto the scene comes another. That keeps the excitement moving. It keeps things "young."

Lexington focused on nine firms as IBM's primary strategic competitors in the ET and/ or PC printer (PCP) markets: Apple (PCP), Brother (ET/PCP), Canon (ET/PCP), Epson (PCP), Hewlett-Packard (PCP), Olivetti (ET/PCP), Panasonic (ET/PCP), Smith-Corona (low-end ET), and Xerox (very-high-end ET). (See Exhibit 24.17 for 1988 ET competitive data.)

THE CURRENT SITUATION

By 1989, IBM was clearly a serious competitor in the personal computer printer and electronic typewriter businesses. It marketed both product lines through high-quality worldwide authorized dealer networks. Manufacturing was consolidated at one of the most highly automated manufacturing and development facilities in the world. According to industry analysts, IBM's development process and computer-integrated flexible manufacturing system gave it cost leadership in state-of-the-art personal computer printers, electronic typewriters, secretarial workstations, keyboards, and related supplies, and provided it with satisfactory margins and profits. Moreover, the shift from a direct sales force to independent dealer organizations, while requiring considerable learning as it was implemented, appeared to have been accomplished successfully and to be having a positive impact on the market. With NDD, through its dealer networks, and its equivalent in the IBM World Trade Corporation calling on customers, there were not many information technology opportunities for which IBM did not have a chance to compete.

EXHIBIT 24.18
Typewriter Niches

	PORTABLE	BASIC	MID-RANGE	HIGH-END	CRT
Use	Light duty	Low volume	Medium volume	High volume	High volume
Features	Small size Little function	Auto center & underline 13.2-inch carriage	Faster print speed Longer carriage	1- or 2-line display Storage revision	WP software use Diskettes may run DOS
Price range	< $400	$400–$700	$700–$1200	$1200–$1700	$1700 +
Major brands	Brother, Canon, SCM, Sharp	Brother, Canon, SCM, Sharp	Canon, Panasonic, Xerox	Canon, Panasonic, Xerox	Canon, Olivetti, Panasonic, Sharp, Xerox
IBM	None	Personal WW $645	WW/10 $935	WW/30 $1195 WW/50 $1495	WW/70 $1795 PTS $2895

Note: WW = wheelwriter; PTS = personal typing system.

Moreover, IBM had in 1988 begun shipping a wide range of new typewriters, including its first CRT display typewriter. According to most analysts, IBM now had a product line stronger than that of any competitor, with marked superiority in certain ranges. The intention was to fill every office niche, from basic to high-performance CRT display models (see Exhibit 24.18).

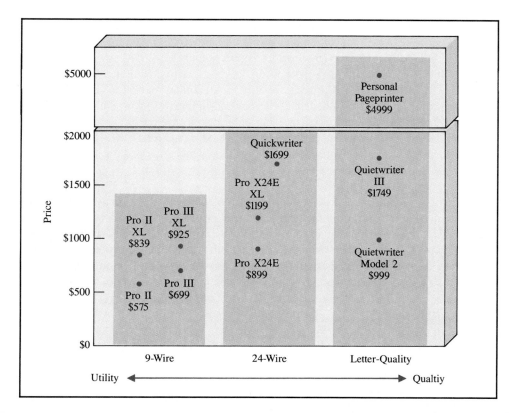

EXHIBIT 24.19
IBM Personal Printers

533

The PC printer line had also recently been expanded and significantly upgraded with introduction of the very well received[14] Proprinter II® and III®; the Quickwriter® dot-matrix printers; a new line of Quietwriter® printers utilizing proprietary heat-transfer technology; and the Personal Page Printer II® laser printer, with exclusive software capabilities designed for publishing and business professionals. Following these introductions, IBM had the broadest and, in many respects, most advanced product line in the industry (see Exhibit 24.19).

CONCLUSION

In assessing the progress made since 1982, Lexington officials felt that their organization had made considerable headway. But competition was still tough and, in many managers' view, likely to get tougher, while the future of the ET in an increasingly computerized world remained uncertain.

Two recent developments had served to bring these strategic issues into bold relief. First, IBM analysts had noted that a large (and apparently growing) segment of the office typewriter and PC printer markets was composed of buyers (often small businesses), whose needs for advanced features, customer education, and customer service were quite limited. According to industry data, customers of this type were increasingly buying established brands (e.g., Brother, Canon, Smith-Corona, Epson) of ETs and PC printers through discount stores and office superstores that offered prices considerably lower than the full-service dealers through which IBM sold. There was currently a proposal before Lexington management to offer older models (life cycles for ETs and PC printers were currently about eighteen months) through such channels, while granting ATDs and PCDs exclusivity on new models until such time as they would be supplanted by more advanced models. The bases for this proposal were: (1) the assumption that customers served by dealers and those served by mass merchandisers were discrete markets with distinct needs and little overlap; and (2) the supposition that IBM's cost structure for incremental production volumes of fully amortized models would be exceptionally low.

A number of IBM officials opposed this proposal, citing as their reason potential problems with IBM's image and dealer relations. A counterproposal to draw increased traffic from this segment to IBM dealers through an intensive advertising campaign in media targeted at smaller businesses was currently being developed.

The second concern had recently been highlighted by a correlation of the advertising plans of Lexington and the Entry-Systems Division (which was responsible for IBM's PC business). Currently slated for the June 12, 1989, issue of *Business Week*, for example, were separate advertisements for IBM ETs and PCs (see Exhibit 24.20). According to one Lexington official, these ads, besides being confusing to potential customers, raised significant questions concerning the relationship between IBM's typewriter and PC businesses. Indeed, this official wondered about possible conflicts between Lexington's new Personal Typing System® (see Exhibit 24.21), which was marketed through ATDs, and lower-end models of the Entry-Systems Division's Personal System/2® product line, which were sold by IBM's direct sales forces and PCDs.

---

[14] The Proprinter III, for example, earned a *PC Week* rating of "A," and comments like "What the Proprinter III does better than its competition is handle paper" and "The styling is square and so is the deal, at a price of $699." *PC Magazine*, in its fifth annual printer issue, gave the twenty-four-wire dot-matrix Quickwriter (most competing dot-matrix printers used only nine wires and offered much lower resolution) its "Editor's Choice" award as the top printer in its category.

EXHIBIT 24.20
Advertisements that appeared in *Business Week*, June 12, 1989 (Personal Computer Ad)

"It seems so simple now."

"I come in one morning, and there it was, big as life. A computer on my desk. IBM, no less.

"But this is one secretary who didn't have time to learn a computer. My VCR was hard enough.

"Then I found a note on it saying, 'Just turn it on.'"

The Solution: We've been working hard to help one of our most important customers: People who are new to computers.

As a result, our computer systems are easier to learn than ever. The IBM Personal System/2® even has a step-by-step tutorial that can help make sure that beginners don't stay beginners for long.

It's just one more way IBM is learning about your needs, and bringing you the best solutions.

IBM Personal System/2 is a registered trademark of IBM Corporation. © 1989 IBM Corporation.

EXHIBIT 24.20 Electronic Typewriter Ad

Test our Wheels.

IBM Wheelwriter Typewriters
Model 50 & 70 Series II

And you could win some of your own.

Grand Prize
1989 Camaro RS Convertible

If you want to get on track to higher office productivity, IBM has your Wheels—the Wheelwriter® Series II Typewriters. Test-drive the Wheelwriter 50 or 70 in your own office. It's free. Discover why Buyers Laboratory Inc. rated the Wheelwriter 50 an "ideal tool for word processing and statistical typing," and the Wheelwriter 70 the "Most Outstanding Display-based Electronic Typewriter" of the year "that offers a wide range of excellent word processing capabilities."

Give the Wheelwriter the green light and you could get even more—up to a $250.00 trade-in allowance on an IBM Correcting Selectric® II or III Typewriter.

Plus, when you choose a Supplies Agreement, you'll get two print-wheels from IBM absolutely free.

When you take the Wheelwriter 50 or 70 for a spin, you'll be eligible to win the Grand Prize in the Test Our Wheels Sweepstakes—a 1989 Camaro RS Convertible. 2,500 First Prize winners will also receive a pair of stylish Ray-Ban Wayfarer® sunglasses. **For details on how to arrange for a free test and complete sweepstakes information, contact your participating IBM Business Partner— Authorized Typewriter Dealer or call 1 800 IBM-7257, ext. 176.* But hurry, offer ends July 31, 1989.**

IBM

®IBM, Wheelwriter and Selectric are registered trademarks of International Business Machines Corporation. Wayfarer is a registered trademark of Bausch & Lomb. *No test necessary.

Courtesy of IBM.

*The workstation that
works the way you do*

IBM Personal Typing System/2
and IBM Personal Typing System/2-286

**Advanced word processing
with the ease of a typewriter
and the power of a PC**

Switch from word processing to typing—
and back again—just by pressing one
key. Or move from word processing to a
whole range of PC applications in seconds. It's that easy to juggle all your daily
office jobs with the IBM Personal Typing
System/2.

Whether you are an executive secretary
in a large corporation or work out of
your own home, you'll find that the IBM
Personal Typing System/2 will help
speed you through your daily tasks and
produce professional-looking documents every time.

Like the original Personal Typing System,
the new system is actually three extraordinary machines in one. It's an advanced
word processor. It's a self-correcting
typewriter that also functions as a letter-
quality printer. And it's a powerful personal computer. The system also has
expanded connectivity so you can
attach it to a host or link it with IBM
Personal System/2s® in a network.

That's not all. For those who need extra
processing speed and IBM OS/2® migration capability, there's the IBM Personal
Typing System/2-286.[1] It has a powerful
80286 microprocessor plus 1Mb of
memory. And if you need more, you can
easily expand to 4Mb.

Press the hot key to productivity. The
Personal Typing System/2 is designed
to work the way you do—handling all
kinds of tasks and interruptions easily.
Say your boss needs a mailing label at
the last minute, and you're in the middle
of word processing a long report. All
you do is press the hot key to switch into
typing mode. Then you type the label, hit
the hot key again, and go right back to
where you left off. All without wasting
time or motion.

*Take advantage of new software solu-
tions.* Along with your Personal Typing
System/2, you get an expanded software package filled with solutions to a
host of administrative problems. You
can use it to handle tasks ranging from
scheduling to calculating to creating
formats for forms you fill in repeatedly.
In fact, the new software includes an
advanced forms application you can
use to create formats for such complex forms as medical records or insurance policies.

Get a fast start on word processing.
Even with all these features, the IBM
Personal Typing System/2 is still easy to
learn and use. There's no complicated
setup. You can begin word processing
almost as soon as you sit down. The
menu-driven system offers you help
every step of the way, and all word processing functions—like Block, Merge
and Spell—are printed on the keys. You
can retrieve a document, add new paragraphs, or delete sections with a few

IBM

537

EXHIBIT 24.21
(continued)

IBM Personal Typing System/2
and IBM Personal Typing System/2-286 at a glance

Machine numbers	6907	6908
Processor	8086 microprocessor, 8 MHz, 0 wait state	80286 microprocessor, 10 MHz, 1 wait state
Memory (RAM) **On system board** **System maximum**	 640Kb 640Kb	 1Mb 4Mb
Integrated functions	64Kb permanent memory (ROM), MultiColor Graphics Array (MCGA) port	64Kb permanent memory (ROM), Video Graphics Array (VGA) port
	RS232C serial port, Centronics parallel printer port, pointing device port, keyboard port and diskette controller, clock	
System expansion	Two full-size PC XT option card slots	Two full-size PC AT option card slots
Operating system	DOS 3.3 or 4.0	DOS 3.3 or 4.0
Storage **Standard**	 One 1.44Mb 3.5-inch diskette drive	 One 1.44Mb 3.5-inch diskette drive
Optional	A second 1.44Mb 3.5-inch diskette drive or 20Mb fixed disk drive	A second 1.44Mb 3.5-inch diskette drive or 20Mb or 30Mb fixed disk drive
Text/graphics	MCGA supports CGA mode and provides up to 256 colors (from a palette of over 256,000) and 64 shades of gray (monochrome)	VGA supports CGA, EGA, MCGA modes and provides up to 256 colors (from a palette of over 256,000) and 64 shades of gray (monochrome)
Display modes	All CGA and EGA modes plus: 320 x 200 pels x 256 colors—all points addressable 640 x 480 pels x 2 colors—all points addressable 8 x 16 character box—16 colors (text)	
Secretarial keyboards	IBM PS/2 Enhanced Keyboard with 101 keys, including 12 function keys and 3 lighted mode indicators; or IBM PS/2 Space Saving Keyboard with 84 keys; both labeled with secretarial functions	
Supported displays	IBM Personal System/2 Color Display 8513 and IBM Personal System/2 Monochrome Display 8503 with 12-inch tilt-and-swivel pedestals and 25-line x 80-character screen	
Supported printers	IBM Correcting Wheelwriter Printer 6902 (with 30 cps impact bidirectional daisywheel); IBM Correcting Quietwriter Printer 6903 (with 40-60 cps nonimpact resistive ribbons); other printers, without correction capability	
Communications support	IBM Token-Ring Network PC Adapter, IBM PC Network Adapter II, IBM PC Network Baseband Adapter, IBM 5250 Emulation Adapter, IBM 5520 Emulation Adapter, IBM 3278/79 Emulation Adapter	
Power supply	50-watt	81-watt
Size **Processor**	 Approx. 5.8"H x 16"W x 10"D (147mm x 406mm x 254mm); 18 lbs. (8.2 kg)	
Keyboards	Enhanced: Approx. 2"H x 19.4"W x 8.3"D (51mm x 492mm x 210mm); 5 lbs. (2.3 kg) Space Saving: Approx. 2"H x 16"W x 7.5"D (51mm x 407mm x 190mm); 4 lbs. (1.8 kg)	
Displays	Monochrome: Approx. 12.3"H x 12.6"W x 12.2"D (312mm x 321mm x 311mm); 18.8 lbs. (8.5 kg) Color: Approx. 12.3"H x 12.6"W x 14.5"D (312mm x 321mm x 362mm); 23 lbs. (10.5 kg)	
Printers	Correcting Wheelwriter: Approx. 8.5"H x 21.3"W x 14.4"D (216mm x 541mm x 367mm); 28 lbs. (12.7 kg) Correcting Quietwriter: Approx. 8.5"H x 21.3"W x 14.4"D (216mm x 541mm x 367mm); 22 lbs. (10.5 kg)	
Applications software	Word processing, with enhanced forms; plus secretarial applications, including typewriter and basic forms, mail and phone lists, phone lookup, scheduler, day's schedule, information management, calculator	

1. What major forces and developments shaped the office typewriter market and industry as they existed in 1989? What was IBM's traditional position in this market? Why had this position undergone change in the 1980s?

2. What were the essential ingredients in IBM's strategy for office typewriters and PC printers in the 1980s? How did this strategy develop over time?

3. How would you characterize IBM's position in the office typewriter and PC printer markets as of 1989? What do you consider to be the major strengths and weaknesses of this position?

4. How do you expect the office typewriter and PC printer markets to develop in the 1990s? What will be the implications for IBM's strategy and position in these markets?

5. What would be your strategy going forward?

25

MARKETING STRATEGY, ANALYSIS, AND DECISION MAKING IN THE FUTURE

The first twenty-four chapters of this book have presented a process of analysis, decision making, and implementation based on in-depth understanding of underlying marketing phenomena (customer behavior, life cycles, segmentation, positioning, market response, and competitive behavior) and three distinct levels of marketing analysis (Levels I, II, and III). We have described state-of-the-art issues in key decision areas such as new products, maturing products, product-line strategy, and worldwide corporate marketing, and have demonstrated how decisions in these areas can be integrated into a comprehensive marketing plan and implemented effectively. The underlying paradigm and decision-making skills presented in this book are intended to equip you to be an effective marketer in the future as well as under today's business conditions. Although we anticipate many changes in underlying marketing phenomena, the marketing environment, and marketing techniques, we expect the basic lessons of this book to retain their validity.

In this chapter, we describe briefly the major trends we see in such underlying phenomena, analytic support systems, and environmental factors. To meet the challenges raised by these and other developments, you will have to be sensitive to such changes and be creative, adaptive, and agile in response. Anticipating and responding to change is, in fact, one of the primary characteristics of the effective marketer.

TRENDS IN UNDERLYING MARKETING PHENOMENA

Customer Decision Making

In the future, customers will have access to more comprehensive information and be required to make decisions about increasingly complex products and services. As they find it more necessary to use heuristics to simplify their decision processes, it will be even more important for marketers to know how to model customer information processing in meaningful ways. Customers will demand quality to a greater degree; they will be skeptical of unsupported claims and products that fail to deliver. The importance of brand reputation or equity will grow as consumers reward firms that consistently demonstrate high value (i.e., benefits relative to price).

The technology of purchasing will change as more and more homes and virtually all businesses acquire high-function computers with broad-band telecommunications capabilities that allow access to a range of customer information and business-to-business links, including data bases and expert systems to assist in the purchase process.

Life Cycles

Life cycles will become shorter as technological change accelerates, competitors imitate successful innovations more rapidly, and customer tastes grow ever more fickle. Windows of opportunity for new products will become narrower, and aggressive strategies to stimulate diffusion of innovation and establish a leadership position before competitive imitation occurs will gain in importance. Rewards for pioneering will multiply as customers favor innovators in their cognitive processing and pioneers become more adept at exploiting their first-mover advantage throughout the life cycle. Firms will need to be skillful at managing all phases of the life cycle. Profit management in the mature phase will be more significant because there will be less time to harvest the rewards of risk taking and innovation. As the number of new market opportunities declines, firms will make greater efforts to rejuvenate categories rather than let them deteriorate. Understanding the causes of the dynamics in each phase of the life cycle will be critical.

Segmentation

While new growth markets will certainly emerge in the future, most markets in advanced economies will grow relatively slowly. As such markets enter the later phases of their life cycles, competition will intensify. Microsegmentation will become increasingly common, with overlaps resulting in a sometimes confusing array of products and services. Firms will target smaller niches that have not yet been saturated with competitive alternatives. As such segments become more and more narrowly defined, finding and selecting advertising media and channels of distribution to reach them efficiently will pose an exceptionally difficult challenge.

Firms will have to be creative in using demographic, geographic, attitudinal, usage, and product data to define segments. Overlap among products and potential cannibalization will be growing concerns. While advances in flexible manufacturing will facilitate more product variety, managing the highly complex product lines that result will be a formidable task. Geographic segmentation within product lines will be a common marketing strategy, with regional managers coordinating multiple product lines and interfacing with category or brand managers who are responsible for a given product or product line across regions.

Positioning

Not only will there be more segments to deal with, but the task of positioning within segments will become more complex. Viewed in perceptual mapping terms, many markets will show a proliferation in the number of dimensions on the product map. After basic customer demands for efficacy and quality have been met and competitive products approach parity on these dimensions, competition will focus on increasingly subtle dimensions, with benefit segmentation (based on differences in customers' valuation of the dimensions) growing in importance.

With more segments and a wider variety of positioning options, consistency in positioning across segments will be especially important. Given the potential overlap between segments and the relative unavailability of opportunities to isolate individual segments by media or channel selection, achieving such consistency will be hard. Many companies will use overall umbrella positioning strategies, with elaborate positioning variations within segments, to minimize this problem.

Market Response

The recent heavy use of promotional price cuts as a competitive weapon will decline as a result of better data (e.g., from supermarket scanners) on the profitability of such promotions and a growing recognition that the competitive dynamics provoked by such promotions greatly diminish their positive impact on either market position or profitability. While promotion will remain a significant variable, emphasis will shift to nonprice variables, such as product features, advertising, and customer service. Firms will develop new marketing tools as they search for market advantage. One company, for example, is experimenting with shopping carts with TV screens that advertise a product as the shopper passes its shelf position in the supermarket, while others are seeking more efficient and effective ways to issue coupons to their most potentially profitable customers. Industrial marketers will seek competitive advantage through marketing innovations such as use of video conferencing for making sales contacts, personal portable video cellular phones for sales and customer service support, and on-line computer links with key customers.

One consequence of greater segmentation will be augmentation of the power of distribution channels. With more products and brands competing for customer attention, wholesalers and retailers will often act as gate keepers rather than conduits, controlling which products potential customers see and the amount of point-of-sale support they receive. ''Value-added remarketers (VARs), which integrate products into benefit propositions targeted at small segments with specialized needs, will become an increasingly important distribution channel in many product categories (they are already common in the computer industry). Solution marketing and selling to microsegments will be standard marketing practice as we move into the twenty-first century.

Competitive Behavior

A number of factors will lead to an intensification of competition. One of the most important will be the continuing saturation of traditional markets. In an effort to sustain growth despite such saturation, more ''foreign'' competitors will enter domestic markets and more ''domestic'' manufacturers will seek new markets in both their own and other countries. As the ensuing global competition weeds out weaker firms, survivors will be either ''lean and mean,'' exceptionally creative, or most likely, both. Market opportunities will have to be pursued rapidly and effectively because only the quick, the innovative, and the aggressive will succeed.

Even as competitive intensity increases, leading firms will become more adept at anticipating the responses of their competitors. Self-defeating price wars will be less common. Instead of engaging in prisoner's dilemmas and mutually destructive competition, firms will tacitly cooperate on price and promotion and seek competitive advantage based on superior understanding of customer needs and effective management of the innovation process to meet those needs.

TRENDS IN ANALYTIC SUPPORT

As the underlying marketing phenomena grow more complex, rich data bases and powerful analytic tools will become more available. Level II techniques, more powerful and yet comprehensible to well-trained line managers, will be widely accepted tools of the trade.

Level III analysis will be routinely required for major high-risk decisions where comprehensive models and extensive data have high payoff potential. Marketing science analysts will be better trained; not only will they have Level III skills, but they will also be able to appreciate Level I and Level II analysis and to implement it effectively.

Level I analysis will continue to be critical. As problems get more complex, defining the problem and specifying the "real question" will be a crucial managerial task. Both qualitative and quantitative customer research will help to frame issues, but direct contact with customers will, if anything, be even more important.

More and better data (comparable to scanner-based transactional data available today in packaged goods) will become readily available to marketers in most industries and advanced countries. This trend is already evident in the financial services, pharmaceutical, and industrial supply industries, and shows signs of spreading to consumer durables and standardized industrial products. This rapid proliferation of data will create a data glut, as it already has in packaged goods, leading to the development of "intelligent" decision support systems that convert the data into useful information.

There will be massive progress in computers, networks, models, statistics, and user interfaces. Managers will use the computer as a tool to support their decisions, but most will not spend hours in front of terminals, even though they will have the skills necessary to engage in elaborate computer-based analyses. Instead, they will rely on intelligent software and skilled analysts to translate data into action recommendations. Essentially, the computer and/or the analyst will present the manager with consultant reports that describe the marketing situation in one or more existing or potential segments and lay out decision alternatives for consideration.

CHANGES IN THE STRATEGIC DECISION-MAKING ENVIRONMENT

Improved analytic capabilities will help us to cope not only with more complex underlying marketing phenomena but also with the profound and rapid environmental changes likely to occur in the decades ahead. Changes in global competition, technology, and society itself will have significant implications for the formulation and implementation of marketing strategy.

Global Change

The emergence of the world as a single market may result in considerable expansion of international trade and investment and the role of multinational and even global companies. A smaller number of larger firms will dominate most markets. As firms segment the world market demographically and psychographically, competition will focus on worldwide rather than national market segments. Only those firms with global capabilities will have the economies of scale and resources necessary to compete effectively. Strategic alliances among firms will become increasingly common as firms strive to develop worldwide capability in marketing, production, and engineering.

The global nature of competition will eliminate the need for a separate concept of international marketing. *All* marketing will be international. In virtually every product category, the world will be the market, competition will be global, or both. Effective marketers will develop the skills necessary to manage the heterogeneity of both the global marketplace and the global strategic group in which they will compete.

Within this framework dominated by giant, global firms, small companies will flourish by targeting niches in the markets of a limited number of countries or perhaps only their home country. These enterpreneurial companies will succeed on the basis of nimble innovation and outstanding marketing skills and strategies. The world will remain a large, diverse market, offering numerous opportunities to firms and individuals who can identify a need, create a market, and satisfy their customers.

Technological Change

New technologies will present major opportunities for growth. R&D expenditures will expand both absolutely and relatively, as they come to be viewed as a major factor in obtaining long-run strategic advantage. As in the computer industry today, firms will race to be first with the next technological advance, to create products based on that advance, and to earn as much profit as feasible before competitors clone the innovation or the new technology becomes obsolete.

While not all markets will undergo a technological revolution, disciplines such as information technology, materials science, and biology will prove to be so pervasive that they will affect a multiplicity of markets. Technological change will present risks and opportunities to virtually all firms. Innovators will earn premium profits as margins on established products are forced down by intensifying competition.

The successful management of technological change will require close linkages among marketing, R&D, and manufacturing. Successful firms will need to be outstanding at both technological innovation and marketing. Successful product design will begin with an understanding of customer needs, the benefits technology can provide, and likely customer responses to various combinations of product and nonproduct attributes. Products will be created by talented engineers working closely with lead users to craft benefit packages that exploit advancing technology at price trade-offs attractive to customers.

Social and Political Change

The coming decades are likely to be characterized by profound social and political changes. Since such changes are difficult to forecast, successful firms will be those that remain flexible and employ adaptive strategies. Several leading American companies that had made large commitments to projects in the People's Republic of China, for example, found their strategies in a near shambles following the 1989 attacks on the students in Tiananmen Square. Although most forecasters still believe in the potential of the Chinese market, it appears that the U.S. companies caught in the recent turmoil had few plans for such a radical contingency. Equally surprising was the tearing down of the Berlin Wall in 1989 and the opening of Eastern European and Russian markets in 1990.

Some developments are easier to anticipate and predict than those in China. Europe is certainly going unify into a large and more powerful economic entity, although the implications for Japan, the United States, and Europe itself, are far from clear. Will economic warfare develop among these regions, leading to a replacement of the trend toward globalization by one toward regionalization? Or will global companies ultimately call the tune, leading to competition on a worldwide market-by-market basis? It is likely that the multinationals will have considerable freedom to create markets, but still, there will be constraints. For example, local production may be required. This is true in autos now and will be typical of other industries in the future. Negotiations between trading partners and company alliances will be required to tap the potential benefits of multinational global markets while meeting the restrictions established by local political interests. Given the uncertainties involved, the wise firm will monitor such developments and plan for a number of contingencies.

Environmental pollution and the rise of the ''green'' parties; problems with education, third world debt, minority rights, drugs, AIDS, and crime; rapid changes in Eastern Europe, continuing pressures for détente and nuclear disarmament; and the growth of newly industrialized countries are just a few of the other issues that are likely to impact strategies significantly. The successful firm will be diligent in monitoring such developments and in analyzing the threats and opportunities they create.

Most firms will experience more direct social and political effects in such areas as labor relations, government regulation, monetary and fiscal policies, and expectations concerning social responsibility and ethics. Adding to the challenge, the various countries in which major firms will be doing business will probably have different and often conflicting policies and expectations in these areas.

CONCLUSION

The net effect of these changes will be a worldwide competitive environment subject to dramatic changes in technology and in social-political structures. A set of ''world-class competitors'' will emerge—companies that have survived intense rivalries, rapidly changing technology, and a turbulent environment. They will produce very high quality products at low costs. The Japanese quality advantage of the 1980s will disappear in the 1990s as firms in other countries catch up. Cost advantages will be rare as all of the leading firms in an industry use the same manufacturing technology and off-shore production sites, and global financial markets minimize differences in the cost of capital.

Strategic marketing skills will improve as leading firms seek to create competitive advantage through segmentation and positioning. Marketing in the 1990s will build upon the quality movement of the 1970s and 1980s. *Customer-driven organizations* will dominate, creating utility for customers through a coordinated total commitment to produce, sell, distribute, and service their products so that they fully deliver promised benefits to customers in their target market segments. *Total customer satisfaction* will require total support from top management, and the shared belief by all employees in all functions that success will come only if they satisfy their customers' needs better than competitors do.

Firms will develop high levels of customer service. They will seriously try to understand what the customer really needs and/or wants. Account management teams and special key account liaisons will become more common. Industrial component manufacturers, for example, will increasingly engage in marketing research and missionary selling at the level of the final buyer or user, rather than confining such efforts to their OEMs or distribution channels. Consumer products manufacturers will find it necessary to offer ''total satisfaction'' guarantees to assure customers that they will receive the benefits that have been promised to them. The primary task of marketing strategy will be to win customer loyalty by offering a truly superior bundle of satisfaction.

Some firms will achieve an initial advantage through the early adoption of new strategic marketing techniques such as those outlined in this book. In time, however, other firms will catch up as they are forced to be responsive to customer needs and behavior. Firms will find themselves at parity in most strategic factors, and will compete on what are essentially level playing fields, rather than those tilted to favor particular companies or countries.

In this world of structural parity, competitive advantage will largely be based on differences in ability to innovate. Innovation in products and services, as well as in the execution of strategy, will be the key to success in the twenty-first century. This capability will be necessary in all aspects of the firm's operations, with marketing likely to be in the forefront. The marketing fundamentals presented in this book provide a foundation for such innovation, but you will have to be creative in developing innovative marketing strategies and tactics based on these fundamentals, and in extending the qualitative and quantitative techniques you have learned. You will need to monitor your market and overall environment constantly, and always be ready to advocate and implement change.

We have provided the concepts and tools you will need. But your success will ultimately depend on your own vision, courage, and creativity, and on the strength of your commitment to deliver total satisfaction to your customers.

QUESTIONS FOR DISCUSSION

1. What are the five most important things you have learned from this text and these cases?

2. Look five years ahead and describe how the marketing environment will be different from what it is today. Now look ten years ahead and describe that environment.

3. Assuming analytic support tools will gain power and acceptance in the future, how will you keep pace with these developments? What role will they take in your formulation of marketing strategy?

❋ 4. What specific programs can an organization put in place to sense changes in the market or in competition?

5. What changes in the underlying phenomena of marketing will present the greatest threat to existing businesses? What changes will present the greatest opportunities?

6. How will the balance of power work out between countries that want to protect jobs and local heritage and multinational companies that want access to global markets?

REFERENCES

BUSINESS WEEK. 1989. "Stalking the New Consumer." August 28, pp. 54–62.

CAPON, NOEL, JOHN U. FARLEY, AND JAMES M. MULBERT. 1987. *Corporate Strategic Planning.* New York: Columbia University Press.

DEAN, J. W. JR., AND G. I. SUSMAN. 1989. "Organizing for Manufacturable Design." *Harvard Business Review* 67: 28–37.

DERTOUZOS, MICHAEL L., RICHARD K. LESTER, AND ROBERT M. SOLOW. 1989. *Made in America.* Cambridge, MA: The MIT Press.

KOTLER, PHILIP. 1986. "Megamarketing." *Harvard Business Review*, March/April: 117–124.

SAMLI, A. C., K. PALDA, AND A. T. BAVIEER. 1987. "Toward a Mature Marketing Concept." *Sloan Management Review*, Winter: 45–51.

SHANKLIN, W. L., AND J. K. RYANS, JR. 1986. "Organizing for High-Tech Marketing." *Harvard Business Review*, November/December: 164–171.

STAR, STEVEN H. 1989. "Marketing and Its Discontents." *Harvard Business Review*, November/December: 148–154.

WEBSTER, FREDERICK E. JR. 1988. "Rediscovering the Marketing Concept." *Working Paper.* Cambridge, MA: Marketing Science Institute.

COMPANY INDEX

NAME INDEX

SUBJECT INDEX

557